Blackburn
College

Library
01254 292120

GREEN AGAINST GREEN

THE IRISH CIVIL WAR

Michael Hopkinson

Gill & Macmillan

Gill & Macmillan Ltd
Hume Avenue, Park West, Dublin 12
with associated companies throughout the world
www.gillmacmillan.ie

© Michael Hopkinson 1988, 2004
First published in 1988
This edition first published 2004
978 07171 3760 2
Index compiled by Helen Litton
Printed in Malaysia

*The paper used in this book is made from the wood pulp
of managed forests. For every tree felled, at least one tree
is planted, thereby renewing natural resources.*

A CIP catalogue record for this book is available
from the British Library.

5 7 6 4

*To my mother and my
late father*

Contents

PART V. THE WAR'S END

PART VI. THE POST-WAR PERIOD

It was an episode which has burned so deep into the heart and mind of Ireland that it is not yet possible for the historian to approach it with the detailed knowledge or the objectivity which it deserves and sooner or later must have. So many of the divisions and hatreds that were to scar the political and social life of Ireland for the next two decades—and are visible even today—stem from those months of internecine warfare that charity and the interests of truth alike demand a certain reticence about events which are still felt so profoundly and yet so little understood in their inner meaning.

F. S. L. Lyons, *Ireland since the Famine*, first edition (1971)

Preface

THERE has been a wealth of detailed and stimulating writing, particularly in the last twenty years, on many aspects of the Anglo-Irish Treaty and Civil War period. No satisfactory history of the war, however, has been written. This book aims to adopt a fresh and scholarly approach and to place the conflict in a wide twentieth-century Irish context.

My research was greatly aided by the availability during the last fifteen years of a vast amount of new primary material, representing all aspects of the Treaty and war. In many respects, moreover, the 1980s is a better decade for writing about the Civil War than the 1960s, during which the two previous war histories were written. The last two decades have seen considerable changes in Irish politics and society, which have aided new historical approaches and perspectives. The old Civil War issues—of constitutional status and Anglo-Irish relations—no longer dominate Irish politics; passions resulting from the conflict have cooled somewhat with the death and retirement of many war veterans. The young of the Twenty-Six Counties today are much less likely than earlier generations to wish to identify emotionally with the war. Meanwhile the concentration of so much attention on the Northern question since the late 1960s has produced a great revival of interest on historical aspects of the North and changed attitudes to the North by some Southern historians and politicians. The present crisis in the North has thrown a sharp relief on the 1920-23 period when many similar issues were faced.

Because of the lack of crucial archives, F. S. L. Lyons felt that no definitive history of the war could be written. That remains true. A considerable volume of government and military material either remains unavailable or no longer exists. My concentration on personal collections, British government papers and, to a lesser extent, on oral evidence is an acknowledgment of the lack of state archival material in the Twenty-Six Counties. Disappointing also has been the attitude of the Stormont authorities who prevented me from gaining access to almost all relevant papers in the Public Record Office of Northern Ireland, some of which have been worked on by other historians. Readers are even prevented from consulting correspondence relating to the wedding present the Northern Ireland government gave to the then Princess Elizabeth!

There are many technical and intellectual difficulties in writing on the subject: it does not lend itself to a chronological and narrative approach. Developments were highly complex and confusing; the writer is often forced to describe chaos. The war had an ill-defined beginning and end; the fighting was erratic, extremely confusing and highly regionalised. The subject requires sympathy and understanding for a range of diverse attitudes, and a knowledge of the background and developments in the South and North of Ireland, in Britain and in Irish-America. On the period's sundry delicate and controversial incidents—the assassination of Sir Henry Wilson and the death of Michael Collins, to quote the two most notorious examples—the historian has to act as something resembling a detective.

It is hardly surprising that a bitter, incestuous conflict in a small country, which saw neither compromise nor reconciliation at its end, has been extremely difficult for Irish historians to write about in a detached manner. Many personal memoirs of the Irish revolutionary period—those of Michael Brennan, Dan Breen and Tom Barry, for instance—have very little to say about the Civil War: it was far easier for them to write about the Anglo-Irish conflict.

To study the conflict is necessary for an understanding of the establishment of the Free State—in that context reticence can no longer have any virtue. Many of the war's events—the executions and the Kerry atrocities, for instance—are extremely unpleasant to write about; to do so can only be justified by a wish to place them, as far as possible, in the context of the conflict.

I have adopted an analytical approach, while providing the necessary chronological base, and have written separate chapters on the North in order to bring out Northern themes more clearly and to facilitate the account of Southern affairs by making it unnecessary to switch frequently to developments on the other side of the border. I have placed a heavy emphasis on regional developments. Too much Irish history has been written from a Dublin- or Westminster-centred perspective, frequently in conjunction with an over-concentration on 'high' politics. My own work on the regions is necessarily incomplete, and there is a need for detailed local studies.[1]

Only the kindness and generosity of considerable numbers of people have made an ambitious project possible. My greatest debts in Dublin, during several long stays, go to Michael and Judith Hutchinson and family, and to Rodney and Susan Thom and their family. In Dublin also, James McGuire, Peter and Isobel Fox and Maeve Bradley were the most helpful of friends. Many there also gave valuable advice: Tom Garvin, who read an early draft of the opening chapters, Dr León Ó Broin, Arthur Mitchell, John McColgan, David Fitzpatrick, Michael Laffan, Ronan Fanning, the late Professor T. D. Williams, the late Professor R. Dudley Edwards, Dr Risteárd Mulcahy and Mrs Rita Childers. Michael MacEvilly has been of invaluable assistance and has saved me from many errors relating to the war in the west. Of Civil War contemporaries, the late Colonel Dan Bryan, the late Máire Comerford, Dr T. O'Reilly and the late Dr C. S. Andrews gave generously of their time. I am also very grateful to the staffs of the UCD Archives, the National Library, the State Paper Office, the Public Record Office and the Records Department of TCD. Special thanks are owed to Kerry Holland at the UCD Archives, and Commandant Peter Young. Dr Garret FitzGerald kindly gave me permission to work on his father's papers. So much of my interest in Irish history was stimulated by Professor F. S. L. Lyons; I was as saddened by his tragic death as were so many other Irish specialists.

In Belfast, Peter and Mary Blair and Peter and Belinda Jupp gave warm friendship and hospitality. I am grateful also to Peter Smyth, Dr A. T. Q. Stewart, Professor J. C. Beckett, Jennifer Fitzgerald and Paul Bew. The staff of the Public Record Office of Northern Ireland strove to assist me despite the attitude of Stormont to scholars in twentieth-century Irish history.

In England, John O'Beirne Ranelagh, Charles Townshend and Josie Howie gave valuable help, and I owe much to the staffs of the Public Record Office at Kew, the House of Lords Record Department, the British Library, and the British Museum Newspaper Library. Ian and Jenny Gibbs gave generous hospitality. In Scotland, I have been helped by Professor D. A. G. Waddell, Professor R. T. Campbell, Dr Robin Law, Dr John McCracken, Dr Neil Tranter and Dr Iain Hutchison, among my colleagues. I am thankful also to the staff of Stirling University Library and the National Library of Scotland, and to the Inter Library Loans facility. My greatest debt at Stirling has gone to the friendship and help of Dr Richard Holt, Fiona Crayton Hutchison, Kim and Bryan, and to Bernie McDougall. My students over many years in the Irish history course at Stirling have helped to keep my interest alive.

My thanks go also to the University of Stirling for allowing me sabbatical leaves for working on this book, and to the Twenty-Seven Foundation for an invaluable award. The typing of a vast, cumbersome and chaotic manuscript has been nobly and efficiently undertaken by Fiona Crayton Hutchison and Margaret Dickson.

Fergal Tobin has been the most warm, informed and long-suffering of editors. Colm Croker has done a magnificent job as copy-editor, saving me from so many sins and omissions. My greatest debt of all is owed to the support of my mother and my late father.

Michael Hopkinson
Stirling, January 1987

List of Illustrations

Between pages 180-181

On 8 May 1922, a meeting of pro-Treaty and anti-Treaty officers at the Mansion House, Dublin sought to avert the threatening civil war. Their efforts were only temporarily successful. *Left to right:* General Sean Mac Eoin, Sean Moylan, General Eoin O'Duffy, Liam Lynch, Gearóid O'Sullivan and Liam Mellows.

Arthur Griffith, Eamon de Valera, Michael Collins and Harry Boland after the signing of the 'election pact', 18 May 1922.

Michael Collins speaking in front of O'Donovan's Hotel, Clonakilty, Co. Cork, on the last day of the election campaign, 15 June 1922.

The opening shots of the Civil War, fired from Free State 18-pound field artillery supplied by the British government. This gun was stationed at the junction of Bridgefoot Street and Usher's Quay, just across the Liffey from the Four Courts.

The ruins of the Irish Public Record office after the Free State bombardment of 30 June 1922. The Republican garrison had converted this part of the Four Courts complex into a munitions factory with the cellars underneath being used to store explosives. The Free State bombardment caused a fire which reached the cellars and the consequent explosion destroyed priceless historical records and documents, some of them dating back to the twelfth century.

A general view of the Four Courts immediately after the surrender of the Republican garrison, 30 June 1922.

Free State troops in a Lancia armoured car distributing bread to Dubliners who had been unable to get food on account of the fighting in the vicinity of O'Connell Street, 3 August 1922.

Sean O'Mahony T.D. (*left*) and Miss Mary MacSwiney, sister of the late Terence MacSwiney, Lord Mayor of Cork, attending the funeral of Cathal Brugha.

The track of the Dublin/Blessington steam tram was torn up by Republicans. Here it is being repaired while Free State troops stand guard.

General Prout outside his GHQ in Carrick-on-Suir, 4 August 1922.

Free State army troops with a Lancia 'chicken coop' armoured car at Claregalway, Co. Galway, August 1922.

Free State troops man a roadblock on the Charleville Road, just outside Limerick city, July 1922.

Unloading an 18-pound field gun at Passage East, Co. Cork, 1922.

Michael Collins's coffin being placed on a gun carriage outside the Pro-Cathedral, Dublin, prior to the funeral procession to Glasnevin Cemetery.

The Earl of Mayo's house burned by Republicans during the latter days of the Civil War, 29 January 1923.

The photographs reproduced between pages 180 and 181 appear with the kind permission of the copyright holder, George Morrison, and first appeared in his book *The Irish Civil War: An Illustrated History* (Gill and Macmillan, 1981).

Ireland, general map

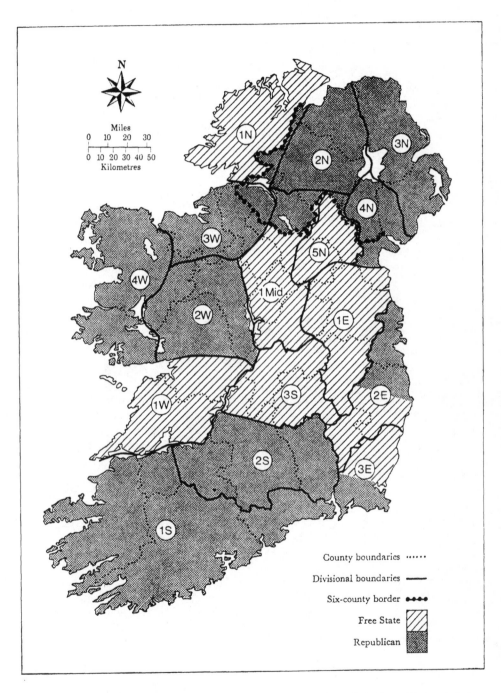

The Civil War split in the IRA, spring 1922. Each IRA division is indicated by a circled number and letter. 1s is the First Southern Division, etc.

1

The Background to the Treaty Divisions, 1912-1918

THE Irish Civil War resulted directly from the divisions in the twenty-six counties of the south and west of Ireland over the Anglo-Irish Treaty of December 1921. It does not follow, however, that in looking for the causes of the conflict attention should be confined to the immediate circumstances relating to the Treaty and the political and military split which followed it.

Many, writing from a stance fuelled by the bitterness of civil war, have put the blame for the divisions on individuals. In his summing up in the Sinn Féin Funds Case of 1948 Judge Kingsmill Moore commented: 'For a quarter of a century political life in Ireland [has] been poisoned by an eagerness to lay the blame for the civil strife which broke out in 1922 on the shoulders of this person or that.' Eamon de Valera has frequently been held personally responsible for the war by many writing from a pro-Treaty stance: General Richard Mulcahy and the historian P. S. O'Hegarty held that without de Valera's influence in provoking widespread opposition to the Treaty, there would have been no break in what Mulcahy depicted as the glorious unity in Irish nationalist ranks which had existed in the 1917-21 period. De Valera, and many of his Republican supporters, held that Arthur Griffith and Michael Collins were to blame for what followed by signing the Treaty without referring it back to the Dáil cabinet in Dublin, and by failing to strive for further concessions which could have preserved republican unity. Frequently responsibility for creating Irish nationalist disunion has been attached to Lloyd George's machiavellian tactics at the end of the Treaty negotiations, in particular his threat of an immediate resumption of intensified war if the Treaty was not signed there and then. The British government's refusal to amend the Treaty in the six months following its signing, and their liberal supply of arms to the Provisional Government, were seen as the immediate cause of the war by many Republicans—for them perfidious Albion was still responsible for Irish ills. From all these perspectives, therefore, the key developments which led to the Civil War took place at, and in the half-year after, the Treaty's signing, and it followed that the war was considered unnecessary and avoidable.[1]

Short-term factors were extremely important in determining the course and character of political and military divisions. The war's underlying causes, however, must be sought for in longer-term considerations stemming from the amazingly rapid changes in Irish nationalism and in Anglo-Irish relations between 1912 and 1921.

*

The Irish Parliamentary Party's quest for a Home Rule settlement of the Irish question appeared close to fulfilment in 1912. With the Liberal government's survival dependent on Irish members, and the House of Lords' veto removed, the Home Rule Bill seemed assured of passage. The constitutional nationalist tactics of wringing concessions from the British government by the application of pressure in the Westminster parliament appeared to have finally succeeded; to judge by the electoral evidence, furthermore, the aim of a devolved government for Ireland appeared to be widely accepted by the population throughout most of the country. The rival nationalist tradition of physical-force republicanism, as represented since the 1850s by the secret Irish Republican Brotherhood organisation, had become virtually moribund by 1906. Although the IRB revived to some extent under a new and more active leadership between 1906 and 1912, there appeared no foreseeable prospect of physical-force rebellion, let alone of a complete separation of Ireland from Britain. By the end of 1918, however, the prospects for the rival nationalist strands had been completely transformed. The general election of December 1918 had obliterated the Irish Parliamentary Party, which had consequently been replaced as the institutional representation of nationalist opinion by a coalition of advanced nationalist elements, brought together under the convenient and dramatic umbrella title 'Sinn Féin'.

How can this collapse of the Parliamentary Party's position be explained? The dominant position assumed by constitutional nationalists in 1912 was based on insecure foundations: in the post-Parnell period the party had been riven by internal disputes and challenged by the various elements of what became known as the 'new nationalism'—organisations such as the Gaelic League, the Gaelic Athletic Association and Arthur Griffith's Sinn Féin Clubs, all placing a heavy emphasis on cultural revival. Although there was little proof of effective political opposition to the Parliamentary Party, by 1912 many of the 'new nationalist' organisations held a great attraction for those who later took over the leadership of Irish nationalism. The most important element in undermining a Home Rule settlement, however, was the militant resistance of Ulster loyalists, which by 1914 had made it extremely unlikely that a devolved system of government could be implemented without some form of partition. The example set by Unionists in the north-east, and the delay this meant for the passage of the Home Rule Bill at Westminster, had an immediate effect on the South. In response to the Ulster Volunteer Force, the Irish Volunteers were set up in November 1913 on similar military lines, and soon claimed a membership of 175,000 from a broad band of the Southern Irish population. The IRB infiltrated the Volunteers by taking key positions in its organisation, and a large number of arms were soon landed at Howth. Thanks to the North, the gun had re-entered Irish politics. The Volunteers grew so rapidly that Redmond, the Parliamentary Party's leader, was forced to link his party to them. The outbreak of the First World War resulted in a suspension of the Home Rule Bill for the duration of that conflict and a split in the Volunteers—the majority, under Redmond, supporting the war, and the minority, under Eoin Mac Néill, opposing it.

At the start of the war the majority of Southern Irish opinion was in favour of Irish participation, but only on the implicit understanding that a Home Rule settlement for all of Ireland would be granted at the end of the conflict. Support for the Parliamentary Party, therefore, was conditional on the successful passage of a

Home Rule Bill—if the British government did not succeed in producing such a settlement, Redmond's party would lose its *raison d'être*. The next crucial development in leading to the transformation of Irish nationalism was the Easter Rising of 1916.

The rising was planned secretly by the Military Committee of the IRB. Mac Néill was deliberately kept in the dark, and even many parts of the IRB were in ignorance of much of the planning. The insurrection only occurred after the collapse of a plan to bring in German arms, and, with a few minor exceptions, was confined to an occupation of prominent buildings in Dublin; the rebels won little support at the time and displayed organisational and tactical ineptitude. Nevertheless, the manner in which the rising was put down, and the executions, internment and martial law which followed it, helped produce an ever-increasing sympathy for the ideas of those who had led the rising. Those ideas, so vividly and dramatically articulated, particularly by Pearse and Connolly, became yardsticks by which future Irish nationalists were to be judged.

The British government's failure to achieve a Home Rule settlement during complex negotiations in late 1916 and early 1917, and the prevalence of talk of possible partition, did much to further the demand for a much greater degree of independence than had been considered as a practicable possibility before 1912. Evidence of that came in the dramatic Sinn Féin by-election victories during 1917. That does not mean, however, that there was a consensus within the south and west of Ireland on the need for complete separation from Britain, nor that there was any agreement on whether Irish independence should be achieved by military or political means.[2]

Given the background, it is not surprising that the Irish revolution was improvised, between 1916 and 1921, in a highly confusing manner: its speed and direction was often dictated by local developments rather than by means of control from Dublin. The aftermath of the Easter Rising saw major institutional changes within Irish nationalism. The public organisations, Sinn Féin and the Volunteers, were reorganised within a short time of each other in the autumn of 1917. The convention that founded the new Sinn Féin met on 25 October. Before that Arthur Griffith's Sinn Féin movement had been more notable for the influence of its ideas than for the size of its membership; the power of the name it bequeathed to the new emerging coalition proved of vastly greater significance than Griffith's unpopular support of the dual monarchy concept and his stress on passive resistance. Nevertheless, Griffith's policy of abstention from the Westminster parliament, to be adopted by the new party at the next general election, and to be followed by the establishment of an Irish government and parliament, provided an excellent basis for uniting the various elements of advanced nationalism in the short term. Crucial, also, to the popular appeal of the new Sinn Féin was Griffith's agreement that he should be replaced by de Valera, the sole surviving commandant of the rising, at its head; the emotional force of the memory of the Easter Rising was thereby related to the new political nationalism. De Valera had turned his back, though not publicly, on both the IRB and the philosophy of martyrdom which underlay the rising, and was well placed to provide pragmatic leadership for an ill-defined, broad nationalist coalition. The new Sinn Féin contained, among other elements, old Parliamentary Party members at non-leadership level, dissatisfied with the apparent impotence of the old party; Griffith's followers; those wishing to relate Irish nationalism to social and, more particularly, land protest; and IRB members, eager to infiltrate public movements.

The key compromise made to ensure unity at the 1917 Sinn Féin Convention was an amendment to the constitution stating that a republic should be the declared aim of the organisation, but that once independence had been achieved, a referendum should decide what form of government should be adopted by the new state. De Valera was to testify that it was the furthest they could persuade Griffith to go towards recognition of the republican aim. The hardline republican Cathal Brugha vigorously objected to the compromise. In his historical account of the Sinn Féin movement Judge Kingsmill Moore said that the reorganised Sinn Féin represented the 'desire to obtain the maximum amount of independence which it was possible to win', and that this 'formed the real bond between all members . . . not any hard and fast adherence to a Republican ideal'.

Less than a month after the Sinn Féin Convention the Volunteers were reorganised under a GHQ based in Dublin. De Valera became President of the Volunteers, seemingly unifying in his person the military and political movements. Members of the IRB, after failing to gain control of the Sinn Féin executive, gained the dominant positions on the Volunteer staff.

On the surface, therefore, by the end of 1917 the national movement, both public and secret, appeared united. The cultural revivalism of the post-Parnell period of Irish history had been triumphantly politicised; members of the Volunteers worked hard for Sinn Féin victory at elections; all seemed agreed on the Sinn Féin policy of abstention from Westminster and the search for recognition of the claim to independence by means of appeal to international opinion, with the Republic as the ultimate ideal. Lloyd George's clumsy and ultimately futile attempts to impose conscription on the Irish population during 1918 put the seal on Sinn Féin's growth in popularity, when even the Parliamentary Party and the Catholic hierarchy were seen to back Sinn Féin's tactics and attitude.

The Sinn Féin party's unity and coherence, however, was a very superficial one. There was no political control of the Volunteers, who continued to be governed by their own executive. The fact that the growth of the physical-force side of Irish republicanism long predated any republican political organisation proved a major problem for the Sinn Féin party between 1917 and 1921, and for the Provisional and Free State governments in the early years of Irish independence. There was no tradition of political control of armed nationalism; nor had there been any experience of effective centralised control over armed movements.[3]

The institutional confusion was made worse by the continuing importance of the IRB. In independence struggles there are often severe problems relating to the existence of secret societies whose purpose and character are different to those of the public movements. In Ireland this was made more apparent by the long tradition of secret physical-force movements—both agrarian and political. The IRB organisation had an ambivalent and often divisive relationship with the Volunteers and the Sinn Féin party. The IRB continued, up to 1919, to claim to be the existing government of the Irish Republic and to demand the paramount loyalty of its members throughout the period up to the Treaty.

The ill-defined institutional relationships and the speed of the organisations' growth made for an increased importance for individuals: much depended on personal initiative and character. The leadership elite emerged very quickly and was, for the most part, a very youthful one. In 1914 Michael Collins was working in an office in London, and de Valera was teaching mathematics; five years later they were both internationally known figures. They owed their prominence to different, and potentially rival, power bases. While de Valera was the public leader in nationalist ranks, Collins held a dominant position in the Volunteer GHQ and the IRB. Many in the Volunteers and the IRB developed a keen personal loyalty to Collins, while Brugha and Austin Stack, for instance, became closely tied to de Valera.[4]

The advanced nationalist cause continued to flourish through 1917 and 1918, as demonstrated by the Sinn Féin triumph in the general election in December 1918, The abstention of the Labour Party, together with the Irish Parliamentary Party's failure to contest many seats, gave an exaggerated impression of the size and nature of that victory, impressive as it was. It was extremely unclear, however, what precisely people were voting for when they voted for the new party. Many Sinn Féiners admitted that the vote represented a criticism of the Irish Parliamentary Party and the failure of the British government to deliver on Home Rule, rather than an expression of enthusiasm for the republican idea. During the campaign there was no mention, naturally enough, of the need for military force to win independence. Collins said that the 1917 by-elections were 'not won on the policy of upholding a Republic, but on the challenge it made to the old Irish party', and admitted that the 'declaration of a Republic was really in advance of national thought'. Mary MacSwiney, the hardline Cork republican, declared that she felt the vote in 1918 was against the Parliamentary Party rather than for the Republic. Griffith affirmed that 'they elected us not as doctrinaire Republicans, but as men looking for freedom and independence'. Seán O'Faolain, the novelist and short story writer, wryly reviewing his own youthful idealism, concluded: 'The policy of Sinn Féin had always been since its foundation that simple formula: Freedom first; other things after.' At whatever cost to ideological coherence, unity had to be preserved and divisive issues avoided.[5]

2

The Anglo-Irish War,
January 1919–July 1921, and the
Truce Period

(a) THE POLITICAL ASPECT

AFTER the general election of December 1918 the Sinn Féin leadership immediately implemented the policy of abstention from the British House of
Commons, the establishment of the Dáil and republican government, and appeal
to the Paris Peace Conference. The limitations of that strategy, however, were soon
demonstrated. There was no possibility that the Peace Conference would agree to
consider the Irish case: it could only be concerned with territory directly relevant
to the world war, and other major powers were not to risk harming relations with
Britain by pressing the Irish cause publicly. The ministries of the Dáil government
developed slowly, and one consequence of abstention from Westminster was a
decline in publicity for Irish nationalist politicians.

While the Sinn Féin political cause lost momentum, the Volunteers, particularly in South Tipperary and Cork, took their own independent initiatives. It was
the small-scale and infrequent military actions against the RIC which led the
British government to ban the Dáil from meeting and to proscribe nationalist
organisations.[1]

As the war intensified during 1919 and 1920 the military part of the nationalist
movement came to dominate their political colleagues; this development was
assisted by Collins and the army leadership managing to evade arrest in May 1918,
when many of the political leaders were imprisoned. The IRB triumvirate of
Collins, Harry Boland and Diarmuid O'Hegarty appear to have controlled
nominations to the Dáil.

Key men held rank in both the military and political organisations, creating
confusion and dispute as to precisely where authority lay. Responsibilities
frequently overlapped, leaving considerable scope for tension between the leaders.
Collins, to quote the most important example, was Director of Organisation and of
Intelligence in the Volunteer GHQ; he was also Minister for Finance in the Dáil
government and the President of the Supreme Council of the IRB. Nominally,
Mulcahy, as Chief of Staff, and Brugha, as Minister for Defence, were Collins's
superiors in the army. Brugha, however, had little role in the day-to-day running of
military affairs. Colonel Charles F. Russell later declared of Collins: 'He was
everything', and Collins's reputation as the crucial figure during the war provoked
the considerable resentment of Brugha, and Stack, the Minister for Home Affairs.

The political leadership was to be far less prominent during the war than Collins. Griffith spent a part of the period in prison, and, despite his substituting for de Valera as Acting President of the Dáil government while de Valera was in the USA, he was not a key figure during the conflict. After de Valera escaped from Lincoln prison in March 1919, thanks to Collins's IRB contacts, he strenuously sought for a safe-conduct to enable him to present the Irish cause in Paris; when that failed he switched his diplomatic attentions to the USA and left for there in June 1919, smuggled across as a stowaway on a liner, again with the help of Collins's men. De Valera was not to return until December 1920.

In the United States de Valera raised considerable funds and spoke at an impressive number of hugely attended mass meetings in sundry cities and states. He inevitably failed in his major purpose of winning recognition for the Irish Republic from the United States government. The greatest importance of de Valera's stay in the United States, however, was that it removed him from Ireland for the majority of the Anglo-Irish War and revealed how ineffective his policy of political and diplomatic pressure proved in practice. While he was away Collins's dominance grew more apparent.[2]

The amount of success the Dáil government had in establishing its authority has often been exaggerated. The Dáil met infrequently and only with great difficulty; many of its members were unable to attend meetings because of imprisonment or participation in the war. The republican courts, frequently made out to be the government's success story, had great problems in functioning when the war intensified. A Home Affairs memorandum of August 1921 admitted that the death and arrests of justices meant that courts had fallen into abeyance in many areas. Kevin O'Higgins held that the useful work of the courts was limited to 1920, and Michael Collins said that courts in South Cork did not meet for eight or nine months. Collins's plans to collect taxes failed, as did his land annuity boycott idea. Admittedly the Irish military effort often prevented the British government from performing its duties, and elections installed Sinn Féin county councils. The effective working, however, of the Dáil government remained questionable—a matter for propaganda and later for historians keen to simplify a muddled situation.

The even partial exercise of civil government was only possible in many respects, and particularly that of the police, because of the army's initiative. Richard Mulcahy commented that 'It would be a disastrous thing if the country got the impression that the army was running the country.' Desmond FitzGerald, who held office in the republican government during the Anglo-Irish War, affirmed: 'In the late war against the British we had to put more or less unlimited powers into the hands of our soldiers.' As a direct consequence of the war, Sinn Féin Clubs declined dramatically; they met sporadically and were increasingly dominated by the IRA. William T. Cosgrave, the Minister for Local Government, spoke of 'the almost complete disappearance of the Sinn Féin organisation'. Ned Broy, one of Collins's key intelligence men, recollected: 'There was a time towards the end of 1918 coming into 1919 when the IRA were asked to join Sinn Féin Clubs so as we could elect army men who would move faster than Sinn Féin were doing. We had visualised that Sinn Féin were a very slow-moving organisation compared to the IRA.'

During the war there was increasing contempt shown by the military for politicians. In May 1919 Collins wrote to Stack: 'The position is intolerable—the policy now seems to be to squeeze out anyone who is tainted with strong fighting ideas.' Soon after he commented that

> We have too many of the bargaining type already. . . . It seems to me that official SF is inclined to be ever less militant and ever more political theoretical. . . . There is I suppose the . . . tendency of all Revolutionary movements to divide themselves up into their component parts.

No doubt with de Valera in mind, Collins stressed: 'The job will be to prevent eyes turning to Paris or New York as a substitute for London.' Collins was later frequently to berate Stack for the inefficiency of his department.

De Valera recollected in the Dáil that 'there had been a necessary clash between the civil and military sides' of the Dáil government and pointed out that civil government had been extremely difficult to run during the war. P. S. O'Hegarty, the future civil servant, maintained that Collins's department was the only one that functioned properly. Liam Lynch, the O/C of the 1st Southern Division, and Richard Mulcahy, from their different viewpoints, were convinced that the politicians had failed to give adequate support to the army. Lynch wrote:

> We must admit that all civil organisations, county councils, Sinn Féin Clubs and all other organised bodies were an absolute failure during the last phase of hostilities. If anything, they were a burden on the army—why even the civil government failed.

Mulcahy affirmed:

> No single Government Department has been the slightest assistance to the Army and some of them have been a serious drag. . . . The Army can no longer afford to dissipate any of its energy bolstering up Civil Government without getting a return in kind. The plain fact is that our civil services have simply played at governing a Republic, while the soldiers have not played at dying for it.[3]

The Dáil government attempted to assert control over the IRA during the war. Brugha, no doubt thinking of the implications for the IRB, got through the Dáil a resolution insisting that men in the army take an oath of loyalty to the Dáil government. Ernie O'Malley, however, recalling his time as O/C of the 2nd Southern Division, recorded his IRA colleague Séamus Robinson's opposition to the oath and had no recollection of taking it himself. On his return from the United States, de Valera stated that the Dáil took full responsibility for all military actions. That, however, was for public consumption at home and abroad. Politicians, as Darrell Figgis complained, remained in ignorance of military developments, although only in rare cases—that of Roger Sweetman, for example—did they publicly dissociate themselves from IRA activity.

During 1921 de Valera sought a change in tactics away from ambushes, which he felt were having a negative effect on international opinion, to the occasional larger confrontation with British forces. He apparently played a part in the planning of the dramatic but disastrous attack on the Custom House. De Valera's knowledge and views on military matters were derided by Collins and Mulcahy, and he had little contact with the army.[4]

(b) THE MILITARY ASPECT

The Anglo-Irish War has often been written about in terms of widespread arms raids, heroic captures of police barracks and dramatic ambushes. The war was, however, largely confined to a relatively small part of the twenty-six-county area, and the aims and achievements of the IRA were very limited.

At best the IRA achieved a military stalemate which prevented the British from administering the south and west. Collins wrote:

> We had prevented the enemy so far from defeating us. We had not, however, succeeded in getting the government entirely into our hands, and we had not succeeded in beating the British out of Ireland, militarily. We had un-questionably seriously interfered with their government, and we had prevented them from conquering us. That was the sum of our achievement. We had reached in July last the high-water mark of what we could do in the way of economic and military resistance. We had recognised our inability to beat the British out of Ireland.

Mulcahy declared, during the Dáil Treaty debates, that the IRA had not succeeded in driving the British from even a 'fairly good-sized police barracks'.

The war was part-time and episodic. Tony Woods, of Dublin No. 1 Brigade, commented: 'Between the scraps, it was an extraordinary unreal war, part-time civilians and youngsters, pitched against a real army.' The historian Frank Pakenham described it as 'an odd sort of war.... Each side ... made its own precedents and used all methods judged essential for victory, in so far as seemed expedient in view of world opinion and in so far as its own humanity permitted.' With Black and Tan reprisals in mind, the IRA's Assistant Chief of Staff commented: 'We have not beaten the English in spite of their being disciplined, but largely because they were not.' Seán Mac Eoin, the IRA leader in Longford, admitted that whatever the IRA had achieved had been by bluff and their intelligence system.

During 1921 British pressure, increasingly applied where it mattered in Munster, was making life extremely difficult for the IRA. Collins's intelligence system in Dublin and Britain had been broken up; Mulcahy confirmed that had it not been for the truce of July 1921, plans would have gone ahead for another Bloody Sunday to ease the pressure from British intelligence agents. The number of raids on police barracks greatly slowed down in the first half of 1921, following the police's retreat into larger town barracks from more isolated ones. The over-ambitious attack on the Custom House in late May 1921 greatly weakened the Dublin No. 1 Brigade of the IRA and demonstrated numerical and organisational weaknesses. Internment and imprisonment, often of key men, meant the IRA was probably down to an effective fighting force of around 2,000 by the time of the truce, when about 4,500 men had been interned and about 1,000 were serving prison sentences. The IRA's numbers had never been substantial; and the highly mobile flying columns used in the later stages of the war were much more effective than the old ineffective imitation of a regular army system.

The IRA's fighting potential was limited by a gross shortage of arms and ammunition, which had become chronic by the time of the truce. Hopes for large-scale arms landings from Italy and the United States during 1921 were not realised. Mulcahy declared in July 1921 that armament was 'approximately 3,000 rifles plus shotguns plus about 50 machine-guns of various kinds and very little ammunition'. Seán Ó Muirthile, a key figure in the IRB, recorded Collins saying that 'We had not an average of one round of ammunition for each weapon we had.' Though the IRA activist and historian Piaras Béaslaí's claim that Liam Lynch had informed GHQ that the south was unable to carry on the fight was contradicted by Florrie O'Donoghue, the old Cork IRA leader and writer, Mulcahy confirmed that Lynch's correspondence to him showed considerable anxiety on the arms and ammunition question.

In June Collins was warned of British plans for imposing martial law throughout the south and west and for greatly increased troop numbers. A truce for a secret, loosely organised force was fraught with problems, but was regarded as necessary by those in Dublin best placed to judge the overall position.[5]

To a great extent the Anglo-Irish War was a Munster and Dublin city affair. After Seán Mac Eoin's arrest and the consequent decline in military activity in his isolated stronghold of Co. Longford, Collins wrote: 'Cork will be fighting alone now.' Patrick Hogan, later the Free State Minister for Agriculture, claimed, no doubt with some exaggeration, that no shots were fired in the war in twenty of the twenty-six counties. There were frequent complaints from GHQ and the 1st Southern Division of the inactivity of sundry areas and the failure to take the pressure off the fighting areas. An tÓglach, the official organ of the IRA, when praising the war effort in Munster, commented on 1 March 1921:

> In other parts of the country...things are still very unsatisfactory. It effects no credit on the Volunteers in these districts that they should leave the gallant men of the South to bear all the brunt of the enemy's activities and thus help to make the military problem much simpler for the enemy.

A considerable proportion of Mulcahy's voluminous correspondence as Chief of Staff was taken up with his urgings for weaker areas to show more activity. Recruitment to the IRA in many areas was low, the effect, it seems, of unwillingness to serve and the revival of emigration in 1920. The active force was remarkably small, which later explained much of the bitterness revolving around those who joined in large numbers after the truce. Only in 1921 did GHQ send young organisers out to work on weaker regions. A teenage Seán MacBride was sent to Wicklow, Andy Cooney to Kerry, and Tod Andrews to Donegal.[6]

A large proportion of the west saw very little fighting, except at the end of the war. Ernie O'Malley commented, after a conversation with Michael Kilroy, a Mayo IRA leader: 'He always talks as if the West had been fighting all the time whereas it was April or May 1921 before a policeman was shot in West Mayo.' Mulcahy confirmed that Mayo only saw action from the spring of 1921. Tom Maguire, another Mayo leader, admitted: 'We had several ambushes at which nothing occurred.' In addition, Ned Moane, of the West Mayo IRA, commented that not a shot was fired in Connemara during the war. Galway saw very little activity, and Mulcahy was consistently critical of the failings of the IRA in Sligo and Roscommon.

The story of large-scale inactivity applied to much of the midlands and the area north of Dublin, together with the prosperous farming areas of Kildare, Carlow and Wicklow. Even more disappointing to GHQ were Kilkenny, Waterford and

Wexford. The Waterford IRA leader Pax Whelan commented: 'There were two Bde Staffs in East Waterford with bickering and robbery and nothing being done to fight the British.' Even within Munster, IRA size and effectiveness varied from area to area. West Clare was much less active than the rest of the county. Kerry, for all its fighting reputation, saw only patchy activity and much disorganisation and internal conflict within the IRA. Michael Fleming and Willie Mullins, of Kerry No. 1 Brigade, told Ernie O'Malley: 'In our area it was not until 1921 that fellows did act on their own . . . about attacking patrols or barracks. This shows that the area was very much behind hand.' John Joe Rice, O/C Kerry No. 2, related: 'I spent all my time tramping from one company to another, fixing disputes and squabbles.' Bertie Scully, of Kerry No. 1, pleaded that Kerry 'was actually tuned up to fight when the Truce came'.[7]

Remoteness and independence from Dublin were not useful attributes when it came to fighting the Anglo-Irish War (though they were in the Civil War). Distance from Dublin or other centres made organisation extremely difficult, particularly with communications affected by the war. Mulcahy constantly complained of the lack of reports from remote areas. What was happening in large areas of the west was often a matter of mystery, during both the Anglo-Irish War and the Civil War.

When western officers complained to Collins that they were receiving no arms they were brusquely told to achieve captures by their own initiative. Arms, however, as Florrie O'Donoghue pointed out, were much more difficult to capture in the later stages of the war than they had been early on, when the Munster brigades had made the majority of their captures. The reorganisation of the Volunteers in many parts of Munster in the two years following the Easter Rising placed them in a better position than elsewhere to show activity throughout the war. Geographical features of particular areas, as well as the existence or not of a fighting tradition, may well have contributed to the development of the IRA. J. J. Rice commented on the great differences between the 'glen' and 'flat' people in Kerry. The former had a rugged, independent fighting tradition, while the latter were much more likely to allow considerations of peace and prosperity to dominate.[8]

The nature of guerrilla warfare involved a great emphasis on localism and secrecy. Often areas knew little of what was happening elsewhere and had infrequent contact with GHQ. Central direction of military operations was minimal, although it increased somewhat during the war. The Volunteers had been reorganised after the Easter Rising in the localities; the formation of a GHQ in Dublin had followed those local initiatives. The drilling and hunger-strikes in Clare and raids on police barracks in West Cork were the inspiration of leaders like Michael Brennan and Liam Deasy. Ernie O'Malley wrote: 'GHQ issued general instructions, but our operations were our own.'

Centralised control was less likely because of the untrained character of the Volunteers, who in most cases elected their own officers and raised their funds by means of levies. Rice said that in his area in Kerry the brigade levy was at the rate of 2s 6d per cow, and he added: 'In Kenmare we took the PP's bullock for sermons he preached against us.' Among the GHQ staff only J. J. O'Connell and Emmet Dalton had experienced regular military training. Training only became a regular feature during the truce. Tod Andrews reminisced about his days in the Dublin

IRA: 'We had ... neither the facilities for training nor the inclination to discipline. I did not regard the IRA as an army in the accepted sense nor did I regard the struggle with the British Government as a war. It was terror and "tyranny tempered by assassination".' The historian David Fitzpatrick has written of the IRA in Clare that very few 'can remember the procedure by which they were appointed officers'. GHQ did not possess the wherewithal to pay local brigade officers and was wary of trying to exercise too much control. Mulcahy commented, in his convoluted style, on the problem of trying to direct guerrilla warfare:

> It has to be considered against weak area spots, lack of leadership spots, personal conflict at leadership level, local displeasure or grievance in relation to GHQ. The adequacy or otherwise of GHQ direction. . . . What more did local units expect in the provision of arms through GHQ? . . . At the general level I had to ask men to do less than might reasonably be expected lest I might frighten off the weak ones . . . I might cramp the initiative of the good ones.[9]

There was frequent criticism of GHQ for lack of support. O'Donoghue recorded that Liam Lynch's brigade 'did not get six or seven rifles from GHQ during the whole of the Tan War, notwithstanding that when it had reached a crisis in 1921, rifles were collected from the Dublin Brigade for the ostensible purpose of arming the Southern Brigades. They did not come to the 1st Southern Division.' Whatever direct contact there was between GHQ and the localities came by infrequent visits by local IRA leaders to Dublin. Cork Volunteer leaders resented that, until the truce, no GHQ representative visited them. While in Kerry, Andy Cooney said he gained 'a bad impression of GHQ who were not able to keep in touch with their areas'. Such contact, however, was extremely difficult to achieve.

The growth of guerrilla warfare was unplanned; it was the product of numerous local initiatives. The famous Soloheadbeg ambush, which began the guerrilla conflict, produced disapproval from GHQ—Mulcahy later describing it as tantamount to murder. In the war's early stages GHQ urged caution in military activities; An tÓglach only advised on the spread of guerrilla warfare tactics after they had become widespread in many areas. Decisions to stage ambushes or to attack police barracks had to be made on the spot. GHQ relevance was limited either to criticising the details of such activities or to making general comments on the lack of action in various areas.

The character of the conflict exacerbated divisions between the attitudes of GHQ in Dublin and the fighting men in the provinces. Cork column leaders, like Tom Barry and Seán Moylan, were quick to label their divisional O/C Liam Lynch and Mulcahy as 'pen-pushers' rather than fighters. The tensions were heightened by personal animosities which had a much greater effect than in a conventional army. Mulcahy had abrasive relations with the South Tipperary Brigade leadership and with Seán Hegarty in Cork No. 1 Brigade.[10] Despite his good personal relations with Collins and Mulcahy, Liam Lynch declared that in the Anglo-Irish War GHQ 'showed all-round inefficiency, and gave very little help to the country'. Mick Leahy, of Cork No. 1 Brigade, told Ernie O'Malley that '95% of the GHQ staff were a crowd of fossils'. From his differing perspective, Mulcahy stressed that Dublin should be the top priority in the war effort.

The lack of institutional control, whether political or military, together with the importance of local initiative in guerrilla warfare, meant there was a considerable reliance on local leadership. The military leader became the hero of his locality, the personification of Irish nationalism and often a force in local government. O'Malley wrote: 'Many of us could hardly see ourselves for the legends built up around us.'[11]

During 1921 GHQ sought to set up a divisional system, though it was established in only a few areas by the time of the truce. Divisionalisation was meant to improve communications between GHQ and the localities and to increase co-operation between the brigade areas. Mulcahy related that the British military pressure of early 1921 had driven GHQ to use divisions, and he admitted: 'In a field in which there were so many areas with individualistic feelings and certain personal rivalry, it took patience and time in getting the idea accepted and the men in command found.' It would have been surprising, as shown by the resistance of some brigades to the founding of the 1st Southern Division, if divisionalisation could have overcome local particularism and led to sharing of arms between areas.

Schisms within the IRA during the post-Treaty period became an extension and prolongation of the particularism, chaos and confusion. The stronger areas resented any GHQ or political attempt at control. The weaker regions were equally resentful of GHQ attitudes.[12]

(c) THE IRB

With the founding of the Dáil and the growth of the Volunteers, many argued that the IRB's usefulness was over; Ernest Blythe, who had been an IRB man and a TD and was subsequently a member of the Provisional Government, held the exaggerated opinion that it 'did little after 1916 except generate envy and suspicion among non-members'. The Easter Rising's failure had weakened the IRB, and former members, notably de Valera and Brugha, thought that the emphasis should be on public organisations. Brugha and de Valera held that the new government could only impose its authority over the military if IRB influence was ended. Brugha affirmed: 'As Minister of Defence it was my duty to safeguard the army from being directed and controlled by a secret society whilst it appeared nominally under my charge.' During the Anglo-Irish War the IRB changed its constitution to accommodate recognition of the Dáil government. Mulcahy, a member of the Supreme Council, recollected that after March 1918 the IRB issued no orders on military matters.

Many IRB circles met infrequently during the Anglo-Irish War, although there were regular meetings of the Supreme Council and executive. Given its organisation by cells, which increased local particularism and created enormous problems of communication, the IRB was always to be a shadowy organisation, and the Anglo-Irish War made this even more apparent. J. J. Rice recalled that, at a 1st Southern Division meeting, all those present were IRB members, but 'we looked upon it as a kind of secondary business of no real importance. It was or would only be of use if we had to go underground again. I don't think we had circles, or meetings even.' Many veterans of the war thought that regular army work reduced the secret society's importance.[13]

To a considerable extent Collins achieved his dominant position by using his control of IRB resources and contacts as a base for his intelligence and arms smuggling systems. Mulcahy testified that IRB men formed the core of the IRA's intelligence system, and Collins's notorious 'Squad', who acted on his own orders, were all IRB members. The organisation's sources in British and American ports controlled arms purchases and communications.

IRB influence varied greatly between areas. The large majority of Cork brigade officers were members, while the organisation seems to have had little influence in Tipperary and the west. In Munster there was a deliberate policy of recruiting key officers—Liam Deasy recalled that 'we put any man of importance in West Cork into the IRB'. In such areas, therefore, the movement was meant to act as a kind of revolutionary elite. While Florrie O'Donoghue, an important Munster IRB man, estimated that membership did not exceed five per cent of the IRA, he affirmed that the IRB's significance was less in its numerical strength than in 'the character, integrity and loyalty of its personnel, in the soundness of its water-tight organisation, and its genius for working inside and through other organisations'. IRB men dominated the IRA's GHQ staff; such control was much less easily achieved in the provinces.

Regional variations in IRB organisation and importance were reinforced by the movement's secrecy—provincial leaders in many cases did not know who leaders in other areas were and may not even have known that Collins was President of the Supreme Council at the time of the truce and Treaty. La Brady, a Leix IRB man, told Ernie O'Malley: 'You knew your own area and the men but nothing else in the IRB.' When Andy Cooney was sent down in 1921 from GHQ to straighten out a confused situation in the Kerry No. 1 Brigade he was given a frosty reception and was told, by one of the few men who spoke to him, that the key to understanding the Kerry IRA was in the IRB strength there. Cooney was not, however, at liberty, according to the IRB's constitution, to reveal his IRB membership outside his Dublin circle or to transfer his membership to Kerry.[14]

(d) THE TRUCE PERIOD

The Anglo-Irish truce, bringing an end to the war, was signed on 11 July 1921. It produced widespread rejoicing, but brought out many of the implicit tensions within the nationalist movement. Piaras Béaslaí wrote: 'At this time all the seeds of the later disorder and bloodshed were sown.'

The loose, ill-defined control of the nationalist movement had been apparent in the undercover negotiations with the British since late 1920. Father O'Flanagan, the Vice-President of Sinn Féin, became a target of strong criticism from Collins and others for conceding too much ground without consulting key figures in the Dáil cabinet in the informal negotiations of December 1920. At that time the situation was complicated by the absence of Griffith and de Valera. The British government were unsure who they should be negotiating with, as well as being concerned whether they could justify talking with gunmen. Mark Sturgis, a British official in Dublin, complained: 'If we want to talk to Ulster there's Craig or Carson, but when we want to talk to SF it's a heterogeneous "collection" of individuals who thanks largely to our own activities are not even collected.' By June 1921 it was clear, however, that negotiations could not begin without the compliance of both Collins and de Valera, the two critical figures.

The truce allowed opinion in the country at large, particularly the church and press, to express the desire for peace and compromise. Circumstances since the close of 1918 had prevented a whole range of voices from being heard. Sinn Féin was the single party represented in the Dáil. Ernie O'Malley recorded being reprimanded by Brugha for saying that 'we had never consulted the feelings of the people'. Brugha pointed out: 'If so, we would never have fired a shot. If we gave them a strong lead, they would follow.' Press and clerical condemnation of Volunteer atrocities were made the less important by the reaction to the excesses of the Black and Tans and Auxiliaries. Local and personal loyalties, together with the threat of intimidation, made it unlikely that the guerrilla warfare tactics were to be widely questioned. The Dáil, as de Valera admitted during the Treaty debates, represented only a part of opinion within the Twenty-Six Counties; its infrequent and ill-attended meetings went on in secret destinations unknown to the electorate. There was, furthermore, what the historian Charles Townshend has described as a strong Robespierrist tendency among Sinn Féin, which disposed the leadership to tell people what they should be thinking, rather than making any attempt to discover and represent what they actually were thinking. That is well illustrated by de Valera's famous comment during the Dáil Treaty debates: 'Whenever I wanted to know what the Irish people wanted I had only to examine my own heart and it told me straight off what the Irish people wanted.' De Valera, however, was more aware of popular attitudes than many of his colleagues were. After the truce it was much less easy for popular opinion to be ignored by the Sinn Féin leadership.[15]

The truce period greatly heightened problems of discipline and control in the army. *An tÓglach* admitted: 'The conditions produced by a prolonged period of truce in Ireland undoubtedly involve serious disadvantages ... in the case of an army such as ours.' Erskine Childers commented: 'Few of us perhaps realised the enervating effect of a long truce on a section of the army and on a war-weary people.' The army's leadership frequently commented on discipline problems resulting from the transition from secret, self-contained flying column activity to peacetime. Tom Barry estimated that there was 'at least a 30% deterioration in our effectiveness and our structure and our morale'. Mulcahy often reprimanded various brigade areas, and Lynch told Mulcahy: 'I assure you that ye at GHQ have not a full knowledge of what discredit the army is brought to in some areas. . . . At the moment we are dealing with such situations in East Waterford and North Kerry.'

Initially in many areas IRA men were fêted. Brighid Lyons Thornton, an old Cumann na mBan member, recalled: 'We were all happy and excited with the truce. We went mad. . . . It was like the Mardi Gras.' Problems however, soon emerged concerning the relationship between the army and the populace. During the war it was not sensible to complain about the commandeering of goods or compulsory levies by IRA order. When such activities continued during the truce they produced considerable opposition. Mulcahy persistently pointed out that compulsory levies should no longer be taken and warned of the consequences if the public was insensitively treated.

The IRA remained highly localised and part-time, although training camps were widely established and Mulcahy arranged a display of IRA strength in the Dublin hills for the benefit of the international press. The resources were still not available for the Volunteers to become a regular army. During the truce de Valera suggested to Collins that levies should be replaced by payment from Dáil government funds. Collins answered that it wasn't realistic—aware, no doubt, that de Valera's plan would have led to greater political control of the army. Michael Brennan, the O/C of the 1st Western Division and the dominant figure in both the Clare IRA and county council, reflected: 'While the army is so dependent on the good will of individuals we can never have proper efficiency.'[16]

Although the truce was generally obeyed, frequent maverick activities, which, particularly in South Tipperary, proved a major embarrassment to Collins during the Treaty negotiations, demonstrated how loose central control over the army remained. There was also increasing resentment of military interference in civil affairs.

The problem of army discipline and cohesiveness during the truce was made worse by the vast increase in IRA numbers. By the beginning of November 1921 nominal IRA strength was listed as 72,363, while at the end of the Anglo-Irish War Mulcahy had put the active IRA force at around 3,000 men, most of whom were in Munster. Many old flying column men resented the prevalence of those who came to be called 'trucileers', particularly those of them who were former British army men. Several were later to complain that no limitations were imposed on IRA membership.

Tensions within the IRA were also caused by differences of attitude to the truce and its prolongation. Men in the provinces had not been consulted about the end of hostilities. Many in the southern divisions admitted that a breathing-space would be useful, but thought there was no reason to end the fight. Mary MacSwiney wrote of the negotiations: 'Most of us looked upon them as a mere gaining of time for the Army. The men wanted a rest. They wanted Arms and Ammunition and the summer was a very bad time for our kind of fighting.' Tom Barry testified that the truce's announcement appeared like a bolt from the blue, and the impression that the truce was only temporary went uncontradicted by GHQ. Michael Brennan recalled that Collins, Mulcahy and Gearóid O'Sullivan of the GHQ staff 'emphasised that they didn't expect the Truce to last very long'.[17] IRA men were told to remain on a war footing and were encouraged by the considerable rise in arms importations. Dublin control, whether exercised through the political leadership or the GHQ, for many in the IRA remained shadowy. Meanwhile there was little for IRA men in the provinces to do. General Macready, Commander-in-Chief of British troops in Southern Ireland, commented: 'The rank and file of the IRA are losing popularity in many places owing to the fact that numbers of them have done no work since July 11th, but are billeted in good houses and practically live on the country.' IRA membership was a means of earning a living. Seán Moylan, an IRA leader in North Cork, bluntly declared in the Dáil on 26 April 1922:

> I am a gun-man. During the war, the British called me leader of a murder gang. These men have been out of employment, without a smoke . . . badly clad, and—we are not all pussy-footers—in want of a drink too. That is the fault of the men who told us that the Truce was a breathing stage.[18]

There was considerable uncertainty during the truce, however, how long employment in the IRA would last, and whether it could be reconciled to the re-establishment of civil government. The period of truce and negotiations saw great tensions between the political and military leadership of the nationalist movement. The truce gave Brugha and de Valera the opportunity to raise controversial issues relating to the control of the IRA, and particularly to Collins's and the IRB's role within it.

Before the truce Brugha had persistently complained about the methods by which the IRB had purchased arms in Scotland, hinting at corruption. The 'Scotch accounts' issue resulted in a meeting in early 1921 at which de Valera sought to restore harmony between the GHQ staff and the Minister for Defence. Mulcahy later related: 'I said that I felt I couldn't be any longer responsible for the morale or the esprit de corps or the safety of the Staff if Cathal was carrying on in the way in which he was carrying on.' Two other issues during the truce worsened relations. Brugha complained at being kept uninformed about the killing of Mrs Lindsay and her butler as spies by the IRA in Cork. Mulcahy and Collins, however, were as unaware of it as Brugha. Brugha also took up the question of Collins's intelligence unit's threats to a Mr Robbie who worked in the Yost Typewriting Company of Dublin. The issues, though representing the unco-ordinated and loosely approved character of much IRA activity, were most important in the role they played in bringing to a head tensions within the Sinn Féin leadership.

Brugha's letter to Mulcahy of 6 September demonstrated the personal bitterness involved. He wrote:

> Before you are very much older, my friend, I shall show you that I have as little intention of taking dictation from you as to how I should reprove inefficiency or negligence on the part of yourself or the D/I [Collins] as I have of allowing you to appoint a Deputy Chief of Staff of your own choosing.

He then reproved Mulcahy for 'inability to maintain harmony and discipline among the staff'.

When Mulcahy refused to obey Brugha's instructions Brugha called for his resignation. Mulcahy sent the correspondence to de Valera, and another peace meeting was held. Mulcahy stayed in office, but problems intensified, with Brugha insisting on the right of Austin Stack, his personal and ideological soulmate, to attend GHQ meetings. Stack was nominally Deputy Chief of Staff, having been appointed to that post in 1917, but he had played no part in military affairs during the war. Meanwhile Brugha used Liam Mellows, as Director of Purchases, to challenge Collins's control of arms sources. During the Treaty negotiations Brugha was thought to be encouraging arms purchases in Britain, which caused a considerable embarrassment for the Irish negotiators and was against the truce terms. Mulcahy and M. J. Costello (later the Free State army's Director of Intelligence) thought that Brugha was in touch with certain disaffected sections of the army which had poor relations with GHQ; notable among these was Brugha's and Stack's old friend Paddy Cahill, who had recently been sacked by GHQ as O/C Kerry No. 1 Brigade. During the Treaty negotiations Brugha told Mulcahy that GHQ had no role to play in them.[19]

The tensions culminated in de Valera's attempt to reorganise the army. At the Dáil cabinet meeting of 15 September 1921 de Valera proposed that the army 'be put on a regular basis'. The cabinet in late November affirmed: 'The supreme body directing the Army is the Cabinet. The immediate executive representative of the Government is the Minister of Defence who is, therefore, Administrative

Head of the Army. The M/D is a civilian.' All army appointments were to be sanctioned by the Minister for Defence, who was to have the power of nomination and veto.

New commissions were to be sent to all officers, and the oath to the Dáil was to be retaken. No changes were proposed among the GHQ and divisional staff, except for Eoin O'Duffy's replacement by Stack as Deputy Chief of Staff. These moves were made while Collins was taking part in the Treaty negotiations, and GHQ members were unconsulted before the commissions were issued. Collins scoffed that the business reminded him of Napoleon, while Mulcahy speedily demanded that de Valera meet the GHQ staff. To emphasise his desired relationship to the army, de Valera in November and December toured army units in the west with the Minister for Defence and the Chief of Staff.

The army reorganisation plan united GHQ and the regions in opposition to it. Liam Lynch refused his commission as O/C 1st Southern Division, and O'Duffy lost his temper at de Valera's meeting with GHQ members on the matter. The plan proved unsuccessful, although the Treaty's signing prevented the issue from coming to the test. O'Duffy remained in his post, and the oath was not re-administered.[20]

3

The Treaty Negotiations

(a) THE BACKGROUND

FOLLOWING hard upon the military truce, negotiations began between the British government and the Sinn Féin leadership, which lasted through many complex stages until the signing of the Anglo-Irish Treaty in the early hours of 6 December 1921. The decision to embark on talks, and the negotiations themselves, posed enormous problems for the cohesion of the Sinn Féin movement, and the circumstances surrounding the Treaty's signing brought all divisions to a head.

It was made clear during the negotiations that there could be no question of recognition of an Irish Republic. Irish membership of the Commonwealth and allegiance to the Crown at its head was a *sine qua non* of the talks.

To negotiate with any positive intention, the Sinn Féin leadership had to acknowledge that the war had not been, and could not be, won. De Valera warned of the plenipotentiaries' task: 'You are asking them to secure by negotiations what we are totally unable to secure by force of arms.'[1] The claims of the past could not easily be reconciled with the realities of the present. Many, however, who had been involved in the struggle for independence since 1916 proved extremely loath to recognise the need for the necessary accommodations.

The Sinn Féin leadership also had to come to terms during the negotiations with the existence of partition. While the Dáil government claimed to govern all thirty-two counties, the Government of Ireland Act of 1920 had established a separate Northern government. The Northern parliament met for the first time on 22 June. Talks between Sinn Féin and the British government only began—and this was not a coincidence—when the constitutional status of Northern Ireland had been established. During the negotiations the North's civil service was formed and its own security forces—the notorious Specials—had already been established. Mark Sturgis commented: 'My view [is] that the handing over on the 22nd to Ulster of many of the executive functions, including unfettered control of the "B" Specials Constabulary, makes Ulster the danger point after that date.'

There was never any possibility that the status of the Northern Ireland government would be altered by the talks. Physical coercion of the North had been ruled out publicly by both the British government and the Sinn Féin leadership; change could only come, therefore, through the consent of Craig's government. Towards the end of the Anglo-Irish War the British had arranged a secret, inconclusive meeting in Dublin between Craig and de Valera; once attempts to bring them together again failed, it was clear that the Six Counties could not be a party to the negotiations.

Craig did not object to any settlement between the South and Britain, as long as his own government's position was unaffected; he stressed to Lloyd George on 29 July that he regarded the 1920 act as a final settlement and that he would only negotiate with Sinn Féin if de Valera recognised the existence of the Northern government. He concluded that it 'cannot... be said that "Ulster blocks the way"'. Near the end of the Treaty conference Craig told his parliament that any settlement could in no way compromise or sacrifice Ulster's rights. The Northern Unionists had not wanted their own government in the first place, but once power had been devolved to them it was unthinkable that it should be surrendered to participation in an all-Ireland government.[2]

The Northern question played a strange, shadowy role during the talks. Many on the British side warned that it would prove the major problem in reaching any settlement, and members of the Dáil cabinet frequently reiterated their desire to make it the crunch issue. Once Northern refusal to co-operate in any concept of a united Ireland, however loose, was made explicit in early November, it was clear that either negotiations had to break down on the issue at the South's behest, or some means had to be found to evade it, thereby allowing other issues to be tackled. Before the negotiations began there was talk of local option and the potential exclusion of Tyrone and Fermanagh as means of compromise. Despite the melodramatic activity relating to the North during the negotiations, particularly at their end, the question was always likely to be avoided. For the British and Dáil governments the Northern issue was used as a bargaining counter during the talks, and was not regarded as a problem capable of being settled there and then.

The Sinn Féin leadership's stance on the Northern issue before the negotiations, and in their early stages, appeared to indicate no hope of compromise. When urging de Valera to begin talks with Lloyd George, Field-Marshal Smuts, the South African leader, despaired of the unreality of de Valera's views on the North. De Valera told Smuts: 'Unless the North-East come in on some reasonable basis no further progress can be made. An Ireland in fragments nobody cares about. A united Ireland alone can be happy or prosperous.' It was argued that the Northern question was a superficial one: agreement could be reached between loyalists and nationalists once the British presence was removed. De Valera told Lloyd George that the Ulster question

> must remain... for the Irish people themselves to settle. We cannot admit the right of the British Government to mutilate our country, either in its own interest or at the call of any section of our population. We do not contemplate the use of force. If your Government stands aside, we can effect a complete reconciliation.[3]

At an early meeting of the Anglo-Irish conference Griffith talked of granting safeguards to the loyalists, to encourage them to enter an all-Ireland parliament. George Gavan Duffy, a member of the Irish delegation, affirmed that if the British government stood aside, there would be no difficulty. Assuring the Sinn Féin representatives of his benevolent neutrality, Lloyd George pointed out that prospects of Ulster Unionist co-operation were considerably less likely than the Southern delegates appeared to believe. He reminded them of Gladstone's and Asquith's failure to achieve an Irish settlement, pointing out that

> They with the instinct of trained politicians saw that Ulster was the stumbling-block. They got the whole force of the opposition concentrated on

Ulster. Ulster was arming and would fight. We were powerless. It is no use ignoring facts however unpleasant they may be. The politician who thinks he can deal out abstract justice without reference to forces around him cannot govern. . . . The first axiom is whatever happened we could not coerce Ulster. . . . I am glad that De Valera has come to the conclusion . . . that force is not a weapon you can use. It would break in your hands. We should have a terrible civil war.

Lloyd George at another session concluded: 'We do not care in the slightest degree where Irishmen put Tyrone and Fermanagh, but it is no use making peace with you if we are going to have civil war with Ulster.'

Beneath the surface of public statements, however, there was an awareness among some of the Sinn Féin leadership of the barriers that Ulster loyalism provided to unity. De Valera's views on the North had grown markedly more pragmatic since his stay in the USA. In a speech to the Dáil on 22 August 1921 de Valera completely ruled out any thought of coercion on both practical and moral grounds. If there was to be any hope for unity, he argued, the north-east would have to be regarded as a special case. If the Republic were recognised, 'he would be in favour of giving each county power to vote itself out of the Republic if it so wished'. Characteristically Collins approached the issue bluntly, declaring:

What was the use of talking big phrases about not agreeing to the partition of our country? Surely we recognise that the North-East corner does exist, and surely our intention was that we should take such steps as would sooner or later lead to mutual understanding.

During the Dáil Treaty debates Ernest Blythe, one of the few Ulstermen in the assembly, argued that the ruling out of coercion made it impossible to achieve an 'absolutely united Ireland'.

The new pragmatic Sinn Féin Northern policy was also demonstrated by the appointment of a committee to advise the conference delegates on Unionist views and the means for accommodating them. They commissioned reports which made much of the reportedly progressive attitudes of Belfast businessmen to the prospect of an all-Ireland parliament, if only more tolerant attitudes—particularly the removal of the Belfast boycott—were shown by the South towards them. Erskine Childers, the most hardline of republicans on defence and constitutional status issues, was arguing for a flexible Northern policy. During the negotiations the Sinn Féin leadership talked of the need to provide strong safeguards for the North, amounting to federal status with considerable autonomy allowed.

The Sinn Féin change of attitude to the North had been arrived at too late. It was a last-minute adjustment to the demands of negotiations, and there was no attempt to spread such ideas through the rest of the movement. Despite public protestations of the overriding desire for unity, the Southern struggle for independence had taken place independent of the Northern question and, to some extent, at the expense of it. J. J. Walsh, a future member of the Free State government, argued during the Dáil Treaty debates that they had been striving for a Republic for only three-quarters of Ireland. The claim to have established an Irish Republic made Irish unity the less likely. The IRA in the North had been little supported; Mary MacSwiney was to bemoan the fact that so little opposition was offered to the establishment of the Northern parliament. The most effective way to have expressed opposition to the Government of Ireland Act's establishment of partition would have been through continued Southern participation in the Westminster parliament. Moreover, the cultural and economic philosophy of Sinn Féin, and particularly the application of the Belfast boycott, greatly reinforced the division between North and South. Emphasis on Gaelic revivalism, economic pro-tectionism and the Catholic Church was hardly likely to attract the Northern loyalist to membership in an all-Ireland parliament. In January 1922 Sandy Lindsay, from Balliol College, Oxford, told Mrs Childers that

> Absolutely everything that de Valera has said to the NE he has with the best intentions said the thing most calculated to put their backs up. I think that now you are preserving the unity of the South and West at the expense or making impossible or delaying for a long time the unity of the whole of Ireland.

Sinn Féin attitudes implied that they placed a stronger priority on independence for the twenty-six counties than on unity for the thirty-two counties: it was unlikely that they would, despite talk to the contrary, regard the Northern question as the make-or-break one during the negotiations.[4]

The British government were prepared to go far to satisfy Southern views on the North—the constitutional issue and not the unity one was the breaking-point for Lloyd George. Government and civil service attitudes had become progressively less sympathetic to Unionist attitudes. Lloyd George told his cabinet in early September: 'The feeling here for Ulster is not so strong as in 1913-14. Lots feel a bit annoyed about Ulster, think them unreasonable, narrow.' In contrast with the situation in the pre-war period, Ulster was not going to be backed beyond a certain point: the 1920 act was seen as satisfactory in preserving the loyalist position. Sir George Younger, the Conservative Party chairman, wrote: 'Any intractable attitude on the part of Ulster [would] be bitterly resented. . . . While there will be no coercion of Ulster if she disagrees, there is a strong feeling that she ought in the interests of the Empire and of Great Britain to make every reasonable concession to secure a settlement.' J. P. Croal, editor of *The Scotsman*, told Bonar Law on 11 November 1921 that there would be 'very little public support anywhere for sup-porting Ulster up to the hilt, especially after Sinn Féin had abandoned the Republic'. Craig was to complain that only Balfour, and to a lesser extent Churchill, were real friends to loyalist interest in the coalition cabinet.

With physical coercion ruled out, however, Lloyd George's power to deal with the Northern question was strictly limited. The moral and economic pressure which Lloyd George placed on Craig to join an all-Ireland parliament had to be applied carefully for fear of arousing Tory susceptibilities and adding to diehard support. Both the existence of the Northern government and the Tory majority within the coalition provided a veto on an All-Ireland settlement.

To negotiate effectively, Lloyd George had first to satisfy his own cabinet, and that consideration led to the placing of Churchill, Austen Chamberlain and Lord Birkenhead on the negotiating team. Up to mid-November Lloyd George was acutely concerned by the fear of plots against him. His worries focused particularly on what he regarded as Churchill's unreliability, and on the danger of opposition to any Irish settlement centring on Bonar Law, who had close contacts with Ulster Unionism. Austen Chamberlain told the Irish negotiators: 'You are not aware of the risks we are taking with our whole political future. We are bound to do it, as a coalition, but do not believe it is plain sailing.' Shortly after, when expressing his concern about truce violations, Lloyd George reminded them: 'We are taking great political risks. The life of the Government is put in issue by our proposals.... To end the feud is worth the risk of our political life, but these incidents will make it impossible.' C. P. Scott, the owner of the *Manchester Guardian*, stressed to Collins how hard Lloyd George had worked to bring the Tories into line during the conference. He wrote that Lloyd George 'alone of all the statesmen ... who had taken the Irish question in hand was in a position to "deliver the goods"'. When Collins replied that he could afford to think only of Ireland, Scott reminded him: 'You have got to think of our politics if you want to get anything done.'

At all costs Lloyd George wished to avoid the Northern question becoming the dominant issue during the negotiations: if that happened, it would imperil the unity and existence of the coalition government. The Prime Minister also warned of the dangers of appearing too inflexible with regard to the six north-eastern counties, and particularly over Tyrone and Fermanagh with their Catholic majorities. He wrote:

> If the Conference broke down on the determination of the Government to retain these two Counties within the area of the Northern Parliament, the issue thus raised would be one far less favourable to us than if the break came on the refusal to accept British Sovereignty and Empire. It would not be possible to unite public opinion in support of the maintenance of the two Counties within political Ulster, whereas loyalty to the Throne and the Empire would command universal acceptance.

All members of the coalition could agree on the offer of Dominion status with defence safeguards—that was not easily to be turned down by the Irish negotiators without alienating much sympathy, at home and abroad.[5]

(b) THE COURSE OF THE NEGOTIATIONS

De Valera took immediate personal control of the negotiations in July with his visit, together with other Sinn Féin leaders, to London, where he held private discussions with Lloyd George. De Valera realised that he had to prepare the Dáil for necessary compromise, making clear he was not a doctrinaire republican. He was to tell the Sinn Féin Ard-Fheis of October:

> The problem is to devise a scheme that will not detract from Irish freedom.... What may happen I am not able to judge, [but] you should realise the difficulties that are in the way, and the fact that the best people might legitimately differ on such a scheme. The worst thing that could happen would be that we should not be tolerant of honest differences of opinion.

De Valera saw himself back in the position he had taken up in 1917—the conciliator in nationalist ranks, the political strategist and diplomat who would, hopefully, unite all elements within the Dáil cabinet and find a formula to accommodate Irish republicanism to the prospect of necessary compromise.

De Valera's long absences and Collins's dominance during the Anglo-Irish War meant that de Valera was to find it difficult to assume a controlling role in nationalist ranks. During the early stages of the negotiations, however, de Valera ably preserved unity within both cabinet and Dáil.

De Valera's early talks with Lloyd George amounted to elaborate verbal sparring sessions—not surprisingly, given the character of the two participants. On 20 July the British government forwarded the offer of limited Dominion status for the Twenty-Six Counties, which the Dáil cabinet quickly turned down. Arthur Griffith, however, appears to have revealed strong interest in the terms.

There followed a prolonged correspondence between Lloyd George and de Valera. Between 21 July and 30 September fifteen telegrams and letters were exchanged which centred on the need to find some form of words on the identity of the Dáil government which would enable a full conference to begin. De Valera was unwilling to cede Irish sovereignty before the negotiations began, while the British government was loath to allow the conference to start on an unconditional basis.

Meanwhile de Valera warned the Dáil that any renewed war would be much harsher than the earlier fighting, involving something akin to a Sherman's March. Lloyd George, though he threatened the renewal of an intensified war, was convinced that de Valera was bluffing in rejecting the 20 July offer, and thought that Sinn Féin would be unwilling to break on the constitutional issues.

Eventually a form of bland words was concocted to enable the conference to take place. It was agreed that the conference should discuss 'how the association of Ireland with the community of nations known as the British Empire may best be reconciled with Irish national aspirations'. The first session of the conference was held on 11 October.[6]

It was very likely that any settlement would provide major problems for political and military unity. While strongly aware of the need to preserve unity in nationalist ranks, de Valera achieved precisely the opposite. The personal and institutional tensions existing before the truce were compounded by de Valera's choice of delegates. The Irish negotiators were appointed neither for their personal suitability nor for their potential effectiveness as a team. When choosing the delegation, de Valera kept in mind the need to appease the various elements within the Sinn Féin coalition. Griffith was chosen to represent the Sinn Féin constitutional approach, Collins the army and IRB, while Robert Barton and George Gavan Duffy, together with Erskine Childers as secretary, were meant to represent de Valera's interests and to act as a check on Griffith and Collins. Neither Barton nor Duffy were leading figures within Sinn Féin, and that also applied to Eamonn Duggan, who during the negotiations unfailingly supported Griffith and Collins. De Valera told Joe McGarrity, his close American supporter, that Duffy and Duggan were 'more legal padding'. The British delegation soon concentrated their attention on Griffith and Collins and formed a dismissive view of the remaining Irish negotiators.

From considerations of experience and negotiating ability—which were bound to be lacking in most of the Sinn Féin leadership—de Valera and Griffith were the obvious men to present the Irish case. The delegation's problems were to be compounded by Griffith's bad health which at times caused him virtually to hand over leadership to Collins. Collins admitted that his temperament and experience were completely unsuited to complex diplomatic manoeuvring: he often stressed that he had little patience with legal and constitutional niceties. Unity within the delegation could best have been achieved by de Valera undertaking its leadership. When de Valera announced his non-participation Cosgrave commented that it was equivalent to leaving your best player in reserve. At the Dáil cabinet meeting following the signing of the Treaty Barton put much of the blame for the division on de Valera's selection of delegates. He stated that they had not been 'a fighting delegation' and that they had been given no clear instructions. Art O'Brien, the Sinn Féin Representative in London, also usually sympathetic to de Valera, criticised the President for not attending the conference and not ensuring a more united delegation.[7]

De Valera's strategy led to clashes between the delegation and the remainder of the Dáil cabinet in Dublin. Sensibly de Valera had decided not to place Brugha and Collins on the same negotiating team, and in any case Brugha and Stack had refused to go. The chief representatives of hardline republicanism in the cabinet, therefore, remained at home with de Valera. Cosgrave was the only member of the cabinet staying in Dublin who was to prove a supporter of the Treaty.

De Valera was to argue that by staying at home he could prepare attitudes, particularly Brugha's and Stack's, for any compromises. He was to claim also that Griffith and Collins were appropriate men to win concessions from the British.

From Collins's perspective, however, de Valera appeared to be putting Griffith and himself forward as scapegoats. They were to have to make the compromises which would produce talk of apostasy and sellout. Collins wrote that he was doing what his cabinet colleagues 'knew must be done but had not the moral courage to do themselves'. Before the negotiations Collins's relations with de Valera had been far from close. They had clashed over de Valera's strange attempt to get Collins to go to the USA on a fund-raising tour soon after de Valera's return from there. Whether de Valera was resentful or jealous of Collins's dominant position within the nationalist movement is a less relevant, and less demonstrable, consideration than the different interests they represented. The decision to send Collins to the conference brought Collins's resentment and suspicion to a head. He protested strongly about his appointment—arguing, on the same lines as de Valera, that he should be held in reserve as the bedrock of republicanism at home. After being exposed to publicity during the conference Collins might be unable to retrieve the position he had held in the Anglo-Irish War.

It appeared that de Valera fully anticipated divisions within the delegation. When Gavan Duffy returned to Dublin to complain about Griffith's and Collins's secret sub-conference meetings with the leaders of the British delegation, de Valera took no action. De Valera's strategy was based on the delegation's promise that they would refer back any settlement to the Dublin cabinet for agreement before they signed it. The negotiators would be allowed to use whatever tactics they thought best because of their accountability to Dublin. Before the negotiations began de Valera told the Dáil that the Irish delegates should not be 'tied . . . hand and foot' by dogmatic instructions. There was, however, a crucial inconsistency between the pledge to refer back any settlement and the full plenipotentiary powers given the delegates. At the start of the Dáil Treaty debates de Valera admitted that the plenipotentiaries had not exceeded their powers by signing the Treaty without consulting Dublin first. It was to be difficult for de Valera to keep in adequate touch with the negotiations. Griffith obeyed instructions by frequently reporting to him, and Childers also was a regular correspondent. At key points in the negotiations, however, particularly when Griffith or Collins was closeted with Lloyd George, Birkenhead or Tom Jones (the Prime Minister's secretary), the rest of the delegation, and the Dublin cabinet, were often kept in ignorance of developments.[8]

Divisions amongst the delegation quickly became apparent once they arrived in London. Collins, surrounded by his IRB men, stayed in Cadogan Place, separate from the rest of the delegation in Hans Place. After a few plenary sessions Griffith and Collins requested sub-conferences eliminating other members of their delegation. The British were keen to agree—they had quickly become as suspicious of Childers's influence as Griffith was. Tom Jones commented on 26 October: 'I thought it important that the next British document ... should be shewn in advance to Griffith and Collins so as to secure as much agreement as possible before it gets into the hands of Childers.' Collins said during the negotiations: 'The advice and inspiration of C is like farmland under water—dead.' Childers transmitted to de Valera Barton's and Duffy's annoyance about being excluded, and his diary account of a discussion amongst the delegation of their draft defence proposal of 21 November gives a vivid flavour of the bad humour:

> A.G. [Griffith] attacks me about *Riddle of the Sands*—says I caused one European war and now want to cause another.... It is exactly like arguing with the British.... Bob [Barton] protests about Trade. I about Defence. A.G. insolent to me about secretary altering drafts. I protest and virtually threatened resignation. He climbs down.

Relations became tense also between the delegates in London and the rest of the cabinet in Dublin. Griffith and Collins often complained that their major problem was not with the British negotiators but with Dublin. Their feelings were intensified by their accurate suspicions that Childers was privately relaying his account of developments to de Valera. Collins wrote to John O'Kane, a London friend: 'From Dublin I don't know whether we're being instructed or confused. The latter I would say'; and he commented additionally: 'Not much achieved. Principally because PM recognises our overriding difficulty—Dublin, plays on that.' Soon Griffith was telling Collins: 'We stand or fall in this together.' Collins's frustration went further than complaints of confused instructions and interference from Dublin. He again confided in O'Kane, referring obliquely to de Valera: 'I was warned more times that I can recall about the ONE. And when I was caught for this delegation my immediate thought was of how easily I walked into the preparations. But having walked in I had to stay.' Collins told Barton that he had been sent to London in 'an attempt to manoeuvre him into an impossible position where he would be if there was a breakdown'.[9]

Soon after the start of the conference all the Irish delegates complained of de Valera's interference. On two occasions—a telegram to the Pope complaining about a message from George V to the Pope, and a letter to the delegation which firmly ruled out any possibility of any settlement involving allegiance to the Crown—de Valera had acted independently. On the second issue Collins had threatened to abandon the delegation, and Griffith sent a strong protest to de Valera insisting on their powers as plenipotentiaries. Relations were worsened by the lack of definite instructions given. Much to Griffith's embarrassment, for instance, he had to argue the case on the North at the start of the conference before the policy on that issue had been drawn up.

De Valera sought to achieve unity within Sinn Féin and a reconciliation of Irish and British constitutional demands by his External Association policy. He had slowly formulated the notion of accepting membership of the Commonwealth, and the British Crown's position at its head, only in regard to external affairs: Irish sovereignty would be preserved in domestic affairs. As shown by the subsequent evolution of the Commonwealth—and particularly the Statute of Westminster of 1931—the idea had considerable coherence and attraction. In the political and ideological climate of 1921 it had no hope of success. Dominion status was the ultimate of British concessions.

External Association had considerable limitations also as a means of unifying the Sinn Féin movement. It was not easily understood: the Republic was far easier to relate to, and far more attractive than the notion of the externally related Dominion. Before and after the Treaty de Valera's brainchild proved unpopular with hardline republicans, to whom there could be 'no other law'. De Valera regarded Brugha's acceptance of External Association as justification for his decision not to attend the conference; Brugha assented, however, more out of loyalty to de Valera than from conviction.[10]

All the Irish delegation in London—some with more conviction than others—were prepared to submit External Association to the British, but Griffith and Collins were fully aware of the British refusal to move beyond Dominion status. De Valera's choice of delegates and his External Association negotiating stand were to fail badly, and this placed him in an extremely awkward position at the end of the negotiations when a compromise was achieved but not the one he desired.

It soon became apparent during the conference that the constitutional status and Northern issues would cause the most concern. The defence issue took up a considerable proportion of the time at the start of the talks but played little role in the crucial parts of the conference. British complaints of truce-breaking, compulsory IRA levies and the continued sitting of republican courts proved of considerable embarrassment, particularly to Collins, but Lloyd George's threats to end the conference on these matters should not be taken at face value. Fiscal and economic issues figured little: the crucial concessions on them were made at the very end.[11]

After two weeks of the conference no progress had been made on the key issues, and Lloyd George was soon to be faced with a vote in the House of Commons on a diehard resolution critical of the negotiations, and also with the possibility of being placed in an embarrassing position by the forthcoming Liverpool conference of the National Conservative Association. The Prime Minister was aware that the Irish delegation would only show flexibility on the constitutional issues if there was progress on the Northern issue; that, however, would bring Lloyd George up against the rock of Ulster loyalist intransigence.

To enable the conference to proceed, Lloyd George resorted to tactical manoeuvres, well suiting his talents. He turned the difficulties he faced to his advantage by playing the one set of circumstances off against the others. Thus by stressing his problems with the Northern loyalists and the Conservative Party, he strove to wring concessions out of Griffith and Collins. It was pointed out to them that Irish concessions on Dominion status would enable Lloyd George not only to put more pressure on Craig to join an all-Ireland parliament but also to gain support for his efforts in cabinet and Commons. When Griffith proved flexible, potential Tory opponents of an Irish settlement were told of the reasonableness of the Irish stance. In turn, Craig, under acute pressure from Lloyd George, was told that by agreeing to come into an all-Ireland parliament he would facilitate a speedy end to the conference. If the conference broke up, the implication was that it would be Craig's responsibility.

Lloyd George's pressure was first applied on Griffith and Collins. At meetings in late October they were told that if they would give reassurances on constitutional issues, it would enable Lloyd George 'to smite the Die-hards' and he 'would fight on the Ulster matter to secure essential unity'. Griffith's positive answer gave Lloyd George what he regarded as the necessary leverage for dealing with the diehards in the Commons and with Craig. While Lloyd George greatly exaggerated his domestic difficulties for the purpose of impressing Griffith, Griffith's assurances did impress Chamberlain and Birkenhead and eased progress within the conference. The problem of winning concessions from Craig, however, proved insurmountable.[12]

Craig was called to London, and the advantages of Northern membership in an all-Ireland parliament were forcefully put to him. Initially Craig seems to have shown some flexibility, but on return to Belfast took the hardest of lines, going so far as to claim Dominion status for the Six Counties. In a memorandum to the Northern Ireland government the British government argued that Dominion status for all Ireland would mean a loyal South and that the powers of the Northern government would remain the same. It was stressed that civil war was the likely consequence if the North did not follow this advice and that the financial consequences for the North would be alarming. When Craig rejected the offer on 11 November his government reached a nadir of unpopularity with British politicians.[13]

Up to that point in the complex manoeuvring the Sinn Féin tactics of making a priority of the Northern issue appeared to be working: it seemed that any break in the negotiations would be the North's responsibility. Griffith reported to de Valera:

> If 'Ulster' proves unreasonable they [the British government] are prepared to resign rather than use force against us. In such an event no English Government is capable of formation of a war-policy against Ireland. The tactical course I have followed has been a to throw the question of Ulster against the questions of Association and the Crown. . . . The British Government is up against Ulster and we, for the moment, are standing aside.

Griffith assured de Valera that he had not compromised on External Association, and de Valera expressed satisfaction at the developments. After Craig's final refusal Griffith triumphantly reported: 'The "Ulster" crowd are in the pit they digged for us, and if we keep them there, we'll have England and the Dominions out against them in the next week or two.' Correct about the Northern government's unpopularity at Westminster, Griffith was over-optimistic about the Southern position in the negotiations.

Northern intransigence was preventing any attainment of the 'essential unity'

Griffith was seeking. Some other means had to be found to secure progress, and Lloyd George's attention switched back from Craig to Griffith. Even before Craig's refusal, Jones, at Lloyd George's behest, was sounding Griffith out about the possibility of a Boundary Commission which at some undefined time after an Anglo-Irish settlement would modify the border. Jones told Griffith and Collins that non-acceptance of the commission idea would bring about the breakdown of the conference and the end of the coalition government, which would very probably result in a government headed by Bonar Law. Griffith related: 'We said that it would be their proposal—not ours, and we would not, therefore, be bound by it but we realised its value as a tactical manoeuvre and if Mr Lloyd George made it we would not queer his position.' Lloyd George wanted something firmer than that and extracted a written promise that Griffith would not obstruct the tactic.

Though Griffith had been cautious in his dealings with Lloyd George, the Prime Minister had outmanoeuvred him. Lloyd George plausibly commented: 'We are after a settlement—that was our objective. Not out for manoeuvring.' Griffith's agreement to the Boundary Commission made it impossible for him, and hence the rest of the Irish delegation, to break on the Northern question. Lloyd George had succeeded in removing the North as the logjam issue and had reassured himself on Tory support, in the coalition government and in the Commons, for a prospective settlement. Chamberlain's and Birkenhead's strong support of Lloyd George helped considerably to nullify potential opposition at the Liverpool conference—they had been impressed by Griffith's concilatory attitude. Lloyd George had exaggerated the threats to the coalition to win the further concessions from Griffith. It appears that Lloyd George had hopes of getting Craig to agree to an all-Ireland parliament, and was genuinely annoyed by Northern loyalist attitudes. He was very happy, however, to settle for second best in the form of Southern agreement to the Boundary Commission, the more so because Griffith failed to force him to define it more clearly. From a longer perspective, however, the real beneficiaries of these developments were the Northern government. They had called Lloyd George's bluff, which Griffith had singularly failed to do.

The agreement over the Boundary Commission had been made only with Griffith, who had not kept either the other members of the delegation or the Dáil cabinet informed. This proved the most important example of the Irish delegation's failure to cohere. Meanwhile the negotiations carried on as if nothing had changed on the crucial issues. Lloyd George, however, could proceed with much more confidence.[14]

On 22 November the Irish delegation, in response to a draft British treaty, drew up a memorandum along the lines of External Association. The Northern question was put to the side—the Irish delegates (apart from Griffith), like the Dáil cabinet members in Dublin, remaining under the impression that it could be used again as the crucial issue at the end of the conference. In response to the Irish demands, Lloyd George talked in terms of the collapse of the negotiations, but again was reassured by personal contact with Griffith and Collins. Attention centred on whether there could be any reconciliation between Dominion status and External Association. In answer to the argument that Ireland, with its history and its geographical closeness to Britain, could not possess in practice the independence of other Dominions, the British delegation suggested the Canadian status clause, which explicitly related Irish constitutional status to that of the rest of the Dominions.

It had become clear to Lloyd George that the major difficulty was to get the rest of the Irish delegation to support the assurances Griffith had given on constitutional issues and the Boundary Commission, and to prevent Dublin influences from hardening the delegation's position. Childers's diaries tell of the irate refusal of Barton, Duffy and Childers to allow Griffith to agree to allegiance to the Crown. A British cabinet meeting on 5 December concluded that 'There were indications that the division of opinion which had manifested itself among the Irish Representatives in London, also existed in the Irish Cabinet.' The British delegation was fully aware of the divisions within Sinn Féin; this goes a long way to explaining Lloyd George's tactics at the end of the conference, and why he would not allow the Treaty to be referred to Dublin.

From late November Lloyd George strove to bring matters to a head. On 30 November he forwarded to the Irish delegation what he described as final terms. Originally his idea had been to submit the terms to Craig at the same time, but Griffith and Collins persuaded him to give them a first look at the document, which would enable them to consult the Dublin cabinet.[15]

On the first weekend of December the Irish delegation returned to Dublin with the draft treaty—the first time since the beginning of the negotiations that all the delegates and the Dáil cabinet had met together. In a confused meeting all tensions surfaced.

At the start of the meeting discussion centred on whether the terms offered were the most that could be won. Griffith, Duggan and, to a lesser extent, Collins thought that the British would not concede more, while Duffy, Childers and Barton argued that major concessions could still be achieved. Griffith stated his willingness to accept recognition of the Crown, while de Valera stressed his opposition to any form of allegiance. De Valera implied, however, that with amendments on the constitutional issue, a settlement might still be possible. The meeting was considerably soured when Brugha attacked the way that the negotiations had been conducted in sub-conferences and commented that the British had picked the weakest men in the delegation for that purpose. Griffith rose quickly to the bait, demanding a withdrawal of the allegation.

Brugha shrewdly argued that a split within the cabinet on the treaty terms would quickly polarise the country. It was considered whether de Valera should attend the conference at that late stage. This was ruled out when Griffith pledged that the delegation would come to no final decision before consulting again with the Dublin cabinet. The meeting ended with considerable confusion as to whether de Valera's suggestion of a substitute oath meant that External Association should be tried again on their return. Collins, after the meeting, complained to Tom Cullen, a member of his old 'Squad', that he didn't know where he stood. Crucially there was no discussion on what the delegation's tactics should be if Lloyd George refused them time to consult their Dublin colleagues before signing the Treaty, and if he threatened war. Ernest Blythe later argued during the Dáil Treaty debates that the delegation had been totally unprepared for the threat of war. No substitute Northern clause to the British one was offered, although it was stressed yet again that the delegation should press the Northern question and use it to break on if necessary. The lack of any reference to Ulster in the Irish reply to the draft treaty further convinced Lloyd George that the Northern question would not prevent a final settlement.[16]

The embittered and inconclusive cabinet meeting made the Irish negotiators even less of a 'fighting delegation' than they had been before. No agreed document had come out of the meeting to set against the draft treaty. The Irish side was ill-prepared for Lloyd George's final assault. Griffith, Duggan and Collins did not travel with the other delegates, returning to London by a separate boat and train. Collins refused to go with the rest of the delegation to present External Association terms to the British; Griffith did go, though with extreme reluctance. Jones accurately reported to the British delegation that Collins was '"fed up" with the muddle'. At the meeting Griffith went through the motions of arguing a case he knew had no hope of succeeding, and discussion was abruptly terminated when Duffy blurted out that their problem was in coming into the Empire. Although the British delegates at that time were talking in terms of dark despair, recourse was immediately taken to personal negotiations with Griffith and Collins. The British concluded from Collins's absence from the abortive session that he could see no point in putting forward External Association again.

At 1.30 a.m. on 5 December Jones met Griffith. He reported afterwards to Lloyd George that Griffith and Collins

> had been completely won over to belief in your desire for peace and recognised that you had gone far in your efforts to secure it. . . . This belief was not shared by their Dublin colleagues and they had failed to bring them all the way, but were convinced they could be brought further. In Dublin there is still much distrust and fear that if the 'Treaty' is signed they will be 'sold'.

If only, Griffith argued, some agreement could be won from Craig to 'a conditional recognition, however shadowy, of Irish national unity', a settlement would be generally accepted in the Dáil. After that, with Griffith's backing, it was decided that Lloyd George should see Collins. If Collins would agree to British terms, the conference could still be brought to a positive conclusion.

Collins was reluctant to meet Lloyd George and, uncharacteristically, arrived late. Lloyd George was at his most conciliatory, confirming, it seems—from Collins's account—Collins's hopes that the Boundary Commission would cede to the South the entire counties of Tyrone and Fermanagh and parts of Down and Armagh and would lead, by force of economic circumstances, to the end of the Northern government. Lloyd George also showed a willingness to be flexible over the wording of the oath—an issue Collins had been working on with the IRB Supreme Council. Whether these assurances led to Collins's decision to accept the Treaty is unclear; Lloyd George could feel, however, more encouraged about Collins's attitude.

By 5 December, the last day of the conference, Lloyd George had every confidence that Griffith would sign the Treaty, and he also had reason to be optimistic about Collins's and Duggan's attitude. The problem was Barton's and Duffy's likely opposition, and that of the remainder of the Dáil cabinet in Dublin. This background explains Lloyd George's insistence that the Treaty be signed there and then, without prior consultation with Dublin.[17]

When the delegations met on 5 December Lloyd George stressed that all the Irish delegates had to sign. He held out the additional carrot of fiscal autonomy.

When Griffith pressed the Northern question Lloyd George—much to the amazement of the rest of the Irish delegation—raised Griffith's earlier undertaking regarding the Boundary Commission. The question of personal honour stopped Griffith in his tracks. Finally, in the most melodramatic moment in modern Anglo-Irish relations, the Prime Minister held up two letters, one of which was to be sent post-haste to Craig. One contained news of the Southern Irish acceptance of the Treaty terms, the other reported the rejection of those terms. The delegates were given two hours to decide. The alternative to their acceptance was laid down as renewed war.

The Sinn Féin delegation returned to Hans Place. It was in the taxi then that Collins told Barton of his intention to sign; up to then the rest of the delegation had been unaware of Collins's attitude. At the tense meeting which followed Barton became the key figure. He, unlike Duffy, was a member of the Dáil cabinet, and thus the pressure built up on him. Barton went into conclave outside the room with his cousin Childers, who reminded him of what Mrs Childers would think of Barton giving way. Barton went back to join the delegation and announced his reluctant decision to sign. Duffy followed Barton's lead. The delegation returned to Downing Street, and, with a few minor adjustments, the Treaty was signed. For the first time in the conference the British delegates shook hands with their Irish counterparts. The Irish, however, could hardly have felt like shaking hands with each other.[18]

Argument since has centred on two issues: whether Lloyd George was in earnest about the threat of war, and why the Irish delegates failed to call his bluff, and test his sincerity, by insisting on their right to refer the Treaty to Dublin before deciding whether to sign. Was it a question of the wiliest of political schemers out-witting confused and disunited opponents?

Lloyd George's threat of war was a tactical ploy, a means by which to place intolerable stress on Barton and Duffy. If they did not sign—as both Lloyd George and Griffith pointed out during the final meeting—they personally would be responsible for the consequences. Griffith and Collins surely knew that Lloyd George was bluffing on the war question. Earlier in the negotiations Collins commented: 'No need at all to be excited as . . . they will not return to war with any haste.' The Prime Minister had assured Collins of his willingness to allow the Treaty to be considered in Dublin before signing, and had intended, they knew, to inform Craig of the Treaty's contents then. Soon after the Treaty's signing Mark Sturgis commented: 'The terms accepted are . . . little different to the terms rejected [in July], and it was a big bluff up to the last minute with even the faithful Andy [Cope] sucked in.' The *Daily Chronicle*, which represented Lloyd George's views, argued that a breakdown at the conference would be followed not by war but by more negotiations.

With a view to the opposition to be surely encountered again in the Dublin cabinet, Griffith and Collins thought it best to sign first and face the consequences. They were convinced that they had achieved as much as they could have at the conference, and that a settlement would receive general support in Ireland; they were much less sure, however, about the Dáil and army. Before the Treaty's signing Collins had been at pains to square the IRB Supreme Council by getting them to agree to an amended oath. It appears that Griffith and Collins agreed with Lloyd George that the time was opportune for the issue to be forced. For his part,

Lloyd George did not allow the Treaty to be referred to Dublin because he was aware of the consequences if he did—more opposition, and an intolerable prolongation of already repetitive talks.

A discussion between Collins and Griffith during the conference gives support for this interpretation. Collins said to Griffith:

> How best to reconcile our ideas with the fixed ideas at present held by certain members of the Cabinet? I will not agree to anything which threatens to plunge the people of Ireland into a war—not without their authority. Still less do I agree to being dictated to by those not embroiled in these negotiations.

Griffith replied:

> It is not so much a question of whom dictating to whom. It is a question of the powers invested in us as representatives of our country. . . . Sooner or later a decision will have to be made . . . and we shall have to make it whatever our position and our authority.

Barton wrote: 'By the time the crisis came with the final decision to sign or refuse, Griffith and Collins had already made up their minds. . . . It is unlikely that they were prepared to accept authoritative advice.' Griffith and Collins, Barton continued, 'where prone to stress the fact that we were plenipotentiaries and would possibly have resented the idea that they should appeal for direction'. That direction, however, as events had shown, was singularly unforthcoming. Collins, Griffith and Duggan probably did not insist on first referring the Treaty to Dublin and failed to communicate by phone with their colleagues because they had no wish to do so. It is surprising, however, that Duffy, Barton or Childers did not suggest the use of a phone during the final hours.

Despite the intense melodrama of 5 December, events then had only confirmed realities that had long been apparent. If there was to be a settlement, the Northern issue had to be pushed to the side, and there was no possibility that the British delegation would allow an advance on Dominion status. Lloyd George's tactics—devious as they were—had allowed a positive conclusion on terms as good as could be offered in the circumstances of that time.

British reaction to the Treaty was jubilant. Apart from the diehard chorus of the *Morning Post*, the press was universally favourable. The political neutralisation, in a British context, of the Irish question was Lloyd George's great achievement at the conference. Overwhelmingly the Conservative Party accepted the Treaty; it was Austen Chamberlain who was to defend it from Craig's attacks. The Treaty gave new life to the coalition. Ireland had done much to weaken Lloyd George's reputation in the post-war years; it now represented his greatest coup. Tom Jones commented: 'This was the one topic on which the Liberals could criticise our Coalition policy—our Irish policy, and here we've got rid of it.' When the coalition eventually broke up in the autumn of 1922 the new Conservative and Unionist government accepted the bill establishing the Irish Free State government.[19]

4

The Treaty Split

THE Treaty was only approved in the Dáil after a bitter and prolonged three-week debate. By that time, and exacerbated by the Dáil Treaty debates, political and military divisions had emerged which endangered the Treaty's prospects. Each nationalist institution—the Dáil cabinet, the Dáil, the Sinn Féin party, the IRA and the IRB—split on the Treaty question. Florrie O'Donoghue commented: 'National unity was broken at the top. No power under heaven could prevent the split from spreading downwards.'[1] Both leaders and institutions were to prove unable to avert the breakup of nationalist unity.

(a) THE POLITICAL REACTION TO THE TREATY

The circumstances of the Treaty's signing ensured that there would be a political split. After the cabinet meeting of 3-4 December de Valera resumed his inspection tour of military units in the west, implying that he felt no immediate developments were in the offing. Initially, when hearing that agreement had been reached in London, de Valera took it that External Association had been achieved; on being shown the terms, however, he was aghast and talked of being insulted by the failure to consult. Clearly de Valera had been caught by surprise; and his strategy of preserving unity in Sinn Féin ranks had been ruined. His reaction was a slow and confused one which, as he and other anti-Treatyites were to admit, helped to yield the initiative to the wave of pro-Treaty opinion which very quickly made itself heard.

The cabinet meeting which immediately followed the delegation's return concentrated on the way in which the Treaty had been signed without the cabinet's authority. It took Cosgrave's urgings for de Valera to agree to hear the delegation's account of what had happened. Griffith's and Barton's arguments that they had only signed under conditions of extreme duress did not allay de Valera's, Stack's and Brugha's feelings that their trust had been abused.[2]

There was much talk of the need for the political and military opposition to the Treaty to assert itself immediately. It was argued that de Valera should sack the members of the cabinet returning from London, or, more drastically, that the delegates should be arrested on their return. De Valera showed sympathy with such arguments, but argued that they would not be wise options to take: agreement to such courses of action would have been entirely out of character. In a letter to Joe McGarrity, de Valera wrote: 'I have been tempted several times to take drastic action, as I would be entitled to legally, but then the army is divided and the people wouldn't stand for it, and nobody but the enemy would win if I took it.'

De Valera had hopes of there being a majority in the cabinet, and then in the Dáil, to oppose the Treaty, which would make it necessary to renegotiate. He seems to have expected that Cosgrave would oppose the Treaty—Cosgrave had expressed his opposition to the oath in the original draft treaty. Cosgrave's vote in favour proved decisive in the Dáil cabinet. De Valera then publicly declared his firm opposition to the Treaty. The political issue of the Treaty's acceptance or rejection was left to the Dáil.[3]

The Treaty's signing was the decisive event which led to the Civil War. No document could have more effectively brought out into the open divisions in the philosophy and leadership of the Sinn Féin movement. If it had offered a little more or a little less, it may well have unified opinion for or against it. Moreover, the terms demonstrated profound differences of attitude between general opinion within the Twenty-Six Counties and the political and military leadership of the nationalist movement. The ensuing developments fully revealed the lack of effective relations between the various nationalist institutions which prevented any controlled, disciplined response to the Treaty.

Popular support for the Treaty extended throughout the Twenty-Six Counties, although it was much stronger in the more prosperous east than in the west. Only one newspaper in the whole country declared itself anti-Treaty. The *Cork Examiner* on 28 December asserted: 'The flowing tide in favour of ratification of the Peace Treaty is submerging all opposition in its course.' Similarly, the *Irish Times* on 9 December affirmed: 'The whole Nationalist Press and, as we believe, the vast majority of Southern Irishmen have accepted it with joy.... Now Mr de Valera steps between Ireland and her hopes.' A total of 328 statutory public bodies declared themselves by 5 January in favour of the Treaty's terms; only five declared against. The chorus of approval also applied to labour organisations, Chambers of Commerce and farmers' organisations. Church leaders were enthusiastically pro-Treaty. Bishop Fogarty of Killaloe wrote to Childers: 'The Peace Treaty to my mind is marvellous.... I congratulate you all.' The Archbishop of Cashel declared: 'The people of Ireland, by a vast majority, are in favour of the Treaty, and in a democratic country the will of the people is the final court of appeal.' The election results of June 1922 were to demonstrate a considerable pro-Treaty majority, although the ninety-five per cent in favour talked about in the Dáil debates by Arthur Griffith and others was a considerable exaggeration.[4]

The popular support for the Treaty, however, was somewhat ambivalent. There was clearly a great desire for peace and normality and a strong feeling that the terms offered were the best that could be expected. There was, though, little enthusiasm expressed, and deep reservations were felt about the constitutional and Northern issues. General Macready reported to the British cabinet that there was little 'outright enthusiasm'. A university student, Celia Shaw, recorded in her diary: 'We heard tonight Ireland is a Free State and every English soldier to be out of Ireland in 6 months.... Not a flag, not a bonfire, not a hurrah.' Acceptance of the Treaty was a practical matter—the other option was far worse. The *Kilkenny People* commented that the 'alternative to ... Self-Determination is ... Self-Extermination', and Dr MacRory, Bishop of Down and Connor, said: 'I do not think that it is possible for us to get anything better at present, and I think there is no dishonour in bowing before the facts and accepting the better when the best is unattainable.'

The Treaty's fate, however, was to be decided not by popular will but by organ-isations—military and political—which did not have a close, clearly defined relationship with the huge majority of the Irish population. Michael Collins commented to his fiancée about the Treaty's prospects: 'The country is certainly quite clearly for it but that seems to be little good, as their voices are not heard.' A report for the British cabinet commented on 'the almost universal desire for peace on the part of the Southern Irish people', but thought there would be no prospect of the people's will 'overriding the decision of their elected representatives'.

The Dáil was an unsatisfactory assembly to decide on the Treaty's fate. TDs had been chosen from Sinn Féin and IRA activists; many interests, labour and Southern Unionists for example, were unrepresented. A few TDs were influenced by opinion expressed in their constituencies over the Christmas adjournment of the Treaty debates. De Valera wrote to McGarrity on 27 December:

> Had the vote been taken on Thursday last when the Dáil adjourned it was thought we might have got a majority of one or two against the treaty. But the press is hard at work throughout the country trying to get the local public bodies, County Councils etc. to pass resolutions in favour of the treaty—and the Church is also hard at work.

Tom Maguire reported the pressure put on him during the adjournment by his parish priest in Mayo, which the priest admitted had been inspired by the bishop and by Dean D'Alton in Ballinrobe.[5] It was six months before the electorate was consulted, and even then, by means of the Collins-de Valera election pact, the Sinn Féin leadership attempted to prevent the people's will from being expressed.

It became clear in the Dáil debates that the Treaty offered more than enough to satisfy the pragmatists within Sinn Féin ranks: many, led by Arthur Griffith, held that the Treaty represented a desirable settlement. Others—most notably Michael Collins—held that the Treaty represented a basis from which further concessions could later be won.

Collins's and Mulcahy's support for the Treaty developed from the premise that a military victory could not be achieved. Collins reminded the Dáil that the dis-appearance of British 'military strength gives us the chief proof that our national liberties are established'. He argued that the only alternative to the Treaty was to renew war: 'Are we simply going to go on keeping ourselves in slavery and sub-jection, forever keeping on an impossible fight?'

Repeatedly Collins stressed his lack of concern with theoretical debate over abstract constitutional issues and symbols, which served often as a euphemism for his impatience with de Valera's arguments. In August 1922 he wrote:

> The true devotion lies not in melodramatic defiance or self-sacrifice for something falsely said to exist, or for mere words and formalities, which are empty.... What we fought for at any particular time was the greatest measure of freedom obtainable at that time.

J. J. Horgan, writing to Childers from Cork, argued:

> It is not common sense or common justice to plunge Ireland back into warfare and ruin because England will not act on principles of abstract inter-national justice, which really have no existence or application in real world politics.... Eighty per cent of the people would accept the terms as they

stand. I know of course that Ireland is permanently partitioned but what other result could you expect from the events of the last two years. That door has been slammed, banged and bolted long ago and can only be opened by an era of constructive politics on this side of the Boyne. . . . I don't want this big chance of a real peace between England and Ireland to be frittered away in a wordy dispute about abstract theories.

Arthur Griffith affirmed: 'It is the first Treaty that admits the equality of Ireland. . . . We have translated Thomas Davis into the practical politics of the day.' Piaras Béaslaí despairingly urged during the Dáil Treaty debates that they get a grip on realities, and quoted the Young Irelander John Mitchel: 'I do not care a fig for Republicanism in the abstract.'

Frequently during the Dáil debates Griffith and Collins argued that the essential compromise with the British government had come with the decision to negotiate—an autonomous republic could not have been on the conference agenda. It was stressed that a return to war could not be justified for the difference between the Treaty and External Association—and that the British government was scarcely likely to be more sympathetic to External Association in future than they had been at the London conference.

It seems that some supporters of the Treaty—most notably Michael Collins—had considerable reservations about the document they were in public defending. Even Kevin O'Higgins, to become the most hardline of Free Staters, admitted that the Treaty had many flaws and no one pretended that it didn't have blemishes. Collins's agreement to the Treaty may well have been a short-term manoeuvre meant to expedite the achievement of a non-partitioned, fully independent Ireland. Jimmy Leahy, of the Mid-Tipperary IRA, quoted Collins as saying: 'Do you think I'm not as good a Republican as Liam Lynch and Liam Deasy? My idea is that if we can get our own army we can tell the British to go to hell.' Childers said the IRB Supreme Council went pro-Treaty because the 'idea was to wait until Great Britain was in difficulties and then to strike again. This was Michael Collins's creed and one he preached widely among the IRB and the army. The Republicans held that this was treachery to Ireland and also to England.' Collins reminded the IRB that his first loyalty was to them. Peadar O'Donnell, the veteran republican socialist, correctly stressed that Collins remained a born conspirator—if he was impatient with constitutional formulae, he was also reluctant to abide by the strict terms of the Treaty.[6]

Republican opposition to the Treaty during the Dáil debates was well summed up by Mary MacSwiney, who stated that it was an issue of right and wrong, not of peace and war. To support the Treaty was to desert the principles of 1798, 1848 and 1916. Mary MacSwiney continued: 'I ask you to vote in the name of the dead to unite against this Treaty and let us take the consequences.' Mrs Pearse denied during the debates that her son Patrick would have accepted the Treaty, and the widows of Tom Clarke and Mayor O'Callaghan of Limerick took a similar line. Religious symbolism was sometimes used to make this point. Harry Boland talked of an 'apostolic succession'; Austin Stack in his Dáil speech invoked his Fenian forebears; Liam Mellows affirmed: 'The delegates . . . had no power to sign away the rights of Ireland and the Irish Republic.'

Two long-lived contemporaries, Tod Andrews and Seán O'Faolain, in later years looked back on what they came to regard as their naïve idealism. Tod

Andrews declared: 'I was in thrall to Pearse; to the standards of Cuchulainn and Fionn.' Seán O'Faolain argued:

> If I were asked what exactly the Republican ideal could do for this old, beloved Ireland and for these poor that could not be done under the constitution of the Irish Free State, I would not have quite known how to say it. . . . I had nothing to guide me but those flickering lights before the golden ikons of the past . . . with a deep suspicion that the men on the other side were letting material things get in the way of principles . . . or realism, smother ideas, and that the upshot of their canny policy of compromise would be to destroy all our symbols. . . . When I met and worked with a number of our 'idealist' leaders in Dublin they struck me as being half crazed by the impossible task of holding to their ideals in a pragmatical world.

The declaration of the Republic at Easter 1916 and its ratification by the Dáil in January 1919 had made it impossible for many to compromise. In his summing up in the Sinn Féin Funds Case Judge Kingsmill Moore commented on 'the symbolic and transcendental appeal' of the Republic:

> Independence and a republic had for so long been considered as essentially the same thing that numbers now found it difficult to conceive of one without the other. . . . Throughout history a flag, a song and a story have counted far more than the arguments of philosophers. With the tricolour, the Soldiers' Song, and the shout of 'Up the Republic' the battle had been fought, and now it seemed impossible to accept the first two without the third.

Anti-Treaty leaders like Mary MacSwiney on the political side, and Rory O'Connor on the military, constantly reiterated that the oath to the Republic had been taken and there could be no compromise on that. Individual reasons for being anti-Treaty may well have been extremely complex, and many changed their minds; but upholding the Republic could always be offered as the ultimate justification. As the historian Ronan Fanning has observed, the dogmatic character of Irish republicanism was ill-suited to the give-and-take of parliamentary assemblies. The various compromises suggested during the Dáil debates on the Treaty were brusquely refused.[7]

De Valera's opposition to the Treaty was more complex than that of most anti-Treatyites. Despite his stressing at the end of the Dáil Treaty debates that the issue was one of 'black and white' and that the principles of 1916 should be maintained, de Valera adopted a detached position from that of the Republican diehards. De Valera's central preoccupation had been unity. He declared during the debates:

> My task was to try to get by negotiations something which would satisfy Britain, something which would satisfy what I may call the left wing of the Cabinet and something which would satisfy the right wing. The left wing of the Cabinet was for an isolated Republic for the most part but I pulled them over a bit. . . . While I was pulling along that wing, the other wing got away from me.

His hesitant initial response to the Treaty left de Valera in a poor position to direct events. During the private sessions at the start of the Dáil Treaty debates, in a vain attempt to recover control, de Valera submitted his 'Document No. 2', which amounted to a rewriting of the proposals he had submitted during the London negotiations. When it became clear that Document No. 2 had little Republican support and could provide no basis for compromise he withdrew it. As Joseph Connolly, the Sinn Féin 'consul' in New York, was to point out, de Valera had abandoned the Republic during the negotiations and at the start of the Dáil debates, and returned to it when his tactics failed.

De Valera admitted that there was little difference between the Treaty and his alternative, while arguing that Britain would not go to war for the difference. In return the pro-Treatyites claimed that the Irish population would be much less willing, or desirous, of going to war for the difference. Seán O'Faolain commented: 'Perhaps the main reason for Mr de Valera's defeat was that he was and always remained too subtle a politician for common understanding.... His idea of "external association" certainly puzzled most people.'

Some have attributed de Valera's opposition to the Treaty to what P. S. O'Hegarty called 'wounded vanity'—a resentment of the fact that he had lost control of events. De Valera's resort to self-pitying justification towards the end of the Treaty debates appears to give support to that. T. Ryle Dwyer has written that de Valera's attitude was 'influenced by his determination to show that he, not Collins, was the real Irish leader'. Ronan Fanning has argued that de Valera 'opposed the treaty not because it was *a* compromise but because it was not *his* compromise—not, that is, a compromise which he had authorised in advance of its conclusion'. This interpretation, however, underrates de Valera's sincerity and his later long pursuance of 'external association' ideas. He had expressed during the negotiations a willingness to compromise on sovereignty only if the Northern question was settled on favourable terms. Wishing to renegotiate with the British, de Valera tried to ensure that fellow anti-Treatyites separate themselves from the IRA. It was to prove, however, impossible for de Valera to distance himself from the military opposition to the Treaty, or for him to direct general opinion.

A few individuals dominated the Treaty debates, in which personal animosities and bitterness played an important part, culminating in the vicious attacks launched on Collins by Brugha and the South Tipperary IRA leader Séamus Robinson. Some Republicans were convinced that Brugha's speech lost them key votes. Problems were exacerbated by the shapelessness of the debates and by confusion over standing orders. It had not been intended that the Treaty vote would be delayed for three weeks. Muddle and bad feeling resulted from de Valera's submission of Document No. 2 in private session and his subsequent withdrawal of it. When Griffith caused a copy of the document to be published in the press it exacerbated an already charged situation, as had de Valera's emendation of his original proposal.

On 7 January 1922 the Dáil narrowly—by 64 to 57—voted in favour of the Treaty. A confusing debate followed concerning the constitutional position of the Dáil and de Valera's position as President. De Valera pointed out that the Dáil had no right to disestablish itself. Griffith and Collins stressed their personal affection for de Valera and their willingness to support his remaining as President. De Valera, however, insisted on standing down in order that a separate vote be taken on the issue. Griffith was elected President by an even narrower majority—60 to 58. Griffith then gave assurances that the Dáil government would remain in existence until the establishment of the Free State, despite the setting up of the Provisional Government. Meanwhile Mulcahy affirmed that the army would remain that of the Republic.

The conclusion of the Treaty debates was a mixture of conciliation attempts and the expression of personal abuse. While de Valera expressed his desire that all opposition be of a constitutional character and his willingness to play a positive role in the Dáil as long as it continued to act in line with republican principles, Collins put forward his idea of a joint Committee of Public Safety. On the other hand, when the anti-Treaty TDs temporarily abstained from the Dáil as a protest against Griffith's election Collins shouted out: 'Deserters all to the Irish nation in her hour of trial.' Countess Markievicz retorted: 'Oath-breakers and cowards.' Soon after, when Childers questioned Griffith on the constitutional status of the Dáil, Griffith snarled: 'I will not reply to any damned Englishman in this Assembly.' Earlier non-public divisions had become all too explicit.

The agreement to the existence of two governments heralded five months of constitutional and political confusion. It was clear at the end of the Treaty debates, and was to remain so up to the outbreak of the Civil War, that the Dáil could no longer act as a constructive or unifying institution. Instead it became the national forum for political division. The failure to preserve political unity meant that the IRA's attitude became decisive.[8]

(b) THE MILITARY REACTION TO THE TREATY

Even if the political response to the Treaty had been a unified one, the IRA could not easily have become reconciled to compromise. The IRA had not been prepared for the Treaty; James O'Donovan, the Director of Chemicals, complained that the majority of GHQ members were not kept posted on developments in London. The IRA had little room for political sophistication; they had been firmly under the impression that they had been fighting for a united Irish Republic. It seemed to many in the army that the claim for a Republic had been watered down as a result of politicians taking over direction of the movement after the truce. Collins was the only national leader with the potential to condition military attitudes to any settlement; de Valera had little relevance to the army. Collins exercised an effective influence—particularly with regard to GHQ, which went overwhelmingly pro-Treaty—over many parts of the army. Without his personal influence, it is most unlikely that the Treaty could have been put into effect: the Provisional Government's army would have been stillborn. Many testified that 'what was good enough for Mick' was good enough for them. Mary MacSwiney told Joe McGarrity in the spring of 1922: 'I deal with Collins only because he is alone responsible for the split. All the young men who follow him—the young soldiers of the IRB—would not have followed Griffith two steps. But they believed and still believe in Mick.' Michael Hayes, TD for the National University, commented: 'It was through the influence... of a small number of people like Collins and Mulcahy... that many officers and men stood fast by the government and the treaty.' Collins's pro-Treaty stance, however, meant he was unable to influence the IRA majority, for instance in his own West Cork, and he became for some a tainted figure.[9]

Both sides during the Dáil Treaty debates avoided the question of the army's constitutional status: the new Minister for Defence, Mulcahy, and the previous one, Brugha, gave assurances that the IRA would preserve its republican identity. At the cabinet meeting following the Treaty's signing de Valera said that 'he would not discuss Army opinion. . . . The Army . . . was the instrument of the Civil Gov and must obey the decision of the Dáil.' On 10 January de Valera asked GHQ members about their attitude to political developments. They promised allegiance to whatever government was formed, but the army in the provinces was already dividing. P. S. O'Hegarty recorded that Mellows and Brugha, just after the Treaty's signing, travelled through the south and west encouraging army units to go anti-Treaty.

It soon became evident following the Treaty that little political control could be exercised over the IRA. During the Dáil debates IRA actions provided considerable embarrassment. The Cork No. 1 Brigade ordered Cork TDs to oppose the Treaty—an action denounced by de Valera in the Dáil. Kay, the London *Times*'s special correspondent, who had written reports form Cork and Clare emphasising widespread acceptance of the Treaty, even within the IRA, was kidnapped in Dublin and taken down to Cork to be interrogated by the leaders of No. 1 Brigade. He was made to revise his opinions in another article—it seems Collins's urgings played a part in his release. During the Dáil Treaty debates Séamus Robinson stressed the desirability of military independence of all political influence.[10]

Military autonomy was constantly affirmed. Frank Aiken, the O/C of the 4th Northern Division in 1921 and 1922, commented: 'We were great believers then in the power of the gun alone to cure all our evils'; Seán Moylan, a North Cork IRA leader, stressed that he was responsible 'only as a soldier'; and Seán Hales, West Cork IRA man and TD, claimed that it was the soldiers who had 'won the fight' and not the politicians. Liam Lynch told his brother: 'The army has to hew the way to freedom for politics to follow.' When Arthur Griffith told Seán MacSwiney in the Dáil that he was not to be intimidated by a gunman, Seán Moylan pointed out that Griffith wouldn't have been present if it hadn't been for such gunmen.[11]

It is hardly surprising that such a localised and independent body as the IRA made a confused, undisciplined response to the Treaty. Much of the military reaction to the settlement can be related to the intense local particularism of the pre-truce IRA, and the differing perspectives on the Anglo-Irish War by the various areas. Broadly speaking, the areas which had seen most fighting during the Anglo-Irish War tended to be anti-Treaty: they had seen the struggle in military terms and remained during the post-Treaty period intensely suspicious of Dublin's attempts at control, whether political or military. The stronger fighting areas during the Anglo-Irish War—notably Cork and South Tipperary—had resented what they saw as lack of support, financial and military, from GHQ for their efforts. They had been critical of GHQ attempts to direct their activities, but also complained that no representative from GHQ had visited them during the hostilities. Liam Lynch told the Chief of Staff:

> Officers and men here realise that the Government, GHQ Staff and the Army in the rest of Ireland outside the Southern Divisions and the Dublin Brigade have outrageously let them down. When the Free State comes into existence GHQ can be responsible for discipline which I have grave fears will be hard to maintain.

Reflecting in his old age on the events of this period, General Mulcahy asked Liam Deasy, the old West Cork IRA leader: 'Did the isolation of the Southern Divisions have the effect of divorcing them from the important national issues which bore so closely on the Independence Movement?'

The Cork IRA had kept a wary eye on the London negotiations by means of representatives on the spot. Seán Hegarty, O/C Cork No. 1 Brigade, complained to the Chief of Staff of excessive drinking and partying amongst the Irish delegation. The old tension between Dublin and Cork, together with Mulcahy's and Collins's strained relations with men like Hegarty and Tom Barry, enhanced such local particularism. Emmet Dalton declared that Cork never forgave itself for not getting involved in 1916 and 'have been getting even with Dublin ever since'. Ernie O'Malley had just as unsympathetic views, writing: 'There was a bumptiousness in the Cork temperament. They resembled the Gascons; quick and volatile, but they seemed too conscious of their qualities; as if they were surprised at possessing them.' Liam Deasy's and Liam Lynch's good personal relations with Collins and Mulcahy did not prevent them from opposing the Treaty. In a note informing Deasy of his lone opposition to the Treaty at the 11 December meeting of the IRB Supreme Council, Lynch added a postscript expressing his continued affection for Collins. The 1st Southern Division's speedy publication, on 10 December, of their opposition to the settlement was probably explained by their earlier knowledge of developments through IRB sources. There had been no time for them to be influenced by any political opposition.[12]

During the post-Treaty period the 2nd Southern Division continued its independent line. Ernie O'Malley, the O/C, had little choice other than to follow the independent line of the brigades nominally under him. There had been resentment at being upbraided by Collins for the South Tipperary Brigade's arms raid on British hutments during the London conference. During the Dáil Treaty debates Séamus Robinson, the O/C of South Tipperary, complained of how little help had been forthcoming from GHQ during the Anglo-Irish War. Mulcahy lamented that IRB influences were as unable as GHQ to influence South Tipperary.[13]

Less active military areas during the Anglo-Irish War were equally resentful of GHQ attitudes. Mayo and Sligo, for instance, had been often strongly criticised by Mulcahy and Collins during the Anglo-Irish War for their lack of activity and for their regular requests for arms and, in Sligo's case, independent efforts to obtain arms in Britain which interfered with the IRB supply links. Mulcahy put the anti-Treaty stance of some areas down to a desire by their leadership to atone for earlier inactivity. GHQ's removal of the O/Cs of the South Roscommon and Kerry No. 1 Brigades intensified antagonism to Dublin control there. Mayo's attitude to the Treaty was complicated by their complaints of lack of financial support from GHQ. Mulcahy claimed that Mayo officers changed their mind on the Treaty, and asserted that while they had been in favour of the settlement he had given them £1,000 for payment of troops there.[14]

There have been sundry explanations of why some inactive areas during the Anglo-Irish War took an anti-Treaty line and became very active in the Civil War. O'Malley put it down to the fact that many senior officers in such areas went Free State, which gave more able junior officers their opportunity to improve the IRA there. The historians Rumpf and Hepburn have sought an explanation in the continued importance of land protest in the west after the Treaty. Common to strong and weak IRA areas was resentment of attempted Dublin control. Distance from Dublin heightened local particularism. The Treaty and Civil War period brought to a head questions of who was to control the army, and by what means the army could become the servant of the state rather than its master. Military developments in the Treaty period are best understood in the context of the difficult transition from a decentralised, volunteer army to a professional unit firmly controlled by government.

There were, however, considerations which made for a considerable reluctance to allow the split to develop. For many there was an extreme reluctance to break the bonds of republican unity which goes a long way to explaining the length of time it took for military divisions to become defined. Mary MacSwiney commented: 'I think it is a great pity that the army business did not take place all over the country just after the Treaty was signed.' Mark Sturgis wrote shortly before leaving Dublin Castle with his British colleagues: 'I wish they would lose no time ... getting the IRA into uniform so that all may know who's who and what's what.'[15]

IRA attitudes were often strongly conditioned by particular circumstances in a locality where the Treaty was signed. During the Anglo-Irish War the Clare IRA had been notoriously divided, largely as a consequence of the feud between the Barrett and Brennan families. To deal with that, GHQ had divided Clare into three separate brigades. Throughout the war Mulcahy had consistently complained of Clare localism and ineffectiveness. Michael Brennan, the O/C of the East Clare Brigade, admitted: 'We were as busy fighting amongst ourselves as we were busy fighting the enemy.' Just before the Treaty it was dubiously claimed that the differences within the Clare IRA had been patched up. Brennan became O/C of the new 1st Western Division. When Brennan went pro-Treaty, despite his old strained relations with GHQ, the majority of the Clare IRA followed him. Frank Barrett took the opposite line; Liam Manahan, of the East Limerick IRA, put this down to Brennan's IRB influence, and to the Barretts in Mid-Clare resenting Brennan's appointment as divisional commandant.

In many localities personal considerations, loyalties and animosities had considerable relevance to choices made over the Treaty. Bertie Scully, of Rosbeigh, held, in common with some of those in Kerry No. 2 Brigade, that Scarteen O'Connor's maverick decision to go pro-Treaty was explained by his resentment at his replacement during the 'Tan War' as brigade engineer. IRA attitudes to the Treaty in East Limerick appear to have had much to do with the old clash between IRB and non-IRB elements. The individual decision by the popular Jerry Ryan in Mid-Tipperary to support the Treaty caused many to follow his lead there, and so break up the anti-Treaty solidarity in that area. Mick Burke, of Cork No. 1 Brigade, told Ernie O'Malley that Mick Leahy's court martial of some men in East Cork helped to explain why some of the IRA there went Free State.

Personal influences also played a strong role in the Dublin IRA's attitude. Relations between GHQ and the Dublin Brigade had deteriorated strongly after the death of Dick McKee, the old O/C, and Peadar Clancy, his deputy, on the Bloody Sunday weekend of November 1920. These problems came to a head over the confused planning, and disastrous outcome, of the Custom House attack in late May 1921. Mulcahy was to explain the fact that a majority of Dublin No. 1

Brigade opposed the Treaty by reference to the change in command. Significantly, the only battalion in No. 1 Brigade to support the Treaty was the 2nd Battalion, whose O/C was Tom Ennis, who had poor relations with Oscar Traynor, the brigade O/C. Paddy O'Connor, a pro-Treaty member of the brigade, commented that in the 3rd Battalion 'The best of the Bn. were secured by Seán MacMahon [a member of GHQ].' Another member of the brigade, Seán Smith, observed: 'The men in the Company went F/S but they did so because Tom Ennis went Free State.' Tom Burke, of the 2nd Battalion, stressed: 'The personality of Tom Ennis swung the battalion.' Men, however, did not always follow their leaders. In the Tipperary No. 1 Brigade only the brigade staff went pro-Treaty, and most of Cork No. 1 Brigade did not follow Seán Hegarty's and Florrie O'Donoghue's belated neutral stance. In Wexford, by contrast, contemporaries commented: 'Each Bn. O/C practically brought his whole Bn. with him.'[16]

(c) THE IRB AND THE TREATY

Many leaders of anti-Treaty opinion attached considerable importance to the IRB's role, and Collins's control of the organisation, in enabling the Treaty to pass in the Dáil and for gaining support for it within the IRA. De Valera ascribed his defeat to Collins 'getting the IRB machine working' and concluded: 'Curse secret societies.' Mary MacSwiney and Cathal Brugha held that IRB pressure was responsible for a number of TDs, said to be around forty, supporting the Treaty in the Dáil. Harry Boland, a member of the Supreme Council, told Luke Dillon, a leader of the reorganised Clan na Gael in the USA: 'There has not been in Irish History a greater betrayal than that perpetrated by the SC and the IRB. The majority of the Executive are in Arms in the field against the Free State, the rank and file is all right...' The pro-Treaty members of the organisation, however, argued that the IRB had always used the appropriate means to advance the cause of Irish independence, even if that temporarily meant the abandonment of the demand for a Republic.

In a vote as close as that on the Treaty many factors could be claimed to have proved decisive. Loyalty and admiration for Collins were probably as important as Collins's presidency of the Supreme Council in explaining his influence. Moreover, the IRB split badly over the Treaty and failed, in common with every other nationalist organisation, to give a coherent lead.[17]

The meeting of the Supreme Council on 11 December showed eleven members in favour of the settlement and four against. The resulting circular declared that the Supreme Council was in favour of ratification, but individual TDs were given freedom to vote whichever way they wanted. A Supreme Council circular of 12 January 1922 was even more cautious, saying that the organisation would not make its views plain until the Free State constitution was published. Later in January the South Munster IRB division confirmed its opposition to the Treaty and effectively cut itself off from the Supreme Council's control, refusing to circulate instructions. An extraordinary meeting of the organisation's city and country leaders with the Supreme Council failed to heal differences. Seán Hegarty complained that the IRB failed to give a lead and, in reply, Mulcahy admitted some 'wobble' in the instructions of 12 January. Retrospectively Mulcahy wondered if it would have been better to have issued an unequivocal order to support the Treaty. Liam Lynch told Joe McGarrity that the rank and file of the IRB went anti-Treaty, but that the majority of the governing body went the other way.

Far from acting as a strong controlling influence, the IRB disintegrated over the Treaty. The historian John O'Beirne Ranelagh has pointed out that from February 1922 the organisation ceased to function nationally. IRB divisions, however, only mirrored military, political and regional ones.

For important military leaders, like Mac Eoin and Michael Brennan, the IRB link helped to consolidate support for Collins and the Treaty. Collins had striven, through Seán Ó Muirthile's activity, to reorganise the IRB at the end of the Anglo-Irish War and during the truce. Considerable IRB pressure was placed on various individuals at the time of the Treaty. Tod Andrews claimed that Collins had placed Thomas O'Sullivan as O/C of South Wexford because of his IRB status, and later strove to influence him to accept the Treaty. It seems also that at the time of the Treaty the IRB held out the prospect of another function of secret societies—the provision of jobs for loyal members. Dennis Quill, of Listowel, told Ernie O'Malley: 'The IRB were placing men for jobs...just before the Treaty was signed and later.'

The fact that very few of Dublin No. 1 Brigade were in the IRB made it more difficult for GHQ to influence them—the reverse applied to Collins's close control over the 'Squad' and GHQ. Collins's meeting in the autumn of 1921 with Cork IRB men, when he warned of the complications of the negotiations, and his failure to fulfil his promise to consult them before any final decision was made, further embittered their attitude. According to Seán Maginiss's account, the IRA in Tullamore went anti-Treaty despite Gearóid O'Sullivan's attempts to bring IRB influence to bear. Of the South Tipperary Brigade, Mulcahy commented: 'Persons like Robinson and Breen had as little opinion of IRB activity as they had of GHQ.' The IRB loyalties of many key men in Munster, however, did not prevent them from opposing the Treaty.[18]

(d) SOCIAL CONSIDERATIONS AND THE TREATY RESPONSE

The complete dominance of political, constitutional and military considerations during the Anglo-Irish War and the Treaty divisions makes it extremely difficult to demonstrate a social basis for the divisions that led to the Civil War. The various elements of the 'new nationalism' may have had radical political and cultural aims, but such radicalism stopped there. The alliance between James Connolly's republican socialism and physical-force republicanism was limited to the immediate circumstances of the 1916 rising. Sinn Féin's early association with agrarian protest, in 1917 and early 1918, was short-lived. Michael Brennan commented: 'I hadn't the slightest interest in the land agitation, but I had every interest in using it as a means to an end...to get these fellows into the Volunteers.... Up to that they were just an unorganised mob.' Soon, however, both the Sinn Féin party and the IRA revealed their conservatism and their reluctance to alienate any potential supporters. The standing committee of Sinn Féin on 23 February 1918 expressed its opposition to unauthorised land seizures and cattle-drives. The republican courts became used as a means to defend property rights: farmers' interests became predominant. Ernie O'Malley commented: 'The movement as a whole was hostile to labour claims even though labour had helped to prevent conscription, had not contested the last election, and was now refusing to carry armed troops.' Labour gained little in return for their support of nationalist ends during the period 1918-21. L. J. Duffy, a union leader, declared: 'Sinn Féin sought, secured and acknowledged the ready co-operation of the Labour Movement during the Anglo-Irish War. But the Labour Movement entered into the compact as a vassal rather than a co-partner.' Furthermore, the circumstances of guerrilla warfare hindered greatly the strength and relevance of the labour movement, and involvement of labour in the conflict was minimal. The Dáil at its foundation had bowed to labour interests by passing the Democratic Programme in a watered-down form. Seán O'Faolain wrote that the Democratic Programme 'was listened to and discussed for precisely twenty minutes and fifty seconds, and then buried forever. In any case, its terms were of a purely pious and general nature that committed nobody to anything in particular.'

The Dáil Treaty debate concentrated overwhelmingly on political and con-stitutional issues. When Thomas Johnson, the Labour Party leader, was given permission to introduce a resolution on the worsening economic outlook a committee on the subject was formed, but almost immediately the issues were pushed to the side. Irish labour and union leaders, while generally pro-Treaty, made little attempt to lead opinion during the Treaty conflict, casting themselves rather as attempted peacemakers.

Peadar O'Donnell, who consistently during his long life criticised the failure of Irish republicanism to relate its aims to socialism, wrote of the anti-Treaty leaders:

> They were the stuff that martyrs are made of, but not revolutionaries, and martyrdom should be avoided. We had a pretty barren mind socially; many on the Republican side were against change. . . . The city-minded Sinn Féiner was darkly suspicious of the wild men on the land. . . . Pure ideals were used as a mask and a blinkers to direct the movement away from revolution.

O'Malley commented: 'We were at the political stage. We had not the faculty for thinking things through sufficiently.' Even Liam Mellows, who was heavily influenced by Connolly, concentrated during the Dáil debates on political and constitutional issues.[19]

Enthusiasm for the Treaty was much greater among prosperous farmers and businessmen than it was among small tenant farmers and farm labourers. A remote situation and a backward economy corresponded often with an attitude that was at best lukewarm to the Treaty. It is difficult, however, to relate social protest and grievances in the regions to political developments at the centre. Resistance to the Provisional and Free State governments often represented opposition to the attempted establishment of central government in general, whether British or Irish.

5

The Irish Question in the United States

THE Treaty and Civil War periods caused a vast fall in the membership and importance of exile nationalist organisations in the United States, and also in the relevance of the Irish question in American politics.

The Irish cause in the USA had been on the decline long before the Treaty. Donal O'Callaghan, TD, reflecting on earlier exaggerated propaganda, commented that 'It was all a myth talking about 20 millions of their people in America. There never was more than half a million in the Irish movement in America'; and de Valera admitted that the Irish question in the USA was of far more significance at a local, than at a national, political level. Mulcahy pointed out how disappointing the amount of arms shipments from the USA had been during the Anglo-Irish War. Congressional resolutions on Ireland, which created so much stir, never went beyond expressions of mere sympathy for the Irish cause; James T. Carroll, of Columbus, Ohio, wrote to Mary MacSwiney: 'I confess I could never see any impress that we made on legislative bodies, either state or National.' The Irish cause was of importance in Washington only when it related to domestic American political considerations, most notably with the Irish-American role in opposing American entry into the League of Nations. Once the League issue was settled in March 1920, there was a sharp falling off in Irish-American activity and the amount taken in fund-raising, despite the strong intensification of the Anglo-Irish War at that time.

The Irish-American cause had also been hindered by divisions within the movement's leadership during 1920 and 1921, exacerbated by de Valera's stay in the USA. Clashes over many issues between de Valera himself and John Devoy and Daniel F. Cohalan, the leaders of the public Friends of Irish Freedom and the secret Clan na Gael, led to de Valera forming a rival public organisation, the inelegantly named American Association for the Recognition of the Irish Republic, while Harry Boland and Joe McGarrity established the 'reorganised Clan', which was Philadelphia-controlled, in contrast to Devoy's New York-based institution. A membership of 750,000 was extravagantly claimed for the AARIR, but much of its organisation was loose and decentralised, and its leadership was chosen because of massive wealth rather than for any long-term commitment to the Irish cause.[1]

During the Treaty negotiations Irish-Americans had no choice other than to leave matters to the Irish and pledged themselves to stand by the Dáil's decision on any settlement. That policy was left in tatters, however, when the Sinn Féin leadership split on the Treaty. Leading Irish-Americans reacted with bewilderment as to why the earlier unity had not been preserved.

The majority of articulate American opinion, that of journalist and politician, looked upon the Treaty as a blessing and a cause for huge relief. The traditional Irish sore appeared to have been removed from Anglo-American relations. The *Boston Globe* rejoiced that

> The settlement which now seems assured is the settlement of a world problem, for Ireland was irritating the conscience of all mankind.... The sanguine may even dare hail the birth of the Irish Free State as the most auspicious event since the gallant Lee passed over his sword to Grant at Appotomax.

James J. Phelan, a well-known Boston banker, immediately following the Treaty's signing, sent a telegram to the Lord Mayor of Dublin declaring:

> Thank God peace has come. This I believe is the feeling of all true friends of Ireland and England the World over. I have always believed that the Irish question has to be settled by the Irish in Ireland. For the first time in centuries the sun's rays of freedom shine upon the Irish.

Not surprisingly, de Valera's speedy denuniciation of the Treaty terms shocked and dismayed the general chorus of favourable response. The *New York World* described de Valera as 'a master of claptrap', and the *New York Times* declared that 'Mr De Valera is too late. The world's approval and supporting opinion for the agreement is now too strong to be overcome.' General American response was less concerned with technicalities as to whether the Treaty should have been referred to Dublin before it was signed, or whether it strictly conformed to republican ideals, than with what seemed to them the favourable terms it offered, with the prospect of an end to the age-old vexed problem. If Irish objections to the Treaty had focused more on the Northern question, there would probably have been a more critical American response.

The general favourable American reaction made it difficult for Irish-American organisations to oppose the Treaty. The exile nationalist cause was left, as a result of the settlement, without much of its *raison d'être*; the newspaper headlines it had once so easily gained were lost for ever. Irish-American disputes after the Treaty took on an increasingly internecine character. Active Irish-American supporters of the nationalist cause were depressed by the fact that they were largely unconsulted over the negotiations. Joseph Connolly, the Sinn Féin 'consul' in New York, said that 'It was a difficult job to get them to understand that, as things were in Dublin, little or no attention was being given to Irish-American thought or opinion. Little or no news came to me officially regarding the crisis nor did I expect any.'

Initially almost all those active in Irish-American organisations received the Treaty positively, though usually with reservations. Joe McGarrity wrote in his paper, the *Irish Press*: 'Ireland's sovereign independence is acknowledged by the British Cabinet and their action is approved by Britain's King. This much is certain.' Harry Boland, who was organising a new bond-selling campaign in the USA, immediately announced his approval. McGarrity's and Boland's tone, and that of others close to de Valera, suddenly changed after de Valera had announced his opposition to the terms.[2]

Reactions to the Treaty from the FOIF and Clan na Gael was also less than straightforward. It would scarcely be expected that the hardline Fenian Devoy would accept a settlement which fell short of the republican ideal. Neither, however, could Devoy and Cohalan line themselves up behind their old opponent de Valera in opposing the Treaty. Instead they poured scorn on Lloyd George's motives in making the settlement, and on de Valera's for opposing it; in so doing they gave qualified support to the Provisional Government. The FOIF convention, embarrassingly timed to take place on 10 December, welcomed the Treaty as a measure which would advance Ireland along the road to a Republic. Devoy wrote to Michael Collins in February 1922:

> Although they remain Republicans our best men here under existing conditions, favour giving the Free State a chance to do what it can for Ireland. Personally I am utterly opposed to de Valera's attempt to upset the Free State agreement. . . . It is grotesque for de Valera to talk of his loyalty to the Republic. . . . Adhering unalterably to my life-long Republican convictions, my earnest hope is that in such a struggle you may win, believing that the defeat of de Valera's selfish campaign is absolutely necessary to Ireland's dearest interests.

In September 1922 de Valera told McGarrity that 'Cohalan and Devoy sent over an envoy, I am told, promising support to the party if I were deposed.'

The confused reaction by the Irish-American leadership exacerbated the depression in exile nationalist circles. An FOIF circular of 1923 admitted: 'The deplorable conditions which existed during 1922 and part of 1923 naturally had a most depressing effect on the friends of Ireland in the US and led to confusion of political thought as to the future course which Ireland could or should pursue.' By mid-1922 Joseph Connolly spoke of the cause in America as having plummeted 'from an all-high rating to a near zero'. As the situation worsened and turned in on itself at home, so the cause was made more difficult in America.[3]

Between the Treaty and Civil War many leading figures in Irish-American organisations, like Frank P. Walsh, the labour lawyer, and Joe McGarrity, remained non-committal, seeking to act as mediators in the divisions in Ireland. Initially Walsh declared that 'All of us Americans should keep quiet at least until the Dáil has acted, until a plebiscite has been taken.' Contrary to his later fixed support of de Valera through the 1920s, Walsh wrote: 'I cannot help but feel that the treaty is a big step forward, and puts mighty weapons in our hands for the final consummation of Ireland's complete freedom.'

The leaders of the reorganised Clan, Joe McGarrity and Luke Dillon, were reluctant to throw their full support behind the anti-Treaty cause. Dillon was extremely unhappy that Boland used money, sent over for IRB purposes, to help set up the Army Executive in March. Mary MacSwiney became extremely critical of the failure of McGarrity and his colleagues to provide financial support for the resistance to the Treaty, and of their attempts to achieve compromise. She wrote to McGarrity on 29 April:

> I cannot tell you how grieved I am that you above all people should be refusing us your whole-hearted support on the ground of forcing a unity where no unity is possible except on our basis. If you really wanted to bring about unity you can do so by giving, and getting others to give, adequate financial support to those who are standing for the Republic. And the reason is this: the treaty party know we have no money. Collins hopes that in a short

time he will be able to get the upper hand—if we are kept without financial help.... I know you are genuinely afraid that any money subscribed now will only foster Civil War. There you are mistaken: if Collins and Griffith felt that we would get financial support they would come to terms.... If we had a million pounds we could save the Republic without any fear of Civil War, yes we could even with half of that.... I know all you have done in the past. Ireland has not had a better friend. But you have failed us now when if *you* had only stood firm on the Republican side we would have been sure of victory. What you are prepared to do in the future is no good if you help to turn down the Republic now.

In February McGarrity visited Ireland on a peace mission and was impressed by Collins's determination to avoid civil war. He concluded that the bond between the old fighting men was 'a great safety-valve at the present time'. McGarrity was to claim that his mediation, through his IRB contacts, had helped to produce the Collins–de Valera Pact.[4]

The six months following the Treaty saw an enormous decline in the AARIR and the FOIF. The AARIR had not had time before the Treaty to establish a clear identity of its own; and it never recovered from the Treaty. Frank P. Walsh, one of its leading members, admitted that the AARIR was 'shot to pieces' during 1922, and Rossa F. Downing, another prominent figure in the organisation, estimated its membership dropped tenfold after the Treaty. J. C. Walsh, an Irish-American journalist, told Stephen O'Mara in May that the AARIR was virtually non-existent in every place he had visited in the mid-west. Those problems were exacerbated by tensions and splits between the various state organisations.[5]

The AARIR's national leadership took a line independent from de Valera. Edward Doheny, the multi-millionaire oil magnate who was national president of the organisation, enthusiastically supported the Treaty and could not see the need for the continued existence of the AARIR. His successor, James E. Murray of Montana, strongly counselled against any involvement in domestic Irish political issues; in the summer Murray wrote that the organisation 'is completely disorganised and demoralised and in view of the chaotic state of affairs in Ireland, there is no immediate prospect of rehabilitation'. In September Murray resigned. Prospects had been no brighter for the FOIF after the Treaty—it was recognised by neither side in Ireland, and its neutral stance meant that it had little relevance.

The Irish-American cause was weakened further by confusion over whether the IRB Supreme Council recognised Devoy's Clan or Dillon's and McGarrity's rival organisation. Collins showed a great reluctance to break with Devoy and told Mulcahy that he regretted Boland's authorisation of the split in the Clan. At the same time, however, Collins was negotiating with McGarrity over institutionalising the link with his organisation. The division and weakening of the IRB at home made the issue a largely academic one. It was ironic, in view of de Valera's frequently expressed distaste for secret societies, that much of his future American support came from secret society sources.[6]

In March rival Sinn Féin delegations came to the USA to present their views and, in the anti-Treaty case, to seek financial support. Both delegations arrived aboard the *Aquitania* on 17 March 1922; James O'Mara led the pro-Treaty delegation, and Austin Stack the rival one. At the last moment Irish-American leaders attempted to place $100,000 at the disposal of both delegations for use in the forthcoming elections, in return for cancellation of the visits. McGarrity and his old exile nationalist colleague Dr William Moloney were among those who made the offer, and the money was to be provided by Doheny and other rich Irish-Americans. After Collins and de Valera were consulted the money was refused—they stressed that it was for the Irish people to finance their own elections.

James O'Mara told Collins that to 'Americans the advent of contending parties in Ireland was as welcome as an outbreak of smallpox'. The *New York Times* commented:

> It is our right to make it plain to them that they are most unwelcome. . . . If it is to be an Irish battle we do not want it transferred to these shores. It is of course not war, but the sinews of war, that the invading Irishmen have in mind. But if Americans, even the bulk of Irish-Americans, were to say what they really think, it would be to cry out to the two sets of Irishmen impartially: 'A plague on both your houses.'

After the excitement of their arrival the rival delegations' visits created little stir in the American press or in Irish-American circles. O'Mara's stay proved short, and he was replaced by Timothy Smiddy, who was the first Irish envoy received by the American government.[7]

6

The Political and Constitutional
Background in Early 1922

INTRODUCTION

I T took six highly confused and tense months for the divisions over the Anglo-Irish Treaty to result in civil war. During that period sundry attempts to settle the political and military divisions, or at least to postpone them, failed. On all sides, however, there was a reluctance, right up to the Four Courts attack, to concede that war was inevitable. The Treaty left many issues open to debate and interpretation; such ambiguity made it the less likely that divisions would quickly come to a final test.

The precise process by which the Treaty was to be legislatively implemented, and the Free State established, had been left vague with regard to the timetable and constitutional authority involved. Unclear also was the relationship the Free State constitution would have to the Treaty, and whether the constitutional authority for that constitution would lie in Dublin or London. Until the legislation setting up the Free State could be passed, both in the British parliament and in the Dáil, a Provisional Government was established. The only authority for the Provisional Government's existence was the Treaty. Meanwhile Republicans claimed that the Dáil could not be legislated out of existence and that the authority for any assembly had to come from the Irish people themselves, and not from British legislation. As long as the Second Dáil and the Dáil government remained in existence, and the constitution was being drafted, there was hope of some compromise being worked out.

While the constitutional issues remained undefined, British troops were leaving the Twenty-Six Counties and the RIC was being disbanded. The transitional government lacked the resources and the necessary acceptance to supply effective government. There were great difficulties in establishing a police force and a settled court system. The Provisional Government's weak position was well described in a famous retrospective comment of Kevin O'Higgins. He summed up the government as

> simply eight young men in the City Hall standing amidst the ruins of one administration, with the foundations of another not yet laid, and with wild men screaming through the keyhole. No police force was functioning through the country, no system of justice was operating, the wheels of administration hung idle, battered out of recognition by the clash of rival jurisdictions.[1]

(a) THE BRITISH GOVERNMENT'S ATTITUDE

During the treaty negotiations the British government had been in the driving seat. Once the Treaty was signed, attention shifted to the Irish context—where the British government could not control events.

The coalition government had not anticipated the opposition to the settlement within the Twenty-Six Counties. They were over-impressed by the favourable public response and had overrated Collins's control of the IRA. As early as February 1922, however, a British government conference on Ireland admitted, with reference to developments on both sides of the border, that 'the fate of the agreement was trembling in the balance'.

Lloyd George gave Churchill the day-to-day supervision of Irish issues by appointing him chairman of the Provisional Government of Ireland Committee, which met for the first time on 27 December. Irish affairs were supervised by the Colonial Office.

British military and political leaders realised that before the Free State could be established any direct British intervention in Southern Irish affairs would be counterproductive and would result in a reunification of republican opinion, which would destroy the Treaty settlement. Lionel Curtis after a visit to Ireland on behalf of the Colonial Office, concluded that he was optimistic about the settlement 'in the long run provided that we can manage to keep clear of intervention'. He continued:

> The most dangerous weapon the extremists hold is their chance of creating a wave of feeling by committing a series of atrocities which will force intervention and throw us back where we were in 1920. The only precautions we can take are to reduce so far as possible the targets against which they can aim.[2]

There were great problems over troop evacuation. The PGI Committee originally planned that all troops should leave by Easter. General Macready was apprehensive about the army's position and feared that attacks would be made on the troops with the intention of provoking them into retaliation. On 31 December he wrote: 'I am more than ever convinced that unless troops are withdrawn from Southern Ireland with the utmost despatch ... they will find themselves in a very difficult and unpleasant situation.' Troops were soon concentrated in a few centres, as was the RIC, to lessen the danger of attacks on isolated units. The pace of troop evacuation became a barometer of the military and political situation within the Twenty-Six Counties. Thus in February, at the height of the border troubles, evacuation was halted. Churchill realised that while the fate of the Provisional Government, and hence that of the Treaty, lay in the balance, some troops must remain in Dublin in case there was a need for direct British reintervention. In April he declared: 'We shall certainly not be able to withdraw our troops from their present positions until we know that the Irish people are going to stand by the Treaty, neither shall we be able to refrain from stating the consequences which would follow the setting up of a Republic.'[3]

However alarmed the British government was about developments in the south, they had to wait until the constitution was drafted, and the election held, before they could insist on their will being observed. The historian John McColgan has written: 'The British, especially their officials dealing with Ireland, maintained a kid-glove attitude towards the Provisional Government. With tact and caution they dealt with the revolutionaries-turned-constitutionalists, doing everything possible to make the way politically easier for them to carry out their parts in implementing the Treaty.' Up to June, therefore, Churchill had to curb his natural impatience, and, in public, support had to be given to the Provisional Government. Privately Churchill was often in despair. In the midst of the border disturbances of February he complained to his wife: 'Ireland is sure to bring us every form of difficulty and embarrassment, and I expect I shall have to bear the brunt of it in the House of Commons.' Later he commented:

> Telegrams arrive constantly from both the Northern and Southern Govern-
> ments. These theatrical Irishmen are enjoying themselves enormously, and
> apart from a few cruel things vy little blood is shed. . . . Our position is a vy
> strong one, *so long as* we adhere to the Treaty. . . . We must not get back into
> that hideous bog of reprisals, from which we have saved ourselves.

The need to preserve the Treaty settlement meant that blind eyes were turned to Collins's aggressive Northern policy and to the Provisional Government's failure to deal with armed opposition within the Twenty-Six Counties. Churchill, in the Commons, went along with pro-Treaty claims that the IRA remained under the Provisional Government's authority and that their military supporters remained in the majority. In the privacy of the cabinet room, however, doubts were fre-quently expressed about the ability, or willingness, of the Provisional Government to deal with the worsening position. British policy in the first six months of 1922 for the most part contrasted vividly with the ineptitude and inconsistency displayed during the Anglo-Irish War period, and showed, by British standards with regard to Ireland, a fairly sophisticated appreciation of a highly complex situation. The Treaty negotiations had acted as an education in Irish affairs for major political figures and had modified some attitudes, most notably Birkenhead's; there was a genuine appreciation of Griffith's stern desire to achieve a settlement, and a con-fidence in his commitment to stand by the Treaty. Appreciation of the Provisional Government's position was aided by the regular despatches of Alfred Cope, the British Assistant Under-Secretary in Dublin, who was always finding a silver lining in any development, however depressing.[4]

(b) CONSTITUTIONAL AND POLITICAL ISSUES

British and Irish signatories to the Treaty hoped that the constitutional and political processes by which the Free State would be established could be completed by the early summer of 1922. The Treaty was comfortably ratified by the end of March in both Houses of Parliament, despite fear of problems in Ireland encouraging diehard resistance within the Tory Party.

Following the Dáil's approval of the Treaty, the Southern Ireland parliament (i.e. the pro-Treaty members of the Dáil, together with the four Dublin University representatives) met on 14 January to ratify the Treaty formally, elect a govern-ment and agree to the transferring of some powers. It was the only time that assembly transacted any business. Confusingly, some members of the Dáil govern-ment became Provisional Government ministers. There was no attempt to spell out the relationship between the two governments. Collins became Chairman of the new government, which Griffith did not join.

A Provisional Government cabinet meeting on 30 January declared that there should be a general election 'at the earliest possible moment'. In early February British and Irish representatives agreed on mechanisms for transferring authority. Collins told the British representatives that the Dáil would be dissolved early in March and an election held in mid-April, with the constitution passed by the new Dáil in June. Revealing his insecurity, Collins commented: 'If they did not have an election till after the Constitution was drafted, the Treaty would be beaten in Ireland.' Collins had hopes, therefore, that the constitution could be drawn up after the Free State had been established, which would give scope for constitutional compromise on a republican basis unaffected by British constraints. At the first meeting of the Provisional Government's Constitution Committee in late January Collins declared that their work would be more important than the Treaty.

The British government in effect ignored the continued existence of the Dáil government and the constitutional ambiguity involved. They did not insist, until the election, that the Provisional Government should owe its authority to its own parliament. Such tolerance was only to apply to the transition period before an election and the drafting of a constitition.[5]

From the Dáil Treaty debates onwards there were many attempts to achieve some kind of constitutional compromise. The basis for all peace attempts was that the Dáil, and its government, should be allowed to remain in existence. On the evening of 5 January, while the Treaty debates were still proceeding, a committee, five from both sides, met at Seán T. O'Kelly's house. Of those assembled, only Liam Mellows expressed opposition to the terms suggested. It was agreed that if, as they expected, the Dáil voted in favour of the Treaty, de Valera should remain as President; that the Dáil should be the ultimate authority; and that only members of the Provisional Government should be called upon to declare allegiance to the Treaty. Griffith and Collins agreed to these suggestions, but de Valera turned them down; they were not forwarded to the Dáil. Towards the end of the Treaty debates Collins urged the formation of a Committee of Public Safety and a procedure whereby the Provisional Government should come into existence without a vote on the Treaty—the issue would be decided at the election. Eoin Mac Néill put forward a compromise based on the preservation of Irish sovereignty, but that also was not supported by de Valera. All those proposals amounted to a postponement of the issues involved by an avoidance of the fundamental question of constitutional authority.[6]

No discussion on the establishment of a dual system of government seems to have taken place; it emerged, rather, in consequence of the narrow vote approving the Treaty, and of the desire to avoid a complete break. Florrie O'Donoghue, from a Republican stance, depicted the establishment of the dual government as the master-stroke of pro-Treaty policy, enabling its creators to build up the Provisional Government and army behind the camouflage of the continued existence of the Dáil. O'Donoghue argued that the two governments created confusion and worsened antagonisms. 'If Dáil Éireann had been extinguished by the vote on the Treaty,' he argued, 'the issue would have been much more clear-cut, and many of the subsequent efforts to maintain unity would have taken a different direction. Despite Republican hopes, time was on the side of the pro-Treaty party.' By contrast, P. S. O'Hegarty depicted dual government as disastrous for the Provisional Government, and representing an appeasement of the opposition which led to weak government, thus making civil war more likely. Griffith warned during the Treaty debates that the setting up of two governments would create chaos.

Dual government helped prevent a complete polarisation of views and postpone armed conflict, although it could hardly have led to effective government and, furthermore, ensured that Dáil meetings would be dominated by questions of constitutional authority and definition, often amounting to a replay of the Treaty debates. At least it meant that no rival government was set up. In practice many of the Dáil ministries soon ceased to function, and its members were invited to attend meetings of the Provisional government. Ronan Fanning has observed: 'This led to the practical, although unofficial, fusion of the two systems of government; and the Dáil cabinet met as a separate body for the last time on 28 April.'[7]

The same desire to postpone awkward constitutional and political issues was revealed at the Sinn Féin Ard-Fheis of 22-23 February. At that meeting, after Richard Mulcahy had requested an adjournment to prevent a vote on the Treaty and thus a complete split, it was agreed that the election should be delayed for three months, and that the constitution should be published before the election, with the implicit assumption that the constitution would be of a republican character.

It has long been held that the Ard-Fheis compromise resulted from a pro-Treaty desire to avoid defeat by preventing the issue coming to a vote. Childers noted in his diary that he was convinced that there was a Republican majority 'evidently present'. Mary MacSwiney told Seán Hegarty: 'When Collins saw he had a majority against him... he put up the unity plea to stave off the vote.' The standing committee of Sinn Féin, elected in January, however, was heavily pro-Treaty. Eleven pro-Treaty members were elected with three anti-Treaty members and one who had not made his position clear. The number of votes cast for the pro-Treaty candidates was 455, and 151 for the remaining four. There was, therefore, very probably a pro-Treaty majority at the Ard-Fheis.[8]

The February compromise made clear the weakness of the Provisional Government's position. The *Irish Times* commented that the government 'wanted a period of truce so badly that it was willing to pay a heavy price for such relief' and argued that Griffith and Collins had secured 'a temporary freedom from open attack, from the danger of snap votes in Dáil Éireann, where their majority is precarious, and from the threats of mutinous sections' of the IRA.

Not surprisingly, there was considerable unease in British government circles. At a British conference with Irish ministers on 26 February Churchill expressed fears that a postponed election would lead to the Treaty breaking down and to the drawing up of an unacceptable constitution. Griffith, however, explained that the constitution would have to be accepted by the British government, and Churchill expressed himself satisfied by assurances that the constitution 'will be framed within the 4 corners of the Treaty in consultation between the co-signatories. The Provisional Government, not the Dáil, will make the Constitution, and the Treaty and the Constitution will be put by the PG to the Irish people early in June.'[9]

On the Republican side there was criticism of de Valera's desire to compromise at the Ard-Fheis, and many suspected that time would be to the Provisional Government's advantage. Kathleen O'Connell, de Valera's secretary, wrote in her diary: 'The vast majority were Republicans. What a pity a decision wasn't taken. We could start a new Republican Party clean. Delays are dangerous. Many may change before the Ard-Fheis meets again.'

The will and personalities of de Valera and Collins appear to have completely dominated the Ard-Fheis. De Valera expected defeat at an election and hoped that over the three-month period agreed on he could win the Provisional Government around to the need to revise the Treaty. For such a policy to succeed it was crucial that the old political institutions remained intact—only within Sinn Féin and the Dáil did he retain any authority. At the Sinn Féin Funds Case in 1948 de Valera said his aim had been to preserve Sinn Féin as an all-embracing national organisation while there was any hope of unity. 'Sinn Féin', he declared then, 'was so to speak common ground until there had been . . . a definite decision as . . . to whether the Treaty would be in accordance with the constitution or not.'

Collins feared that an election would produce the military confrontation he wished to avoid at almost all costs. The time won by the agreement could be used to strive to achieve common ground on the constitution and to concentrate on the North and army unity issues.[10]

Sinn Féin continued to disintegrate during early 1922. The political scientist Tom Garvin has pointed out that the February assembly was effectively that of a rump party. Outside of the Dublin area the military was dominating the Sinn Féin organisation. Pro-Treatyites appear to have stopped attending meetings, which meant that by the time of the next Ard-Fheis, in May, there was, by default, a Republican majority. In March, as if in recognition of his failure to keep Sinn Féin united, de Valera set up his own political party, Cumann na Poblachta, which had little success (at the Sinn Féin Funds Case hearings de Valera was unable to remember when it ceased to function). The political divisions had helped to nationalise, and make more coherent, the general opposition to the Treaty, and political leaders retained some personal influence. From February on, however, the initiative in anti-Treaty affairs was in the hands of the IRA, which was little influenced by the political side.[11]

7

The Military Split

THE problem of preserving army unity would have been difficult enough in a static military situation, considering the divisions in the IRA over the Treaty. The situation was made infinitely worse, however, by the speedy British troop evacuation, which meant that evacuated barracks were taken over by local IRA units regardless of their Treaty attitude—and the new government had no choice but to agree to this. Large areas were dominated by anti-Treaty units: the most effective and experienced parts of the pre-truce IRA went anti-Treaty, with the exception of Brennan's command in Clare and Mac Eoin's in Longford, and elements, though not the majority, of the old Dublin No. 1 Brigade. Listowel and Skibbereen were the only barracks in Munster occupied by men supporting the Provisional Government. Mulcahy was to admit: 'We had not preserved the fabric of our organisation in ... Sligo, Mayo, Leitrim ... '

Before the new government, therefore, could build up any reliable military force a large proportion of the country was potentially outside their control. To contest the taking over of posts was to risk civil war. Unless some compromise was achieved on the constitutional issues, the establishment of government authority over all the Twenty-Six Counties would have to involve forcible takeover of Republican areas or, much less likely, Republican surrender.[1]

(a) THE ANTI-TREATY IRA

In terms of numbers and experience, the anti-Treaty members of the IRA had the advantage in the first months of 1922. That was the most likely period for successful military opposition to the Treaty. The opportunity, however, was not grasped: the anti-Treatyites showed a failure of coherence and purpose which was to bedevil their efforts during the Civil War. Frequently Republicans warned of the dangers of delay and thought that the pro-Treaty leadership were deliberately adopting a policy of prevarication and postponement while they built up their forces. Many pressed for action to take advantage of a situation which was not likely to continue. Young IRA leaders like Andy Cooney urged that an attempt should be made to capture Beggars' Bush barracks soon after the Provisional Government forces had established themselves there. Any armed clashes that occurred were, however, not part of any general plan. A Republican propaganda document published during the Civil War argued:

> Like the Republican political party, the Army of the Republic lost opportunity after opportunity since December last and wasted its strength in unavailing efforts to secure unity and peace. Our efforts and anxiety were

utilised by our opponents to gain time to strengthen their position, to undermine the Republic, and finally to strike us unexpectedly in the back.

Even the most intransigent parts of the anti-Treaty leadership, as represented
by Rory O'Connor and Liam Mellows, were reluctant to bring matters to a
military confrontation. The crucial 1st Southern Division, and particularly its
Cork leadership, sought continually to find some reconciliation with the GHQ
leadership. The old decentralised structure of the Volunteers told against post-
Treaty republican unity and direction. Maurice Walsh, of the 1st Battalion,
Dublin No. 1 Brigade, commented: 'In this country there were men in charge of
Divisions who were a law to themselves. They felt that they were responsible for
driving out the British.'[2]

The majority of divisional officers and three GHQ members met on 10 January
to formulate their anti-Treaty policy. They affirmed that the army had been established under its own executive, and that allegiance to the Dáil had only been
granted on the condition that the Republic be upheld. It was argued 'that the
action of the majority of the Dáil in supporting the Treaty involving the setting up
of an Irish Free State was a subversion of the Republic and relieved the Army from
its allegiance to An Dáil'. At that meeting Liam Lynch declared his intention of
cutting his division off from GHQ. Those there demanded that an Army Convention meet by 5 February and set up a Military Action Committee, later called
the Army Council.[3]

In response to the demand for a Convention, Mulcahy affirmed the need to keep
the army under the Dáil's control and told the Dáil cabinet that permission should
not be granted for the Convention. He did, however, agree to a meeting between
GHQ and anti-Treaty officers on 18 January. Ernie O'Malley recalled that he
attended that meeting with two guns under his coat. During the discussion Liam
Pilkington, O/C of the 3rd Western Division, declared his desire for separation
from GHQ, and Jim O'Donovan, the Director of Chemicals, accused Collins of
being a traitor. It became clear, however, that Mulcahy and Lynch were working
for some kind of compromise. Frank Aiken, O/C of the 4th Northern Division,
represented another voice for compromise, advocating delay of a Convention until
the publication of the Free State constitution. Mulcahy suggested that the holding
of a Convention should be delayed for two months, and meanwhile that a
'watchdog committee' should be set up to ensure that the interests of a republican
IRA should not be departed from. Some were sceptical of this committee's usefulness, including O'Malley, who, although appointed, never attended its meetings.
Nevertheless, two members from each side of the Treaty division were chosen for
the committee, which appears to have achieved little. When Mulcahy told them,
at the end of that meeting, that they would remain the army of the Irish Republic,
Rory O'Connor commented that the name alone would not make it so.[4]

It is clear from his change of mind on the Convention issue that Mulcahy only
agreed to a compromise with extreme reluctance. He told the Dáil in April: 'At a
time when the enemy was beginning to evacuate the country, I gave in to the
holding of a Convention.' Mulcahy knew that there was a considerable basis in the
IRA's history for demands for an independent Army Executive. He conducted the
18 January meeting with no reference to either the Provisional or Dáil governments. The agreement to the holding of a Convention was confirmed in February.
Again the Dáil and its cabinet were merely informed of the decisions and did not

take any part in making them. Desmond FitzGerald, the Minister for Publicity in the Provisional Government, complained of Mulcahy giving the impression that the Dáil cabinet had agreed to the holding of the Convention when he recalled it was decided 'not to bring it before the Dáil for fear of jeopardising the Free State' at a time when the bill establishing that state was passing through the British parliament. Mulcahy told the Dáil cabinet that 'the proposal is one which if given effect to will consolidate and strengthen the Army', but admitted: 'I would prefer that this Convention could have been avoided, and I don't accept any responsibility for the fact that it is forced to take place, but I do accept responsibility for recommending to the Dáil that in the circumstances permission . . . shall be given.' Tendentiously Mulcahy went on to argue that the setting up of an Army Executive would not take the army away from the Dáil's control.[5]

While anti-Treaty IRA leaders accepted that Mulcahy was in earnest about the Convention, and Mulcahy abided by the agreement that local units should take over barracks from the evacuating British troops, there was no cause for matters to be brought to a test. All that had been gained, however, was time.

The demand for an Army Convention had linked the desire for IRA units to continue to exercise local autonomy with the political demand for the Republic. Regional particularism was encouraged by the weakness of both GHQ and anti-Treaty leadership in those months. Nowhere was that better shown than in the case of the 2nd Southern Division, which on 16 January voted not to recognise GHQ. O'Malley admitted that his decision, as O/C, to support this line of action was connected with his desire to restore unity in his division and to assert his position within it, so leading, he hoped, to 'effective control and discipline'. When reprimanded by GHQ, the division refused to send any representatives to Dublin, and GHQ instructions against the taking of compulsory levies were ignored. O'Malley told a Cork officer that his division was acting by itself and struggling to exist. Commandeering remained rife, particularly in South Tipperary. When the Clonmel *Nationalist* refused to publish IRA proclamations it was suppressed and its machinery dismantled. The separation from GHQ increased the urgency for funds and military equipment: the Custom House in Clonmel was raided, as were military and police barracks, most notably the Clonmel RIC barracks, where 293 rifles and one armoured car were among the material seized. British military reports frequently dwelt on the lawlessness of South Tipperary and regarded it as the prime example of the Provisional Government's failure to assert its authority.[6]

(b) THE ESTABLISHMENT OF THE PROVISIONAL GOVERNMENT ARMY

It was vitally necessary for the security of the Provisional Government that loyal troops take over evacuated barracks where possible. It soon became necessary, therefore, to establish a Provisional Government army. As early as 12 January Mulcahy reported to the Dáil cabinet that they were faced with 'the necessity of arranging for taking over certain barracks, say Beggars' Bush, from the English and for the quartering and training of Irish troops to act as care and maintenance parties'. It was decided 'that such troops should be loaned from the Defence Dept and that the cost of their clothing and maintenance shall be defrayed out of the funds of the Provisional Government'. In the hope of preserving army unity, these plans could not be publicly admitted. O'Malley commented: 'I knew from the conversation I had with Ginger [J. J.] O'Connell that a Free State Army would be built up. I had no longer any faith in Collins or Mulcahy. They would use the army for their own purpose and slowly our men would either be absorbed or would return to their farms, business or universities.'

The army consisted of units almost entirely from outside Munster and the west, and of new recruits. Not only did the majority of the IRA go anti-Treaty, but many retired from the army. Only those agreeing to support the Treaty were admitted to the new army. Its first regular unit consisted of reliable Dublin men who took over Beggars' Bush barracks in March after being earlier installed in Celbridge barracks. Meanwhile the anti-Treaty IRA followed a policy of infiltrating the new army in the period up to the Army Convention.

The size of the force was initially small. A memorandum talked of plans for building up a small regular army of 25,000 from reliable IRA units, to be trained at Beggars' Bush and sent to take over local barracks. Training was to be based on a British War Office manual. It was admitted that the unit which took over Beggars' Bush barracks was 'very raw and untrained'. There were complaints about the lack of regular pay. The greatest problem was the lack of well-trained officers. A memorandum stressed: 'When the Regular Army started it was not possible to confine the number of Officers to the proportion required for a regular Army but any Volunteer officer who was Pro-Treaty and willing to join the Army was appointed an Officer.' Seán MacMahon, the Quartermaster-General, testified: 'We had got officers and other people who never got out of the backroom or the cellar and the old way of working that we had in 1921. . . . We found it very hard to get some of them out of it.' At the start of the Civil War, according to the Adjutant-General, the army had only six men who could drive a Crossley tender.[7]

The new army's weakness meant that considerable independence was granted to local commands and their O/Cs. Throughout the whole Civil War period local O/Cs appointed officers in their own areas. James Hogan wrote, after his retirement as Director of Intelligence in the Free State army: 'The Irish Army started on a territorial basis like feudal armies, and the feudal and baronial mentality is by no means dead in this country. . . . To give undue powers to individuals or Commands is to feed and stimulate such instincts.' Gearóid O'Sullivan, the Adjutant-General, admitted the considerable powers given to the GOCs, but said it had been necessary. For Charles F. Russell, who was in charge of aviation and then railway protection during the Civil War, each O/C was 'a kind of chieftain' and was only theoretically responsible to GHQ.[8]

The problems of the Provisional Government army in its early days were to be well revealed at the start of the Civil War. MacMahon recalled: 'When this task was over in Dublin we had to turn our faces to the Country and it was then, and not till then, that the realisation came to us that [we] were in for a long struggle and we began to look around for an Army.' Any intelligence system was confined to Dublin. To start with, uniforms had to be manufactured in Britain; of necessity, goods were not purchased in a regular way, and recourse was often made to commandeering. The old guerrilla warfare habits were to die hard. Emmet Dalton described the new army as 'a rag-tail and bobble-tail one'.

The lack of experience in the army also applied to the General Staff. Only J. J. O'Connell, the Deputy Chief of Staff, and Emmet Dalton had adequate training (the former with the USA army, the latter with the British forces during the First World War). Even Eoin O'Duffy, who was not given to modesty, admitted his lack of military experience and knowledge. Given the fluidity of the situation, it is not surprising that a fifth column element existed within the new army. Mutinies were a frequent occurrence, usually resulting from problems relating to pay and rank, which were exacerbated by the absence of military law.[9]

There were enormous problems involved in the transition from a volunteer, locally based guerrilla force to a regular, professional, government-controlled army. That particularly applied to the members of Collins's old 'Squad'—men like Liam Tobin, Tom Cullen, Jim Slattery and Frank Thornton—who seemingly went pro-Treaty, in the first place, because of personal loyalty to their 'chief'. They had formed a clannish unit during the Anglo-Irish War directly under Collins, had been a key element in Collins's intelligence system and what Colonel Charles Russell called the 'shock troops' of the Volunteers. The interim report of the 1924 Army Enquiry concluded of Tobin's group: 'Their training and experience in pre-Truce warfare was not calculated to help them to adapt themselves readily to the conditions of ordinary routine work.' They reacted badly to the establishment of a regular army with, in many cases, new men being brought in over their heads. The Tobinites resented O'Duffy taking over as Chief of Staff and had little respect for Mulcahy. At a meeting at the Gresham Hotel in Dublin in June they passed a motion of no confidence in the General Staff. Gearóid O'Sullivan recorded: 'Many subsequent mutineers never suffered from over-respect for discipline. . . . Were it not for the personal influence of . . . General Collins many of them would not be in our Army today', and concluded that since 1922 'some of them had marked themselves out as being opposed to authority of any kind in the Army'.[10]

J. J. O'Connell, the Deputy Chief of Staff, related his attempts to build up the army. O'Connell held that a small national force should consist of old, reliable IRA men and that their task should be to build up a line of stable garrisons preventing any spread of anti-Treaty areas. Barracks in Limerick, Templemore, Naas (which was to be used as a training base) and Kilkenny were to be taken over by reliable troops, even if that meant going back on Mulcahy's promise to hand over barracks to local IRA units regardless of their political allegiances. O'Connell, however, appears to have been over-optimistic about the size and effectiveness, together with the likely loyalty, of pro-Treaty troops. O'Sullivan, the army's Adjutant-General, gave a graphic illustration of the position in the spring of 1922:

> At that time we were in Beggars' Bush I did not know but the man in the next office would blow me up. . . . The idea was to build up a line of forts by fellows who might blow up the forts themselves. . . . On one occasion the late Chief of Staff and myself had to hold the Bank of Ireland for a few hours, because everybody had left it.

Mulcahy commented: 'We were dealing with a difficult situation where you did not know where loyalty lay and you had to handle the threat of what was a secret society.'[11]

(c) THE LIMERICK CRISIS

The government policy of allowing local IRA units, of whatever political complexion, to take over barracks broke down in Limerick.

The crisis there began as a local affair—a continuation, it seems, of pre-Treaty tensions between the Limerick city IRA and neighbouring units. Rival units contested the right to take over barracks from the British forces, who began to evacuate Limerick in late February and continued to leave until the process was completed on 25 March. A Mid-Limerick Brigade resolution of 18 February affirmed their loyalty to the Republic and independence from GHQ.[12] Faced with the prospect of the loss of Limerick, the Provisional Government decided that it was too important to lose. For the anti-Treaty IRA to have taken over the city would have been to directly link control of Munster with that of the west. Mac Eoin's command, based in Athlone and stretching from the midlands to the west coast, and Brennan's in the 1st Western Division, based in Clare, would have been left dangerously isolated. It was decided to order Brennan to occupy the evacuated barracks with men from his command, supported by loyal troops from Dublin, including some of Collins's old 'Squad'. As a response anti-Treaty forces moved into Limerick, led by men from O'Malley's 2nd Southern Division, and soon including men from all the strong fighting areas. The *Irish Times* reported that Limerick had become a rallying-point for anti-Treaty forces, and O'Malley claimed at one stage that they had eighteen posts.

O'Malley's plan for a speedy takeover of all Provisional Government positions, however, miscarried. He gave pro-Treaty forces in the Castle barracks, led by Collins's old henchman Jim Slattery, twelve hours to leave, but Rory O'Connor refused O'Malley's request to send engineers for his planned assault. Despite O'Malley's warnings that the Provisional Government would take posts all over the Twenty-Six Counties if the IRA did not act decisively, the rest of the anti-Treaty leadership showed no inclination for a military showdown. O'Malley wrote to Rory O'Connor on 9 March: 'Tell Séamus Robinson to adopt a stiffer attitude. Am seizing some rather important positions today. . . . Will be ready to knock hell out of the others in two or three days' time.' Little more than a flexing of military muscle resulted, however, and J. J. O'Connell reported the great reluctance of both sides to fire the first shot. Old friends made reluctant fighters. O'Malley reported that 'Free State Units in three Barracks said they would not fight against me—at one time they had worked under me.' Michael Brennan was quoted as saying: 'I have just had lunch with the opposition, and we are all perfectly friendly.' The *Cork Examiner* commented: 'Meanwhile the county life flows smoothly, and the people, reassured by the good behaviour of the invaders, are not inclined to take the whole business too seriously.'[13]

It became apparent that the Republican forces, in terms of equipment and men, held the advantage. Brennan demanded more arms, even asking for a tank and contrasted his resources with the opposition's. He reported:

> There are 800 mutineers here at present all armed with rifles and most of them with revolvers also. They have a splendid transport service—we have practically none. . . . Robinson told me yesterday that they propose putting three or four thousand men here. I propose cutting down my garrison here but increasing my reserves outside. . . . As it is a foregone conclusion that the mutineers will be able to lock us in I propose cutting down the Limerick garrison to 500 reliable men. . . . Some of my men have too many associations with the Mutineers to be properly reliable, hence my anxiety to get 100 good men from KcKeown [sic]. The 3rd Southern is too near things to be thoroughly reliable.[14]

The Limerick crisis became a major test of the Provisional Government's will to govern. Arthur Griffith urged that all the barracks be taken, and initially, according to Ernest Blythe, who was present at the meetings, he was backed up by Collins in 'a lukewarm way'. Mulcahy, however, effectively vetoed such plans by warning that 'the Pro-Treaty Forces were not yet ready from the point of view either of psychology or even of military training to carry out satisfactorily the suggested operations'. Military logic won the day within the government—the new force, given its apparent weakness and the dangers of desertion, was not ready for a decisive test. Furthermore, Mulcahy's original strategy of occupying barracks in the city with outside troops had failed, and the only recourse to be had was negotiation with his old colleagues.

The Republican leadership was as desirous for compromise as Mulcahy. O'Donoghue related that Liam Lynch regarded the situation as 'a disgrace to both sides', and Lynch was more proud of his role in producing a settlement, he declared, than any successes he had achieved in the Anglo-Irish War. De Valera was also greatly alarmed and on 6 March wrote to Mulcahy begging him to intercede. By the time de Valera's letter arrived Mulcahy and his adjutant were on their way to Limerick.[15]

The initial peace move was made by Mayor O'Mara, who, on behalf of a committee set up in the city, travelled to Dublin to plead with the various leaders. Lynch was wrong to say that O'Mara's peace mission failed. Griffith took an intransigent line and insisted that Republican forces must withdraw before there could be any settlement. When O'Mara said that he 'almost thought it would be better to burn the Barracks than to risk a continuation of the situation', Griffith replied: 'That would not solve the difficulty, which is that these men challenge our authority and right.... A worse disaster than a continuation of the present situation would be the overthrow of the Dáil and the Provisional Government.' Despite Griffith's firm stance, the next day O'Mara saw Mulcahy and O'Duffy, and the outline of a settlement was arrived at.

The proposals were that the police barracks should be held by the Limerick Corporation; outside troops should return to their own areas; and a small maintenance party of local troops, under Lynch's authority, should be left to occupy two military barracks. The settlement, 'fixed' in Dublin, had to be then sold to men like Ernie O'Malley and Tom Barry in Limerick. At Mulcahy's suggestion, Liam Lynch and Oscar Traynor travelled overnight to Limerick with the terms. J. J. O'Connell disapprovingly recorded that the agreement was arrived at in Beggars' Bush mess: 'All I was able to do', he said, was to arrange for an officer 'to drive Lynch and a colleague to Limerick'. On 11 March Rory O'Connor wrote to Erskine Childers about the terms:

> They have been agreed to by Mulcahy—Lynch and Stephen O'Mara conveyed this to Limerick.... The matter is settled at this end. If the Limerick officers accept this the whole incident is closed. If it has not been accepted in Limerick, you may take it for certain that there will be no further negotiations, and in fact fighting on the lines decided upon will have already commenced when you receive this note.

Soon a messenger told O'Connor that the proposals had been accepted. Oscar Traynor recalled:

In King John's Castle we saw Brennan who tried to bluster as he said he was going to fight and he was puffed out in his uniform like a peacock. . . . We had an awful job with Barry. . . . We saw fellows lying in numbers and rifles sticking out. . . . We were successful in getting people to call it off. Eventually they marched off singing and carrying their guns. We had to try and impress on Barry that there would be fighting at some time.[16]

The crisis had developed spontaneously and had been settled by Anglo-Irish War leaders, reinforced by their IRB loyalties, which on both sides represented what little basis there was for centralised control of local units. General Macready described the events as resembling a 'comic opera', but they had serious implications. As a Republican source claimed, the Limerick agreement represented a considerable climbdown by the Provisional Government. Collins continued to be alarmed by the Limerick situation, as shown by his later abortive attempts to get Churchill to arrange for the remaining British troops to postpone their evacuation. The affair had caused considerable alarm within the British government. Churchill wrote to Collins: 'You seem to have liquidated the Limerick situation in one way or another. No doubt you know your own business best, and thank God you have got to manage it and not me.' J. J. O'Connell regarded the agreement as a sellout and a disastrous blow to his plans to build up the Provisional Government army. A meeting of loyal pro-Treaty troops protested against the Limerick compromise and concluded:

Without the attendance of all the members of GHQ Staff and in consultation with officers not entitled to be present a decision was taken . . . which the people of Ireland seem to regard as something nearly approaching capitulation to the mutineers, and which, we have reason to think, tended to cause demoralisation amongst units loyal to GHQ.

The pro-Treaty quartermaster of the Mid-Limerick Brigade, Seán Hurley, who had been imprisoned during the crisis for attempting to take over barracks and had then gone on hunger-strike as a protest, also complained, writing: 'The mutineers regard the present arrangement as a victory over GHQ.'[17]

In the prevailing military circumstances, it is difficult to see what else the Provisional Government could have done. In the short term, the Limerick crisis led to increased tensions before the Army Convention. The battle for Limerick was postponed until July. The crisis was soon followed by confrontations over the evacuated barracks in Templemore, Birr and Renmore which again illustrated the weakness of the Provisional Government army.

J. J. O'Connell regarded Templemore as an important part of his planned line of strong Provisional Government posts, and he strove to ensure its loyalty while anti-Treaty troops were otherwise engaged at Limerick. The local Templemore unit had yet to declare its allegiance. Jimmy Leahy, the local O/C at Templemore, however, refused to admit outside troops to the barracks, even when O'Connell arrived. Leahy told O'Malley that he had tried to obtain rifles from Mulcahy with a view then to holding the barracks for the Republic. Later, in April, O'Connell sent an armoured car to Templemore, only to have it lost to the anti-Treaty forces. O'Duffy recorded: 'I got ready a force to go to Templemore after the car. All that was possible was for an officer and the driver to steal into the

Barracks and dismantle some minor parts.' Men from the pro-Treaty 1st Eastern Division, who had been involved in the attempt to take over Templemore, were sent to deal with a similar situation at Birr and took joint occupation of the barracks with Seán Gaynor's local men. At the end of March Gaynor took over the barracks and disarmed the 1st Eastern men. Gaynor, the acting O/C of the 3rd Southern Division, put the discontent in Birr barracks with the Provisional Government down to the lack of regular pay, and had asked the troops which side they wished to support before his action. Again O'Duffy, who was having a frustrating spring, went down to deal with the situation and was refused entry to the barracks. A similar affair occurred at Renmore, where 200 Provisional Government troops, who again had been part of an occupying force, were disarmed. GHQ once more did not feel their position was strong enough to attempt to regain control.

At a time coincident with the holding of the Army Convention, the weakness of the new army's position had been strikingly illustrated in key parts of the strategically important south midlands. The British government was concerned, particularly after the loss of the armoured car at Templemore, that arms it had been handing over to the Provisional Government were not ending up in reliable hands. At the end of March Churchill told Cope: 'There can be no question of handing over further arms until we are assured that persons to whom they are entrusted will use them with fidelity to Irish Provisional Government and will not allow them simply to pass into Republican hands. Such episodes', he added, 'tend to cramp my style.'[18]

(d) THE ARMY CONVENTION

The Limerick crisis and the other disputes over barrack occupation had made it clear to anti-Treatyites that the Provisional Government was building up an army of its own. In the Dáil, in March and April, Mulcahy came under fierce pressure on the question. Brugha eagerly quoted Churchill as having said in the House of Commons that the IRA were acting under the orders of the Provisional Government. Mrs O'Callaghan complained of Mulcahy: 'I cannot see how he has maintained the Army as the Army of the Irish Republic. Under his management, it has split into two camps and it is very hard for the plain people to follow the position.' Mellows claimed that a Free State army 'was being superimposed upon the Army of the Republic'.

The worsening military situation led to the Provisional Government reconsidering whether the Army Convention should be allowed to proceed. They feared that if permission was granted, the strength of anti-Treaty troops would become apparent and the government would be greatly embarrassed by the virtually certain declaration of army independence which would be made at the meeting. It was already clear, from the results of brigade elections of delegates to the Convention, that there was to be a considerable anti-Treaty majority. With such considerations in mind, Griffith issued an order on 16 March banning the Convention. It stated that the proposed Convention would 'endeavour to remove the Army from under the control of the Government elected by the people, which is Dáil Éireann. Such a purpose is illegal.' The Dáil cabinet meeting which discussed the order asserted that the Dáil should be 'the sole body in supreme control of the

Army and that any effort to set up another body in control would be tantamount to an attempt to establish a Military Dictatorship'. Mulcahy ascribed the need for a ban to political influences which had destroyed the army's unity. The greatest political influence, however, was the Treaty.[19]

Even after the banning order, Mulcahy had hopes of a rapprochement with the anti-Treaty parts of the IRA through contact with Lynch and the 1st Southern Division. He told Collins that, while opposed to any talk of a military dictatorship, Lynch felt that the Convention should insist on the Army Executive having full control over the IRA. Mulcahy hoped that if Lynch agreed not to interfere with an election, and if some form of compromise was achieved over the army's constitutional status, there could yet be an avoidance of a complete split. Mulcahy met with 1st Southern Division leaders at Mallow on 20 March. It was suggested then that brigade and divisional commandants meet with the GHQ staff to elect a council to 'frame definite proposals for associating the IRA with the Government elected by the Irish people'. Lynch agreed to this and to the postponement of the Convention until 16 April, but added that recruiting for the Civic Guard should be discontinued. The 1st Southern Division, as shown by a resolution they framed on the subject at the Convention, felt very strongly about the need for the IRA to retain control of policing. On 21 March the Dáil cabinet turned down these terms. Mulcahy was to complain that Lynch failed to deliver on his promise to bring the resolutions to his divisional council. There was still, nevertheless, considerable scope for negotiations between GHQ and the 1st Southern Division, as was to be demonstrated in the post-Convention period.

Meanwhile Rory O'Connor seemingly appointed himself leader of the anti-Treaty military cause. On 22 March he held what soon became a notorious press conference. When asked then if the army would forcibly prevent an election being held, O'Connor said: 'It will be in its power to do it'; and in answer to a question on whether there was to be a military dictatorship, he replied: 'You can take it that way if you like.' O'Connor claimed to represent eighty per cent of the army, and asserted that 'There were times when revolution was justified and the army had overthrown the Government in many countries in that way.' He argued that it was impossible to give allegiance to any government, affirming: 'If a Government goes wrong it must take the consequences.' O'Connor concluded by stating that he didn't understand the Treaty and hadn't read Document No. 2.[20]

The Convention itself, which met on 26 March, was something of an anticlimax following the dramatic build-up. Mick Leahy recorded that his men from Cork went to the Convention 'in battle formation with full equipment and an armoured car'. The Provisional Government took no action against the meeting, apart from Mulcahy's announcement that those attending it should receive no more support from GHQ. According to O'Donoghue's notes, taken during the roll-call at the beginning of the Convention, 223 delegates attended. A detailed breakdown of the representation shows the high proportion from the south and west: 54 of the delegates came from the 1st Southern Division and 28 from the 2nd Southern Division, while a total of 69 delegates attended from the four western divisions. Four GHQ officers were present. An evaluation of what proportion of the IRA attended is complicated by the fact that some went as uncommitted observers. With Frank Aiken's approval, therefore, two of his 4th Northern Division attended, although they still followed their division's neutral stance. The areas most heavily represented were where the IRA had been strongest during the Anglo-Irish War.

Eoin O'Duffy soon claimed that the bulk of the army remained loyal to the Provisional Government. He argued that in twelve of the sixteen divisions seventy-five per cent supported GHQ, and in the remaining four divisions between thirty and fifty per cent. O'Duffy concluded, with a desperate optimism: 'GHQ was never in a stronger position than now, enjoying as it does the loyalty and confidence of a fairly equipped, well-trained and well-disciplined Army, which has the respect and devotion of a grateful people.' O'Duffy's attempt to demonstrate that there was a split between the attitudes of officers and the rank and file in the Southern and Western Commands was tenuous. O'Connor immediately replied to O'Duffy's claims, pointing out that 52 of the 73 IRA brigades in the country had attended the Convention, and that 'The numerical strength of one division alone, which was fully represented, amounts to one quarter of the whole army in Ireland.' The turnout at the Convention was firm evidence that Mulcahy had been correct to stress the vulnerable position of the new army at the time of the Limerick crisis.[21]

Predictably the Convention reaffirmed the republican status of the army and agreed that the army should be brought back under the complete control of its Executive. The members of the new Executive were chosen by the Convention, and it was decided to draw up a new army constitution. It also resolved that the Belfast boycott should be reimposed, that dog-licence money could be collected by the IRA, and that the new Civic Guard should be boycotted in the way that the old RIC had been. A motion to prevent a general election was discussed and widely supported, before being referred to the next Executive meeting.

Beneath the surface the Convention revealed disharmony and a lack of coherent purpose. There was a row about who should chair the assembly, and frequent complaints were made by Cork men about their not being sufficiently represented on the new Executive. Oscar Traynor recalled that he threatened to resign from the Executive over Liam Lynch's complaints. Joe O'Connor, of Dublin No. 1 Brigade, claimed that the anti-Treaty IRA never recovered from these divisions, and declared: 'The First Southern had threatened us with 30,000 men.'

Many criticised the lack of definite decisions made. Tom Maguire, the O/C of the 2nd Western Division, later commented: 'We were undecided . . . because the last thing we wanted to do was to start to shoot. We would have done anything to avoid that', although he felt that nearly fifty per cent of the delegates were for strong action against the Provisional Government.

The Convention went far to clarify an extremely confusing military situation: nobody could pretend after it that the IRA was one body. It greatly heightened tensions over the occupation of barracks and led to a great increase in commandeering and bank raids. Financial problems for the anti-Treaty IRA were intensified, as they now were deprived of any GHQ assistance.[22]

Events before, during and after the Convention served to associate the new Executive with military dictatorship and censorship. Tod Andrews strongly criticised O'Connor's press conference (together with many of his later utterances) and the wrecking of the presses of the *Freeman's Journal* after it had published an account of the Convention's proceedings. He saw them as grave mistakes, as giving the impression that people 'were liable to be pushed around at the whim of young IRA commanders. Discipline was rapidly deteriorating in the local units of the

IRA. People began to feel unsafe of the enjoyment of their property and their freedom of movement.` The anti-Treaty IRA was showing a disregard for general opinion. Thanks to the association of anti-Treaty units with commandeering, looting, censorship and compulsory levies, the Provisional Government was increasingly able to use the virtues of majority rule and law and order as major planks. Before the Convention the anti-Treaty side had been able to argue that the Provisional Government had undermined stability by the subterfuge of building up its army under the camouflage of the IRA. From the Convention onwards the anti-Treaty IRA got most of the blame for the worsening disorder and the increasingly apparent threat of civil war.[23]

8

De Valera and the Military and Political Developments

THE period between the Treaty and the end of the Civil War represented Eamon de Valera's political nadir. Bishop MacRory commented: 'Since the Treaty he had apparently got no status.' He was able to exercise little personal authority over events; his claim to national leadership became increasingly tenuous. Concentration by historians and contemporaries on de Valera's responsibility for the Civil War can be explained less by any consideration of his actual importance at the time than by his later dominance, for so long, of Irish politics, and by his leadership before the Treaty.

De Valera had become an increasingly isolated figure striving behind the scenes to win back his influence. He had significance in making the anti-Treaty cause publicly understood, in personifying it as the best-known figure on the Republican side, and in making the issues appear national in scope. His Treaty revision policy, however, had no hope of success because of British insistence on the terms of the Treaty, which meant, ultimately, that Griffith and Collins could not compromise. Meanwhile, to maintain his position as the nominal head of the Republicans, de Valera could not be seen to oppose pure republican philosophy or the IRA.

De Valera had deep reservations about the Army Executive's independent line. During the Civil War he admitted, in private correspondence, that he regretted declaring support for Rory O'Connor at the time of the Four Courts attack, and he had been a firm opponent of autonomous IRA activity. At a meeting of anti-Treaty TDs during the Treaty debates it was decided that 'no action should be taken likely to lead to violence or civil war'. It was agreed 'provisionally that should the Army fall under the control of the Provisional or Free State Government the best course for members of it who refused to come under that control would be to leave the Army and become members of Republican Clubs'. Childers recorded in his diary on 14 January: 'The President—with Rory O'C at 6. Army question. Convention? P. [de Valera] against.'

Rory O'Connor admitted that the Four Courts had been taken without consulting, or even informing, de Valera. O'Connor and his staff, Childers recorded, 'decided to act independently of political leaders henceforward', and though they held de Valera 'in respect and trust', they were convinced that only the army could deal with the situation. Mrs Childers, writing to de Valera in 1940, recalled this and commented: 'Later, talking with Erskine and me, you confirmed this statement that Rory and the others had not consulted you. What grave apprehension you felt and how anxious were the days that followed...' De Valera admitted in the Dáil that he had no control of the army.[1]

The series of notorious speeches de Valera made in March and April should be seen in the context of his diminishing influence. At Thurles, where a meeting was attended by Séamus Robinson and 700 men of the Tipperary No. 3 Brigade, de Valera warned: 'If the Treaty were accepted the fight for freedom would still go on and the Irish people instead of fighting foreign soldiers would have to fight the Irish soldiers of an Irish Government set up by Irish men.' In an even more controversial speech at Killarney de Valera said that if the Treaty was accepted by the electorate, IRA men 'will have to march over the dead bodies of their own brothers. They will have to wade through Irish blood.' The *Irish Times* talked of de Valera's contempt for democracy. The London *Times* expostulated: 'Mr de Valera's wild speeches in the South of Ireland have shocked the whole country. They indicate a rapid change in his attitude for some little time ago he was protesting that the will of the electors must be respected.' Time after time in the Dáil de Valera was to be reminded of how his speeches in the spring of 1922 contradicted his affirmation during the Treaty debates that a constitutional way should be found to resolve their differences.

Though de Valera, as he explained in his letter to the *Irish Independent* protesting about misrepresentation, meant his speeches as warnings of civil war rather than incitement to it, he nevertheless showed an amazing insensitivity to the effect his speeches would have and to the inevitability of their being misunderstood. The historian J. M. Curran has commented that the Irish people were all too well aware of the dangers of civil war and did not require further warnings. De Valera may well have been trying to force Griffith and Collins to compromise, but instead had placed himself in a very embarrassing position.

De Valera's struggle to retain his influence had led him to appear to reject majority rule and constitutionalism, which, in normal circumstances, represented the basis of his political philosophy. De Valera told John J. Hearn, an Irish-American activist: 'Events here since 1921 have tended to make it difficult to distinguish between fundamental principle and mere policy.' In an interview with the *Evening News* de Valera claimed that the views of the military and political opposition to the Treaty were identical. 'If there is a movement toward a military dictatorship,' he commented, 'it is because the present Executive of Dáil Éireann has broken its pledge to maintain the authority of Dáil Éireann and the Institutions of the Republic.' He went on to say that a free election would only be held if the British threat was removed, and that the army was providing a necessary check against the abandonment of the Republic. More controversially still, when de Valera refused Griffith's and Collins's attempt to sign a pledge opposing intimidation at the election, de Valera said that there were 'rights which a minority may justly uphold, even by arms, against a majority'. Such arguments, however, stemmed from the exigencies of the moment.

De Valera's complex position was made the more difficult to understand by his tendency to cloak political compromise and ambiguity in the language of principle. His wordy utterances, moreover, led easily to caricature and confusion. To interpret the complexities of de Valera's language and mind became, and was long to remain, a national pastime. It was difficult to ascribe ordinary politicians' considerations to the much revered and abused Chief.

During the whole Civil War period there was never any prospect of de Valera's strategy being accepted, either in London or by all his Republican allies. The consequence was an increasingly marginal role for him.[2]

9

Military Developments after the Army Convention

THE setting up of a separate Army Executive made the struggle for evacuated posts a far more open affair. Many fence-sitters on the Treaty issue within the army declared their views. The confrontations over the barracks at Birr and Renmore coincided with the holding of the Convention; a succession of such struggles followed in April in 'frontier' areas in the midlands and the east. The government was particularly worried about the Dublin area and set up a separate 2nd Eastern Division to help deal with any threat. Although the Provisional Government troops were in the minority in Dublin No. 1 Brigade, no barracks were ceded there to the anti-Treaty forces.

It was in Dublin, however, that the Executive forces staged their most dramatic coup. On the night of 13 April men from Dublin No. 1 Brigade, on the orders of the Executive's Army Council, took over the Four Courts building in Dublin as Republican military headquarters. Various other buildings were occupied in the city—the Fowler Hall, the Ballast Office, the Masonic Hall and Kilmainham Jail among them. Some of the buildings were used for work connected with the Belfast boycott: the Kildare Street Club, for example, housed Belfast refugees. The taking over of the imposing Four Courts building was the most symbolic of acts and dramatised the failure of Provisional Government authority. There was no military strategy involved. The Four Courts Hotel, which was vital to any defence of the Four Courts, was quickly given up because, it seems, it was owned by Stephen O'Mara, the Mayor of Limerick, whom they had no desire to offend. The Republican garrison, consisting, among others, of men from the South Tipperary Brigade, became a kind of revolutionary vanguard. The uncompromising presence of Rory O'Connor, Liam Mellows and Ernie O'Malley dominated the Four Courts occupation, and they issued intransigent press statements from there. On 14 April Mellows, as secretary of the Army Council, sent peace terms to the Secretary of the Dáil laying down the basis of their claims, which included the disbandment of the Civic Guard, an undertaking from the Dáil to meet all the army's financial liabilities, and an agreement that no elections would be held 'while the threat of war with England exists'. The Executive warned that these terms represented 'probably the last' hope for the Dáil to take 'this matter out of the hands of the Cabinet' and 'of saving the country from Civil War, now threatened by those who have abandoned the Republic'.[1]

The Four Courts occupation hugely alarmed British government circles. While Alfred Cope repeatedly pointed out to Churchill that any pro-Treaty attempt to seize the building would be counterproductive, he could not hide how effectively it demonstrated the weakness of Collins's and Griffith's position. While Churchill in public stated that Collins's cautious policy was the correct one, he complained informally: 'I do not understand why they do not ring them round and starve them out.' Macready told Churchill on 16 April: 'It is vitally important to avoid a general conflict, because it is probable that Rory O'Connor ... hopes to embroil British Troops in order to bring about unity in the Irish Republican Army against a common enemy.' Churchill replied: 'I entirely approve of the arrangement you have made with the Provisional Government about our troops. Intervention in any form would be a most grave act which only the supreme emergency could justify.' No response was made even to the killing of three British soldiers in Co. Cork in April, although Macready was unhappy, remarking that Churchill had decided not to take a hard line so as not to embarrass the political situation. After that Macready was additionally keen to speedily evacuate barracks in Cork, but that was prevented by Collins's failure to give an assurance that pro-Treaty troops would take over.

As early as 5 April Churchill was warning: 'A point might come when it would be necessary to tell Mr Collins that if he was unable to deal with the situation the British Government would have to do so.' Between April and June economic and military subcommittees of the cabinet met and drew up contingency plans for any breakdown of relations with the Provisional Government. The preferred plans were for a limited economic blockade and for an occupation of the waterways from Co. Donegal to Co. Louth in order to prevent any threat to the North.[2]

Despite the establishment of the IRA Executive, local initiative remained the dominant characteristic of anti-Treaty actions. Many were interested in the occupation of barracks from the point of view of gaining supplies, particularly as the possibility of GHQ arms and financial assistance was at an end. There was no coherent policy with regard to the occupation of barracks. The failure of anti-Treaty forces to take over various barracks was often due less to the effectiveness of the pro-Treaty forces than their own lack of a sense of direction. Con Casey, who had moved to the 1st Eastern Division from Kerry No. 1 Brigade, commented on the failure of Executive forces to take over Drogheda and Mullingar and complained of the lack of leadership from GHQ. Leo Henderson, of Dublin No. 1 Brigade, also said: 'There was no lead from anywhere.' Though Ernie O'Malley was greatly encouraged by the occupation of the Four Courts and thought it might lead to the end of the policy of drift, he was soon dissatisfied again. He declared: 'There was no attempt to define a clear-cut policy. Words ran into phrases, sentences followed sentences.... A drifting policy discussed endlessly in a shipwrecked way.' Paddy Mullally, of North Kildare, commented: 'The Executive at the time of the attack on the Four Courts was appointed from the whole country, yet here you were stuck in the Four Courts. There were no orders given to the country as to what they should do.'[3]

The anti-Treaty IRA had considerable success in arms raids, particularly the major coup resulting from the taking of arms from the naval vessel, the *Upnor*, which was travelling, according to official British documents, with 400 rifles (rather than 2,000, as was claimed), together with 700 revolvers and, among other material, 25,000 rounds of ammunition. It left Haulbowline dockyard for Portsmouth, but was intercepted by the *Warrior*, which had been commandeered by the local IRA under Seán Hegarty at Queenstown harbour. Most of the arms on the *Upnor* were escorted to Ballycotten, where they were taken away by 200 lorries. Alfred Cope immediately reported to Lionel Curtis, of the Colonial Office, on 5 April concerning the rumours that more arms had been taken than was officially admitted, commenting: 'I have heard of one battalion of insurgent IRA being offered 500 rifles from the "Upnor scoop".' Collins quickly charged the British naval forces with collusion, while British sources talked of pro-Treaty troop complicity in the incident. Churchill brusquely reminded Collins: 'You have claimed and assumed the responsibilities which we are relaxing and there the burden rests.' Curtis concluded that the 'elaborate conspiracy' revealed Provisional Government control of that area of Cork 'to be practically non-existent'.[4]

Following the South Tipperary Brigade's raid on Clonmel RIC barracks in late February, the British cabinet were told that 'The capture of arms had put the rebels in relatively a better position than the forces of the Provisional Government.' On 2 March a large number of arms had been landed from Bremerhaven at Helvic Head, Co. Waterford. Such developments led to the Provisional Government stepping up their demands for arms supplies from Churchill at the time when the British government were becoming greatly alarmed concerning the Provisional Government's stability.

A series of incidents during April and early May demonstrated the indecision of anti-Treaty military policy, the highly localised nature of the divisions, and the Provisional Government's weak position. The various confrontations between rival forces bore a remarkable resemblance to each other. Frank O'Connor, the writer, who in his youth was an IRA man in Cork, later described these events:

> On all such occasions the demonstration seems to have been solely with the purpose of starting a parley and declaring a truce, and, in most of these, excitable priests rushed from general to general, and the generals, straight from the paternal farms, sat at large tables and read maps and gave interviews; sometimes the two parties came to blows, there were shots fired and arrests made. Then there were fresh demonstrations and ultimatums, and fresh parleys and fresh newspaper interviews, in which the contending generals made it quite clear that it was the other fellow with his unreasonableness and bellicosity who was intent upon plunging the country into civil war. It was the beginning of a campaign which would make the position of the Provisional Government intolerable, [and]...but for its tragic consequences would have been exceedingly funny.

What deaths did occur seem to have been accidental, as in the case of Brigadier-General Adamson of Athlone. Adamson had been leading a party of officers from Custume Barracks in Athlone who had gone to the Royal Hotel, which was held by anti-Treaty forces, to commandeer a motor-car. Adamson was shot while in the car. Following the shooting, the leader of the anti-Treatyites there, Seán Fitzpatrick, agreed to Mac Eoin's order to evacuate the Royal Hotel. Thomas Johnson, the Labour Party leader, justifiably asked why a car had been commandeered before Adamson's shooting. The enquiry on the Adamson affair broke down in disorder and feuding over who was responsible for the killing. While Collins was convinced he knew who was responsible, Republicans continued to place the responsibility on the men in Adamson's guard.[5]

In the sundry confrontations of April much depended on bluff on both sides. J. J. O'Connell argued that where the Provisional Government held a garrison strongly it was not lost. Much depended, however, on the strength and popularity of the local leadership. Twice on successive days in Athlone, Mac Eoin, aided by the temporising activity of local priests, persuaded armed Executive forces to evacuate the Royal Hotel. When the soldiers guarding the Bank of Ireland building in the centre of Dublin mutinied, shortly after the Army Convention of 26 March, the quick thinking of Vinny Byrne, who was in command of them, prevented a complete collapse by insisting, gun at the ready, that only those stating definite loyalty to the government could remain. He was rescued at the last moment by Beggars' Bush reinforcements. While the mutiny was in process Oscar Traynor was outside the building ready to occupy it with a force from his Dublin No. 1 Brigade. According to J. J. O'Connell, only six of the fifty men there had been prepared to declare their loyalty to GHQ, and a new guard had to be enlisted. After that anti-Treaty IRA plans to storm Beggars' Bush, by means of collusion from within, proved stillborn.[6]

At Mullingar a potential armed clash was nipped in the bud by an exchange of prisoners. Walter Mitchell, of Offaly No. 2 Brigade, complained of the anti-Treatyites' abrupt termination of their attempts to take over the barracks: 'They had to get out or lose what guns they had. . . . We were, in effect, being stood down.' Tod Andrews, who had been sent to reorganise the Eastern Division, spoke with dismay of Michael Price's abortive attack on the Auxiliaries who were evacuating Gormanstown Camp. Price had undertaken it on his own initiative, without reference to the division's command. Of the Eastern Division, Andrews concluded: 'Having visited several areas I discovered that, except for Leixlip and Mullingar, there was very little left to organise.'

The final, and largest, armed confrontation between the Army Convention and the army truce was the Kilkenny crisis of early May. It resembled a smaller version of the Limerick crisis of March. Supported by men from South Tipperary, anti-Treaty forces in Kilkenny took over various positions in the city, including Ormond Castle and the City Hall. Hastily the Provisional Government sent 200 men from the Dublin Guard by train who retook the buildings. There was much firing but few casualties. Just when an outright military confrontation appeared on the cards an agreement was patched together in Dublin whereby the barracks in the city were to be shared by the rival IRAs.[7]

The anti-Treaty IRA had not been as successful in capturing barracks during April as they had been at Templemore, Birr and Renmore. Athlone stayed uneasily in Mac Eoin's control, and the Provisional Government still remained dominant in the area around Dublin.

Military tension also focused on political meetings. Meetings addressed by Collins and Griffith became an opportunity for the anti-Treaty IRA to show their strength. Collins wrote to Joe McGarrity on 5 April 1922:

> The Opposition policy is making it almost impossible for us to hold useful meetings. The crowds assemble all right, but 20, or 30, or 40 interrupters succeed in most places in preventing the speakers from being heard. That apparently is the official policy accompanied by blocked roads and torn up railways to prevent the excursion trains from bringing the people to our meetings.

Collins concluded that he feared civil war was close at hand.

Collins gave speeches at that time deep in areas dominated by the anti-Treaty IRA. On 14 March he travelled to Cork, where, together with the Deputy Lord Mayor and Seán Mac Eoin, he was refused entry to the republican plot in the cemetery by twelve armed men. Later, at a meeting in the city, attended by 50,000 according to Collins's estimate, shots were fired. Collins thought there were 'no more than a dozen' doing the shooting. Meanwhile a train bringing people to the meeting was held up at Mogeely station on its way from Midleton to Cork. In early April Collins was prevented from speaking at Dungarvan when the train on which he was delivering his address was driven off while he was speaking. He was eventually forced to speak from a hotel balcony. In a tense meeting at Castlebar Collins was prevented from being heard. Potentially even worse problems faced Collins when he was due to speak at Killarney on 22 April and Tralee the day after. In both cases the meetings were proclaimed by the local IRA. At the last moment, however, IRA forces in both localities were confined to barracks as a result of last-minute agreements. At Tralee Collins declared that neither the Treaty nor the Republic were worth the risk of civil war.'[8]

The tensest of all these public gatherings was that addressed by Arthur Griffith on Easter Sunday, 6 April, in Sligo. Liam Pilkington, the local division's O/C, had proclaimed the meeting. Republican troops poured into Sligo, taking over buildings and preparing to carry out the order. In response, Mac Eoin led Provisional Government troops from Athlone to the town and took possession of the jail; on the day of the meeting he was joined by J. J. O'Connell and more troops. All the ingredients for an armed confrontation seemed established. Before his departure from Dublin, Griffith left a letter with friends in case he did not return. At the last moment, however, Pilkington decided not to enforce the ban. Griffith arrived at the meeting with Mac Eoin in an armoured car and was surrounded by troops while speaking. No shots were fired.

The Sligo affair was seen as a failure by many Republicans. Frank Carty, a Sligo IRA leader, called it 'the flop'; to some Pilkington had proved an Irish version of the grand old Duke of York. The British government, however, were encouraged by the Provisional Government's determination to go ahead with the meeting. Mark Sturgis told Churchill that the meeting represented a personal triumph for Griffith, and the London *Times* concluded: 'We find it difficult to hold that a stronger handling of affairs would not prove, as it proved at Sligo, the more profitable policy.'[9]

10

The North, from Treaty to Attack
on the Four Courts

THE Treaty heightened tensions in the North and proved a prelude to a greatly
increased level of violence—particularly on the border and in Belfast—in the
six months following. For loyalists the prospect of the Boundary Commission
produced strong fears that an attempt would be made to alter radically the area of
jurisdiction of the Northern government; for nationalists expectations had been
raised. The Treaty, furthermore, made Southern politicians more sensitive to the
interests of the North's minority population and increased the enormous stress the
Northern government placed on security considerations, with the greater use of
the notorious Special Constabulary. While the coalition sought to implement the
Treaty terms as they applied to the Six Counties, there was an increasing
divergence between British government views and those of the Northern government.

In loyalist opinion the constitutional status of Northern Ireland could not be
changed—the Treaty only related to Britain and Southern Ireland. It followed
that the British government should provide the necessary financial and security
force backing as the Northern government strove to maintain its stability.
Loyalists, however, felt intensely suspicious of the British government's intentions.
On 15 December 1921 Craig warned Austen Chamberlain:

> So intense is local feeling . . . that my colleagues and I may be swept off our
> feet. . . . Loyalists may declare independence . . . seize the Customs and other
> Government Departments and set up an authority of their own. Many
> already believe that violence is the only language understood by Mr Lloyd
> George and his Ministers.

The majority of the British cabinet, together with key civil servants in the
Colonial Office and the Treasury, became alarmed by the ever-increasing
demands made on British sympathies and the British exchequer by Craig's government. To help stabilise the Provisional Government's position and ensure the
passage of the Treaty, the coalition was aware of the need to appear reasonable
and flexible on Northern issues. Craig expressed to Lord Devonshire, the new Conservative Colonial Secretary, at the end of the coalition government's time in
office, his dissatisfaction with the support he had received from Westminster and
commented: 'There is no doubt that the late Government was inspired by a desire
to concentrate attention on the Irish Treaty rather than on the Act of 1920.' He
concluded that the coalition government's policy had been controlled by a deter-

mination not to upset 'the susceptibilities of the Irish Provisional Government or of imperilling the passage of the Treaty through the Parliament in Dublin'.[1]

(a) THE BOUNDARY COMMISSION

Through the promise of the Boundary Commission the Anglo-Irish Treaty side-stepped direct consideration of partition. In public Collins insisted that they had been assured the commission would grant to the South, at the least, Tyrone and Fermanagh and part of Down and Armagh; following such a settlement, Collins declared that 'the general trend of development, and the undoubted advantages of unity, would have brought the North-East quietly into union with the rest of the country, as soon as a stable, national government had been established into which they could have come with confidence'. Elsewhere Collins affirmed: 'We have faith in these silent forces of mutual interests, of economic persuasion, of intercourse, for the union of Ireland.'

There is no proof that members of the British negotiating team gave definite assurances that the commission's findings would be favourable to the South. Discussions on the subject with Collins and Griffith during the negotiations, as well as public statements around the time of the Treaty's signing, were meant to expedite the settlement and encourage its acceptance in the Twenty-Six Counties. Lloyd George affirmed in the Commons: 'There is no doubt, certainly since the Act of 1920, that the majority of the people of the two counties [Fermanagh and Tyrone] prefer being with their Southern neighbours to being in the Northern Parliament.' Lloyd George went on to stress that while against coercion of the North, he was also opposed to the Northern government coercing any part of its own population. At the same time, however, Lloyd George told his cabinet that the commission 'would possibly give Ulster more than she would lose'. Birkenhead and Churchill were soon to point out vigorously that Collins was giving a misleading impression of the amount of territory to be involved.

The commission, and the deliberately vague way in which the clause was phrased, was a device by the British negotiators to allow the conference to reach a successful conclusion and to put the Northern issue into cold storage. In 1923 a government reply to a question in the House of Commons from Captain Wedgwood Benn on when the commission was to be established stated: 'The question is tiresome at the moment and stirs a dog we hoped would sleep.' Surprisingly, Article XII was allowed to remain ambiguous by the Irish negotiators. Judge O'Byrne warned Griffith about the consequences of the qualifying phrase which declared that the boundary would be readjusted 'in accordance with the wishes of the inhabitants, so far as may be compatible with economic and geographic conditions'. There was imprecision also about when the commission should sit. It was decided at a conference between British and Irish ministers in early February 1922 that the commission should meet once the North had formally opted out of the Free State following the establishment of the Free State government. Lloyd George commented: 'I am glad the legal gentlemen have come to an agreement. It postpones the Ulster issue and we can get out of the present bad atmosphere.'[2]

Collins and many of his colleagues had little faith in the Boundary Commission: Collins had only agreed to it as a means to end the negotiations. To accept the commission was a means of saving face: the Southern government could claim that Irish unity had only been delayed. Kevin O'Shiel, a member of the Southern Boundary Commission, told his government in May 1923:

> The late General never made any secret of his distrust in the Boundary Commission as a means of settlement per se. He used frequently to remark that, 'the Boundary Commission settled nothing'. He realised that even after the Boundary Commission had sat and made its decisions, and even if these decisions conceded to us our ultimate claim, there would still be an 'Hibernia Iridenta' to disturb the peace of future generations.

O'Shiel argued that there would in addition still be the problem of the loyalist population. He continued: 'Though the territory of Saorstát might be broadened, the gulf between Saorstát and these populations would also be broadened.' O'Shiel concluded that Collins aimed to achieve unification by other means than the winning of more territory by means of the commission. Collins told the IRA's 2nd Northern Division that 'Although the Treaty might have [seemed] an outward expression of Partition, the Government had plans whereby they would make it impossible. . . . Partition would never be recognised even though it might mean the smashing of the Treaty.' Mulcahy told the North-Eastern Advisory Committee that with regard to the North they had accepted the Treaty in order to destroy it. Kevin O'Higgins bluntly declared: 'I wonder if anyone here, or in England, or in North-East Ulster believes very strongly in the Boundary Commission as a piece of constructive statesmanship? I don't.' The commission could, however, be used as a weapon in post-Treaty negotiations with London and Belfast.

The Republican opposition had little alternative policy, as shown by de Valera's implicit acceptance of the commission in his Document No. 2; his strong criticisms came later.

The *Belfast Newsletter* made the most salient point when declaring that the Northern government still ultimately had control of its own boundaries. As the Southern and British governments had declared against coercion, the border could not have been changed without the Northern government's compliance. The North was always to refuse participation in the Boundary Commission and was intensely alarmed about the prospect of its meeting. When reviewing border developments, Craig said on 26 May: 'The Boundary Commission has been at the root of all evil.' A few days earlier he had affirmed: 'What we have now we hold, and we will hold against all combinations.'[3]

(B) JANUARY–MARCH 1922

In the three months following the Treaty a succession of incidents on the border and riots in Belfast led the British government to show acute concern for the settlement's fate.

On 14 January some of the Monaghan Gaelic football team were arrested in Co. Tyrone on their way to Derry to play in the final of the Ulster championship. They included Major-General Dan Hogan, O/C of the 5th Northern Division, and a number of other IRA men. Documents were found on them relating to plans to release three prisoners due to be executed in Derry jail. The IRA responded on 7 and 8 February by kidnapping forty-two prominent loyalists in Fermanagh and Tyrone, who were held as hostages for the footballers. Soon after a number of A Specials, journeying by train from Newtownards to Enniskillen, clashed with IRA men at Clones station, in Southern territory: four were killed and several kidnapped. There was inevitable disagreement as to who had fired the first shot, and Collins pressured Churchill for an enquiry. General Macready was strongly critical of the decision to send the Specials, at that time of all times, through Southern territory.

Craig asked Churchill whether there was 'any legal obstacle to our sending a flying column of 5,000 constabulary to recover the kidnapped Loyalists'. He suggested that for every individual kidnapped from Northern Ireland 'a portion of Southern Ireland adjoining the border will be occupied by British troops and retained at any rate until the safe return of the kidnapped person'. Churchill immediately warned that such action would lead to military confrontation and told Craig that 'Violent measures would do more harm than good and might entail the resignation of the Irish Provisional Government, thus creating chaos and leaving the extremists in control.' He added that precipitant action could endanger the captives. At the same time Churchill told Griffith: 'If your people are going to pop into Ulster and take off hostages every time the Northern Government enforces the law in a way you dislike there will be reprisals and we will have a fortified frontier and we will have to put there Imperial troops because they would be more impartial than Northern Ireland troops.'[4]

As a consequence of these developments, the British government suspended troop evacuation in the South and talked of the possible need for martial law in Northern Ireland; Churchill and Chamberlain urged Craig and Collins to secure release of the various captives. The Derry prisoners were reprieved and the Monaghan footballers reluctantly released by Craig, who stressed that no more releases should be requested on political grounds and that the Southern government must recognise the authority of Northern Ireland courts. Neither assurance was forthcoming. By 16 February Collins had arranged for several of the kidnapped men to be released; his role in these events, however, had gone well beyond that.

The crisis over the Monaghan footballers had seen the formation of a united IRA Northern policy—usually ascribed to March. An Ulster Council Command was established, with Aiken at its head and Mac Eoin under him. An exchange of arms between pro- and anti-Treaty units was talked about but only implemented two months later. The newly formed council planned the kidnapping raids of early February with the approval of Mulcahy, Collins and O'Duffy. Tom Ketterick, a West Mayo IRA man, recorded that Collins and O'Sullivan sent him to Coolaney to arrange for the taking of hostages. Collins, hardly surprisingly did not 'publicly . . . accept responsibility for these raids, but put them down to "natural reprisals" by indignant comrades of the men detained by the Northern Government'. Collins claimed he was making efforts to allay unrest and violence, concluding that the Provisional Government 'are making every effort to get the situation under control'. Over the next few months the kidnapped men were released in stages—the pace being dictated by Collins's attitude to developments in the Six Counties.[5]

Churchill responded to the border troubles by establishing the Border Commission on 16 February, with British, Northern and Southern liaison officers to report to each other on developments. Churchill told Collins: 'I suggested this Commission in the first instance only as an alternative to drastic steps which Parliament would otherwise expect me to take for securing the area of Northern Ireland.' The number of British troops was increased on the border, but the major responsibility there was left dubiously to the Specials. The commission, however, never proved effective and by late April had completely broken down. Macready commented: 'To those who knew anything of two of the component parts of the Commission, the IRA and Ulster representatives, the scheme was foredoomed to failure, though no doubt it looked very attractive in Whitehall. . . . From the first, in spite of the loyal efforts of the British officers, the whole affair was a farce.'[6]

The aggressive IRA policy on the border continued in March. Following raids on Belcoo, Maghera and Pomeroy barracks, the London *Times* commented: 'The news from Monaghan, Tyrone and other parts of the Ulster border grows steadily worse—we hear no news of the border commissions which [were] set up a month ago in the hope of easing the tension. For the moment the situation has passed beyond their control.' In the ensuing days the *Times* talked of 'a state of guerrilla warfare' having developed on the border—'A ring of steel soon will be stretched between the Mourne Mountains and Lough Foyle.' The attack on Belcoo barracks was by the pro-Treaty 1st Midland Division: Seán Mac Eoin, the O/C, advertised his involvement by appealing in Mullingar for volunteers for the border action. Macready later reported on the discovery of papers relating to the South Fermanagh Brigade demonstrating that in April and May the brigade 'was administered by and took orders from the 1st Midland Division'. Meanwhile Collins had been involved in a proposed IRA Belfast city guard.[7]

March saw in Belfast a number of outrages and reprisals by the IRA and Specials, of which the killing of the MacMahon family was the worst example. Frequently violence on the border interacted with that in Belfast (on the day after the Fermanagh and Tyrone kidnappings there were some particularly bad incidents in Belfast), and riots and disorder in the city often appeared as an almost instantaneous response to political developments. As on the border, basic issues relating to security, and who should provide it, underlay the Belfast violence. The phasing out of the RIC meant a greater dependence on the Specials while the RUC was built up. Even General Sir Henry Wilson, who in March became security adviser for the Northern government, and Major-General A. Solly-Flood, his nominee as head of the Northern Ireland security forces, were very critical of the Specials' organisation and discipline. From the loyalist perspective it was justly considered that the IRA was acting as more than a protective force for the minority community: the Northern government possessed documents demonstrating the role of pro-Treatyites as well as anti-Treatyites in attempts to undermine the Northern Ireland state. For the loyalist community security interests were crucial for the province's survival; by contrast, most of the nationalist population could not accept the security system and its legal basis.[8]

(c) THE CRAIG-COLLINS PACTS

A false hope that an agreement between North and South could be arrived at within the Treaty terms was produced by a meeting between Craig and Collins on 21 January in London. The conference resulted from Churchill's faith in direct talks between men whom he regarded as pragmatic and reasonable, aided by, as Churchill pointed out, the tactful British role of supplying mutton chops. An accord was achieved on specific, limited issues, which became known as the first Craig-Collins Pact. It was decided to settle the boundary issue by mutual agreement and to forgo the Council of Ireland which had been a provision in both the 1920 Government of Ireland Act and the Treaty—surprisingly Craig suggested a meeting of representatives of both governments, and Collins, with the Northern minority in mind, wished to widen that to all elected representatives. While Collins undertook to end the Belfast boycott, Craig promised to do all he could to enable the return to the shipyards of those Catholic workers who had been expelled in 1920. The pact was enthusiastically received in London and Dublin. Collins concluded: 'The result of our meeting has been that North and South will settle outstanding differences between themselves. We have eliminated the English interference.' Such optimism was soon shattered at a second meeting in Dublin in early February where Collins's and Craig's views on the boundary question were shown to be as wide apart as ever. The pact ran the risk for the Southern government that they would be depicted as implicitly recognising the Northern government; Collins, however, stated during a meeting with Northern minority representatives that 'non-recognition of the Northern Parliament was essential—otherwise they would have nothing to bargain on with Sir James Craig'. Collins was to find it impossible to end the Belfast boycott, and unemployment levels made the shipyard provision in the pact unrealistic.[9]

The British government's faith in direct negotiations was not ended, however. In late March, at the height of the post-Treaty violence, Churchill brought members of the Northern and Southern governments together, again in London. The Provisional Government of Ireland Committee concluded on 25 March that the 'present situation would rapidly lead to further outrages and then to civil war unless the British Government intervened. . . . Outrages in Belfast meant trouble on the border, and Belfast would not be pacified unless a meeting took place between Craig and . . . Collins.'

The meeting produced the second Craig-Collins Pact, which owed much also to Griffith, O'Higgins and Churchill. This agreement on 30 March 1922 was the last attempt before the 1960s and 1970s to reform radically the Northern Ireland governmental system in a manner designed to satisfy the Catholic minority and with the approval of the Southern government. Among the pact's complex provisions, Collins agreed to use his authority to stop IRA activity in the North, and to release those kidnapped in border incidents. Craig undertook to do his best for expelled Catholic shipyard workers and to release some political prisoners. Committees were to be established to conciliate disputes and hear complaints, to deal with policing problems in troubled areas and attempt to achieve an adequate representation of Catholics in the province's security forces, and to administer a British government grant for new schemes giving employment to both Catholics and Protestants. At Churchill's behest the pact's first clause melodramatically read: 'Peace is today declared.'

Despite the overwhelmingly favourable press response in Britain and Southern Ireland, the agreement exacerbated problems rather than solved them. The immediate aftermath was a train of outrages and unrest in Belfast causing an exceptionally long and acrimonious correspondence between Collins and Craig on how the pact should be applied, and between them and Churchill, who acted as a sympathetic referee, urging them to be reasonable and to meet again. The only committee set up by the pact which worked at all effectively was the Relief Committee, which was concerned with less sensitive political issues. Other parts of the pact soon collapsed. The agreement failed because it concerned itself with effects rather than causes; it did not, therefore, deal with partition or the possibility of the Catholic minority recognising the Northern government. Whatever optimism among politicians there had been about the pact derived from the British side. As so often in Northern Ireland, talk of solutions led to an acceleration of violence.[10]

The lack of commitment to the pact among representatives of the Northern Catholic minority and members of the Provisional Government was graphically demonstrated by the discussions of the North-Eastern Advisory Committee, which had been set up in February to inform the Southern government of Northern nationalist opinion. The committee's members regarded the London agreement as a means to apply pressure on the Northern government and wring concessions from them. On 15 May they debated whether the Southern government and the Northern Catholic minority should formally declare that the pact had collapsed. Kevin O'Shiel argued that to do so would be to play into Craig's hands. 'Let them carry on', he urged, 'half-hearted negotiations with Craig and whilst continuing to be as civil to him as Craig pretends to be with us actually harass him in his Pact plans until such time that he agrees to work the whole Pact.' O'Shiel concluded: 'The most unpleasant thing to Craig is not the breaking of the Pact but the pretending on our part of keeping it on.' Collins argued at this meeting that the agreement offered the opportunity to press the British government for an enquiry concerning atrocities in the North and prison releases. At the meeting of the committee on 11 April O'Duffy affirmed that 'they were not observing the Pact in Belfast and activities were carried out by our side', and Mulcahy argued that to 'carry out all its [the Treaty's] terms will ultimately unify the country and destroy the Northern Parliament'. Dr McNabb, a Northern member of the committee, stressed: 'They are only going to recognise that Parliament [the Northern one] in as much as it helps them to beat it.'[11]

(d) THE JOINT IRA OFFENSIVE, APRIL–JUNE 1922

During April it appears that IRA activity was reduced so as not to be shown responsible for shattering the second Craig-Collins Pact. When it became clear that no worthwhile gains would result from the agreement plans for a Northern offensive were stepped up. Evidence for the joint IRA policy is sketchy and heavily dependent on oral evidence. It is a very sensitive and controversial subject because of the mistrust, secrecy and confusion involved, and its virtually total failure.

Plans were laid—with Collins and Liam Lynch heavily involved—to despatch north a large consignment of arms. To avoid detection by the British government of pro-Treaty IRA involvement, arms supplied from Britain to Collins's government were swapped with arms from anti-Treaty units, so that no guns with

British serial numbers should be discovered in the North. Volunteers were requested from Southern counties to stiffen the Northern IRA. Seán Lehane went from Co. Cork to take charge of the 1st and 2nd Northern Divisions; he was to be based in Donegal, with Charlie Daly, from Kerry, as his second-in-command, and a number of other 1st Southern Division officers. Their purpose, Lehane recorded, was to assist Aiken in his activities against the Specials and the Crown forces. It appears that the recruits for the North came from anti-Treaty units, while the financial resources were provided by the pro-Treaty GHQ. Seán Mac Eoin's Midland Division was to co-operate in the attacks.[12]

The offensive proved a dismal failure. Ineffective communications between the divisions caused utter confusion concerning the widespread activities scheduled for 19 May. A member of the North-Eastern Advisory Committee claimed that the plans had been common knowledge in Dundalk public houses a few days before the proposed starting date. An attack on Musgrave Street barracks in Belfast on 17 May, for the purpose of capturing two armoured cars, miscarried, and it appears that attempts were then made to call off the planned actions meant for two days later. Countermanding orders, however, did not reach some areas. Some attacks on police barracks did take place in the 3rd Northern Division; there was one on Shane's Castle in Co. Antrim and widespread burning and property destruction in Belfast. Roger McCorley, a Belfast IRA leader, was to complain that the 1st and 4th Northern Divisions failed to act, and Tom MacAnally, also of the 3rd Northern Division, recorded: 'We had little association outside of ourselves, and we had no faith in other areas.' MacAnally complained that the 2nd Northern Division did not do 'a damn thing'. In the west of the province matters had been complicated by tensions between pro-Treaty and anti-Treaty units, culminating in an armed clash between them at Newtowncunningham. Controversy also arose over the arms swap. Liam Lynch complained publicly that Beggars' Bush had failed to send all the swapped arms north, and O'Duffy was forced to reply. Thanks to that, and the capture of documents, pro-Treaty IRA involvement in the operation was known to the British authorities.[13]

The failure of the joint offensive was always likely given the weak position of the IRA within the Six Counties. The advantages the IRA had possessed during the Anglo-Irish War in the south and west did not exist in the six north-eastern counties, where IRA organisation was loose and dispersed, the population mostly hostile, and the existence of IRA brigades threatened by both Specials and the British army. Séamus Woods, the O/C of the 3rd Northern Division in the Civil War period, pointed out the futility of an aggressive IRA policy in Belfast, where the minority population was highly vulnerable to reprisals. Woods commented that respect for the IRA in Belfast 'had been won not so much out of sympathy with our National aspirations . . . but more on account of the part the Army had played in defending the minority against organised attacks by uniformed and non-uniformed Crown forces'. The IRA's position in the North was made worse by independent activity from anti-Treaty units, which the pro-Treaty IRA frequently regarded as ill-judged and as provoking reprisals.[14]

Prospects for the joint army policy were further hindered by Northern IRA complaints that they had been insufficiently consulted by their Southern counterparts, as over the ending of the economic boycott. Moreover, both pro-Treaty and anti-Treaty leaders did not make clear the precise aims of their Northern policy.

Roger McCorley claimed that the purpose of the attacks had been to bring down the Northern government, and a 2nd Northern Division report spoke of Collins's plans for ending partition, even if it meant the smashing of the Treaty. Conversely, Mossy Donegan, of Cork No. 3 Brigade, thought the plans he was involved in were only intended 'to be of nuisance value' and to 'produce a political or a diplomatic effect'. Kevin O'Shiel attributed considerable responsibility for the offensive's collapse to Collins. He related that Collins tended to come 'to quick decisions without consulting many', and complained of the absence of a coherent Northern policy. He continued:

> Whilst I was urging a policy of peaceful do-nothingness in Northern Committees the two branches of the IRA were actively making united preparation to invade the North East in alliance and were only called off at the last moment because of some sane man's intervention. The Army, for a long time, had one policy and the civilians another, or rather a series of policies that changed as quickly as the circumstances upon which they were founded.

Pro-Treaty politicians remained in ignorance of Collins's and Mulcahy's support for an aggressive Northern policy, as Cosgrave testified in the Dáil in September. In all probability the May offensive was nothing more than an attempt to embarrass and destabilise the Northern government, while having the useful additional role of aiding the search for army unity.[15]

The collapse of the joint army policy had disastrous consequences for the IRA, particularly in the 3rd Northern Division. The Specials staged an effective raiding policy, and a considerable amount of information on the IRA reached the security forces. A raid in April on the Belfast IRA's liaison office at St Mary's Hall revealed the names of 'practically every officer in the Division'. After the assassination on 22 May of William Twaddell, a Belfast MP, some 350 IRA and Sinn Féin members were arrested, and a proclamation declared all republican organisations illegal. A Belfast Brigade report concluded: 'Under the present circumstances it would be impossible to keep our Military Organisation alive and intact, as the morale of the men is going down day by day and the spirit of the people is practically dead.' General Macready reported that 'The disorganisation of the IRA caused by the action of the Police since 22 May has been greater than was supposed. The majority of the IRA gunmen of the North [were] either wiped out of the Six Counties or are in hiding.' An IRA memorandum reported that

> After a period of over five weeks the demoralisation has practically completed its work. . . . The position in No. 2 and 3 Brigades of 3rd Northern Division today is that the Military Organisation is almost destroyed [and the enemy] believe that they have beaten the IRA completely in Antrim and Down. . . . The people who supported us feel they have been abandoned by Dáil Éireann, for our position today is more unbearable than it was in June 1921. . . . Today the people feel that all their suffering has been in vain and cannot see any hope for the future.[16]

The Northern IRA offensive alienated many of the minority population. A Southern government report from Newry stated that relations between all elements of the community had been good until the barracks was attacked in

May; nationalists and Sinn Féiners had considered the aggressive policy 'futile and foolish'. The report concluded: 'The only result of the attack was to embitter feeling and place the Catholic population at the mercy of the "Specials".' The aftermath of the IRA offensive was to leave the minority population more exposed than ever to reprisals. Large numbers were arrested, and many of the IRA were forced to cross the border. The IRA's future in the Six Counties appeared very bleak even before June's depressing developments, though arms exchanges continued up to the Four Courts attack.

The British government had chosen, in the interests of the Treaty, to cast a blind eye to the offensive. That tolerance did not extend to June, when adherence to the Treaty was insisted upon explicitly.[17]

The last overt throw of the joint army offensive caused the Belleek–Pettigo crisis of late May and early June 1922. Clashes between Specials and IRA men in that portion of the Fermanagh–Donegal border running between the closely adjacent villages of Belleek and Pettigo resulted in British troops taking over the area, which included some Southern territory. British artillery was used on Pettigo, where seven pro-Treaty troops were killed, six wounded and four taken prisoner. For the next few months British troops remained in a neutral zone from which both Specials and IRA had to retire. Collins virulently complained about the taking of Pettigo, demanded an enquiry, which was refused, and denied any pro-Treaty involvement. Joe Sweeney, however, who was in command of pro-Treaty troops in the region, admitted that his men had raided homes across the border which they had orders to burn if arms were found. Collins expressed annoyance with Sweeney for allowing his troops to become involved in the crisis. There appears, however, to have been little substance in Craig's claims that the IRA action was intended as a prelude to attacks on Strabane and Derry.[18]

The frequently hysterical reaction to these events in London, Belfast and Dublin had much to do with the timing of the crisis. It occurred while Griffith and Collins were in London facing British complaints on their draft constitution, and when the Northern and British governments were intensely suspicious of Provisional Government intentions following the Collins–de Valera pact.

The crisis caused considerable tensions within the British government. Lloyd George's sense of frustration with how the Northern question was acting as a block to the Treaty settlement increased as he became extremely alarmed about the dangers of military confrontation resulting from a minor and confusing clash. The Prime Minister became convinced that Churchill was overreacting and reminded him that 'Our Ulster case is not a good one.' He warned of the dangers of alienating Dominion and world sentiment and enjoined:

> Let us keep on the high ground of the Treaty—the Crown, the Empire. There we are unassailable. But if you come down from that height and fight in the swamps of Lough Erne you will be overwhelmed. . . . We have surely done everything that Ulster can possibly expect to ensure its security. Fifty-seven thousand armed men ought to be equal to the protection of so small a territory. If they require more they can get them. It is our own business as a great Empire to be strictly impartial in our attitude towards all creeds.

Lloyd George was greatly relieved when the crisis quietly subsided after the speedy and largely painless British occupation of Belleek.[19]

(e) JUNE 1922

The Belleek–Pettigo crisis and the constitutional question produced a reappraisal of the Southern government's Northern policy. On 3 June 1922 they 'decided that a policy of peaceful obstruction should be adopted towards the Belfast Government. . . . No troops from the twenty-six counties either those under official control or attached to the Executive should be permitted to invade the Six-County area.' Pressure from the British government and army, together with the IRA's weak position in the North, forced Collins to retreat from his aggressive outlook. In an interview with the *Daily Mail* Collins commented:

> I think my attitude towards Ulster . . . is not understood. There can be no question of forcing Ulster into Union with the 26 counties. I am absolutely against coercion of the kind. If Ulster is to join us it must be voluntarily. Union is our final goal, that is all.[20]

While there was no longer a direct military threat to the Northern government, their position was still a vulnerable one. With the constitutional question settled and the Fermanagh border threat removed, most within the British cabinet became sympathetic to the establishment of a judicial enquiry into Northern security questions which, it was hoped, would encourage the Southern government to adhere to the Treaty terms. Craig, however, continued to talk of a Southern plot to destroy his government, and tensions between the British and Northern governments were exacerbated by incidents such as the firing on British soldiers by loyalists in East Belfast in early June and killings associated with Specials in Cushendall. Craig was reminded by the British government of the responsibility of Specials for some reprisal murders, and that the previous six months' figures for dead and wounded Catholics considerably exceeded those for Protestants. It was stated that it might be necessary for the British government to become more directly involved, and the possible imposition of martial law in Belfast was discussed in the British cabinet.

The logical consequence of such anxieties would have been for the British army to take over prime responsibility from the Specials for policing the border and to have introduced martial law for Belfast and other parts of the North. By early June it had become apparent that a mixture of political pressure from the Southern government and the background of IRA activity and loyalist reprisals could help to undermine the stability of the Northern government. It seemed that the coalition government's attempt to defuse the Northern question by means of the Treaty and the Craig–Collins Pacts had failed. The British government was reluctantly facing the need to intervene directly in Northern developments and to redefine the powers of the Northern government. In early June Churchill confided to representatives of Catholic businessmen from Northern Ireland: 'Either the North and South must join hands to establish the will of the hard-working mass of Irish people, or England must again intervene and establish order or Ireland would slide into complete anarchy.' Such a situation did not recur until the 1970s. Eventually the British cabinet decided to send a civil servant, S. G. Tallents, to Belfast to report on the reasons for the second Craig–Collins Pact's failure and to consider whether there was need for a general judicial enquiry. By the time Tallents had reported, the Civil War had begun and the North had become considerably more peaceful.[21]

In the Twenty-Six Counties during June Northern considerations came perforce to be neglected. The key problems related to the election, the Treaty terms and the IRA opposition; the partition issue had to be postponed. Only with regard to education does the non-recognition of the Northern government policy seem to have been applied. Eamonn Donnelly, a Northern nationalist spokesman, declared that a meeting of the Sinn Féin standing committee 'did not decide on any policy for the North-East', and held it was 'a matter for the people living in the Six-County area to decide on a policy'. The situation was complicated by problems of communication between the South and the Northern minority—of finding out precisely what they desired and who should speak for them. British policy, as Churchill regretted, had helped Collins appoint himself as spokesman for the Northern minority, but much Northern opinion, notably the MP Joe Devlin's constitutional nationalist supporters, favoured adopting a more flexible attitude towards the Northern government and parliament. Three Catholic businessmen warned Collins of the amount of support among the minority population for recognition of the Northern parliament. The North-Eastern Advisory Committee, moreover, emphasised problems in relating minority opinion in Belfast to that of the agrarian west of the province. There was a growing feeling, during the whole Civil War period, of detachment from the South by Northern Catholics. Cahir Healy, a leading nationalist spokesman in the west of the province, declared: 'We have been abandoned to Craig's mercy.'[22]

Collins, Mulcahy and O'Duffy had attached a much greater importance to the North than that which generally applied in Southern Sinn Féin circles. While the desire for national unity was continually reaffirmed on all sides, there remained a considerable amount of apathy in the South concerning the North. There had been attempts during the Treaty negotiations to understand and make concessions to Northern Unionism. There was, however, over-optimism concerning Northern willingness to join an independent Irish state if local autonomy was allowed. Eoin O'Duffy declared: 'The position of the Six-County Nationalists has been treated with complete indifference by the rest of Ireland, except at Election time, or when it served party purposes to exploit it.' Seán Milroy, one of the few Sinn Féin TDs with a Northern background, said in the Dáil in September 1922: 'There is as little appreciation in Dublin and the South of the state of mind, and habit of thinking, and the point of view of the people in the North as there is in the North of the people in the South.' That impression was reinforced by the choice of Southern TDs to fight Northern seats in Six-County elections. For all the Irish talk of unity, the emphasis had been on the winning of independence for the Twenty-Six Counties, and then on the Treaty division as it applied to the South. The Belfast boycott, far from undermining the Northern government, reinforced Northern determination to stay aloof from the South. Little account, moreover, was taken in the South of how their economic independence would serve to entrench partition—Loughnane, Cope's successor in Dublin, commented that Southern politicians had given no thought to the consequences of the establishment of a customs barrier between North and South.[23]

11

Social and Governmental Problems

THE vast amount of social dislocation during the first half of 1922 should not
be seen purely in the context of political and military divisions over the
Treaty. Much of the lawlessness of the whole Civil War period should be put down
to the weakness of both central and local government. After two years of guerrilla
warfare and chaos in civil government and administration there were great
problems in ensuring widespread acceptance of any government, and this would
have been so even if the Treaty settlement had been unopposed.

Not only was the legitimacy of the Provisional Government and its army widely
challenged, but there was considerable confusion as to precisely where
government authority lay. Tod Andrews related that he could not understand the
difference between the Provisional Government and the Dáil government, and a
British report commented: 'It is obvious that the dual role which members of the
new Government are compelled to fill... is attended with grave practical dis-
abilities, particularly in the matter of maintaining law and order.'

The new government was necessarily preoccupied with immediate questions
relating to the threat of civil war. There was little opportunity to establish the basis
of ordered government. The police and courts would have to be established during
the Civil War. The *Irish Times* of 2 February said of the government: 'It is
established in office, but not in power. Its machinery for the enforcement of law
and order does not yet exist on any adequate scale. The hasty—far too hasty—departure of the British troops confronts it with administrative and economic
problems of the gravest kind.' Less sympathetically the London *Times* commented
on 6 February: 'It has done hardly anything as yet to fill the gap left by the
departure of the Crown forces.' O'Higgins relayed to the Dáil the Labour Party's
concern that there were 130,000 unemployed at a time when there was so little civil
jurisdiction.

The vacuum left by civil government was frequently filled by the military. IRA
men continued to play a dominant role in many communities. Seán Moylan spoke
in the Dáil of his role as IRA commandant in North Cork:

> In one particular village, I put up a notice on Friday evening that I would
> come to the parish on Sunday to collect the dog tax.... I collected £47, and
> the people willingly paid me.... That is the extent of my robbery. I am not
> ashamed of it.... In doing things like this, I am standing up for and
> defending the Republic.

Compulsory levies continued to be made, post offices were raided for funds,
newspaper distribution often interfered with, and the train services frequently dis-

rupted. The government referred in the Dáil to 331 raids on post offices between 23 March and 19 April, and 319 attacks on the Great Southern and Western Railway by armed men between 1 March and 22 April. Mulcahy pointed out that much was 'done under cover of the declaration of the Belfast Boycott'. The organised raids on branches of the National Bank (the Provisional Government's bankers) on 1 May, when nearly £50,000 was taken, took place by order of the Army Executive. Concern was expressed not only about the anti-Treaty IRA's actions. Thomas Johnson wrote to Mulcahy on 27 April complaining of overactive pro-Treaty troop activity in Dublin, and particularly the shooting of Michael Sweeney, a Republican prisoner. Johnson concluded: 'Our protest was and is directed, not only against individual acts . . . but mainly against the ascendancy of the military forces in the public life of the country.'[1]

Southern Unionists regularly brought to the British government's notice their deep concern about social and economic conditions. Lord Midleton told Churchill of the 'mischief which is being done by the withholding of rent':

> The farmers who have purchased their tenancies had begun in the last two months to pay their instalments again . . . but the general spirit of Bolshevism, which is being cultivated by the revolutionaries all over the West, will undoubtedly land the Provisional Government in further difficulties, while the land-lords in the districts affected are living on their capital and have not the money to pay their labourers.

While despairing of the will and effectiveness of the Provisional Government, Midleton was critical of the rapid evacuation of British forces. He told George V of an 'extremely grave' situation:

> The hasty withdrawal of British troops, against which your Majesty's Government were repeatedly warned, has left the South of Ireland without any force to preserve order and even if individuals were made amenable, there are no courts sitting effectively to deal with them. . . . The mutiny of the IRA is probably the least serious element in crime.

Plans were laid to establish, if necessary, a Committee of Public Safety, to consist of prominent Dubliners including the Provost of Trinity College, the President of the Chamber of Commerce, and the Lord Chancellor. Midleton warned that 'If matters go on unchecked as at present, by two months from now it will be beyond the power of the Provisional Government to restore order, without prolonged struggle.' In meetings with a Southern Unionist deputation Griffith agreed with their pessimistic view of the situation. 'Mr Griffith', the minutes of the meeting recorded, 'said they were most anxious to press forward to a better state of things, but they had not had up to now the requisite power. . . . They were training four thousand police at Ballsbridge and would need more force, but they had not the legal power at present which they would receive under the Treaty Bill.'[2]

The lack of government authority contributed to the revival of land seizures and disturbances in the first six months of 1922. There was widespread withholding of land annuities and many examples of cattle-stealing. These months also saw some seizures of factories, although many attempts to set up co-operative factory movements swiftly collapsed. The land disturbances went on throughout the Civil War period; as during the Anglo-Irish War, it was often difficult to distinguish between agrarian protest and armed resistance to the state. Initially the anti-Treaty Army Council showed some interest in relating its aims to those of land protest: local commandants were instructed 'to seize certain land and properties and hold them in trust for the Irish people'.

Absentee landlords were to be a particular target, and Divisional Land Courts were to be established with funds which had been seized and placed in the hands of the Congested Districts Board. No action, however, followed. Liam Mellows and Peadar O'Donnell were lone voices in the anti-Treaty leadership ranks urging the breakup of large estates. Mellows, however, in a speech at Ballinasloe just before the June election, condemned the seizure of land as a sectarian reprisal. The Provisional Government took a strong line against agrarian disturbance, but was in no position to enforce such a policy.[3]

Policing was a particularly sensitive issue. The first successes for the Volunteers during the Anglo-Irish War had been in greatly reducing the effectiveness, morale and recruitment of the RIC; no police force had replaced them, and what republican policing there had been during that conflict had been done by members of the IRA. After the Treaty split there were to be enormous problems for any police force to win acceptance of their position, not only because of the political divisions, but also because of the long background of non-application of the law in many areas. The RIC was disbanded after the Treaty, and the old republican police force was terminated in late January. By the end of March the RIC had been withdrawn from nineteen out of the twenty-six counties and had been concentrated in one or two centres in each of the remaining seven counties. The anti-Treaty IRA was to be extremely reluctant to relinquish control of policing to any new force, as was shown by the vigorous opposition from the 1st Southern Division to the new Civic Guard during army unity negotiations.

The early history of the Civic Guard represented virtually a complete failure. Collins concluded on 7 August 1922 that

> We are not in a position to repose confidence in the effectiveness of the Civic Guard as a body to maintain ordinary law. . . . It is not necessary for me to illustrate this by pointing to the wretched Irish Republican Police system, and to the awful personnel that was attracted to its ranks. . . . The lack of construction and the lack of control in this force have been responsible for many of the outrageous things which have occurred throughout Ireland.

When O'Duffy was offered the headship of the Civic Guard in the autumn of 1922 he wrote that it 'stands very low in the estimation of the people. It would be difficult to retrieve its position.'[4]

The Civic Guard was established on 21 February. As with the army, taking over police barracks was greatly complicated by uncertainties with regard to the political loyalties of those taking over. Mulcahy admitted in the Dáil on 26 April: 'Owing to the secession of some senior officers this work of policing has suffered very much in some parts of the country.' Simon Donnelly, the Chief of Police in its early days, left the force to establish a Republican police force and took with him a considerable amount of material relating to the force. The Civic Guard could only be set up in pro-Treaty areas. There were problems also relating to the employment in the force of some old RIC men, which created so much resentment that there were open mutinies at the training barracks in Kildare in May and June and entry to the barracks was refused to Commissioner Staines. There were complaints, furthermore, of the taking of so many positions in the force by Clare men. In June Ernie O'Malley led a successful raid for arms on the Kildare head-quarters of the Civic Guard, aided by support from mutinous officers.

In view of the problems within the new force, a commission was set up by the Provisional Government. While the commission's findings laid the major blame for the problems on the mutineers, they pointed to sundry weaknesses within the organisation. The commission concluded that the force should not have been armed and that Michael Staines, as a TD, should not have been appointed to a senior post; it also criticised the leadership's handling of the alarming disorder within the force.

As a consequence of the commission's report, the Civic Guard was disbanded by the Provisional Government on 18 August. O'Shiel concluded that 'there was a state of grave insubordination, and lack of discipline among the men, and that, as at present constituted, the Civic Guard could not . . . be organised into a compe-tent Police Force'.[5]

12

The Search for Unity

BOTH pro-Treaty and anti-Treaty leaders were profoundly aware of the danger of civil war. In March and April 1922 Collins often warned in speeches that they were on the brink of conflict, and Seán MacEntee declared in the Dáil late April: 'We are now upon the verge of Civil War in Ireland. Let there be no mistake about that.' Labour leaders, the church and press all left the population in little doubt of their fears for the immediate future. Labour Party peace attempts culminated in the Mansion House Conference of 26-29 April, when they proposed a return to the Dáil's sovereignty, the unification of the army, the establishment of a police force under civilian control, and a revised electoral register. Talks, however, broke down on Collins's insistence that an election or plebiscite be held on the Treaty issue. Civil war would only begin when one or both sides took decisive, unequivocal action. Until that happened there was a desperate search for both political and military unity.

The Army Convention in March and the sundry clashes and disturbances of April did not end attempts to produce army unity. Instead they resulted in increasingly frantic attempts to bring the two sides together. The army unity talks of May and June should be seen as a continuation of the peace efforts between Mulcahy and the 1st Southern Division just before the Convention. The Convention had revealed Liam Lynch's and his colleagues' unease at talk of military dictatorship, and Seán Hegarty, Florrie O'Donoghue and Tom Hales (of the West Cork IRA) were later to resign from the Army Executive over their opposition to plans to interfere with the election. The Cork contingent on the Executive offered as an alternative to a resolution on the election issue that army unity talks should commence. Because the rest of the Executive realised how crucial the Munster IRA's support was to them, the election resolution was deferred.

Moves for army reunification began in April within the IRB. Through the personal contacts and loyalties involved, the IRB represented, as Liam Mellows observed, the most convenient medium for such negotiations. Any agreement achieved, moreover, would serve the beneficial purpose also of restoring IRB unity. Earlier in the year the Clan na Gael leader Joe McGarrity had made a peace effort through IRB contacts.[1]

A final, post-Treaty joint meeting of the IRB's Supreme Council and its divisional centres was held in Dublin on 19 April. A majority of those present were against the Treaty. La Brady, a Leix IRB man, recalled Collins at this meeting 'taking down on a piece of paper who were for and who were against the Treaty and he found that the majority were against him'. O'Donoghue suggested that the organisation be used as a means to prevent civil war. Collins supported

O'Donoghue's suggestion, and a committee of six, equally representative of the rival Treaty attitudes, was appointed to draw up proposals. Liam Lynch laid down hardline minimum terms insisting on the Republic and an independent Army Executive, the disbanding of the Civic Guard with the IRA to do all necessary policing, no election until the British threat of war was removed, and an undertaking by the Dáil to deal with the army's financial liabilities. There was, it appears, an agreement to speed up moves towards a republican constitution, and to allow again purely local occupation of evacuated barracks, as well as on the need to prevent the commandeering of cars, and on the continuation of the Belfast boycott. The next day, however, Seán Ó Muirthile recorded that the anti-Treaty side, prompted by the men in the Four Courts, took an intransigent line, and no statement was agreed. O'Donoghue, by contrast, related that the committee broke down after four meetings when Lynch demanded guarantees about a republican constitition.

Though the IRB peace effort was unsuccessful and the organisation continued to decline, IRB influences had much to do with the later attempts at army unity, which were made through different channels. Mulcahy was to record Collins's opinion expressed a few days before the attack on the Four Courts:

> What a pity it was that the Organisation could not stand solid on the Treaty position, and advance from there, building up the social, economic and national life of the country. He referred to his statement that the Treaty was freedom to achieve freedom, and appeared convinced that complete freedom could be achieved without further recourse to Arms.

Ó Muirthile, the IRB's key organiser, recorded: 'The remnants of the IRB endeavoured to bring about unity right through the spring of 1922 as long as there was a hope left, and even on the eve of the outbreak of Civil War further efforts were made to avoid a physical conflict.'[2]

The starting-point for both the army and political unity talks of May and June was the army officers' statement of 1 May. The statement was signed by Seán Hegarty, O/C Cork No. 1 Brigade; Dan Breen, of the South Tipperary Brigade; Humphrey Murphy, O/C Kerry No. 1 Brigade; Florrie O'Donoghue, of Cork No. 1; Tom Hales, O/C Cork No. 3; and Seán Boylan, O/C 1st Eastern Division. Their appeal began by warning of the imminence of what 'would be the greatest calamity in Irish history and would leave Ireland broken for generations'. They suggested an acceptance of the Treaty as the basis for army unification, a non-contested election, and the formation of a coalition government following the election.

The initiative had arisen from meetings between the officers and Collins, together with Mulcahy in one instance. All but one of the signatories (Boylan was the exception) had taken an anti-Treaty stance. They were all IRB men. Sean Moylan, another important figure within the 1st Southern Division, attended the meetings which drew up the appeal, but did not sign it. He and Liam Lynch could not accept the Treaty as a means of furthering peace hopes, but they were just as reluctant to make a complete break with GHQ. Moylan had prepared earlier peace terms, when it was recorded: 'Seán stated that he had the wind up as to what things were drifting towards. He worried not about himself, but about others being shot and about he shooting others.'

The officers' document demonstrated the lack of central control and coherence within the anti-Treaty IRA. It was published without reference to the Executive, which immediately denounced it. Important individuals within the key division had effectively declared their independence of the Four Courts.[3]

On 3 May Seán Hegarty, although not a TD, was allowed to address the Dáil on the officers' initiative.

> You have [he declared] two sections of the army in Ireland and . . . for many months feverish activity on both sides, and putting arms into the hands of men that never saw a gun. . . . For the last week little conflicts have occurred here and there, most of them in places where there never was anything done when hostilities were on. Let that progress and once the south gets into it there is nobody can stop it.

Hegarty thought there was no choice other than to accept the Treaty, for civil war would not produce a Republic, but rather 'England . . . coming back in'.

The officers' appeal was immediately denounced by Liam Mellows as 'another political dodge'. It did, however, get the peace process started in the Dáil. Seán Moylan said that he was still 'very anxious to accept, if possible, an assurance that the Treaty can be made a step to the Republic, that the Constitution, when drafted, will prove that this assurance is correct'. After Hegarty had suggested an army truce de Valera affirmed: 'I believe that peace can be got.' When, however, Griffith urged de Valera to use his influence with the anti-Treaty IRA de Valera replied: 'The Army has taken up an independent position in this matter.' At the end of the debate the Dáil set up a committee to work on political peace proposals along the line of the officers' document; army unity talks went on independently.

The army unity talks had begun on 4 May, and a joint committee, representing both sides of the army, drew up truce terms which were to hold until 8 May, when they were extended to give more time for the negotiations. The early talks foundered on the Treaty issue. Eoin O'Duffy recorded the objections of the men in the Four Courts to the proposals his side were making based on the 1 May appeal: 'Unless an agreed election meant that the Dáil continued as the Government of the Irish Republic and was solely responsible for the entire administration of the country (Ulster included) they would not accept it.' The anti-Treaty representatives held that the unity proposals avoided 'the cause of split in army which they allege is the Treaty'. Lynch told O'Duffy: 'Since the Truce was declared no satisfactory effort had been made to discuss a basis for Army unification. Progress is impeded by Officers of the Committee on your side not being willing to discuss the vital matters at issue.' Impatient at the time taken during the negotiations, Lynch warned on 15 May: 'Negotiations must cease if a definite understanding for agreement is not reached.'[4]

Meanwhile the Dáil committee used the officers' document as a starting-point. It soon became apparent that the anti-Treaty members could not accept the first clause, providing for the acceptance of the Treaty as a basis for unity. The memorandum which Harry Boland placed before the committee to represent the Republican viewpoint insisted that the Dáil remain as the supreme governing authority, that no issue (meaning the Treaty) should be decided by the election, and that in the period pending the finalisation of the constitution a President and Council of State should act as the sole executive. The Provisional Government was to act purely as a transitional commission with no executive function; the army would be controlled by an Army Council, and the Minister for Defence would be elected by a new Army Convention.

Seán Mac Eoin suggested they lay aside the Treaty issue for the moment and proceed to other issues relating to the representation of pro-Treaty and anti-Treaty elements in the proposed election panel and coalition. This led to a considerable argument about whether representation in the panel, as the pro-Treatyites argued, should be in the proportion of six to four in favour of the pro-Treaty side or, as the anti-Treatyites wished, the proportion be unchanged from that in the Second Dáil. Boland reluctantly agreed to the pro-Treaty proposition, but Mellows said he wished to have nothing to do with such haggling over seats and stressed that he was only concerned with the fundamental issues. He bluntly declared that the purpose of a coalition for him was to provide a means to 'evade the Treaty.' Eventually discussion turned back to the Treaty issue and broke down on it, despite the army officers being called in to redraft their clause on that question. The committee told the Dáil on 11 May that they had failed to reach an agreement, but they still struggled on with the talks until 17 May. Boland continued to think that the seats problem had been the only question which separated them, and declared that it was 'quite compatible with our position to work in Coalition with the men who claim that they are Republicans but who have a different policy to achieve that end'.[5]

At that time a delegation from Newry, led by Frank Aiken, the O/C of the 4th Northern Division, visited Dublin to put pressure on both military and political leaders to sink their differences in view of the deteriorating situation for the IRA and the Catholic minority population in the Six Counties. They argued: 'Should the split unfortunately become final, our people in the North are bound to be influenced by the issues in the other counties, and our forces will be divided and disheartened, so that we are bound to succumb to the powers opposed to us.' Another letter from Newry pointed out: 'We consider that perhaps we have a clearer perspective on the national situation than you in Dublin, and we ask you before finally breaking to at least hear what we have to say.'

Both sides in the army dispute agreed on the Northern offensive. At one stage, as Rory O'Connor pointed out in a Civil War propaganda document, Mulcahy admitted that the presence of the anti-Treaty IRA in the Four Courts acted as a useful camouflage for their Northern policy. During the unity talks 'some one suggested', O'Connor wrote, 'the evacuation of the Four Courts, and Mulcahy laughingly said that as long as we held that place, the war against NE Ulster would be attributed to us. We, of course, had no objection.' O'Connor concluded that this was the real reason why they were not asked to evacuate the Four Courts building. Although the Northern question provided a major stimulus for unity hopes right up to the attack on the Four Courts, it also created tensions between the two sides as each side blamed the other for the failure of the offensive.

On 17 May the day after the delegation from Newry had met with leaders from both sides, Collins pointed out the consequences of disunity in the South for their Northern policy and triggered off renewed hopes of an agreement by a conciliatory tone in the Dáil.

> If a Coalition Government [Collins declared] is formed here on a basis of good-will [and] carrying through, let us say, the advantages of the Treaty

position ... we shall be on the road to a united Ireland. It is well known what my opinion is about a united Ireland. ... The next line-up in Ireland must be for a united Ireland.

Collins went on to say that now that they had rid themselves of 'practically all' British agents, 'the one thing for us to do now is to consolidate the position, having in view the unity of Ireland'. He concluded by warning about the British: 'It will be easy for them to return if we start slaughtering each other.'[6]

De Valera immediately said he was pleased with Collins's speech and that he regarded it as a positive test of sincerity for the coalition idea. He admitted that the Republicans were in a minority and agreed on the need for stable government. Collins and de Valera were then closeted together for three days to attempt some form of compromise. The discussions between Collins and de Valera, as shown in a memorandum by Collins, looked certain to break down quickly. Collins insisted on a working majority for the pro-Treaty side in any election pact and coalition government, and that recognition of the Treaty be the basis for any agreement. De Valera argued that that would be unnecessary and that the reliance instead should be on good faith. Both Collins and de Valera referred the issues to their respective parties. While de Valera reported that his colleagues insisted on the then representation in the Dáil being maintained at the election, Collins said that some members of his party 'thought he ... had gone beyond the limit of concession. He further felt that he had what was practically unanimous support in making any arrangement that the position of securing and maintaining the Treaty allowed'. Collins concluded that 'The position of the Opposition was that any advantage that might be gained from a Coalition would simply be used to destroy the Treaty position. This he could neither accept himself, nor recommend to his party, and from this stage it was quite clear that no agreement could be reached.'[7]

While Collins and de Valera talked, Griffith and O'Higgins, the two political heavyweights in the Provisional Government, made speeches in the Dáil which did not augur well for compromise prospects. Griffith emphasised that the paramount need was for an election and declared:

It is time this humbug ceased. ... We have offered everything that could be offered short of giving away the indefeasible right of the Irish people to pronounce on the issue before them. ... If men will come with force of arms against us to attempt to prevent the Irish people expressing their opinion, all we can say is we are prepared to meet them on that issue.

O'Higgins, after denouncing de Valera's speeches at Killarney and Thurles, declared his pleasure at the failure of the Dáil committee's deliberations. 'Personally', he affirmed, 'I am glad that no such oil-and-water and wolf-and-lamb Coalition was agreed upon.' At that point Mulcahy, no doubt much to Griffith's annoyance, urged that Collins and de Valera resume their talks. Collins, however, was pessimistic, commenting: 'I do not believe we could agree upon recommendations. ... We had pleasant conversations, but they did not result in anything.'

On 19 May Collins had been complaining of de Valera being impossibilist; a day later he signed the pact with him. On both sides of the Irish Sea the agreement appeared like a bolt from the blue. Thomas Jones had written to the Prime Minister on 17 May: 'Up to the time of writing ... there is no likelihood of agreement between Collins and de Valera. This is good news as what I most feared is an agreement in which Collins would be still further paralysed and the constitution compromised.' After the pact was signed the London *Times* commented: 'In no other country . . . save Ireland could the political situation have undergone such an astounding development.'

There is no evidence explaining why Collins made the *volte-face*. British observers, however, spotted the important role Harry Boland played in bringing about the agreement. Because of his closeness to de Valera and Collins, and his political skills, Boland was ideally placed to act as a go-between. He was to tell Joe McGarrity haw hard he had worked for unity, and that he was quite happy with the pact. Ernie O'Malley claimed that when Collins was resisting signing the agreement, Boland had persuaded him to do so.

The pact's terms were close to Boland's earlier proposals in the Dáil Peace Committee. A national coalition panel for the election was agreed upon 'on the ground that the national position requires the entrusting of the Government of the country into the joint hands of those who have been the strength of the national situation during the last few years'. The proportion of candidates chosen for the panel was to be according to their then strength in the Dáil. The agreement also made provision for a coalition executive following the election, to consist of a Minister for Defence and nine other ministers in a proportion of five to four in favour of the majority party. In event of the breakdown of the government a general election would be held. The insistence in one clause that non-Sinn Féin candidates be allowed to stand on equal terms in the election was the only issue within the agreement that Collins actually stood firm on.

There was no reference to the Treaty in the pact. On issues relating to the election and the constitution Collins appeared to have given way. Technically, as Frank O'Connor pointed out in his biography of Collins, the agreement amounted to 'a complete give-away of the Treaty position'. On the day after the pact was signed it was unanimously approved by the Sinn Féin Ard-Fheis, and Collins was cheered to the echo there when he declared that 'Unity at home was more important than any Treaty with the foreigner, and if unity could only be got at the expense of the Treaty—the Treaty would have to go.' It was reported that at the meeting 'enthusiasm and happiness prevailed'. Liam Lynch told Liam Manahan: 'Collins was back with his own crowd and . . . he would definitely remain that way.'[8]

To the British government the pact was the final straw in a whole series of pre-varications by the Provisional Government. Churchill concluded that the pact 'is obviously designed to prevent the transfer of political power from the Sinn Féin and IRA organisations to the Irish electorate, by healing the split in these organisations. The two parties agree to simply monopolise power. The one inducement offered to the public to accept the agreement is the hope of escaping from anarchy.' The Colonial Secretary also told the cabinet: 'It was an agreement full of disaster; it prevented an expression of opinion on the Treaty; it gives the Provisional Government no further representation of strength or authority from the Irish people; it left the Government in its present weak and helpless position.' Churchill had earlier concluded that 'We were witnessing in Ireland a process of rapid disintegration.' He criticised the Irish government for living 'far too much in the narrow circle of their own associates and late associates, and they think only of placating the obscure terrorists who spring up one after another all over Ireland'. Churchill claimed that he had been repeatedly assured by Collins that he was about to act decisively against the 'mutineers', and, as a result, the British government had supplied more war materials. He then refused to hand over any more arms and halted the evacuation of British troops.

It seems that Collins signed the pact without consulting his political colleagues. The action ended Collins's close alliance with Griffith which had been central to the achievement and acceptance of the Treaty. Griffith never again called Collins by his Christian name. Ernest Blythe related that when the agreement came up in the cabinet Griffith took two frosty minutes to motion his assent; Griffith, he added, had been driven to despair by the 'wait and see' attitude of the military leaders. Griffith scathingly commented: 'If we were not prepared to fight and preserve the democratic rights of the ordinary people and the fruit of national victory, we should be looked upon as the greatest set of poltroons who had ever had the fate of Ireland in their hands.' Eoin Mac Néill commented on the pact: 'It seemed to me to mean nothing less than depriving the people of the right to vote.' Blythe felt it had nothing to recommend it, and that only the clause permitting non-Sinn Féin candidates to be nominated prevented the election from being a complete farce. The cabinet was faced, however, with a *fait accompli*. Officially the cabinet justified it in terms of restoring order to allow the election to take place. It was affirmed that

> They were not prepared to wage war against Bolshevism sheltering under the name of Republicanism, and it was essential that there should be unity of the political forces in the country to cope with disorder. . . . It should be made quite clear that the Provisional Government are determined to stand by the Treaty.

Mulcahy was to admit that the quest for army and political unity went further than he would have desired to move. O'Higgins took a less sympathetic view, saying that the 'toleration' and 'magnanimity' shown had caused him to think that 'in the whole history of our country there never was a more despicable period'.

The Republican opposition appeared to have won far more from the pact than the Provisional Government. On closer examination, however, it is clear that the agreement amounted to little more than a postponement of the issues. The *Sunday Times* wrote that the Provisional Government had 'as yet no legal existence, and Mr Collins has no power to employ a policeman or a soldier. . . . He will have a month longer to organise his force and so ensure a fairly free election. It will be seen, therefore, that de Valera has not gained so much as at first apparent.' The agreement could only be successful if a constitution satisfactory to all sides was published before the election. Harry Boland told Joe McGarrity on 30 May: 'The whole game is now in the hands of Mr Collins. We shall see how he will act. I, for one, would like to think that he will direct all his actions towards the Republic.' A week later Boland commented:

> We hammered out an agreement after very hard and strenuous work and for the moment everything is harmonious!!!—how long it will last I know not. . . . If we can work out a successful constitution . . . all may yet be well, if not I shall begin to despair.

Seán T. O'Kelly saw the constitutional issue as a matter of how far Collins could take Griffith along with him.

The success of the agreement depended on Collins's ability to put it into effect, and that needed the help of his political colleagues and, more important, the tolerance of the British government. Meanwhile elements in the Republican opposition were extremely unhappy about the pact, seeing it as an attempt to mislead them and secure the Provisional Government's position. Mary MacSwiney had warned Boland and McGarrity about dealing with Collins:

> The main point is that Collins declares he is going to have a Republican Constitution and if L. George objects he will fight him on it. Now if he is sincere in that, why is he risking Civil War on the acceptance of the Treaty?... Collins is undoubtedly a clever man, and I am sorry to say an unscrupulous one but do you think for an instant that he can beat L. George in the game of duplicity?

Of Boland, Mary MacSwiney wrote: 'Poor Harry! For a long time he believed in Mick, believed that Mick and de Valera could be brought together...' In retrospect, de Valera told Ernie O'Malley 'that signing the pact was the worst day's work he did for the Republic'.[9]

It appears that both Collins and de Valera signed the pact as a last attempt for them to try to control events. De Valera's role had become peripheral, particularly since the Army Convention; if the pact's proposals could be put into effect, an attempt to revise the Treaty could be made along External Association lines. By signing the pact de Valera was trying to re-establish the position of Sinn Féin, and his own leadership position within the nationalist movement. Sinn Féin had, however, already disintegrated; de Valera was to say of the pro-Treaty members of Sinn Féin that 'by keeping away from the organisation' they 'were allowing Sinn Féin to die'. De Valera made repeated efforts to get the election postponed by demanding that the electoral register be changed.

General Macready was to depict the pact as a clever scheme to enable the election to take place; after that the terms of the agreement could be ignored. The pact should, however, be seen as an expression of the weakness of both Collins's and de Valera's positions, and also as a product of their overriding desire to avoid a civil war which would represent the death-knell of their hopes. In private Collins called the pact a wartime emergency measure; by signing it he was putting off the day when fundamental choices would have to be made.

Collins's actions since the Treaty had revealed a consistent desire to compromise on the constitutional issue, and an impatience with being made to conform narrowly to the Treaty terms. The important elements in his desire to compromise were his respect for his old military colleagues, together with his concern about the Northern question. In a scribbled note on the compromise Collins wrote: 'Above all Ulster.'[10]

After the Collins–de Valera Pact the army issues could be divorced from the political ones. James O'Dwyer, a member of the Dáil Peace Committee, argued that once political terms had been agreed, army unity should be no problem. The *Cork Examiner* asserted: 'The unification of the Army should now be a matter easy of accomplishment.'

The signing of the Collins–de Valera Pact produced immediate gains in the army talks. On 26 May it was agreed that there would be no more commandeering of cars or private property, that commandeered cars would be returned to their owners, and that some of the occupied buildings in Dublin (though not the Four Courts) would be evacuated. A 'tentative Army Council' was set up to enquire into army unity proposals and 'the question of unity of command'.

Despite some obscurity concerning the chronology and precise character of developments, it is clear that the talks came close to success on matters relating to army organisation in the period between the pact and the publication of the constitution on 15 June. Five on the Army Council agreed on a memorandum which became the basis for the discussions. It suggested that all ranks and positions in the army should be held as of 1 December 1921. Ex-soldiers of other armies were only to be employed 'ordinarily' in training or advisory capacities; organisation of the proposed army was to be in Lynch's hands as Deputy Chief of Staff; divisions were to be recruited and controlled locally; and the army was to be kept as small as possible. Local antagonisms created by conflict over occupation of barracks were to be dealt with 'by drafting in officers native to the area who are at present serving in other districts'. It was stated that 'no man' was 'to be victimised because of honest political views'.

The question of the personnel of the proposed new Army Council proved difficult. Mellows complained that much time was taken up with haggling over appointments. Although the pro-Treaty representatives rejected the proposal that de Valera should become Minister for Defence in a coalition government, they proved remarkably flexible on the matter of proposed appointments for the Army Council. It was proposed that the majority of the posts should be given to anti-Treaty men. When this was conveyed to the Provisional Government cabinet, objection was raised and Diarmuid O'Hegarty was added to the list. For some time the anti-Treaty insistence on filling the Chief of Staff position provided a barrier to progress in the talks. Lynch threatened to terminate talks on this question, but Mulcahy and Lynch manoeuvred round the roadblock by providing for two Deputy Chiefs of Staff, Lynch and Deasy, the former to be in charge of organisation in the new army. The anti-Treaty side was also given to believe that after a short time O'Duffy would resign as Chief of Staff and be replaced by Lynch; O'Duffy had sent a letter of resignation when he thought army unity was in sight. In effect, also, the Army Council was to have control of the appointments of the Minister for Defence and the Chief of Staff. On 8 June Lynch wrote that in the event of his being appointed Chief of Staff

> I am prepared to guarantee...that I will do my utmost to maintain...stability and will not endeavour to overthrow the administration of the govt. to be formed as a result of the elections of 16 June even though Mr de Valera or any of his party do not become members of that Govt., this guarantee to cover the period during which the constitution is being considered and until a further election has been held and a Govt. formed.[11]

Any assurances that Lynch could give, however, were not supported by the majority of those in the Four Courts. Mellows was concerned that Mulcahy and Lynch were trying to 'fix' matters in the absence of Rory O'Connor. Finally the proposals were submitted to the Army Executive on 14 June and comfortably rejected. Mulcahy stated then that negotiations were at an end and that any further steps would be a matter for the new coalition to handle. The Executive's reply, also on 14 June, declared that talks must cease, that the Executive was to take action to maintain the Republic 'against British aggressors', and, meanwhile, that there were to be no offences against Beggars' Bush forces. Even after 14 June talks between Beggars' Bush and Lynch and his entourage went on, and the unity proposals were submitted to the Army Executive on 18 June. By that time, however, the constitution had been published, the election had taken place, and the prospect for a coalition government was nil.[12]

Throughout the talks there had been a great desire by men like Lynch, Deasy and Moylan to find a settlement. Moylan repeatedly declared: 'There's going to be no f...... Civil War'; and Lynch wrote to his brother before the talks:

> If we fail at the election, I hope to have the Army united under an Executive and not giving allegiance to any party or Government. . . . If we can force the Treaty party to draw up a Republican Constitution we are A1 again. This I consider possible.

There appears to have been general optimism during the talks, even within the Four Courts, probably based on the combined Northern policy. Sheila Humphreys, an old Cumann na mBan worker, recorded that Mellows told her, a week before the Four Courts attack, that both sides were going to sink their differences on the North.

The delicate negotiations had not been aided by the *Cork Examiner*'s publication on 29 May of another of Rory O'Connor's outspoken press conferences. He now stated that the achievement of the Republic had only been postponed by the truce and that plans for attacks on the North were ready. Again he made it clear that de Valera 'has nothing to do with the Army' and argued that the popular will should not be expressed through parliamentary channels. He claimed that Republicans controlled three-quarters of the arms and that it was their seizure of the Four Courts that had forced Collins and de Valera to make peace moves. Seán Hegarty immediately protested to the *Cork Examiner* about O'Connor's claim to speak for and to be head of the army.

Problematical also was the reaction to the army negotiations of politician members of the Provisional Government. Mulcahy told Hegarty: 'I ... have created consternation amongst the Government by letting them know I have more or less agreed to an agreed Army Council the majority of whom were more or less in arms against the Government until a day or two ago; and of whose general attitude they have absolutely no guarantee at the moment.' Mulcahy's and Lynch's chief concern, however, was with hardline Republicans. Mulcahy concluded: 'Apart altogether from any Government trouble of this kind which can fairly easily be overcome, I am afraid that we will be driven to call a meeting of all Divisional and Brigade Commandants and putting the situation up-to-date before them, in order to force the hand of some of the more impossible people.'

The planned personnel of the Army Council demonstrated how the army unity talks represented an attempted rapprochement between the old GHQ leadership and the 1st Southern Division, based on the personal regard between Lynch and Deasy on the one side, and Mulcahy and Collins on the other, and reinforced by IRB contacts. Hegarty's poor personal relations with Mulcahy did not prevent him from being a powerful positive influence. During the early stages of the unity talks Mulcahy agreed to evacuated barracks being handed over to Cork No. 1 Brigade; he reported that Hegarty 'suggests that the basis of understanding in the matter . . . be that of general good faith and harmonious working'.[13]

The large concessions made during the army talks greatly disturbed some of the Provisional Government side. J. J. O'Connell wrote: 'Lynch had very great influence with certain members of GHQ which was hard to understand seeing that he himself and his senior officers were known to be to a man hostile to the Government.' O'Connell noted that IRB men dominated the proposed Army Council, with Lynch having a crucial role. 'Certain it is', he commented, 'that members of GHQ like myself . . . and the Director of Training, had not any such influence at all. Gradually one got to feel that one was up against a stone wall, and that Lynch and what he stood for were being given a free hand. And as it fell out all the efforts to placate Lynch were unavailing.' O'Connell went on to complain that the army organisation proposals amounted 'in effect to giving the mutineers control . . . Organisation, Training, and Intelligence were entrusted to them.' On 22 May there was a meeting of Provisional Government army officers dissatisfied with developments, and on 23 May O'Connell tendered his resignation, which was not accepted, on the issue of the demotion of some ex-British officers.[14]

Retrospectively many anti-Treaty leaders thought that the Provisional Government had been deliberately playing for time while building up their army and had been aiming to encourage dissension in anti-Treaty IRA ranks. Moss Twomey, representing the young hardline IRA man's viewpoint, commented that the talks took seven weeks when they should have taken seven days, and that meanwhile 'the enemy' were 'preparing to wage war'. Liam Lynch complained that 'Before hostilities opened we had too much of this humbug, which was very much to our disadvantage.' A letter written by Emmet Dalton on 10 May appears to give some credence to this opinion. 'I write to know', Dalton enquired, 'would it be possible to prolong the truce negotiations until the 19th inst. by which time I believe I could have the British cleared out of the Curragh, Cork and part of Dublin.' The Provisional Government was in a vulnerable military position at the time of the talks and had every cause to be concerned about the wisdom of attempting a decisive stand against the military opposition. That does not mean, however, that the government representatives were not in earnest about desiring army unity. Collins and Mulcahy made considerable concessions: a large amount of autonomy to the Army Executive was granted in the proposals, and there was little provision made for centralised or political control of the IRA. Mulcahy, speaking in the Dáil in September 1922 (when at last the issue came to be debated), admitted they may have been 'finessing with honour' during the talks. He justified the proposals as not desirable in themselves but necessary at the time, and said that the government had misgivings about how far they had gone to appease the opposition.

The army unity talks demonstrated vividly how far the thinking on both sides of the army was conditioned by purely military considerations. A pro-Treaty military leader commented:

> It will be a good thing if we can make peace with the soldiers—but we cannot abandon our own position or be deflected from our own course by politicians who are trading on the soldiers' attitude. Politicians have no power apart from the soldiers' threat of war. . . . Only conferences of any value are

conferences with soldiers to get them to see this in order that civil war may be avoided, and that the shame of suppressing our own people by force may be avoided. This really the object, not to decide whether or not an election should be held.

Ó Muirthile observed of Collins:

He had no great regret regarding the loss of De Valera's friendship, nor no great fears of the opposition he alone could offer. . . . He did not worry too much either about parting company with others of his political colleagues. . . . What troubled Collins most was the split in the Army. There were men in the Army that he would go almost any distance to satisfy. He would rather, as he said to me more than once, have one of the type of Liam Lynch, Liam Deasy, Tom Hales, Rory O'Connor, or Tom Barry on his side that a dozen like De Valera. These were men of great energy and patriotic outlook down through the . . . Anglo-Irish War, and they had been faithful subordinates as well as personal friends, and the thought of turning the guns on such men was abhorrent to Collins.

The talks failed because their proposed compromise was incompatible with the Treaty. Old army loyalties and the desire for army unity did not end with the Four Courts attack, however.[15]

13

The Constitution

THE Collins-de Valera Pact coincided with the completion of the projected Free State constitution. At that time developments in the North, culminating in the Belleek-Pettigo crisis of early June and demands for an enquiry into killings and disorders in Belfast, had reached a new intensity. With the election imminent, the coherence and purpose of the Provisional Government was put fully to the test.

Before the signing of the pact Republican political leaders realised that the constitution would be the vital test of Collins's intention to make an effective compromise. While Seán T. O'Kelly and Harry Boland were moderately optimistic of a republican document being accepted by the British, Mary MacSwiney felt that such an eventuality 'could not be obtained under the Treaty'. Republican leaders maintained their demand that the constitution be published before the election: the electorate would then be able to judge the full reality of the Treaty settlement. Churchill meanwhile reminded Cope on 8 May 1922: 'It is of the utmost importance that I should receive a draft of the Constitution before it has been finally settled by the PG', so that it could be confirmed that the document was in conformity with the Treaty. Both the Republican opposition and the British government, therefore, insisted on the constitution being published before the election as a test of the Provisional Government's intentions.[1]

The unamended constitution—the product of three separate drafts—represented the desire to establish Irish sovereignty and to eliminate the role of the British Crown in Irish affairs. Hugh Kennedy, the government's chief legal adviser, argued that such aims were not incompatible with the Treaty terms, but James Douglas, a member of the Constitution Committee, admitted that the constitution had been framed along the lines of de Valera's Document No. 2, which had provided 'That the legislative, executive and judicial authority of Ireland shall be derived solely from the people of Ireland.' Douglas argued that Ireland under the Treaty 'had not become a British Dominion. Ireland is another country, and her nationality and her sovereignty are not of recent growth.' Patrick Hogan, the Minister for Agriculture, affirmed:

> The Constitution should be enacted first and the Treaty ratified afterwards. . . . Our position is and should be that we are a Sovereign Nation. The Constitution itself should be the Constitution of an independent Sovereign Nation.

Professor Alfred O'Rahilly, a major figure in the drawing up of the document, emphasised the electoral advantages that would accrue if 'England' was left 'as much as possible out of the picture', and continued:

Attention should be concentrated on the Constitution which Ireland is making for herself for her future well-being, and not on the terms of the Treaty, which, by defining our relations with England, secured peace and freedom to establish our own Government on our own lines.

The constitution, written after over three months' work in committee, eliminated an oath to the Crown, removed the role of the British Privy Council in appeals, and made no mention of the Crown's executive authority. The document also had a provision for the inclusion in a new government of external ministers who would not have to take an oath to support the Treaty. It was therefore claimed that 'The system we have adopted has taken away every excuse the Anti-Treaty Party may have for non-participation and non-co-operation in building up Ireland.' From the start of its work the Constitution Committee had been instructed to concern itself with democratic authority, rather than with Anglo-Irish relations which had been the work of the Treaty. If, however, they thought that interpretation of their role would be accepted by the British government, they were being vastly over-optimistic. The historian J. M. Curran has written: 'The only explanation for Collins's optimism is that his legal advisers were breathing the rarified air of constitutional theory, untainted by political realities, while he himself ignored these realities because of his desperate desire for a Republican Constitution.'[2]

All the British government's worst fears were confirmed by the constitution. Suspicions were further aroused when Collins showed extreme reluctance to come to London when summoned there by Lloyd George after the signing of the pact with de Valera. Lloyd George told Griffith and Collins on 27 May that their constitution was a republican one with 'a thin veneer', a 'complete evasion' of the Treaty. Tom Jones, who had been generally sympathetic to the Provisional Government, agreed that the document 'knocked the Treaty end-ways'. The Treaty settlement appeared endangered, and the government's worst fears about Collins realised. It was at that point that the Prime Minister became directly involved in Irish affairs for the first time since the Treaty's signing. Jones related that when he met with Collins and Griffith, as a preliminary to their second conference on 1 June with Lloyd George, he found Collins in a 'most pugnacious mood' and talking of going back to fight with Mulcahy and Mac Eoin. Jones also recorded that during their discussions Collins was keen to switch the subject to the North, away from the constitutional issues. During dinner with his colleagues at the time Jones recorded Lloyd George as describing Collins as 'a wild animal—a mustang'. Jones said that 'Curtis had very neatly compared negotiating with Collins to writing on water and the P.M. had added "shallow and agitated water".' Lord FitzAlan, the Lord Lieutenant of Ireland, expressed his distrust of all the Irish government, with the exception of Griffith, and Chamberlain was similarly hostile to Collins.[3]

During his two meetings with Griffith and Collins, Lloyd George returned to his basic position of the Treaty negotiations. He made a distinction between the parts of the Collins–de Valera Pact which, although distasteful to British government eyes, were not, strictly speaking, in contravention of the Treaty, and the issues directly relating to the constitution. At a meeting of British signatories to the Treaty on 26 May Lloyd George said that 'The one thing on which the British Government could fight was Allegiance to the King. On this they would get the whole British Empire behind them.'

The Irish representatives were faced with six issues on which the British government held the draft to be at variance with the Treaty. The British government insisted that the Crown must have genuine authority and not be just a symbolic link between the two countries, that the Judicial Committee and appeal powers of the Privy Council be acknowledged, that any constitution must include an oath to the Crown, and that Northern Ireland's position be recognised. Finally it was made clear that the provision for external ministers could not be tolerated. Lloyd George concluded that they were back to the issue of Free State or Republic, and Chamberlain affirmed that the Provisional Government had to choose between appeasement of de Valera and support for the Treaty. On 31 May Churchill told a concerned House of Commons, while Griffith and Collins sat in the Strangers' Gallery, that a Republic could not be tolerated. He warned: 'In the event of such a Republic it will be the intention of the Government to hold Dublin as one of the preliminary essential steps to military operations.'[4]

When Lloyd George met Griffith and Collins on 1 June he stressed the imperative need for the constitution to be made to conform to the Treaty, which he said 'had represented the extreme limits to which Parliament would go'. The Prime Minister asked whether the Provisional Government 'were prepared to recognise that under the Treaty the Irish Free State must be inside and an integral part of the British Commonwealth'. Collins and Griffith indicated their willingness to abide by the Treaty, although Jones recorded Collins as saying 'that they were not prepared to have the English Common Law forced upon them'. Lloyd George pointed out that the issue was between republican and monarchical institutions. Before Collins and Griffith left Lloyd George made one of his theatrical appeals: 'If the Treaty perished,' he stated, 'not only Irishmen but friends of Ireland in this country would be stricken with sorrow. If it went through, the names of all the signatories would be inscribed in letters of gold.' The bluff of the Irish representatives had therefore been called on the same fundamental issue as it had been on 5 December 1921.

While Collins, in grumpy humour, caught the boat back to Dublin, Griffith remained to supervise Kennedy's detailed work of amendment of the constitution, carried out in collaboration with Lord Hewart, representing the British government. Griffith soon gave a reassuring reply on all six points contested by the British government. He agreed that it was not enough for the constitution to make it a question only of 'external association' with Britain. On 9 June British ministers were told that Kennedy had 'given way' on all major matters. Griffth reported to Collins that 'I am pretty well satisfied that the best that can be obtained in the Constitution in the present circumstances is being obtained in the least obnoxious form.' Lloyd George commented: 'The British Government had delivered the ultimatum and to their surprise the Irish had agreed. At first, it looked as if they were going to fight it out, but they had surrendered completely.'[5]

The amended constitution, nonetheless, put the emphasis far more on Irish internal authority than on the British Crown's role. O'Higgins pointed out that the document 'contains the trappings, the insignia, the fiction and the symbols of monarchical institutions, but the real power is in the hands of the people'. In order to meet British and Irish demands, contradictory intentions were juxtaposed within the same article. The President of the Free State's Executive Council was to be appointed by representatives of the Crown, but only after nomination by the

Dáil. The constitutional historian Leo Kohn has summed up the document as 'essentially republican. . . . The monarchical forms paled into insignificance in the light of the formal enunciation of the principle of the sovereignty of the people as the fundamental and the exclusive source of all political authority.' The forms, however, with regard to the monarchy, the Privy Council and the Governor-General had been preserved, and that was what mattered both to the British government and to the Republican opposition.

Collins was later to contend that if the Republican opposition had been less active, a more satisfactory constitution could have been achieved. The British Government was made the more intransigent, it was argued, by their perception of what was happening in the Twenty-Six Counties. O'Higgins noted: 'Every time we crossed to England to negotiate points consequential on the Treaty, things happened here that were meant to be mines under our feet.' Churchill seemed to give evidence for that view when he said following the Collins–de Valera Pact: 'As no Election of value is contemplated we are in a position to be much more searching in our examination of the Constitution.' O'Higgins was correct to stress, however, in the autumn of 1922: 'Had circumstances here been other than what they were, I do believe that we could have got a more pleasantly worded Constitution, but I do not believe that in any important point of substance we could have got a better Constitution than we in fact have got.'

Given his decision to sign the Treaty and his impatience with abstract constitutional questions, it was inconceivable that Collins would break with the British government on the issue of the constitution. That reality, however, did not prevent him from trying his luck on a question which, if it had been resolved on favourable terms, could have avoided final confrontation with the Republican opposition. At least he had succeeded in postponing the confrontation. There never was any doubt that Griffith and other politicians within the Provisional Government would readily accede to British requirements over the constitution. The retreat on the constitution issue, however, ended any hope for the Collins–de Valera Pact and drew a predictable reaction from Republican ranks. For Harry Boland, Collins had been forced to undermine the pact once Lloyd George had 'raised hell with them'.[6]

14

The June Election and the Assassination of Sir Henry Wilson

THE constitution was eventually published on the morning of 16 June—election day. It is unlikely that if it had been made available before, it would have significantly changed the result of the election. There could have been little time available between completion of redrafting of the constitution and the election, but for it to make its first appearance in the newspapers on election day was bound to produce a cynical reaction. Griffith's comments to the British government, six days before polling, suggest he was not keen to allow much time for analysis of the document. He said that 'A promise had been given to publish the Constitution before the Election, but he did not know if the other side would insist on the carrying out of this promise. The Constitution need, however, only be published a day or two before the Election.'

British insistence on the constitution confirmed that a coalition government was not practical politics, although it did not seem to have ended Harry Boland's hopes. A government with 'external ministers' included could not be formed with British compliance.

The other part of the Collins–de Valera Pact—the holding of a non-contested election—had broken down before 16 June. The fact that the election saw Proportional Representation used for the first time ensured that voters were able to express their pro- and anti-Treaty preferences. Newspapers, moreover, made the electorate well aware of the Treaty stance of Sinn Féin panel candidates, by stating their attitude alongside their names. That non-Sinn Féin candidates were all pro-Treaty made it easier for the voters to express their views on the settlement.

The anti-Treaty side campaigned far more vigorously for the panel than did the government candidates. Griffith and Collins in particular could plead that they were otherwise engaged on government business, but they showed little desire to speak on coalition platforms. De Valera was resentful that Collins refused to join Austin Stack and himself on a speaking tour to Cork. Many anti-Treaty TDs, moreover, showed enthusiasm for the pact because it increased the likelihood of their holding on to their seats: they were aware that their representation in the Second Dáil greatly exceeded their support in the country at large.[1]

Two days before the election Collins made a speech in Cork which has often been depicted as amounting to a deliberate destruction of the pact. Collins told his audience that he expected them to vote for the candidates they thought best of, regardless of whether they were on the panel or not. It is unclear, however, whether Collins meant to terminate the agreement—on the following day he made a speech in Clonakilty in which he urged voters to support the pact in the spirit in which it was made. The historian Michael Gallagher has pointed out that considerably less press publicity was given to Collins's Cork speech than has often been claimed. The speech does not mean that Collins had been insincere in signing the pact, but rather that he realised the constitution had ended any prospects for that compromise. The pact agreement completely broke down in Monaghan, where Eoin O'Duffy and Ernest Blythe, the pro-Treaty candidates, urged their supporters to give their third-preference choices to independents rather than to the anti-Treaty Sinn Féin candidates.

The pact had represented the ultimate example of Sinn Féin claims to speak for the spirit of the nation. Republicans were deeply critical of the clause in the pact allowing non-Sinn Féin candidates to stand at the election, and in some con-stituencies considerable pressure, moral or physical, was applied on them to withdraw. Dan Breen, who stood as a joint pro- and anti-Treaty candidate in South Tipperary, induced the Farmers' Party's candidate there to step down, but was unsuccessful with the Labour candidate, Dan Morrissey; Con Collins, while campaigning for Sinn Féin, complained that he had never heard of Morrissey and had never met him in prison or at an ambush. Sean Etchingham, a Sinn Féin panel candidate in Wexford, accused the Farmers' Party there as consisting of Orangemen and Freemasons. Denis Gorey, for the Farmers' Party, and William O'Brien, for the Labour Party, were to protest against the amount of intimidation used against their candidates at the election. Some of the independent candidate's agents were kidnapped in Sligo on the day of the election.[2]

However many caveats are entered (the state of the register and Collins's breaking of the pact, for example), the election demonstrated that there was a very large pro-Treaty majority. Pro-Treaty panel candidates won 239,193 out of the 620,283 votes. Anti-Treaty candidates won 133,864, and non-panel candidates 247,276.

The anti-Treaty Sinn Féiners would have done considerably worse if there had not been an election panel: anti-Treatyites were more likely to have voted the straight party ticket than pro-Treaty Sinn Féin voters were. Only in Sligo and East Mayo did anti-Treaty candidates win a majority of the votes. The Republican side received less than 22 per cent of the first-preference votes; no anti-Treaty candidate headed the poll in a contested constituency. Pro-Treaty candidates overwhelmingly dominated the result in Leinster, where anti-Treatyites won only five out of forty-four seats. In Co. Dublin the anti-Treaty poll was a mere 9.3 per cent. Republican candidates also ran poorly in the three Ulster counties and in Cork city. In Munster the pro-Treaty vote represented a small overall majority, while the Republican vote was narrowly in a majority in Connaught. The low turnout, of less than 60 per cent, would appear to be more due to the number of uncontested constituencies than to intimidation or the fear of it.

The election was notable for the very large non-Sinn Féin vote. For the first time since 1918, when the Labour Party had not contested the election, the Irish electorate had been given an opportunity to express their opinion; a high proportion of the vote represented a protest against Sinn Féin and their manage-ment of affairs both during and after the Treaty negotiations. While campaigning, Cosgrave had argued: 'I think that both sides in the Dáil are perfectly satisfied that they had made a mess of things throughout the entire country, and that mess should be settled by those who made it.' On 10 June Kevin O'Higgins had pointed out to members of the British government that 'already there was a healthy revolt against the pact' and 'a clamour for representation of particular interests'. A provincial journalist said of the Labour candidate in Louth–Meath that he did so well because he was the only candidate 'who gave the electors a chance of breaking the old chain of silence that has bound them since 1918'. Farmers' Party candidates were successful in all but one of the constituencies where they stood, and ten of the twenty-one independent candidates were elected. Labour won 29.4 per cent of the votes cast, and would have done even better if they had put forward more candidates. The fact that Labour candidates did particularly well in constituencies where their candidate was the only non-panel one would suggest that the party's vote was partly a protest one against Sinn Féin arrogance. T. J. O'Connell, the future Labour Party leader, was later to argue that a considerable proportion of former Parliamentary Party voters allied themselves with the Labour Party in 1922 (after the end of the Civil War their vote moved, more in line with their socially and economically conservative views, to the pro-Treaty government party). The success of non-Sinn Féin parties and candidates was primarily a Leinster and Munster affair. It was more difficult for candidates to stand in remote constituencies, and a considerable proportion of seats in the west were uncontested.

The result did not represent a vote of confidence in the Provisional Government—still less an expression of resistance to Republican ideals. Instead it demonstrated a popular realisation of the need for stable government, and the acceptance of realistic compromise with regard to Anglo-Irish relations. The electorate had at last been able to show that social and economic issues and, more particularly, the desire for settled conditions were of greater import to them than the endless debate over constitutional symbols and authority.

The election had an important role in legitimising the Treaty and the status of the Provisional Government. Although it did not prevent the Civil War, it greatly helped to facilitate the establishment of the Free State government during and after the war. It linked the government with the causes of majority rule and legitimate, democratic authority, and, through the Republicans' apparent resistance to the electorate's judgment, caused the opposition to be associated with non-acceptance of stable, legitimate government. In fact the pre-election pact had not intended the adoption of such political ideals; indeed, an ambivalent attitude to democracy was also shown by the decision of the government to attack the Four Courts before the new Dáil could sit.

The election result, together with the constitution's publication, clarified the political and military situation within the Twenty-Six Counties. The search for political and military unity, by means of an agreed constitution, a non-contested election, and a coalition government, had been rendered impossible on all three counts.

The British government drew what appeared to them the obvious conclusion that it was time for the Provisional Government to assert its authority. Whatever excuse there had been for delay and compromise no longer applied. The election result, and the fact that the election was held at all, represented a success for the politicians within the Irish government. Griffith had won the democratic authority he had so long demanded. Prospects for the Treaty settlement and for

Anglo-Irish relations appeared enormously improved. The British government could draw great relief and satisfaction. After the gloom relating to the constitutional and Northern issues of early June, the wheel seemed to have turned full circle. Collins's stock had markedly risen.[3]

It was at that point, with a dramatic timing never bettered, even in Irish history, that on 22 June two IRA men in London, Reginald Dunne and Joseph O'Sullivan, assassinated Sir Henry Wilson. Wilson had been trailed on a journey to unveil the war memorial at Liverpool Street Station. No opportunity offered itself for Dunne and O'Sullivan until Wilson arrived back at his home in Eaton Square, where he was shot between the taxi and his front door. Two policemen were also shot during the assassins' attempted escape; however, they were surrounded by a vengeful crowd and were soon arrested. The prospects for their getting away were not aided by O'Sullivan's wooden leg, the product of a war wound.[4]

The testimony of many of those who were involved in the events surrounding the affair suggests strongly that Collins was directly implicated. Written evidence, unsurprisingly, is not forthcoming, but oral testimony abounds. Joe Sweeney, the pro-Treaty military leader in Donegal, recorded meeting Collins shortly after the assassination. He told Ernie O'Malley: 'Collins told me that he had arranged the shooting of Wilson.' Sweeney said of Collins: 'He looked very pleased.' Frank Thornton, one of Collins's old 'Squad', recalled that the killing was carried out on the direct orders of GHQ. Mick Murphy, of Cork No. 1 Brigade, said that when in London he had been asked to take part in the plot, explaining: 'They had instructions then from Michael Collins to shoot Wilson.' Some have argued that the orders were given before the Anglo-Irish truce, but statements from Collins's intelligence agents point to fresh instructions being given in June. It is clear also that Dunne had seen Collins in Dublin in early June and had spent some time closeted with him. Shortly after the assassination de Valera told Art O'Brien that the Provisional Government was 'covering up' about the affair.[5]

Dunne—a key figure in the London IRA—had taken a neutral line on the Treaty and had a great personal attachment to Collins. He had come under increasing criticism from within the London Irish organisations for his Treaty attitude: the Cumann na mBan there had sent him some white feathers. Dunne commented that he hoped that Wilson's shooting would help towards the reunification of republicans in London and Ireland. Dunne had problems finding a companion for the task—Liam Lynch remarked that it was unfortunate that O'Sullivan did not possess two sound legs.

The planning for the assassination was made through Collins's old London IRB network—loyal Collins supporters, like Sam Maguire and Dunne, who had doubts about the Treaty but none about Collins's intentions. They hoped that unity in London and Ireland could be restored with one dramatic stroke. If the orders had come from Collins, he could not have admitted it in the context of the beginning of the Civil War—to have done so would have wrecked his relations with the British government and with his colleagues in the Provisional Government. Hence when Dunne and O'Sullivan were executed the impression had to be given that Wilson's shooting was their own personal responsibility. In letters to the *Sunday Press* in 1953 O'Sullivan's brother complained that the two men's memory had been besmirched by the failure of any Irish government since to declare that they had acted under instructions.

It is possible that both Collins and members of the Four Courts Executive were involved in the planning of Wilson's assassination. When Dunne was in Dublin earlier in June he had seen Rory O'Connor, as well as Collins, and both sides were implicated in the attempt to spring Dunne and O'Sullivan from prison. Dinny Kelleher, a Cork IRA man who was actively involved in the escape planning, told O'Malley that both Collins and O'Connor were connected with the planning of the shooting. The evidence for such Four Courts involvement is very slight, however. Ernie O'Malley, who was a very prominent figure in the Four Courts at the time, had no memory of any such planning.

Collins's cabinet colleagues knew nothing about any role Collins might have had in the assassination's planning. Mulcahy was incensed when Liam Tobin told him about it. Ernest Blythe recorded Griffith's dismay when told about Wilson's death, and although Blythe did not think Collins was responsible for the orders, he felt that Collins, who was present at the time, knew more than Griffith did.

The motive for Wilson's killing is not hard to find. Seán Moylan remembered Collins saying that Wilson had been a thorn in his side and had made a procurement of arms more difficult. General Macready pointed out that Wilson's role in the North was exaggerated—he was not in charge of the Specials and was critical of them, but he was the most famous and vociferous loyalist critic of the Treaty and of British policy since. He was the most obvious of scalps for the gunmen, and the one, outside the British cabinet and the royal family, likely to win the most publicity. By Wilson's shooting, moreover, Collins may have hoped to reassure Northern IRA units that their cause was not forgotten at a time when they were in a very depressed state. What is more difficult to explain is why, at the very time when Collins had turned his back on the search for an agreed constitution and a coalition government, he was apparently involved in an action which, if his complicity was discovered by the British government, would have endangered his career and the Treaty settlement.[6]

British suspicions about Collins and the assassination must have been aroused by a document found on Dunne, which, while referring to IRB matters in Britain, stated that 'The "Big Fellow" ... would arrange an election.' It may be safely assumed that someone in government circles knew who the 'Big Fellow' was. The British government was eager to place responsibility for Wilson's shooting on the men in the Four Courts, who provided a useful cover for Collins, but they must have had their suspicions about Collins.

Collins's involvement can be explained by consideration of his background and the emphasis he placed on the Northern question and on army unity. He remained a conspirator, attached to his IRB colleagues rather than to his government colleagues. Throughout the first six months of 1922 he had been actively involved in an aggressive Northern policy which ran directly counter to the Treaty and the need to establish sound relations with the British government. If he had run the risk of the British discovering his connection with Wilson's assassination, the same was true of his involvement in the February kidnapping of loyalists and the arms exchange and attacks on the North between March and May. The policy and action is of a piece. The hysterical language of his protests to the British government about outrages in Belfast and on border issues should be taken at face value—the expressions of a mind that related closely to that of the Catholic minority, and particularly the Northern IRA, and had a deep hatred of loyalism.

If the order was given to kill Wilson at the most sensitive of all times for Anglo-Irish relations, it demonstrated again that Collins placed the Northern question, and the importance through that issue of restoring IRA and IRB unity, ahead of adherence to the Treaty terms. Dinny Kelleher recorded meeting Collins at the end of the Treaty negotiations, and Collins saying: 'We have the bloody Treaty... and I don't know whether they'll take it or not in Dublin but we can march on the North.'[7]

There never was any prospect that the British government would respond favourably to the Provisional Government's plea that Dunne and O'Sullivan be reprieved from execution; as a loyal secret society man, Collins must have felt a deep moral responsibility for them. Collins sent two close associates, Joe Dolan and later Tom Cullen, to London to investigate escape possibilities; meanwhile the Army Executive, probably at Liam Lynch's behest, sent various Cork IRA men over, led by Dinny Kelleher and including Frank Cremins and Billy Aherne, on the same mission. The Cork men talked of schemes to capture the Prince of Wales at Bournemouth, and of capturing his sister and using her as a hostage, but neither scheme got off the ground. A plan was also hatched to blow up the van carrying Dunne and O'Sullivan from Brixton prison to their trial, but again nothing resulted. The split within the IRB in London, the outbreak of the Civil War, and the decline of Collins's old intelligence system, rendered such plans more difficult. Many of Collins's old IRB men in London by that time had returned to Ireland: there were apparently no friendly warders in Brixton. In the end no escape effort was attempted, and Dunne and O'Sullivan were executed.

The British government's reaction to the assassination was immediate and out-raged. Frances Stevenson, the Prime Minister's private secretary and mistress, commented in her diary on Lloyd George's reaction: 'It will put the whole Irish question back into the melting-pot again. D [Lloyd George] had been warned by Shortt [the Home Secretary]' of 'dangerous Irishmen in London, and S advised him not to go to Chequers, but we had been rather inclined to discount the warning at this juncture. However Shortt was right.' Two conferences of British ministers talked about the possibility of there being a general conspiracy. A search for Irish suspects in the London area was begun, and parliament debated the possibility of introducing passports for those travelling between Ireland and Britain. The government decided that General Macready be brought over to discuss measures to be taken, and that a letter be sent to Collins stating that the Four Courts occupation and 'the ambiguous position' of the IRA could no longer be tolerated. It was pointed out that evidence had been found on Dunne con-necting the IRA with the killing.

The most immediate consequence of Wilson's assassination was that it focused attention back on the Four Courts; it greatly added to British impatience with the Provisional Government. There was within the British cabinet a desire to respond by some definite action. Macready recorded that he found the Prime Minister and certain ministers 'in a state of suppressed agitation in which considerations of personal safety seemed to contend with the desire to do something dramatic as a set-off against the assassination... on the previous day'. Kevin O'Higgins regarded the assassination as 'simply another barrel of oil on the flames'.

Wilson's death had greatly increased tensions, although, surprisingly, it did not provoke widespread reprisals in the North. It served to speed up enormously the developments in the next few crucial days.[8]

15

The Attack on the Four Courts

THE tensions between the officers of the 1st Southern Division and the Four Courts leaders came to a head at the Army Convention of 18 June. The resulting split was to greatly weaken the anti-Treaty cause nine days before the Four Courts attack.

At the Convention Liam Lynch tried to put forward his army unity proposals which had been rejected by the Army Executive. Before the motion could be put to the vote Tom Barry put forward a dramatic resolution stating that unless all remaining British troops left Dublin within seventy-two hours, they would be attacked. It appears that O'Connor and Mellows had severe doubts about the practicability of the motion. Barry's resolution gained a majority, but when the vote was contested a second ballot saw it narrowly defeated. O'Connor then declared that he would leave the Convention if Lynch's proposal was put before them, and following a call from Seán MacBride, approximately half of the delegates left the Mansion House for the Four Courts. Joe McKelvey—latterly the Belfast O/C—was elected Chief of Staff in Lynch's place. The 1st Southern Division men returned to the Clarence Hotel.

No incident better illustrated the lack of effective central control within the anti-Treaty IRA. It was remarkable that Lynch should still see any prospect of army unity after the publication of the constitution, and that Barry's impractical motion should win so much support.[1]

The British conference of ministers, which met the day after Wilson's assassination, with General Macready in attendance, decided on a policy of retaliation. Plans were laid for British troops to take over the Four Courts on the following Sunday (25 June) or the day after. The attack was to involve the use of tanks, howitzers and aeroplanes. When asked about the plan's feasibility, Macready said it would present 'no great difficulty', but expressed concern at the possible political effects of such a move in potentially rallying opinion to the Republican side; he told Lloyd George that civilian casualties could not be avoided. Discussion centred not on the purpose, or likely results, of such an attack, but on whether Sunday or Monday was a better day for it. The situation was complicated by Collins's absence in Cork, which meant the British government was unable to get a quick reply to their ultimatum.

At a meeting on 24 June the British government made a definite decision to go ahead with the attack on the following day. They held that Collins's reply had not given a definite enough commitment on ending the Four Courts occupation. A proclamation was drawn up for publication after the proposed attack, and Lord Beatty, the First Lord of the Admiralty, was to arrange for ships to be sent to

Kingstown to take prisoners away from Dublin after completion of the action.[2]

On the day of the proposed operation the order was withdrawn as a result of what amounted to military cold feet. It appears that Macready had developed stronger doubts than he had expressed in London; he sent Colonel Brind to London to warn of the potential consequences of the operation. Brind pointed out to ministers that many of the Republican leaders would not be in the Four Courts if the attack was carried out on the Sunday. He warned of the dangers of unifying Republican opinion and the likelihood of reprisals on British troops. The military leaders cast doubt on the intelligence reports which had provided the basis for the British government's reaction. It had to be admitted in the cabinet that the evidence found on Reginald Dunne did not prove Four Courts complicity in Wilson's assassination, although the cabinet feebly concluded that 'it was by no means improbable'. Macready and Brind advised that the Provisional Government should be given another chance to clear the Four Courts.

The orders were rescinded at the eleventh hour. Ships on their way to Kingstown were hastily redirected. It was decided that Churchill should write to the Southern government pointing out that the Treaty could not be proceeded with unless the Four Courts was cleared. When the coalition government fell in October, Churchill ordered that all copies of the proclamation that had been prepared for issue after the attack should be destroyed.

If the British had attacked the Four Courts, events would very probably have taken a hugely different turn: the basis of the cautious post-Treaty policy, which had allowed for a tactful withdrawal from the southern twenty-six counties, would have been shattered. Macready argued that 'Panic and a desire to do something, no matter what, by those whose ignorance of the Irish situation blinded them to possible results, was at the root of this scheme.' As it was, the British government was able to take a comfortable back seat during the Civil War. The nearly disastrous response to Wilson's assassination must be put down to extreme impatience: Macready thought that Churchill's 'feverish impetuosity' lay behind it. Long-term doubts in the British government about the Provisional Government's reliability were made explicit. Macready, for his part, was to conclude in his memoirs: 'I have never ceased to congratulate myself on having been instrumental in staving off what would have been a disaster from every point of view, except the actual capture of the buildings.'

The British threat had been a real one, and the Southern government was aware of the intense pressure on them to act. Churchill told Collins on 7 July that 'We had reached the end of our tether.' Compromise with the Republican opposition was no longer an option. Commenting on Churchill's warning speech in the Commons of 26 June, the London *Times* declared: 'The moment has at last come for Mr Collins to choose which path he shall take. There are only two paths—that of the Treaty and that of anarchy.'[3]

It is unclear precisely when the Provisional Government decided to attack the Four Courts. The scarcity of evidence is explained by the acute sensitivity of the subject, both at the time and since. Before the projected British attack on the Four Courts was decided upon there had been a meeting of British military officers with Griffith and Emmet Dalton at which the possibility was discussed of material being loaned to the Provisional Government forces to enable them to attack the Four Courts. It appears that it was on 26 June that the Provisional Government cabinet virtually decided to make a definite move.

On 27 June an army unit under Frank Thornton, one of Collins's old 'Squad', was ordered to intercept a Republican raiding party on Ferguson's Garage in Lower Baggot Street. Ferguson's was a branch of a well-known Belfast firm, and the raid was in accordance with the Belfast boycott. As the joint army policy on the North still applied, Thornton was as surprised by his instructions as was Leo Henderson, the organiser of the raid and the boycott, to be arrested. Thornton expressed his embarrassment to Henderson. Ernie O'Malley immediately urged that an officer of similar rank on the other side be kidnapped in retaliation. J. J. O'Connell, the Deputy Chief of Staff, was chosen as his whereabouts were well known, and after his capture had been successfully carried out O'Connell was accommodated in the Four Courts during the bombardment and siege.

That evening the Dublin City Guard took up their positions around the Four Courts in Chancery Place, Bridewell Street and the Four Courts Hotel. Paddy Daly, with a force of men from the Dublin Guard, was in charge of positions in the vicinity of the building, and the 2nd Eastern Division formed a cordon around it. Meanwhile a unit under Commandant Bolster was sent to attack Fowler Hall, which had also been occupied by an anti-Treaty garrison. At 3.30 a.m. an ultimatum was given to those in the Four Courts to evacuate the building; the bombardment's opening had evidently been delayed for a few hours by a small mutiny in the Provisional Government army. The attack began at 4.15 a.m. with rifle response from the Four Courts to the shells which were fired at quarter-hour intervals.[4]

In their official pronouncements at the time the Provisional Government put the decision to attack the Four Courts down to the need to respond to the reapplication of the Belfast boycott and to O'Connell's kidnapping. The events of 27 June were depicted as the final straw with regard to Republican resistance to the state. That explanation is weakened, however, by Mulcahy's admission that the decision had effectively been taken before O'Connell's arrest. In the Dáil sessions of September 1922, when there was the first opportunity to debate the issue, Mulcahy and O'Higgins argued that the attack's timing was explained by the need to respond to intelligence information concerning an imminent Republican coup. The threat of Tom Barry's Army Convention resolution, it was argued, was about to be implemented by an attack on British troops. The evidence, however, for this was not forthcoming, as Thomas Johnson pointed out, although isolated attacks on British troops were increasingly likely. The coup explanation reads like a retrospective rationalisation, designed to deal with criticism during the Civil War.

There is no difficulty in explaining why Griffith and O'Higgins, and their political colleagues, supported the Four Courts attack. The decision was a necessary affirmation of the right to govern by democratic authority and the need to stand by the Treaty. Griffith had desired an attack on Republican forces since the Limerick crisis of March; O'Higgins regarded the six months up to June as a demonstration of continual weakness. There was nothing to be gained, except cosmetically, in waiting for the new Dáil to meet in early July; to do that would only lead to more prevarication and delay.

The political side, however, could not move without military support. Ernest Blythe was to argue that the decision to attack the Four Courts was almost automatic once Collins had accepted the need for it.[5]

Collins's agreement to the Four Courts attack was only given with extreme reluctance; it represented a bowing to immediate circumstances. Mulcahy recalled that when he told Collins on 26 June that they would have to fight, Collins replied that the decision should be left until the morning. The British government had made it plain that the choice for the Southern government was between dealing with the Four Courts garrison and, failing that, allowing the British to return. There is no evidence that Collins had knowledge of British plans for the taking of the Four Courts, but he must have been in little doubt of the earnestness of British government warnings. Pressure from the British government thus determined the context of the developments. This is not to ignore Collins's impatience with that pressure, and his anger with Churchill's speech in the Commons on 27 June, which amounted to an ultimatum; Collins declared that Churchill could do his own 'dirty work'. The Southern government did not wish to be seen to be responding to British pressure, and once the Four Courts bombardment had begun the British government understood the need to ascribe the action to the Southern government's own initiative. Cope emphasised to Curtis on 27 June: 'There must be no suggestion that Collins is prompted to take action at request of British Government. Such a suggestion would do infinite harm.' Churchill's reply affirmed: 'I will of course make it clear that action is spontaneous.'

One of Collins's major reasons for supporting the Treaty had been to achieve British troop evacuation—the last thing he wanted was to risk British reoccupation. He must have been deeply alarmed about the prospect of provocative attacks from the Four Courts on British troops, which might eventually have forced Macready's hand. The political pressures, from both Whitehall and within his own cabinet, were proving intolerable for Collins. His double game of, on the one hand, public support for the Treaty and, on the other, private adherence to traditional republican aims could no longer apply in the post-election context.[6]

Collins's decision was probably affected by his knowledge of the split in anti-Treaty IRA ranks. Attempts to heal those divisions were, it seems, not known to Collins and, in any case, had not been concluded by the night of 27 June. The hope was that Lynch and his 1st Southern Division would not join the conflict and that little further action would occur after the fighting in Dublin had ended. Gearóid O'Sullivan is reported to have said that the conflict would be over 'inside a week or ten days'. Such an interpretation is supported by Mulcahy's decision to allow Lynch and two Cork colleagues to leave Dublin during the fighting. This argument, however, should not be carried too far. From any consideration of Lynch's character, Collins and Mulcahy must have been aware that decisive action against the Four Courts would be likely to bring the Munster IRA out against the Provisional Government army. They knew only too well how anti-Treaty forces controlled Munster and Connaught. Collins admitted to Mulcahy that it would have been difficult to gain sufficient support within the army for the attack if it had not been for J. J. O'Connell's kidnapping. O'Connell's popularity had, Mulcahy argued, aroused opinion against the Four Courts Executive. The Provisional Government army was in no position at that time to fight a prolonged war, and was to show weakness enough during the Dublin action. The military decision to support the Four Courts action had been taken extremely hastily and with no enthusiasm. Collins's options had finally run out. He must have hoped that the fighting could be limited in both duration and geographical extent, but could have had no expectation of either.[7]

If the opening of the Civil War was in no way planned for, or desired, by Collins and Mulcahy, the same is true of the Republican side. Florrie O'Donoghue wrote: 'Despite six months of talk of the possibility of civil war no one had allowed himself to believe it to be inevitable, and no plans existed on either side for conducting it.' When calling off the army unity talks, the Army Executive had made it clear that they desired no conflict with Provisional Government troops, but only the removal of British troops. General Macready reported later: 'Information in our possession . . . goes to show that Rory O'Connor thought that British troops would be employed in forcing him to evacuate the Four Courts, and that, after consideration, it was decided that resistance to British troops would be good propaganda.' The same report stated that 'the ultimatum of the Provisional Government came as a surprise, and that the mines which destroyed the Four Courts had been laid previously with a view to resistance against the British attack only'. No plans were made to resist any attack on the Four Courts, and it seems that no attack was expected until the last moment. Hopes remained until the eleventh hour of unity on the Northern question—more troops were to be sent north. No adequate measures were taken to safeguard the Four Courts. A Republican publicity document, reviewing the origins of the Four Courts attack, admitted: 'As a result of our desire not to provoke any hostilities with Free Staters, the obvious things for defence of Four Courts was [sic] not done . . . from a strictly military point of view.' There was firm opposition to any thought of firing the first shot: a scheme to occupy the buildings surrounding the Four Courts was turned down on the grounds that it would have been offensive action. There was no prospect, however, that there would be any surrender to the Provisional Government ultimatum.[8]

There was little communication between the Four Courts and the provinces. Tom Maguire, the O/C of the 2nd Western Division, commented on their complete ignorance in the west of developments in Dublin. What strategy there was remained based on the Four Courts. O'Donoghue noted: 'The Executive never fused into an effective unit. It never had a common mind or a common policy. There was not time.' By the time of the attack the situation resembled the Easter Rising in its sacrificial character and lack of planning. Within Dublin there was no satisfactory contact between the Four Courts garrison and members of the Dublin No. 1 Brigade outside the building. These weaknesses were made worse by the division in anti-Treaty IRA ranks resulting from the Army Convention of 18 June. Meanwhile the Republican political leadership were left in complete ignorance of developments: de Valera was only told about the Four Courts attack on his way into Dublin.

The Army Executive entered the Civil War because war had been declared on them; this applied as much to O'Connor and Mellows as it did to Lynch and Deasy. For all the confusion and mixed emotions involved, the Four Courts attack served to clarify the situation. The conflict was now that of Free State *versus* Republic; the issue was that of whether the Treaty terms were to be implemented or not. The Labour Party executive at the time was correct to attribute responsibility for the reunification in Republican military and political ranks to the Provisional Government's action. Although Churchill argued that resolute action towards the Four Courts men would make it easier in future to follow a path to Irish unity, all realistic hope ended on the night of 27 June for joint initiatives on the North. The taking of the Four Courts proved a far from straightforward business. It took three days and nights of heavy shelling, culminating in a full-scale assault and the occupation and destruction of part of the building, before the surrender came.[9]

During the first day of the attack the British government became alarmed. General Macready reported: 'No progress was made during the 28th June by the attackers, and though breaches were made by guns in the southern walls of the building the young and inexperienced Free State troops are reported to have been much discouraged at the lack of early success.' On that day Churchill told Cope: 'We think it quite impossible to let matters stop unfinished.' There was still the possibility, it appeared to Churchill, that the British would need to complete the task themselves. Cope replied: 'It is possible for Provisional Government to win through alone, if they get the 300 shells quickly. This is very regrettable that we should interfere, but it has got to be one thing or the other.'

Prospects were hindered by the inability of Provisional Government troops to use the two eighteen-pound guns loaned for the bombardment by the British forces. During the shelling Collins urgently looked for ex-gunners with First World War experience, and plans were made for British troops to give training in the use of artillery. The position was so desperate that Dalton, who was in command of the attack, had to take over one of the eighteen-pounders himself for three hours. Under pressure from Dalton to supply more ammunition, Macready recorded:

I agreed to send him fifty rounds of shrapnel, which was all we had left, simply to make a noise through the night, as he was afraid that if the guns stopped firing his men would get disheartened and clear off. . . . About every quarter of an hour during the night a shrapnel broke up against the walls of the Four Courts, making much noise but doing no harm.

The eighteen-pound guns were ineffective against the strong walls of the Four Courts, and the British government urged that their offer of sixty-pound howitzers be accepted. The Provisional Government army leaders showed no enthusiasm at the prospect of using such artillery. By that time British troops in Dublin were showing a contempt for the proceedings, made worse by the accidental shelling of British military headquarters in Phoenix Park. When Dalton went there to apologise he was nearly hit by shells aimed in the wrong direction. While Collins's demands for more arms and ammunition grew increasingly desperate, Macready showed no desire to hand over large resources to a force about whose motivation and effectiveness he was extremely sceptical. Churchill, on the other hand, was even keen to loan the Provisional Government as much as they wanted. He instructed Cope on 28 June: 'Tell Collins to ask for any assistance he requires and report to me any difficulty that has been raised by the Military.'

General Seán MacMahon, the Adjutant-General, was to comment on the untrained character and exhausted state of the troops during the Four Courts attack; he pointed out that many of them had never handled a rifle before. By the end of the siege many were falling asleep at their posts and were, MacMahon related, only kept in the fight by their officers' urgings.[10]

On the second day of the attack Churchill was warning Macready that it might become necessary for the British army to take over. Even Cope was pessimistic, reporting:

This is not a battle. Rory is in the Four Courts. Free Staters are in houses opposite each firing at the other hundreds of rounds with probably remarkably few hits. A few hundred yards away the people carry on their ordinary business.

It seemed, during 28 and 29 June, that the fate of the Treaty lay in the balance. Churchill held that aerial bombing might become necessary, which he told Collins could not be done by untrained Irish pilots but would have to be in the hands of British ones. That would entail, he argued, painting the planes in Free State colours 'to show that they were an essential part of your forces'. Cope commented that if Dublin was not effectively cleared, 'the PG is lost. They are quite certain that to accept the assistance of British troops would be fatal.' He became increasingly alarmed that sympathy for the men in the Four Courts would increase the longer the bombardment took. Given the total failure, however, of the Republicans to plan for likely military contingencies, there was no way that the attack could ultimately fail, provided the troops remained at their posts.[11]

Even before the attack there was considerable disagreement between Dublin No. 1 Brigade and the Four Courts leadership about the tactics to be pursued. The leadership of No. 1 Brigade was opposed to the defensive occupation of buildings. Tod Andrews wrote that he had

> little confidence in the Dublin Brigade as a relieving force for the beleaguered garrison because the best of the officers were either pro-Treaty or if they were anti-Treaty were already inside the Four Courts. The senior anti-Treaty officers of the Brigade who were left could hardly be said to be over endowed with qualities of leadership. . . . I could not believe we were going to indulge in such a foolishly futile military exercise.

Oscar Traynor recorded that it had been his aim to prevent the staging of another Easter Rising. He wanted an adoption of guerrilla warfare tactics and a breaking up into columns. Traynor sent out emissaries to localities relaying news of developments and asking for help, but got replies only from Séamus Robinson in South Tipperary and the Belfast O/C. Traynor favoured the occupation of a ring of buildings around the Four Courts to prevent access to the Provisional Government troops. Ernie O'Malley said of Traynor: 'His whole attitude about O'Connell Street and the holding of Dublin in June/July was to hold the area until relieved from the country.' Traynor, however, failed to implement his ideas.

Dublin No. 1 Brigade was mobilised on the evening of 27 June, but disbanded at midnight following misleading advice. Emmet Humphreys recorded that orders reaching his battalion headquarters instructed each company to operate armed patrols within their own area. 'There seemed to be no question', Humphreys commented, 'of co-ordinating our operations with adjoining companies or with the battalion as a whole. . . . It never has been made clear why such a co-ordinated move was not ordered for the first day's fighting.' Meanwhile unsubstantiated rumours circulated about relief columns marching to their assistance from the south.[12]

The position in Dublin was made more confused by the overlapping authority within the Four Courts. Paddy O'Brien, of Dublin No. 1 Brigade, was O/C within the building, but Joe McKelvey, Lynch's replacement as Chief of Staff, together with Mellows and O'Connor, represented the Army Executive's leadership. When

O'Brien was badly wounded during the fighting, Mellows willingly yielded command to O'Malley because of the latter's war experience.

O'Malley had strongly urged that the buildings around the Four Courts be fortified. He recorded, with over-colourful but probably precise recollection, that he had told O'Brien they were like 'rats in a trap'. The separate parts of the Four Courts building made it difficult to achieve satisfactory communication within the building during the attack. O'Malley described the conditions endured by the occupants:

> It seemed a haphazard pattern of war. A garrison without proper food, sur-rounded on all sides, bad communication between their inside posts, faulty defences, girls bringing ammunition from attackers, relieving forces on our side concentrated on the wrong side of the widest street in the capital.

During the bombardment O'Malley urged that tunnels be built as a means of escape, and Rory O'Connor suggested the sewers be used, only to learn that they were flooded. O'Brien and others argued that members of the Executive should be evacuated from the building, with the Dublin No. 1 Brigade men preserving a garrison. In the end, however, the only policy followed was a demonstration of Republican intransigence and protest. The attack culminated with the explosion of two mines, laid beforehand by the Four Courts men in the archives department of the building, which was then being used as their munitions centre. A Provisional Government report commented that the second explosion caused a column of smoke to rise two hundred feet into the air. Most of the contents of the Public Record Office were destroyed by the explosion. Fire spread rapidly through the building, and the position of those inside became untenable.[13]

Even under the appalling circumstances following the explosions, Mellows and O'Connor remained implacably opposed to any thought of surrender. Debate centred, it appears, on Pearse's notions of blood sacrifice. With the building collapsing around them, however, Mellows, O'Malley and O'Connor had to agree, with extremely heavy hearts, to Traynor's order that a surrender be made for the sake of the outside areas. It is unclear why Traynor's authority should have overridden that of the members of the Executive within the Four Courts.

Among surviving Republican participants in the Four Courts action there has been widespread agreement on the total lack of planning displayed. Ben Doyle commented: 'The whole thing was taken in a half-hearted slipshod manner.' Seán Smith recorded that 'We could see Staters going around in lorries, but we had no actual orders to fire on them.' Maurice Brennan concluded: 'Eventually I felt that the disunity was against any chance we had. . . . I had no heart in it.'[14]

16

The Dublin Fighting

DURING the Four Courts bombardment the Dublin No. 1 Brigade took over buildings in various parts of Dublin, but not in a manner that made any coherent military sense. To start with, the brigade headquarters were established in Barry's Hotel, which was on the north side of the city and very poorly placed for any projected relief of the Four Courts. Pressed for fresh accommodation, Traynor took over, on 29 June, the Hammam and Gresham Hotels, together with two neighbouring hotels, on the east side of O'Connell Street—the wrong side for any communication with the Four Courts. Isolated buildings were also taken on the city's south side, for instance on the South Circular Road and in York Street and Dolphin's Barn, but only two buildings on the west side of O'Connell Street were occupied. Liaison between the Four Courts and O'Connell Street was dependent on Máire Comerford, the most energetic of Cumann na mBan workers, and her bicycle.[1]

Members of Dublin No. 1 Brigade in the O'Connell Street hotels were soon joined by the Republican political leaders. During the fighting Seán T. O'Kelly arrived at the headquarters at the Hammam Hotel armed with nothing more than an umbrella. De Valera met with Brugha and Stack, together with the leadership of the 1st Southern Division, and decided to give public support to the Army Executive and to rejoin the IRA as a private in his old battalion. He released a press statement declaring:

> English propaganda will strive to lay the blame for this war on Irishmen, but the world outside must not be deceived. England's threat of war, that, and that alone, is responsible for the present situation. In face of England's threat of war some of our countrymen yielded. The men who are now being attacked by the forces of the Provisional Government are those who refuse to obey the order to yield—preferring to die. They are the best and bravest of our nation, and would most loyally have obeyed the will of the Irish people freely expressed, but are not willing that Ireland's independence should be abandoned under the lash of an alien Government.

The *Irish Times* stated that de Valera 'has associated himself openly with the men who are firing on Irish homes. . . . What does he expect to gain? His political cause is hopeless.' Privately, however, de Valera showed enthusiasm for the Lord Mayor of Dublin's and the Labour Party's peace initiative, although his favourable disposition was to incur the disapproval of Brugha and Stack. De Valera's deep reservations about the tactics used are well shown in a note he sent to Brugha. 'The Brigade', he wrote, 'has disengaged from the very foolish type of battle into which it had been drawn and will now be able to engage in operations more suited to its training and equipment.' Any decisions taken during the O'Connell Street fighting seem to have had little to do with the political leadership. Erskine Childers wrote to his wife shortly after the fighting in Dublin had ended:

> Have just seen Bob [Barton]—depth of depression and hopelessness. Says we can't do anything. Dev I think has collapsed.... Frank [Gallagher] and I... fear general cave in. Trying to get them to form a nominal Gov at least and act strongly. No *one* leader alas!... There is a truce in one district already but details very vague. Dev says we should surrender while we are strong I believe.[2]

The Republican occupation of the east side of O'Connell Street appears as militarily pointless as the Four Courts occupation had been. Emmet Humphreys, who was in Harcourt Terrace during the fighting, commented: 'We were becoming more and more frustrated at the fact that we were achieving nothing whatsoever.' General Macready reported that by 3 July nearly all the Republican strongholds to the south of the Liffey had been taken. All attention, and most Republican personnel, became centred on O'Connell Street. The four hotels on O'Connell Street were linked up by smashing through their connecting walls. The billiard room in the Hammam Hotel became the hospital.

The Provisional Government attack on the O'Connell Street Republican strongholds began, somewhat ineffectively, with heavy rifle and machine-gun fire, which was hindered by the enemy's heavy sandbagging of the floors. Soon armoured cars with artillery, under cover of Lancia cars, were brought in, and the Republicans were progressively forced to evacuate various buildings. They had to use Red Cross cars as a cover for their firing. The Adjutant-General reported: 'Brigadier Daly reports that they are the dirtiest lot of fighters he ever saw.' The Labour peace terms—for a truce and a meeting of the Dáil—were turned down on the grounds that all Republican arms had first to be surrendered.[3]

On 5 July a white flag was hoisted above the Hammam Hotel, only to be followed by a burst of firing at Commandant O'Connor's men when he went to take the surrender. By that time it was reported that 'The whole block of buildings from Findlater Place to the corner going down to Marlborough Street Cathedral [is] in flames.' The casualties in the Dublin fighting amounted to sixty-five killed and twenty-eight wounded, while the property destroyed has been valued as between £3 and £4 million.

Before 5 July it had been decided to evacuate the Republican headquarters, and de Valera and others were smuggled across the river to Mount Street. The last to surrender were a group under Brugha's leadership. After he had ordered his men to surrender and seen them all off the premises, Brugha ran out of the building, gun at the ready, and was instantly shot down. He died that evening in the Mater Hospital. Not knowing the extent of Brugha's wounds, de Valera had written to him:

> I had no idea in view of the plan agreed on that you would attempt to hold the Hotels as long as you did. We were all extremely anxious. If your wound is not too serious however your magnificent fight will give you added prestige and obtain for your counsels in the army the respect they are entitled to but which vile slanders were bringing to a discount in some quarters.

De Valera reproached Brugha, pointing out they could ill afford to lose him, and concluding:

> You were scarcely justified . . . in taking the risk you ran—and we were all more than vexed with you—But all's well that ends well. And the opening of the campaign otherwise not to be dreamt of by us gave [*sic*] a definite beginning.

Loyalties to either side were in many cases extremely loose. Seán Harling recorded that during the action in Dublin he joined the anti-Treaty side solely because he met up with some old friends. The Republican garrisons must have been extremely unclear as to who precisely they were taking orders from. On the pro-Treaty side, Martin Walton commented: 'Collins asked for a roll-call of the men he could depend on if they had to make an attack, and there was quite a large number, seven or eight hundred. But later on when he wanted to throw a ring around the city, a lot of those men refused to do it. They hated the idea of shooting their old comrades.'

The Republican evacuation of Dublin was improvised with no sense of what was to follow. Tom Ketterick commented: 'No plan only to be pulled out of bed and get out as best you could. We kept our arms.' In that last sense the evacuation was successful. The surrender at the Four Courts had ensured that some of the Republican leadership would be imprisoned through the early stages of the Civil War, unless they managed to escape. Rory O'Connor and Liam Mellows remained in Mountjoy Prison until their execution in December. Tom Barry, who had been arrested entering the Four Courts disguised as a woman, was in prison until his escape in August. The leadership, thus, was greatly weakened at the start of the conflict. Ernie O'Malley, together with Seán Lemass, escaped from Jameson's Distillery immediately after the Four Courts surrender, in a manner which demonstrated something worse than carelessness on the part of the guards. O'Malley recorded that O'Connor and Mellows passed up the opportunity to escape.[4]

Meanwhile O'Duffy, on Mulcahy's orders, had allowed Liam Lynch, Liam Deasy and Seán Culhane to leave Dublin after they had been arrested during the fighting. When intercepted on their way south, they were allowed to proceed by Prout's officers in Kilkenny. Considerable controversy later developed over whether Lynch and his colleagues gave any definite assurances that they would not participate in subsequent fighting in return for their safe-conducts. Provisional Government propaganda claimed that Lynch dishonoured an agreement, while Lynch and Deasy argued that there had been no understanding in the first place. Culhane, for his part, related that, as a result of their meeting with O'Duffy (who, he remembered, 'had more gold braid on him even than Franco'), 'the assumption was that when we got down to the South we would not start a rumpus and we had a freer hand then'. Mulcahy must later have regretted his leniency; his decision again demonstrated his desire to avoid a break with the 1st Southern Division. The release would, he hoped, enable Lynch and his colleagues to bring pressure on other areas to stay out of the conflict.

Lynch's and Deasy's release helped ensure that the Republican military effort was henceforth to be decentralised. The anti-Treaty IRA leaders of the Four Courts, who for the previous six months had followed a completely different policy and attitude to Lynch and his colleagues, were in prison and in no position to control events. The 1st Southern Division leaders threw their weight behind military resistance to the Provisional Government, but only after returning to their own localities. When Lynch issued a public statement affirming that he had taken over the position of Chief of Staff again, he ordered all men to return to their command areas. This was contradictory to the Dublin-centred policy followed up to then by the Army Executive. At the very beginning of the Civil War all the emphasis had been on Dublin; soon Dublin was to be largely neglected, and was never again to be the scene of major hostilities during the Civil War. The fighting in Dublin had been muddled and inconclusive; its result, however, turned attention away from the capital to the provinces.[5]

Meanwhile the British government and cabinet, after all their anxiety during the Four Courts bombardment, expressed satisfaction and relief at the developments. Churchill told Collins, shortly after the end of the fighting in Dublin: 'I could not have sustained another debate in the House of Commons on the old lines without fatal consequences to the existing governing instrument in Britain, and with us the Treaty would have fallen too. Now all is changed. Ireland will be mistress in her own house.' Birkenhead told the House of Lords: 'I am even bold enough . . . to say that at the moment the situation is more hopeful than it has been at any moment since this Treaty was come to.' Nevertheless, the British government realised it was important not to be seen to be jubilant for fear of providing evidence in support of Republican propaganda that they had promoted the whole conflict. Churchill, in a famous letter to Collins, told him: 'If I refrain from congratulations it is only because I do not wish to embarrass you. The archives of the Four Courts may be scattered but the title-deeds of Ireland are safe.' Any threat of Britain having to intervene militarily in the Twenty-Six Counties appeared to be over.[6]

17

The Military and Political Background to the Fighting

AT the beginning of the Civil War the Republican side appeared to possess many advantages. Munster and the west were almost completely dominated by the Republican IRA. By contrast with the Republican volunteer army, which was fighting for the separatist ideal, the Provisional Government army was, for the most part, a mercenary one, recruited extremely hastily and fighting for a limited aim. For the first weeks of the war the anti-Treaty side had an advantage in numbers outside Dublin and were much better armed than they had been during the Anglo-Irish War. A Provisional Government source at the time estimated Republican IRA numbers as 12,900, with 6,780 rifles. As men were not attested, and as it was extremely difficult to differentiate between active and purely nominal membership, these figures must be treated with extreme caution. The number of Provisional Government troops at the beginning of the conflict is also uncertain: while 9,700 were said to have taken the oath to the government at the time of the Four Courts attack, General Seán MacMahon, the Adjutant-General, thought their numbers amounted to approximately 8,000. Provisional Government units were heavily concentrated in Dublin; they were ill-equipped to carry the war to the provinces, and large areas of the country had few, if any, pro-Treaty forces. An alarmed Alfred Cope told Lionel Curtis on 29 June: 'No one can say what line the P.G. troops in the country will take under pressure, for it must be remembered that all the leading men of the P.G. side are in Dublin.' By contrast, Republican military forces were concentrated in their own areas and thus enjoyed all the potential advantages that followed from knowing both the land and the people.[1]

In retrospect, however, it is clear that if Republican arms were to be victorious, it would have had to have been a quick victory. In time Provisional Government superiority in arms, numbers and resources would tell—and large consignments of arms were regularly supplied to them by the British government, including the artillery which proved crucial in urban fighting while the Republican side remained dependent on arms captures. Between 31 January and 26 June 1922 the British government had supplied 11,900 rifles, 79 Lewis machine-guns, 4,200 revolvers and 3,504 grenades. By the middle of August the British government had parted with eight eighteen-pounders. On 2 September Cope reported that 27,400 rifles, 6,606 revolvers, 246 Lewis guns and five Vickers guns had been supplied.

The longer the war continued, the more unpopular the fighting would become to the majority of the population. In July Harry Boland admitted: 'There is no doubt that the people in the main is [sic] against us at present, believing that we are to blame for the present state of affairs.' In much of Ireland the advantage Republican forces had in fighting in their own localities was neutralised by the hostile public reaction to the war. A large proportion of the population dreaded the return to guerrilla warfare, with its blight on social and economic life. The Republican side could never afford to forget that they were fighting against the popular will, as demonstrated in the June election. Their effort was also to be greatly hindered by the fact that the other side often had an inside knowledge, stemming from the common Anglo-Irish War background, of their haunts, fighting methods and personnel.[2]

Throughout the Civil War the Republicans were to be hamstrung by considerations of local particularism and the lack of any coherent central direction. Both sides had been appallingly badly prepared for war, but that was to be of more consequence on the Republican side. Johnny McNoy, of the 4th Northern Division, observed: 'I felt that the crowd in [the] Four Courts were making no effort to avoid war and making no preparations for it.' Séamus Robinson recalled: 'There was no plan. The only orders I was given was [sic] that I must not advance, nor must I retreat into Cork.' The confusion in the Four Courts was reflected in the provinces. P. J. McHugh related: 'I was in Cork City when I got the news about the Four Courts. I came to the Divisional Headquarters at Mallow for I thought the Cork men would not move on Dublin. There was no one there to decide what to do one way or the other.' It was left to local units to make their own decisions whether to join the conflict, and to decide on the tactics to be pursued. There was, it appears, considerable doubt in Dublin as to whether the various areas would respond to the fighting in the city and so enlarge the conflict. Andy Cooney recalled: 'I was...convinced that the Four Courts would be the only protest that would be made outside of South Tipperary.' The decentralisation can be explained, in part, by the extreme difficulties in communication once the fighting had started; contact with the provinces was only kept up by the heroic efforts of Cumann na mBan couriers, who appeared to possess most of the car drivers in Republican ranks, and who provided chauffeurs for Liam Lynch, de Valera and others. Nothing, however, can excuse the lack of communication between Dublin and the other areas in the period preceding the Four Courts attack.

The long-held conviction of many, especially in Cork, that the Treaty divisions would not result in fighting between fellow-countrymen, ill prepared them for war. The prospect of civil war was so terrible, and the immediate background to the Four Courts attack so confused, that few could come to terms with its reality once it began. The Four Courts attack acted as a catalyst for both the military and political side of the Republican movement. It did not lead, however, to any greater coherence, or to a clearer articulation of political or military strategy. Because of the imprisonment and dispersal of the Executive members, and the danger of capture, it was impossible for an Executive meeting to take place until 16 October.[3]

Peadar O'Donnell, in common with many Republican contemporaries, was to complain of the leadership failings of Liam Lynch and Rory O'Connor. He said of Lynch: 'As he travelled south, while the Four Courts attack was in progress, his only message to us was that he was not thinking of war, but of peace.' During the decisive early stages of the war the Republicans tended to respond to events rather than to initiate them. They fought a defensive war when the situation cried out for bold initiatives. The policy turned out to be, although it was never actually stated, to hold their own areas and not to move back on Dublin, nor to reinforce weaker areas. Many warned against a defensive policy. Séamus Robinson claimed that he told Lynch: 'Liam . . . its absurd to stay in your own areas, for they'll take us piece-meal.' Joe O'Connor, from his Dublin No. 1 Brigade perspective, also criticised the strategy: 'It was a rotten proposal that we should withdraw all our forces and hold Munster without any opposition to the P/G in other areas.' The same point was made, from the other side, when General O'Duffy commented: 'The enemy has already lost much by not taking the initiative and operating throughout the whole country while our strength was, more or less, dissipated in the capture of Dublin.'

It was often claimed during the early stages of the war that the Republican IRA established a fortified line between Limerick and Waterford, guarding Republican Munster. Liam Deasy wrote on 9 July: 'We are getting down to a systematic plan of defence. At the moment we are engaged in stretching that important line Waterford to Clonmel taking the River Suir as a line.' At one time it was argued that the line ran along the River Suir, at other times the Blackwater. Such a vast stretch of territory, however, was impossible to defend without far more numerous, and vastly better trained and disciplined, troops than the Republicans possessed. Mick O'Hanlon commented: 'There was really no defence . . . of an area of country'; and Frank O'Connor depicted the holding of the line as existing more in the Republicans' minds than in reality. O'Connor had been stationed at Ashill Towers, near Kilmallock, where he noted that 'the front line was our pride and joy' but that the men 'melted away' on Sunday to attend mass. He wrote: 'Anyone who knew his Ireland would have guessed that on that fine summer morning our whole front was being pierced in a dozen places.'

When the various Republican barracks, on the so-called 'line', came under pressure from Provisional Government troops there was no attempt to hold it. Time after time, when major confrontation appeared imminent, the Republicans evacuated and burnt their garrison buildings in important centres, such as Sligo and Castlebar in the west, and Clonmel and Waterford in the south. Most crucially, they vacated Limerick after little fighting, and Cork city with no resistance. The way that Lynch moved his field headquarters from Mallow to Limerick, then to Buttevant, and then to Clonmel, served to mirror the confusion and indecision of Republican military policy. That indecisiveness greatly weakened the Republicans' morale and lowered their faith in their leaders. On 21 July Ernie O'Malley, who by that time was second-in-command to Lynch, asked Lynch: 'Could you give me an outline of your Military and National Policy as we are in the dark here with regard to both?' Moss Twomey, who was close to Liam Lynch throughout the Civil War, produced a memorandum which was strongly critical of the defensive tactics adopted. 'There is too much talk', he wrote, 'of our waging this latest war . . . as a "Defensive" war, and only because we were, and are being, attacked. Suppose Collins now gave an order to his forces to "Cease Fire" should we cease too?' Never in the early part of the war did Republicans adopt a planned aggressive policy; whatever initiatives were taken by the Republican side in the first weeks of the war only emphasised the lack of any planning. Poor relations between divisions and tensions within various localities made it the more difficult to achieve an effective combined Republican IRA effort. Séamus Robinson recorded one reason for poor relations between the 1st and 2nd Southern Divisions:

> Seán Hyde lost his eye near Carrick during the split between Liam Lynch and the Four Courts. He and others were in uniform and the attackers took them for Staters. Liam Lynch wanted me to hand the men who had taken part in the attack on Hyde over for court martial by the First Southern but I refused. I might have handed them over to another Division for trial but certainly not the First Southern.[4]

The Republican military side also faced appalling problems of achieving disciplined organisation within their ranks—difficulties enormously exacerbated by the sporadic and dispersed character of the fighting. Liam Lynch often admitted these defects. Con Moloney, the anti-Treaty IRA's Adjutant-General, wrote to divisional O/Cs on 27 July 1922: 'Organisation is bad in most areas, Coys are not paraded, Council meetings etc. are not being held and reports are not being forwarded.' He also commented: 'It is unfortunate that Divisions and Brigades have not [at] any time brought their staff up to final strength. . . . This more than anything else is telling on us now that the fight is on.' A substitution policy was slow to be put into effect in a number of areas where many officers were imprisoned. Local O/Cs were frequently concerned when key officers were required to work elsewhere in a division. The Waterford IRA, which suffered dire problems in finding reliable and efficient officers, complained that Mick Mansfield was working elsewhere when he was desperately needed in the Waterford Brigade. Tom Hales, from his West Cork base, wrote to Liam Deasy, his divisional O/C, about his fears concerning the consequences of men from the West Cork Brigade being transferred to work on the division staff. He pointed out:

> I . . . need not impress you that the main key to success is organisation with unified control. It was England's game in the past to bust our organisation, it is also Collins and Cos only hope of success. No individual effort counts when organisation is gone.

Ernie O'Malley was frequently to complain that the vast Northern and Eastern Command area, to which he was appointed in July, existed only on paper. He commented that he had often to replace a member of staff arrested 'with a boy who had succeeded in escaping that same day from a prison or an internment camp'.[5]

An effective intelligence system is of paramount importance in guerrilla warfare but, here again, Republican failings were demonstrated. When appointing Seán Hyde as Director of Intelligence in early September, and thus switching him from the Western Command, Liam Lynch admitted that 'Our Intelligence system is in great need of organisation, and there are several matters which have been neglected.' Special services, generally, were weak, and the lack of trained engineers was particularly crucial. O'Malley reported on 21 July: 'I have no report of operations since 12th inst. I have no reports from the Engineer, as I am without one.' In the following month he commented:

> The enemy like ourselves lack general tactical knowledge and usually could be surprised just as easily as we can. I was preparing a memo on protection but I have always doubted whether these memos have been put into

practice: officers smile when they receive them and immediately go and get all their armed men caught owing to not putting common sense into practice.

The chaos in Republican military ranks is well illustrated by David Robinson's account of his time with various units in the south. Robinson, an old friend of Childers, who had considerable fighting experience with the British army, looked askance at the irregular habits and wrote: 'The thing that interested me most while staying in that barracks was that if anybody wanted to go on leave they just went without asking for permission.' Another major difficulty for the Republican military effort was their inability to hold prisoners for any length of time—to have done so would have involved an impossible expense, apart from problems arising from the absence of suitable accommodation. It was difficult enough for Republican forces to provide for themselves, let alone for their captives.[6]

Finance was also to prove a major problem. While they occupied Cork city the Republicans controlled the revenues from customs, and they benefited from levies and commandeering during the occupation of many areas, but by early September Lynch was reporting: 'We are very short of cash, as enemy issued orders to Banks to refuse to release funds which they discovered were ours.' Meanwhile the London *Times* reported on 23 August that 'The temporary injunction of the Supreme Court of the United States which restrains the Irregular leaders from drawing upon funds collected in that country for the Republican cause has struck directly at the most sensitive part of their organisation.' Looting and commandeering became a necessary means for the Republican forces to survive, but served also to increase their unpopularity. Attempts to establish Republican police and civil agencies proved incapable of successful attainment.

Two further factors weakened the Republican military effort. First, some of the key leaders in the old IRA who had originally taken an anti-Treaty stance abstained from participation in the fighting. Thus Seán Hegarty and Florrie O'Donoghue, two leaders of the 1st Southern Division, remained neutral. Hegarty, who had supported decisive military action shortly after the Treaty's signing, told Lynch: 'No other course was open to Griffith and Collins except to attack Rory O'Connor in the Four Courts.' In another crucial centre of Republican strength, the 4th Northern Division, Frank Aiken only lined his men up behind the anti-Treaty forces in September, after the early fighting was over. Secondly, Republican forces showed an unwillingness, particularly in the early stages of the war, to fire on old colleagues. Tom Maguire recorded: 'In the beginning our fellows would not kill the Staters.' George Gilmore told Ernie O'Malley: 'I had a desire not to kill the enemy, all of our men had it to some extent, and the officers who were operating against us were our own former friends. We never tried to kill.' An officer in Mid-Clare reported to his brigade commandant the story of a failed ambush: 'Just as the car came on to the trench, Ignatius O'Neill came off the car, so any of them did not fire, as I will tell you the truth they find it hard to fire on Ignatius or Tosser.'[7]

The coming of the Civil War completed the collapse of the Sinn Féin party, and meant again the subjugation of political opposition over the Treaty to purely military considerations. War necessarily meant a decline in political activity: political meetings could not be held.

By 11 June 1923 only sixteen Sinn Féin *cumainn* remained in existence; the r at the beginning of 1922 had been 1,485. Reviewing Sinn Féin decline during the Civil War, Judge Kingsmill Moore concluded in the Sinn Féin Funds Case: 'Such few *cumainn* as carried on their meetings seem to have acted as unarmed auxiliaries of the irregular forces, meeting secretly, subject to frequent raids, and with their most prominent members in and out of prison.' The Sinn Féin staff in Dublin were dispensed with in July, and the standing committee did not meet after November 1922. De Valera's and Stack's attempt to reorganise Sinn Féin at the end of the year proved unsuccessful.[8]

While Republicans abstained from the Dáil there was no public forum in which the political leadership could present their views. Once the occupation of towns ended, and with it control of the *Cork Examiner* and other newspapers, there was no hope of their cause being represented in the Irish press. De Valera's only recourse was to have secret interviews with foreign newspapermen. The Republican political cause was further weakened by ideological divisions. While Mary MacSwiney remained close to irreconcilable military opinion in Cork, de Valera waited for a favourable opportunity to relaunch his External Association idea. Once the war had started, however, there was no option for all anti-Treatyites but to fall in behind the full Republican demand as expressed in arms; any disagreements about ends remained underground, and talk of compromise only re-emerged at the close of the conflict.

The precise whereabouts of political leaders could not easily be discovered, as they were so frequently on the move. De Valera took up a military post in South Tipperary, but was of little relevance to the fighting. The political leaders suffered all the hardships of the military men—the threat of capture, the uncomfortable living conditions—while not being in a position to exercise any leadership. De Valera complained: 'We have all the public responsibility, and no voice and no authority.'

Harry Boland took up a military role by filling a staff position in the South Dublin Brigade. He soon had to lie low in the Dublin hills—it was from there that he wrote to Joe McGarrity on 13 July. 'It may very well be that I shall fall in this awful conflict,' he told McGarrity, but concluded: 'I am certain we cannot be defeated even if Collins and his British Guns succeed in garrisoning every town in Ireland.' Having striven so hard for compromise, no one was more aware of the bitter irony of the fight against recent close colleagues: 'Can you imagine', Boland asked McGarrity on 25 July, 'me on the run from Mick Collins?'

On 30 July, while in the company of Commandant Griffith, Boland was shot at the Grand Hotel in Skerries; he died in hospital on 2 August. There was a bitter debate as to the circumstances of Boland's shooting—over whether he was deliberately shot while resisting arrest. Collins frequently stressed his desire to find out the full facts. Boland's death was timed as if to symbolise the death of the Sinn Féin organisation which he had done so much to build up.[9]

Loathed by the enemy and distrusted by many of his own side, Erskine Childers struggled, through the early stages of the war, to find some useful role. During the fighting in Dublin he unavailingly attempted to maintain the publication of *Poblacht na h-Éireann War News*; the presses of the propaganda sheet, however, were raided, and Childers was forced to lead a fugitive, peripatetic existence in Cork and Kerry. Throughout his time in Munster Childers was cut off from Dublin news; his movements remained a mystery to pro-Treaty and British sources. He succeeded, on a fairly regular basis, in producing a southern version of his paper, and while the Republicans were in control of Cork city he helped to edit the *Cork Examiner*. After the pro-Treaty occupation of Cork, Childers retreated, trailing around with him a printing-press loaded onto a pony and trap.

For much of that time Childers was accompanied by David Robinson. To the local people they made an incongruous pair—the ascetic, ailing Childers, and the tall, monocled Robinson who resembled a character from a P. G. Wodehouse novel. Robinson wrote of Childers:

> Every one loves him, especially the people in the cottages who vie with each other wherever he goes to do him a kindness and make him comfortable as possible. Usually however he prefers to sleep on an old sofa or in a chair to sleeping in a bed which astonishes the people. . . . In one case something I did was put down to him—I think the local people thought that the only person with an English accent in the Army must be he.

Early in September Childers recorded his despair in his notebooks:

> Impossible . . . to get anything done here. . . . I stick on in the obstinate determination somehow to galvanise these people into life, but it may fail any moment. . . . Picture me in a remote cottage, without even a bicycle . . .

Later Childers revealed that he was spending his time digging potatoes and reading Mazzini, whom he found 'poignantly relevant to our situation today—the same discouragements and hopes, illusions and spiritual realities'.

The Republican military leadership in the south showed little desire to give Childers and Robinson a military role. Robinson affirmed: 'Erskine had no connection with the army good, bad or indifferent.' Frank O'Connor recorded the general indifference of the column men to Childers, and the failure of the leadership in Cork to act on suggestions that Childers should escape the government's vengeance by being smuggled away to the continent. The Irish and British press, however, were to persist in describing Childers as the mastermind behind the guerrilla warfare. O'Duffy thought that Childers was in control of the fighting in July and August in Co. Limerick, and British government sources eagerly sought evidence of his activity and influence. The *Irish Times*'s special correspondent affirmed on 6 September that 'There is no doubt that Mr Childers is the chief military brain among the irregulars.' The London *Times*'s obituary of Childers said that his 'cool, calculating brain and knowledge of the art of war was behind the Republican military effort'. In a statement defending his position, issued from prison on 17 November, Childers referred to

> the mass of prejudice which has gathered round me and, what is more important, the cause I represent. . . . I have been held up to scorn and hatred as an Englishman who, betraying his own country, came here to lecture and destroy Ireland. Another and viler version is to the effect that so far from betraying England I have been actually acting as the secret instrument of Englishmen for ruining Ireland.

Pro-Treaty leaders, notably Arthur Griffith and Kevin O'Higgins, were as obsessed with Childers's English origins as were Republicans with the pro-Treaty army's employment of former British soldiers.[10]

Many felt that it was a mistake for the military leadership to pay little regard to political considerations, and criticised the failure to set up a Republican government at the start of the war. While such a government could not have functioned, its establishment would have helped to define the purpose of the Republican military effort and would have provided a focus for Republican unity. By the time a government was set up in October the military cause, and hence the Republican one, was lost. The neglect of political considerations also weakened the legitimacy of the Republican cause; following the June election there was a lack of clarity about precisely what were the constitutional and political aims of the Republicans. To general opinion the war appeared to resemble an army mutiny, and the logic of the position adopted by the Army Executive seemed to amount to military dictatorship. Father Donnegan told Ernie O'Malley that a Republican government should have been formed in January: 'We are without a government—nothing more in the eyes of the world than murderers and looters.' Moss Twomey asked of the Army Executive:

> Have they any definite policy outlined beyond fighting it out? We say we are out (a) to maintain the Republic (b) to get control of the Army. These are very vague and ambiguous terms and should be defined beyond possibility of misunderstanding. The Executive should some time define their objects, as it is generally believed they have no policy, and it is difficult to dispel or despise this view.

Relations between the Republican political and military leadership were extremely poor in the early stages of the war. De Valera told Michael Colivet: 'The old contempt for civil or semi-civil work apparently persists.' Rory O'Connor wrote to O'Malley from Mountjoy Prison in early September: 'Congratulations on your fight. I am certain you can win but for God's Sake beware of the compromising mind of the diplomats.' Liam Lynch was the fiercest opponent of what he regarded as political interference. The simplicity of his republicanism, and his optimism concerning the war's outcome, contrasted vividly with de Valera's pessimism and pragmatism. Lynch often stated unequivocally during the war that no other considerations than the purely military should be allowed to obtrude. In early September Lynch told Liam Deasy: 'I know of no alternative policy to present one of fighting we could adopt.... At present it is a waste of time to be thinking too much about policy; we should strike our hardest for some time, and this would make the question of policy easier to settle.'[11]

Three days after the evacuation of Fermoy ended the Republican occupation of towns and barracks in the south de Valera wrote sadly in his diary:

> Went for a walk in a field. Meditation. Any chance of winning? If there was any chance, duty to hold on to secure it. If none, duty to try to get the men to quit—for the present. The people must be won to the cause before any successful fighting can be done. The men dead and gloomy—just holding on. How long will it last?... This situation has not been brought about by my will, nor could my will end it. It has been brought about by a blind and ruthless disregard of the essentials of peace and it will continue as long as those conditions are wilfully ignored.

Tod Andrews recalled receiving a letter from Lynch 'saying that deV prepared to call off the civil war and I recollect that if he did that L.L. intended to repudiate him'. O'Malley was authorised to write to de Valera and inform him of Lynch's view. Mick Mansfield recalled that de Valera's attitude was that it was 'too much to expect the men who fought the last war to fight each other'.

De Valera wrote to Joe McGarrity on 10 September about the war:

> There can be no glory and no enthusiasm. . . . Worst of all, there seems to be no way out of it. . . . I am almost wishing I were deposed for the present position places upon me the responsibility for carrying on a programme which was not mine. . . . If the Free State should become operative, and . . . the present physical resistance fails, I see no programme by which we can secure independence but a renewal of the Sinn Féin idea in a new form . . . *Ignoring England* . . . acting as if Document 2 were the treaty . . .

No such policy, however, was practicable until the war was long over. Cosgrave commented at the end of October that de Valera 'was not worth arresting as the irregulars no longer took orders from him'. There were rumours in August that Lynch wished Childers to replace de Valera as leader of the Republican Party. Con Moloney, the anti-Treaty IRA's Adjutant-General, grew alarmed about de Valera's pessimism and wrote to Ernie O'Malley on the need for Austin Stack to see de Valera. He stressed:

> This is very important as when de Valera was leaving GHQ on the 15 August he was most pessimistic and regarded our position as hopeless. He even at that time contemplated taking public action which would ruin us. At that time the Military Situation was not encouraging certainly but it has improved immensely since. . . . He must be told we are so certain of success that we ask that no action be taken by him or Republican Party which would weaken us and may even rob us of victory.

Lynch was convinced that only the army would remain faithful to the Republic. He told Deasy: 'Surely Republican Party are not expected to face any responsibility as regards this war, and I hope they realise this?' On another occasion he wrote, also to Deasy: 'I am not over-anxious as to co-operation of Republican Party. Of course they are doing their best, and I consider in sufficiently close touch . . . in Dublin. You know D.V.'s mind.' He informed O'Malley: 'Consider that a statement drafted by political side would have to run on many points different to military one. Besides, the Army has its mind made up to total separation from England; I do not think this also can be said of party.'

Lynch's suspicion of political influences applied also to rejection of Liam Mellows's urgings from Mountjoy Prison for support of the Democratic Programme, and Mellows's advocacy of an alliance between workers and republicans. Con Moloney told Ernie O'Malley:

> Personally I think the only questions we should bother about are purely military ones. Questions of Democratic Politics etc., are not for us. Of course we should if possible handle Civil Administration, but we should very carefully distinguish between such Administration and what are purely social problems. These latter are matters to [be] dealt with by a Government properly elected when this Republic has been set on a firm foundation.[12]

The Provisional Government army proved an extremely problematic vehicle for establishing the new government's authority. The army was very poorly prepared for armed conflict. An appeal for recruits was immediately made at the start of the war, and on 3 July permission was granted by the Provisional Government cabinet for the raising of an extra 20,000 men to serve for six months. By 17 July the strength of the army was said to be around 15,000, which implied that 5,000, at least, had joined since the Four Courts attack. On 26 August the government gave authority for an army strength of 35,000, which included the Volunteer Reserves.

A War Council and an improvised military command structure were formed in early July when it became apparent that hostilities were spreading to the provinces. Collins wrote to Griffith demonstrating how the military leadership dominated: 'It would be well, I think, if the Government issued a sort of official Instruction to me nominating the War Council of Three, and appointing me to act by special order of the Government as Commander-in-Chief during the period of hostilities.' Collins was relieved of his government duties and became Commander-in-Chief; Mulcahy remained as Minister for Defence and again became Chief of Staff; O'Duffy took over control of the newly formed South-Western Command. The three of them formed the War Council—which was, however, never to meet again after they had established it. Five command areas were set up. The Midland one, with Seán Mac Eoin in command, took in the old 2nd, 3rd and 4th Western Divisions, together with much of the midlands. The South-Western Command consisted of Clare, Limerick, Kerry and Cork. The Eastern Command area, under Emmet Dalton, was made up of the old 4th and 5th Northern Divisions, the 1st and 2nd Eastern, Carlow, and the North and South Wexford Brigades. The South-Eastern Command included Kilkenny, Waterford, and South and Mid-Tipperary, under General Prout; and the Curragh Command, to be headed by J. J. O'Connell, incorporated the old 3rd Southern Division.[13]

The huge majority of the new army possessed no military knowledge and experience and must have been motivated by consideration of the regular pay when enlisting, rather than out of any commitment to the pro-Treaty cause. Throughout the war, and particularly in its early stages, there were frequent denunciations, both within and without the army, of the standard of the troops, and particularly the lack of sound officers. O'Duffy and Collins complained of the appalling quality of troops from the Curragh Reserve. Prout's 2nd Southern Division was heavily criticised in the strongest possible terms by Mulcahy and others for lack of discipline and competence, while Emmet Dalton, when in command of Cork, was heavily critical of the situation there. In mid-September Diarmuid MacManus, who held high office in the army, described the military knowledge of average junior officers as 'absurdly nil' and stressed the need to employ ex-British soldiers. In a memorandum to Collins, Mulcahy urged the use of sound men who had served in the British army.[14]

In view of the hasty formation of the army, it was hardly surprising that it was difficult to instil in it the disciplined methods of a regular army. At the start of the war General Seán MacMahon estimated that only 6,000 of the army were armed, and he commented that 'not even that number were fully uniformed or equipped'. A large proportion of them, he recalled, had never handled a rifle. He recollected:

'Men were taught the mechanism of a rifle very often on the way to a fight.'

At the Army Enquiry of 1924 many witnesses from the old GHQ staff admitted the weakness and chronic problems of the army in its early days. Mulcahy testified that recruitment had been unchecked and free, and 'taken without any strict enquiries as to character'. He affirmed:

> It will be readily realised that a large proportion of the criminal element found its way into the Army . . . and needless to say the Government service on account of the pay involved was the more attractive. Old soldiers, experienced in every kind of military wrong-doing, were placed under the command of officers necessarily inexperienced and the resulting state of discipline is not to be wondered at.

No provisions for a disciplinary code in the army were made until 1923, and an inspection staff only started effective work in the last stages of the war. Plans for men to be trained at the Curragh went unrealised during 1922. Gearóid O'Sullivan recollected that men were taken into the army without proper medical examination and the signing of any attestation forms. Accommodation for recruits was often inadequate. The army's journal, *An tÓglach*, said that the army was forced to do a good deal of its work 'in a rough-and-ready way'.

Seán Ó Muirthile, who took over the Quartermaster-General's position in early 1923, after the post had lain vacant for three months, recalled the chaotic functioning of the department in the first part of the war. Colonel Charles Russell concluded that 'The Quartermastering of the Army was simply diabolical. . . . When I was in charge of the Railway Corps I had two enemies, one was the Irregulars and the other was the QMG.' There were, furthermore, frequent complaints about the non-payment of wages and accounts. Mulcahy admitted that men had often been forced to rely on their own resources, which often led to commandeering; he said also that there had been only primitive means of accounting and checking supplies. Frequently local populations were to find it difficult to distinguish between the anarchic activities of Provisional Government and Republican forces. Mulcahy told the Dáil: 'You could not sit down in Dublin and make a contract for tea, and guarantee that Major-General Dalton would get his 5 lbs per week for his treaty men in Inchigeela.' Many troops had to wear civilian clothes because of the lack of available uniforms. Gearóid O'Sullivan told the Army Enquiry that they had to purchase khaki cloth from Britain, 'got it dyed green, and had it made into uniforms with all possible speed'.[15]

Problems were made worse for the new army because of the poor communications produced by the war, and the necessity to allow local commands to exercise considerable autonomy. Professor Hogan told the Army Enquiry that 'Our organisation generally speaking was not of a very high level. Our communications were not very good, an area . . . had to fight for itself, to depend on its own resources to a great extent, and decentralisation under these circumstances was almost inevitable.' The army in its early days was, in effect, a collection of local units with little effective control from Dublin. Often there were poor relations between army commands. O'Duffy and Emmet Dalton were to have an acidic relationship within the South-Western Command, and in Tipperary Blythe commented: 'Jerry Ryan does not pull well with the Dublin group.' In the circumstances considerable power had to be allowed to GOCs in the various areas.

The loose structure of the old Volunteer force made it extremely difficult for many to adapt to the demands of a regular army. As Cathal O'Shannon pointed out, 'You cannot always make a good officer in anything like a regular army out of a good guerrilla fighter.' The employment of former officers of the British army became necessary to staff the special services. The useful employment of many members of Collins's old 'Squad', men like Liam Tobin, Tom Cullen and Frank Thornton, became a major problem during the Civil War. Collins had initially put Tobin, together with some of his old colleagues, in charge of the new Intelligence Department in Oriel House, but soon became unhappy about the failure there to establish an efficient service. It was then decided to send some of them to Cork with Dalton's expeditionary force, while others would be sent to Tipperary, in the hope that they would respond better to the discipline of fighting. That, however, only produced fresh problems. In the south they had the opportunity to negotiate with leading Republicans, and they were resentful of Joe McGrath's appointment as Director of Intelligence, and also of other appointments which they regarded as their preserve. Collins had admitted that his old Squad members constituted a major problem and had even debated sending them on a mission to the USA. Collins's death greatly exacerbated these problems. The attitude of others within the command structure was also heavily influenced by their personal attitude to Collins and by their former role in the Anglo-Irish War. This applied, for instance, to Emmet Dalton and Tom Ennis, who were keen to negotiate with leaders of the Republican forces and were progressively unhappier with their work in Cork.

Many had joined the army heavily motivated by loyalty, for instance to Collins or to their local O/C. They had been assured that the Treaty was but a stepping-stone to the old republican ideal. It became increasingly difficult to maintain that position. Michael Brennan told GHQ of the feelings of the men in his own 1st Western staff: 'We all here have been very worried for some time past at the prospect of finding that the Free State was the end for which we fought, not the means to that end.'[16]

When the Third Dáil met in September, Mulcahy was frankly to admit many of the problems faced in setting up the army, but also complained of political and civil administration failings at the time of the Treaty and since. He affirmed: 'Let us see our courts re-arise . . . let us see our police there and then the army will very soon find its own place.' Mulcahy reminded the Dáil 'that the Army is no better than the people it comes from'.

Both the civil and military sides were faced with huge problems in establishing a reliable and extensive prison system. A considerable part of Provisional Government cabinet minutes for the first few months of the war were taken up with problems relating to the provision of suitable prison accommodation and the appointment of reliable prison governors. Complaints about overcrowding in prisons, and the behaviour of prison guards, became a regular feature of Republican propaganda in the course of, and after, the war.

During the Dublin fighting Alfred Cope told the British government: 'I have got two hundred cells ready in Mountjoy prison.' A major riot by Republican prisoners caused the jail to be put under the control of the military, and, evidently at Cope's suggestion, Diarmuid O'Hegarty was relieved of his duties as Secretary of the Executive Council to become governor of the prison. Referring to such appointments, Gearóid O'Sullivan later commented: 'You had to . . . get men whom you could trust, not because they had any particular ability.' Leading Republicans were moved to a more secure area at the centre of the prison. Soon, however, thirty members of the Mountjoy guard resigned after some prisoners had been fired on, and the government asked for eighty men to be supplied from the army to act as an additional guard, and for an armoured car.

At first many prisoners were released on signing a form pledging them not to take up arms again against the government. That served to keep the number of prisoners down, although it meant that many were captured for a second time. A government meeting on 10 July agreed that 'while it might be advisable to keep some of the leaders in custody for the present, no good purpose would be served by retaining large numbers of the rank and file, and that the public should be prepared by careful propaganda for an early general release'. As the war lengthened and became more bitter, however, attitudes to prisoners had to harden and there was an urgent desire for more prison space. Soon Kilmainham was turned into a military jail under Seán Ó Muirthile—a good example of Collins's desire to find jobs for his IRB colleagues. The British authorities made Gormanstown Camp available for internees. As the number of prisoners increased to 5,000 by September, there was urgent discussion of the need for more accommodation. Talks went on with the British for the use of either St Helena or the Seychelles as possible internment centres. News of this was leaked by a secretary in the Home Affairs Department. Cope commented about the Seychelles idea: 'I wish we could find a place with less glamour.' Eventually space for a total of 12,000 prisoners was made available at the Curragh, which ended talk of such exotic venues.

Republican complaints about overcrowding soon centred on Limerick prison about which the Bishop of Limerick complained in November. A government source stated that overcrowding in jails was inevitable, and that 'The conditions existing in Limerick are described as being particularly bad and it is feared that there is danger of an epidemic there. . . . It is also stated that prisoners in certain areas are being released simply because there is no accommodation for them.' Limerick prison provided for much of the west and south; usually it held 120, but by November there were over 700 housed there, with sometimes six to a cell, and the need for some to sleep in corridors.[17]

Tension between civilian members of the Provisional Government and the army was apparent from the early days of the war. While Collins and Mulcahy concentrated on their military duties the rest of the government demonstrated different attitudes to the fighting. The cabinet showed increasing impatience with Collins and Mulcahy for not supplying them rapidly enough with information on military developments. It became apparent also that the cabinet was taking a harsher attitude to censorship and the manner of depicting their opponents than Collins wished. On 25 July Collins wrote to Cosgrave:

> I am sorry to have to concern myself with this matter but I think it very necessary that our Press Organs should be very reticent in their tone about both active Irregulars and Political Opponents. Much of the criticism lately has been inclined towards abuse. This is not good from our point of view, and it is not the best way to tackle them. That many of them deserve to be abused I know well to be correct, but it is not those people who are the real driving

force in the campaign. The men who are prepared to go to the extreme limit are misguided, but practically all of them are sincere. Our propaganda should be on a more solid and permanent basis even if what may look to be advantages have to be sacrificed.

Meanwhile Collins asked Desmond FitzGerald to ease the press censorship.

From the start of the war military considerations had to be paramount. Collins, McGrath, O'Higgins and Fionán Lynch were discharged from their civil responsibilities to serve in the army. The War Council had no definition, it appears, of its relationship to the government. Lionel Curtis, following a visit to Dublin in early September 1922, reported to the British government 'that the Civil Government in Dublin had not acquired a thorough control of the military machine which it inherited from Sinn Féin'. Lord Midleton relayed the opinion of a Treaty supporter that the Provisional Government 'have a vague war policy but absolutely no civil policy'. Departments, he argued, had ceased to function because it was claimed they were too busy with the war, and he also commented on Cosgrave's total reliance on Collins. Cosgrave admitted to Sir Samuel Hoare that 'owing to the inadequacy of their machinery they would take ten times longer to do things than would be needed by the British administration'. Collins continued to be the key figure in the government; he missed few cabinet meetings, and the British government addressed their important correspondence to him.

The Civic Guard was reconstituted in September, and only two months after the fighting had started was the possibility of sending police forces out into proscribed areas mooted. O'Higgins admitted in the Dáil when replying to criticisms about the activities of Oriel House:

> There is no use claiming that there should have existed in that institution what did not exist in any other phase of national life at that time—discipline. There was indiscipline in the country from top to bottom. Was there any force or department in which it could be said that the standard of either efficiency or discipline was high?

Republican courts were only sporadically functioning and were soon to be replaced by a new system. In the early Civil War, furthermore, leading civil servants assumed dominance in their departments, little influenced by their ministers whose attention was elsewhere.[18]

The position of the new government was weakened by the fact that the Third Dáil could not meet until early September—before that time its meetings had to be often postponed because of the military situation. Until the constitution was submitted to the Dáil in September and the Free State came into existence in December, the government appeared to lack authority as well as security. Until September there was no public means of criticising the military effort. When the Dáil convened, Thomas Johnson complained about the army's performance, declaring: 'The spirit of militarism is still rife.' Members of the government, notably Kevin O'Higgins, shared such views but could not express them.

It is doubtful if Griffith's death from a cerebral haemorrhage on 12 August led to any significant changes. Griffith had been ill for some time and, apparently, had become a less important influence in the government. His death, however, alarmed the British government, Macready describing him as probably the only genuine 'Free Stater' in the government. In assuming the responsibilities of President, William Cosgrave could not at the outset make up for the loss of Griffith's authority and personal stature, but the combination of Cosgrave and O'Higgins put into effect much of what Griffith had stood for, and with considerably more energy than Griffith had been showing.[19]

The War in the Localities:
July–August 1922

THERE was little possibility that fighting in the Civil War could have been limited to the conflict in Dublin that followed the Four Courts attack. The course of the war was initially determined by the pattern of barrack occupation by pro-Treaty and anti-Treaty forces. To establish its authority over all the Twenty-Six Counties, the Provisional Government had to rely on its army to end the anti-Treaty occupation of barracks in Munster, the west and other key areas. Use of the army became the crucial precondition for the establishment of the new state. Only after nearly a month could the army's leadership feel at all confident in sending forces to deal with the heart of Republican strength in the south and west. The first concern of the Republican side was to take over pro-Treaty-controlled barracks in anti-Treaty areas; accordingly their forces soon concentrated on places like Skibbereen and Listowel in Munster, and Sligo town in the west. They also sought to gain complete control of towns where both sides occupied separate barracks: Limerick was the prime example. Attention was to centre also on areas which had declared no definite allegiance, for instance Co. Wexford and Frank Aiken's 4th Northern Division. Both forces at the start of the conflict lacked confidence as to the reliability of some areas nominally supporting them.

(a) BLESSINGTON AND WEXFORD

Not for the first time in Irish history the postscript to fighting in Dublin occurred in the Dublin and Wicklow hills. While the confrontation in O'Connell Street was still in progress a column of over a hundred men from South Tipperary, led by Mick Sheehan, had stationed themselves in the village of Blessington, taken over buildings, and commandeered transport and provisions. They had represented the sole practical response to Oscar Traynor's plea for relief forces to come to the aid of Republicans in the capital. They were soon joined by units, numbering over two hundred men, from the South Dublin Brigade and from Kildare, and by men escaping from Dublin, notably Oscar Traynor and Ernie O'Malley.[1]

Ben Doyle recalled that at the end of the fighting in Dublin there was talk of 'Blessington legions who were going to march on Dublin'. On arriving in Blessington, however, on 6 July, Traynor reported:

> I find things rather mixed up. Boland is working like a hero, but Brig. A. McDonnell has retreated from the whole Eastern portion of his area, leaving

it in the hands of the enemy. . . . Unless some Officer of superior command is sent immediately to Dublin or district, things may get into a state of chaos.

The South Dublin Brigade had failed to cut roads in the vicinity which would have prevented enemy troops from advancing. While he remained convinced of the need to restart hostilities in Dublin, Traynor saw no possibility of advancing on the capital from Blessington. He said that there was a 'kind of' Provisional Government cordon around the city which was sufficient to hold up any Republican attempt to advance. He instructed those still in Dublin: 'Let the stuff come along by the means I supply and let the men take the tram to Terenure, and get to me at this post on foot and unarmed. This is the only possible hope of reaching me.'

Traynor realised that no aggressive policy could involve the Blessington men. He said that he had met 'Tipp men who were very anxious to get home' and who were 'completely out of their element'. Of the rest, Traynor related: 'I broke them up into small parties and told them not to hold towns . . . to hit and get away.' Advances on Brittas and Ballymore Eustace saw sixty Republicans captured at the former, and thirteen at the latter. When Provisional Government troops advanced from the Curragh, Dublin and the coast, the Republican forces dispersed. On 8 July a Republican report declared:

> It is useless in holding out in position any longer. Blessington is taken and our organisation broken in Area. Reports are reaching here of a big encircling movement from Naas to Curragh, and it is only nonsense to let them get our arms. I recommend to dump all arms in safety; give all men some rations, and let every man mind himself.

The Provisional Government troops arriving at Blessington had no battle to fight.

Gerry Boland, Andy McDonnell and one hundred other Republicans were arrested at Blessington. Some of the Tipperary men went with O'Malley on his expedition to Wexford, and the Dublin men drifted back to the city. George Gilmore commented: 'The lads filtered back from Blessington and nearly all of them stayed at home and were arrested for they had no leadership either from Bn. or from the Bde. . . . There was practically no one left in our Bn. There was a terrible spirit of defeat after Blessington.'[2]

O'Malley had originally aimed to lead a force back to Dublin from Blessington; he had received inaccurate reports of men from the 2nd Southern Division taking Kilkenny town, and had expectations that they could join up with the Blessington units before advancing on the capital. O'Malley urged Lynch 'to send mobilised columns up country to attack posts simultaneously before the Free State could recruit and consolidate'. After the breakup of the Republican units in Blessington, O'Malley led a force which quickly took over the major towns of Co. Wexford. At Enniscorthy, after some fighting and the intervention of priests, O'Malley agreed to release some captured Provisional Government troops, veterans of the Anglo-Irish War, on the condition—soon broken—that they would promise not to take up arms against the Republicans again.[3]

There was little coherent strategy about O'Malley's movements and, seemingly, little expectation that the towns in Wexford would be held for long. The confusion was increased by Seán Moylan's strange expedition with a column of 230 men from Cork to New Ross. Séamus Robinson felt that Moylan's move was meant to represent the first step in a Republican offensive, leading to a convergence from all directions on Dublin. Robinson recalled: 'When we were in Clonmel... Seán Moylan sent me word... that they were moving up towards Dublin along the East Coast. I sent back to arrange for the West to meet and advance.' Moylan's immediate intention was to link up with O'Malley's force. He notified O'Malley: 'Have arrived here in New Ross with 230 men, propose dividing them into 3 columns and advancing towards Wexford. Suggest that you also advance and try to get your column into touch with mine.... I believe that our job is to finish this Beggars' Bush Column here in Wexford before tackling anything else.'

Moylan's expedition proved a sorry failure. His men soon made themselves unpopular in the locality—Pax Whelan, the O/C of the Waterford Brigade, saying of them: 'They stayed a day or so in New Ross and they commandeered everything they could lay their hands on.' Madge Clifford, Liam Lynch's future secretary, related: 'Moylan wouldn't let in the men to Wexford for fear they'd starve them.' Moylan told O'Malley: 'We are without a base, transport, food, or Intelligence. The local Volunteers seem to be practically non-existent, and the few men we've met have been very little assistance to us.' Moylan saw no point in his and O'Malley's columns remaining in the area and affirmed: 'The only method of successfully combatting [sic] the Free State here is by guerrilla tactics, small local columns of snipers and obstructionists.' To have attempted to hold barracks in the area 'means giving away rifles, and ruining whatever little moral [sic] is left'. He ended by informing O'Malley: 'I am therefore taking my fellows back to concentrate on Thurles, Nenagh, and perhaps Kilkenny.... I hate leaving here but I can see no use in having a column here which has no knowledge of the country, and which would be blind and useless.' Whelan concluded on Moylan: 'He marched them up to New Ross. And he marched them down again.... Moylan's army didn't march. They went up and down by special train.' The expedition was a prime example of the failure of Republican troops to work effectively outside their own areas.[4]

A pro-Treaty Wexford expeditionary force was meanwhile raised, under Colonel-Commandant Keogh and Brigadier Slattery, which comprised 230 men and sixteen officers, with 150 rifles, one piece of artillery, two armoured cars, two Lancias and four Lewis guns. They left on 6 July. Republican troops evacuated Enniscorthy and Wexford by 8 July, and pro-Treaty posts were set up in Enniscorthy, Wexford and New Ross. It was reported on 7 July that O'Malley's men had left in a charabanc and car in the direction of Carlow. A Provisional Government army report commented: 'There are forming Flying Columns. We have no intention bothering about these, for of all the crowds in Ireland, the Wexford Brigades are most assuredly the most pitiful and helpless.' Any hope of a successful south-eastern strategy had, therefore, soon ended for the Republicans.[5]

(b) DUBLIN

On returning to Dublin, following his Wexford sortie, O'Malley was appointed Assistant Chief of Staff by Liam Lynch, on 10 July, and given a vast command area over the north and the east. O'Malley had little knowledge of large areas of his new command and felt he would have been better employed in the 2nd Southern

Division, which was far more likely to see fighting. O'Malley and Traynor were extremely critical of what they saw as Lynch's neglect of the capital. During the Dublin fighting Traynor had written to Lynch: 'I note remarks about keeping route to South open. If route to South is more important than the holding of Dublin, then you can keep the men.' Four days later, while marooned in Blessington, Traynor stressed: 'I regard the continuance of activities in Dublin as the most essential thing for the present and am prepared to take the risk.' O'Malley told Liam Deasy: 'I think. . . . that GHQ must recognise that the enemy are much stronger in Dublin and that it is not so much use making the South unbearable for them if they have the Capital.'[6]

The position of Dublin No. 1 Brigade had been greatly weakened by the fighting in Dublin and the retreat from Blessington. The outlook for the Republican IRA in the capital was to remain a bleak one. Arrests were frequent, partly because old colleagues knew where they were to be found. John Cullinan recalled: 'It was difficult to stop at home for Dan Bryan our former I/O knew us all and he also knew all our haunts. I didn't stay at home.' Battalion and company organisation in the city had been broken up, and it took several weeks before a flying column could be set up in South Dublin. Cullinan commented: 'As a Bn. we were then down and out for there was great dissatisfaction at the loss of arms and the lack of thought about . . . the use of men and . . . our arms. . . . It took us a long time to get a few revolvers together, and there were no bombs to be had.' When a column was formed George Gilmore said that 'We had nothing to do . . . save to exist.' Traynor was arrested on 27 July, together with a number of other senior officers, and O'Malley admitted that 'Petty jealousy, insubordination and organised opposition have prevented columns, which I instructed to operate, from doing anything active.' Tod Andrews summed up the situation in characteristically blunt manner: 'Things were hopeless in Dublin. Only a few young fellows active.' O'Malley reported to Lynch on 6 August: 'One has to be patient here but certainly the circumstances are most peculiar and it is very difficult to counteract enemy espionage. Dublin is very severely tried.'

Activity was mainly limited to street ambushes and sniping of posts. *An tÓglach* in January 1923 commented that 'Properly speaking, there has never been an attack on a military post in Dublin City since their surrender in O'Connell Street . . . It has not entered the wildest . . . dreams of the Irregulars that they could capture or hold any position in Dublin City at any time since July.'[7]

On the night of 5 August the Republicans planned to isolate Dublin city by destroying bridges and blocking communications. Men from Cork were brought in to help. It was unclear, however, what the plan would have led to if it had succeeded. In the event a document giving details of the plan was found on Liam Clarke, of Rathfarnham, who had been captured shortly before. As a result, the Intelligence Officer of the 2nd Eastern Division reported: 'In North County Dublin we picked out likely bridges and sent patrols to same. In nearly every case the Irregulars were found in the act of tearing up the bridges. We captured 104 Irregulars including the officer in charge, Pat Sweeney. There was practically no damage done in North County.' Christy Smith told O'Malley: 'It was the Bridges job that crushed the Dublin Brigade'; for Tod Andrews it was a 'complete failure with the most active elements in the Brigade being captured in the course of the operation'.[8]

There followed a more ambitious project, which twice failed to come to fruition, to take a plane from Baldonnell Camp, with which it was intended to bomb the Government Buildings in Dublin. Tod Andrews, who was given the task of dropping the bombs, wrote in his autobiography:

> The pilot selected to fly the plane was a man who, having reached the diaconate with the Columban Fathers at Dalgan Park, had left the Order to take part in the Civil War. 'The Deacon' as he was always referred to by us was, if his story was to be believed, something of a universal genius. I do not know who checked his credentials; it is quite possible that nobody did. He had, it was said, flown with a mixed British and French squadron in defence of Verdun. He had been decorated, it was said, with the Croix de Guerre by Marshal Pétain. He had, it was said, the British Distinguished Flying Cross.... When I was introduced to him as his bombadier, I found a cheerful, expansive, confident and friendly man. He did not impart to me the confidence he so obviously felt. I discussed plans with him; how high, how low we would have to fly over Government Buildings, how did we aim our bombs, would we need any special clothing? For all the questions he had pat answers, but when I asked if he had checked whether the tide would be in or out when we came to land on Merrion Strand, he admitted that he had forgotten. My confidence unsurprisingly shrank.

After being postponed once, for a week, the project was again called off at the last possible moment because, it was claimed, of insufficient numbers assembling. It was to have involved men from Paddy Mullally's Kildare column and a group of collaborating Provisional Government soldiers inside Baldonnell. Mullally was left to reflect on his ignorance as to what had gone wrong, and Christy Smith complained of men having to wait around endlessly.[9]

(c) LIMERICK

Even before the fighting in Dublin was over it became clear that Limerick city would become the next crucial centre for concern. In retrospect, both Republican and pro-Treaty participants held that the struggle for control of the city decided the war. Michael Brennan argued that 'the whole Civil War really turned on Limerick', and, on the other side, Seán MacSwiney confided to Liam Deasy: 'After Limerick, I personally did not believe that we could attain a complete military victory. Prior to Limerick I did think we could win in the field.' O'Duffy stressed: 'We cannot afford a defeat in Limerick as we may have to fight the whole 1st Southern in Limerick.'

If the Republicans had gained control of Limerick, Brennan's command in Clare and Galway and Mac Eoin's in Athlone—the two vital pro-Treaty areas outside the Dublin region—would have been completely isolated. Republican success in Limerick and the south-east could have become a springboard for a move on Dublin.

At the start of the war Republican forces possessed the majority of the barracks in Limerick city; they took over prominent buildings and held most of the surrounding areas, excluding East Clare. Mac Eoin's Athlone Command was cut off from the city by the Republican control of many barracks in North Tipperary,

Leix and Offaly. The Republican units in Limerick were soon considerably strengthened by units from Cork and Kerry, who moved through East Limerick to the city. These men had little problem clearing West Limerick on their way to the city, although the post at Foynes had to be set on fire before the pro-Treaty garrison surrendered. When a clash was threatened between local Provisional Government units and the advancing force, a hastily arranged meeting at Broadfoot between Deasy and Donnchadh O'Hannigan, the pro-Treaty O/C, resulted in a truce, signed on 4 July, which left the way open to Limerick for the Republicans. O'Hannigan's readiness to settle was influenced by his old connection with Lynch and Deasy—he had command during the Anglo-Irish War of the neighbouring flying column to Lynch's North Cork one, and they had close IRB ties. Before entering Limerick the Republican forces took the picturesque village of Adare after a short fight.[10]

Republican numbers in the city then amounted to over 700, and considerably outnumbered the 400 troops of the 1st Western Division, under Brennan, and the 4th Southern, under O'Hannigan, who had 360 rifles between them. Liam Lynch set up his headquarters in the New Barracks and had a full experienced staff with him, including key men like Seán Moylan and Liam Deasy.

The strong Republican position in Limerick did not, however, lead to any aggressive policy, nor did it end peacemaking activity. O'Hannigan and Brennan met frequently with Lynch, with a parish priest acting as the intermediary, and Frank Aiken soon arrived on his own personal peace mission. Hearing rumours of truce conferences in Limerick, O'Duffy sent Diarmuid MacManus to the city with instructions to prevent any further peace talks and to report on the situation to GHQ. Nothing better revealed the lack of communication between Dublin and the provinces at the start of the war, and how insecure GHQ felt about the allegiance of men like Brennan. To reach Limerick MacManus had to dress as a tramp and take a circuitous route through Clare. He arrived to find Brennan and O'Hannigan heavily involved in negotiations with Lynch. MacManus told Lynch that he had been instructed to commence military operations and affirmed that 'no . . . agreement, even if signed, could be admitted by GHQ and these Officers had no authority whatever to enter into such an agreement'.

MacManus was nevertheless alarmed at the vulnerable position the pro-Treaty troops were in, and reported to GHQ: 'I found the morale of the Divisional Staff extremely low. All ideas centred on (a) How best an attack from the enemy could be postponed or avoided by compromise and agreement, and (b) How long we could . . . hold out when besieged.' Though he wanted to take the offensive, he had doubts about the reliability of the troops and felt that any attack would have to await the arrival of reinforcements. MacManus warned that 'Unless Rifles and armoured cars arrive within 24 hours of now, 10 a.m. 6/7/22 we will be in very grave danger of disaster.' He concluded:

> I feel confident that I can finish off and capture the whole of the Executive in this area in a few days. There is, however, this real danger. Comdt-Gen Brennan is seriously anxious for a truce and an agreement. He may come to an understanding with Lynch and when I repudiate it, resign, and probably a large part of his Division with him. This is only an impression I have, but none the less a definite one. Lynch seems to have established an influence over him by soft words, and says the matter is a Munster one, and once

Munster compromised Ireland will follow. . . . Hannigan, however, is not fooled, and is the brightest spot in the situation.

While MacManus ordered some limited offensive action to improve the pro-Treaty position, he did not prevent a truce agreement being arrived at between Brennan and O'Hannigan with Lynch on 7 July.

The Limerick agreement 'in the interests of a united Ireland, and to save our country from utter destruction' called for a meeting of the relevant divisional commandants from both sides, which would take place 'as soon as Seán MacKeon [sic] can be got into this Area'. Brennan and O'Hannigan 'as a guarantee of good faith' promised that they would hand in their resignations if an agreement was not arrived at as a consequence of the projected meeting. It was agreed which buildings the pro-Treaty forces should be allowed to hold, and that the anti-Treaty forces should withdraw to barracks. GHQ in Dublin, however, had no intention of allowing a new army unity meeting to take place: at that time a definite policy was being worked out in Dublin for the reoccupation of Munster.[11]

It is unclear what motivated both sides in making the Limerick truce. It was in the interest of the Provisional Government to play for time before reinforcements of men, arms and ammunition arrived. Brennan later explained his policy by his desire to prevent a Republican advance on Dublin: he worked out a strategy to mislead the Republicans as to the number of arms his troops possessed in the city. Frank Aiken, however, gave a different view of Brennan's motivation. He recorded that when hostilities started he berated Brennan for going back on his agreement with Lynch. Brennan claimed, however, according to Aiken, that the decision to fight had not been his, and Aiken quoted him as saying: 'I don't see how serious fighting can take place here, our men have nothing against the other lads.'

Liam Lynch claimed that the Limerick truce represented a major success. He wrote: 'I expect we will control from the Shannon to Carlow in a day or two' and added that the agreement

> gives us a very considerable military advantage, as with a comparatively small number of troops held up at Limerick, we have been able to ensure that at least 3,000 F.S. troops are also held up. Had we to fight in Limerick, our forces that are in Limerick would not only be held there for at least 10 days, but we wouldn't be in a position to re-inforce Wexford–New Ross Area nor could we hope to attack Thurles. The most we could do would be to harass Kilkenny.

When hostilities started in the city Lynch felt that the Republican offensive, in both South Tipperary and in the south-east, was harmed. Seán Hyde, who was one of the prominent Republican officers in Limerick, however, attributed Lynch's unwillingness to fight to his trust in O'Hannigan and his dislike of civil war. He related that 'The Blessed Sacrament was produced on the table and they agreed not to attack each other.' Paddy Coughlin, a Mitchelstown IRA man, also recollected that 'Liam Lynch did not want a war.' Lynch hoped that he would by his tactics take not only Brennan and O'Hannigan but also Mac Eoin out of the conflict. The truce policy can thus be seen as an attempt to consolidate Republican control of Munster and to limit the spread of the war, leaving scope for an agreement with the Provisional Government based on revision of the Treaty and the constitution.

The vast majority of the leadership of the Republican forces in Limerick, however, were for an aggressive policy. On 6 July Seán Moylan told Liam Deasy:

> I must get one hundred riflemen ten machine-guns and crews sent on from Cork 1 and Kerry at once. The Staters are in force—well equipped and I must hold the offensive.... There is no use in fooling with this question any longer. Send on the men and let us get on with the war.... What about sending a few hundred grenades.

Seán Hyde recalled telling Deasy: 'This is a game of ping-pong. If we don't take them on today we'll have to take them on tomorrow.'

The delay brought about by the truce enabled Provisional Government forces to build up their strength and caused the men in the Cork and Kerry units to become deeply disillusioned. 'Time was needed by the enemy,' Seán MacSwiney commented. 'To gain time they gave pledges which they broke when it suited their purpose.' Frank Bumstead, of Cork No. 1 Brigade, recalled: 'Liam Lynch and his bloody Truce ruined us in the Civil War.' Mick Leahy, the new O/C of Cork No. 1 Brigade, said that Limerick 'finished our fellows . . . the waiting there demoralised the men'. Mick Sullivan, from Ballyvourney, said that he became 'thoroughly disgusted . . . we were kept there for 3 weeks'. He went on to criticise their leadership: 'I could see our incompetence and limitations for this type of fighting for we had no military man between the whole lot of us.' MacSwiney declared that 'the honesty of purpose of our leaders and their belief in the honesty of purpose of the enemy' was what lost Limerick for the Republicans.[12]

On 11 July a consignment of arms, with 150 men and the same number of rifles, was sent to Limerick from Dublin via Galway and Clare. That day Brennan sent Lynch formal confirmation of the truce's termination, with the shooting of a pro-Treaty soldier in the city used as a pretext. Later in the day Seán Hyde reported to Deasy:

> The situation here has got very serious during the last hour or so. FS troops have swarmed into the City like bees and occupied practically all the posts we had last week.... Already casualties have been reported among our men who were raising barricades.... The enemy have a plentiful supply of armoured cars and steel-plated lorries.

Lynch told O'Malley: 'The second agreement reached at Limerick has been broken by the enemy.... I believe ... we will eventually ... have to destroy all our posts and operate as of old in Columns.' Lynch switched his headquarters from Limerick to Clonmel before the pro-Treaty attack began.

A further arms convoy was needed, however, before the Provisional Government forces could attack with any confidence. Mulcahy recommended that artillery be sent to Limerick with one Rolls-Royce armoured car, ten Lewis guns and 10,000 rounds, 400 rifles and 40,000 rounds, two Lancia cars, four military lorries and 400 grenades. O'Duffy went with the convoy and established his headquarters at Killaloe, across the Shannon from Limerick.[13]

The Provisional Government attack on Republican positions in Limerick city began on 19 July, after an eighteen-pound gun had been placed on Arthur's Quay ready to fire on the Strand Barracks. The fighting assumed many of the characteristics of the Dublin conflict. Mulcahy and O'Duffy had decided that an artillery attack on the Strand, Ordnance, New and Castle Barracks should be followed by a storming of them. The struggle for the Strand Barracks saw the only serious fighting. Nineteen shells were fired at the front of the building, followed by fourteen at the back. O'Duffy described the storming of that barracks as 'the finest operation in the present war'. The Republican forces burnt the remaining barracks and retreated south. The confrontation was over by 21 July. Casualties were light: eight Provisional Government soldiers were killed, and twenty wounded; between twenty and thirty Republicans were killed. Apart from the barracks, there was little damage to property. The Provisional Government troops, however, failed in their aim to prevent the Republican forces escaping.

For Republican units in Limerick the policy of truce and evacuation was not easily understood. They had been in the stronger position, but that advantage had been dissipated by Lynch's policy. Mick Murphy, of Cork No. 1 Brigade, commented: 'We came back to Buttevant, but why we didn't know.' Jamie Managhan, another Cork No. 1 officer, recalled of the withdrawal: 'There was pandemonium.... Our men from Limerick were completely demoralised.' The Republican retreat meant that the Provisional Government now controlled the estuary of the Shannon and could requisition boats for patrolling the coast and transport units to other parts of Munster. Republican units in Clare and the midlands were henceforward cut off from their Munster colleagues.[14]

Co. Limerick, particularly East Limerick, was to prove a much greater problem for the Provisional Government troops than Limerick city. During the last two weeks of July and the first week of August the area south of the city, most notably the Bruff–Bruree–Kilmallock triangle, saw the heaviest continuous fighting of the Civil War, at times even approximating to what could be called line fighting. The area had considerable strategic importance, as it controlled the routes, rail and road, to Kerry and Cork from Limerick city; it was the barrier to a pro-Treaty advance on Munster from the north.

During the Limerick city crisis the Republicans had been taking control of important garrisons in East Limerick. Kilmallock and Caherconlish had been taken on 13 July; the Republicans claimed to have captured 150 men at Kilmallock. Meanwhile the whole pro-Treaty brigade staff of East Limerick, numbering forty-seven, were captured on 12 July and taken to Tipperary barracks. General Séamas Hogan admitted in a report to GHQ on 15 July:

> The situation in East and West Limerick is not good. Flying columns from each are passing through and Commdt. Hannigan does not seem strong enough to cope with them. He is short of rifles, and until he has more will not be able to check movements to and from Cork. I have found it rather difficult to wean Hannigan from the idea of holding posts in East Limerick. I instructed Commdt. Hannigan only to hold posts that could resist any attack.

Hogan's opinion was that it had been a mistake to have held Caherconlish and Kilmallock.

Kilmallock, with the large house of Ashill Towers as headquarters, became the centre of Republican concentration. Many Cork and Kerry men established themselves there after the evacuation of Limerick city. O'Duffy reported that pro-Treaty troops held only Rockbarton and Bruff in the county, and estimated the total strength of the Republicans in the county, including the city, as 2,030 rifles.

He concluded: 'The irregulars still outnumber us by 727 Rifles.' The Republicans had with them in the Kilmallock area an armoured car, the *River Lee*, which, in the words of Jamie Managhan, 'cruised around like a labourer's cottage'.

There was little sense of overall direction in the Republican ranks. During the fighting around Kilmallock, Con Moloney, the Adjutant-General, told O'Malley: 'Deasy is, more or less I/C operations,' Seán Murray, of Cork No. 1 Brigade, thought 'the men had no intention of holding a line'. Problems of local particularism, moreover, continued to weaken the Republican effort. The O/C of the Limerick Brigade reported that the East Limerick column 'refused to operate under Cork, as they would much prefer to operate in their own divisional area. They let our men down badly; it was impossible to get anything from them.' The units encountered supply problems. Murray recorded that 'they had to scrounge for themselves', and Deasy admitted that they had to demobilise men because they couldn't feed them.[15]

Once he established himself in Limerick city, O'Duffy assembled plans for an advance by various units to the south and west in order to free the county of Republican forces and to clear the path for a land invasion of Munster, to be carried out simultaneously with various landings on the coast of Kerry and Cork. Brennan's 1st Western men were despatched back to Clare to clear the situation there, while 200 men under Brigadier Keane were to proceed south-west to remove the Republicans from Rathkeale, Askeaton, Foynes and Newcastle West, and then to move on to Kerry. Meanwhile O'Hannigan and W. R. E. Murphy, who was to be O'Duffy's second-in-command, were to concentrate on the Bruff–Kilmallock area. O'Duffy was confident that his plans would lead to the breaking of the Republican resistance throughout the entire south. He was soon to be disillusioned.

On 26 July O'Duffy reported serious reverses during the advance on the Kilmallock front. Commandant Cronin and forty-seven of his men were captured near Thomastown on 23 July after a five-hour engagement, as a consequence, O'Duffy held, of disobeying express instructions not to advance south of Kilmallock. On the day before that a pro-Treaty force of thirty had been surprised and captured between Kilmallock and Bruff. As a consequence of such reverses, O'Duffy ordered that they should not advance south of a line north of Kilmallock until the rest of Limerick had been cleared and further reinforcements had arrived. Intelligence sources were reporting that 500 Republicans were in the Kilmallock area and that 1,000 were based in Buttevant, ready to come to their support. O'Duffy concluded that 'practically the entire forces of the Irregulars are arraigned against us', including their best fighting men.

O'Duffy put most of his problems down to the poor performance of his troops, and their lack of resources. On 4 August he wrote:

> We are operating in large areas with nothing better than a Rifle. I estimate that the Irregulars have 4 Lewis Guns in this Command for our one. In Limerick City at the moment there is not a single Lewis Gun. . . . As regards Rifles, the last rifle is distributed and I have none for recruits coming in.

He stressed the need for transport—they had no touring cars available, and not a single motor-bike—and concluded: 'As it is, our troops have to scrounge on the countryside. This leads towards indiscipline and is unfair to the people.'

Looking back on the struggle for the Kilmallock area, O'Duffy told Mulcahy:

> We had to get work out of a disgruntled, undisciplined and cowardly crowd. Arms were handed over wholesale to the enemy, sentries were drunk at their Posts, and when a whole garrison was put in clink owing to insubordination, etc. the garrison sent to replace them often turned out to be worse, and the Divisional, Brigade, Battalion and Company officers were in many cases, no better than the Privates. To get value out of these the Command Staff had to work very hard—18 hours out of 24 . . . as there was always fear we might lose some of the posts through treachery, as actually happened on two occasions.

Some of the Bruff garrison deserted to the Republican side on 20 July, and troops at Foynes gave up the post there on 29 July. O'Duffy's particular venom was reserved for the men sent him from the Curragh Reserve. He reported Commandant Keogh's view: 'The Reserve are absolutely worthless, at least 200 of them never handled a rifle before.' On another occasion O'Duffy wrote: 'Half of them are now in clink, or have deserted altogether.'

The unreliability of the pro-Treaty forces enormously encouraged the Republican forces. Moloney reported of Deasy: 'He is confident of success, as any time his forces have met in this area, the enemy ran away.' Liam Lynch told O'Malley that: 'After experience of East Limerick for last few days where we captured 76 prisoners and where enemy show no fight we are convinced of our future success in open country.'[16]

The Republican control of the Kilmallock area, however, could only be temporary. Moloney admitted on 2 August: 'Up to yesterday we have had the best of the operations there. There will I fear be a big change there now as the enemy have been reinforced very considerably.' There had been considerable fighting in Bruff and Bruree, in which Republican forces had more than held their own. The Provisional Government forces had taken Bruree after a strong attack from two directions, only for fighting to start up again there three days later. Earlier the Republicans had successfully attacked Bruff.

The reinforcements for O'Duffy's forces arrived at the same time as the sea landings in Cork and Kerry, which ensured that there would be no final battle for Kilmallock. On 4 August a pro-Treaty force consisting of over 700 men, together with an eighteen-pound gun and an armoured car, left for the Kilmallock front, while other units moved west towards the Kerry border. On the following day there was only limited fighting before Kilmallock was entered. By that time the Cork and Kerry men had left for their home territory, following the pro-Treaty landings at Fenit and Cork—a small garrison had been left behind in Kilmallock and offered little more than a token resistance. Lynch reported to O'Malley concerning Co. Limerick: 'Owing to developments in Cork . . . our forces on this front have been reduced, and are forming into columns.'[17]

Republican forces had captured Patrickswell on 2 August, but were to evacuate it when pro-Treaty forces advanced on their march to the Kerry border. Some resistance was offered to that advance at Adare on 4 August, but was swiftly ended by the use of an eighteen-pound gun. There was little damage to the valuable property in Adare, although there was a hole in the church tower where Republican soldiers had been ensconced with machine-guns. The pro-Treaty troops moved on to Rathkeale, which they took the same day, despite the desertion of some of the Curragh Reserve men. The Republicans evacuated Newcastle West, where they burnt the castle.

In the end the struggle for Co. Limerick had represented little more than a Republican delaying action. It had also provided a striking exhibition of the Provisional Government army's considerable limitations.[18]

(d) CLARE

Clare played little part in the Civil War. The county's isolated geographical position had aided active resistance during the Anglo-Irish War, but also meant that once pro-Treaty troops had taken control of Limerick, by early August 1922, Clare Republicans could have minimal contact with those in the 1st Southern Division and the west.

During the fighting in Limerick, and later in Kerry, Clare pro-Treaty forces played an important role. The 1st Western Division, together with the men of the Dublin Guard, were the only Provisional Government units singled out for praise by General W. R. E. Murphy of the South-Western Command and by journalists on the spot. While Michael Brennan and his units were in Limerick Republican forces took control of various centres in Mid-Clare and the west of the county—notably Kilrush and Kilkee. There was a rapid evacuation of those towns when Brennan applied a sweeps policy in early August. Many Republican leaders were captured; Frank Barrett remained at large, but was to spend much of the war outside Clare.

There is very little material available on the brief fighting in Clare. Some captured correspondence, however, gives a sharp insight into the confused nature of the conflict, and the difficulty of finding out precisely who was on each side. On 22 July Seán Hennessy, the Republican O/C of the 4th Battalion of the 4th Brigade in Ballyea, reported: 'The Free State Batt Commdt [M. Frawley] . . . has promised to do all he can for us—he has done a little already in helping to get the fellows desert from the Workhouse and bring out some stuff.' He further noted: 'The Comp Capt at Milltown and Lahinch are neutral and have refused to take arms or assist the Free State Bgde Comdt.' Two days later, however, Hennessy reported the arrest of three of his best officers and concluded that Frawley was not on their side after all.[19]

(e) WATERFORD

Soon after taking over as Commander-in-Chief Collins made plans for his troops to attack Waterford city. On paper this appeared to entail many risks. Waterford was surrounded by the strongly Republican areas of South Tipperary and Cork to the west and south-west. The location of Waterford city made it difficult to attack—to occupy the city entailed first of all crossing the River Suir, which promised to be a very difficult exercise. The city, however, was to be taken extremely easily, and was to prove the base for future advances from the east on the so-called Republican 'line' and on the Republican headquarters at Clonmel and beyond. With the taking of Waterford, the war in that area was effectively over. Frank Edwards, a Waterford Republican, commented that following its capture 'the area of activity moved on from Waterford very quickly. . . . For us it had hardly started when it was over. It then became something that we read about in the newspapers.' Even by the standards of the Civil War, the fall of Waterford demonstrated an extreme unwillingness on the part of the Republicans to fight, and a complete failure of co-operation between the various anti-Treaty forces. General Macready concluded: 'In no case, whatever may be said beforehand, do the Republicans stand and fight to a finish.'

Since the start of the war Waterford had been occupied by around 200 anti-Treaty IRA troops, who had taken possession of barracks, together with public buildings such as the post office and the jail. Republican sources soon warned that the city was one of the first likely places for the Provisional Government to attack. The divisional O/C reported on 9 July: 'The first landing I anticipate is Waterford, a possible objective being Waterford City.... We have arranged for the mining of landing stages and the holding of a line through Mount Congret to Tramore. A reserve force to act between Mount Congret and City is also being provided for.' An inspector of the Local Government Department in Waterford observed that during the Republican occupation 'Each night the rail bridge is drawn in anticipation of an attack from Kilkenny. The Republicans are in a state of nervous tension, and rumours of an attack on the city causes great apprehension in their ranks. Desertion is frequent, and every precaution is being taken to stop it.' The inspector had been told by 'several leading citizens that Waterford will not put up a fight when the Free State troops advance'.[20]

The state of the Waterford Brigade was hardly conducive to an effective defence of the city. In July its O/C, Pax Whelan, told the O/C of the 1st Southern Division that it was important that he come to the city as quickly as possible because of the 'serious situation' in the brigade. 'Two most important officers', he wrote, 'have sent in their resignations, and I cannot see my way to carry on. Bring capable man or two to take charge.... Reasons for resignations, won't take part in civil war.' The columns from Cork and Tipperary who were sent to aid in the defence of Waterford quickly formed a dim view of their Waterford colleagues. Seán Culhane reflected that 'Everything...in Waterford was chaotic.' Whelan complained also that there was a considerable shortage of guns and that ammunition ran out during the pro-Treaty attack.[21]

Collins's arrangements for the taking of Waterford laid down that men from the Curragh and the Thurles–Templemore area should link up with Prout's Kilkenny command units. The men from the Curragh, however, did not arrive. Collins arranged that 500 rifles, together with machine-guns, were taken on the pedition. Meanwhile he sent his old henchman Frank Thornton to report on the .uation at Kilkenny. Thornton arrived just after Prout's men had left on 17 July ır Waterford and became alarmed about the situation he found. He reported: The situation is rotten here. There is absolutely no organisation in any branch. Commdt. Prout evidently did not expect any attack from the rear and made no preparations to meet it.' Thornton complained that Prout had advertised his departure and had made it easy for Lacey's and Breen's South Tipperary columns to cut communications between Kilkenny and Waterford and to prevent reinforcements arriving from Kilkenny.[22]

Blocked roads, and a near confrontation at Nine-Mile House, delayed the expedition's journey to Waterford, but the attack on the city proved to be far easier than could have been anticipated. The Waterford Brigade had failed to occupy

Mount Mercy, which overlooked the city and provided an excellent base from which Republican-held buildings in the city could be shelled. Republicans had raised the bridge over the river, but pro-Treaty forces solved that problem by sending across a small party in rowing-boats, who then took over buildings in the city as a bridgehead and lowered the bridge to enable the rest of the expedition to enter the city, which they did with a little hindrance from Republican firing. There were very few casualties.[23]

By that time the Republican IRA in Waterford were completing their evacuation. The ease with which the city was taken is explained more by Republican failure than by the effectiveness of the strategy adopted by Provisional Government troops. The Cork and Tipperary men failed to effectively support the Waterford forces. In response to Whelan's pleas for help, Deasy had ordered a column, under Pa Murray, to go to Kilmacthomas. He admitted, however, that he could not afford to send with them more than the 5,000 rounds of ammunition and the grenades he had despatched. Murray's column, however, did not reach Waterford in time. The Republican Intelligence Officer reported on 24 July:

> A Cork Column under P. Murray was delayed deliberately three hours in Dungarvan, on their way to Waterford. When they reached the suburbs... they were not allowed to advance into the city, in spite of the fact that the fight was raging at the time.... All... of the Waterford Bde. consider they have been let down by the O/C and as a result great unrest exists among them.

Whelan complained that the requested machine-guns and ammunition reinforcements had not arrived, and that 'The first column from Cork came up as we were just evacuating, but they didn't want to fight.' The Cork columns retreated to their home base when they saw that the Waterford units were evacuating the city, and Whelan was soon to report on the unauthorised disbandment of some of the Republican IRA battalions in Waterford. Whelan reported to Lynch that

> The Cork column complained of the lack of co-operation by our Bde. and that they had no proper scouts to keep them informed of enemy movements. This meant that the line Mount Congret to Knockeen was vacated. The Cork Columns returning to their Units and the Waterford Column returning to Portlaw and leaving a clear line for the enemy to advance as far as Kilmacthomas.

The projected attack on the pro-Treaty forces from the rear by Dinny Lacey's and Dan Breen's South Tipperary men failed to materialise. South Tipperary columns under Kennedy, Sheehan and Lacey, with one from Cork under Jim Hurley, had advanced through Carrick, Piltown and Mooncoin and had linked up with a hundred men, led by Breen, in Mullinahone. Apparently, however, an unauthorised attack by Michael Sheehan's column on pro-Treaty troops at Mullinavat alerted the enemy to the danger. After the Waterford troops had vacated most of their posts there was little that the South Tipperary columns could do in Co. Waterford, and so their attention switched back to domestic territory. Meanwhile reinforcements, including 500 more rifles, for the Provisional Government troops arrived aboard the *Helga*. The cautious Prout, however, delayed his advance on Carrick and Clonmel.[24]

(f) THE MIDLANDS

The situation for Provisional Government troops in Limerick, and for Mac Eoin's command in Athlone, was made much more difficult by the Republican control of large areas of the midlands. The 1st Eastern and 3rd Southern Divisions had been weakly led and organised by both the Provisional Government army and the Executive IRA. Andy Cooney, who had been the anti-Treaty O/C of the 1st Eastern Division, had despaired of the area and lost touch with it by June. To improve the work of the anti-Treaty forces in the 3rd Southern Division, Seán Moylan was appointed to command it, but he spent very little time there and resigned early in the war. It is not surprising, therefore, that there was little co-ordinated action in these areas at the start of the conflict.

In the first two weeks of the war the Republicans held all the main posts in Offaly. Pro-Treaty sources said that 300 Republican IRA troops were in Birr, based in Crinkle Barracks, and had taken over the railway station and the three hotels in the town. They had also broken the railway line between Birr and Roscrea. In Tullamore Republicans had occupied the jail, constructed a tunnel from the police barracks into Daly's Distillery, and mined the roads out of the town. The position in North Tipperary and Leix at the beginning of July was more confused, with both sides holding positions of strength. Nenagh, the chief town of North Tipperary, was taken by Provisional Government forces on 3 July, as a con-sequence, it appears, of one of their officers being shot. It took an occurrence as serious as this to provoke hostilities. The Republicans decided to pull out of Nenagh and burn the barracks before the pro-Treaty troops arrived in force. Dan Gleeson commented: 'There was no cohesion and no plan of campaign. We had arrived to support Nenagh only to find they were leaving it.' Gleeson also recol-lected: 'We had evacuated Roscrea. . . . After that we were fooling around here and there, not too sure of what action we should take.' Portarlington and Mountmellick were vacated by the pro-Treaty forces so that their position in Nenagh could be reinforced. In the 1st Eastern Division area, Devlin Barracks in Mullingar had been taken by pro-Treaty forces, and the Republican brigade staff there had been captured.[25]

During the first week of the war Mac Eoin made some tentative steps to move from Athlone to deal with the Republican areas between there and Limerick. He took the barracks in Clara, but appears to have moved no further, preoccupied with the major problems his command faced in the west. The initiative for pro-Treaty action in the midlands thereafter came from GHQ in Dublin. Collins ordered columns from Maryborough and Roscrea to move on Tullamore and Birr and clear Offaly of Republican-held barracks. At the same time the new Curragh Command was formed. Before the pro-Treaty forces arrived in Tullamore and Birr the Republicans evacuated them. Walter Mitchell commented: 'We had burned the barracks at Tullamore and retreated from it. Most of the lads seeing we were not prepared to make a stand, dispersed and went home.' Before that the men from the 3rd Southern Division had held these towns with little confidence. Seán Gaynor, who had been in charge at Birr, told Séamus Robinson: 'The situation in this Division is pretty bad. In the fight in Nenagh our men had to retire and now in flying columns. We are very short', he continued, 'of rifles. . . . The sooner you can send us strong reinforcements the better.' Gaynor's appeal to Robinson was unavailing.[26]

Mac Eoin reported to Collins on 31 July: 'In the Midland Divisions all posts and positions of military value are in our hands.' The Republican resort to guerrilla warfare in the midlands provided many problems for the new army, however. Republican columns were particularly active in late July and August in Offaly. Railway, road and telephone communications were frequently broken, and there was an attempt to blow up Birr courthouse. Columns were also active in the Birdhill area of North Tipperary. The worst reverse for pro-Treaty forces in the area came with the Maryborough ambush of 28 July. Two separate columns had been sent by different routes to deal with a reported mine at Tonduff. One of these units was ambushed on their way there; a mine exploded and shots were fired, resulting in the death of Commandant-General McCurtain and Commandant Collison, the chief officers in the Leix–Offaly area, and Captain Gantly. Three others were seriously wounded. The second column of pro-Treaty troops captured twenty-four of the ambushers, and solitary confinement was ordered for the prisoners. Before this incident the conflict in the midlands had taken on the air of shadow-fighting. Walter Mitchell recollected: 'A few weeks after the start of the Civil War, we got orders in our area not to fire upon the Staters. We were to fire over them. . . . They were trying for a truce.' The fatal ambush brought to a head criticism of the performance of pro-Treaty forces in the area.[27]

Collins visited the Curragh Command on 7 August on his way to Limerick. He reported:

> The entire organisation and command is defective and, in my opinion, has been defective from an old date. There is no real grasp either of the actual forces in the area or of what is required to be done by these forces. The general outlook is casual; discipline, I should say, is bad; the officers, while good as individuals, lack any grasp of their duties.

He went on to criticise the lack of sufficient equipment and arms and finally ordered that Commandant-General Price should take charge of the area and make a complete inspection of it. An earlier report of 23 July had noted that O'Connell, the O/C at the Curragh, and McCurtain had little knowledge of their command; it concluded: 'The Command is not working satisfactorily. There is no cohesion, and there can consequently be no co-operation in activities.' There had, moreover, been notorious examples of indiscipline. Some prisoners in Roscrea were found in possession of arms, and as a result of this lapse some of the prison guard were placed under arrest. Some pro-Treaty troops were sentenced to twelve months' imprisonment for stealing supplies of Guinness from a Banagher store. On 9 August Ernie O'Malley wrote: 'The areas in the 1st Midland are weakly held by the enemy. If some of the Western Divisions crossed the Shannon now and again they could help to make things rather hot for the enemy there. The local FS troops are of very poor quality and would be very easy to beat.'

On the Republican side, O'Malley was frequently to complain of his lack of any organisation in the midlands. He commented: 'I cannot get in touch at all with the remnants of the Athlone Brigade', and in September he complained of men from Offaly requesting arms from him independently of their brigade officers. North Tipperary, in common with the south of the county, fought the Civil War on an individual basis, with column leaders acting largely independently of each other. Seán Gaynor recalled: 'Each one of us was to go down and was to fight in his own area.'[28]

(g) THE WEST

A loose pro-Treaty control in the west was only exercised in South Roscommon and parts of Co. Galway. Almost all the IRA in Mayo, Sligo and West Galway had gone anti-Treaty. Liam Lynch had great faith in the prospects for Republican arms in the west, but little knowledge of events there. Ernie O'Malley wrote to Lynch in September: 'Have you sent an Officer to the West? If not, I think it advisable that you should do so; as they are so much out of touch that it is essential that they should be brought into touch with recent developments and thought in the Southern Divs.' Meanwhile Mac Eoin's vast pro-Treaty Athlone Command had responsibility for the entire western area north of Galway and south of Donegal and was frequently to be overstretched. The news of the Four Courts attack caught the anti-Treaty IRA in the west by surprise and produced a divided response from the leadership on the best strategy to be adopted. While Liam Pilkington and the officers of the 4th Western Division advocated a non-aggressive policy towards the Provisional Government and a continued offensive against the North, individual brigade and column leaders, notably Frank Carty in Co. Sligo, urged that hostilities should be started immediately, with a view to moving on Athlone after remaining pro-Treaty centres had been cleared in the west. Tom Carney, the Republican column leader in East Mayo, related: 'When the F Courts was attacked everything was in chaos here ... The night of the Four Courts a Div meeting was held in Sligo ... Carty was fighting on his own for destruction at once but Brian MacNeill was discussing his idea that all available men and arms should march at once on the North. Most of the Divisional officers were in favour of this plan.' Soon Carty was supported by Michael Kilroy, who arrived back in his West Mayo Brigade area from Dublin, and by Carney's East Mayo Brigade. The North Mayo Brigade also supported Carty's offensive policy.

The war for the Republican IRA in the west, as elsewhere, was a matter of individual initiative and local column action. Jim Hunt, of Gorteen, explained: 'You supported a man from your own area'; and Mark Killilea remembered: 'Mick Kilroy always carried his plans in his own head.' Animosities between leaders were carried over from the pre-war period. In Sligo there had been long-term tension between Carty and Pilkington, which had intensified after what Carty regarded as Pilkington's failure to prevent Griffith's Easter meeting in Sligo town. Ernie O'Malley remarked on the tensions within the Republican IRA leadership in the west: 'This explains a good deal of Irish history—the bickering of the chiefs ... and their various allegiances determined by their local enmities.' The failure to co-ordinate policy and to communicate effectively with GHQ ended any hope of an offensive policy being adopted in the west. The conflict in the west was to remain an isolated one.[29]

Conflict started in places like Collooney and Sligo town where isolated pro-Treaty barracks were vulnerable, and at Boyle, which was garrisoned by both sides and represented a gateway to the west from Athlone for Mac Eoin's forces. On 2 July Republican forces attacked the pro-Treaty post in Boyle workhouse, and the ensuing firing resulted in the death of Michael Dockery, the Provisional Government army's O/C there. A protracted struggle for posts in the town continued for the next three days, with an armoured car, the *Ballinalee*, used on the pro-Treaty side. On 5 July the Republicans retreated when Mac Eoin arrived with an eighteen-pound gun, and they quickly formed columns around Ballaghaderreen and Charlestown.

During the first days of the war a military confrontation appeared extremely likely in Sligo town. The pro-Treaty forces held some posts but were considerably outnumbered by the Republicans. Surprisingly, in early July the anti-Treaty forces left the town and burnt the barracks, leaving Mac Eoin, who was there on his unfortunately timed honeymoon, to help put out the fire. Tom Scanlon, of Ballina, commented: 'We wouldn't attack the Free State. Our orders were to evacuate the town and to burn the barracks.' For the rest of July the town was extremely insecurely held; on 11 July pro-Treaty sources complained of their weak position there and the poor arming of their troops. The Republicans occasionally retook posts in the town during the month. On 21 July Commandant Séamus Devins demanded the surrender of the Provisional Government troops in Sligo. Bishop Coyne of Elphin urged the pro-Treaty O/C, Martin Fallon, to comply with the order and, on Fallon's refusal, suggested an exchange of prisoners, which Devins turned down. Again Republicans failed to back up words with actions. Mac Eoin wrote at the time: 'It is very difficult to understand the civilian population of Sligo, as one day they would appear with you and the next day against you.' No doubt, however, the people were understandably very confused.[30]

Republican units had no problem in exercising control over much of Co. Sligo during July. They quickly staged a successful attack on the isolated pro-Treaty post in the Market House at Collooney. Carty claimed that thirty-four prisoners were taken in Collooney with arms. Men from the North and East Mayo Brigades had joined with Carty's Sligo men and attacked from Tobercurry on 1 July. A lorry containing pro-Treaty forces was successfully ambushed at Carrickagat. The Collooney area became the base for Mayo and Sligo Republicans who favoured an aggressive policy. The Mayo brigades , there agreed with Carty to act independently of the division. It was the middle of the month before pro-Treaty forces returned to the Collooney area in any strength, only for them to receive a major reverse at the Rockwood ambush on 13 July, in which five pro-Treaty men were killed, four wounded, and two Crossley cars taken. The prime capture was the *Ballinalee*, which became a major roving weapon for the Republicans. After that reverse Mac Eoin himself took command of a force of 400 which took over Collooney after a four-hour attack and captured some of of Frank O'Beirne's column, along with a claimed seventy prisoners.

After the loss of Collooney, Carty decided that all towns should be evacuated; henceforward the Republicans operated in columns. The war in Co. Sligo, though more intense than in many places, was to conform to the general pattern. Carty admitted that from mid-July there was no large-scale activity for some time and that various planned ambushes did not come off. Meanwhile the pro-Treaty offensive caused the divisional staff to become committed to the war, and the Mayo men in the Collooney area returned to their home areas.[31]

Republican columns in Sligo concentrated from mid-July on three areas. Carty's men continued to be active in the Tobercurry area and to retreat into the Ox Mountains when pressed. Another column, under Ned Bofin, proved active throughout the war in the Arigna district in the hilly north-east. Pilkington's divisional headquarters was at Rahelly House, north of Sligo town, and columns operated in that area.

Meanwhile Michael Kilroy's men controlled West Mayo, Kilroy having insisted on the three columns there coming together. They used the area around Westport as their base. Tom Maguire's columns controlled the Ballinrobe area. There was little combined action, however, and no plans for an offensive policy which went further than the support given to Carty's men on the other side of the Ox Mountains. Tom Maguire commented: 'In the beginning our fellows would not kill the Staters.'[32]

The Provisional Government's resistance to Republican control of much of the west began in earnest with the landing of the Westport expedition on 24 July. It was the first of the major coastal landings of the war and demonstrated doubts about the viability of attempts to occupy enemy territory by using purely land communications. Intelligence reports, based on information gained from priests in West Mayo, had led Mulcahy to believe that Kilroy and Maguire would resist the landing force. The *Minerva* left Dublin on 22 July under Colonel-Commandant O'Malley, carrying 400 men, 600 rifles, one eighteen-pound gun, one armoured car and 150 bicycles. The extra rifles would be given to men recruited after the landing. Initially the landing was delayed as the boat was thought to be too long for disembarkation purposes. GHQ suggested that the landing be at Limerick or Tralee instead, but eventually it was decided to risk the Westport landing. Before the main force disembarked forty men were sent to capture the Rossmoney coast-guard station, where they captured the garrison of eleven men and released forty-eight prisoners, including Commandant Reynolds. The main force occupied Westport unopposed, receiving an enthusiastic response from the residents. Immediately the eighteen-pound gun was recalled for duty elsewhere, but the armoured car was retained. With a garrison left in Westport, the expedition moved on to Castlebar, which had been taken on 25 July by forces under Tony Lawlor, Mac Eoin's second-in-command. Lawlor had earlier led a large force on a long march, which had involved the taking, without fighting, of Castlerea, Ballinrobe, Ballyhaunis, Claremorris and Ballaghaderreen.[33]

The Republicans had retreated from the major towns and headed for suitable guerrilla warfare bases, such as the Ox Mountains. Some were critical of the failure to oppose the pro-Treaty landing. Tommy Heavey, of Ballina, recollected that they had talked for months about the possibility of a landing at Westport, but claimed that Kilroy had been too preoccupied in building up his bomb factory to put up an adequate defence. Meanwhile Clifden was captured by Provisional Government troops on the night of 14-15 August; the Republicans burnt the Marconi station there preparatory to retreating. There was also an abortive attempt by some of Bofin's column in the Arigna area to arrange a truce with Provisional Government forces in Boyle; it led to the arrest of the Republicans involved, on orders soon countermanded by Commandant-General Farrelly. This incident served to harden Republican attitudes, as admitted by the pro-Treaty Intelligence Officer.

After pro-Treaty troops had moved from Castlebar to take Ballina the *Irish Times* enthusiastically reported on 31 July: 'Here in the West the war seems to be over. The capture of Castlebar and Westport, following the swift and sweeping advance of the national forces sealed the fate of the irregulars.' This was to prove a hugely premature judgment. Collins in early August implied that there was still much to be done by his establishment of a new Western Command. He ordered that thirty of the small posts were to be immediately abandoned; twenty-two garrisons and four columns, amounting to 2,100 men, were to remain in the new division. Excess troops were to be ordered back from the west to train at the Curragh. This represented an adjustment to the demands of guerrilla warfare. The problem was not the number of the troops, but their quality and their deployment. Collins stated there were 2,234 troops in the new Western Command area, and Mac Eoin admitted that there were around a thousand men about whose whereabouts he was uncertain. The Western Command remained a vast one, and was still to be controlled from Athlone.

Mulcahy was to be extremely critical of Mac Eoin's slowness to implement Collins's orders following expressions of opposition to the evacuation of small posts by small traders in some towns. Mulcahy stresseed 'We are simply going to break up what we have of an Army if we leave it any longer in small posts, and do not give it proper military training. We are also going to leave it at the mercy of any small band of Irregulars with a "punch" in them.'[34]

(h) DONEGAL

Nowhere was the Civil War a more bitter and forlorn affair than in Co. Donegal. Volunteers from the 1st Southern Division, led by Seán Lehane and Charlie Daly, were still in the county at the start of the conflict, committed to what they thought was still a common policy against the North. There were also IRA units from the west of the Six Counties who had crossed into Donegal to avoid being rounded up.

The attack on the Four Courts depressed and confused the IRA in Donegal; the situation was made worse for them by the fact that Lehane and Daly were in Dublin. Daly reported from the Clarence Hotel:

> The Army question is in a worse mess than ever, and everybody is sick and disgusted. The worst of it is that people on our side have made a muddle of the whole thing. We don't know where we stand at present and so far as we in Donegal are concerned I don't see that we have any business being there any longer. We will probably go back there for a few days to wind up affairs and then go home for some time.

Daly returned to his headquarters at Glenveagh Castle to a highly disorganised situation, while Lehane only got back to his base two weeks after the war had started, having had to walk from Sligo to North Donegal.

While Lehane had been away the pro-Treaty forces had taken over Finner Camp, Ballyshannon and Buncrana, thus clearing routes to the south and ensuring that the Republicans and not themselves would be isolated in the remote north-west. After the pro-Treaty attack on Carndonagh and Buncrana the Republicans retreated to Raphoe; the brigade columns of No. 1 and No. 2 Brigades of the 1st Northern Division were captured. Joe Sweeney, who was in command of the pro-Treaty forces, was clearly unhappy about the prospect of confrontation and hastily arranged a peace meeting with Daly. Sweeney proposed that the southerners in Donegal should be allowed to leave with their arms, but Daly would not agree to prohibiting his men from serving in other parts of the Twenty-Six Counties. Meanwhile O'Duffy laid out plans for rounding up the rest of Donegal. 'Our immediate objective', he reported on 3 July, 'is to surround the stretches of country occupied by the enemy from Glenveagh to Lifford, and from Buncrana to Derry city and drive the enemy into their posts.' O'Duffy hardly needed to add: 'It is not considered necessary to send Artillery to Donegal.' Sweeney did, however, make a strong appeal for the use for a few days of an armoured car.

Charlie Daly's despatches at the time give excellent (and sad) testimony of the impossible position for the Republican forces. Daly reported that his column was hopelessly outnumbered and that the men were living in dreadful conditions:

> The country is so assuredly poor that we could hardly get enough to eat. We were often glad when we could get potatoes and salt, or a bit of bread and a drop of tea.... No matter what side their sympathies were with they were always hospitable.... We held back from taking life as long as we could, although we got plenty of provocation.

On another occasion Daly wrote: 'We had something over 100 men at the start but most of them were very poor stuff.... Some of them were spies and traitors.... In the course of a few weeks we were left with only 30 men and nearly all of them were strangers to the county.' Their only option was to divide into small groups, and to operate in different areas. Daly concluded that: 'We could have got across Donegal Bay into Sligo at any time, but we didn't want to give up here [when] there was the faintest chance of carrying on.' Many, however, were captured, and one of the Cork men, Jack Fitzgerald, recorded his forsaking the unequal struggle and going off to join Ned Bofin's column in the Arigna area of Sligo–Leitrim. Lehane confessed to Daly: 'I believe our work here is impossible. We have to steal about here like criminals at night; and it gets on ones nerves.' He admitted they were 'faking fight'. Lehane was very critical of the poor support he had received from the local people. 'They want money and ease,' he commented.[35]

The decision for all Republican columns to evacuate Donegal was postponed for as long as possible. At the end of July Ernie O'Malley informed Liam Lynch about the situation in Donegal: 'I understand that men are starving and are very much in need of money. I have sent on some.' On 24 September O'Malley reported: 'No local organisation worth speaking of.... There is a small flying column left in the west of the County and another small one of about 5 or 6 men round about Castlefin area.' O'Malley concluded that Lehane's men would be of more use in the fight elsewhere than clinging on for mere survival in Donegal.

Eventually, early in November, Lehane was ordered by O'Malley to abandon Donegal. Before that Daly had been arrested, together with his small column. His execution in March 1923 at Drumboe Castle, together with Tim O'Sullivan, Seán Larkin and Dan Enright, was a terrible postscript to the combined Northern policy.[36]

(i) CORK

Cork Republican IRA men very reluctantly entered the war and showed little commitment during it. P. J. McHugh commented: 'The Cork men had no interest in the Civil War', and Florrie Begley declared: 'We had no heart in the Civil War.... When the attack on the Four Courts was over the fight should have stopped.' Many Cork veterans of the period confirmed that they had only entered the war because the news from Dublin had forced their hand. Liam Lynch stressed on 1 September 1922: 'The remainder of the country I am sure looks to the 1st Southern for a lead.' If Cork had played the crucial role during the Anglo-Irish war, its failure to fight in earnest during the Civil War was just as important.

In early July, after a three-day confrontation, the one remaining pro-Treaty post in Cork was taken at Skibbereen. Many anti-Treaty Cork IRA men were involved in the frustrating occupation of Limerick and the Kilmallock area, and also in the abortive attempt to prevent the fall of Waterford city. Many were exhausted by the time they were suddenly recalled to deal with the Provisional Government landings in their own territory. Jamie Managhan, of Ballyvourney, confirmed that their men who had been in Limerick 'were completely demoralised'.[37]

During the Republican occupation of Cork customs money was appropriated, and the *Cork Examiner* was taken over and edited by Frank Gallagher. The Ford factory, however, was left untouched. Republican leaders frequently warned of the threat of coastal landings, and mines were laid at various potential landing places. Eamon Enright, of Cork No. 1 Brigade, commented: 'We had a huge area and a wide perimeter, too wide to be adequately held.' A Treaty supporter in Cork city reported that the Upper Harbour was mined up to Passage West, but did not think the Republicans would defend the city once attacked. He also commented that the best anti-Treaty forces were involved elsewhere, and that only inexperienced, less committed men remained in the city. The writer concluded: 'The tactics in Cork and Kerry will be most likely guerrilla tactics. There will be no fighting on a big scale, consequently a concentration in Cork city is unlikely.'[38]

The idea of coastal landings was Emmet Dalton's. He took charge of the expedition to Cork aboard the *Arvonia*, which had been commandeered for the purpose, and sailed on 7 August. Two other ships set sail for Union Hall and Youghal. An armoured car and an eighteen-pound gun were part of the equipment carried. Five hundred men, most of them raw recruits, went with Dalton to Cork; the Union Hall party consisted of 180 men, that to Youghal of 200. Dalton's landings policy involved enormous risks. Michael Hayes, the Ceann Comhairle (Speaker) of the Dáil, told Mulcahy that Dalton took Cork by breaking 'all the rules of common sense and navigation and military science'. Frank O'Connor pointed out: 'Technically, a landing from the sea is supposed to be one of the most difficult of military operations, but as we handled the defence it was a walk-over.' Dalton admitted that he had no detailed knowledge of the coast, and that the disembarkation of a large force in hostile territory is extremely difficult.

Originally Collins had pressed the British government to hand over forts held by them under the terms of the Treaty. When this request was refused it was decided to make the landing close to the city at Passage West.

The commander of British naval forces in the area, H. C. Somerville, admitted that he aided the Cork landing by informing Dalton of the position of mines in the approach to Passage West. Dalton found it necessary to point a gun at the ship's captain to ensure that the landing went ahead. As at Youghal and Union Hall, the landing was virtually unopposed. The Republican garrisons in the vicinity had been caught unprepared while men who had been involved in Limerick and Waterford were in the process of returning. Tom Crofts recalled: ' The lads at Passage had been line fighting for weeks and they had been brought back there without sleep. There was very little opposition to the Free State. . . . The bulk of the men were in Kilmallock and they were our best men.' Mick Leahy admitted that the 'poorest type of our men [were] there to oppose the landing', and Donald Barrett, of Cork No. 1 Brigade, said: 'The Staters were not expected so soon and there was a panic.' Dan ('Sandow') O'Donovan claimed that they had identified Passage as the likely landing place, but that their men were asleep when the pro-Treaty forces landed. The tone of Liam Lynch's correspondence at the time, and the fact that the advance of Dalton's men into Cork was strongly contested at Rochestown and Douglas, indicates that there was no preconceived plan to evacuate the city. Lynch told O'Malley: 'Bodies of our troops have been rushed to these places to delay and contest their advances.'[39]

The resistance at Rochestown and Douglas came from men returning from Limerick and from Mick Murphy's men, who had hastily come back from Waterford. 'I commandeered a train', Murphy recalled, 'and we brought the train back to Cork. . . . We threw our crowd in front of the Staters but we couldn't stem them. We had about 80 men.' Murphy's men put up considerable resistance at Douglas, but were ordered back to Ballincollig, on the other side of the city, by Tom Crofts. Eight pro-Treaty soldiers were reported killed during the fighting, which went on for three days.

After Douglas there were no more problems for the Provisional Government troops on their way into Cork city. Meanwhile the Republican forces, in extreme and confused haste, evacuated the city, hardly having time for the obligatory burning of barracks. It appears that the decision to retreat was taken at virtually the last possible moment. Republican units dispersed in a highly improvised fashion towards Macroom. While the decision to evacuate preserved Republican strength intact by avoiding a confrontation with pro-Treaty artillery, it represented an unheroic defeat. Pa Murray, one of the most effective of Cork column leaders, commented: 'When we left Cork City I thought the whole thing was finished.' He told Liam Lynch that this was the time to end the war. The evacuation represented the culmination of the Republican defensive policy since the Four Courts attack. Dalton reported:

> It is hard to credit the extent of the disorder and disorganisation that was displayed in the retreat. The amount of damage done to the city by mines and fires is not really as bad as it seems, because most of the positions that were destroyed have little value other than as military positions.[40]

Following the enthusiastic reception given them in Cork city, Dalton split up his forces and ordered a clearing up of routes to the north and west. They had no need to fight as Buttevant and Fermoy, the Republican centres on the road to the north, were evacuated, and in the west Macroom, Bantry, Clonakilty, Inchigeelagh and Kinsale were soon taken. The *Irish Times*'s special correspondent reported on 16 August: 'The advance is becoming swift, but the retreat, or, as I should prefer to call it, the disappearance, is swifter. Of the thousands of irregulars who occupied Cork County a month ago, there is no trace.' Dalton had originally expected that the Republicans would hold a line in the north of the county, but it soon became clear that the evacuation of towns in Cork had led to the adoption of guerrilla warfare tactics. A general report on 22 August commented:

> The Irregulars in Cork and Kerry are still more or less intact. Our forces have captured towns, but they have not captured Irregulars and arms on

anything like a large scale, and, until this is done, the Irregulars will be capable of guerrilla warfare.... Our present dispositions leave us particularly exposed to guerrilla warfare.... Our forces are scattered all over the Command area.... It is easy to isolate our posts.

Nevertheless, the retreat of the Republicans into the mountain fastnesses had a demoralising effect on their morale. Many gave up the armed struggle at that time: some temporarily, some for good. Liam Deasy admitted: 'Many of the men just returned to their homes.' Seán O'Faolain, who was among those who evacuated Cork city, wrote that it 'left us under no illusions as to the army's capacity to form another line of battle, and ... there was nothing left for the majority of them to do but to scatter, go into hiding, slip back at night into the city like winter foxes'.[41]

(j) KERRY

Kerry was to prove the most difficult of the counties for the Provisional Government to establish its authority over during the Civil War. The vast coastline and mountain fastnesses made Kerry extremely difficult to control. At the beginning of the conflict, however, developments took on a similar pattern to those elsewhere. The Kerry IRA, in common with the rest of the 1st Southern Division, had supported the army unity talks of April to June 1922; while the huge majority had gone anti-Treaty, personal divisions continued to cause problems. Humphrey Murphy, who had only recently taken over as O/C Kerry No. 1 Brigade, still had difficulty dealing with Paddy Cahill's supporters around Tralee. In July a new battalion, under Cahill, was formed; on 13 July Murphy reported to Cahill: 'The Division does not approve of the formation of a new Battalion in Tralee District.' To start with, Kerry showed as little enthusiasm and preparedness for the conflict as other areas. Murphy wrote: 'I have offered Tadhg Brosnan Vice O/C ship of Brigade and he has refused to accept as he says he is most needed in his own Battalion Area [based on Castlegregory on the Dingle peninsula] where, when he came back from Cork, he found only ten who were willing to fight the Free Staters.'

Pro-Treaty military support at the beginning of the war centred on Listowel, where Provisional Government troops occupied the workhouse. On hearing of the Four Courts attack, men from Kerry No. 1 and No. 2 Brigades immediately moved on Listowel. A small fight on 29 June resulted in the surrender of pro-Treaty troops with their rifles and Lewis guns; local priests expedited the surrender. Johnny Connors, one of the Kerry No. 1 officers, commented: 'We just opened fire and they surrendered.' The Republican forces then moved on through Abbeyfeale, Newcastle West and Rathkeale to augment the Republican presence in Limerick city. John Joe Rice, the O/C of Kerry No. 2, said of the Rathkeale capture: 'There was no fight for there was no one to fight, for all the F/S had gone to Limerick.'[42]

Kerry men were to be active in the struggle for the Kilmallock area and in some of the Tipperary fighting. Their reaction to the evacuation of Limerick city was as bitter as that of the Cork men. Tom McEllistrim, the O/C of a Kerry column in Limerick city, recalled: 'The fellows were fed up. "What's the use of carrying on a fight when we ran away in Limerick" they said. I knew the war was over when we left Limerick.' At the time when the most active Kerry Republicans were involved in Co. Limerick the Provisional Government forces embarked on their policy of bringing in troops by sea.

On 15 July Paddy Cahill had warned Murphy of the danger of coastal landings. 'A landing of troops may not be so far-fetched especially if the Free State troops are strong at Limerick, and I need not remind you that Fenit, Dingle and Tarbert are likely places.' While a section of O'Duffy's men were clearing the region between Limerick and the North Kerry border General Paddy Daly landed at Fenit on 2 August with 500 men. Only some of Cahill's battalion showed any resistance. Many criticised the failure to mine the pier at Fenit. By that time the Kerry Republicans in Co. Limerick were hurrying back in a disorganised state. P. J. McHugh, a Cork man with the Kerry columns, said: 'They were at 6's and 7's planning away all of them, but nothing was being done. I was with John Joe Sheehy and with Humphrey Murphy, and we finally retreated having done nothing.... There was no attempt made to prevent a landing in Kerry.' Soon after, another landing, consisting of a smaller force of 240 men from the 1st Western Division, arrived at Tarbert and moved through Ballylongford and Listowel, garrisoning them on the way through, to link up without any problems with the Tralee force.[43]

There should have been many dangers involved in landing isolated forces on different parts of the coast, but the Republican IRA was in no state to resist effectively. Daly had encountered some opposition at Sammy's Rock on the way into Tralee. Problems were encountered also with Johnny Connors's recently returned men when Daly's men moved on Farranfore, south of Tralee. The total pro-Treaty casualties in these operations were eleven dead and 114 wounded. Connors recalled his own experience when he returned to the Tralee area: 'I went on', he said, 'by train to Ballymullen to find our men there in the greatest state of funk and disorganisation I ever saw high-ranking officers.' Connors was told by Murphy to draw back from an engagement with invading forces. 'There was no plan', he commented, 'just a firing of ammunition.' Following that, the Kerry units returned to their own areas and regrouped for a form of fighting for which they were much better suited.

On 11 August another sea expedition took Kenmare. The 200-strong expedition was under Commandant Scarteen O'Connor, one of the very few officers from the South Kerry area who had gone pro-Treaty. They were allowed to land unopposed, despite the Republican presence around the town and in the coastguard station. Rathmore and Millstreet were taken after the Kenmare landing, and O'Connor sent 100 men on to occupy Valencia and Cahirciveen, with the additional object there of making the transatlantic cable safe. Daly had advanced on Killarney and Killorglin at the same time as O'Connor's landing. By mid-August the pro-Treaty troops had occupied the main centres of population in Kerry. The war, however, was only beginning in the regions controlled by the Kerry No. 1 and No. 2 Brigades.[44]

(k) SOUTH TIPPERARY

It was clear at the start of the Civil War that the 2nd Southern Division, and particularly the No. 3 Brigade area in South Tipperary, would prove a major problem for the Provisional Government forces. The area was almost completely held by the Republican IRA; it provided the most formidable barrier against any pro-Treaty advance into the rest of Munster and was an obvious threat to the Provisional Government posts in Kilkenny. There was considerable potential for Tipperary Republican columns taking the initiative, but in fact that never occurred.

The lack of unity within the division and the failure to co-operate with other areas proved as evident during the Civil War as it had in the Anglo-Irish War. Seán Fitzpatrick commented that his Tipperary No. 3 Brigade was 'a little Republic of its own' and that the O/C, Dinny Lacey, was not on speaking terms with the divisional O/C, Séamus Robinson, during the early part of the war and refused to take orders from him. Two of Lacey's battalions refused to co-operate with him. Around his Nine-Mile House base Dan Breen showed characteristic independence of spirit. Nobody, it appears, took much account of any instructions from Liam Lynch, and the position was further complicated during July when prominent Republicans, including de Valera and Childers, arrived in Clonmel. As early as 10 July Lynch complained of the lack of organisation in the 2nd Southern Division; the war remained there a matter of every column for itself. Beneath the chaos and all the stories of near confrontations, the South Tipperary Republicans showed an extreme reluctance to engage in armed conflict.[45]

At the start of the war Thurles, held by Jerry Ryan's isolated pro-Treaty troops, became an obvious target for Republican forces. In order to secure a base for an attack, Lacey's column took Urlingford barracks, in Co. Kilkenny, without difficulty, but some of his men were ambushed outside Mary Willie's public house shortly after, and two of them were killed. At that time Liam Lynch was optimistic about the prospects of taking Thurles and Kilkenny town, which, he argued, the truce in Limerick made possible. Ryan, in Thurles, desperately asked for reinforcements from Kilkenny. The Thurles, attack, however, failed, apparently because of the lack of a genuine offensive commitment. Meanwhile Republican forces decided to evacuate Templemore barracks, the third largest in Ireland.

By the time pro-Treaty forces were assembled for the Waterford expedition the opportunity for a Republican offensive had been lost. Mick Sheehan's column returned to South Tipperary from their exhausting and frustrating time in Blessington and Wexford, and Lacey's and Breen's columns were clearly happiest in their own areas. There was no chance for Séamus Robinson to put into practice his view that an advance should immediately be made on Dublin. South Tipperary columns played a role in hindering the pro-Treaty advance on Waterford, but avoided any major confrontation. Lacey, who had been in charge of the columns during the attempted Waterford defence, retreated to Carrick-on-Suir as his base, with Breen's column holding part of the area between there and Waterford city.[46]

During July the leading towns in South Tipperary, most notably Carrick-on-Suir and Clonmel, were strongly held by the Republicans. De Valera was active in both these towns as Director of Operations for the 2nd Southern Division. There was a considerable amount of commandeering: over £20,000 was reported to have been seized from Clonmel barracks during the occupation, and 100,000 gallons of petrol was estimated to have been taken. Whiskey, commandeered from bonded stores, was sold by the Republicans. Séamus Robinson issued a general circular that all arms and lorries should be seized. A circular of 15 July from the South

Tipperary Brigade, urging the need not to antagonise the local population, demonstrated Lacey's awareness of how unpopular they might become, as did the reprimand he gave to Cork men in the area for looting in Ballingarry. The burning of local creameries in the area caused particularly strong and widespread hostility. Different attitudes were taken by Robinson and Lacey to the co-operative creamery in Tipperary town—which flew a red flag during the Republican occupation; Paddy O'Halloran, of the South Tipperary Brigade, asserted that its burning at the time of the evacuation 'ruined us in the locality'.

Despite the extent of their occupation, the Republicans became increasingly insecure. Both Clonmel and Cashel were evacuated, and the barracks partly burnt, when inaccurate rumours of the Provisional Government army's approach circulated. The final decision to evacuate both Carrick and Clonmel appears to have been made only at the last moment; there was little attempt to make a stand.

The Republican occupation became more unpopular as pro-Treaty forces neared the various towns. The local townspeople demonstrated against the destruction of the old bridge at Carrick, and numerous other bridges in the area were broken up in early August.[47]

The pro-Treaty advance on South Tipperary came from both Limerick and Waterford. With a view to an eventual advance on Clonmel from the north, a force led by Jerry Ryan moved from Templemore; it consisted of 250 men of the Dublin Guard and 100 Tipperary men. Ryan's men successfully surprised Republican forces in Golden on 26 July. Three days later there was an unsuccessful attempt by Republicans, estimated as numbering 400, to retake the village. Their columns, however, advancing from three directions, failed to synchronise their movements; furthermore, they jammed a Lancia car on a bridge, were fired on by a Provisional Government field gun, and, to conclude the sorry story, one column from Cashel marched straight into a position held by pro-Treaty troops, and twenty-six of them were arrested. Following the Golden incidents, some of the pro-Treaty force, under Paddy O'Connor, made a daring and successful attack on Tipperary town—a rare example of Provisional Government troops attacking without the use of artillery, armoured car or machine-guns. After two days of fighting the Republicans evacuated the town and retreated to the Clonmel area.[48]

After taking Waterford, Prout's troops had been ordered to move quickly on Carrick-on-Suir. Prout, however, delayed his advance and started out on 24 July. Prout's force consisted of 600 men, armed with field pieces, trench mortars and machine-guns. At the same time a detachment under Commandant McCarthy set out from Kilkenny to clear up the Callan and Mullinahone area before joining up with Prout in Carrick.

Advance intelligence had told Prout of the activity of Dan Breen's column, estimated at 200, though more probably about seventy, in the Mooncoin and Windgap area, and the blocking of roads between Fethard and Carrick. The same sources estimated the number of Republican troops in Carrick as 400. Prout's appeals for more arms and his cautious advance suggest considerable apprehension. Lacey soon ordered his columns, numbering 100 men, and Breen's to withdraw from Piltown back to the Three Bridges area, where the pro-Treaty troop advance into Carrick was strongly contested. Fighting began on 2 August on a semi-circular front following the bend of the river and in heavily wooded country. The Republicans used Killorney House, the home of a Carrick businessman, as their base, but were eventually driven out of the area by artillery and machine-gun fire, following the turning of Lacey's right front. They fled across the Suir to the Kilmacthomas area, allowing the Provisional Government troops to make an uncontested and popularly received entry into Carrick on 3 August. Prout's units were joined there four hours later by McCarthy's men, who had encountered some resistance in the Windgap area. On 4 August Cashel was evacuated by the Republicans.

The pro-Treaty force, having gathered a considerable crop of recruits in Carrick, left for Clonmel in two columns on 8 August. They advanced to the north by Ballykeale and Ballypatrick because the main road was mined. Again Lacey's columns were involved in delaying actions at Kilcash and Ballypatrick, while Breen's men operated from the slopes of Slievenamon. The final resistance was made on 9 August at Redmondstown, when once again the use of the eighteen-pounder was needed to cause the Republican columns to fall back towards the Nire valley. Clonmel was entered on the evening of 9 August. The *Irish Times* commented: 'With Clonmel in the hands of the national troops, it is now only a matter of days until the activities of the irregulars throughout the County Tipperary are brought to an end.' However, although Cahir and Fethard were soon occupied, which meant all the towns in Tipperary had been evacuated, this was a grossly optimistic judgment. After the Redmondstown resistance Lacey ordered the adoption of guerrilla warfare tactics—each column was to fight in its own area. Some observers thought the Republican columns in Tipperary might fall back on Cork and make a stand there—a view that overrated both their desire to fight and their willingness to leave their own areas and co-operate with other units. Liam Lynch reported to Ernie O'Malley on 9 August: 'Since yesterday all the 2nd Southern Division forces have been ordered to form into Columns, and while contesting the enemy advance they are also to operate on his rear. All the Barracks in this area have been destroyed. Clonmel was burned this morning.'

A mere six prisoners had been taken by pro-Treaty troops on the advance into Clonmel. The South Tipperary columns survived largely intact for the guerrilla war stage of the conflict. The clumsy evacuation of the South Tipperary towns had hardly raised Republican morale, however. Liam Deasy concluded of the defence of Carrick and Clonmel that it was 'to say the least, weak but let me hasten to add that not one area in Munster at that time could boast that their campaign was anything better'.[49]

(1) THE 4th NORTHERN DIVISION

The chaos and confusion of the early Civil War is nowhere better illustrated than in the 4th Northern Division. In terms of men and arms, no division of the anti-Treaty IRA outside Munster was better placed to adopt an offensive policy against the Provisional Government. Tod Andrews reported that 'From what Aiken says the position of this area from the point of view of arms, equipment, and men and moral support, is as good as any in Ireland.' Aiken's retaking of Dundalk and its large military barracks on 14 August 1922 represented one of the major Republican coups of the war. The division, however, remained neutral for over two months, and never was to play an important role in the Republican effort.

Between the Treaty and the Four Courts attack Aiken had striven to remain aloof from the developing split and to concentrate on the Northern question. After the start of the war Aiken was very critical of the Republican tactics, but hoped that a compromise could be achieved by amendment of the constitution, and by the meeting of a new Army Convention. A meeting of the division at the end of June supported this policy, an on 6 July Aiken wrote to Mulcahy urging a truce. While Mulcahy could not satisfy his wishes, he gave Aiken safe passage to enable him to see Liam Lynch in Limerick. Aiken recalled telling Mulcahy that

> if ordered, I would not attack the Executive forces, but, on the other hand, I thought the Executive should quit, and if I had to leave his army I would not fight him, because the fight would only ruin the country without gaining any ground for the Republic. When leaving him I said I would try and get Comdt. Gen. Lynch to quit.[50]

While Mulcahy clearly had some sympathy with Aiken's peripatetic peace efforts, O'Duffy had long had a testy relationship with Aiken, and in the spring had tried to arrange for pro-Treaty troops to take over barracks in Dundalk held by McKenna's local brigade which supported the anti-Treaty IRA but accepted Aiken's authority. On 7 July O'Duffy ordered Johnny McNoy, who was in command during Aiken's absence, to take over two barracks in Dundalk. O'Duffy also ordered that Northern Unionist hostages, still held in Dundalk, be released.[51]

A meeting of the division's staff on 15 July reaffirmed their neutrality and ordered that all arms should be concealed with a view to being used, in future more favourable circumstances, in a Northern attack. To press that policy, Aiken, with members of his staff, revisited Mulcahy in Dublin, who promised to circulate their views to other members of the government. On his return to Dundalk, Aiken and 300 others were captured by Provisional Government troops who had managed to gain entry into the barracks. Aiken recorded in disgust:

> At 5.30 on the morning of the 16th I awoke with two Thompsons at my nose. An officer who had been reduced for inefficiency, some men who were under arrest for drunkenness, opened the gates and so—Brilliant Victory of National Army! 300 Irregulars arrested! Not a shot fired!

Aiken demanded parole to see Mulcahy and told him that he could not sign a document pledging his division to refrain in future from any attack on property or government forces. Mulcahy replied that he could not order their release, but would change their status from prisoners to that of 'confined to barracks'.

Dan Hogan, the O/C of the 5th Northern Division, had acted on his own initiative in capturing the Dundalk barracks. When Aiken was refused, on 18 July, parole for himself and his men, Mulcahy commented at the bottom of Aiken's letter of protest: 'What exactly is charge against A . . . Who are the officers with him and what are the charges against them?' While Mulcahy appeared prepared to allow Aiken his neutrality, O'Duffy wished to force his hand. Aiken was left to ponder the difference between Dick Mulcahy, his old colleague, and Richard Mulcahy, the Minister for Defence, and concluded: 'Its quite plain to me that there's somebody wants to goad our Division into resistance.'[52]

On 27 July Aiken and his colleagues escaped after the walls of Dundalk prison were successfully mined. Soon after that, Ernie O'Malley sent Tod Andrews, his young organiser, to the Dundalk area to try to ascertain Aiken's position. While

Aiken reluctantly allowed Andrews to join him in the attack on Dundalk barracks. Andrews did not return with any assurance of intent from Aiken to join the Republican side.[53]

Three hundred Republicans were estimated to have been involved in the attack on Dundalk barracks on 14 August. McKenna's men joined in, McKenna himself being killed in the action. Two mines were used, and it was claimed that 400 rifles were taken, amongst considerable numbers of other arms. It was reported that four died and fifteen were wounded on the pro-Treaty side, while on the Republican side two were killed and thirty wounded. Two hundred and forty Republican prisoners were set free. As in the case of all such Republican successes, the taking of Dundalk did not provide a base for further positive developments. The released prisoners went back to their different areas, though some were recaptured on the way. Aiken called for a truce at a meeting in the town square. Three days later Hogan's forces recaptured Dundalk without difficulty—they had correctly anticipated that Aiken had no intention of holding the town. Aiken's men split up into columns in order to operate in the mountainous border areas.[54]

By September Aiken's hand had been forced. His eventual adherence to the Republican side, however, had more to do with Provisional Government intransigence than his own desires. Aiken showed unwillingness to take charge of a new integrated 4th and 5th Northern Division command, and Lynch and O'Malley were critical of Aiken's defensive outlook, particularly as they were aware of the amount of arms and ammunition he had captured at Dundalk. On 3 September O'Malley wrote to Lynch that Aiken

> seems to be pressed in against the Border between F.S. and Specials and his policy seemingly is to allow things to quieten down in the North Louth area so that he can again resume the offensive when things are quiet—this, I think, is a mistaken policy... as it would be much better... if he supplied technical assistance to Brigades in Monaghan and Cavan and hold up the pressure in Louth County.

Given Aiken's acute pessimism concerning the war's prospects and purpose, his cautious policy was scarcely surprising.[55]

The Opening of the Guerrilla Phase
of the War

ON 5 August Collins sent Cosgrave a highly optimistic memorandum on the general military situation. He claimed that despite the activity of localised columns in the west, no 'definite military problem' confronted them outside the 1st Southern Division area. If it had not been for Munster, he argued, the Dáil could have been summoned 'and the questions of Police, Courts, and the necessary punishments for people found guilty of breaking Railways, cutting telegraph wires, looting, carrying arms unauthorisedly, etc. settled. The Army would simply then have to co-operate with the Police, and would be able effectively to do this.' As for the south, Collins asserted:

> The immediate military problem that confronts us is not so much the military defeat of the Irregulars... as the establishing of our forces in certain principal points... with a view to shaking the domination held over the ordinary people by the Irregulars. The establishing of ourselves in a few more of these positions would mean the resurgence of the people from their present cowed condition, and the realisation by the Irregulars that they had lost their grip on the people and that they could not hope to last. An immediate demoralisation of the Irregular rank and file would be the result.

The special correspondent of the *Irish Times*, one of the journalists then allowed to travel with the troops in the south-west, wrote on 15 August that if the pro-Treaty forces moved quickly, the war should have been over in three weeks.

Such hopes, however, were to be disappointed. It soon became apparent that the Provisional Government army had only superficial control over large areas. Mulcahy's stated policy of preventing 'enemy troops evacuating Barracks in possession of Rifles and Ammunition and reverting to guerrilla warfare' had failed. O'Duffy admitted on 22 August that although the Republicans had been driven from their bases, they were still 'more or less intact' in Cork and Kerry. 'Our forces', he affirmed, 'have captured towns, but they have not captured Irregulars and arms on anything like a large scale.' Guerrilla warfare tactics were to prove much more difficult to deal with than the Republicans' ineffective hold on the towns had been.

Con Moloney, the Republican IRA's Adjutant-General, on 19 August issued an operation order stating: 'Owing to the attacks of the enemy in superior numbers, our troops will now be formed into Active Service Units and will operate in the open. ... Where possible also, a small A.S. Unit shall be formed in each town, the men to be armed generally with small arms and bombs.' Deasy and Moloney laid down that the emphasis should be on small columns, the minimum number of each unit not exceeding thirty-five men. This, it was argued, would lead to easier direction, facilitate the finding of accommodation, and lessen the danger of large-scale losses. The columns were to obstruct communications and to attack isolated posts and enemy forces when they left their bases. Deasy declared that 'only the very best and most experienced men' were to join the columns, men 'whose record in the late War with the English was such that absolute reliance can be placed on them'. The instructions implied that many of the remainder were to be released from active service; already, however, many had taken that decision for themselves.[1]

By early September various pro-Treaty sources admitted that guerrilla warfare tactics were proving successful. In many areas Provisional Government troops controlled little more than the towns, and large-scale sweeps of Republican mountain fastnesses had little effect. Republican raids on towns were frequent, and the interference with communications threatened to undermine confidence in the Provisional Government's stability.

Between September and December a kind of military stalemate existed. Republican successes were limited, and even these were not followed up. The lack of observable progress, however, reflected badly on the government. The special correspondent of the *Irish Times*, Theodore Kingsmill Moore, wrote from Limerick on 20 September: 'Ever since the radical change in strategy made by the irregulars in August it has been increasingly difficult for the national Army to strike any blow of immediate effect.' Unless there was to be a quick improvement in the Provisional Government army and an increase in its size, Kingsmill Moore feared that there was to be a long, protracted conflict.

The slow progress must be related to the failings of the Provisional Government army. Even a well-disciplined and trained army would have faced major problems dealing with guerrilla warfare. The pro-Treaty troops were looked upon as outsiders in many localities and rapidly lost any initial popularity when bills were not paid and they appeared to be living off the locality. Sympathy could easily swing back to local Republicans. The army acted as the only police and law-enforcement agency in many areas, though it was extremely ill-equipped to do so. Had it been a more effective force, it might well have decisively moved against the remnants of the Republican units before guerrilla resistance had intensified and become more effective.

Provisional Government army sources were prone to exaggerate the effectiveness of Republican tactics and the coherence of their planning. Emmet Dalton wrote of the improved Republican resistance he had come up against in Cork:

> Seeing how unwieldy their big numbers were they split into three Categories — 'X', 'Y', and 'Z'. They collected all arms and munitions for redistribution, they selected their best fighting men, placed them in 'X' Class, armed them very well, appointed good Officers, split them into Columns of from 10 to 30 and gave them definite Areas in which to operate. They put their next best men in 'Y' class, disarmed most of them, sent them back to their own Areas, instructed them to organise, do Intelligence work, destroy Roads and Railways, keep up odd sniping operations and always be in a position to co-operate with Flying Columns entering their Areas. The men

whom they placed in 'Z' Class were of the poorest type, and for whom they had little use, they disarmed them and told them to go home, take up civil employment and be ready to be mobilised again at any time.

In September Dalton argued that, as a result of such reorganisation, the Republicans had regained the offensive in Cork.

They have now adopted [he wrote] a type of warfare, of which they have years of experience. They now operate over territory which they know. They are now better armed and better trained than they were against the British. In short, they have placed me and my Troops in the same position as the British were a little over a year ago.

Dalton's account represented a far too clear-cut picture. Republican actions were determined more by necessity than by conscious planning. The units were, in most localities, considerably better armed than at the end of the Anglo-Irish War, but did not have the same commitment or motivation or level of popular support as then.

General orders counted for little when related to harsh local circumstances. Special service appointments went frequently unfilled. Deasy wrote on 13 September to brigade O/Cs in his 1st Southern Division: 'There are indications that in many instances A.S.U.s are not properly staffed, receive no regular directions, are not supplied with the necessary local or other intelligence, carry out no systematic method of attempted ambushes, or other forms of attack.' Reports from the west and other areas were rarely received on a monthly, let alone a daily basis as Lynch had required. Frequently the Republican GHQ remained in ignorance of developments in localities, and it seems the location of GHQ itself was unknown to most Republicans. In such circumstances much continued to depend on local initiative. There is rarely any evidence of Republican local units responding to central direction, either from their division or GHQ, and the vexed problem of communication between fighting units in a guerrilla war was never resolved. Little attempt was made to aid weaker areas; for example, despite Deasy's and Lynch's urgings, arms dumped in Cork were not sent to the 1st Western Division.

For all the explicitness of Deasy's and Moloney's orders on the size and make-up of columns, the numbers and character of the units varied greatly. In the autumn the adjutant of the 1st Southern Division argued that small battalion columns had proved ineffective, and a large divisional column was established for a brief period. In most cases the fighting units became progressively smaller. When he went to investigate the situation in Mid-Tipperary, Deasy observed: 'I found it consisted of Paddy Leahy and a few individuals: no organisation left but a few individuals who were doing their best.'

Within the ranks of the Republican IRA there were many critics of the small-column policy adopted. O'Malley thought that large-scale confrontations and the taking of large posts would have been of much greater publicity value; the temporary capture of small posts in the south and west had little overall military significance. Tom Barry was to hold much the same opinion. David Robinson, commenting on the failure to follow up the capture of Kenmare, claimed that it resulted from 'a growing disinclination to take chances, essential in fighting of this kind, which was the inevitable result of long weeks of inaction between ... attacks, always fatal to guerrilla troops'.

Many Republicans embarked on the guerrilla stage of the conflict with little hope of success; in Cork, for example, several of the leaders felt that an end should have been called after the fall of Cork city. In large areas, much of the midlands for instance, the guerrilla phase of the war hardly existed. Column activity was most widespread and effective in remote areas, often in mountainous regions difficult of access, such as South Kerry and West Mayo, where central government authority was most difficult to establish, and where much of the community had a vested interest in the non-functioning of that government. In fertile, prosperous and more central regions, by contrast, guerrilla activities were bound to alienate public sympathy. With no prospect of military victory, and with men in columns often having to live in the most uncomfortable conditions in mountain retreats and dugouts, the highest premium was placed on determination and loyalty. These qualities were not to be as forthcoming in the Civil War as they had been in the Anglo-Irish War.

There were major Republican successes, notably the capture of Kenmare on 9 September, and Ballina three days later. They had the consequence of undermining public confidence in the Provisional Government army at the time when the Third Dáil was about to assemble; in addition, they produced large arms hauls and confidence boosts for the Republican side. Such successes, however, were not followed up, and a number of other attacks on, for example, Killorglin, Macroom, Newcastle West and Bandon ended in failure. The greatest Republican success, however, occurred on 22 August at Béal na mBláth in West Cork in an incident which continues to plague the Irish historical memory.[2]

The Death of Collins

MICHAEL Collins, with a convoy of troops, left on an inspection tour of the South-Western Command on 11 August. His journey was interrupted when he returned to Dublin to attend Griffith's funeral on 16 August. Before Collins recommenced his tour by journeying to Cork city on 20 August many commented on how ill and depressed he appeared.

Collins's correspondence with Cosgrave from Cork and his personal notebooks demonstrate his concern about the restoration of civil government and the necessity to terminate the operation of Republican bank accounts. It appears strange, however, that Collins should risk a journey to one of the strongest areas of Republican resistance. Such a visit could surely have been left to other, less vital men. Before he left for Cork both Joe Sweeney and Joe McGrath had urged Collins not to go there. Plentiful oral evidence suggests that Collins's visit had other purposes. Before leaving, Collins had sent Frank Thornton on ahead to arrange for safe-conducts to be granted for Deasy, Lacey and Breen, among others, to see Collins. Thornton, however, was badly wounded in an ambush outside Clonmel before he could make any arrangements. Some Republicans, including de Valera himself, believed that Thornton had been sent down to kill de Valera. Séamus Robinson recorded that he had been approached about arranging a meeting between Collins and Deasy, and Thomas Malone, of East Limerick, claimed that Collins had approached him in Maryborough jail suggesting a peace meeting with himself, Tom Hales and Tom Barry. While in Cork Collins met with Seán Hegarty and Florrie O'Donoghue, who were potential mediators between the two sides. Liam Deasy told Ernie O'Malley that Collins 'saw Seán Hegarty and Florrie the night before he was killed' and was to have met Deasy himself on the following evening. O'Donoghue related that he met Collins on the 22nd. At the same time as Collins was travelling through West Cork, de Valera was meeting Deasy near Béal na mBláth and urging peace negotiations. There is no evidence, however, that there was any prospect of a meeting between de Valera and Collins.[1]

Collins's meetings with old colleagues do not demonstrate that he was about to give away the Provisional Government's position, or that peace was possible. They represented, rather, his desire that some form of accommodation could be arrived at by which Republicans would lay down their arms, while retaining their principles intact. This is confirmed by some of Collins's personal jottings suggesting that the Republicans should be given an opportunity of 'Going home without their arms', provided they accepted 'the People's verdict'. He stressed: 'We don't ask for any surrender of their principles', and argued that the government had already demonstrated their determination to uphold 'the People's rights'. He concluded:

'We want to avoid any possible unnecessary destruction and loss of life' and 'We do not want to mitigate their weakness by resolute action beyond what is required.' If the Republicans did not accept his terms, 'further blood is on their shoulders'. Paddy O'Connor, a leading pro-Treaty officer from Dublin, testified that Collins opposed O'Duffy's plans for a large, determined sweep of his command. 'Collins didn't want them streamrollered,' O'Connor recollected. Collins's journey south represented a despairing attempt to mend fences before the war became widespread and embittered. He was relying again on his old personal and institutional ties, particularly his IRB colleagues.[2]

An outline of events on the fateful 22 August can be pieced together from pro-Treaty and Republican sources. In the early hours of the morning Collins, accompanied by Emmet Dalton, left Cork city in a convoy consisting of a motor-cycle scout, an open Crossley tender, a touring car, in which Collins and Dalton travelled, and an armoured car bringing up the rear. On a tour of West Cork posts on their way to Bandon they passed through the remote valley of Béal na mBláth. Aware of the likelihood of roadblocks, they stopped there to ask the way of Dinny Long, of Cork No. 2 Brigade of the Republican IRA, who was acting as sentry for a council meeting of his brigade. In hostile territory it was indiscreet for Collins and Dalton to advertise their presence. Plans were made for an ambush in this ideal terrain in case the convoy returned by the same route. Some sources suggest that there were two attempted ambushes during the convoy's tour of West Cork, and Collins is said to have been warned at Rosscarbery of the unreliability of some of the men accompanying him.

At 8 p.m. the bulk of the Béal na mBláth ambush party decided to retire, thinking that the convoy had chosen another route back to Cork city. A number of them went to a nearby pub, among them Liam Deasy and Tom Crofts, Deasy's successor as divisional O/C. A small party of five stayed behind to clear a mine and a barricade. While doing that they heard the sound of the motor-cycle leading the convoy and swiftly took up their ambush position. Against Dalton's wishes, Collins ordered the convoy to stop when it was fired upon and left his vehicle, returning the fire for what appears to have been at least half an hour. It was undoubtedly a mistake for two such senior officers to stop and involve themselves in this type of fighting. Moreover, no attempt was made to outflank the ambushers. Near the end of the shooting Collins was hit by a bullet which left a gaping wound in the back of his neck. He died soon afterwards, and was the only fatal casualty on either side. Once the ambush party had been forced to retreat, the convoy, with Collins's body draped over the armoured car, made an extremely uncomfortable and confused journey back to Cork city.[3]

For the years since speculation has run riot on the subject of Collins's death, frequently leading to spates of correspondence on the subject in Irish newspapers, in addition to the publication of two books devoted to the subject. Some Republican contemporaries have had strong doubts about the authenticity of the traditional version that Collins was killed by a bullet, perhaps a ricochet, fired by one of the ambushers. It has been argued that the ambush did not take place, that Collins was killed by a man in his own convoy, or by a British intelligence agent who had infiltrated himself into Collins's entourage and found the ambush a convenient cover. Lately it has been claimed that one of two Republican soldiers returning home to Kerry from duty in Cork city was unintentionally responsible for the shooting when they came upon the ambush.

There were certainly suspicious circumstances. Collins's convoy had been too loosely chosen; the route taken was an extremely strange one; and Jock McPeake, the Scottish gunner of the armoured car, was later to join the Republicans and hand over the car to them. It appears, however, that McPeake's gun jammed during the ambush when he was responding to the ambushers' fire. Dalton was later to leave the army, and his various accounts of the ambush revealed many inconsistencies. There have been many examples, on both sides, of failure to speak up on the subject. Testimony from Republicans has come from men like Deasy and Crofts who had left the ambushing party and not from those who actually participated in the fighting. Given the extreme sensitivity of the events, however, the reluctance to comment is not surprising.[4]

The sundry conspiracy explanations, all based on circumstantial evidence, have owed much to the inspiration of spy literature and a Republican desire to restore Collins's reputation. It has not been convincingly explained, nor could it be, why either those on his own side or the British authorities should wish to kill Collins. Nobody supporting the Treaty could think their cause would benefit from Collins's removal. Immediately after Collins's death the British government became highly alarmed by the danger it presented for the future stability of the Provisional Government, although they had considerable reason to be suspicious of Collins's intentions. Any implications that Emmet Dalton was involved in a conspiracy appear patently absurd, given Dalton's closeness to Collins and how devastated he was by his death. If Dalton was a former officer in the British army, so too were Tom Barry and many others on the Republican side. Collins may have signed the Treaty in order to destroy it later, and he remained, as Peadar O'Donnell stressed, a conspirator determined to retain his IRB contacts; but that does not mean that any conspiracy must lie behind his death.

Analysis of the shooting and evidence relating to Collins's wounds is inconclusive. Liam Lynch received a report from Liam Deasy which ascribed Collins's death to the ambush attack. While regretting that his old colleague had died, Lynch criticised the failure to lay mines for the ambush. The members of the ambushing party were evidently unaware until the next day who had been killed.

Collins's death can be put down to his devil-may-care attitude — his decision to journey through hostile territory in a large convoy, the inadequate choice of the members of the convoy, and the tactics he adopted in the ambush. For all the debate about ballistics and entry and exit wounds, and the use of powerful historical imaginations, it matters more that Collins was killed than how he was killed. Concentration on the events at Béal na mBláth has, moreover, often meant a failure to place them in the overall context of the war.[5]

Collins's death threatened a major crisis for the Provisional Government. Initially, to judge by their negotiations with William O'Brien, the government did appear to suffer from a crisis of confidence. Though they privately regretted the killing, Republican leaders regarded it as a major opportunity. Liam Lynch told Deasy of the need to raise the volume of their warfare to take advantage of the situation. Mulcahy moved quickly into the leadership breach in the army—making a morale-raising speech at Collins's funeral and urging against reprisals. To stabilise the position, many officers were not given permission to leave their posts for the funeral. In such an untrained and poorly disciplined army the threat of large-scale reprisals at such times was ever present. Some unauthorised killings did take place, but they were few and isolated. In the long term, however, Collins's death made the war a harsher, nastier affair and led to a greater degree of commitment and ruthlessness on the Provisional Government side, culminating in the executions.

The government had lost its one popular leader—the man who had made the Treaty's acceptance a probability. He has been all too easily glamourised, both by contemporaries and by historians; yet he remains, of all modern Irish national heroes, the one with whom ordinary people feel the greatest affinity. De Valera's appeal lay partly in his detachment and his remoteness; Collins, by contrast, was a back-slapper and a drinking companion. Both Cosgrave and Mulcahy were to admit that they also were vastly different characters from Collins—they could not hope to achieve Collins's personal appeal. Collins had dominated the army and government so much that he was clearly going to be difficult to replace. Though possessing much of Collins's dynamism and strength of purpose, O'Higgins was never to be remotely as popular.

As Collins was only thirty-one at the time of his death, there has been much debate about whether he would have matured into a major statesman if he had lived, or whether he would have become a military dictator. He had shown considerable impatience with politicians and negotiations, often telling friends that he had little aptitude for politics. He did have definite administrative talents and great gifts of communication. He had demonstrated no desire to establish a military dictatorship. Collins had little consciousness of any need for wide-ranging social and economic change, despite being a severe critic of some aspects of Irish society. Major parts of his speeches were taken up with a simple articulation of Gaelic revivalism.

Although they were genuinely alarmed about the possible consequences of Collins's death, British politicians and civil servants were to be relieved that they no longer had to deal with what Sir Samuel Hoare described as Collins's 'film-star attitudinising'. They were to contrast Cosgrave's straightforwardness and reliability with Collins's stridency. Anglo-Irish relations were to improve under Cosgrave and O'Higgins. The Northern government had every reason to be grateful for Collins's death.

Collins could, perhaps, have helped to heal wounds within the Twenty-Six Counties—many believed that he would not have allowed an executions policy. He might well, however, have increased tensions between North and South in the post-war period. Meanwhile, for many old volunteers in the army the loss of their leader meant that their position appeared to be threatened, and it increased their fears that the old republican ideals were to be ignored.[6]

The Establishment of the Third Dáil

THERE appears to have been no opposition to Cosgrave replacing Collins as Chairman of the Provisional Government. Ironically, considering Mulcahy's future poor relations with O'Higgins, the latter is said to have preferred Mulcahy for the leadership. Cosgrave had come to the fore because of his administrative record in Dublin local government. Many had been quick to point out he had no military experience. Cosgrave himself admitted to Craig, at their first meeting in late 1922, that he regarded himself as no leader of men, and much of the initiative within the government was assumed by O'Higgins. Cosgrave did act, however, as a tactful, stabilising influence in the establishment of the Free State. Mulcahy continued to act as both Commander-in-Chief and Minister for Defence; there was no other military representation in the cabinet, although McGrath still had close ties with the army.

The government felt secure enough to allow the Dáil to meet on 5 September. A. Belton, a leading Southern Unionist, told Lord Midleton early in October: 'I really believe that the assembling of the Dáil and the progress already made with the Constitution has done more to damage the Republican forces than any action taken by the Free State Army.' At last the political authority of the government could be asserted and the Second Dáil laid to rest. Cosgrave's government put a heavy stress on its authority— circulars to the press ordered that the government should be referred to as 'The National Government' and not 'The Provisional Government', and that the Republican opposition, of all shades, should be known as 'Irregulars'.[1]

After much debate within Republican ranks only the aged Laurence Ginnell attended the first meeting of the Third Dáil, and he was rapidly ejected when refusing to desist from repeated enquiries concerning the constitutional status of the assembly. Republican abstention meant that the only source for criticism of government within the Dáil came from the Labour Party, whose TDs, particularly Thomas Johnson and Cathal O'Shannon, performed a useful though powerless role.

The first major business for the new Dáil was the passage of the constitution. Demands came from Labour TDs for an explanation of the developments which had led to the drawing up of the document earlier in the year, and questions were asked as to how many changes had been made from the original Irish draft. It is hardly surprising that answers were not forthcoming. O'Higgins admitted, however, that the government would have preferred a different document. Despite abortive attempts by the Irish government to secure British agreement to changes in the preamble, Alfred Cope reassured Curtis that they had 'no intention

On 8 May 1922, a meeting of pro-Treaty and anti-Treaty officers at the Mansion House, Dublin sought to avert the threatening civil war. Their efforts were only temporarily successful. *Left to right:* General Sean Mac Eoin, Sean Moylan, General Eoin O'Duffy, Liam Lynch, Gearóid O'Sullivan and Liam Mellows.

Arthur Griffith, Eamon de Valera, Michael Collins and Harry Boland after the signing of the 'election pact', 20 May 1922.

Michael Collins speaking in front of O'Donovan's Hotel, Clonakilty, Co. Cork, on the last day of the election campaign, 15 June 1922.

The opening shots of the Civil War, fired from Free State 18-pound field artillery supplied by the British government. This gun was stationed at the junction of Bridgefoot Street and Usher's Quay, just across the Liffey from the Four Courts.

The ruins of the Irish Public Record office after the Free State bombardment of 30 June 1922. The Republican garrison had converted this part of the Four Courts complex into a munitions factory with the cellars underneath being used to store explosives. The Free State bombardment caused a fire which reached the cellars and the consequent explosion destroyed priceless historical records and documents, some of them dating back to the twelfth century.

A general view of the Four Courts immediately after the surrender of the Republican garrison, 30 June 1922.

Free State troops in a Lancia armoured car distributing bread to Dubliners who had been unable to get food on account of the fighting in the vicinity of O'Connell Street, 3 August 1922.

Sean O'Mahony T.D. (*left*) and Miss Mary MacSwiney, sister of the late Terence MacSwiney, Lord Mayor of Cork, attending the funeral of Cathal Brugha.

The track of the Dublin/Blessington steam tram was torn up by Republicans. Here it is being repaired while Free State troops stand guard.

General Prout outside his GHQ in Carrick-on-Suir, 4 August 1922.

Free State army troops with a Lancia 'chicken coop' armoured car at Claregalway, Co. Galway, August 1922.

Free State troops man a roadblock on the Charleville Road, just outside Limerick city, July 1922.

Unloading an 18-pound field gun at Passage East, Co. Cork, 1922.

Michael Collins's coffin being placed on a gun carriage outside the Pro-Cathedral, Dublin, prior to the funeral procession to Glasnevin Cemetery.

The Earl of Mayo's house burned by Republicans during the latter days of the Civil War, 29 January 1923.

of dealing fast or loose with either the Treaty or the Constitution neither have they any doubt that the Treaty is the governing instrument'.[2]

The first session of the Third Dáil coincided with increasing evidence of widespread guerrilla warfare and heavy criticism of the Provisional Government army's ineffectiveness. Many members of the government had long felt that insufficiently stern measures had been taken against armed resistance, and with the increasing evidence of army casualties, culminating in the loss of Collins, the military leadership dropped their opposition to a tougher policy.

The Public Safety Bill was introduced into the Dáil on 27 September. It set up military courts which were given powers, including that of execution, for sundry offences, for instance the possession of arms and the aiding and abetting of attacks on government forces. Eoin Mac Néill, the Minister for Education, argued that the army's failings were the reasons for the execution policy. On 3 October an amnesty was offered for those willing to hand over their arms and accept the government's authority. There was little positive response to the offer. On 12 October a press statement announced that the military courts were to come into operation three days later.

The Public Safety Bill represented a turning-point: it ushered in a harsher period of the war and provoked the formation of a Republican counter-reprisal policy. The adoption of such a controversial strategy was not to be influenced by any political constraints, given a censored press and a government-dominated Dáil. When the bill was introduced Ernest Blythe stressed that the reluctance to take life had weakened their case. Mulcahy was convinced by then that compromise was out of the question. He was to quote General Crozier on the necessity for any army to have the right to execute, and said of the executions: 'There can be no question but that I personally was the ultimate and supreme authority for these, and at all times accepted the supreme responsibility.' The bill came under fire from Labour TDs for its implications of military dictatorship. Johnson and O'Shannon complained of such powers being given to an undisciplined and inexperienced army and warned that the measures would result in more support for the Republicans. Cosgrave replied by saying:

Although I have always objected to a death penalty, there is no other way I know of in which ordered conditions can be restored in this country, or any security obtained for our troops, or to give our troops any confidence in us as a Government. We must accept the responsibility.

The bill caused considerable strains in the army, and there was particularly strong opposition to executions in the Cork Command. General Seán MacMahon told the 1924 Army Enquiry:

The carrying out of executions was perhaps the most severe test of our troops. In an Army such as ours which had been built in a hurry without the necessary training, and which had no time or means for fostering discipline, it made us think carefully as to how the first executions should be carried out. It was proposed that the first execution should be carried out by a Squad of Officers as so much depended on it at the time and we could not afford to run any risk of our men refusing to carry out the work. It was, however, decided that a firing squad would be picked from the men of the best unit we had in Dublin and that proved successful.

The potential for military dictatorship was present while the army remained the only expression of government power and authority in many areas of the country. In this context Mulcahy's opposition to any notion of military dictatorship was extremely important. Mulcahy was to prove sensitive to what he regarded as political interference in the army's sphere, but insisted that the army should remain the servant of the government. Paddy O'Connor commented: 'Mulcahy believed always in law. Once I said to him I have taken over the military and civil jurisdiction of Tipperary. Within a week the Guards were moved in to Co. Tipp. He didn't want the military to take over civil authority so he'd clear us out as soon as an area was ready.'[3]

The government's authority was given powerful support by the Catholic bishops in their joint pastoral of 10 October. The pastoral was timed to coincide with the amnesty period and the application of the Public Safety Bill. The pro-Treaty attitude of the church hierarchy had been evident throughout the year — they had issued statements supporting the government and had been consulted about some of the clauses in the constitution. The Catholic Church's relationship to revolutionary nationalism had been an awkward one, particularly on the question of the use of physical force. Support for opposition to pre-Treaty government had come from church leaders only because that government was an imperial one. Now that the government was Irish and had popular approval, the church could enthusiastically support the established order. Even so, the pastoral went further in its denunciation of the Republican opposition than most would have expected. The bishops declared:

> They carry on what they call a war, but which, in the absence of any legitimate authority to justify it, is morally only a system of murder and assassination of the national forces—for it must not be forgotten that killing in an unjust war is as much murder before God as if there were no war.

The pastoral stressed that the people had the clear duty 'of supporting the national government, whatever it is'. To continue to resist government would result in excommunication; many priests were to deny the sacraments to prisoners. Given the support for the Republicans by many young clerics, the policy laid down in the pastoral was very difficult to enforce, and the pastoral was weakened by being seen as the work of the Catholic hierarchy in Ireland, rather than as emanating from Rome.

Many were to point out that the pastoral lacked balance—there was a notable absence of any criticism of Provisional Government army actions in the document. De Valera regarded the pastoral as a personal affront. He told Archbishop Mannix, the staunch Australian Sinn Féiner: 'The late pronouncement of the hierarchy here is most unfortunate.... Never was charity of judgment so necessary, and apparently so disastrously absent. Ireland and the Church will, I fear, suffer in consequence.' In its implicit attempt to make the Republicans social outcasts, the document made the war the more bitter. It apparently did nothing to change the minds of active Republicans; some commented, however, that the social ostracism engendered by it had its effect on wives and parents.[4]

Peace Initiatives

GIVEN the extreme distaste that so many on both sides felt for the war, and the alarm of neutrals, it is hardly surprising that there were frequent attempts to find some kind of peace formula.

In the early stages of the conflict peace attempts tended to be the preserve of public organisations. On 13 July 1922 representatives of opinion in Cork city suggested to the leadership of both sides that the Second Dáil should reconvene in Cork if possible, or, failing that, in Dublin. Not surprisingly, given the fact that the proposal ignored both the Treaty terms and the election, the anti-Treaty leaders were agreeable, while the Provisional Government firmly rejected the offer. Following the pro-Treaty occupation of Cork, the People's Rights Association, composed of prominent citizens, submitted changed terms to General Dalton, which reflected the weakened Republican position. They recommended an amnesty for Republican troops, together with the recognition that all opposition should henceforth be on constitutional lines; the handing over of Republican arms and munitions to a mutually agreed committee; and the framing of a new constitution. Similar proposals provided the basis for peace efforts in many other parts of the country.

The constitutional and political issues at stake, however, were not amenable to such compromise—that had been all too clearly demonstrated in the six months before the Four Courts attack. A truce could only have been agreed to if there had been a major reverse for pro-Treaty arms; and if there had been any likelihood of military defeat, there was a considerable prospect of direct British military reinvolvement.

There was always the possibility that depressing developments would lead to a weakening in the Provisional Government's resolve. That appears to have happened shortly after Collins's death. It was at this time that William O'Brien, the labour leader, on 2 September recorded Cosgrave and Mulcahy telling him that if the Republicans disbanded, they could keep their arms 'and the government would not molest them'.[1]

At that time also a meeting between Mulcahy and de Valera took place on 5 September as the result of the urgings of Monsignor Rodgers, an American priest. Both Mulcahy and de Valera acted on their own initiative in going ahead with the meeting. Mulcahy claimed that he had only agreed to it after much pressure and after he had been given to believe that de Valera had changed his views. Of his cabinet colleagues, he told only Eoin Mac Néill about the meeting. De Valera was to comment on the irony of their issuing safe-conducts for each other.

It became apparent during their discussion that there was no basis for agreement. De Valera wrote in his diary: 'Couldn't find a basis. Mulcahy was looking for a basis in acceptance of the Treaty—we in revision of the Treaty.' In his account of the meeting Mulcahy noted that de Valera had admitted that 'personally he would tend to be led by reason but as long as these men of faith like Rory O'Connor taking the stand that he was taking, that he ... was an humble soldier following after'. Mulcahy was to tell the Dáil that de Valera's argument represented 'a very specious plea'.

For de Valera and Mulcahy the meeting represented the end of any hope for compromise. De Valera told Joe McGarrity that it was no longer possible for him to retain any hope for his policy of Treaty revision proving practicable. Thereafter he was to take a more intransigent public stance. Mulcahy was to depict the meeting as the incident which caused him to support the establishment of military courts with the power to execute.[2]

As the war intensified, peace moves increasingly took the form of clandestine meetings between old comrades in arms, with priests often acting as intermediaries. Leaders of the pro-Treaty occupying force in Cork—for instance Emmet Dalton, Tom Ennis and Liam Tobin—had been noted for their personal allegiance to Collins, whose death made them all the more determined to find some compromise. Seán Murray, a Republican IRA officer in Cork, referred in September to 'a lot of peace talk going on which I nor anybody else cannot stop.... And the peace talk did not come from me, but men of higher rank.' By September Ennis, together with Charles Russell, another leading pro-Treaty officer, had, with Dalton's approval, established contact with Tom Barry and Liam Deasy. Deasy commented on his attitude: 'We saw no purpose in any more of our fellows being killed.... The Civil War had gone far enough, as I would have agreed with Dev's views in August.'

Liam Lynch, however, remained suspicious about the peace feelers, and did not share the pessimism about military prospects so rife in the Cork anti-Treaty forces. He insisted that the ultimate Republican aim be adhered to and that his authority should be paramount. Lynch thought that Dalton's and Ennis's actions represented a weakening of pro-Treaty resolve; he wrote to Deasy on 6 September: 'I do not believe the moment has arrived for negotiations, just yet, unless F.S. see futility of their actions. Our position is vastly improving every day. We are all of course anxious for Peace as early as possible.' When Mary MacSwiney brought up the question of External Association, Lynch in another letter told Deasy: 'We are better see the thing through now.... We cannot have even External Association with the British Empire.'

The clandestine meetings, however, continued. At a meeting in September set up by Father Duggan at Crookstown, near Cork, Ennis and Russell met Deasy and Barry. Ennis and Russell suggested peace terms among which were the disbandment of both armies and the formation of an independent Army Executive. They proposed also: 'The Army to be the servant of the Government, only in so far as the better government of the country is concerned (Maintenance of Law and Order etc.).' Russell concluded that 'they [i.e. he and Ennis] would go to Dublin to attempt to enforce their proposals on the M Defence; if they failed in this they would attempt to organise the Officers in the Free State Army who still possess an Irish-Ireland outlook, to leave the Free State Army.' He related his fear that men of a pro-British outlook would take over the Provisional Government army.

These proposals were placed before the IRA Executive meeting on 16 and 17 October and produced an enthusiastic response. Even Lynch was positive, saying:

> This shows a vast improvement in the enemy attitude, and our Military successes, and general development of the situation in our favour, will soon bring the enemy to realise the actual position and thereby recognise the National Honour. ... If an Irish Constitution is drafted which destroys the Treaty, that is, places Ireland outside the British Empire, it will settle the matter. ... The control of the Army, and restoration of Officers is only a secondary consideration. ... I realise peace may come quicker by leaders meeting, even before now, but there is no use in officers not in supreme authority meeting.

By that time, however, such peace proposals were completely unrealistic—the Provisional Government's position had hardened, the Dáil was sitting again, and the constitution had been passed to the British government's satisfaction.

Informal peace talks continued between rival military units into the new year. Such efforts were promoted and supported by the 'Neutral IRA', as well as by individual clergymen. The 'Neutral IRA' was founded in December 1922, and Florrie O'Donoghue claimed a membership of 20,000, although he admitted its organisation was necessarily loose. It consisted exclusively of pre-truce IRA men and was led by Seán Hegarty and O'Donoghue. The Neutral IRA had a Republican bias on political and constitutional issues; the widespread publicity concerning their search for a month's truce, however, was used by pro-Treaty sources to weaken Republican resolve. Despite their lobbying of public bodies, they had no hope of success. In March 1923 O'Donoghue wound up the Neutral IRA, saying its purpose was incapable of fulfilment. Some surviving sections of the organisation, however, remained active in peace moves throughout the war.[3]

The Formation of the Republican Government

THE prospect of the Third Dáil meeting in September produced a debate among Republicans on whether their TDs should attend, which soon widened into a debate on whether a Republican government should be formed. Much of the comment on these issues implied a criticism of Lynch's reluctance to consider political and social issues, and his opposition to the holding of a meeting of the Army Executive. Despairing of his frustrating existence in Dublin, Ernie O'Malley frequently asked his Chief of Staff for clarification of the anti-Treaty IRA's political, social and military aims; he also urged that effective communications be established with de Valera and the political party, and that Lynch should help to achieve this by switching his GHQ to Dublin. In late September O'Malley told Lynch: 'We consider it imperative that some sort of a Government, whether a Provisional or a Republican or a military one, should be inaugurated at once. . . . It is indeed time to turn our attention to a constructive policy.' A letter from Oscar Traynor and other Republican military leaders in jail expressed their wish for a meeting of anti-Treaty TDs who should elect a new President; if such action was not taken, they threatened to withdraw their support from the party. Meanwhile Liam Mellows stressed the need for a Republican government which would revive the Democratic Programme. He wrote:

> Republicans must be provided with a rallying centre, and the movement with a focussing point. The unemployment question is acute. Starvation is facing thousands of people. . . . The situation created by all these must be utilised for the Republic. The position must be defined. Free State—Capitalism and Industrialism . . . Empire—Republic—Workers—Labour.

In another letter Mellows was severely critical of the military leadership. He argued that

> During the past six months we suffered badly because responsible officers in their desire to act as soldiers, and because of an attitude towards 'politicians' acquired as result (in my opinion) of a campaign directed towards this end by old GHQ, could only judge of situation in terms of guns and men. Even from a military point of view it ought to have been apparent to such men that every situation and advantage—no matter of what nature—should be availed of to gain victory.

Lynch was sceptical of the need to consider such questions. He said of Mellows: 'I fear his ideals prevent him from seeing the same military outlook as others at times.' De Valera was also opposed to the establishment of a Republican government: while naturally in favour of its desirability, he did not regard it as feasible at that time. Furthermore, he was concerned about the army's dominance. In long letters to the Republican TD, Charles Murphy, de Valera revealed his deep unhappiness about the war. This correspondence was captured and triumphantly published in the press as evidence of the division in Republican ranks. De Valera began his letter of 7 September by recommending against the Republican TDs attending the Dáil, 'both from the points of view of principle and expediency', and stressed that the Second Dáil was not legally dissolved and could not therefore be legally replaced by any new assembly. On 12 September he wrote:

> I have opposed the setting up of rival Govt. solely because of our obvious inability to maintain it. . . . If we were now in the position we were in when we held a portion of Cork I'd certainly favour it. But again we cannot maintain it. . . . The position of the political party must be straightened out. If it is the policy of the party to leave it all to the army . . . the obvious thing for members of the party to do is to resign their positions as public representatives. . . . If I do not get the position made quite clear, I shall resign publicly.

On the following day de Valera put forward to Murphy the various alternatives. These were, firstly, that 'The Republican Party . . . take control, acting as legitimate Dáil'; secondly, that 'The Army Executive take control and assume responsibility'; and, thirdly, that 'A Joint Committee be formed to decide policy for both'. He held the first alternative to be constitutionally the correct one, but could not foresee it winning 'from the Army that unconditional allegiance without which our Government would be a farce'. Rory O'Connor's 'ultimate repudiation of the Dáil,' he continued, 'which I was so foolish as to defend even to a straining of my own views in order to avoid the appearance of a split, is now the greatest barrier that we have'. He maintained that

> Even if we had the allegiance we have not the military strength to make our will effective; and we cannot, as in the time of the war with the British, point to authority derived from the vote of the majority of the people—We will be turned down definitely by the electorate in a few months time in any case.

De Valera concluded that the only practicable policy was for the Army Executive publicly to accept all responsibility, which would answer pro-Treaty propaganda that Republican politicians were behind the military resistance. He claimed that he would have resigned before if that had not carried with it the danger of prejudicing the Republican cause.

In his correspondence with Murphy, de Valera firmly rejected the possibility of a joint executive. In the following month he was to change his mind. The reasons for his *volte-face* are unclear. In all probability his agreement to the government's formation was a bowing to pressure from both military and political Republicans, and an attempt to avoid an undermining of the Republican cause by splitting the movement. Throughout the war he was extremely unhappy about his relationship to the Army Executive, and the formation of the Republican government only served to paper over divisions.[1]

Lynch eventually agreed to an Army Executive meeting, held at Ballybacon, near Tipperary town, on 16 and 17 October. After a policy of substitutes for captured Executive members had been agreed, military developments since the Four Courts attack were reviewed and the Cork army officers' peace terms considered. The meeting unanimously agreed to the formation of a Republican government, with de Valera as 'President of the Republic and Chief Executive of the State'. As a result of the Executive's request, a meeting of Republican TDs on 25 October agreed to form a cabinet.

> to be temporarily the Supreme Executive of the Republic and the State, until such time as the elected Parliament of the Republic can freely assemble, or the people being rid of external aggression are at liberty to decide freely how they are to be governed and what shall be their political relations with other countries.

There was no prospect that the government could actually function, as de Valera was to admit. The air of unreality was well demonstrated by de Valera's appointment of Seán Moylan to his cabinet, unaware that he had recently been sent as the IRA's representative to the USA. Some of the cabinet members were in prison. Stack testified that the financial resources for the political side were virtually nil. In his choice of cabinet de Valera emphasised his desire to appease military interests. He informed Art O'Brien: 'I intend the personnel of the Executive to be, as far as possible, those who have direct influence on the Army Executive. We will thus run less risks of duality of control.' The formation of the government did not make de Valera more sanguine. He told Joe McGarrity:

> The setting up of the Government should have been done long ago—but the members of the Army Executive are far apart and meetings are difficult. . . . I do not care what Republican government is set up so long as some one is—only I will not take responsibility if I do not get the corresponding authority to act in accordance with my best judgement. If the Army think I am too moderate, well let them get a better President and go ahead.

The old tensions therefore remained.

Soon after the formation of the government Mary MacSwiney, then on hunger-strike in Mountjoy Prison, was given by de Valera a lecture on the need to take practical stances. He stressed to her 'the difference between desiring a thing and having a feasible programme for securing it'. Mary MacSwiney concluded: 'The Republican Government has been kept alive and that is the most important thing.'[2]

The First Executions

A month after the Public Safety Bill had come into operation the British government was showing increasing scepticism as to whether the Irish government intended to put all the powers into effect. On 17 November the first executions took place—of five unknown men who had been caught with arms in Dublin. The executions produced an immediate hostile reaction from Labour TDs and others in the Dáil. O'Higgins replied to the protests by stating that the executions were meant as a deterrent and were not vindictive. This exchange occurred shortly after Childers had been arrested, and a remark made by O'Higgins during the debate fuelled suspicions that the first executions were intended, in de Valera's secretary's words, as 'a forerunner for Childers' execution'. O'Higgins declared:

> If you took as your first case some man who was outstandingly active or outstandingly wicked in his activities the unfortunate dupes through the country might say, 'Oh, he was killed because he was a leader' or 'He was killed because he was an Englishman'.[1]

The formation of the Republican government had given de Valera the opportunity to find a role for Childers. Mrs Childers wrote that Childers was summoned back to Dublin to act as Minister for Publicity. He made an appallingly uncomfortable journey from the south-west with David Robinson, only for them to be arrested at Childers's cousin Robert Barton's family house at Annamoe, Co. Wicklow, on 10 November. Childers was captured with a small automatic on him, which had been given to him by Michael Collins. That provided the evidence needed for his execution. There was never any doubt that the military court would find Childers guilty, as he technically was, and his execution was only delayed until 24 November by his pleading *habeas corpus* in order to aid some other prisoners. It was at this time that Winston Churchill made an attack on Childers as crude as O'Higgins's. Churchill referred to Childers as 'a mischievous and murderous renegade'.

Childers died with grace and heroism, writing to his wife:

> I believe God means this for the best for us, Ireland and humanity.... I triumph and I know you triumph with me.... Dead I shall have a better chance of being understood and of helping the cause—I am, as I sit here, the happiest of men.... If only I could die knowing that my death would somehow—I know not how—save the lives of others—arrest this policy of executions.... I see big forces rending and at the same time moulding our people in affliction.... I hope one day my good name will be cleared in

England. . . . I die loving England and passionately praying that she may change completely and finally toward Ireland.

Earlier Mrs Childers wrote to her husband: 'I will be with you if you are called to climb Calvary and to stand beside Christ. I will carry the cross with you.' De Valera, writing to Mrs Childers, restated the 1916 credo: 'From the blood of martyrs will spring the Ireland we seek to build.'

Childers had played an obsessive role in opposing the Treaty, and some of his ideas, particularly on defence issues, were to be proved exaggerated and erroneous. De Valera told Joe McGarrity that Childers's death was 'a big blow—not so much on account of what he was doing immediately before then, but because of what he could do under new conditions'. Through the murky circumstances surrounding his execution, Childers assumed an importance he had not possessed since the signing of the Treaty.[2]

The first executions caused Liam Lynch to change his attitude to reprisals. On 28 November he addressed a letter to the Ceann Comhairle (Speaker) of the Dáil threatening 'very drastic measures' against those who had voted for the Special Powers Resolution, and two days later a general order was sent out to Republican IRA units to kill listed categories of Provisional Government supporters. Lynch argued that up to that time the Republicans had abided by the rules of warfare, but that now they had to respond to the ultimate provocation. Henceforward the war had the character of a vendetta on a national scale. As a consequence of the developments, government members lived in siege conditions at their offices, while their movements were studied by potential assassins. Mulcahy was the only minister who continued to live at home.[3]

There appears to have been little desire to put the reprisals policy into effect, and Lynch had reservations about the implications of his own orders. The lack of effective action can be put down partly to the consciousness that reprisal killings would produce more executions and prove a death sentence for many Republican prisoners. Local units adopted their own attitudes and were intensely aware of the effect reprisal killings would have on the cause in their communities. On both sides, moreover, the reluctance to kill old comrades persisted. Frank Henderson, of Dublin No. 1 Brigade, told Ernie O'Malley of his resistance to reprisals:

> Prominent supporters of the Free State government and Parliament were to have been shot, and it was left to officers in charge of each area who was to have been shot. . . . I didn't like that order. . . . I could have shot Eamon Duggan and Fionán Lynch, for they went home every night drunk but I left them alone. . . . Seán McGarry was often drunk in Amiens St and the boys wanted to shoot him and the Staters there but I wouldn't let them. . . . I think the execution of Rory O'Connor and the others may have stopped a continuation of our shooting. It was very hard to get men to do the shooting and I don't think they'd have done any more shooting.

For the rest of the war there was frequent talk about projected assassination of government ministers, but no action after 7 December. The death of the pro-Treaty TD James McGarry's young son in December, after his house had been burnt down, acted as a warning of how disastrous a reprisals policy could be.

Just once, on 7 December 1922, the reprisal orders were acted upon. Members of

Dublin No. 1 Brigade killed Seán Hales and wounded Pádraic Ó Máille, the Leas-Cheann Comhairle (Deputy Speaker) of the Dáil, outside Leinster House. Hales, a pro-Treaty TD, was the brother of Tom Hales, a West Cork brigade leader, who had been one of the party which ambushed Collins's convoy. On the following morning four of the Republican prisoners in Mountjoy Jail, Rory O'Connor, Liam Mellows, Joe McKelvey and Dick Barrett, were executed after a cabinet meeting had explicitly authorised their deaths as a reprisal.

There could be no pretence that these executions were carried out under the Public Safety Act. All four men had been captured during the Four Courts attack and had been in Mountjoy since that time. They were chosen, it appears, as representing the four provinces, and all, perhaps significantly, were IRB men. O'Connor and Mellows had been particular *bêtes noires* of the pro-Treaty army leadership over the army unity discussions, and relations between O'Connor and Mulcahy had been particularly acid. Joe McKelvey had been the Chief of Staff in the Four Courts and was the one Belfast IRA leader who had gone anti-Treaty. Barrett was a West Cork man. Mellows wrote in his last letter:

> I shall die for Ireland—for the Republic; for that glorious cause that has been sanctified by the blood of countless martyrs throughout the ages. The Republic of Ireland is assured and before long all Irishmen . . . will be united against Imperialist England—the common enemy of Ireland and of the world.

There has been considerable debate ever since about who in the cabinet was responsible for the orders to execute the four. It appears that Mulcahy took the initiative, and that McGrath and O'Higgins were the last to give their consent.

The reprisal executions produced a shocked reaction. The London *Times* commented on 9 December: 'The British Government never adopted such drastic measures, even in the darkest days of the fighting before the Truce.' Thomas Johnson declared in the Dáil: 'I am almost forced to say you have killed the new State at its birth', and Cathal O'Shannon described it as the worst crime in Ireland in the previous ten years. O'Higgins argued, in reply, that all government was ultimately based on force, and defended his own position by stating: 'Personal spite, great heavens! Vindictiveness! One of these men was a friend of mine.' (Rory O'Connor had been the best man at O'Higgins' wedding.) No argument could detract from the fact, however, that these were killings of untried and unconvicted men.[4]

There were to be no further attempts during the war to assassinate TDs. Despite the fact that Lynch issued orders widening the targets for reprisals, attention turned to kidnapping Senators and burning property. Pax Whelan admitted that the executions lowered Republican morale, and Tom Smith said: 'The effect of Rory O'Connor's execution on the men outside was complete depression.' Michael Sheehy, of Leix, related that: 'The effect of the executions was gloom and depression, and a general atmosphere of who is next for it.' From a pro-Treaty perspective Paddy O'Connor told Ernie O'Malley: 'The executions broke your morale. There is no doubt of that.'

The only possible justification for the executions was that they were a deterrent that aided the establishment of elected government and shortened the war. The executions could not be said to have decided the war—there was no prospect of

Republican victory by that time. They appear, however, to have played a role in reducing Republican military activity. Liam Deasy was to list the executions and reprisals as one of the reasons for his desertion of the military cause in February. With regard to a wider perspective, however, the executions policy ensured that the Free State would be tainted from its birth with the blood of Republican heroes and former colleagues. The Provisional Government's crime was seen by many ex-colleagues as being personal and ideological.[5]

On 6 December, at the height of the storm over the executions, the act establishing the Free State completed its passage in the House of Commons. As surely as night followed day, the Northern government immediately exercised its option of separate existence.

The British Government and the Early Civil War

THE war's opening had not seen an end to the British government's anxieties. Its members became increasingly concerned about the ability of the Provisional Government army to prosecute the war successfully, and sundry observers relayed their fears about the army's limitations to the British government and commented on the half-hearted manner in which the war was being conducted. General Macready recorded that British troops regarded the pro-Treaty units with 'amused indifference', and Lionel Curtis reported in January 1923 that the Free State government 'have been terribly hampered by the inefficiency of their Army'.

In the early stages of the war there was a deep suspicion of Collins's motivation, and increasing alarm about rumours of informal peace talks. On 25 August Curtis informed Churchill of Collins's secret negotiations in Scotland for arms, and concluded:

> It was just because of this kind of thing that personally I felt a sense of relief when I heard that Collins had paid what you just described as a debt that he owed. I don't believe that the PG would ever have shaken off the habit of conspiracy in which they were bred, so long as he remained at their head. Under Cosgrave I believe that there is a real chance that they will. This incident will enable you to bring him face to face with the issue at a moment when of all others it is most ... necessary that the PG should make a fresh start in life as a civilised government.

Nevertheless, Griffith's and Collins's deaths produced an understandable unease in Whitehall about the Irish government's stability—a British secret service report, which embarrassingly became available to the Irish government, told a disconcerting story about the state of the pro-Treaty army after Collins's death. But while unease about the army remained, the British government was convinced that Cosgrave and O'Higgins were in earnest about implementing the Treaty. Curtis reported in January: 'Individually, as well as politically, Cosgrave's Government is showing the most remarkable courage.'

Any fears that the new government in Britain from October would mean a change in Irish policy were soon dealt with by Bonar Law's assurances on the maintenance of the Treaty position. L. C. M. S. Amery, who was to become First Lord of the Admiralty in the new Conservative government, stressed that the 'earnest desire for national stability imposes on the Government, and indeed on every citizen, whatever his personal feelings may be, the duty of fulfilling this Country's treaty with the Irish Free State. . . . It is the Government's intention to approach its future relations with the New Dominion with patience and forbearance.'[1]

The British position had become an uneasy and impotent one: the former administrators were now forced to adopt the role of acting as defence counsel for a regime they had many reasons to be unhappy about. Even Cope warned Churchill not to paint the Southern Irish picture in too 'roseate colours' when Churchill thought it necessary in October to reply in parliament to concern about the war. The great concern of British policy was still the establishment of a stable government for the Twenty-Six Counties, and with that end in mind no limits were set on the munitions sent over to support the pro-Treaty military effort. For all the public show of faith in the Irish government's position, there was a continuing debate within the British government about contingency plans if a Republic was declared, and 5,000 British troops were kept in Dublin, fulfilling what Macready described as a 'watching brief'. Churchill admitted in October that the evacuation of British troops could worsen the Provisional Government's position. Macready, however, was uneasy about the vulnerability of his troops to attack and felt that their numbers were too small to perform any useful role in an emergency. The British troops were frequently subject to sniping from Republicans with the intention of provoking a response which could reunite the rival Irish forces. The establishment of the Free State in December meant the departure of the remaining British troops. By that time the British government had been further reassured about the Irish government's intentions by the Dáil's enactment of the Public Safety Bill. Cope told Churchill: 'They are now going to take the gloves off.' In December Lionel Curtis reported that all British newspapers, from the *Manchester Guardian* to the *Morning Post*, were in favour of the executions.[2]

The Southern Unionists and the Civil War

IN the long term, the part of the population which suffered most from the revolutionary period were the Southern Unionists, particularly those of them who were large landowners. Their estates and houses were extremely vulnerable targets in the midst of guerrilla warfare; to attack them could be justified on both nationalist and social protest grounds. A considerable number of houses had been burnt during the Anglo-Irish War—in Cork it was reported that 'Our only fear was that, as time went on, there would be no more Loyalists' homes to destroy.' A pamphlet concluded: 'The evidence shows... how greatly the burnings have increased since the evacuation by the British forces took place and the Free State Government assumed office. It will be observed that in fifteen weeks the total number of burnings had exceeded that of the whole previous year.' Con Moloney's instructions to Republican columns in July 1922 authorised that Unionist property should be commandeered to accommodate their men; this had in fact already occurred in many cases. Provisional government concern that the splendours of Unionist houses, and the treasures within them, should be preserved failed to save, for instance, Lismore Castle in Co. Cork from being burnt in September 1922. The worst spell of attacks on Unionist property was in the early months of 1923. In January and February the houses of thirty-seven Senators were burnt to the ground, including Oliver St John Gogarty's Connemara mansion at Renvyle. Senator John Bagwell's house near Clonmel was burnt on 9 January; on 1 February Moore Hall, the ancestral home of Senator Colonel Maurice Moore in Co. Mayo, was totally destroyed; and two weeks later the home of Senator Sir Bryan Mahon was burnt down at Ballymore Eustace, Co. Kildare. These were but a few of many examples.

It is not surprising that Southern Unionists felt under a state of siege and that there was much talk of emigration. The high level of post-First World War agricultural prices had encouraged many to stay, but considerable numbers left. Between 1911 and 1926 the Protestant minority in the Twenty-Six Counties fell from 10.4 per cent to 7.4 per cent of the population.[1] Mark Sturgis reported to Churchill in April 1922 that an old hunting friend of his, Nigel Baring, 'has now had his house raided and burgled for the third time and has announced that he is giving up the hounds, selling his horses at Sewell's next month and clearing out of the country'. He continued: 'This step is something like a bombshell for the farmers in a wide district, and should do much to stimulate local public opinion against the forces of anarchy.' Colonel O'Callaghan-Westropp, in Clare, felt they should be 'given the option of being expropriated by the State and given safe conduct out of Ireland, if they so elect, before the Government of Ireland Act comes into force. . . . Those who elect to remain in Ireland would then do so at their own risk and have no grievance, which would be a relief to the new Irish Government.' During the truce and early Civil War periods there was much talk of schemes for the British government to evacuate Unionists; Mark Sturgis, for instance, debated in July the possibility of using British warships to evacuate Protestant refugees from the south and west. Such plans, however, were never implemented.

The fact that many Southern Unionists had sought to make accommodation with the new nationalist forces did not ease their position. Lord Midleton was deeply resentful that his work in bringing about the truce of July 1921 had not been subsequently reflected in any gratitude expressed by Irish nationalist leaders. Midleton wanted the British government to make future supplies of munitions to the Provisional Government conditional on the Irish government implementing his proposals for rectifying civil order problems. A British army infantry brigade intelligence summary commented in August 1921: 'Loyal Munster men see only years of trouble ahead—years with no light behind. The retribution for the victims of cowardice and betrayal is truly terrible.'[2]

Midleton was frequently to complain of the lack of safeguards for Unionists in the new state, and to point out that Griffith had failed to deliver on his pledges with regard to the Senate's powers in the Free State constitution (as a consequence of which he refused to accept an offer of a seat in the Senate). In resigning from his position as Chairman of the Anti-Partition League on 24 November, Midleton summed up his many frustrations and alarms. 'We have now been "dished" all round,' he wrote. 'Lloyd George went back on his pledges, Griffith's soft words have borne no fruit'; and he went on to complain that the Senate had been given fewer powers than any second chamber he understood to exist. He concluded that his discussions with the Provisional Government 'make it clear that *persuasion* goes for little with no power behind it. . . . Hence my desire for relief from further responsibility in Ireland.'

Unionists became most alarmed about the failure to restore settled conditions. Another pro-Treaty observer was quoted by Midleton as saying:

> I am unable to understand how such a big movement as Sinn Féin can [be] led by such small men. Substantial people in Dublin and elsewhere realise that there can be no peace under the existing regime and that unless there is some intervention of force the country will be bled whole. A member of the Dáil said last week 'The English had the capacity to govern us but not the will—we have the will but not the capacity'.

Other leaders of Unionist opinion adopted a more positive line towards the new government, particularly after Collins's death when they detected a change of character in the leadership. As Directors of the Bank of Ireland, Andrew Jameson and Henry Guinness backed the government financially and accepted nomination for the Senate. Belton told Midleton, after talking with Cosgrave: 'I think he is desirous of co-operating with the best elements of all parties of the country and his one desire is to see a prosperous, progressive, and, if possible, united Ireland.' A delegation of prominent Unionists, including Dr John Bernard, the Provost of Trinity College, and Lord Desart, met Cosgrave on 20 October and reported that they were impressed by Cosgrave's determination to restore stability:

He certainly seemed very anxious to meet us as far as possible, and said over and over again that he attached the greatest importance to keeping us in the country. All I can hear about him and O'Higgins is favourable. This seems to be the general opinion.

Gogarty demonstrated his support for the government by offering to loan them his Rolls-Royce car for military purposes. There was, however, to be no way back to any position of political power for the Unionists; any role they were offered was a grace-and-favour one.[3]

The Civil War and the Railways

THE most successful aspect of Republican military policy was their attack on the railways. During the Anglo-Irish War IRA action against the rail system had been infrequent, as it was feared that it would alienate public opinion and hinder their own war effort. There were to be no such restraints during the later conflict, when a Free State politician was to comment: 'There never has been a case of any country in which such a fierce attack was made on its Railway system.' Ireland had a highly developed rail network, and many areas were heavily dependent on it; the system could ill afford the war's effect when motorised transport was expanding rapidly.[1]

During the war's first phase the Republican policy against the railroads was intended to block the movement of pro-Treaty troops and supplies to Munster and the west; later the purpose was to prevent the functioning of government. A GHQ staff meeting in late July issued orders for the destruction of the lines from Limerick Junction to Tipperary and from Waterford to Carrick-on-Suir. Liam Lynch also ordered that railway workers be instructed not to repair trains or lines. The Great Southern Company directors, fearing reprisals, were soon rejecting government requests to reopen many of their lines. The anti-Treaty North-Eastern Command told the Irish Engineering Union on 3 August 1922:

> Owing to the use of railways by the 'Free State' Headquarters for the conveyance of troops and war material and for purposes of Army communication, the destruction of railways under 'Free State' control is an essential part of our military policy. Unless absolutely essential we are reluctant to interfere with those services which are a convenience to the civil population. This decision has, however, been forced upon us by reason of the fact that the chief work of the railways at present is army work; that the railway authorities give allegiance to the so-called Provisional Government, and that organised Labour has, up to the present, freely co-operated in assisting the 'Free State' and the British Government in their attempt to exterminate the Republican forces.[2]

Lynch was critical of the patchy implementation of the policy, but by August all routes to the south and west were non-functioning. In particularly notorious incidents, a prison train was ambushed on 24 July at Killurin, Co. Wexford, with some of the prisoners escaping, and an armoured train was destroyed at Inchicore, in Dublin, near the end of July. In August the destruction of the historic bridge over the Blackwater at Mallow ended any hope of a speedy resumption of services between Dublin and Cork. Local community leaders pointed out to the

Republican leadership the disastrous social and economic consequences such an action would have for the area; in reply, de Valera argued that it was a military necessity. The first months of the war saw a particularly heavy offensive on the rail system in South Tipperary, the Dundalk region and the Silvermines area of Co. Limerick, all key strategic communication areas. For almost all the war there were minimal rail communications in Kerry and the far west.[3]

With any hope of a conventional military campaign long over, the Republican Director of Engineering on 29 December emphasised the need for 'bringing Railways to a standstill, as on this to a great extent depends the success of our campaign'. Liam Lynch reminded his colleagues that 'a hundred bridges blown up was just as effective a blow... as a hundred barracks blown up'. In January the army were unhappy that the Great Southern and Western Railway Company had released details revealing the extent to which their property had been damaged. That report revealed that during the previous twelve months the lines had been damaged in 375 places, 42 engines had been derailed, 51 over-bridges had been destroyed, together with 207 under-bridges, 83 signal cabins and 13 other buildings. In the same month the stations at Sligo, Ballybunion and Listowel were wrecked.[4]

The task of railroad repair and protection only began in any coherent manner from October, with the formation of the Railroad Protection and Maintenance Corps under Charles Russell. In the early stages of the war the government had feared that such a protective policy would only provoke Republican attacks. The corps was largely made up of rail workers and navvies, who were paid at very favourable rates; for many to repair the tracks meant the restoration of their regular jobs. Units of the corps were sent out to specific problem areas: work began with the line between Clonmel and Thurles, followed by lines in Co. Cork. A training camp was established at Baldonnell. In early April 1923 Cosgrave said that there was only one serious dislocation in the country. The corps established blockhouses at all important bridges, signal cabins and stations. Use was made of improvised armoured trains, consisting of Lancia cars attached to the roofs of railway carriages; later in the war, swivel turrets were used to enable the machine-gunners to fire in all directions.[5]

The Railroad Corps had definite success in reopening lines. It won much praise in the Dáil, where William Davin, a Labour TD, said that the units had saved the country millions of pounds. Some of the success can be put down to the unwillingness of Republican forces to risk the large-scale attacks which would have been necessary to overcome the sizeable strength of Free State protective forces, and also to the general decline of Republican military strength and purpose. Russell admitted at the Army Enquiry in 1924 that his units had enormous problems with quartermastering, which greatly limited the effectiveness of their work. He complained:

> Every boot, every uniform, every cap and every gun that I drew from him [the QMG], I drew with the greatest possible difficulty. There was no appreciation at all of the difficulties in commanding a corps and there was no assistance from the Supplies Organisation to make sure that you had enough supplies. ... The thing was so bad at times that I was really ashamed to inspect the men. Their feet were out of their boots; they were verminous and they had no change of clothing and no overcoats and so forth.

Russell related an incident where his men were needed to deal with Republican activity on the line between Athlone and Mullingar: 'I prepared troops . . . to try and outwit them. I had the troops standing to in the Griffith Barracks and they were just short of caps and leggings and rifles.' As a result, the men could not set out, and the Republicans blew up a bridge and a goods train. Russell testified that such problems persisted up to the end of the war; he complained that all the commands 'threw all their "dud" officers, as they called them, into the Railway Corps—every one of them'. Soon after the ceasefire there were major discipline problems within the units, particularly concerning officers fearing demobilisation, and there were instances of shootings and of absence without leave.

Many areas continued to suffer from rail destruction throughout the war. In a report on the Cork Command prepared in January, Seán Ó Muirthile concluded:

> The closing down of the Railways out of Cork to the west and north of the area is responsible for a very serious economic position. The people are almost entirely dependent on road transport, and if even goods trains could be run, the position would not be quite so bad. The Railway Maintenance Corps have begun work on the smaller lines out of Cork . . . but in the immediate future, there seems very little hope that the people will be facilitated in this matter.

There were particularly bad problems during the early months of 1923 in Co. Wexford, where local civic leaders complained of how long it took to send units of the corps to the area. It was only after the end of the conflict that all the Cork and Kerry lines were reopened. A Free State army report of 26 May affirmed: 'This week witnesses the practically complete return of the Railway Systems to normality. Every line in the state is open to traffic with the exception of the line from Waterford to Mallow and Rosslare and in the extreme South two small branches from Skibbereen to Schull and Baltimore.' At best the Railroad Corps had been a successful example of damage limitation.[6]

The War in the Localities:
September 1922–January 1923

(a) CORK

NOWHERE was the stalemate character of the war better illustrated than in Cork. Tom Crofts, the O/C of the Cork No. 1 Brigade of the anti-Treaty IRA for most of the conflict, commented that there was no worthwhile fighting.

Emmet Dalton told Mulcahy that he had been surprised by the lack of Republican resistance following the arrival of the pro-Treaty troops. He wrote that the enemy were 'crowded into positions of a barren nature without a base for supplies', and considered that their position 'was next to hopeless' in view of 'the poor nature of the country and knowing that all communications, roads, railways, etc. were broken'. Dalton concluded: 'There was one obvious course for us to take and that was to harass them, keep them moving.'

Dalton admitted that the pro-Treaty forces allowed the Republicans to regroup by not moving decisively against them. The troops, he reported, soon lost their popularity in many areas, and he was especially critical of the insufficient transport provided for them. He further complained that he was being forced to spend too much time on civil administration, and by early September was requesting permission to establish martial law. Dalton felt that O'Duffy's failure to co-operate with him was the major cause of his continuing problems: 'I maintain', he wrote, 'that if his [O'Duffy's] men from Banteer, Millstreet, Killarney and on the Blackwater line had pushed in and cooperated with me, the fight would now be over.' O'Duffy, for his part, put the failure down to the ineffectiveness of Dalton's command. The projected large-scale sweep of the west Kerry and West Cork Republican mountain strongholds was postponed from late August and proved ineffective when it was attempted in mid-September.[1]

By early November Dalton was even gloomier. He felt that public support for his troops had considerably declined; there were, he stated, more Republicans in Cork than at the time of the June election. He reported:

> One may travel 70 to 80 miles in part of the county without meeting even one Free State soldier.... The serious business of the Army—an old friend of yours says is junketing, dancing and flirting. I can't endorse this... statement because I believe that lack of transport—cohesion—organisation are creating the necessity for the soldiers, particularly in Cork, to find some means of occupation; they naturally choose the fascinating one.... I am beginning to lose hope. As a whole excluding some honourable examples,

there is no zeal—no dash—no organisation or determination, but only lack of discipline.... In Cork, we are going to be beaten unless we wake up and at once. The state of things is very bad—it is my plain duty to say so.

Tensions in the army became apparent soon after their arrival in Co. Cork. There was considerable resentment about the employment of former British army men who had been recruited after the occupation of the towns; in late August the divisional adjutant reported fears that the Dublin Guard had been responsible for letting men into the army 'some of whom ... were suspects during recent hostilities against the British Government'. The projected execution of three Republicans in December was put off because of the opposition of some officers, and Andy Doyle reported Ennis's refusal to have any Republicans executed in his area. Cork was to remain almost entirely free of executions.[2]

Problems in the army in Cork were greatly exacerbated by Collins's death and the circumstances surrounding it. Mulcahy was to put the genesis of the army mutiny of 1924 down to 'those who either deserted their posts in Cork after Collins' death, or had to be taken out of Cork because of their inability to deal with the situation there, and of their colloguing with the irregulars'.

Despite Dalton's feeling that the Republicans had won back the initiative, the work and organisation of the Republican columns was far from efficient, and their attacks were infrequent and usually unsuccessful. Their most effective work was in breaking communications, but Republican sources were to admit that even that was only patchily applied as was the order forbidding the use of motor vehicles. Paddy O'Brien, of Liscarroll, commented: 'When a general order was given ... one area carried it out and the other didn't.' Tom Crofts recollected that 'Sandow' O'Donovan had a plan to poison the River Lee when the first execution took place, but was told by Liam Deasy to hold his hand. Republican military organisation in Cork city was ruined by a large number of arrests which, Republican commentators admitted, limited them to occasional sniping in the evening.[3]

A review of the Cork brigades at a divisional meeting on 30 October concluded:

> Cork 1 Brigade is disorganised, and will take a lot of pulling up, Cork 3 is also in a very poor state. We find it impossible to get any Brigade still working.... Cork 4 is keeping together pretty well but the enemy are not travelling through the area except in very large numbers. Cork 5 is in a good state, and the morale of the men is good.... The Deputy O/C stated that Cork 2 is very weak.

It was admitted that the organisation was very weak in most brigades, finance was lacking, and the munitions factory non-functioning. Problems were also created by desertions, as reported in the Bantry area during September, and by men moving out of their own areas without permission. Even in the comparatively active West Cork Brigade, Tom Hales was referring in September to a 'disheartening situation'. Around Ballyvourney, the centre of column activity, Paddy O'Sullivan commented: 'We were a kind of a broken-up army.' Many thought that the amount of peace talk affected commitment.[4]

The Republican effort in Cork was considerably weakened by the degree of local particularism and the failures of co-operation between brigades and divisions. Seán

MacSwiney wrote from Ballingeary on 16 October to the divisional adjutant: 'It looks as if 5th Brigade can't distinguish between a loan and a gift. The Lewis gun which they sent to Div Column was taken from the armoured car. They still have the Vickers and another Lewis which you asked us to give them.' When Seán Murray complained of David Robinson's activities in his area, he told Deasy: 'I am doing my best and don't want to be interfered with. . . . If the 5 Brig. want Protection from me they might give us a hand with our armour car.'

On 30 August there was an attack on Bantry lasting several hours; the Republicans captured several posts in the town before the killings of Gibbs Ross, the O/C of Cork No. 3 Brigade, and three other officers led to a retreat. The attack on Macroom on 2 September with the armoured car, the *River Lee*, appears to have consisted of little more than ineffective sniping for over seven hours. A planned assault on Inchigeelagh, to be led by David Robinson, never took place, apparently as a result of the refusal of a column to turn up at the appointed time because of their cynicism about Robinson's tactics, which involved dressing men as tramps and using children to surprise the garrison. For many this became one of the comic events of the war.[5]

It took Tom Barry's escape from prison in September, and his short-run formation of a large divisional column in Cork, for there to be successful raids, in late October, on the small posts of Ballineen and Enniskean in the south-west of the county. Barry, however, soon switched his attention to Tipperary and Kilkenny. The one area where there was comparatively frequent armed confrontation was around Ballyvourney. Ballyvourney was often taken and retaken, and the region continued to be one of the chief Republican strongholds in the country, and a safe retreat for many from all southern areas. In November Jock McPeake handed over to the Republicans the armoured car, the *Slievenamon*, which had been in the Collins convoy on the fateful 22 August, and it was soon used in attacks in the area.[6]

For all the ineffectiveness of the Republican military effort, problems continued within the Provisional Government army. In November Dalton left the command in mysterious circumstances. Before that, in late September, he had gone to Dublin to be married and, evidently, had returned to his job with no great fervour. There was great difficulty experienced in finding a new Cork GOC. The original idea was to move Murphy from the Kerry Command to the Cork one, but that was blocked by the opposition of many Cork officers. The Adjutant-General, Gearóid O'Sullivan, offered to take the job himself, but that also was rejected, while Séamus Hogan refused the appointment. Seán Ó Muirthile took over the command for a short time in January 1923 before David Reynolds was appointed.[7]

(b) KERRY

The guerrilla phase of the war was more extensively and bitterly fought in Kerry than anywhere. On 17 September 1922 Liam Lynch commented: 'The development of the campaign has been more rapid and satisfactory in Kerry than in any other area. Kerry has given a lead to the Division, and indeed to the whole of Ireland.' He regretted, however, that the Kerry No. 3 Brigade, in the flat, prosperous farming region of the northern part of the county, was so backward and inactive compared with the other two brigades.

While pro-Treaty troops continued to occupy strong posts in the Kerry towns, the countryside of the centre, south and east of the county was dominated by the numerous Republican columns, particularly in the hilly and mountainous areas. By August O'Duffy's second-in-command, General W. R. E. Murphy, a veteran of the big offensives of the First World War, adopted a policy of large-scale sweeps. These were to provide few positive results. On 26 August a convoy of a hundred men operating between Tralee and Killorglin was ambushed, and their O/C. Captain Burke, killed, during a two-and-a-half-hour fight; it was reported that they were ambushed nearly every mile of their road home. Another column, under Commandant J. McGuinness, was ambushed between Killarney and Rathmore on 10 September; seven troops were killed, and five shells had to be fired before the Republicans retired. In mid-September Murphy ordered plans for a large convergence of over 600 troops by sundry units, from all directions, on Ballyvourney. This manoeuvre was intended to deal with Republican concentrations in East Kerry and West Cork, but the prospects for its success were ruined by the capture of Murphy's instructions. As a result, Liam Lynch ordered all columns (among them Erskine Childers, together with his printing-press) to leave the area.

From mid-September pro-Treaty troops in Kerry found it necessary, as they did in Mayo and Sligo, to close small, isolated posts and to operate their own flying columns from the larger garrisons. Murphy, who took over the command from O'Duffy in early September, was soon to demand more men and transport for what he had come to realise was an extremely difficult task.[8]

While Republican units in Mid-Kerry were confined to particular localities, such as the Castleisland area and the Ballymacelligott and Farmer's Bridge regions near Tralee, large parts of the No. 2 Brigade territory were untouched by pro-Treaty troops. Loo Bridge, the key to communications into West Cork, and Morley's Bridge, on the Kenmare to Killarney road, and similar centres, were held as permanent Republican posts. The *Irish Times*'s special correspondent wrote at the end of the September that

> Beyond the occupation of some of the more important towns, the national forces have been able to do very little. Enemy columns several hundred strong can move along the hills in full view and complete impunity. Vessels can reach the coast with arms and supplies for the irregulars and peaceful trading ships are frequently attacked and relieved of their cargo. A ship load of petrol was lately run into Tralee and unloaded, while a strong attack on the national troops made them powerless to interfere.

Communications of all kinds were frequently broken for long periods; in late August O'Duffy admitted that he was forced to rely on the sea to keep in touch with other areas. The Tralee ship canal was blocked by Republicans, while there was no hope of train services resuming in Mid- and South Kerry.[9]

The ambushing of pro-Treaty troop convoys on the Kerry main roads became regular. One source likened the road between Tralee and Castleisland to that between Jerusalem and Jericho. Columns of twenty-five men, quartered between Ashill and Farmer's Bridge, operated against convoys on the Tralee–Killorglin and Tralee–Killarney roads, and units from the Ballymacelligott and Farranfore areas performed the same role on the Tralee–Castleisland road from their bases on the Stack and Glanaruddery Mountains. In the north-east of the No. 1 Brigade area there was regular harassing of enemy communications from Abbeyfeale by Republicans based in the Castleisland and Knocknagoshel regions. Troops had to journey in convoys of over a hundred men, with Lancia cars often accompanying them.[10]

The war was made the more bitter in Kerry because of the pro-Treaty dependence on outside troops—a mixture of men from the Dublin Guard, who were the most numerous, and northerners, from their Curragh headquarters, and men from the 1st Western Division. Paddy Daly, who was to take over the Kerry Command in January and who led the contingent from the Dublin Guard there, was reported as saying when he left Dublin: 'Nobody asked me to take my kid gloves to Kerry and I didn't take them.' From early in the war there were frequent rumours about troops attacking prisoners. Problems were made much worse for the pro-Treaty forces in Kerry by the support for the Republican IRA from large sections of the population. Tralee was a particularly strong Republican town, with a voiciferous and numerous branch of the Cumann na mBan. Theodore Kingsmill Moore, probably in ignorance of Republican support in Mayo and Sligo, commented: 'Alone among the counties in Ireland Kerry has a population of whom a very large number are, covertly or openly, in favour of the irregulars.' John Joe Rice recollected that even pro-Treaty sympathisers were willing to provide accommodation for his men. 'In Scartaglin, Glenflesk, Glenmore you could move around as freely as you liked,' he affirmed.[11]

The degree of Republican success in Kerry should, however, not be exaggerated. Theirs was a defensive, holding policy. Republicans were increasingly concerned about the availability of a continued ammunition supply and saw the need, for morale purposes, of taking a large post. Poor communications and old tensions between Republican leaders prevented effective co-operation between regions. The columns in the Dingle peninsula stayed in their area undisturbed until November and did not seek to involve themselves with activity elsewhere. Columns generally remained small, and activity part-time. The brigade adjutant for Kerry No. 2 gave an excellent, if awkwardly written, description of the problems faced by Republican columns:

> Under the present circumstances Officers cannot take...steps to punish men for disobedience....We have only to get on as best we can without driving men, and be satisfied with those who are willing to work....Many cannot go home and do wholetime Army work without creating the ill-will of their families who in most cases are not of independent means....Let us take for example a Company of 60 men — 10 of them are on Active Service, Rifle men, 10 are engaged on wholetime special services, 10 are hired servants and have families to support, 10 are small farmers' sons or only sons, who cannot spare any time and are lukewarm, 10 may be fairly well off but have friends in the opposite forces and cannot be trusted, and 10 have the grievance of having done wholetime...during the late war and were not taken into Barracks. When a Section Commander tries to get his section of men who are comprised of a mixture of these I am sure that he will find it difficult. Active service is now the only work they will spring to and the Battn. Staffs do not want much paper work. As regards daily reports I think a report of operations as they occur would be as much as we could do.

Humphrey Murphy made an outraged response to divisional demands for more organised work: 'For God's sake', Murphy pleaded, '... give ye typewriter and your index finger a rest for a few weeks, because the harvest being generally late in my Brigade, the crop of I/O's is not yet mature and the harvesters are few.' Murphy admitted that 'We have to keep shifting our H.Q. owing to the poverty of the people in the most suitable places, want of finance and proper supplies etc. I now have only one Lewis Gun in Brigade, one having been captured in Tipp., one captured in Castlemaine, and one having been left at Div. H.Q. during Kilmallock operations.'[12]

As the Cork Republican Stan Barry remarked, most of the fighting in Kerry was formless and very limited in magnitude. However, the capture of Kenmare on 9 September and the abortive attack on Killorglin on 27 September were large-scale incidents by Irish Civil War standards.

The Republican capture of Kenmare is an excellent example of the war's strange mixture of tragedy and something resembling comic opera. The aim of the attack appears to have been to take provisions from ships and arms from the pro-Treaty garrison. The operation's success owed little to careful planning, or to disciplined column activity. David Robinson, who was involved in the operation, concluded that there was 'insufficient information... insufficient forces and ... what appeared to me to be a lack of assistance or enthusiasm on the part of the Brigade Staff'. Only half of the thirty men supplied from the Cork No. 1 Brigade arrived, because of rumours of a pro-Treaty attack on Ballyvourney. Eighty-four men were involved in the operation—their task made much easier by the fact that a considerable number of the pro-Treaty garrison were away on sweeps, and because their officers were living separately from the men. The commandant of the pro-Treaty garrison in Waterville attributed the loss of Kenmare to thirty of the garrison deserting. Very little resistance was shown by the dispersed garrison, based mainly in the National Bank, the library and the workhouse.

At the start of the attack a body of Republican troops under 'Sailor' Dan Healy broke into the shop of Tom 'Scarteen' O'Connor, the pro-Treaty O/C in the town. When O'Connor appeared at the top of the stairs, reportedly unarmed, he was shot dead, as was his brother when he attempted to come to his aid. Liam Lynch praised the fact that the enemy O/C was prevented from rallying and organising his troops; many, however, were left with a sour feeling after what they regarded as a particularly ugly incident.

Republicans then tunnelled through various houses into what they thought were the pro-Treaty headquarter buildings. David Robinson criticised the lack of intelligence and reconnissance work, which meant that considerable time was taken up boring their way through to the post office, only to find it unoccupied by troops; they also failed to realise that the Lansdowne Arms was not used as a barracks. Scouting appears to have been non-existent. Liam Lynch complained that six of the men were drunk during the expedition. Following the taking of the bank, Robinson commented that some men showed more interests in the contents of that building than in moving on to take the library. Once the bank was occupied, however, pro-Treaty troops came down the main street waving a white flag. Seán Hyde, who led the attack, said that it lasted nine and a half hours.[13]

J. J. Rice told Liam Deasy that their total captures at Kenmare were 110 rifles and two Lewis guns, together with 20,000 rounds of .303 ammunition; of that,

4,000 rounds were ordered to be given to Cork No. 5 Brigade, and another 5,000 rounds were sent to Ballyvourney. The six battalions of Kerry No. 2 Brigade were handed 2,000 rounds each; before that ammunition had been reduced to fifteen or twenty rounds per man. During the attack 120 pro-Treaty prisoners were taken, including a younger brother of Kevin O'Higgins. They soon had to be released. Rice concluded: 'This capture has put us in a good position. . . . There are no idle rifles in the Brigade area.' He could not, as requested, give any rifles to Cork No. 2 Brigade. 'No day passes', he wrote, 'without a fight of some description, and I cannot spare a single rifle out of the Brigade unless I want to have a fearful row, which I do not wish, now that everything is working smoothly.' Rice later told Ernie O'Malley: 'Kenmare kept us going', and it clearly did much to expedite the extensive column activity of the next few months in his brigade area. The National Army uniforms taken at Kenmare were to prove useful in attacks on other posts.

The Kenmare coup enormously raised Republican morale, but little attempt after it was made to move on the other main centres of population in the Iveragh peninsula. Reinforcements were quickly sent by the government to the garrisons at Cahirciveen and Valencia.

On 10 September men from the 6th and 8th Battalions of Kerry No. 1 Brigade and from West Limerick took Tarbert, claiming to have captured forty rifles. During the same period Abbeyfeale was briefly taken, but such Republican successes in the north of the county were isolated events.[14]

The attack on Killorglin demonstrated much of the same failure of the Republicans' planning and co-ordination as that at Kenmare, but with much less happy results for them. A force of possibly 500, led by Seán Hyde and Humphrey Murphy, failed to overwhelm a garrison of sixty Clare men. The attempt to burn down the main barracks and to rush other buildings proved abortive. Hyde was to complain that some of the sections converging on the town failed to take up their positions. David Robinson, who was once again engaged in the attack, criticised the vagueness of the arrangements made—he had been left behind and had to take a pony and trap to Killorglin. 'The attack was a total failure', Robinson concluded, 'and we returned at night fall with a lot of wounded and killed.' British intelligence sources claimed that twenty-three Republicans were killed and thirty wounded during the operation, but Robinson, by contrast, stated that only two were killed, fifteen wounded, and fourteen captured. One of the Republicans who surrendered, John Galvin, admitted under interrogation that he had earlier killed a pro-Treaty officer during an attack on a bridge at Castlemaine. Next day Galvin's body was found in Ballyseedy Wood, near Tralee. Robinson commented on this: 'I cannot believe that Mulcahy would tolerate it for a minute, but I wonder would he take enough trouble to find out the real truth?' Key elements in the local population regarded the attack with no great relish. An American hotel owner warned that he would complain to the United States government if his sick wife was disturbed, and it was reputedly the local priest who sent for pro-Treaty reinforcements. Some Republicans attributed their failure partly to the fact that they were unaware that pro-Treaty troops were billeted in different houses. After the attack had lasted twenty-four hours, mainly consisting of sniping, pro-Treaty reinforcements arrived from Tralee.[15]

The Killorglin failure evidently made Republicans reluctant to attack town posts on a large scale. Further improvements in the Kerry situation for the pro-Treaty forces, however, came only in late November and December after considerable reinforcements had arrived. A successful sweep of the Dingle peninsula, which had often been postponed, was made, and leading members of the important Ballymacelligott column were arrested. In early December Kenmare was retaken; prominent Republicans like Tom McEllistrim, Tadhg Brosnan and Paddy Cahill were reported inactive. In December, just before he left the command, General Murphy reported little Republican military activity, but protested about the absence of any effective civil authority in the county. Murphy concluded:

> The Irregular organisation here is well-nigh broken up.... The capture of Kenmare will dispose of their last rallying ground.... We are still 250 men short of the 1,000 I budgeted for. With those we could put posts in Barraduff, Beaufort and Glenbeigh and one in Kilgarvan.... Then you can mark off Kerry as finished. In fact it is nearly as even now.

Murphy was refused the 250 reinforcements he requested because of the need for men in Dublin at the time of the final British troop evacuation. In fact he proved vastly over-optimistic: the south and east of the county continued to be dominated by Republican columns.[16]

(c) THE 2nd SOUTHERN DIVISION

South Tipperary, together with Cork, represented the most disappointing of failures for Republican military policy. The sundry columns remained active, but few Republican military initiatives were taken. Micky Fitzpatrick, one of the local leaders, commented: 'There was no offensive action and there was no fighting at all from the first week of July.' While praising the captures of Kenmare and Ballina, Liam Lynch wrote: 'I am urging the 2nd Southern ... which are so well armed to at once concentrate on the capture of some posts.' For the most part, the column men retired to the recesses of the Nire valley and the Glen of Aherlow, making sporadic moves out to ambush pro-Treaty troops and to block communications. After making a tour of inspection, Liam Deasy commented on the pro-Treaty forces: 'In many villages and important towns in 2nd Southern (outside of S. Tipp) garrisons of 25 are holding—no wonder they [the pro-Treaty troops] can concentrate on South when these conditions exist.'[17]

Throughout the war Republican military leaders in South Tipperary continued to operate as individuals. It appears that Dinny Lacey, the O/C of No. 3 Brigade, still refused to take orders from Séamus Robinson, the divisional O/C. Meanwhile other battalion and column leaders in Lacey's brigade area, for example Jerome Davis, took their orders directly from the division, not from Lacey. When Robinson organised a truce with Tom Carew, the pro-Treaty commandant in the Clonmel area, it was soon broken by Lacey's staging of an ambush of some of Carew's troops at Woodruffe, in which Carew and his driver were hurt. The situation was still further complicated by Lacey's policy of shifting some men from their own areas. Fitzpatrick concluded: 'Nobody knew who was in charge.'

Fitzpatrick commented on Lacey's stubborness, and on the fact that he was inarticulate. Lacey did, however, have a much stronger reputation as a fighter than Robinson, and he took a hard line on any looting by his men. Like O'Malley before him, Robinson appears to have exerted little control over his division. 'We were hanging around Clonmel,' Fitzpatrick recalled, 'but we wanted to break up and to do something but Séamus was not giving us orders to do anything.' By October Liam Lynch was intending to place Tom Barry in charge of operations in the 2nd Southern Division, observing: 'Splendid opportunities are being neglected for want of proper direction in this area.'[18]

Of all pro-Treaty commands, Prout's in the south-east got the worst publicity during the first half of the war, and it had extremely strained relations with GHQ. In December 1922, when Prout requested GHQ to supply more arms, he received the reply: 'Your officers and men are letting us down at a critical moment and throwing away the fruits of months of work.'

A Provisional Government army report of 13 October stated: 'Indiscipline is reported to be common amongst our Troops, especially in the Clonmel District. . . . A deputation—consisting of the Mayor and Town Clerk—recently interviewed Major-General McGrath. They reported a very serious condition of affairs in this area—charging our men with drunkenness etc.' A Callan priest told Cosgrave that Prout 'is too weak as well as too guileless to handle traitorous or semi-mutinous Incompetents. . . . The local clergy and local leaders would in most cases be only too delighted to help, but they seem completely ignored.'

The worst developments in the command came in early December with the Republican capture of Carrick-on-Suir, followed in quick succession by that of Callan, Thomastown and Mullinavat in the south-western part of Co. Kilkenny. On 13 December Tom Barry led an attack on Carrick by about a hundred Cork and Tipperary men. The pro-Treaty garrison was surprised and the town easily taken. Phelan, the Free State army's Intelligence Officer for the area, put Carrick's capture down to the lack of discipline of the pro-Treaty troops and the failings of the local O/C, Captain Barrett. The Republicans seized 107 rifles, two Lewis guns, one Crossley tender and two touring cars. Uniforms acquired as a result of this operation were later used in the capture of the Kilkenny barracks.

In the course of discussions with the Republicans about a truce the pro-Treaty O/Cs at Callan and Thomastown, Somers and Kerwick, agreed to hand over their posts when their commissions expired on 6 December. Information on the activity of pro-Treaty flying columns had previously been given to the other side by Somers, Kerwick and Captain Kelly, the O/C of Mooncoin barracks. The command's Intelligence Officer reported on 16 December: 'The procedure for betrayal was the same in all cases. He [Somers] entertained the three Garrisons, shaking hands with the Officer in Charge, having a party of Irregulars with him in full National Army Uniform.' After sixty rifles had been taken on 14 December at Callan, where twenty of Somers's men went over to the Republican side, they took Mullinavat and Thomastown. Lacey and Bill Quirke of the South Tipperary leadership were present at the taking of Callan. It was difficult, even for the censored press, to hide the import of these attacks. Stephen Gwynn commented in the London *Observer*: 'Three important garrisons in County Kilkenny were captured without a shot fired, and with no following counter-strokes.'

The taking of these posts did not lead to further successes—despite Barry's reported nebulous idea of moving on to the Curragh. There is no evidence that Barry had taken over as Director of Operations in the 2nd Southern Division, or that he was acting under instructions in taking Carrick; he remained a law unto himself.[19]

These events resulted in complaints against pro-Treaty troops reaching a new pitch, and in GHQ sending Commandant-General Eamon Price to investigate the command. His report noted the 'extreme lassitude' caused by the treacherous behaviour of certain officers and the bad effect of peace rumours. He felt that the principal problem was the lack of initiative shown by the General Staff, and he described the command staff at Kilkenny as a 'nesting ground for "buckshie" Officers'. Price sympathised with Prout and agreed with his frequent demands for more arms, and particularly transport, but was heavily critical of the officers under Prout, describing the intelligence staff as 'indicative of the dry rot which has stolen in here. . . . The intelligence of the Irregulars particularly in the South is pre-eminently superior to ours.' Price recommended the transfer of the command headquarters from Kilkenny to Clonmel, and the bringing in of outside officers and more supplies.[20]

(d) LIMERICK AND NORTH TIPPERARY

In the Limerick and North Tipperary areas of the 3rd Southern Division small Republican columns, usually of a strength of less than twenty, operated in isolated areas, such as the Birdhill region and the area around Galbally and Newport. The overall strength of these units was very limited, and little offensive or co-ordinated activity was shown. Liam Lynch commented that East Limerick was 'one of the slack areas', and the divisional adjutant reported on 13 November: 'West Limerick, after doing such good work at the start, is now over-run with troops, and have lost some good men.' One of the column leaders, Seán Gaynor, admitted: 'Our general attitude was defensive. We were not going out to look for fight.' He pointed out that there was: 'No organised plan in the Civil War. You were left on your own to do whatever you thought you were able to do.' Seán Hynes, of Mid-Limerick, concluded: 'There was no edge to that activity at all.'

From the pro-Treaty troop perspective, it was the familiar story of an inadequate number of poorly trained men failing to finish off the job which would have appeared to have been near completion by early September. A Provisional Government report of 20 November indicated that the Limerick area was very quiet with the exception of the territory around Castleconnell. It stated that

> The Irregulars are not numerous but their leader, Carroll, is uncommonly active and enterprising. They also, combine forces with the North Tipperary Irregulars and always have a perfectly safe and open line of retreat through Newport to the Silvermines. It would be necessary to have a post in Newport to deal with the Silvermines and Castleconnell Area. We have not men enough to establish this Post.

The resort to guerrilla warfare reinforced the local particularism of the various columns. Seán Carroll, the O/C for Mid-Limerick, told Ernie O'Malley that he had moved there in order to link up with the Tipperary men, as he had found it impossible to work with Seán Forde in East Limerick. Matt Ryan and Seán Daly objected to what they regarded as Seán Gaynor's defensive outlook in the Silvermines area, and Paddy Ryan Lacken in North Tipperary was criticised for his unwillingness to retreat from his mountain bases.[21]

(e) DUBLIN

The Republican cause in Dublin city continued to be very depressed. Ernie O'Malley reported on the South Dublin Brigade that 'roughly from 65 to 70 per cent' of the men and ninety per cent of the officers had been arrested, and that 'Vacancies in Officer's [*sic*] ranks have been filled, but, of course, with inexperienced men, and before they have time to settle down in their new positions they are arrested.' The success in destroying an armoured train at Inchicore in July was followed by the loss of three Republican columns the next day. Individual Republicans were vulnerable to the activities of the recently expanded CID, based at Oriel House, who travelled around in mufti. Kit Smith, one of the Republican column men, commented: 'You had to take it that you had no friends.' Accusations were frequently made of unauthorised killings by CID men, for instance of two Fianna boys.[22]

O'Malley spent his time in his elegant retreat at Mrs Humphreys's house in the prosperous Herbert Park area, working on the administrative details of his command, for much of which there was no evidence of its functioning. By September some small columns had been set up which were responsible for a few street ambushes and attacks on property. A projected attack on Oriel House on 30 October was aborted at the last moment; a raid on Wellington Barracks a week later produced some pro-Treaty casualties, but was otherwise unsuccessful; and an assault on Mulcahy's home also failed. A priority target was Mountjoy Prison, but plans to stage a major rescue of key prisoners came to nothing.

In the south of the county a small column had some success in breaking railway communications in the well-to-do outer suburbs of Dalkey, Stillorgan and Foxrock, and the assault on the house of the prominent Unionist Sir Henry Robinson became an early example of the Republican desire to attack conspicuous Anglo-Irish wealth.[23]

Liam Lynch admitted that no large-scale activities were possible in the Dublin area and pointed out to O'Malley that his units should concentrate on destroying communications. In response, O'Malley was to complain about the lack of trained engineers and explosives in his command, a situation not helped by the failure of Russell's munitions factory to start up again after Russell's escape from prison.[24]

On 4 November O'Malley was arrested in an episode which the *Irish Times* described as resembling the plot of an adventure film. It occurred just after he had been asked to take command in the west, an appointment which he was looking forward to enthusiastically. When, in the early hours of the morning, pro-Treaty troops surrounded Mrs Humphreys's house in Ailesbury Road, O'Malley was in his concealed cupboard hideout; but the government troops, with their Anglo-Irish War experience, knew where to find him. Determined to avoid surrender, and against all the odds, O'Malley decided to shoot his way out. During a hefty exchange of fire he was badly wounded and spent the next few months fighting for his life in a prison hospital; a pro-Treaty soldier was killed, and a Miss O'Rahilly, who was staying in the house, was accidentally wounded by O'Malley.

Ernie O'Malley had built up the strongest of reputations as a fighter during the Anglo-Irish War, perhaps second only to Tom Barry's. His military talents had been little availed of since the Four Courts attack. For the rest of the conflict O'Malley thought that he was the most obvious of candidates for execution—but perhaps pro-Treaty leaders were reluctant to execute a badly wounded man with his reputation. By the time of his arrest O'Malley had become extremely pessimistic about Republican prospects in the war and was very critical of the way it was being conducted. He reflected that 'men were being picked up slowly with or without arms and that they might as well go fighting as to be taken like sheep putting up no resistance. . . . A good fight would set a standard.'[25]

(f) THE WEST

West Mayo, Sligo and part of Leitrim remained major problems for pro-Treaty troops throughout the war, and other western areas, notably Connemara and the Tuam region of Co. Galway, proved very difficult to rid of Republican armed presence. Michael Kilroy's columns, operating around Newport, Westport, Castlebar and West Connemara, and Frank Carty's, usually centred in the Tobercurry district, were among the largest and most active Republican forces in the Twenty-Six Counties during the early phases of the war. Early in September 1922 Kilroy was appointed O/C of a new Western Command.

The election results of 1922 and 1923 demonstrated the continuing reservoir of Republican support in the west; there appears to have been considerable public tolerance, admitted by many pro-Treaty sources, of Republican columns encouraged by the unpopularity of government troops, the continuing land-hunger and the traditional suspicion of central government.

The difficulties of extending the government's authority to the remote west were made infinitely worse by the inefficiency of Mac Eoin's Athlone Command, which had to attempt to regain control of the area from the unsuitable base of Athlone. At times a large-scale sweeps policy was attempted, but never effectively enough, nor with the necessary support from the local population. The Republican columns, for their part, never attempted any consistent or coherent aggressive policy; major successes, such as the capture of Ballina in September and Clifden in late October, were not used as the basis for further operations and amounted to little more than raids for arms and food.

The Athlone Command's Intelligence Officer complained in late October that the army had lost a great opportunity to move decisively against the Republican columns after the Westport landing. 'Last July,' he wrote, 'when the National forces reached Castlebar, a force of 150 men would [have] defeat [sic] Kilroy's men in a week if they followed them up. Every day's delay since is adding strength to his force.' Mac Eoin complained to GHQ that a large sweep of Co. Sligo, planned for August, was delayed because of a lack of supplies.[26]

The great strength of the Republican columns was their mobility, local knowledge and roots; they were aided by their geographical isolation and the mountainous terrain—when pressed, they could retreat to the islands and use the sea for transporting supplies. The basic column unit consisted of between twenty and thirty men. A pro-Treaty intelligence report on 1 November said that Kilroy 'has the advantage of knowing the country well together with the impregnable positions'. Many sources claimed Kilroy had from 500 to 700 men under his direct command, although that is impossible to prove, considering the part-time, episodic character of so much of the column work. Kilroy's men ranged far and wide from their headquarters, which were generally north of Newport.

A local pro-Treaty supporter reported on 30 October:

> The people of Newport—with the exception of about 300 are unanimously with them now and in the west public opinion is gradually veering round to the Irregulars simply because not having seen any National troops or any concrete proof that such exist and being fed continuously with 'irregular' propaganda they are simply losing faith in us. This has reference in particular to the Newport, Achill, Belmullet, Bangor Area. In public opinion Kilroy is *the* absolute moving force of the west and the phrase 'Why cannot they Tackle Kilroy' is heard everywhere.

Kilroy's men were able to operate within a very short distance of pro-Treaty garrisons, which were unwilling to engage his men directly. In some of these areas publican licensee duties were collected by Republicans. Kilroy appears to have been sensitive to the danger of alienating public opinion, as was shown by his opposition to the raiding of banks.

Kilroy was best known for his munitions factory—a field of undertaking in which little was done in other areas. Pro-Treaty intelligence reports in October and November revealed that Kilroy had built three armoured cars and was probably working on trench mortars. One report concluded that Kilroy 'seems to be running a kind of Woolwich Arsenal on his own. He has nearly 400 tons of flour and 300 tons of coal.' Kilroy was said to have been making armoured cars out of boilers taken from the Mulranny Hotel and steel plates from the barracks there. A fourth armoured car was said to have been made out of shutters taken at Clifden. In addition, the factory was turning out mines and bombs.

By November pro-Treaty intelligence sources were saying that a thousand troops were needed to clear up the area. They argued that if they were not provided, Kilroy 'will be in a position to clear enemy Garrisons out of Mayo before Xmas. He is able to get a man for every rifle and when he has more Garrisons taken... the chances of ever defeating him will be remote.' Fears at that time, however, that Republican attacks on Westport and Castlebar were imminent proved unjustified. Meanwhile Republican resistance in East Mayo was greatly weakened by the capture in October of Tom Maguire, the divisional O/C, and of Tom Powell and his Ballinrobe column in November.[27]

The most dramatic evidence of Kilroy's strength, and the vulnerability of pro-Treaty posts, came with the capture of Ballina on 12 September. Liam Lynch was to hail this as one of the major Republican triumphs of the war's early stages. The Intelligence Officer for Mac Eoin's command reported that 100 rifles and 20,000 rounds of ammunition were taken from Ballina barracks; he claimed that goods worth £25,000 were looted from shops, and that banks had been raided.

The armoured car, the *Ballinalee*, which had been in action two days before in an attack on Tobercurry, was lent for the Ballina attack. Good advantage was taken of local intelligence as the raid began with an attack on the chief pro-Treaty post at the Imperial Hotel when pro-Treaty troops were at a special mass for a dead colleague. Kilroy related that after the hotel had been taken the Republican officers used the captured pro-Treaty officers 'to force the other posts to surrender'. He commented: 'This may not appear honourable to you but I told the Officers concerned not to forget the hateful tactics by which the Staters murdered their brother officer Ned Hegarty.' In any event, 'The trick succeeded', and the other posts were taken without a shot being fired. A body of pro-Treaty troops under Tony Lawlor was despatched to retake Ballina. The Republicans had left by the time he arrived.

While the Ballina attack was greeted as a Republican triumph, Kilroy was very dissatisfied about the behaviour of his men during the operation, and by the failure to follow the coup up with the capture of other large posts. He stated that their original aim had been to move on to take Crossmolina, Westport and Castlebar as part of a general plan to clear the county of pro-Treaty troops: they then planned to commandeer a train and travel to Athlone.

Kilroy put most of the problems on the Ballina expedition down to drink. He concluded: 'It was dangerous for us to take a lot of our men and even Officers into a town or any place [where] liquor is to be got.' He reported that 'After arriving in the camp . . . I saw a bottle of whiskey in Comdt. Kelly's hand in the midst of Officers whom I thought were to help me in stamping out this terrible evil, and I simply smashed it against the wall.'

When Kilroy heard of Lawlor's advance he evacuated Ballina and returned to his home base via the long coast route. While he concluded that his men were in no fit condition to move on, as planned, to capture other towns, he did give orders to advance on Crossmolina in order to ease the pressure on those still operating around Ballina. On the spread of a rumour that Lawlor was advancing in strength on Crossmolina, this plan was abandoned and the Republican unit involved retreated. During the retreat Kilroy's armoured car sunk in the road. On 14 September his men ambushed a party of forty pro-Treaty troops between Ballycastle and Belderg; the advance guard was captured and sixteen rifles taken. Following the failure of another plan to attack Crossmolina, a large assault was made on Newport on the night of 16-17 September; the town was entered, but was not taken because of confusion over mines. As a result of more Republican pressure on Newport, the Provisional Government army evacuated the garrison there on 24 September.

Kilroy drew extremely depressing conclusions from the frustrating sequence of events following his initial success at Ballina. Gloomily reviewing the situation, he recorded:

> I thought it would be no difficulty for us to collect the total revenue of a large portion of our Command after this week, but instead I am now stuck in the bogs with my cars and machinery that we recaptured from the enemy while the enemy whom we captured are behind us in our Hotel. . . . [I feel] just like a big fool with all my Air Castles tumbled to the ground. . . . Just imagine about 60 rifle men as well as Officers and Special Service and others to spare standing to since Sunday night according to my orders, around Newport, Westport and Castlebar waiting for my arrival and here I am stuck in the Bog of Erris and Tyrawley like a highwayman or an outcast. . . . Just imagine the humiliation of it all, the victorious IRA sooner than tackle a handful of already routed Troops in Crossmolina, to start off for Newport . . . only to end in the bogs of the North Coast road and through the fear of having the Armour Car bottled up in Erris sending her back again in all haste to the 3rd Western Division, and even now I do not know if she has got safely back.[28]

While the Republican units were retreating from Ballina they staged a successful ambush of some of Lawlor's advancing forces in the Ox Mountains, in which Brigadier Joe Ring was killed and Lawlor wounded. Ring had been the only leading IRA officer in Mayo to go pro-Treaty.

The next offensive move by the Republicans was the raid on Clifden in late October, when an armoured car was again used and men from North Mayo and Connemara were involved. The fighting lasted from 7 a.m. to 5 p.m., and nearly eighty of the garrison were captured: Colonel-Commandant O'Malley, the pro-Treaty O/C, refused to surrender until the result was clear. A pro-Treaty intelligence report admitted that Clifden's taking was 'a great coup'. For Kilroy again, however, it had no long-term consequence.[29]

In Co. Sligo Frank Carty's column had become progressively more active since the adoption of guerrilla tactics, and a party of engineers came from Belfast to aid Carty. Rahelly House remained the headquarters for raids on Sligo town and the area around Rosses Point and Ben Bulben, with the numbers there usually amounting to around 150. There were various attacks on Tobercurry by Carty's column, including one on 26 August when thirty rifles were captured; Dromahaire barracks was taken on 4 September when the pro-Treaty garrison surrendered to Pilkington's unit, and Drumshanbo garrison was seized on 14 September after the troops there had been lured into an ambush by false information.[30]

Mac Eoin's long-planned sweep of North Sligo began on 19 September. An encircling movement by several columns was made on Rahelly, aided by men from Joe Sweeney's Donegal Command and troops from Fermanagh. After receiving information of pro-Treaty troops leaving Sligo town, the Republican units evacuated Rahelly and briefly delayed the pro-Treaty advance at Milltown. The Republican plan appears to have been to fall back on Manorhamilton, but their attempt to do so came adrift, perhaps, as Tom Scanlon suggested, because of their not allowing sufficiently for the distance involved. During the desperate Republican retreat their prize possession, the *Ballinalee*, was cornered on a dead-end road at Liscally Bridge, near Grange, and its engine was wrecked by shells from an enemy armoured car. The *Ballinalee*'s crew was forced to retreat up the large expanse of Ben Bulben, where nine were killed, four of them under extremely suspicious circumstances. Among the four were Brigadier-General Séamus Devins, of the No. 1 Brigade of the 3rd Western Division, and Brian Mac Néill, the divisional adjutant, one of Eoin Mac Néill's sons, who had a brother in the pro-Treaty forces. The pro-Treaty Intelligence Officer for the area reported that Mac Néill had been shot through the forehead, Devins through the heart, 'while Banks and Carroll were absolutely mangled by Machine Gun fire'. Mac Néill's name was held back in the immediate press announcement for 'diplomatic reasons'.

It is impossible to be dogmatic on whether the men were shot after surrender, as was widely claimed by Republican commentators. Mac Eoin claimed that the four were shot on their way up the mountain and that their death was necessary in a war context. In early January 1923 one of the pro-Treaty force who had been involved in the operation was reported as giving an account backing Republican claims, recalling that near the top of Ben Bulben, after the four had surrendered, the pro-Treaty officers 'apparently decided to shoot the prisoners, as the members of the party were asked to volunteer for a firing party to shoot them. This the men would not do.' According to the soldier's account, the two captains and four of the former British soldiers remained behind, and the sound of machine-gun fire was soon heard.[31]

The North Sligo round-up meant the smashing of large Republican concentrations. There were to be no more major confrontations in Co. Sligo. Carty's column remained frequently active, a pro-Treaty military report noting on 15 December: 'The District between Collooney and Dromore West has been the scene of great activity by the Irregulars. Frank Carty's columns are hovering round here for the past three weeks, and they hold up all motors passing on the road between Ballina and Sligo.' On 9 December a small Republican force wearing Free State uniforms stormed into the pro-Treaty garrison at Sligo town hall through the main door and escaped with four rifles and 150 rounds of .303 ammunition. One of the Free State troops was killed in the action. Two Republicans—Tom MacEvilly, a Gaelic teacher, and Frank Pilkington, a brother of Liam Pilkington, O/C 3rd Western Division—were later arrested in connection with the attack.

The Provisional Government's GHQ became progressively more impatient with the failure of Mac Eoin's command to clear up Mayo and Sligo. On 19 October Mulcahy told Mac Eoin that he had thought before that the problems were limited to the West Mayo area, but that he had recently had reports of disturbances in the Sligo and the Ballinrobe areas and received numerous complaints about the behaviour and performance of pro-Treaty troops in the west, notably from William Sears, one of the area's TDs, and from various priests. In late September Professor Joseph Whelehan, TD, deprecatingly observed that 'our troops had made absolutely no impression on Mayo', and a Sligo doctor bitterly criticised the troops' failure to make use of a potentially friendly local population in order to gain intelligence information. Mulcahy concluded that if 'the troops had been kept busy and on alert the areas could have been cleared long before. . . . The people of the area feel that no impression at all is being made on the situation, and that they are beginning to whisper to themselves that they have no confidence in "Seán McKeon".' There were frequent complaints about bills being unpaid and goods commandeered by pro-Treaty troops.[32]

The worst kind of adverse publicity resulted from Lawlor's fatal shooting of Patrick Mulrennan in Athlone jail on 6 October. There had been frequent incidents there before, involving Mac Eoin and Lawlor: ashplants had been used to put down disturbances, and shots had been fired over the heads of rioters. Eventually, during further riots, Lawlor deliberately shot Mulrennan, who later died. Mac Eoin defended Lawlor's action. Lawlor sought to justify himself in a letter to his mother, which was captured and proved of marvellous propaganda value for the Republicans. Lawlor wrote: 'I don't believe in shooting as a wholesale medicine but a little is very usefull [sic]. . . . It was a wonderful shot.' He claimed that the jail had been orderly since the shooting. In that letter Lawlor revealed just as unhealthy an attitude to some of his own troops: 'I sentenced eight of my own men to death for kicking up a row but Seán let them off. . . . In a new outfit like ours Discipline must be strenuously maintained at any cost. I don't believe in shooting for vengeance, certainly not.'[33]

Mac Eoin attributed the inadequacy of his troops' performance to lack of support from GHQ. When on 4 September he asked for more supplies he was told that supplies were more urgently needed elsewhere. Mac Eoin informed Mulcahy that the failure to pay the troops regularly had led to the surrender of the Dromahaire garrison; he also complained about local officers being replaced by outsiders—the Civic Guard had, therefore, taken over from the brigade's police chief. Mac Eoin argued that 'Because I stood for a certain thing ... they stood with me.... If GHQ carry on as present ... even my influence with them will be severely tested.' His officers were reporting 'that men have not been supplied with uniform or underclothing or pay some as long as 4 months', and when mutinous troops handed over Charlestown barracks to the Republicans 'it was reported that the garrison said there was no use in fighting for those who don't care to look after us'. From Sligo also came complaints about lack of resources; on 7 November a pro-Treaty officer commented: 'A column of about 50 men under Carty is making a circuit of the Tubbercurry area leaving a trail of blood behind them. It is impossible to follow them up as we are short of ammunition, rifles and Transport.' As late as December Lawlor was gloomily noting that 'So far as I can see there is no Transport in the West.'

Mac Eoin's command was in desperate need of reorganisation and reduction in size; there were considerable grounds for the strictures about lack of supplies. While severely critical of Mac Eoin and Lawlor, Mulcahy could not remove them during such a vulnerable period.

At the end of November a massive attempt was made to clear West and South Mayo and Connemara of Republican columns. The efforts had very limited results, although the prize capture of Kilroy was made.[34]

Christy Macken, one of the Republican column leaders, said that they had received advanced warning of Lawlor's attack and many retreated to the islands to avoid the advancing troops; they did not lose many men. Lawlor declared that five of his troops were killed during the operations, and nine wounded. He also claimed that eleven Republicans were killed, nineteen wounded, and twenty-three taken prisoner. After receiving Lawlor's report on his operations, one GHQ officer considered that it provided 'an explanation of the lousiness of the Western Command. It is not fair to the rank and file to let Lawlor loose like this.'

Provisional Government troops moved from various directions on the Republican strongholds, using Crossmolina and Castlebar as advance bases. They journeyed first to the Newport area, where, in a brief ambush of Lawlor's forces, Kilroy was wounded and captured. Three pro-Treaty officers, as well as two men, were killed. Lawlor admitted, in his eccentric report, that the Republicans had retreated from the area and that they had a much greater knowledge of the countryside. He told Mac Eoin:

> You will have to keep me full of 303 [sic]. I am using it unstintingly, its the only way.... Our Columns have had several brushes with enemy, but, its next impossible to get them in the mountain.... I must have mounted Infantry, you cannot travel the country on foot.... You cannot move faster than $1\frac{1}{2}$ miles an hour, and a scrap delays you from two to twelve hours.

Despite these drawbacks, and problems with food supplies, Lawlor concluded: 'I have broken the back of the Irregulars, but, they are like an eel their bits jump about.' From Newport he force-marched his men to the Mulranny and Glenhest area, where he commandeered whiskey from a store and reported:

> 250 men were in town, and, all had been wet to the waist, most to the armpits fording a river under fire. It was raining, and there were few beds, therefore,

> I gave every man a glass of whiskey, ¼ loaf. ½ tin Bully Beef etc. and made big fires. I am happy to say the men suffered little as a result of their hardships.

Lawlor complained that his instructions to his men to return to their bases only when permission was granted by their O/C were frequently disregarded; he affirmed that if necessary he would take 'disciplinary action, even to enforcing the Supreme Penalty'. Lawlor told Mac Eoin that he was 'enforcing absolute Prussian Discipline here':

> I do not tolerate the least deviation from orders. . . . I am putting a stop to the drinking here, though Poteen is an awful curse. . . . This enforcing of Discipline was a nasty shock to some of the men at first. It must be understood that I am acting as a Governor of Mayo, who has plenary powers, anything less is worse than useless.

From the Newport and Mulranny districts Lawlor's columns moved down by special train to sweep the Ballinrobe area, the South Mayo mountain range and parts of Connemara. By that time Lawlor was admitting that he was imposing forced marches on already exhausted troops. 'I had to absolutely force the pace at times,' he wrote.'. . . The Doctors of course said that three-quarters of the men should be in Hospital but I had to will otherwise. I had to punish men for reporting sick, or else I would have no one left.' Eventually thirty men were transferred to hospital as bad weather caused influenza attacks on top of the exhaustion they were already suffering.[35]

Lawlor's 'big push' produced a highly critical local response. Father T. Brett, CC, Kilmaine, complained that in his village a public house was raided while Lawlor's men were on the Dartry Hills, together with the men of the local garrison, whose assistance they had commandeered. Brett commented on the harsh manner in which Lawlor handled his troops, recounting that a Longford contingent had arrived in Ballinrobe after a long march with only two hours sleep; they were, he wrote, 'most disgusted at the way they were handled by their officers'. Canon D'Alton, the parish priest of Ballinrobe, related that part of Lawlor's sweeping force had failed, despite accurate intelligence information, to take on the Republican units at both Leenaun and Kilmullin; at the latter, when they caught sight of the enemy, 'they retreated, without firing a shot, losing one dead and three prisoners. They would have lost more, but the enemy also ran away, never halting till they got to Maam Cross.' D'Alton was not critical of the troops, however, because by that time they were exhausted and 'in scattered bands, not a few without shoes or stockings'. One officer, he described, 'was left with a party of men in the Dartry Mountains to guard a post while his comrades went forward to reconnoitre. But when the first shot was fired the Volunteer officer took to his heels, taking 20 men with him, and never halted till he reached Ballinrobe. Then he went home to his parents where he remains.'

Following Kilroy's capture, and probably as a result of Lawlor's sweeps, there was a lessening of Republican activity in Mayo during December; the main strength had retreated to Connemara. Lawlor was vastly over-optimistic, however, to claim that 'Another month will finish the West completely except of course for ordinary crimes and offences.'[36]

The extreme poverty of many areas in the far west was important in reducing any prospect of continuous and effective Republican column activity. In early December 1922 C. Ó Gaora of the No. 4 Brigade, covering East Connemara, in the 4th Western Division area, wrote to his divisional O/C:

> Since the commencement of hostilities last June, our ASU's numbering about 80 men, are in a pitiable and most desperate condition in need of proper clothing and feeding, especially since the Winter months. As you will see by the geographical position of our area it is the poorest in Ireland, and the shops in our area which are small did not stock the stuff required by our men, and therefore the necessaries needed could not be commandeered.

Ó Gaora pointed out that their columns were extremely badly clothed and often had to go without any fresh meat. 'The people [who have stood with us] are of the poorest type in Ireland,' he continued, 'and I consider it a crime to trespass much longer on their hospitality.' He concluded that if 'at least' £800 was not provided immediately for their use, 'the fighting spirit of our men will get broken, and the best material in the Brigade will get disheartened in the fight for the Republic'.

On 5 January 1923 the O/C of the West Connemara Brigade gave a similar depressing picture and stressed that if funds were not provided immediately, 'we must cease to function; as my men have neither boots nor warm clothing. . . . Men cannot stand it always being out in cold and wet without overcoats, and in wet feet, minus underclothing, etc.'[37]

Concentration on areas of active Republican resistance, such as Kerry and Mayo, should not obscure the fact that in a large part of the Twenty-Six Counties little military activity of any kind occurred for much of the war. Some counties which had little fighting record during the Anglo-Irish War became active during the Civil War—Wexford and Sligo for example. However, some areas saw little action in either conflict, including the Fingal area, north of Dublin, Meath, Carlow and Wicklow, and much of Co. Kilkenny; in large parts of the midlands and the east Republican organisation was virtually non-existent. Some of the inactive regions were geographically unsuited to guerrilla warfare, as Tom Barry pointed out about the flat land of Offaly, but that could not be said of the mountainous territory of Co. Wicklow. The election results before and after the war demonstrated that there was little public support for the anti-Treaty side in the fertile, prosperous areas around Dublin, which had much to gain by support of the government.

The 1st Eastern Division, to the west and north of Dublin, was a dismal area for Republican arms and organisation. The Meath No. 2 Brigade and the Mullingar Brigade were wrecked by arrests in the early days of the war, and most of the small number left were arrested in ones and twos. The Louth Brigade, and others in the division, retreated when a large pro-Treaty force took Drogheda. Michael Price, who became the divisional acting O/C, wrote: 'The Div. was never properly equipped, for, as you know, 69 rifles were all that were in it at the commencement of hostilities.'

Price talked of 'blank space' in the division which had never been integrated. He reported to O'Malley on his visit to Trim: 'I don't wish to be funny but I believe there is one man in the town with us.' O'Malley and Lynch had little knowledge of the division: two months into the war Lynch was asking what had become of Andy

Cooney, the old divisional O/C, who had in fact been in Mountjoy Prison since early July. O'Malley, however, soon grasped how little base existed for Republican IRA operations in the area. He reported on 24 August: 'The former QM has been acting O/C; in fact, he constitutes the entire staff and is doing very good work.' O'Malley said there were a mere 250 men in the division. As late as September, Lynch urged O'Malley to appoint a new O/C and staff in the division (although he was to disapprove of O'Malley's choice of Price). Arms were then supplied and there was some reorganisation, but the old problems remained.

The one area of the division where there was regular column activity was that covered by Bob Brennan's men in Co. Kildare, where they were assisted by Paddy Mullally's men from Meath. Brennan, however, was captured early in the war, and Mullally's column was taken into custody on 1 December after an armed confrontation on the Kildare and Meath border which resulted in one death on both sides.[38]

29

The Free State—Government and Army: January–April 1923

IN purely military terms, by Christmas 1922 prospects had immensely improved for the government. There had been a diminution in Republican column activities, even in the strongest centres of resistance; key leaders had been arrested, the IRA was incapable of launching any major offensive, and their activities were limited to specific, usually remote, areas. A Free State military report of 21 January 1923 commented on the Republicans:

> With depleted numbers, lack of resources and unified control, and almost complete ineffectiveness from a military standpoint, their policy of militant action is slowly changing to one of sheer destructiveness and obstruction of the Civil Government.

Nevertheless, there was deep concern about prospects for the new state. N. G. Loughnane, the British representative in Dublin, reported, after seeing Cosgrave, that Republican incendiary tactics had 'succeeded in rattling the civilian supporters of the Free State ... more than the Irregulars themselves knew'. The reasons for the pessimism can partly be put down to impatience: since July government propaganda had continually led people to believe that the war would soon be over and that only limited opposition remained to be overcome. Questions were bound to be asked when the conflict dragged on, in its messy way, into the new year. That large parts of the country were approaching normality only made the survival of pockets of Republican resistance the more alarming. There was a deepening frustration about the increasing destruction of property and communications which was threatening to prevent government being effectively established throughout the Twenty-Six Counties.[1]

Concern surfaced within the government when the Executive Council decided on 11 January that some of their members should meet representatives of the Army Council to discuss methods to deal 'with the lawlessness prevailing throughout the country, with a view to bringing it to a speedy end'. All the Executive Council were asked to prepare memoranda on the subject.

Kevin O'Higgins and Patrick Hogan wrote hard-hitting papers expressing acute alarm. O'Higgins argued that they were faced with an opposition which had a vested interest in law-breaking and social dislocation. He wrote: 'Leavened in with some small amount of idealism and fanaticism, there is a good deal of greed and envy and lust and drunkenness and irresponsibility.' Hogan emphasised the activities of the Tenants' Associations, which he likened to the Ku-Klux-

Klan—they were using murder and arson, he claimed, to acquire land. He cited five hundred examples of land seizure, and a dispute at Athy between farmers and labourers which led to the burning of seven farmers' property and the shooting of a farm steward. In the prevailing circumstances, he argued, it was impossible to implement any land purchase or compensation legislation. 'As the first sign of a crumbling civilisation,' O'Higgins wrote, 'the bailiff... has failed, and the system of impounding livestock, pending auction for recovery of a decree, has utterly broken down. It has become impossible to obtain men to act in the capacity of bailiff, and there are large numbers of decrees (Co. Court and High Court) unexecuted in every County.' O'Higgins listed 247 unexecuted decrees in the Cork county court and 141 in the High Court; the figures for Kerry were 908 and 30 respectively, and 272 in the county court in Sligo.

For O'Higgins and Hogan large segments of the population were losing sympathy with the army and government. Hogan wrote: 'In my opinion the civilian population will surrender definitely before long if the Irregulars are able to continue their peculiar form of war.... Two months more like the last two months will see the end of us and the Free State.'

Hogan told the Dáil that 'We are prepared to take rough and ready methods.' 'The Irregulars', he wrote in his memorandum, 'must be beaten and terrorised by the utmost military activity.' Special army units, consisting of men from outside the localities, should, he held, be used to clear the land and implement decrees; legislation should be passed to enable seized land and property to be confiscated by the government. It was also suggested that mobile columns should be recruited to deal with difficult situations in any part of the country, and that considerable attention should be paid to settlement of military accounts and the army's relations with the community. O'Higgins argued that there should be executions in every county, as the news of capital charges in Dublin was having little effect in the provinces. Hogan felt that the unwillingness of local commands to implement execution orders, together with legal obstacles, should be overcome by the passage of further legislation. He concluded that a policy of extensive executions could only be applied for a limited time, 'but within that time they ought to be going with machine-like regularity'.

O'Higgins and Hogan had adopted an exaggerated tone and failed to differentiate between geographical regions—many large areas did not suffer from the problems of Kerry and Mayo. If O'Higgins had implemented some of the measures he advocated, the war would almost certainly have been even more bitter. O'Higgins was to claim that his measures helped to end the war. The Special Infantry Corps, however, which represented the mobile columns idea, was only set up at the very end of the war, and his property and land confiscation schemes cannot be said to have decisively affected the situation.[2]

Despite the Army Council's extension of the powers of military courts in January 1923, including an increase in the categories liable to execution, O'Higgins pressed for yet sterner measures to be taken. When it was suggested to Cosgrave that a proclamation should be issued 'warning that anybody found in arms after a certain date will be summarily shot without the option of being taken prisoner', Mulcahy commented: 'I could not run the possible and consequent dangers.' Cosgrave was told: 'You will never rule this country by adopting idealistic principles, nothing but the ruthless application of the Iron Hand will heal its ills.' In February it was suggested that there should be official reprisals for property burnt, and that internees 'should be kept in confinement for an indefinite period or released only on condition of leaving the country'. After the kidnappings of Senators Bagwell and Gogarty in January, Senators were armed and guarded, and O'Higgins introduced a policy on the arming of civilians.[3]

There was also increasingly strong criticism of the army's performance and leadership, and growing stress on the need to establish the government's control over the military. In the first months of the war the government had been entirely dependent on the army for its survival; any critical thoughts had to be suppressed. In the improved military situation, however, the spotlight was increasingly focused on the army's deficiencies. The army still lacked training and discipline and often appeared to be acting independently of central control; it also appeared to be too much influenced by old personal and institutional loyalties. For their part, the army leadership remained critical of civil government. A memorandum from the Chief of Staff in May 1923 complained of 'lack of everything except the Army. Everyone looks to the Army. No other department makes an attempt to function.' While admitting deficiencies in the army, the military leadership deeply resented what they regarded as ill-informed and insensitive political criticism.

Within the government O'Higgins took the lead in attacking the army's performance. He told the 1924 Army Enquiry that he had been 'far from satisfied that in Cork, Kerry, Leitrim, Sligo and other places, a genuine effort was made to afford the people that protection from violence and outrage which they were entitled to from an organisation of 50,000 costing them eleven million pounds in a single year'. O'Higgins admitted, under questioning, that such a hastily recruited army should not have been judged by the standards of an experienced, professional army, but stressed that 'There should be no conscious or deliberate departure from the standard by which other Armies are judged, but I believe there was such departure.' O'Higgins attributed some of the responsibility for the army's weakness to Mulcahy's failure to stand for 'stern impersonal discipline'. Supplied with information from Colonel Jephson O'Connell, he claimed that IRB membership had determined GHQ and GOC appointments. In common with many others, O'Higgins held that it was wrong for Mulcahy to hold the position of Minister for Defence as well as that of Commander-in-Chief. He commented: 'We have not had a Minister of Defence supervising the Army so much as a soldier in uniform defending the Army, scarcely recognising the right of this Body [the Executive Council] to be very much concerned about the discipline or efficiency of the Army.'[4]

Tensions between politicians and military were increased by the personal antipathy between O'Higgins and Mulcahy. Mulcahy was to describe O'Higgins as 'a frustrating and almost a malicious influence around my work'. O'Higgins showed considerable insensitivity in his criticisms and did not make anywhere near enough allowance for the enormous problems faced by the military leadership. For Mulcahy to have directly confronted many of the tensions would have risked the possibility of further schisms within the army. O'Higgins, moreover, greatly exaggerated the IRB's influence; in fact the IRB now met irregularly, and not at all in many areas, and had only been revived in December 1922 in order to combat Republican attempts to take over the remnants of the organisation. Mulcahy correctly claimed that to have banned any membership of secret societies would have been dangerous in the war context.

There was, moreover, much to be said for the army's leader continuing to act as Minister for Defence. Hugh Kennedy, the Attorney-General, in a memorandum to Cosgrave, argued that because the constitutional status of the army had been ill-defined and the army had exercised considerable independence over its own affairs, Collins's 'vesting of the supreme army command in the head of the civil government had an enormous political value'. He continued:

> It diverted the allegiance of the armed military executive to the civil executive government of the state and, though its effects in this direction may not have been sudden, they have been sure and far-reaching and have enabled the army to be gradually established on a constitutional basis. . . . It would be a grave and dangerous error to undo the work of Collins in this respect. To have a purely civil Ministry of Defence and a completely individual army organisation, to separate again what Collins pulled together, would be in my judgement to risk giving life to some of the troubles of which we have just steered clear, to set the ground for a crop of army irregularism finding in our unfortunate characteristic temperament ready nourishment for a conflict between the purely civil and the purely military.

The war was a crucial transitional phase in military–political relations, and the questions posed were not to be resolved, and then messily, until the army mutiny of 1924. O'Higgins's criticisms were more important in increasing tension between the political and military leadership than in improving the military situation.[5]

General Michael Costello said at the Army Enquiry that every officer admitted that 'there had been an extraordinary improvement in the Army about December until April'. Much of that was put down to the reorganisation of January, Seán MacMahon claiming that by March 'we had grasped every element in the Army'. Tim Healy, the Governor-General, commented to Lord Beaverbrook on 13 January on the Republican resistance: 'Our ability to cope with it becomes daily plainer. The army commands are stiffening in discipline and getting better results.' In February, in a letter to Michael Brennan, Mulcahy stated: 'We are getting some strength and discipline into the Army.'[6]

In the reorganisation many of the old vast commands were split up—most crucially a new Western Command was established, based at Claremorris. A battalion organisation was set up, a training period at the Curragh instituted for some officers, and a disciplinary code laid down for the first time. Any improvement, however, was only relative to the chaotic early days. In March the Dublin special correspondent of the *Manchester Guardian* commented: 'For the first time since General Collins fell I have heard a man speak with enthusiasm of a Free State officer and of his troops.'[7]

Many problems remained. The Curragh training scheme was only introduced on a limited basis, and, like the Inspection Corps, regarded as a dumping-ground for unwanted officers. The problem of surplus officers was only to be faced up to on any large scale after the end of the war. The GOCs retained a considerable degree of autonomy—Michael Costello claimed that the GOCs successfully resisted attempts at the time of the reorganisation to centralise the army more effectively. Inspection reports continued to reveal maladministration and inefficiency. Mac

Eoin's Athlone Command and Prout's Waterford one came under particularly harsh criticism from the newly organised Inspection Corps. Colonel Jephson O'Connell reported: 'In Athlone during April and May, I had seen impotence [and] indolence revered and waste glorified. I had seen the powerlessness of the Higher Command when brought face to face with the actual problem.' His first report on Kerry described 'almost indescribable chaos'. He claimed that 'The two most incompetent and indolent officers occupied the two senior administrative positions.'[8]

In February the CID was moved from Oriel House to 68 Merrion Square. After the early problems connected with the organisation's semi-military character under Liam Tobin, it had come under governmental control in September. In November the Protective Corps had been set up to act as an auxiliary to the seventy-five officers of the CID; it consisted of demobilised pro-Treaty troops and reached a strength of 175 by the end of the war. The Protective Corps's function included the collection of intelligence information on prisoners in the Dublin area and the protection of the houses of ministers. More controversially, the Citizens' Defence Force had been established, consisting of former British soldiers—101 officers and men whole-time, fifty part-time. It was organised on military lines, was semi-secret, and was concerned with guard and intelligence collection duties.

These units were merged in the February reorganisation under Joe McGrath; up to June 1923 approximately 350 were employed. Late in the war the CID claimed to have 2,200 intelligence files on Republicans; interrogation of prisoners produced the bulk of the evidence. The use of so-called 'mouse-trap' raids was thought to be effective; they involved the CID's clandestine occupation of a building and interrogating, and often imprisoning, callers. The CID also used touts, but one of the organisation's reports admitted that they proved of only limited success, 'owing to the counter espionage adopted by the "Irregulars"'. The report continued: 'Most of our "touts" became known after a short time and though in some cases they obtained excellent information on the whole the result of their activities was disappointing. Extreme patience and caution are two qualities required to make a successful tout and these are not qualities for which Irishmen are noted.' The CID sometimes successfully used spies to infiltrate Republican ranks.

In the Dáil Kevin O'Higgins gave credit to the CID's work in helping to end the war, but in the Executive Council he was highly critical of the force's membership. O'Higgins reported that out of 86 CID men, 25 were of a 'good type' and could be transferred after the war into the G Division of the DMP; he held 31 to be 'hopeless', and the remaining 30 to be of adequate standard, who could be disbanded and held on reserve.[9]

The period of army reorganisation brought to a head tensions between members of Collins's old intelligence staff and GHQ. In January a number of officers, led by Liam Tobin, set up their own organisation, to be known extremely confusingly, as either the 'Old IRA' or the 'Irish Republican Organisation'. Tobin and his colleagues deeply resented their exclusion from the IRB's revival in December 1922, and they held that they had not been given positions in the army commensurate with their services during the Anglo-Irish War. Colonel Charles Russell told the Army Enquiry that certain officers had been appointed to 'buckshie' or low-prestige positions during the reorganisation; Tobin, for example, had been commissioned as the Governor-General's aide-de-camp. and Charlie Dalton had become Adjutant of the extremely small-scale Air Service.[10]

The Tobinites focused resentment on the number of former British army officers and post-truce officers in positions of authority. O'Duffy quoted one officer, Tom Keogh, as saying that 'Every fighting man in Dublin is leaving the army if these snobs are kept on.' However, Seán MacMahon, the Chief of Staff, gave figures to the Army Enquiry demonstrating that the number of former British officers in the army was frequently exaggerated. He estimated that ninety per cent of the army's officers had served before the truce. 'Before reorganisation', he declared, 'when we had an army of 55,000 it was made up of roughly 25 per cent post-Truce and 75 per cent pre-Truce.' There was an awareness, therefore, that the army's character was changing considerably.

Much concern was also felt about what were regarded as changes in the army's objectives. At the end of the war General Michael Brennan told Mulcahy: 'We all here have been very worried for some time past at the prospect of finding that the Free State was the end for which we fought, not the means to that end.' Brennan affirmed that his whole command staff in Limerick, except for two, would not have

> lifted a finger for the Free State if they hadn't felt sure that it was the best means of attaining the end for which they fought the British and for which their comrades died. They asked me to assure you and the CGS that they would support by every means in their power your desire to make our Army one worthy of the past,—Irish in its training, Irish in its associations, Irish in its ideals, and *above all* Irish in *its object*.

Tobin's new organisation did not state its demands until after the war. Meanwhile the army leadership had to be extremely wary in its dealings with the various commands: to have confronted the issues directly could well have had disastrous results.[11]

The army throughout the war remained far from being effectively professionalised. An army report in late January stated: 'One cannot be in touch with people outside without noticing a weakening of confidence in the Army, in its ability to carry out its work.' The great advantage the Free State army possessed was its numbers, which built up to over 50,000 by March, and increasingly troops were concentrated in the key areas.

It was only near the war's end that institutional changes were made in the relationship between government and army. On 27 March the Executive Council decided to set up the Supreme War Council; four days earlier they had lowered the army estimates by over £4 million from the £14¾ million originally claimed. In the debate over the establishment of the new committee O'Higgins declared: 'I believe that the present Headquarters Staff has not given to the people the result which they are entitled to'; he went on to say that there were men in the army who would do a better job. For two months the British press had been speculating on changes in the General Staff, with, supposedly, former British soldiers like General W. R. E. Murphy and General Sir Bryan Mahon replacing Mulcahy. However, no personnel changes were made. One cabinet member was concerned that O'Higgins was attempting to appoint his own GHQ staff. It was feared that changes in the army's command could have endangered the army's unity and its loyalty to the state and encouraged Republican resistance.

The Supreme War Council had a civilian majority and was given considerable powers which limited the army's autonomy. It possessed the authority to enquire into the administration of any military department, and it could recommend to the Executive Council the removal of any officer, including generals. The committee had a veto over all military appointments and was 'to exercise a general supervision and direction over strategy subject to the approval of the Executive Council'.

On 28 March, the day after the decision to establish the new controlling body, an outraged Mulcahy wrote to Cosgrave resigning from the Army Council, declaring:

> I realise that yesterday's discussion at the Executive Council implies that the Executive Council felt dissatisfied with the work of the Army, and the general position with regard to the Government, with implications that: 1. The progress made by the Army up to the end of February has not been satisfactory. 2. That the control of the Army is aloof from and is felt to be unresponsive to the Government. 3. That there is some undefined divergence of purpose on the part of the Army, as from the Government.

Cosgrave immediately wrote to Mulcahy persuading him to rescind the resignations. The new committee, however, went ahead, reviewing the military situation, Free State intelligence methods, and the grounds upon which prisoners should be released; they established an enquiry into the killing of Breslin, a Republican soldier, and in late May arranged for a joint military and Civic Guard inspection of certain specified areas. The Supreme War Council set up the Special Infantry Corps, which was immediately given responsibility for the clearance of illegally occupied land in specific troubled areas.

The new committee could have had little significance in bringing the war to an end. Mulcahy held that its establishment unnecessarily took attention away from the measures being taken to bring the war to a speedy conclusion, and that it encouraged disharmony within the army, and between army and government.[12]

The Republicans and the Civil War: January–April 1923

THE first four months of 1923 saw a progressive disintegration of the Republican military effort. Any large-scale military activity was impossible; columns could only remain in existence if small; and arms and financial resources were extremely limited. In mid-February a Cork Republican wrote:

> The Staters have all areas overan [*sic*] and if a Column start off the next you find is a few thousand of the enemy rounding up. Columns cannot exist except in small parties and as jobs are few and far between the rule of the Torch and Can are proved to be more effective. Killing a few of the other side does not count as they can be easily replaced. Making Government impossible is your only chance of success and for the past month it has been more effective than for the six months prior to that.

In areas such as South Tipperary and Cork, where the Republican resistance should have been strongest, peace overtures were most frequent. The conflict had become patchy and localised and scarcely merited the term 'war'. Captures and deaths did much to demoralise the cause: by May over 12,000 Republicans were in prisons or internment camps. The only type of activity possible in much of the country was house-burning and the wrecking of communications. Only in Mayo, the Sligo–Leitrim border country, South Kerry and Wexford was activity widespread, and even there it was essentially a defensive struggle.

The Republican effort became demoralised not just because of the military hopelessness of their position. January saw the greatest number of executions—thirty-four—in any month during the war. The Free State policy of suspending death sentences, on condition that hostilities ended in the localities of the sentenced men, placed intolerable strains on Republicans, both inside and outside jail. It is impossible to estimate accurately how far the executions and hostage policy affected Republican activity. It is extremely unlikely, however, that friends and relatives were not heavily influenced, however much prisoners like Ernie O'Malley urged that their safety should be irrelevant to the struggle outside. The Director of Operations of the 1st Southern Division argued: 'If we intensify war it will mean losing some of our best men who will be executed.' He would not 'stand for it as these were the very best in the late war'. Bertie Scully, of Rossbeigh, Co. Kerry, told Ernie O'Malley: 'It was no good carrying out an operation . . . for our prisoners inside in gaols . . . would have been taken out and shot.' A Republican commented to Liam Lynch: 'All the enemy do now is issue a *threat* of

Execution and the men will give way.' The prison population, therefore, was ruth-lessly used by the Free State to influence the situation outside. Meanwhile many prisoners came to see the futility of the war effort and criticised the tactics being employed.

If military victory had become a Republican pipe-dream, it was nevertheless inconceivable that the war would result in a surrender of Republican ideals. It was also clear that the Free State government would refuse to compromise on constitutional and political issues when in the dominant position. The war continued because there appeared no means of bringing it to an end, either by negotiations or by complete military victory. The only alternative was a Republican ceasefire not involving a surrender of principle, but that was decided on only when IRA resistance had virtually completely collapsed.[1]

Lynch's intransigence, and his refusal to appreciate how depressing the situation had become, was a major cause of the war's continuation. While he was able to exert scant control over events, and often appeared to have little knowledge of developments, Lynch remained the decisive Republican voice regarding peace initiatives. He had the power to call Army Executive meetings and he dominated them on the infrequent occasions they were held. On 9 February 1923 Lynch claimed that the IRA was

> in a stronger military position than at any period in its history. . . . The war will go on until the independence of our country is recognised by our enemies, foreign and domestic. There can be no compromise on this funda-mental condition. Victory is within our grasp if we stand unitedly and firmly.

A few days earlier he had told Con Moloney: 'Though everything seems moving against us, I believe all will be right.' For all his integrity and courage, it is difficult to defend Lynch's failure to face up to realities and to plan accordingly. He continued throughout the remaining weeks of his life to clutch at straws, talking of extending the war to Britain, and of bringing over mountain artillery from Germany which would supposedly decisively change their position, and he had an obsessive belief that the west would save the day. Many Republican contempor-aries have pointed to Lynch's complete lack of sophistication and his lack of experience in anything other than leadership in guerrilla warfare.

Strong criticisms of IRA policy came in a letter to Lynch at the end of January from James L. O'Donovan, the Director of Chemicals. O'Donovan complained of 'an almost complete out-of-touchness with affairs', together with feelings of discouragement and insecurity and 'general impotence in coping with a situation which becomes daily more increasingly grave'. Despite the reprisal orders, he wrote: 'People see the highest enemy Officers... strutting about the same City Hotel two or three times every week!' While against reprisal killings, O'Donovan was appalled by the lack of any kind of effective reaction to the fifty-three executions that had taken place up to that time. While unimpressed by both armies, he emphasised that the Free State 'have numbers and foreign backing we have not'. O'Donovan could see no prospect of anything but defeat in a war of attrition: 'Our man-power [is] proving too weak... the enemy are too well estab-lished and... any further weakness on our side caused by further arrests or executions of our best men will leave us simply a wasted shadow of what was once a glorious little Army of Independence.' He suggested incendiary attacks in Britain, application of a severe economic boycott of British goods, attacks on 'undesirable' financial and economic supporters of the government, and a concentration on jail escapes.

Lynch replied: 'Plainly, I do not want to be receiving such communications as yours. I am about fed up of trying to meet the situation between Govt, Executive, Army Council and Executive Staff.' He admitted that 'Units are not carrying out our detailed instructions', and continued: 'It is all very well to have ideals but we must take effective measures to put them into effect.' He claimed: 'We are continually facing facts. . . . Taking everything into account the general situation is quite satisfactory. . . . The army in all areas is now very well re-organised.'[2]

What de Valera described as the 'biggest blow . . . since we started' came after the arrest of Liam Deasy on 18 January. Deasy had represented the most important example of the Cork IRA's reluctant participation in the conflict. His pessimism was reinforced at the turn of the year by a depressing tour of the 3rd Southern Division, during which he contracted scabies—the dreaded 'Republican itch'. He later told colleagues that he had been preparing for peace negotiations, and was planning to see Lynch about this, when he was arrested in the Galtee Mountains.

When Free State military authorities learned of Deasy's desire for peace they conspired to win the maximum of advantage. Deasy was refused permission to appeal to IRA leaders for peace without first signing a form in which he would 'accept and aid in immediate surrender of all arms and men as required by General Mulcahy'. Deasy insisted that he could not issue orders to men outside, but he agreed to advocate the war's stoppage. 'At 4 a.m. I was informed', he wrote, 'that execution would not be suspended' unless he agreed to a prepared statement. 'After long consideration', he continued, 'I decided on accepting the conditions in the best interest of the country.'

Deasy was given the opportunity by the military authorities to send out a letter to leading Republican officers justifying his position. In the letter Deasy said that he felt the war could continue indefinitely if the negative, destructive policy continued. 'Our hopes', he asserted, 'of advancing the fight to a successful ending and the clearing up of the British were not however so bright.' Deasy explained that he had earlier had hopes that a considerable number of pro-Treaty officers would come over to their side, particularly after the executions, but that he had been disappointed. He had become aware of the increasing Free State military strength, the rate of captures and the loss of popular support for the Republicans. Deasy was very pessimistic about a continuation of the struggle into the summer. While in jail he had become aware of 'the serious situation which the executions have created: viz. reprisals, counter-reprisals'. He was concerned about the danger of the war developing into a matter of vendettas and reprisals and feared that 'the losses on both sides will be so great some other power, probably England, will be called on to intervene and possibly will be welcomed with more enthusiasm than was displayed on her departure'. Deasy concluded that the armed struggle should be stopped in order to benefit the long-term Republican cause: 'If we conserve our forces the spirit of Ireland is saved.'[3]

Deasy's old senior colleagues, for the most part, admitted his integrity but disagreed with his conclusions. Republican ranks closed after Deasy's surrender.

All the recipients of the letter turned down his idea of peace negotiations, although some agreed with his pessimism. Initially it appears that Lynch thought Deasy's letter was a forgery, and many put Deasy's action down to extreme Free State pressure. Lynch issued a statement to officers warning against all talk of compromise, reminding them how favourable the position was. In notes sent to Con Moloney, however, Lynch admitted that Deasy's action had a bad effect on their cause in the south, commenting: 'Prisoners all over south are acting in a horrible manner. Deasy of course played hell with this.' On 5 February Lynch told Joe McGarrity:

> The general situation here up to a few days ago was most satisfactory, and were it not for the Deasy incident . . . I am sure we would have matters all our own way within a few weeks. Owing to this incident it may take us some time to recover from it, but I am certain all will be right again.

Madge Clifford, who was acting as Lynch's secretary, recollected that the Deasy affair affected Lynch very badly and that he was broken-hearted when he journeyed south a short while later. Writing from the USA, Seán Moylan commented:

> Deasy's attitude knocked me silly. I thought he'd be the last man to cave in. It wasn't a question of being able to win with us. Twas that we were right, that we couldn't surrender being right. It wasn't cowardice on his part I know and I have feared greatly the troops must have got hell in the South since I left. I believe however that we can't be beaten.

Seán MacSwiney, of the Cork No. 1 Brigade, wrote to Deasy: 'Your outlook as to the continuation of the fight is shared by practically every one of us. As you say Government can be made impossible.' MacSwiney reasoned that 'Time is on our side now', and he put much faith in the weakness of the Free State army, arguing:

> As a general rule fighting on a large scale is, of course, impossible. We are, however, in a much better position than we were in the last war. . . . We are better armed. We also have a greater belief in our ability to stand up to large forces, and finally, in the South we are rid of the idea that the rest of Ireland never does anything. This feeling, resultant of the actual fighting, strengthens our determination to carry on to victory.

He disagreed with Deasy that either war-weariness or Republican reprisals were widespread, and concluded:

> You believe, for the best interests of the Country, we should surrender now with a view to a fight at some future date. I believe, for the best interests of the Country, that we must carry on. If we surrender now the next war will be worse than this. It is no solution for any one to say that that is the business of the next generation.

Ironically, in view of the peace efforts he was soon involved with, Tom Barry said: 'It was Deasy who put the Tin Hat on us. . . . We were at our very highest level of success . . . when the Deasy Manifesto crippled us.' Deasy was testily received in Mountjoy Prison, where Ernie O'Malley commented: 'I am glad I got to contain myself when he was in my cell, but when he left I went up in smoke.' In 1924 Deasy was to be court-martialled and expelled from the IRA.[4]

Deasy's appeal produced its most demonstrable effect on prisoners. From the hospital wing in Mountjoy, O'Malley admitted that the morale amongst the prisoners was bad: 'Yesterday we went through several kinds of hell here,' he wrote. 'I am afraid the ultimate result will tell against us.' He was strongly critical, by implication, of the resistance in Cork: 'I can see an area poor in man-power and in arms doing little else beyond the destruction of property, but I fail to see why strong areas cannot help the fight from developing into a vendetta.' The Free State authorities ensured that the Deasy letter was brought to the notice of prisoners, and an amnesty period of two weeks was granted for the surrender of arms. Seán McLoughlin, one of the leading Republicans in Limerick jail, claimed that a pistol was held to his head and that they were told that Lynch and other leaders had surrendered. McLoughlin and eleven others asked Michael Brennan to grant parole to four prisoners for them to put peace terms before Republican leaders in the area. Their appeal stated: 'A continuation of the present struggle is waste of blood and has developed into a war of extermination. We think it has gone far enough and ought to stop now.' Similar appeals were made from Republicans in Cork and Clonmel jails. At the meeting of the 1st Southern Division in late February Tom Crofts, Deasy's replacement as divisional O/C, explained that Deasy's action had led some in Cork jail to sign a similar document to Deasy's in order to avoid execution. 'To prevent publicity and a further catastrophe', Crofts wrote, 'six of the prisoners asked for parole with a view to putting the full facts before their superior Officers. The parole was granted and these men appeared before a Divisional meeting and placed the full facts before all. The impossibility of unconditional surrender was fully explained to them and after some discussion the men were allowed to return to prison. It was clearly explained by the prisoners that the men inside, no matter what orders they got from outside would sign Deasy's Document as it was preferable to being executed.' Crofts concluded that to prevent further such problems 'an order re future peace activities by the men in prison was drafted. . . . Men handing in arms came to be treated as traitors and dealt with accordingly. Men signing paper will be treated as deserters.' Some damage had, however, been done. While the worst fears of an avalanche of form-signing receded, there were to be later examples of prisoners agreeing to the Free State's terms, including all of Paddy Mullally's Leixlip column.

Deasy's action did nothing to encourage men in the ranks to fight to the death. John Joe Rice commented: 'It created an air of unreality for we weren't sure which of the important officers would go next.' A Cork IRA man remarked that some of the men 'will get fed up' and 'won't ever have the same confidence in any one of the leaders again'. De Valera thought Deasy's action was the 'worst development yet': in retrospect it can be seen as the beginning of the public collapse in the Republican military position. The affair only dramatised, however, what had long been apparent—a Cork officer commented to Ernie O'Malley that 'We were beaten anyhow.'[5]

Meanwhile the 'Neutral IRA' persisted in attempts to achieve a truce. Archbishop Harty of Cashel, helped by Father Duggan, produced peace terms which, the Dublin correspondent of the London *Times* reported, 'bridge the difficulty of an unconditional surrender in an ingenious manner'. It was suggested that 'pending a General Election, all arms should be dumped under the charge of Battalion Commandants, who will pledge themselves not to allow them to be used in any way against the Free State'; after the election arms and ammunition should be handed over to the government. These proposals were sent to Tom Barry, who put them before a meeting of the council of the 1st Southern Division on 10 February. It was then decided to request that an Army Executive meeting assemble to discuss the terms, and Barry, Crofts and Father Duggan travelled to Dublin to present the division's wishes to Lynch.[6]

Rumours abounded in Republican circles that Barry stayed in the Royal Hibernian Hotel while in Dublin and travelled around freely on a safe-conduct from the Free State authorities. Lynch stressed his opposition to the holding of an Executive meeting, on the grounds that those travelling to it ran a great danger of arrest and that the situation demanded that O/Cs should stay in their own areas. Lynch was very critical that the 1st Southern Division leadership had taken independent initiatives; he referred to Barry 'doing about his worst' on the peace issue. Tod Andrews recorded Lynch sending Barry a sharp letter telling him to desist from negotiations. That, however, did not deter Barry, who journeyed out at night to Lynch's hideout, waking Lynch and his entourage, who must have been convinced that the Free Staters had arrived, and told Lynch, during a harsh verbal exchange: 'I did more fighting in one week than you did in your whole life.' Barry returned to Cork to form a peace committee.

Lynch was sufficiently alarmed about southern developments to attend a meeting of the council of the 1st Southern Division on 26 February. He had been dangerously isolated in Dublin. If Lynch had not been convinced of the hopelessness of the Republican military position in Dublin, he should have become so as he journeyed south. Lynch was accompanied by Dr Con Lucey, his regular assistant, who had the rank of Director of Medical Services, and the young Tod Andrews, who was amazed by Lynch's reliance on him. They were forced to journey as fugitives—first by means of a Ford car, then in a pony and trap, and finally on foot. Their movements were mainly at night, and they were reliant on safe houses away from Free State troop concentrations. For weeks, back in Dublin, de Valera and IRA officers heard nothing from Lynch. Andrews recorded Lynch poring over detailed maps of brigade and battalion areas—although he had no means of knowing whether many of those units still existed. While in South Tipperary, Lynch asked Andrews to journey to Ballingeary to order a halt to peace moves in West Cork. Andrews, however, found himself delayed by an attack of scabies and by the unavailability of transport; he was forced to walk from Aherlow to Ballingeary, which took him eight days. He arrived only to find Lynch there.[7]

As demands for peace negotiations became increasingly frequent, from January onwards, so de Valera assumed a greater prominence. Lynch left it to de Valera to make the public rejection of the Neutral IRA's demands for a truce—the President had his uses to the military leadership. De Valera remained, however, in no position to stamp any authority on the situation. When he resurrected Document No. 2 as a possible means to achieve compromise, in a letter to the press of 17 February, it became apparent that External Association was no more popular with the IRA than it had been thirteen months earlier. Con Moloney expressed his alarm to de Valera about the Ulster clause in Document No. 2 and asked whether the proposals involved an oath to the British Crown. Officers of the 1st Southern

Division made it clear at their meeting on 26 February that they had not been fighting for de Valera's compromise. At that meeting Liam Lynch emphasised that de Valera's subordinate position had not changed. He had consulted the President on the peace terms and the calling of the Army Executive meeting, but stressed that

> The President . . . is always guided by the military situation and the decision of the Executive. . . . The question of Document No. 2 does not arise as the only terms that the Executive could make peace were those of October meeting. . . . Document No. 2 in his opinion was a diplomatic one. The President was of great assistance but had no authority to interfere in Army matters.

When Lynch told de Valera that 'Your publicity as to sponsoring Document No. 2 has had a very bad effect on army and should have been avoided', de Valera replied that the army should either 'leave all political matters to the Government' or, 'If they want to deal with the political question . . . they will have to think intelligently along political lines and discuss the political problems as they would discuss military ones.'[8]

The British and Free State governments were as keen as Lynch to prevent de Valera from having any substantial role. Churchill had warned Cosgrave's government about the danger of a 'sloppy accommodation' with de Valera, writing: 'It may well be that he will take advantage of the present situation to try to get back from the position of a hunted rebel to that of a political negotiator.' The Free State government remained resolutely opposed to any negotiations based on revision of the Treaty. When a Miss Ellis wrote from London expressing her desire for peace, de Valera in reply summed up the depressing position he had been in throughout the conflict:

> My thoughts and sentiments are exactly like yours, but alas our country has been placed in a cruel dilemma, out of which she could be rescued only by gentleness, skill and patience, and on all sides a desire for justice and fair dealing. Instead we find ourselves in the atmosphere of a tempest—every word of reason is suppressed or distorted until it is made to appear the voice of passion. I have been condemned to view the tragedy here for the last year as through a wall of glass, powerless to intervene effectively. I have, however, still the hope that an opportunity may come my way.

To maintain his nominal leadership of the Republican movement, de Valera had to be seen to be in line with the military effort. Replying to Frank Fahy's peace move, he affirmed: 'It is useless to ask Republicans to abandon ideals which I know they will surrender only with their lives.' When de Valera turned down the Neutral IRA's proposals asking for a truce, he argued that 'under the present conditions' a truce 'would not lead to peace. It would be regarded by both sides merely as a breathing-space in which to prepare for a more violent resumption of hostilities.' In a memorandum to his ministers de Valera, while admitting that such a rejection would put public opinion 'strongly against us', stressed that he could not see 'anything of material value' being won by negotiations with the Free State.

Privately de Valera warned Lynch not to be over-sanguine about the military situation, and at the same time he was striving to prepare Republicans for compromises which he knew would have to be made. He told Con Moloney in his most wordy and enigmatic style:

As far as England is concerned I don't see how we can go beyond Document No. 2. As far as the Free State is concerned, there is a wide range from surrender by them to surrender by us. The obvious answer is that our minimum will be the maximum that the conditions of the moment will enable us to obtain. Under conditions which it is possible to conceive the maximum might be as low as zero.

More directly, de Valera reminded Mary MacSwiney of 'the difference between desiring a thing and having a feasible programme for securing it'.[9]

It is easy to sympathise with de Valera in the largely powerless position he found himself in, and because his views have been frequently misrepresented by his opponents. He often, however, committed the same sin of over-optimism for which he criticised the military side. On 5 February he told Joe McGarrity: 'One big effort from our friends everywhere and I think we would finally smash the Free State.' He followed this by stating: 'We have . . . to face the possibility of the British forces coming back and taking up the fight where the others lay it down—But God is good!' The pragmatic and the ideal coexisted uneasily in de Valera's mind—he told McGarrity that he was hopeful of divisions within the Free State government, concluding: 'We are a far more homogeneous body than they are. If this war were finished Ireland would not have the heart to fight any other war for generations, so we must see it through.'

De Valera became unhappy about Lynch's support for widespread reprisals. His own preference was for action to be taken only against those directly responsible for the passage of the executions policy. He warned Lynch:

The policy of an eye for an eye is not going to win the people to us, and without the people we can never win. . . . We must on no account allow our contest to be sullied by stupid and foolish action on the part of individuals who may never look to the consequences, not to speak of the morality or justice of what they are doing.

Such views, however, could not be disclosed publicly, and this allowed Free State propaganda to depict de Valera as being in agreement with Lynch over reprisals. De Valera did support Lynch's determination to extend the war to Britain, stressing that 'The first blow should be concerted and big, followed quickly by a number in succession of other blows.' It appears that violence, which might well imperil the lives of non-combatants, was more acceptable to de Valera in Britain than in Ireland.[10]

The 1st Southern Division meeting of 26 February could not have been franker about the Republican military position and prospects. Representatives of all the brigades agreed that only small operations were possible, and were extremely pessimistic about prospects for a summer campaign. The O/C of Cork No. 3 Brigade admitted that 'In a very short time he would not have a man left owing to the great number of arrests and casualties. It was only a question of time as to how long we were going to last.' Humphrey Murphy, of Kerry No. 1 Brigade, commented that 'The steamrollering of the South would soon finish us.' The depression was shared by divisional officers, Tom Crofts saying:

> The present state of the Division is that we are fought to a standstill and at present we are flattened out. In Cork 1, 3 and 4 Brigades we had 29 killed, roughly 13 posts captured and 6 seriously attacked. If five men are arrested in each area we are finished. The men are suffering great privations and their morale is going.

When faced with such depressing conclusions, Lynch said that he 'quite realised the position in the South and the morale and suffering of the men and Officers'. He nevertheless 'reviewed the position in the rest of the country and although the position of the South was pretty bad he felt the situation in general was very good and held great hopes for the future'. Some of the officers present, however, expressed cynicism about the prospects elsewhere in the country, and Lynch had to agree to hold an IRA Executive meeting. The meeting concluded: 'Impossibility of carrying on and this matter to be clearly put to executive meeting.'

On 8 March Lynch wrote to Con Moloney on Father Duggan's peace initiatives: 'All this humbug will have to be cleared up.' The evidence was accumulating, however, that Lynch was becoming increasingly isolated by his optimism. Con Moloney wrote some notes on 7 March which arrived at many of the conclusions Deasy had come to a month before. He wrote:

> Position not improving. Reprisals and counter-reprisals.... Agree to temporary set aside ideals—but will complete surrender make our position from that point of view any better?...We can't beat enemy militarily. Enemy can't beat us militarily (if officers put more energy into the fight and take reasonable precautions).... The advent of the English is probable, and our morale will by that time be very low, and the war will have been very bitter between ourselves, so both armies will not come together to face England.... Development of open fighting no gain to us.... Course of struggle run—not agree summer campaign if war lasts till then, we will be beaten or very nearly so.

Moloney concluded by saying he favoured compromise and negotiations, as long as the spirit of republicanism could be kept alive. On the same day that he wrote these comments Moloney was captured near his hideout in the Glen of Aherlow, together with two other officers. By that time Lynch knew that the Free State army was aware that an IRA Executive meeting was planned for the 2nd Southern Division area.[11]

By now Lynch was convinced that an Executive meeting was 'of vital importance' to 'put actual Army and general national position', and stressed the importance of placing before the meeting all the evidence available from reports. 'Southern members', he continued, 'have a poor idea of situation in rest of country and cannot believe position is as good as pointed out to them.' Much to Lynch's alarm, reports had failed to reach him from the west; many of the Chief of Staff's colleagues, however, were cynical about his faith in the west, which, it appeared, was not based on firm evidence.[12]

Lynch's hopes also rested on negotiations which had been going on since the beginning of the year in the USA and Germany for a supply of mountain artillery, which became known as the 'Jetter business'. 'Jetter' was the code name for J. T. Ryan, who had been active in arms purchasing work in Germany. It was hoped that artillery could be landed by a submarine on the west coast. As a result of the capture of correspondence relating to these negotiations, the project became known to the Free State and the British governments.

In the correspondence Lynch emphasised that rifles and revolvers were no longer needed and told Seán Moylan: 'The enemy army is now about 80,000 and it is our duty to bring the war to a successful conclusion before summer, if possible. You will realise that even one piece of artillery now would do this. One such piece could be moved round amongst our strong forces and this would completely demoralise the enemy and end the war.' It soon became apparent that there was considerable difficulty over raising the necessary finance in the USA, and Lynch argued: 'I cannot see why it is necessary to spend 100,000 dollars as only a few pieces of small artillery . . . with shells . . . can be got in England at £500 each with shells. Germany is at least 20 times cheaper.' McGarrity warned Lynch against over-expectation, writing on 15 January: 'If the Jetter matter can be got underway in course of a month or two, the scales may turn in our favour. I do not like to build castles in the air. At least I feel it dangerous to talk of projects in mind until they reach a point of maturity which promises results.'

The history of Irish physical-force republicanism is full of the collapse of ambitious Irish-American schemes; the Jetter matter was no exception. At the Executive meeting which took place on 13-14 May Frank Aiken admitted that there was no possibility of purchasing artillery, 'even if we had £50,000' before the middle of summer.[13]

It was decided to hold the March Executive meeting in the area of the Nire valley. Kathleen Barry described her harrowing journey over the mountains with Lynch, Humphrey Murphy and Tom Barry. Tod Andrews reflected: 'How could they decide when they were such physical wrecks?'

The meeting started on 24 March and lasted for four days; because of the threat from Free State troops it was held in several different locations. It represented the first opportunity for IRA leaders to assess their position together since October. At the beginning of the meeting it was debated whether de Valera should be allowed to attend (the President had been made to wait in an adjoining room). He was eventually admitted, but with no voting rights. Nothing could have better revealed the military side's dominance. During the discussions, Bill Quirke, of the 2nd Southern Division, queried Barry's claim that the war was lost. Barry retorted by asking when the last fighting in Kilkenny occurred, to which Quirke replied: '1867.' According to J. J. Rice, the assembly collapsed in laughter.

A resolution proposed that de Valera should conduct peace talks in line with Republican demands, though with the proviso that the Army Executive was to have a veto over any conclusion to these negotiations. A split vote resulted from the resolution. Barry then proposed a motion seconded by Crofts, which read: 'That in the opinion of the Executive further armed resistance and operations against FS Government will not further the cause of Independence of the country.' This was defeated by six votes to five. After this inconclusive result it was agreed that the Executive should reconvene three weeks later; they would then receive reports of de Valera's peace efforts and the situation in the west.

Very probably some who voted against Barry's resolution did so only because they wished to see if the mountain artillery could be purchased and landed. On that issue and over the western reports Lynch had been able to stall, but the auguries did not appear favourable for Lynch satisfying the doubters.[14]

Lynch's fears about the risks of IRA men meeting together were proved correct by the arrests which followed. Information about the meeting had been extracted from Republican prisoners in Dublin, and a large sweep was organised, under Prout's direction, of relevant areas in South Tipperary and Waterford. On 14 April Austin Stack was arrested near Ballymacarbry with peace terms on him accepting the Archbishop of Cashel's proposals for a simple quit and dumping of arms. Stack's projected peace move had not been supported by Seán Gaynor, Frank Barrett and Dan Breen, who had been with Stack before his capture; shortly afterwards Breen was captured in the Glen of Aherlow, and many others were jailed, including Barrett, Gaynor and Andrews.[15]

The most important Republican loss occurred on 10 April. Lynch was with Frank Aiken, Bill Quirke and Seán Hyde on the slopes of the Knockmealdown Mountains, near Newcastle, Co. Tipperary, when surrounded by Free State troops under Tommy Ryan and Lieutenant Clancy. Lynch and his colleagues were carrying only revolvers and automatics and were exhausted by their fugitive existence. The party was fleeing up a hillside when Lynch was hit by a long-range bullet. He died that evening.

Lynch's last message declared: 'I am confident if we stand united that victory is certain, and that in a short time.' Lynch's death removed the last barrier to a Republican acceptance of the need for an end to hostilities. On 11 April the *Irish Times* wrote: 'The National Army has now a position of overwhelming superiority in the field. The militant Republicans have lost their most active leaders. . . . The hour is ripe for peace. The whole country seeks it.' A Free State army report concluded: 'Events of the past few days point to the beginning of the end so far as the irregular campaign is concerned. . . . The general feeling of the people seems to be that the Irregular Organisation, as a whole, is doomed as a result of the recent operations and captures of leaders.' It is difficult to believe that even Lynch's determination to view the most desperate of circumstances with rose-coloured spectacles could have prevented the Executive from bowing to reality.[16]

In April there was considerable controversy and confusion over the visit of Monsignor Luzio, who came to Ireland on a peace mission with the Pope's blessing as a consequence of Republican appeals to Rome. Luzio was cold-shouldered during his visit by the church hierarchy. He stayed in the Shelbourne Hotel in Dublin and conferred with Republican political leaders. The Free State government rejected all Luzio's approaches and saw his visit as implicitly sympathetic to the opposition. On 25 April Luzio was recalled to Rome at the request of the government. The Free State and the church hierarchy had thus asserted their independence of the Vatican.[17]

The War in the Localities:
January–April 1923

(a) CORK

REPUBLICAN units in Cork were largely confined to the mountainous areas near Macroom and Bantry, in the westernmost part of the county. On 2 March Tom Crofts concluded of his No. 1 Brigade area: 'The number of whole time men in the area is 983. In addition you have 8 Brigade staffs and Division staffs. . . . We are absolutely on the rocks.' Cork remained a major centre for peace initiatives, through church intermediaries and the Neutral IRA. In December Liam Lynch had made an approach to Seán Hegarty and Florrie O'Donoghue about reorganising the IRB, and shortly after the end of the war Tom Barry was to attempt to achieve an amnesty by reviving old Supreme Council loyalties.

Free State troops remained in heavy numbers; by early March there were over 5,000 pro-Treaty troops in Cork, considerably more than in any other area of the country. Sixty-four posts were held. It was easy for these troops to concentrate on specific areas. In January Liam Lynch commented on the large enemy presence around the boundary between Cork No. 1 and No. 2 Brigades: 'Mulcahy has realised', he wrote, 'the importance of initiative and his forces are continually on the move, following up our men to our safer areas.' Considerable amounts of arms were dumped by the anti-Treaty units. The Deputy Chief of Staff wrote to Lynch in March: 'It is outrageous that about 1,200 Rifles are in the 1st Southern area of which close on 500 are dumped, yet this Area will not assist weak Areas where opportunities afford for using Arms.'[1]

The Cork IRA leadership had little stomach for the fight continuing. Tom Barry's behaviour demonstrated that he still had considerable faith in his ability to lead columns in offensive action, but saw no purpose in the war continuing in the defensive manner in which it was being fought. On 1 February Tom Crofts wrote to Seán Moylan: 'Liam [Deasy] is a big loss to us. I am practically the only one of the old 1st Southern Division Staff left now. I think the enemy has half his army in Cork and Kerry, but I suppose every area thinks the same. Of course they are not getting things all their own way.' Lynch, moreover, did not help the Cork IRA by sending three of their key men to posts abroad: Moylan and Leahy were in the USA for much of the war, and Pa Murray became O/C in Britain.[2]

The comparative mildness of the Free State army's occupation of Cork may partly explain why there was little resurgence of support for the IRA there. Many Republicans admitted that there were few atrocities; there were few executions throughout the war, and fewer complaints, it appears, than in many other areas, of bad conditions and treatment in jails. Tom Crofts said of David Reynolds, the Free State O/C in Cork, that he 'was decent for he did not want executions'. It was difficult for columns to operate with any safety in Cork city: any action there, as in Dublin, won them little sympathy with a population eager for a more settled economic and social environment. During the later stage of the war there was a discouraging level of support for the Prisoners' Dependants' Fund.

Mick Murphy, one of the column leaders, recollected near the end of the war that they resembled wandering sheep. At no time, however, was there an outright defeat, but rather a progressive wearing down of any will for a continuation of the struggle. At the end of the war Republicans could still billet safely a mere six miles out of Bandon, and many Republican leaders, for instance Tom Crofts and Tadhg O'Sullivan, remained free during the whole war.[3]

(b) KERRY

General W. R. E. Murphy's optimistic remarks about having broken the back of Republican resistance in Kerry—made when he left the command in January 1923—were not proved justified. The south and east of the county, the area covered by Kerry No. 2 Brigade, were uncleared of columns until the very end of the war. Ambushes, raids and the blocking of communications remained frequent occurrences. Little, however, was attempted on a large scale, and attacks on Castlemaine in January, Kenmare in February, and Cahirciveen in March proved expensive failures. Kerry No. 1 Brigade declined considerably in effectiveness during the first months of 1923. Humphrey Murphy admitted that he was hard-pressed to carry on. Cahill's and Pierce's columns were captured; a number of the Kilmoglen column 'signed the form'; and 'Aeroplane' Lyons's column was lost in April. Both the Ballymacelligott and Castlegregory columns were inactive during 1923. On the Free State side, large sweeps continued to have disappointing results—the guerrilla warfare stalemate persisted.[4]

Some of the intensity of Republican resistance in Kerry can be put down to the extreme unpopularity of Free State troops. Complaints and rumours about violence to prisoners and general indiscipline abounded. Free State army inspection reports stressed that Paddy Daly's command left a lot to be desired in discipline and behaviour. The methods used against the troops, however, would have tested the restraint and control of any army. It is difficult to find demonstrable proof for many of the crimes attributed to Daly's troops. Referring to allegations concerning David Neligan, Ernie O'Malley commented that, to the best of his knowledge, none of Neligan's accusers had been actually involved in the incidents concerned. Nevertheless, Daly and his officers failed badly to answer the various charges in a satisfactory manner, and little attempt was made by Free State GHQ to deal with the problems.[5]

The conflict in Kerry will always be associated with the atrocious events of March, which left behind a bitterness remarkable even in the context of civil war. On 6 March at Knocknagoshel, in the north-east of the county, a mine killed five Free State troops, including three officers, and appallingly wounded another. Republican propaganda claimed that the mine had been laid as a deliberate attempt to kill Lieutenant O'Connor, who, it was alleged, had been responsible for the torture of captured Republican soldiers. Following the Knocknagoshel deaths,

Daly issued a memorandum stating that henceforward Republican prisoners would be used to clear mine obstructions. He argued that this was not intended as a reprisals policy, but was 'the only alternative left us to prevent the wholesale slaughter of our men'. Similar instructions had been issued earlier in the war, but the new order was followed, in the next few days, by four appalling events.[6]

At 3 a.m. on 7 March, a party of nine prisoners was taken from Ballymullen barracks in Tralee to clear a mine obstruction at Ballyseedy Cross, three miles away. The prisoners were men recently arrested, and included Paddy Buckley, an old RIC man, who, it was claimed, had been earlier granted a safe-conduct in Limerick by Michael Brennan. According to Republican accounts of the incident, when they reached their destination the prisoners were tied together and the mine was detonated by Free State soldiers. Eight of the prisoners were killed, and it was alleged that shots were fired at the bodies. Remarkably, one of the prisoners, Stephen Fuller, was blown clear by the blast and survived. Fuller was taken to the local IRA dugout, behind May Dalaigh's house at Cnocán, where John Joe Sheehy and his men had heard the explosion. Sheehy immediately publicised the news, contradicting Free State claims that the killings had been the result of an accident while the mines were being tackled. Back in Tralee nine coffins were prepared; to the amazement of the Free State troops only eight bodies were available to fill them. At the funerals the military coffins were broken into and smashed to pieces.[7]

The next day another attempt to get prisoners to clear mines at Castlemaine was foiled when some of the prisoners escaped. On that day also, at Countess Bridge, near Killarney, a mine exploded, killing four prisoners, with again one, Tadhg Coffey, escaping. On 12 March at Cahirciveen five more prisoners were killed by a mine, and some Free State soldiers were reputed to have boasted about the event.

A military enquiry into the grisly events was held by Daly and his deputy, Colonel J. McGuinness, together with Michael Price. They denied that the incidents had been reprisals, pointing out that at Cahirciveen all the mines had been laid by Republicans as part of their plan to take the town. In reply to attacks from Labour TDs in the Dáil, Mulcahy stressed the ugly forms of war that had been used against his troops in the county, saying that 68 had been killed and 157 wounded up to that time. He did, however, admit that the mines could have been checked before they were detonated. Thomas Johnson, in reply, pointed out the suspicious fact that three of the incidents had taken place within twenty-four hours of each other, and added that the prisoners killed had not been found guilty of any offence. He also criticised the composition of the enquiry and pressed for a non-military one.

Daly's order, in itself, does not prove all the Republican claims to be true. P. J. McHugh admitted to Ernie O'Malley that the Republicans had laid the mines at Ballyseedy. After the war, however, a Free State representative, Niall Harrington, investigated the Ballyseedy incident and concluded that it was a reprisal. He was not allowed to publish his conclusions. Lieutenant McCarthy, who later resigned from the Free State army, said of the Cahirciveen incident: 'There was no attempt at escape, as the prisoners were shot first and then put over a mine and blown up. It was a Free State mine, made by themselves.'[8]

The Republican attack on Cahirciveen on 5 March, which preceded these outrages, was repelled first by a counter-attack and then by Free State reinforcements which arrived by sea. Five Republicans were killed in the fighting there, and three on the Free State side. An ineffective sweep of the McGillicuddy's Reeks followed. On 28 March five Republicans who had been captured during the Cahirciveen attack were executed.

In April another tragic and melodramatic event occurred with the siege of Timothy ('Aeroplane') Lyons's column, which had been surrounded by Free State troops and taken refuge in Clashmealcon Caves, north of Kerry Head. After a siege of several days there was shooting as the trapped men attempted to escape. Republican accounts claimed that the rope bringing up some of the Republicans from the caves was deliberately broken, and that mines had been lowered over the cliff and exploded by Free State troops. Three of the Republicans were killed, including Lyons himself. A Free State army report stated that Lyons had been drowned in trying to move to another cave.[9]

Two thousand Free State troops were said to have been in Kerry at the end of the war when Seán MacMahon, the Chief of Staff, led a massive sweep of South Kerry. On 15 April the Republicans suffered a reverse at Glenvar, in which a Free State army report claimed nine Republicans were killed. The report, however, had to admit that an estimated 400 well-armed Republicans were still in Kerry, centred around Loo Bridge, Kilgarvan and, over the Cork border, in the Ballyvourney area. 'The Columns around Morley's Bridge, and eastwards,' an army report commented, 'enjoy a virtual "Republic" as this area has not yet been seriously handled by us.' Just before the ceasefire there were four more executions of survivors of the Clashmealcon Caves affray and men from the Ballyduff area.[10]

(c) THE WEST

While large areas of North and West Mayo and the adjoining border areas of Sligo and Leitrim remained uncleared of Republican columns, it is difficult to understand what grounds Liam Lynch had for possessing so much hope that the west could change the course of the conflict. A Free State military report concluded:

> Despite their very considerable numbers, and ample equipment in Mayo, the Irregulars have not been inclined to indulge in any militant action. Extensive destruction of roads, raiding, looting, and the burning of houses of supporters of the Government is the form their warfare continues to take.

Lynch's ignorance of developments in the west enabled him to inflate the importance of events there.

The major part of the Free State army's resources and energies were devoted, in the spring of 1923, to subduing the south. A large-scale clearance of the far west awaited completion of work in Munster. Mulcahy said, at a Defence Council meeting on 23 April, that Dan Hogan, the O/C of the Claremorris Command, needed more men for his extensive planned operations. A Free State military report of 31 March noted that the Claremorris Command in North and West Mayo was 'perhaps the only one' where Republicans were able to carry out operations on an extensive scale, and that Mayo was 'the only County in the West where anything like the old Irregular regime still holds. . . . North and West Mayo yet present a a problem calling for the employment of a large body of troops and considerable equipment to clear up the area.' At a meeting of the Defence Council in late April O'Higgins asked: 'Did the military intend to leave the situation in the West alone until the Southern operations were over?' It was admitted that Hogan 'had not sufficient troops for the very large area under him'. The ceasefire order, however, was given before it was possible for attention to be switched to the west. There never was to be a final showdown in Mayo and Sligo.[11]

The troops of the new Claremorris Command were disliked as outsiders. Commenting on Hogan's men, one local source concluded: 'The Southern man's temperament is altogether unsuitable for the West here. They are too cocksure and overbearing, and this savagery is unparalleled.' Inspection reports in February gave a depressing account of lack of training and discipline in sundry pro-Treaty posts and of appalling living conditions in many of the billets. A report from Ballyhaunis stated that the posts 'are dirty' and in 'a bad state of repair. The men have no training and the usual consequences follow. Officers in need of training.' Colonel J. J. Slattery, one of the inspectors, commented about the Swinford garrison: 'Undoubtedly the worst I have ever seen' and stated that one of the posts there could be entered unchallenged by anyone. Slattery concluded: 'In Mayo, which is the worst portion of the Command, there are but fourteen Garrisons. Some of these are up to 40 miles apart.' A similar critical story emerged from reports on posts in Co. Galway.[12]

Ned Bofin's column in the Arigna Mountains and small units in the Ox Mountains and the Grange area remained intermittently active. A determined large sweep of the Arigna area in mid-February produced scant results—the *Daily Telegraph* reported that Bofin, who it called the 'Republican De Wet', was married in Leitrim village while the sweep went on.

In early 1923 also there were two incidents in the Sligo–Leitrim border area which produced extremely unfavourable national reaction. On 11 January Sligo railway station was burnt by a party of forty IRA men from the 1st Battalion of the 3rd Western Division. Seven engines were damaged, together with forty carriages, and the station was completely destroyed. The Free State army garrison in the town was heavily criticised for lack of response to the attack until an hour after it had started. In the Dáil Mulcahy admitted that the incident had 'very serious aspects'. The *Irish Times* concluded: 'If ... the garrison lacked neither vigilance nor efficiency, but was overpowered by superior numbers, the condition of the Sligo area is far worse than Eastern Ireland had been allowed to suppose.' On the 12 February the small town of Ballyconnell was raided, during the daytime, by columns from the surrounding Arigna Mountains. Of many such incidents during the war, it produced a particularly critical response in the Dáil and the press. Mulcahy admitted to the Dáil that the region had been a continual source of trouble and that the troops there had proved inadequate. He concluded that political and geographical factors in the Arigna area had prevented it from being cleared up. The London *Times* drew wider conclusions, writing that

> It is common knowledge that the Army is trustworthy only in parts; that a large portion of it, variously estimated, sympathises with the Republican cause; that its movements have over and over again been betrayed before they could be carried out; and that officers and men have trafficked at times in supplies and munitions with the 'enemy'.[13]

At the end of the war large-scale sweeps were proving more effective in the troublesome parts of Mayo and Sligo. In March there was an extensive round-up of the Newport area, and Seán Hyde, the IRA's O/C in the west, admitted on 16 March that the area would be 'completely mopped up' by the end of the month. During the Newport sweep Joe Baker's column was captured, and on 25 March Ned Bofin and many of his column were similarly rounded up in the Arigna Mountains. Christy Macken, O/C of the 2nd Western Division, reported at the beginning of April: 'I understand Major-Gen Hogan is transferring his forces towards your Division [the 4th Western]. . . . He has been rounding up No. 2 Brigade of this Division for the past fortnight.' Macken stated that Hogan's methods involved the setting up of small posts from which areas were heavily scoured, and buildings known to be occupied by Republicans were rushed. Small columns were being used for this, together with relief units. Macken contrasted Hogan's methods with Lawlor's earlier counterproductive use of forced marches.[14]

(d) THE 2nd SOUTHERN DIVISION

There was no effective move made against Republican columns in the 2nd Southern Division until February. Paddy O'Connor, who then took charge of Free State troops in South Tipperary, related that General Prout had been deliberately misled by rumours of Dinny Lacey's and Bill Quirke's desire for negotiations; in consequence, Republican columns had been allowed considerable freedom. From December 1922 the Neutral IRA had been active in the area, and talk of negotiations was frequent, including a meeting between Dan Breen and Michael Brennan at Soloheadbeg early in the new year. Meanwhile the work of Republican columns was confined largely to unco-ordinated burning of property and wrecking of communications. The IRA's Adjutant-General admitted to the Chief of Staff on 12 March: 'We are quite in the dark . . . regarding 2nd S/D not having received reports. . . . I understand their difficulties but it is too much of a good thing that neutral IRA and seven travellers passing through this area know more about it than GHQ or the President.'

By means of threats to public bodies Lacey took the firmest of lines against Free State executions. Moss Twomey told Liam Lynch that 'The enemy has resorted to the destruction of houses as counter-reprisals in the 2nd Southern. Of course if they do this, they will be playing into our hands.'[15]

A witness before the 1924 Army Enquiry commented that in early 1923 'The Tipperary portion of the Waterford Command was . . . the worst area in the country and a most important area to get full control of.' From February onwards the Free State troops put particularly strong pressure on South Tipperary, and with considerable success; Paddy O'Connor and Tommy Ryan were sent to take charge. Free State troops had known of the Republican retreat in the Glen of Aherlow for some time, but only from February did they pour into the region and make it a death-trap. On 18 February Dinny Lacey was killed. This was followed by a confrontation at Ashgrove House and by a sweep of the Mitchelstown–Ardfinnan region and, in the following week, by one of Ballingarry, the Galtees and the Glen of Aherlow. In early March Con Moloney, with some other officers, was captured in his hideout at Moore's Wood, Rossadrehid.[16]

Lacey's loss had a demoralising effect. He was rumoured at the time of his death to have been involved in peace moves. A Free State army report concluded:

Lacey was the toughest leader which [*sic*] could be found in any part of Ireland and for months he controlled a group of large columns and manoeuvred them over the whole area. An operation against the Aherlow Glen ... disorganised Lacey's systematic column work and made them scatter into areas where they could be more effectively dealt with. The killing of Lacey and the capture of the greater part of his own column demoralised to some extent the other columns. ... Since we started transferring troops from one area to another within the Command they have improved wonderfully.

This report overrated Lacey's control over IRA units, but many Republicans agreed that Lacey was one of the most vital of their leaders. Ned Glendon, of Clonmel, affirmed: 'From the time that Dinny Lacey was killed it practically crippled the fight', and Micky Fitzpatrick recollected that there was no serious fighting thereafter.

As a result of the increasing pressure from Free State troops, Republican forces, through March and April, split into progressively smaller units. The situation was made even worse for them when the Army Executive meeting in the area in March resulted in a massive sweep of the Galtees and the Knockmealdown Mountains and in numerous captures.

By April Republican resistance had become a matter of small, scattered bands struggling to avoid arrest in remote areas. Nugent's column, for instance, was forced to retreat across the county border, where its members joined up with Seán O'Meara's column, which operated around Dungarvan.[17]

(e) LIMERICK AND NORTH TIPPERARY

In North Tipperary and Co. Limerick the small Republican columns were limited to a defensive, harassment role. A Free State army report described the situation at the end of April:

Recent events seem to have had a very demoralising effect on the rank and file in almost all districts, and it is only where an outstanding personality like Seán Carroll is at the head of a column, and where a certain local sympathy exists, that they are still holding together. In most districts centralisation seems to have given way to localism, and the larger columns have ceased to operate, their places being taken by smaller columns who work together in bands of 5 or 6.

Key IRA men were captured, for instance Paddy Ryan Lacken and Seán Gaynor, and in late March the Republican units in the Silvermines area were broken up.[18]

(f) WEXFORD

The south of Co. Wexford is a rare example of an area that became more active as the war progressed. The columns of Thomas O'Sullivan, in the New Ross area, and Lambert, around Wexford town, were responsible for extensive destruction of communications, raids on post offices and similar activities and effectively controlled large areas of the countryside. There were strong complaints about the Free

State troops and their failure to deal with the repeated railroad problems, notably around Macmine and Killurin. Lieutenant-Colonel Tommy Ryan, who had been sent by General W. R. E. Murphy to deal with Wexford, recollected that in January and February 1923 'Destruction was being carried out almost daily in Co. Wexford despite the fact that there was [*sic*] at that time 950 troops in the county.' He complained that GHQ and neighbouring commands supplied little support to the troops in Wexford, and also that there was an apparent failure to put into effect Murphy's suggestions for improved troop methods. An officer at GHQ claimed that in Co. Wexford 'We got less assistance from the civilian population than in any other County in Ireland. Our most ardent supporters were a backboneless people.' A number of local notables complained on 19 February that 'In the rural districts the Anti-Government forces are in effective control, and from enquiries made from all sections of the community both in town and country we find there is a progressive tendency towards the belief that the army is neither earnest or efficient in its work.' Another local source commented that by February the people were much less likely to give information to the pro-Treaty troops because they had lost confidence in them.[19]

The Free State army GHQ was sufficiently alarmed about the position in Wexford to switch Paddy O'Connor and Tommy Ryan there after they had completed their work in South Tipperary. Lambert, however, remained active; his answer to the executions of local men was to authorise the killing of four captured Free State soldiers, and he gave severe warnings concerning any future executions. Even as late as the end of April and early May, Free State army reports depicted the situation as unsatisfactory and held that the continued support for Lambert was explained by the unpopularity of the Free State troops. Numerous inspection reports testified that Prout's Waterford Command remained inefficient and undisciplined through the war and after.[20]

(g) DUBLIN

In Dublin the IRA's sorry Civil War story continued during the first months of 1923. The organisation was still disrupted by numerous arrests. Liam Lynch warned Moss Twomey that too much should not be expected from Dublin. Considerable planning and energy went into an attempt on 21 February to destroy income tax offices and documents in various parts of the city. Most of those attacks failed, notably the attempt to burn Jury's Hotel, together with attacks on offices in Merrion Square, Dawson Street and Lower O'Connell Street. Offices in Nassau Street, Upper Gardiner Street and Beresford Place were burnt. A Dublin IRA report stated that of seventy-five men engaged, six were captured. Other activities in the city were few and far between.[21]

In March attention turned to implementation of the general order banning the holding of public amusements. Moss Twomey despairingly commented: 'I am constantly pressing Brigade O/C to take drastic action.... This new Brigade O/C ... appears to be hopelessly out of touch with recent policy. He was un-aware—so he said—of the issue of the most important orders.' The amusement order was only patchily enforced and was effectively countered by a Free State adoption of a strong line against any cinema and theatre managers who complied with the IRA threat. The IRA decided not to incur the inevitable public outrage which would have resulted from an attempt to ban the holding of the Battling Siki–McTigue world championship boxing match, which attracted so much attention at the time.

In South Co. Dublin and Wicklow Nial Boyle, widely known as Seán Plunkett, a Donegal man who had escaped from Newbridge prison, led a mixed column of Northern, Dublin and Wicklow men which was periodically active. Two weeks after the ceasefire Boyle was killed during a Free State army sweep near Knocknadruce, Co. Wicklow. Ben Doyle and Séamus Fox both told Ernie O'Malley that there had been a plan to shoot Cosgrave, Mulcahy and Gearóid O'Sullivan at Greystones, but that this had been foiled by the ceasefire order. There had, however, been strikingly little inclination to implement such reprisal plans during the war.[22]

The North and the Civil War

IT is a major irony that the Six Counties were almost completely untouched by the Civil War. The London *Times* commented on 26 February 1923: 'In every part of Ireland, but Ulster, from the Capital to the wilderness of the Western coast, houses have been reduced to smoking ruins.' Churchill reported to the British cabinet on 3 August 1922:

> In the area of the Northern Government the position had sensibly improved: murders and incendiarism had almost entirely ceased, and a state of quiescence established. This might be due to the fact that the gunmen were engaged in the South.... With their return there might be a recrudescence of outrage, but at the moment life in Belfast had almost become normal.

Wilfrid Spender, the Secretary to the Northern Ireland cabinet, commented that 'Lootings and hold-ups have nearly ceased.... The conflict in Southern Ireland had drawn away many of the most active politicians from Ulster.'

For Northern IRA units the war was the culmination of depressing developments since the Anglo-Irish Treaty. Séamus Woods, the O/C of the 3rd Northern Division, had warned Liam Deasy and Liam Lynch that 'when fighting began between Republicans and Free Staters we could be wiped out in the North'. The war in the South moved attention away from the North; any lingering hope of a joint IRA Northern offensive disappeared. Many in the 3rd Northern Division had emigrated or gone south to avoid arrest. IRA men in the west of the province were ordered to cross the border to Donegal. During July IRA men continued to be arrested in the 2nd and 3rd Northern Divisions, and those remaining were extremely vulnerable to arrest.[1]

Early in the war Mulcahy wrote to Collins urging that they change their Northern policy to a peace one. At a GHQ meeting with Northern officers at Portobello Barracks on 2 August Collins announced that Northern volunteers were to be sent to train at the Curragh; they were to be paid by the Southern government but not forced to join the pro-Treaty army. The meeting decided against military activity in the North unless necessary in a defensive capacity. Woods recorded, however:

> The late C.-in-C. made it clear to us that the Government in Ireland intended to deal with the Ulster situation in a very definite way, and as far as their Division was concerned, every Officer present felt greatly encouraged to carry on the work when we had a definite policy to pursue and an assurance that the Government ... would stand by us.

The presence of Northern IRA men in the Curragh amounted to an admission by Collins that he had failed to make the North the central issue in Southern politics and in Anglo-Irish relations. Tom MacAnally commented: 'Northern men could no longer stay in the North. . . . The IRA there never recovered.' Whatever hope there was of a quick end to the Civil War and a return to an aggressive Northern policy died with Collins. Roger McCorley, the Northern O/C in the Curragh in the early phase of the war, declared: 'When Collins was killed the Northern element gave up all hope.' Of the 524 Northern IRA men who went to the Curragh, 243 joined the Provisional Government army. McCorley led a contingent of them to Kerry, while the bulk of the rest remained in the Curragh. Some returned to the North, where many were arrested, and others eventually joined Republican units.

The Northern IRA had become the refugees of the army split. Not surprisingly, many felt an acute sense of betrayal: some Republicans, viewing the situation from the Civil War perspective, felt that the joint army policy had been nothing but a sham meant to weaken their position. Guns exchanged with pro-Treaty forces were being used against them in Co. Donegal. One of those ordered out of the Six Counties to Donegal, Lieutenant-Commandant E. Conway, told Mary MacSwiney: 'In order to retain unity within the Division we decided to remain neutral and take no part in the fighting in Donegal. . . . I can come to no other conclusion but that the orders about Training Columns to fight inside and the sending in of arms was only to hoodwink us.' Conway went to the Curragh after agreeing to Collins's terms; on his subsequent return to Donegal he was arrested by Joe Sweeney's men.[2]

During the war the Republican side never evolved a coherent Northern policy. Ernie O'Malley, who had the north-east as part of his vast command, had an almost total lack of contact with developments there, particularly before Frank Aiken belatedly joined the Republican side. O'Malley reported: 'The North and Eastern Command existed more on paper than in any other way; the Fourth Northern was the only division that had any cohesion.' Early in September O'Malley asked Lynch: 'I would like to have a definition of our Northern policy.' Of the remaining men in the Belfast area, O'Malley wrote: 'They are absolutely snowed under. I met some of the Sen Officers and they stated they could not do anything in the Divisional Area.' Lynch replied: 'It is too bad how the Dáil and the old GHQ let down our people in the North, particularly in Belfast. I fear we cannot come to their assistance financially.' During the war de Valera advocated only civil resistance in the North. Kevin O'Shiel reflected of the Republicans: 'Although they are waging war against us in the South they have tacitly agreed to leave the Six Counties alone until the findings of the [Boundary] Commission.'[3]

The war produced considerable changes in Southern government policy towards the Six Counties. During the first six months of 1922 Collins's will had dominated and his political colleagues had been kept in the dark about many developments. Early in the war, with Collins preoccupied with military affairs, the government formed a committee to draw up a northern policy. Ernest Blythe, as a member of that committee, wrote a memorandum implicitly criticising the policy pursued since January:

> There is no prospect of bringing about the unification of Ireland within any reasonable period of time by attacking the North-East. Military operations on regular lines are out of the question because of the certainty of active

British support. Guerrilla operations within the Six Counties can have none of the success which attended our operations against the British.... Heretofore our Northern policy has been really, though not ostensibly, dictated by Irregulars. In scrapping their North-Eastern policy we shall be taking the wise course.... The belligerent policy has been shown to be useless for protecting the Catholics or stopping the pogroms.... There is no urgent desire for unity in the North-East and it would be stupid obstinacy for us to wait till the Belfast attitude improved.

Blythe argued that to renew warfare in the North would result in the extermination of the Catholic population within two years. He saw no prospect also for bringing the Six Counties into a united Ireland by economic pressure.

The change in outlook was publicly demonstrated when in December Cosgrave contradicted Northern government claims that the Southern government was desirous of forcing parts of Northern territory into the Free State. 'So far as I know or can discover,' Cosgrave affirmed, 'nobody in the Free State cherishes this crude wish, save that small minority who support the calamitous policy of Mr de Valera and his Irregulars.' Alfred Cope reported to Lionel Curtis at the Colonial Office that Cosgrave

satisfied me that he holds the opinion that the National Army... should deal only with internal troubles and defence and not [be] an army of aggression against the North and I think that given the opportunity which does not present itself at the moment, he is prepared to make a public statement to that effect. I observed that such a declaration would go far towards relieving tension and facilitating the reduction of forces in Northern Ireland.

When complaining in January 1923 of the Northern government's attitude to his own, Cosgrave commented:

Since I have assumed office I have striven to bring about a better feeling between Northern Ireland and ourselves, especially along the inflammable Border regions. I have gone to great lengths to stop all manner of inciting propaganda. I think I can claim that my efforts in this direction have been largely successful.

In contrast to Collins's aggressive letters to the British government on difficult Northern issues, Cosgrave stressed his desire to defuse crises.[4]

Such changes in Southern government policy did not go down well with Northern IRA units. At the end of September Séamus Woods asked whether Collins's outlook had been departed from, adding: 'I take it the Government feel that they are not equal to the task of overcoming the Treaty position with regard to Ulster. If it is their intention to recognise the Northern Government, it is well that they should be acquainted with the present position in Ulster.' Woods bemoaned the poverty-stricken, vulnerable state of the IRA in the North, concluding: 'The breaking up of this Organisation is the first step to making partition permanent.'

The policy of civil obstruction to the Northern government faded away during the war. By the end of 1922 the Southern government had stopped paying the salaries of Catholic schoolteachers in the North who refused to recognise the Northern government. While the Free State government could not advocate recognition of the Northern government, neither did they encourage any non-recognition policy by Northern Catholics. Cope wrote to Churchill on 16 September 1922: 'Mr Cosgrave has been against this stupid interference in the Northern Government's concerns and he is anxious for his Government to get on a proper footing with the North.' Cosgrave's attitude won him plaudits in London and grudging respect in Belfast, but widened the rifts between Northern nationalist opinion and the South. A Free State representative reported from the North in October 1923: 'Again and again I heard the opinion expressed that the Free State took no interest in their position. . . . The Editor of the *Irish News* reminded me that the Catholic minority is today absolutely helpless in the face of the Orangemen.' Peter Hughes declared in the Dáil that Northerners felt their 'interests have been neglected', and Patrick Baxter, another TD, reproachfully observed: 'It struck me . . . many of the Southern, Midland and Western Deputies are not as interested in the North as they might be and should be.'[5]

The war necessarily meant postponement of the Boundary Commission. In January 1923 Kevin O'Shiel pointed out:

> What a ridiculous position we would cut—both nationally and universally—were we to argue our claim at the Commission for population and territory when at our backs in our own jurisdiction is the perpetual racket of war, the flames of our burning railway stations and property and the never-failing daily lists of our murdered citizens.

B. C. Waller, a British government adviser, reported after a visit to the North in December 1922:

> People there are at present just thanking their stars they are out of the trouble in the S. Their own affairs are much better. Even those who expect to see union of some sort in the end are at present inclined to wait and watch.

Only after the end of the war did Cosgrave request that the Boundary Commission meet, and he did so more from a sense of duty than from any optimistic expectation. Many in the Northern minority regarded the delay as another example of British duplicity and Southern apathy. Joe Devlin believed that it enabled the Belfast parliament to 'dig themselves in'. A Free State representative reported on the minority: 'They have lost faith in the Boundary Commission and many of them think it would do more harm than good.' Sir John Anderson, representing the British government in Dublin, reported that 'The belief is prevalent that the [Southern] Government is abandoning all its claims.'[6]

The vastly improved security position in the North and Cosgrave's moderation did not produce any softening of the Northern government's attitude towards the Southern government and to security issues in the Six Counties. At the time of the Four Courts attack Spender expressed scepticism about whether the Provisional Government army was in earnest, and O'Shiel commented on the constant cry in the Northern press that the Civil War was a 'fake' one. Several issues and incidents in the Six Counties during the war revealed a determination to act in accordance with a siege mentality, even when the siege had been lifted. Before he was sacked in the autumn Solly-Flood pressed ahead with extensive military plans, and fears were expressed about the threat thought to exist from the few second-hand planes of the Free State air force! Despite Southern and British government objections,

Proportional Representation was removed in local government elections, and an inflexible attitude was also shown in the carrying out of flogging sentences on IRA prisoners and over the bringing to trial of IRA prisoners on charges dating from before the Civil War. Lord Londonderry, the Minister of Education in the Northern government, declared that: 'With every desire to assist Mr Cosgrave and his Government in the difficult task which they have in restoring law and order in the South, we feel that we can best do so by insuring that law and order are enforced in the North.' Internal Northern considerations were paramount; wider issues relating to the South and to Northern relations with the British government remained secondary considerations. Cosgrave was left to speak 'very sadly about the unconciliatory and unbending attitude of the Northern Govt and pointed to the fact that the pinpricks were all on the one side and the forbearance on the other'.[7]

The Northern premier refused to appoint a Northern representative to the Boundary Commission. Cosgrave described 'the Ulster protestants as the spoiled children of politics' and said 'that they have [been] so long accustomed to get their own way by sheer obstinacy that they have become quite incapable of making concessions'. Cosgrave met Craig twice during the war, but found him unyielding and, Cosgrave recorded, keen only to talk about cricket.

Developments in the Twenty-Six Counties had given the Northern government the breathing-space to firmly establish itself. Meanwhile the British government happily allowed the Irish question to slip down its order of priorities. The Southern conflict had begun the process of taking the Northern question largely out of British politics for half a century. At a meeting of Sinn Féin's standing committee in August 1922 Father Irwin said of the Northern government that 'It would be difficult to abolish it later on if allowed to function now.'[8]

Exile Nationalism: The United States and Britain in the Civil War

THE outbreak of the Civil War and the deaths of Harry Boland and Michael Collins further depressed the Irish-American cause. Archbishop Curley of Baltimore said that Ireland was 'becoming a laughing-stock' and that its American supporters 'have been humiliated by the present state of things'. James E. Murray, the National President of the American Association for the Recognition of the Irish Republic, wrote in July: 'If the people of Ireland are bound to destroy each other and ruin their chances for freedom, it is their funeral—not ours.'

The course of events during the war made it impossible for Devoy, together with the Clan na Gael, to support the government side, but they remained aloof from the anti-Treatyites (Devoy and Cohalan were in fact to show sympathy for the views of Liam Tobin and his 'Old IRA' organisation). During the war Joe McGarrity, his reorganised Clan and much hardline republican opinion in the USA threw their weight, and what was left of their financial resources, behind the anti-Treaty side. The increasing unpopularity of the Free State government, and particularly its policy of executions, did much to harden such opinion. De Valera nevertheless commented pessimistically in January 1923: 'Remember that in the present conditions it is far easier to get money for relief purposes than for any other. Very many of our friends abroad object to give money for "lead" as they say.'[1]

Just before his death Harry Boland emphasised the prime importance of American funds for the anti-Treaty IRA, and he affiliated the reorganised Clan to the Army Executive. It was only after the first phase of the war that an attempt was made by the anti-Treaty leadership to influence opinion in the USA and to reorganise Irish-Americans. In the late autumn Seán Moylan and Mick Leahy, two leading Cork IRA men, were sent over as army representatives, and J. J. O'Kelly ('Sceilg') and Joseph O'Doherty arrived to represent the political side of the movement, together with Laurence Ginnell as the Washington representative; they were supplemented by sundry other visitors, including Austin Stack, Mrs Muriel MacSwiney, Father O'Flanagan and Countess Markievicz. Acute tensions, however, became apparent between Moylan and the Sinn Féin representatives, and also within the political delegation. Moylan complained that the politicians were interfering with his work and were spending money extravagantly—he described Ginnell as 'a damn nuisance'. Ginnell and Muriel MacSwiney were strongly criticised by their colleagues. By January de Valera was despairing of his American representatives, telling O'Kelly: 'There are five or six of you over there, and America is a big place. Surely it should have been possible to secure harmonious working.' To separate the factions de Valera instructed O'Kelly and Father O'Flanagan to switch their fund-raising activities to Australia.

A blunt letter from Moylan about the situation in the USA was captured by the British authorities. 'The trouble here', he wrote, 'seems to be that there are 32 Irelands in America and you'd need a man from every county to make a really successful appeal.' He felt that the AARIR 'is being run in a good many States by a bunch of grafters'. He only had faith in the reorganised Clan. Moylan concluded:

> The story about this being the land of the flowing gold is all rot. I'm always on the run and I shall be under the necessity of holding up a bank if the fellows here don't come across with a more plentiful supply of cash in the near future.[2]

After Deasy's surrender and Dinny Lacey's death Moylan thought that 'there was nothing to be done but to go right home and get plugged'. The reduced expectation of American aid is well illustrated by the low target of $100,000 Moylan set for his fund-raising. After the war Clan members decided that the sensible recourse was to a total reliance on the old method of operating through secret cells. Moylan admitted, however, that such a strategy had 'its limitations' and that it 'cannot touch all the people who are willing to help us and we must get them all'. Clan money helped to finance the 1923 election campaign.[3]

In Britain the Treaty resulted in the collapse of the Irish Self-Determination League and the Sinn Féin movement. The British government's report on revolutionary activities of 16 March 1922 claimed that there had been a decline in the ISDL's membership in England and Wales from 27,000 in early 1922 to 18,000. The League's annual conference in April 1922 decided that a neutral stance should be adopted towards the divisions at home, which Art O'Brien thought would result in 'the organisation' going 'to pieces to a very great extent before another conference is held'. O'Brien admitted that financial support from the branches had been declining since the Treaty had been signed. By early 1923 O'Brien concluded:

> Our well-to-do people are either against us or too timid to be actively with us. . . . The effect of the Treaty has been to frighten them further away from us than they ever were before. Amongst other class of our people here, say the clerical and the civil servant class etc., the vast majority of these have been rendered either hostile or apathetic as a result of the Treaty.

The ISDL had then only about forty branches, and almost all its staff had been sacked because of lack of financial resources.

With the decline of public organisations in Britain, activity was left to the hard-liners—the IRB men and arms smugglers. The London IRB and IRA had been divided by the Treaty—Collins's old network of intelligence men, such as Sam Maguire and Reginald Dunne, remained true to their old leader but came under increasing fire from irate Republicans, and particularly from the Cumann na mBan. The anti-Treaty side made no organised attempt to revive IRA work in Britain until after the first phase of the war. Early in September 1922 Liam Lynch appointed Pa Murray, a Cork column leader with experience in Britain and the

USA, to the position of O/C Britain. Lynch told Deasy that the London O/C 'has now got together the nucleus of an Organisation' and that 'Large quantity [of] supplies are available in England; the whole trouble is in getting them across.' With regard to projected activities in Britain, Lynch thought that 'a war on political leaders, and their leading soldiers would have the best effect' and recognised that 'The Free Staters have an active Organisation in London, which is working against us, and likely to give trouble when we begin active operations.' Lynch put a great emphasis on organisation in Britain, but faced great difficulty in starting operations. On 10 September he admitted: 'We are letting precious time pass by, and should have things going there already.' Murray was unhappy about the vagueness of the responsibilities he was offered, telling Lynch early in October:

> If I were to go there I would like to know what I am expected to do.... Very little was done in England when everyone was with you. Now you have very few on your side—what do you propose to do there? Burn houses—shoot people—what is expected?

Murray took up the appointment, but was correct to be sceptical about the prospects: little was achieved by the reorganised leadership. Murray told Ernie O'Malley of the great difficulties he had faced: he pointed out that the pro-Treatyites 'controlled all the original sources of supply and new contacts and lines have to be built up from zero'.[4]

The Republican organisation in Britain was subject to harassment from British police and intelligence agents and from Free State intelligence units. British and Irish government sources reported that the IRA in Britain had been reorganised in January and that they expected a revival of activity. Such concern resulted in a major move in March against Irish organisations in Britain. Simultaneous raids were made in various centres, and many were deported to Ireland on dubious legal grounds. When questioned in the Dáil about the legal basis for the deportations, Kevin O'Higgins replied: 'None of us lost a wink of sleep as to whether it was or was not a derogation of sovereignty.' A total of 160 were arrested, including 33 in London, 24 in Liverpool and 38 in Scotland. Liam Lynch admitted: 'Our Organisation appeared to be pretty badly hit by arrests. I hope that others will be appointed to replace them and that in the areas where they were arrested our Organisation will not be allowed to drop.' Pa Murray, who, along with the O/C London and the Director of Purchases, escaped arrest, stated that all officers in Newcastle and Liverpool had been arrested. On 5 April Moss Twomey reported to Lynch: 'I am afraid the chances of operations in Britain are now negligible if not altogether impossible.' After *habeas corpus* proceedings those deported were eventually released from Irish prisons, except for nine, including Art O'Brien, who had been alleged by the British government to have been involved in conspiracy against the Free State government.

In February Lynch claimed: 'Our position in America was never better while our Organisation in England has immensely increased.' The reality was that the Treaty and the Civil War had dealt a severe blow to the Irish nationalist organisations in both Britain and America.[5]

The Ceasefire

THE Army Executive met again on 20 April 1923 at Poulacapple, near Mullinahone, The meeting had to be postponed from 10 April because of Lynch's death and the intensive enemy activity in the area.

At the meeting Frank Aiken was unanimously elected Chief of Staff. Aiken was a strange choice given his peripheral role in the war and his sceptical attitude to it. He was one of the few remaining original members of the Army Executive; and, intentionally or not, his appointment improved prospects for the adoption of a more flexible negotiating stand. Aiken was much closer, personally and ideologically, to de Valera than Lynch had been. Liam Pilkington and Tom Barry joined the new Chief of Staff on the Army Council.

Aiken proposed to the Executive meeting that the Republican government and Army Council should 'make peace with the FS "Government"'', on the basis that 'The sovereignty of the Irish Nation and the integrity of its territory is inalienable.' This motion was passed by nine votes to two. Barry and Tom Crofts then put forward a resolution that all armed resistance should be called off, but this received no support and was turned down. A recommendation that the war should continue if their peace terms were not accepted produced a tied vote.

A joint meeting of the Republican government and the Army Council followed, which directed the new Chief of Staff to issue a 'Suspension of Offensive' Order, published on 30 April, and the President 'to issue a Proclamation embodying the terms upon which we were prepared to negotiate peace with FS "Gov"'. The negotiations were placed in de Valera's hands—at that crucial juncture the political leadership was allowed to return to the centre of the stage. P. J. Ruttledge commented that the army was 'passing the buck' to them. A message from the Republican headquarters stated: 'Suggestions as to methods of ending the present struggle will be effectively dealt with by the Government. Such questions do not concern the Army, whose duty is to prosecute the war with redoubled vigour.' Soon Aiken urged support for de Valera's policy of reorganising Sinn Féin Clubs as the best means of furthering the Republican cause.

There was no possibility that the Free State government would agree to the intransigent Republican peace terms. While concessions in the proposals were made on the North—a willingness to withdraw the Belfast boycott policy and a granting of local autonomy to Ulster—no compromise on constitutional issues was offered which could have proved remotely acceptable.[1]

Senators Andrew Jameson and James Douglas—reviving the old Southern Unionist role of middlemen between intransigent opponents—met with de Valera to see if any basis could be found for negotiations. Jameson reported to the government, following a meeting with de Valera on 3 May, that de Valera refused to sign the government document acknowledging the Free State to be the legitimate government. As to the surrender of arms, de Valera 'was afraid he could not get his followers to give them up'. Jameson and Douglas, in response, affirmed that there could be no possibility of the release of Republican prisoners while the arms were 'waiting for them to take up', and that an election could not be held under those circumstances.

During another meeting with Jameson and Douglas, de Valera stated that 'what he wanted was a peace which would enable his followers to return to constitutional action', but that he 'doubted whether his followers would be willing to publicly hand over arms', though they might do so 'if other peace conditions were satisfactory'. This gave Douglas the opportunity to ask how much de Valera was in control of the Republican movement. The President 'stated that he was now in a position to decide on behalf of the whole Republican Party and that he was in this respect in a stronger position than he had ever been before'. He nevertheless admitted that he could not order the army to stop fighting, and that while 'many . . . wanted to simply quit without binding themselves in any way to the future . . . others wanted to carry on until they were dead'. De Valera said that the oath was the only barrier to Republican participation in the Dáil. When Jameson and Douglas suggested a meeting of representatives from both sides, de Valera vetoed the possibility of O'Higgins attending, 'suggesting that he could not trust him', but said he 'would like' to meet Mulcahy and Mac Néill.

Douglas concluded of de Valera that his 'whole bearing . . . was that of a defeated man and his attitude towards me was the reverse of that when I had met him in the old days when he was President'. De Valera was depicted as desperate for an opportunity to return to constitutional action. 'He was very anxious', Douglas wrote, 'to explain how much worse things would have been if he had not been with them and seemed extra anxious to apologise for himself. . . . He is trying to get his followers to hold together as a constitutional party.' Douglas argued that, if 'properly handled', de Valera

> could be made to agree to any reasonable terms which the Government insist upon if anything is given him which will save his face and we both thought that he is speaking the truth when he says that he can now speak for the bulk of the Irregulars. If he is carefully handled in this matter the Government could very greatly strengthen their position whether a formal peace results or not.

O'Higgins warned that there could be no risk of allowing a replay of the conflict. Jameson and Douglas had overrated de Valera's position at the head of the Republican movement—he still could not take most Republicans as far towards compromise as he would have wished. De Valera's peace terms were hastily rejected by the Free State government. De Valera and Aiken had to turn to considerations of ordering a ceasefire.

A joint meeting of the Republican government and army held on 13-14 May instructed Aiken to issue an order to cease fire and dump arms. In the order, published on 24 May, the Chief of Staff emphasised the need to develop Gaelic civilisation and to join the Sinn Féin organisation. On the same day de Valera released a proclamation to the army, which declared: 'Further sacrifice on your part would now be vain and continuance of the struggle in arms unwise in the national interest. Military victory must be allowed to rest for the moment with those who have destroyed the Republic.' Two days later de Valera told Mary MacSwiney, who had been critical of the decision to embark on negotiations:

> You speak as if we were dictating terms and talk . . . of a military situation. There is no military situation. The situation now is that we have to shepherd the remnant of our forces out of this fight so as not to destroy whatever hope remains in the future by allowing the fight to peter out ignominiously.

No ground had been conceded on the constitutional and political issues which had caused the conflict. The Civil War, therefore, ended without any negotiated peace, and in many respects the Twenty-Six Counties remained on a war footing.[2]

35

The Republicans

LEADING IRA men concluded that the military tactics adopted during the war had failed abjectly. Frank Aiken thought they had underrated how far the Free State government would go to put down resistance. Ernie O'Malley held that the war had been fought too defensively, while Aiken argued: 'If we have to fight another war with the Staters, it will have to be short and sweet, and our Units will need to be trained in taking the offensive in large bodies.' He stressed the need to receive civilian support and concluded also that rifles and revolvers were out of date as offensive weapons and should be replaced by explosives and small trench mortars.

No easy military course was available, however, and any future military opposition was increasingly unlikely to win support once the Treaty divisions faded into the memory and the Free State government became consolidated. For long after the war IRA leaders were to disagree on whether future action should be concentrated on the North or in Britain, or whether there should be a union with those supporting socialist aims. During the long debate on these issues many IRA veterans emigrated or retired from the fray. In the short term, the IRA military leadership had no choice other than to support the revived emphasis on political activity.[1]

Free State sources agreed that Aiken's and de Valera's ceasefire orders were generally obeyed: there were to be no armed confrontations of any size from the end of April onwards. This was one of the few examples of the leadership's orders being obeyed by all Republican units; hostilities, however, had already all but ceased in most areas. The orders, therefore, were a rubber stamping of the fact that Republican arms had failed. Meanwhile the Free State search for Republican column leaders and arms dumps continued, and leading Republican military figures, for example Liam Pilkington and Humphrey Murphy, were captured after the war. A Free State military summary of 26 May pointed out:

> Reports point to the fact that in almost every Command their organisation is absolutely broken or else hampered in such a way as to render it almost impossible for them to carry out any major operation. The large number of arrests and captures of dumps during the week is evidence of the effective manner in which the troops are clearing the parts of the country that yet call for attention.

If the armed struggle was at an end—although no one could be sure for how long—the immediate post-war period was to witness a heightening of tension on the many issues which continued to divide Free Stater and Republican.[2]

In their ceasefire proclamations Aiken and de Valera had stressed the necessity to keep the army together, with the implication that the dumped arms would be used again in more favourable circumstances. The military leadership had, however, acknowledged the need to replace military resistance by constitutional methods and political organisation. That did not mean that the old tensions between Republican army and government had been resolved in favour of the latter, but rather that desperate circumstances had forced a temporary recognition from the IRA that circumstances had changed. From May onwards de Valera held a superficially dominant position based on the IRA's weakness, his handling of the peace initiatives, and his good relations with Aiken.

Meanwhile there were major problems relating to political tactics. While diehard Republicans felt a compromise could only be made on the principle that the Second Dáil still existed, de Valera felt some accommodation would have to be made with constitutional and political realities in order to avoid a considerable spell in the political wilderness. It was too early, however, for de Valera to jettison the Republican government, or for Tom Barry to be successful, as he attempted, in getting the Army Executive to agree to an amnesty and a handing over of their arms. Barry's efforts to achieve a rapprochement with the Free State resulted in his resignation from the Executive in July.

De Valera graphically illustrated the dilemma he faced in a letter to Ruttledge in which he wrote:

> We should now continue on the basis that the Republic exists. Temporary military defeat cannot destroy it. ... The difficulty I see is as to whether the Government of the Republic should be kept in existence. There is one very strong reason in its favour ... if the Govt. abdicate the Army is released from its allegiance, with consequences to the nation that we can all clearly visualise.

He contrasted present realities with the ideal of an inalienable Republic:

> We must recognise that as far as the *body* of the Republic is concerned, and its ability to function, it is dead. As regards the soul and spirit and form, that is another matter, and I wish we could devise a programme which would make manifest the existence of the latter without having to carry the weight of the dead body attached. Of course the formal existence of the Republic will continue, with its authority residing in the members of the Second Dáil, and in the Trustee Executive.

To preserve intact the movement and its principles, the pretence of a government thus had to be kept alive.

De Valera strongly, and successfully, urged participation in the general election of August 1923, although he admitted that such action was in effect a contradiction of the policy of non-recognition of the Free State. De Valera wrote about the elections:

> To declare them illegal and to stand aside is dictated by the idea of the continued existence of the Republic, but as a practical political policy to my mind it is not the best. The more progress we make at the coming elections, the more certain will be our victory at the subsequent elections. The

elections give an opportunity for explaining our position and reaching the people, which I think should be availed of. If we do not appear at the elections it will be impossible for us to go ahead with our organisation in an effective manner.[3]

De Valera came out of hiding to address an election meeting on 15 August in Ennis town square. He had explained that he 'took the step of going down to Clare because . . . we came to the conclusion that it was the right way to bring about a termination to a certain state of affairs'. It was in de Valera's interest that if he were to be arrested, it should be while speaking, thereby making the Free State appear as the enemy of free speech. The Free State troops failed to recognise de Valera before he started to speak, although he had rid himself of his beard and moustache disguise the night before. Firing started after de Valera began to address the crowd, and he was immediately seized and whisked off to Arbour Hill prison. Before leaving for the meeting de Valera had remarked: 'As regards Clare, and my recent commitment, enemy action will settle that. Either way, the effect will be good.'[4]

The publicity surrounding de Valera's arrest, and the length of his imprisonment, helped to restore his position at the head of the Republican movement. By putting a heavy priority on his arrest, and going to great pains to guard him closely, the Free State authorities demonstrated that they regarded de Valera as their prime opponent. During de Valera's year-long absence, however, he was unable to exert any direct influence on Republican attitudes, and Mary MacSwiney's abstentionist policy predominated. Writing from jail, de Valera admitted to Ruttledge:

> So far, we have not evolved a political programme which will fully meet the situation. Now that touch is re-established, I will give more thought to this. The people can only be won over by a programme which will remove the present nightmare of war, which they dread. The difficulty will be to get it to fit all the conditions. Meanwhile, there is no immediate hurry for anything specific.

De Valera resorted to suggesting that the old, vague principles of Sinn Féin be applied.

> Press the idea of Sinn Féin everywhere—self-determination, self-respect, self-reliance. The nation to be made self-sufficient as far as possible, economically. . . . We must be the best in the community, and soberest, most truthful, honestest, most hard-working, most Irish and most Christian. When we organise, we can, if it be deemed advisable, engage and pledge ourselves to boycott *voluntary* [*sic*] British goods and North goods. But not for a long time yet.

De Valera could achieve his aims only by participation in the political process. Because of the need to take the oath, however, elected Republican TDs could not enter the Dáil. It was to take over three years from the end of the Civil War for de Valera to found the Fianna Fáil party and to contradict the traditional abstentionist policy by entering the Dáil—a decision that entailed a final break with the IRA. Before then his position was not strong enough to justify splitting the

Republican movement. When the division did occur it was the logical consequence of de Valera's views throughout the Treaty and Civil War period.[5]

Despite the absence of many Sinn Féin candidates and workers in jail, the
election results were unexpectedly good for the Republicans. Cumann na
nGaedheal, the newly formed government party, had 63 candidates elected,
compared with 44 Republicans; of the first-preference votes, about 415,000 were
given to former pro-Treatyites, and around 286,000 for the Republicans. While
Labour successes declined from 17 in the June 1922 election to 14, the number of
Farmers' Party candidates in the new Dáil rose from 7 to 15, and the number of
Independents increased from 16 to 17. Ernie O'Malley described his surprise at
hearing the results in Mountjoy, and was amused that transfers of some of Richard
Mulcahy's second-preference votes helped to get him elected in the North Dublin
constituency.

The election results demonstrated the continuity of Republican support which
had been obscured by the war's unpopularity; they also reflected the bitterness felt
by many at the methods used to win the conflict. Conor Maguire, an election
organiser for the Republicans, noted that 'Our greatest successes have been gained
in the two counties in which the Free State terrorism was greatest, and in which it is
probable that most of our workers were in prison. I refer to Leitrim–Sligo and
Kerry.' The Republicans performed particularly strongly in Mayo, Kerry,
Wexford and Clare. As Rumpf and Hepburn have commented, 'The small-
farming districts of the west...demonstrated their continuing commitment to
Republicanism.' The Republican vote was strongest in districts where over three-
quarters of the labour force worked on the land. This was not because the anti-
Treatyites had eagerly embraced the land issue—they had in fact singularly failed
to do so—but was rather because of the alienation of many from central government authority which the Civil War had intensified. The Republicans did worst in
the more prosperous areas least affected by the war; for example, they won only 17
per cent of the Dublin vote. The Republican vote was disappointing in the cities
generally and in Co. Cork.

While the detailed results gave encouragement to Republicans, the election
legitimised the Free State's existence, in terms of its constitutional basis and its
claim to represent majority opinion in the Twenty-Six Counties. The issues had
not been confused by an election pact as they had been in June 1922; and no longer
could de Valera argue that a meaningful result was prevented by the British threat
of force. Seán MacEntee admitted during a meeting of Republican TDs in
January 1924. 'It could not be said that that election was taken upon a false
pretence. The people had to choose between the Treaty position and a return to
the Republican position.' The election demonstrated that the old Sinn Féin
abstentionist principle was no longer a sensible option; it was now apparent that
the Free State government lacked popularity and could be defeated—but only if
the Republicans found some means of entering the Dáil.[6]

The Post-War Free State Government and Army

IN June 1923 Kevin O'Higgins had warned the Dáil that 'There is going to be a pretty ugly aftermath to this whole business'; earlier he had commented that 'The aftermath of these last ten months is going to be more serious, perhaps, than the last ten months themselves. In many areas you have conditions bordering on anarchy.' The lack of a negotiated settlement, and the dumping of arms, meant there were no large-scale prison releases and no easing of the legislation on public safety. To release the prisoners, it was argued, would risk the reopening of hostilities, and there was the danger of a link-up between disaffected Free State troops, Republican units and Neutral IRA members. It was decided to release the prisoners in stages, according to the danger they were thought to represent. There remained the problem of establishing the government's authority, and that of the courts, the bailiffs, and the Civic Guard, in large, disaffected areas of the country, such as South Kerry and West Mayo. What O'Higgins and Patrick Hogan had called 'passive irregularism'—the seizure of land and stock, for instance—had still to be dealt with, and Gerald Fitzgibbon, TD for Dublin University, told the Dáil that £3 million in income tax arrears remained uncollected. When introducing the new Civic Guard Bill in the Dáil, O'Higgins said that only half the force provided for was being used, and he admitted that 'It has been only with great difficulty that Civic Guard Stations have been established in such important towns as Mallow, Carrick-on-Suir and Claremorris.' At the end of 1923 O'Duffy's police reports depicted considerable law and order problems in many areas.

The introduction of the new Public Order Bill in June demonstrated the Free State government's continuing hard line. Powers to intern, and to seize land and stock, were granted for another six months; flogging was established as a punishment for arson and robbery. The government and army were thus shown to be acting independently of the judiciary. Thomas Johnson argued against driving 'those in opposition to continue their opposition until they are worn out.... A peace ... by repression and only repression, is going to leave these 12,000 men in your hands perpetually until you are prepared to take the risk of letting them out.' Colonel Maurice Moore held that the harsh measures would increase bitterness and told Free State ministers that they had 'shown great courage in a great emergency.... But I do not know that they have shown great wisdom at the same time.... I object to any person in Ireland being made a sort of Pooh Bah or Lord High Executioner, and ordering anybody he likes into gaol.' It was pointed out that the flogging legislation resembled that of the Northern government which Cosgrave's government had heavily criticised.[1]

In answer to claims that conditions had reverted to near normality in many areas,

O'Higgins affirmed: 'When you come face to face with stark anarchy, worse still if it masquerades as political idealism, you have got to be reactionary.' O'Higgins remarked that there seldom had been 'a country more in need of strong central Executive authority than this'. The continuation of a severe, repressive policy for long after the war alienated a considerable body of opinion, and in the long term aided de Valera's prospects for returning to political power. There was often an insensitivity about government policy, and little attempt was made to build up its support throughout the Twenty-Six Counties. The 1922 and 1923 elections had not required the building up of widespread political organisation: the emphasis had been on ensuring the survival of the government.[2]

In the immediate post-war period the major responsibility for preserving public order and the government's authority continued to rest with the army.

There could no longer be any justification for an army of over 50,000 men. The transition had to be made to a trained, disciplined force of a suitable size for a small country; governmental control had to be firmly and definitively established, and the army rid of political influences.

Many witnesses at the Army Enquiry of 1924 testified that improvements made in army discipline since the beginning of 1923 were not maintained after the end of the war. Inspection reports from the various commands continued to paint the gloomiest of pictures. Following a post-war inspection of the Athlone Command, Major-General Séamus Hogan wrote that 'Areas which were well in hand a month ago . . . are retrograding. . . . Wherever improvement is taking place it is apparently due to local officers rather than to the influence of Command H.Q. . . . The Command Staff has not a just appreciation of the military situation. . . . The general attitude of officers is that the struggle is over, and that they can take things easy.' A report on the Waterford Command in July 1923 concluded: 'A state of affairs which we can only describe as scandalous exists.' By the end of the year a large proportion of crimes in the country (though O'Higgins's claim of 95 per cent was greatly exaggerated) were attributed to the army or to demobilised men. At that time complaints came in from the Kerry and Limerick Commands that the senior officers were using as their private property cars commandeered during the war. It was reported, for example, in December that General Paddy Daly was driving around in a six-cylinder Buick, the property of a Mr Leslie of Cahirciveen, who was claiming compensation in the courts. General Michael Costello, the army's Director of Intelligence, wrote:

> There was a time some months ago when, owing to the strain and hardship of active operations, it was frequently inexpedient to enforce discipline with an iron hand. That time is now passed. If the Irish Army is to bear any favourable comparison with other armies the task of inculcating discipline must be immediately undertaken and rigidly carried out.[3]

The worst problems occurred in the Kerry Command. General Daly and two other officers were accused of manhandling two daughters of a local doctor in an incident at Kenmare on 22 June. After an army enquiry Mulcahy argued that there was not enough evidence available for the case to go to a court martial, but many in the government did not agree and felt Mulcahy was shielding his old army and IRB colleagues. O'Higgins angrily declared that 'This thing is in a class to itself. . . . It is going to ring the death-knell of either discipline or banditry'; he also claimed that witnesses to the affair had been placed under arrest on a six-months-old charge. Major-General Séamus Hogan commented: 'The Command has been thrown into a ferment, where discipline has been swallowed up by the Kenmare occurrences which are now the common talk of the Army.' At the end of the year O'Duffy felt that the command 'has lost the confidence of the people of Kerry', and pointed to the army doing nothing to prevent Republican activity around Kilcummin and Scartaglin. To the surprise of many, Daly and his colleagues were not even transferred to another command; the Army Enquiry of 1924 concluded that the handling of the Kenmare case was 'a grave error of judgement'.[4]

The tensions within the army were enormously increased by demobilisation. The aim was to reduce the army from 52,000 in April 1923 to 30,000 or 28,000 by the end of the year, and in the process surplus officers had to be dispensed with. The number of demobilised officers by 15 December 1923 was 763, which left 1,000 still to be demobilised. Criticism focused upon two complaints: firstly, that compared with the ex-British officers, the pre-truce volunteers were treated badly; and secondly, that too much power in the selection process was granted to GOCs. The danger of mutiny was always present. At the Curragh in mid-November seven officers were court-martialled for refusing to sign demobilisation papers 'and claimed that as old members of IRA' they 'couldn't lay down their arms until Ireland' was 'an independent Republic'. Prominent veterans of the Anglo-Irish War complained that they no longer possessed an influence in the army commensurate with the length and value of their service; Tom Ennis and his Dublin entourage, for example, discovered when they returned to the city from the Cork Command that officers from Northern Ireland had the plum positions. David Neligan and Captain Martin Nolan argued at the Army Enquiry that preference in the demobilisation was given to ex-British officers and some from Northern Ireland. Gearóid O'Sullivan, the Adjutant-General, became particularly unpopular because of his alleged bias in favour of ex-British officers. Both Northern Ireland and ex-British officers formed associations to protect their interests. When reviewing the debate over demobilisation, it is impossible to distinguish between what was a protest over loss of jobs or non-promotion and what was a protest over the changed aims of the government. When Tobin, representing his 'Old IRA' organisation, wrote in June to Cosgrave protesting about the treatment of many officers, he put the emphasis on the danger that Collins's principles were being sacrificed. Seán Ó Muirthile emphasised that the problems over demobilisation were caused by the necessarily short time involved, and the fact that the war period had spawned a great number of surplus officers. The difficulties were greatly exacerbated by the size of the unemployment figures, and many were to find it extremely hard to adjust to peacetime conditions.[5]

Criticism, within both the army and the government, focused on the failure of GHQ to tackle the independence of the GOCs and to deal more stringently with dissident officers—a lack of action that was often attributed to Mulcahy's unwillingness to take a firm line with old IRB colleagues. The GOCs complained of not being sufficiently closely consulted about demobilisation; others, however, were of the opinion that they had the decisive influence. The Army Enquiry concluded that Mulcahy and his colleagues had been wrong to allow the IRB to be reorganised during 1923, and that GHQ was too often representing the army's rather than the government's interests. Mulcahy was strongly criticised for responding to Tom Barry's request in June 1923 for a meeting to arrange an amnesty for the Cork IRA based on a revival of Supreme Council loyalties. Barry's efforts proved abortive, and the government were aware of the developments. Mulcahy's tolerance of Liam Tobin's threats of what amounted to mutiny applied also to the government.[6]

O'Higgins became convinced, through Colonel Jephson O'Connell's advice, that the army was controlled by IRB influences at GHQ and among the GOCs. At the Army Enquiry O'Connell quoted one of the GOCs as having commented in June 1923 'that the Army had put the Government in, and the Army, if it wished, would put it out', and recalled Michael Brennan saying that 'the only difference between the Irregulars and ourselves was that we had won'. O'Connell, however, greatly exaggerated the influence of the IRB, about which he had only very sketchy evidence, and O'Higgins, by accepting such information from O'Connell, was acting improperly.

Professor James Hogan, Director of Intelligence of the Free State army, was a particularly strong critic of the amount of power still lying in the hands of GOCs, which he held responsible for many of the army's failings. For him the amount of decentralisation had been understandable during the war, but he also maintained that GHQ should have moved much more decisively to centralise authority after the conflict. Any risk of confrontation, however, with men like Brennan and Mac Eoin, whose continued support was so vital still to the stability of the Free State, would have been fraught with danger. Mulcahy's caution on these issues went well beyond considerations of personal or IRB loyalties, and he had been privately very critical of Mac Eoin's and Prout's commands during the war. Colonel Charles Russell recounted that Mulcahy was becoming increasingly impatient with the GOCs in the post-war period. Mulcahy declared in favour of prohibiting the right for secret societies to exist in the army, but felt that to implement such a ruling immediately after the war would have risked many defecting to the Republicans.[7]

Only after the army had been severely reduced in numbers and transformed into a disciplined, professional outfit, no longer required to perform police duties it was unsuited for, could the long-term problems be resolved. Mulcahy thought that 'Permanent commissions, and reasonable pay for line officers would obviate most of the tendency to discontent.' The Free State was fortunate that there were no major incidents relating to the problems within the army, and the army's relationship to the government and to the Republican opposition, in the post-war period. The Tobinite mutiny was delayed until the spring of 1924 and proved a damp squib; it amounted to little more than the many other desertions and protests which had occurred since the formation of the pro-Treaty army. The mutiny was important, however, in bringing to a final, public issue the tensions between the army leadership and a large section of the government. The army GHQ's move against Tobin and his supporters—in the mysterious Parnell Street raid—was not authorised by the government, and resulted in the forced resignation of Mulcahy and his closest military colleagues. Mulcahy thus paid for his long-term estrangement from his government colleagues.

The army mutiny has generally been depicted as the means by which government authority over the army was finally established. It was Mulcahy, however, who had contributed much to the establishment of a settled government by his staunch opposition to any thought of military dictatorship and by his tactful, delaying policy with regard to difficulties within the army. Colonel Russell emphasised that Mulcahy's had been 'a tremendous task'. 'From the beginning', Russell commented, 'when he had no uniforms and only a handful of men', Mulcahy had 'created an Army out of them. The actual work done...has not been appreciated and could not possibly be appreciated. It was a work of night and day for General Mulcahy and those in immediate association with him.' Mulcahy became the chief victim on the pro-Treaty side of the war's aftermath; though he returned to government office in 1927, it was as Minister for Education. Following the mutiny, O'Higgins's star appeared in the ascendant, and to him has been given the major credit for stabilising the government and ridding the army of political influences.[8]

The Republican Hunger-Strike, October–November 1923

THE retention of 12,000 Republicans in jail after the ceasefire provided a major problem both for the Free State authorities and for the Republican leadership. The prisoners were, in effect, hostages against a revival of Republican hostilities, and there was bound to be considerable debate in government circles concerning the appropriate time to release them. The collapse of Republican resistance lowered morale within the prisons. Séamus O'Donovan wrote:

> In the month or so following my arrest last March, I had to work very hard to combat defeatism and a spirit of non-cooperation with GHQ which was prevalent in that portion of Mountjoy in which I found myself. . . . The events of the last couple of months have left [in] some degree a legacy of soreness and misunderstanding between those inside and outside.

There was evidence also of the regional tensions persisting in the jails. John Cullinan, of Dublin No. 1 Brigade, commented on his prison experience: 'Cork men would only obey their own officers . . . and there was no way of enforcing discipline either.' Republican prison organisation could easily be disrupted by an increase in the rate of releases or by moving leaders to other camps or jails; pressure to 'sign the form' meanwhile intensified.

What went on within the prisons was regarded as of great significance for the Republican cause. In July de Valera sent a dramatic-sounding message to all prisoners, affirming: 'The whole future of our cause and of the Nation depends in my opinion upon the spirit of the prisoners in the Camps and in the jails. You are the repositories of the NATIONAL FAITH AND WILL.' Believing that the real struggle was going on behind the wire, Frank Aiken had to be dissuaded by de Valera from giving himself up.[1]

Problems within the jails culminated in the mass hunger-strike which began on 13 October; it proved an acutely depressing aftermath of the war. The strike originated in Mountjoy and was initially a protest against conditions there, as well as the prolongation of internment. Following the instructions of camp councils, the strike spread to all prisons and internment camps, Republican publicity claiming that at one stage over 8,000 were refusing to take food.

Many were to criticise the decision not to limit the strike to carefully selected individuals—men who could be relied upon to follow the tactic to the end, whatever that might be, and had the physical and psychological constitution to withstand a long strike. Michael Kilroy, O/C of the Mountjoy prisoners, commented on Liam

Pilkington's views: 'It was hard he thought to get a strike to succeed when there were a big number of men on strike. A h/s should consist of picked men only.' When the strike collapsed one of the officers in Tintown No. 3 Camp at the Curragh declared: 'Of course the main mistake was to allow so many men to go in the beginning. Joe Harrington and myself pleaded at the Camp Council for a limit to be put on the number of men (I suggested 700) but this was turned down on the plea that it would rouse a lot of bitterness because some good men were afraid to be overlooked, and also every day we lost we were letting down the boys in the Joy.'

The strike became an ill-defined and poorly planned sympathy one, which imposed enormous strains on individuals and their consciences. There was little clarity about its purpose, or about when it could be called off, by whom, and on what grounds.[2]

The Army Executive and the political leadership were only informed of the strike after it had begun. The Executive left the decision to strike to the individual, while urging that the physically unfit should not participate. In a message to all prisoners on 31 July Aiken stated that any 'prisoner who goes on hunger-strike should realise that he must stick it to the end. . . . A number of them will very probably die in the fight.' He felt that it would 'be disastrous to the cause if, when a few had died, the others left off. The risk of this happening is very great and the possibility should be kept clearly in mind when coming to a decision.' Aiken's warnings were to go unheeded, but once the strike had started he was to support it to the hilt. During the strike Aiken told the O/C of the prisoners in Kilmainham: 'Under no circumstances, even should a comrade die, are you to call off the hunger-strike—of course you have no power to *order* any man off. I believe your fight will do more for the cause than a thousand years war.'[3]

There was considerable unease within the prisons about the decision to strike. Madge Clifford recollected that Stack had told her 'that the whole business of the hunger-strike, its starting, and the swaying of men was . . . an underground and an underhand business'. Frank O'Connor related how his opposition caused him considerable unpopularity, and Peadar O'Donnell concluded: 'No one was ordered on to it, but then no one felt they could stay off it.' It was decided not to ask de Valera to join the strike, and he was in fact unaware that it had begun. There was criticism about the exaggerations of Republican publicity concerning the condition of prisoners. One prisoner complained of *Éire* and *Sinn Féin* printing 'sob stuff which even *we* do not read'.[4]

The strike broke up amidst immense confusion. In the various jails before three weeks were out numbers of men started taking food. After a considerable number of protesters in Mountjoy had broken off the strike, it was decided on 23 November to call it off for the rest. Tom Derrig toured the various prisons on parole to get others to follow Mountjoy's lead. By then, however, many had heard of the weakening of the protest elsewhere and had taken food on their own account. In the Curragh Camp, therefore, the 4th Western men ended the protest independently, their O/C, F. J. McDonnell, giving as the reason for his order that 'the men would break off on their own accord in any case'. Soon afterwards it was recorded that 'a regular . . . stampede took place' and the decision was taken to call off the strike. Considerable resentment was felt in the Curragh Camp when Christy Byrne, the O/C of the prisoners, ordered the discontinuation of the strike and was soon afterwards released. Before the end of the protest two Cork men, Dinny Barry and Andy O'Sullivan, died.[5]

Prominent leaders like Con Moloney and Frank Barrett, who had been strong supporters of the strike, signed the pledge ending their participation in the protest, as did Dan Breen, Seán Gaynor and Leo Henderson. In letters justifying their action Gaynor and Henderson said that they had disapproved of the Army Executive's policy for some time. After a misunderstanding with a government intermediary, David Robinson signed the form, and Stack was involved in negotiations with Mulcahy's agents. One of the Mountjoy prisoners expressed his disgust: 'I stuck it for 27 days and could have gone 27 more, but didn't see any fun for the men who organised it, when they themselves had broken and were taking food.' The Free State authorities used the strike as a convenient opportunity to apply pressure on Republicans to sign the pledge in order to gain freedom from hunger and prison; some argued that they were deliberately misled concerning the numbers of those who had gone off the strike or who had gained release.

The decision to end the protest led to much heart-searching. One of the Cork men wrote: 'I would rather have faced the firing squad than call it off, but there was [*sic*] Divisional Officers ordering their men off.' Another Cork prisoner concluded that it was a 'fiasco of a hunger-strike', but consoled himself by saying that the Cork men in Mountjoy had held fast. Ernie O'Malley, whose poor medical condition was worsened by the ordeal, expressed his feelings in a long correspondence with the widow of Erskine Childers. While on strike he wrote:

> I hope the men will last: I'm afraid some are rather weak but so long as even a few stick it to the end it will save the situation. . . . The country has not had, as yet, sufficient voluntary sacrifice and suffering and not until suffering fructuates will she get back her real soul.

After the strike was called off he reflected:

> I hope God directed us to do the right thing. And now we are beaten and disgraced but I am not beaten in my heart as yet. . . . There is not enough of spirituality in the movement. Dying is so easy compared with coming off; I'm sure the C/S and the others will be disgusted at us. . . . If the men are released before Christmas something has been done.[6]

In the jails it was widely admitted that the strike's collapse had a demoralising effect. Michael Sheehy, of Leix, concluded that there was a 'loss of self-esteem and a mass depression and ill-feeling'. The adjutant of Kerry No. 1 Brigade commented: 'I am afraid it will recoil heavily on us, and it will result in some fellows being in Jail indefinitely. Our position has been considerably weakened for past month.' Remarkably, however, Aiken wrote:

> The strike was really a great success for the Nation. I am very sorry for Ernie [O'Malley] and others who were prepared to go on, but I'm very glad in another way that they are available for the work before us. . . . Don't believe anyone who tells you that the IRA is down and out.

For the Free State government the hunger-strike involved huge dangers. A large number of deaths could well have produced a considerable sympathetic reaction in the tradition of Republican martyrdom. Following the strike there was an increase in the number of prisoners released, but the government decided that a mass release policy would have made it appear that the protest had been a success. In the following months the question of a general amnesty was often debated but always rejected in favour of what was called the policy of 'dribble'. The gradual release of prisoners was only completed in the summer of 1924; after that time only those convicted for criminal acts were retained in jail.[7]

Conclusion

THE Civil War marked the end of what has justly been called the Irish revolution. Since the war the Irish government, of whatever party or coalition, has proved remarkably stable: there have been very few challenges to the state's institutions. The army mutiny of 1924 and the Blueshirt movement of the 1930s were little more than echoes of the earlier conflict. The much-feared accession to power of anti-Treatyites in 1932 produced a crisis only in Anglo-Irish relations—the Dáil and the civil service were to be reassured by de Valera's constitutionalism and conservatism, while de Valera himself was to be impressed by the amount of political independence the Treaty had allowed. The war and its consequences enabled governmental authority to be asserted over the army, the constitutional opposition to separate itself from the IRA, and civil government to be re-established. With the restoration of order, the conservatism and homogeneity of the vast majority of the Twenty-Six Counties population could be asserted. The exclusion of the Six Counties, moreover, and the pre-Treaty experience of local, devolved government greatly aided the functioning and widespread acceptance of the new state.

The Treaty and Civil War period had posed important and intractable questions about the causation and interpretation of events. Observers have frequently and wrongly argued that the war was fought for the difference between Tweedledum and Tweedledee, and too much emphasis has been attached to the responsibility of individuals for the conflict. Once rival IRA units had taken over barracks following the Treaty, a military confrontation was inevitable, and indeed necessary, if the Provisional Government's authority was to be established—only a political compromise on the constitutional issues could have averted fighting, and that was unrealisable. Desmond Williams has pointed out that there was, and has been, nothing peculiarly Irish about political, constitutional and military divisions resulting from a compromise with an old colonial power. There were certain to be enormous problems in establishing central government following a long period of rejection of any authority in so many areas, and in establishing government control of the military. This is not to say, however, that the war, the way it was fought and the bitterness it engendered were necessary or inevitable.[1]

On many counts it is impossible to come to other than negative and depressing conclusions about the war and its consequences. Admittedly the conflict was of short duration and saw no major battles; even military activity on a middling scale was confined to the first two months, and large areas of the country were comparitively unaffected. There are no means by which to arrive at even approximate figures for the numbers of dead and wounded. Mulcahy stated that around 540 pro-Treaty troops were killed between the Treaty's signing and the war's end; the government referred to 800 army deaths between January 1922 and April 1924. There was no record of overall numbers of Republican deaths, which were very likely to have been much higher. No figure exists for total civilian deaths. Curran's and Fanning's suggestions of around 4,000 or 5,000 military deaths in the war are based on conjecture and appear too high. It is clear, however, that casualties were considerably in excess of the number of Irish Volunteers lost in the 1916-21 period.

The war's effect on the economy imposed a major burden on the new government. It has been estimated that the material damage involved amounted to more than £30 million and that it cost around £17 million to finance the war. Property damage easily exceeded that of the Anglo-Irish War. In April 1923 Cosgrave told the Dáil of a more than £4 million deficit built up over the preceding year, which had to be met by borrowing. In that year there had been an expenditure of £7,500,000 on the army and £1,250,000 on compensation. The army estimates for 1923-24 amounted to £10,500,000. There was considerable expense involved in housing the over 12,000 prisoners of the late war and post-war period; by May 1923 there were 27,000 dependants' allowance claims under payment. The estimates for the Civic Guard and the Railroad Protection and Maintenance Corps were both well over £1 million for 1922-23. The collection of taxes and rates constituted a major problem in the most disturbed areas throughout the war and its aftermath. Ernest Blythe remarked in March 1923 that the total of uncollected rates in Co. Clare amounted to around £200,000. Ronan Fanning has written: 'In 1923-24, 30 per cent of all national expenditure was devoted to defence and a further 7 per cent to compensation for property losses and personal injuries. As late as 1926-27 compensation absorbed £1.7 million of the national expenditure of £28 millions and only subsequently did defence and compensation no longer rank among the five heaviest charges on expenditure.'[2]

In April 1923 Cosgrave argued: 'The anticipated deficit for the coming year is, no doubt, serious but it is not such as to cause any misgiving as to the financial future of the Free State and the credit of the country. A large amount of the expenditure is non-recurring, and it is quite clear that on the arrival of settled conditions the revenue of the country will be ample to cover all commitments.' Nevertheless, the war, particularly in its early stages, had a disturbing effect on trade and commerce. For long periods important regional centres, such as Clonmel and Tralee, were cut off from other areas by the destruction of communications. News of the war—the constant detailing of burnt railway stations and bomb outrages—did not encourage investment in the new state's economy, and Cosgrave referred to the contraction in the banks' discounts and advances. During the war Irish banks were reluctant to give loans to the government—although Kevin O'Higgins's biographer has recorded that 'a large contribution from the Bank of Ireland to the Exchequer, at a crucial time, staved off bankruptcy'.[3]

The war's depressing consequences went well beyond casualty figures and considerations of material loss. Pearse's argument—reiterated by many Republicans during the war—that bloodshed had a cleansing effect on Irish nationalism was proved emphatically wrong. As early as 3 August 1922 Frank Aiken quoted an old priest: 'War with the foreigner brings to the fore all that is best and noblest in a nation—civil war all that is mean and base.' The heavily regionalised conflict within such a small country left a permanent scar on the national psyche. The *Kilkenny People* on 15 April 1922 warned:

> Ireland is big enough for great things and great movements, but it is too small for Civil War. Civil War means death and destruction. It means the material ruin of the nation and the moral degradation of its people.

As a consequence of the war, large areas of Kerry and Mayo, to quote the two most obvious examples, were to feel more alienated than ever from Dublin.

Much of the national leadership was lost during the war. Key and loved leaders on both sides died—Cathal Brugha, Harry Boland, Erskine Childers, Liam Lynch, Liam Mellows, Michael Collins—the list could easily be extended. All those named died under extremely controversial and unpleasant circumstances. The greatest bitterness was caused by the executions and unauthorised killings. It was an awful irony that the atrocities and the reprisals of the Anglo-Irish War were exceeded in the later conflict.

A small state in its infancy could ill afford to lose so many of its actual and potential leadership. Following the war many Republicans were excluded from public life, and considerable numbers were forced to emigrate. Employment was unattainable for numerous anti-Treatyites. Much talent, therefore, was lost to the nation, and not merely by means of death. The careers of some of the pro-Treaty side were blighted by their involvement in the war: Richard Mulcahy was never allowed to forget his association with the executions policy, and Kevin O'Higgins was to be a murder victim of the old animosities. The 'small world' character of Irish politics and professional life, applying even in the cities of Dublin and Cork, aided a continuance of post-war bitterness. Members of the O'Higgins and de Valera families were to live in mutual estrangement within a few yards of each other in Blackrock, South Dublin; and many other contemporaries have related that the war ended any social contact with anyone on the other side of the Treaty split.[4]

It was of great consequence that no compromise ended the war. The Republicans only accepted defeat in a military sense; the attraction of their ideology and the partition and constitutional issues remained. Judge Kingsmill Moore commented in 1948: 'Even now Irish Politics is largely dominated by the bitterness between the hunters and the hunted of 1922.' The unchanging character of political debate in the Twenty-Six Counties was further ensured by the fact that the leaders of both major parties were the survivors of the old Sinn Féin leadership, and that many of them, most notably de Valera, were to be so dominant and long-lived. While the Fianna Fáil and Fine Gael parties attracted a wide range of support from diverse elements within Irish society, Irish politicians were to continue to fight the unresolved issues of the Treaty and Civil War period, thankfully with words, not guns.

While questions relating to constitutional status and Anglo-Irish relations predominated up to the Second World War, social and economic considerations took a back seat. The constructive achievements of the first Free State government—the re-establishment of security, the formation of a stable court system and, at the second attempt, of an unarmed police force—were little appreciated by contemporaries. Support for the Labour Party declined, together with the political influence of trade unions, as a consequence of the Civil War period. The socialist element within the Republican opposition became increasingly marginal, while the character of the Cumann na nGaedheal party, and the nature of its support, ensured that its successor, the Fine Gael party, would remain conservative in economic and social affairs. Kevin O'Higgins rejoiced that 'We were probably the most conservative-minded revolutionaries that ever put through a successful revolution.' British constitutional procedures and institutions proved the principal models for the new state; in cultural and economic terms the primary debt was to Arthur Griffith's Sinn Féin philosophy. The narrower, more reactionary aspects of the 'new nationalism', typified by literary censorship, the boycott of Belfast goods and the long-continuing one of British games, came to prevail over the more generous-spirited aspects of the nationalist tradition, which placed an emphasis on international perspectives and the liberal treatment of minorities. Whatever party governed, the church maintained a great importance in Irish politics. As a disappointed Republican, Seán O'Faolain complained about the mediocrity of the new state's leadership, writing:

> I believed in the years after the Troubles that this combination of an acquisitive and uncultivated middle class and a vigorous and uncultivated Church meant that the fight for a republic as I now understood it—that is, a republic in the shape of France or the United States—had ended in total defeat.

Considering the social and economic structure of the Southern population and the influence, over much of it, of the church, it was to be expected that any state established in the Twenty-Six Counties would be conservative. The events and consequences of the Civil War, however, considerably reduced the prospect for forward-looking, let along radical, policies.'

It is extremely unlikely that the war in the South prevented one between Northern Unionist and Southern nationalist. Southern nationalists of all shades had failed to make a priority issue of partition. It was not necessarily desirable that fundamental issues relating to the Six Counties should be swept under the carpet as a consequence of the Civil War. Those questions surfaced again half a century later, when they were no more capable of resolution—indeed, almost certainly less so.

With regard to Southern attitudes towards the North, the war had largely negative consequences. While the conflict did much to stabilise the Northern government's position, it did not lead to any widespread acceptance within the Twenty-Six Counties of the enormous difficulty of ending partition. John Bowman has demonstrated that de Valera, throughout the rest of his political career, continued to sound the old trumpet-call of Irish unity while acknowledging, in effect, that the removal of partition was a long way from fulfilment. The evidence of Southern support for nationalist ends in the North after Collins's death was of a purely rhetorical character.

The war and its consequences saw little softening in Irish attitudes to the British government. Cosgrave and O'Higgins risked popularity at home by consorting freely with British government personnel and by dressing in formal finery to attend a function at Buckingham Palace. Differing attitudes to Britain became one of the chief distinguishing marks between the major parties, even after the oath to the Crown had been removed, the Treaty ports recovered and the Republic realised. The survival in Irish politics of anglophobic attitudes, moreover, did not aid the task of reconciling the Southern Unionist population to the Free State. The worst excesses of anti-Unionist action were confined to the war, but the Protestant population, for the most part, while remaining economically secure, had only peripheral influence, both politically and socially.

The war had an extremely depressing effect on international attitudes to the new Irish state: its course and character seemed to conform to all stereotypes concerning the reputed Irish propensity for disorder, confusion, argument and violence. The issues involved were easily depicted as trifles. C. P. Scott, the owner of the *Manchester Guardian*, commented to Margot Asquith: 'Who would have believed that, having got rid of us, the Irish would start a terror of their own?' Herbert Moran, a Sydney surgeon, recorded his father's reaction when in 1922 he paid a return visit to his homeland. 'For him', Moran wrote, 'this was the final stage of his disillusionment. He could not understand it. So back he turned gladly to Australia. Between him and Ireland there was now more than a world of miles.'

The prevailing memory of the conflict has been of considerable importance in determining the way the inhabitants of the Twenty-Six Counties regard their own state. Failure to come to terms with the war and its consequences, together with the frequent neglect of it as a historical subject, has often proved a barrier to an accurate examination of the new state's foundation; it has also hindered prospects of reconciliation between Ireland and Britain, loyalist and nationalist, as well as Republican and Free Stater.[6]

Notes

The following abbreviations are used in the notes.

CP	Childers Papers	PRO	Public Record Office of England
DD	Dáil Debates	PROI	Public Record Office of Ireland
IFS	Irish Free State	PRONI	Public Record Office of Northern Ireland
MP	Mulcahy Papers		
NI	Northern Ireland	SPO	State Paper Office of Ireland
NLI	National Library of Ireland	TCD	Trinity College, Dublin
O'MN	O'Malley Notebooks	TD	Teachta Dála
O'MP	O'Malley Papers	UCD	University College, Dublin
PG	Provisional Government		
PGI	Provisional Government of Ireland (Committee)		

AAC/S	Acting Assistant C/S	D/O	Director of Organisation
AA/G	Assistant A/G	D/P	Director of Publicity
AC/S	Assistant C/S	FGHQ	Field GHQ
A/G	Adjutant-General	GC-in-C	General C-in-C
AO/C	Acting O/C	GHQ	General Headquarters
B/C	Brigade Commandant	I/O	Intelligence Officer
C of GS	Colonel of General Staff	M/D	Minister for Defence
C-in-C	Commander-in-Chief	O/C	Officer Commanding
C/S	Chief of Staff	Q/M	Quartermaster
DC/S	Deputy C/S	QMG	Quartermaster-General
D/E	Director of Engineering	SNO	Senior Naval Officer
D/I	Director of Intelligence		

In the Irish Civil War, there was much inconsistency on both sides in the abbreviations of military titles and ranks. I am aware that the abbreviations adopted above do not even represent a notional contemporary standard but they are, I hope, used consistently throughout the Notes.

Preface (pp. xi-xiii)
1. Lyons (1971), 463; Brennan (1980); Breen (1924); Barry (1949); Hopkinson (1971).

Chapter 1:
The Background to the Treaty Divisions (pp. 1-5)
1. Sinn Féin Funds Case, PROI, 2B/82/117. Claims of de Valera's responsibility: Mulcahy, 'Notes on Questionnaire', MP, P7/D/45; Mulcahy notes on Béaslaí (1926), ii, ibid., P7/D/67; Mulcahy note, 17 Feb. 1963, ibid., P7/D/1; O'Hegarty (1924), 72, 123. For Mulcahy on unity of Irish nationalism before the Treaty negotiations see his notes on Béaslaí, ii, loc. cit. Republican criticisms of the Treaty's signing and claims of Griffith's and Collins's responsibility: de Valera, *Treaty Deb.*, 271-5 (6 Jan. 1922); Brugha, ibid., 326-9 (9 Jan. 1922); Mellows, ibid., 227-30 (4 Jan. 1922); Mary MacSwiney to Mulcahy, 24 Apr. 1922, UCD, MacSwiney Papers, P48a/235(10): Mary MacSwiney to Joseph McGarrity, 29 Apr. 1922, TCD, MacSwiney Papers, 7835; de Valera to Art O'Brien, 7 July 1922, NLI, Art O'Brien Papers, 8461. Republican

claims of British and Lloyd George's responsibility: ibid.; Childers Diary, notes for meeting of Dáil Cabinet, 8 Dec. 1922, CP, 7814; Childers notes, ibid., 7819; de Valera to McGarrity, 27 Dec. 1921, NLI, McGarrity Papers, 17440; *Poblacht na h-Éireann War News*, from 28 June 1922.

2. For continuation of the Easter Rising's ideas see Count Plunkett and Austin Stack. *Treaty Deb.*, 27-9 (19 Dec. 1921).

3. Kingsmill Moore, Sinn Féin Funds Case. and de Valera's evidence. PROI. 2B/82/118, items 35, 37.

4. For IRB constitution see Mulcahy notes, MP, P7/D/3, 70.

5. Collins (1922), 73, 67; Mary MacSwiney, *Treaty Deb.*, 245-60 (17 Dec. 1921); Griffith. ibid., 335-44 (7 Jan. 1921); O'Faolain (1965), 146.

Chapter 2:
The Anglo-Irish War, January 1919-July 1921, and the Truce Period (pp. 6-18)

1. The vast amount of material in the Mulcahy Papers provides an essential primary source on the Anglo-Irish War.

2. Figgis (1927), 218-21, 245, 246; Mulcahy notes on Béaslaí (1926), ii, MP, P7/D/67; Russell at Army Enquiry, 1924, ibid., P7/C/29.

3. Ministerial Report for Home Affairs Department, 16 Aug. 1921, MP, P7a/13; Casey (1970); O'Higgins, *DD*, 1325-8 (24 July 1923); Collins, *Private Sess.*, 22 (18 Aug. 1921); Fitzpatrick (1977), 171-2; Mulcahy notes on talk with Gen. Costello, 23 May 1963, MP, P7/D/3; FitzGerald, *DD*, 810 (27 Sept. 1922); Kingsmill Moore's summing up, Sinn Féin Funds Case, PROI, 2B/82/117; Cosgrave in Dáil, 17 Aug. 1922, quoted by Mulcahy in notes on Béaslaí (1926), ii, loc. cit.; Broy, 20 Feb. 1964, MP, P7/D/70; Collins to Stack, 17-18 May, 20 July 1919, NLI MSS, 5848; Pakenham (1935), 81; de Valera, *DD*, 24 (18 Aug. 1921); O'Hegarty, *Separatist*, 26 Aug. 1921; Lynch, n.d., MP, P7/D/70; Mulcahy memo on Standing Orders for GHQ, ibid., P7/A/32.

4. Mulcahy notes on Béaslaí, ii, loc. cit.; O'Malley (1936), 115, 116, 145; de Valera press statement, 30 Mar. 1921, *Irish Bulletin*, 4 Apr. 1921; Figgis, 255-61; Murphy (1975), 13; Mulcahy notes on Custom House attack, MP, P7/D/1; Ó Broin (1976), 188; Oscar Traynor, O'MN, P17B/95; Longford and O'Neill (1970), 121.

5. Collins (1922), 102; Pakenham, 37; Mulcahy, *DD*, 143 (22 Dec. 1921); Mac Eoin, ibid., 225, (17 Dec 1921); Woods in *Survivors*, 314-15; report by AC/S, 6 Sept. 1921, on visit to 3rd S. Div., MP, P7/A/25; Mulcahy talk on Collins, 29 Oct. 1963, ibid., P7/D/66; for breakup of Collins's intelligence units see O Muirthile Memoir, 143, ibid., P7a/201; for attack on Custom House see IRA report, 25 May 1921, ibid., P7/A/19, and Mulcahy notes on Béaslaí, ii, loc. cit.; Mulcahy at Army Enquiry, ibid., P7/C/38; P. Hogan, ibid., P7/C/24; Mulcahy notes on Collins, ibid., P7/D/69; IRA report, 25 May 1921, loc. cit.; Pax Whelan in *Survivors*, 139; Hopkinson (1971); Ó Muirthile Memoir, 107, loc. cit.; Connie Neenan in *Survivors*, 240; Mulcahy notes on Béaslaí, ii, loc. cit; Mulcahy address to Donegal Men's Association, 11 Dec. 1964, MP, P7/D/70; O'Donoghue (1954), 173-9; Collins to President, 16 June 1921, SPO, DE 2/244; Sturgis Diary, 4 June 1921, PRO, 30/59.

6. Mulcahy notes on Béaslaí, ii, loc. cit.; Hogan, *DD*, 345 (20 Apr. 1923); Garvin (1981), 122; C/S to M/D, 29 Oct. 1921, MP, P7/A/28; C/S to Kerry 1, 18 May 1921, ibid., P7/A/29; MacBride in *Survivors*, 112-14; C/S to M/D on Cooney, 18 Oct. 1921, MP, P7/A/28; Cooney, O'MN, P17B/107; Andrews (1979), 165, 196-200.

7. O'Malley, O'MN, P17B/101; Mulcahy notes on Béaslaí, ii, loc. cit.; Maguire, O'MN, P17B/100; Moane, ibid., P17B/109; Fleming, Mullins, Rice, Scully, ibid., P17B/102.

8. Examples of Mulcahy's complaints: C/S to Kerry 1, 18 May 1921, MP, P7/A/29; C/S to B/C Mid-Limerick, 4 May 1921, ibid., P7/A/38; C/S to O/C S. Wexford, 6 Apr. 1921, ibid., P7/A/16. Appeal for arms, C/S to B/C Sligo, 6 June 1921, MP, P7/A/19; Maguire in *Survivors*, 281; O'Donoghue (1954), 27, 48; GHQ memo, MP, P7/A/32; Rice, O'MN, P17B/102.

9. For increase in central direction of war effort see correspondence, MP, P7/A, and Fitzpatrick (1977), 227; O'Malley (1936), 340; Rice (second recollection), O'MN, P17B/102; Andrews, 215; Fitzpatrick (1977), 202; Mulcahy notes, MP, P7/D/1.

10. O'Donoghue (1954), 42; Cooney, O'MN, P17B/107; Mulcahy comment on Mac Eoin interview, 15 Jan. 1964, MP, P7/D/3; C/S to O/C 1st S. Div., 25 Apr. 1921, ibid., P7/A/18; GHQ memo on E. Clare and S. Galway, ibid., P7/A/47; An tÓglach, Feb., 15 Apr., 15 Dec. 1919; Barry (1949); for his views on Lynch see below; Mulcahy, 'Notes on Liam Ó Briain's Talk to the 1916-1921 Club', 20 Feb. 1964, MP, P7/D/3; 'Notes on Questionnaire', ibid., P7/D/45; notes on Béaslaí, ii, loc. cit; Mulcahy notes on discussion with Gen. Costello, 22 May 1963, MP, P7/D/3; Mulcahy notes on talk on Collins, 22 Oct. 1963, ibid., P7/D/70.

11. Lynch to Séamus O'Donovan, 31 Jan. 1923, NLI, O'Donovan Papers, 22306; Leahy, O'MN, P17B/108; O'Malley (1936), 317.

12. Memo on divisional idea, with details of divisional officers, MP, P7/A/75; Mulcahy's comments in his notes on Béaslaí, ii, loc. cit.; for resistance to divisionalisation see Barry (1949), 147-9.

13. Blythe, quoted in Curran (1975), 14-23; de Valera to McGarrity, 27 Dec. 1921, NLI, McGarrity Papers, 17440; O'Hegarty (1924); Brugha letter, Irish Independent, 24 Mar. 1922; Mulcahy notes, 29 Oct. 1963, MP, P7/D/3; Mulcahy notes on Liam Ó Briain's talk, ibid., P7/D/10; Prof. Hogan at Army Enquiry, ibid., P7/C/30; O'Donoghue letter, Irish Press, 25 Jan. 1959; O'Donoghue (1954), 17, 188; Rice, O'MN, P17B/102.

14. Collins correspondence on arms supplies with IRB agents in British cities, MP, P7/A/1-11; Mulcahy talk on Collins, 29 Oct. 1963, ibid., P7/D/66; Mulcahy notes on Béaslaí, i, ibid., P7/D/67; Deasy, O'MN, P17B/86; Dan Corkery, ibid., P17B/111; J. J. Rice and Dinny Daly, ibid., P17B/102; Liam Manahan, ibid., P17B/106; O'Donoghue, (1954), 186-9; evidence at Army Enquiry, MP, P7/C/3-43; Brady, O'MN, P17B/116; Cooney ibid., P17B/107; Tadhg Kennedy, ibid., P17B/102.

15. Truce terms, MP, P7/A/2; Béaslaí, ii; Mulcahy notes on Béaslaí, i, loc. cit.; Sturgis Diary, 13 June 1921, PRO 39/50; O'Malley (1978), 25; de Valera to McGarrity, 27 Dec. 1921, NLI, McGarrity Papers, 17440; Townshend (1983), 329; de Valera, Treaty Deb., 274 (6 Jan. 1922).

16. An tÓglach, 11 Nov. 1921; Childers autobiographical fragment, CP, 7821; Barry in Curious Journey, 247; C/S to M/D, 7 Oct. 1921, MP, P7/A/28; Mulcahy to O/C 1st S. Div., 27 Oct. 1921, ibid., P7a/26; Lynch, 7 Oct. 1921, ibid., P7/D/70; Lynch to C/S, 4 Oct. 1921, ibid., P7a/26; Thornton in Curious Journey, 234. Compulsory levies: Mulcahy's warnings, C/S to GHQ Organiser, S. Wexford, 19 July 1921, MP, P7/A/22; Mulcahy to O/C Mid-Clare, 23 Sept. 1922, ibid., P7a/26; M/D to C/S on problem of financing the army, ibid., P7/A/24; Vice-Comdt. Cork 1, 18 Nov. 1921, ibid., P7a/26; C/S to M/D, 17 Oct. 1921, ibid., P7/A/37. GHQ memo 'Improvement of Existing Organisation and Training', ibid., P7/A/43; press cuttings on Dublin hills publicity affair, ibid., P7a/26; Collins to de Valera, 15 Oct. 1921, and reply, 19 Oct. 1921, SPO, DE 2/244; Brennan, 10 Nov. 1921, MP, P7/A/27.

17. For South Tipperary problems see below; Divisional Adjt to all brigades, 1st Midland Div., 24 Oct. 1921, MP, P7a/26; for IRA numbers, with tables of divisional strengths, see ibid., P7/A/27, 32; Mulcahy at Army Enquiry, ibid., P7/C/38; Mulcahy address to Donegal Men's Association, ibid., P7/D/70; captured British report on military situation in Ireland, 1 Oct. 1921, ibid., P7/A/37; Joe O'Connor on resentment of 'trucileers' and British army men, O'MN, P17B/105; Barry (1949), 201-7; O'Malley (1936), 342; Mary MacSwiney to Joseph Scott of Los Angeles, 27 Mar. 1922, UCD, MacSwiney Papers, P48a/116(6); Brennan (1980), 105.

18. For IRA being kept on war footing see An tÓglach, 9 Sept. 1921; Oscar Traynor, O'MN, P17B/98; Macready report for week ending 26 Nov. 1921, CAB 24/131; Moylan, DD, 340 (28 Apr. 1922).

19. Mulcahy memo, n.d., probably Oct. or Nov. 1921, MP, P7/A/29; C/S to President, 19 Oct. 1921, ibid., P7/A/27; Mulcahy notes on talk with Gen. Costello, 23 May 1963,

ibid., P7/D/3; Mulcahy notes, 22 Oct. 1963, ibid., P7/D/70; E. Benson (sister of Mrs Lindsay) to de Valera, 6 July 1921; C/S to Divisional Comdt, 12 July 1921; Publicity Department to M/D, 7 July 1921; Cork 1 to C/S, 11 July 1921, ibid., P7/A/21: summary of Robbie affair, with excerpts from correspondence, including Brugha to Mulcahy, 6 Sept. 1921, ibid., P7/A/22; Mulcahy to de Valera, 19 Oct. 1921, ibid., P7/A/27; Brugha to Mulcahy, 13 Sept. 1921, ibid., P7a/1; Brugha to Mulcahy, 18 Oct. 1921, ibid.; Mulcahy, 12 Oct. 1921, ibid., P7/A/27; Mulcahy talk with Gen. Costello, loc. cit.; Mulcahy notes on Béaslaí, ii, loc. cit.; Bob Briscoe, O'MN, P17B/197; Pax Whelan in *Survivors*, 139; Johnny Connors and Tadhg Kennedy, O'MN, P17B/102: Mulcahy address to Donegal Men's Association, loc. cit.; C/S to M/D, 5 Oct. 1921, MP, P7a/2.

20. Dáil Cabinet meeting, 15 Sept., 25 Nov. 1921, SPO, DE 1/3; statement from M/D, MP, P7/A/37; Collins to Mulcahy, 23 Nov. 1921, ibid., P7/A/82; Mulcahy address to Donegal Men's Association, loc. cit.; Lynch to M/D, 6 Dec. 1921; MP, P7/A/5; O'Duffy to M/D, 24 Nov. 1921, ibid.; P7/A/5; Mulcahy talk on Collins, 29 Oct. 1963, ibid., P7/D/66; Mulcahy to Collins, 17 Nov. 1921, ibid., P7/A/2.

Chapter 3:
The Treaty Negotiations (pp. 19-33)

1. Béaslaí (1926), ii, 281.
2. Sturgis Diary, 14 Nov. 1921, PRO 30/59; de Valera, *DD*, 29 (22 Aug 1921); Collins, *Treaty Deb.*, 35 (19 Dec. 1921); Griffith and Lloyd George at Anglo-Irish conference session, 14 Oct. 1921, CAB 43/4; Sturgis Diary, 4 May 1921, loc. cit.; Lloyd George at cabinet meeting, 12 May 1921, Jones (1971), 68; cabinet meeting, 2 June 1921, ibid., 74, 79-81; Craig to Lloyd George, 29 July 1921, House of Lords Record Dept, Lloyd George Papers, F/11/3-15; Craig, 29 Nov. 1921, *Irish Independent*, 30 Nov. 1921.
3. Sturgis Diary, 15 July, 30 Sept. 1921; Jones to Bonar Law, 7 July 1921, Jones, 90; draft statement, CP, 7785; Irish delegation's memo 'Ulster Status and Powers of a Subordinate Ulster Province', ibid., 7786; de Valera to Griffith, 9 Nov. 1921, CP, 7791; Chamberlain account of meeting with Griffith and Collins, Jones, 146; conference session, 14 Oct. 1921, loc. cit.; Sturgis Diary, 18 Aug. 1921; Cope to Jones, 3 Sept. 1921, Jones, 105; C. P. Scott relaying Smuts's views, 28 July 1921, Wilson (1970), 394-8; de Valera to Smuts, 31 July 1921, Lloyd George Papers, F/45/9-51; de Valera to Lloyd George, 10 Aug. 1921, Jones, 94-5.
4. Conference sessions, 14, 17 Oct. 1921, loc. cit.; de Valera, *Private Sess.*, 28-35 (22 Aug. (1921); Collins, *Treaty Deb.*, 35 (19 Dec. 1921); Blythe, ibid., 193-4 (3 Jan. 1922); for Sinn Féin Northern Committee see first report, 11 Oct. 1921, and draft statement, 15 Oct. 1921, CP 7784; report 'Economic and Political Conditions and Outlook' by Diarmuid Fawsitt, 3 Dec. 1921, and report 'Ulster and Irish Trade Policy' by George W. Russell, ibid.; Bowman (1980), 50-6; Walsh, *Treaty Deb.*, 188-9 (3 Jan. 1922); UCD, MacSwiney Papers, P48a/299(35); Lindsay to Mrs Childers, 20 Jan. 1922, CP, 7849.
5. Lloyd George at cabinet meeting, Inverness, 7 Sept. 1921, Jones, 110; Cabinet Minutes, CAB 23(27); Younger to Bonar Law, 19 Nov. 1921, and Croal to Bonar Law, 11 Nov. 1921, quoted in Cowling (1971), 127; for Craig's attitude to British cabinet see pp. 77-8 below; for Lloyd George's political concern see cabinet meeting, Inverness, 7 Sept. 1921, loc. cit.; Stevenson Diary, 28 Oct., 6 Nov. 1921, Stevenson (1971), 233-4; Lloyd George on Bonar Law and Churchill, 7-8 Nov. 1921, Jones, 154-6; Scott Diary, 28-9 Oct. 1921, Wilson, 402-4; Chamberlain at conference session, 14 Oct. 1921, Jones, 132, 139; Scott Diary, 28-9 Oct. 1921, Wilson, 404-5; Lloyd George at cabinet meeting, Inverness, 7 Sept. 1921, CAB 23(27); see also Jones, 106-12.
6. Jones, 82-92; Pakenham (1935), 71-6; de Valera, *Treaty Deb.*, 101-2 (14 Dec. 1921); de Valera at Sinn Féin Ard-Fheis, Macardle (1937), 500; Childers autobiographical fragment, CP, 7821; Stack in Pakenham, 72; *Private Sess.*, 18 Aug. – 14 Sept. 1921; Pakenham, 77-9; Jones, 93-117; de Valera, *DD*, 34 (2 Aug. 1921); Lloyd George to de Valera, 29 Sept. 1921, Macardle (1937), 478; cabinet meeting, Inverness, 7 Sept. 1921, loc. cit.

7. De Valera to Lord Longford, 25 Feb. 1963, CP, 7848; de Valera to McGarrity, 27 Dec. 1921, NLI, McGarrity Papers, 17440; Sir E. Grigg's note, 24 Oct. 1921, CAB 21/253; Collins to John O'Kane, n.d., quoted in Taylor (1958), 170. For Collins's aversion to politics and negotiations see Collins to J. O'Reilly, 11 Oct. 1921, ibid., 151-2; Collins to O'Kane, 6 Nov. 1921, ibid., 154-6; Collins to de Valera, 12 Oct. 1921, CP, 7790; Collins, DD, 96 (14 Sept. 1921). Cosgrave, DD, 95 (14 Sept. 1921); Barton quoted in Childers Diary, 8 Dec. 1921, CP, 7814; Art O'Brien to de Valera, 10 Dec. 1921, NLI, Art O'Brien Papers, 8425.

8. De Valera to Lord Longford, 25 Feb. 1963, loc. cit.; de Valera to McGarrity, 27 Dec. 1921, loc. cit.; Collins quoted in O'Hegarty (1952), 752; de Valera to Collins, 18 Jan. 1921, SPO, DE 2/448; Béaslaí, ii, 146; Robert Barton's written comments in answer to Andrew Boyle, CP, 7834; Childers Diary, 2, 3, 4, 8 Nov. 1921, ibid., 7814; de Valera, DD, 80-3 (26 Aug. 1921); de Valera, Treaty Deb., 101-3 (14 Dec. 1921); Griffith–Childers correspondence, CP, 7790.

9. Jones, 146-7; Scott Diary, 28-29 Oct. 1921, Wilson, 402; Collins to O'Kane, 30 Nov. 1921, Taylor (1958), 195; Childers to de Valera, 14, 18 Oct. 1921, CP, 7790; Childers Diary, 21 Nov. 1921, ibid., 7814; Collins to O'Kane, 4 Nov. 1921; Taylor (1958), 165; Griffith to Collins, ibid., 166; Collins to O'Kane, n.d., ibid., 171; Barton quoting Collins, O'MN, P17B/99.

10. De Valera to the Pope, Pakenham, 136-7; de Valera to Lloyd George, 25 Oct. 1921, CP, 7791; de Valera to Griffith, 27 Oct. 1921, ibid.; de Valera to Griffith, 14 Oct. 1921, SPO, DE 2/304/1; Longford and O'Neill (1970), 136-7; Childers autobiographical fragment, loc. cit.; Harkness (1969); de Valera to McGarrity, 27 Dec. 1921, loc. cit.; Longford and O'Neill, 154-5.

11. Material included in CAB 43/4 and MP, P7/A/82; detailed evidence in CP, 7850; Defence Committee meetings, 17, 18 Oct. 1921, MP, P7/A/72; British Cabinet Minutes, 14 Oct. 1921, CAB 43/1; Irish memo on defence, 29 Oct. 1921, MP, P7/A/42; Macready to Greenwood, 27 Sept. 1921, CO 904/188(1); Collins to A/G, 18 Oct. 1921, MP, P7/A/82; Collins to Mulcahy, 14 Oct. 1921 (two letters), ibid.; M/D to C/S, 22 Oct. 1921, ibid.; conference meeting, 18 Oct. 1921, CAB 43/1; 6th session of conference, 21 Oct. 1921, loc. cit.; agreed aide-memoire, MP, P7/A/82; Truce Committee, 4th session, 14 Oct. 1921, ibid.; Pakenham, 122-3, 127, 144.

12. For diehard resolution see Hansard, 1480-4 (31 Oct. 1921); Cowling, 122-3; Jones Diary, 31 Oct. 1921, Jones, 151-2; conference session, 14 Oct. 1921, loc. cit.; Griffith to de Valera, 24 Oct. 1921, MP, P7/A/82; Collins to Griffith, 31 Oct. 1921, ibid.; Morgan (1979), 246-8; Cowling, 122-7; Pakenham, 186-8; Griffith to Lloyd George, 1 Nov. 1921, CP, 7790; Griffith to de Valera, 24, 25, 27 Oct., 1 Nov. 1921, ibid.; memo of conversation between Jones and Childers, 28 Oct. 1921, ibid.; memo of meeting of Lloyd George with Griffith, 30 Oct. 1921, and Griffith to de Valera, 31 Oct. 1921, MP, P7/A/82; Jones Diary, 25, 30, 31 Oct. 1921, Jones, 145-7, 151-2; Stevenson Diary, 28 Oct. 1921, op. cit.; Cowling, 124-7.

13. Lloyd George account, 10 Nov. 1921, CAB 23/29; memo from British government to NI government, 10 Nov. 1921; Lloyd George to Craig, 10 Nov. 1921; Craig to Lloyd George, 11 Nov. 1921; Lloyd George to Craig, 14 Nov. 1921; Craig to Lloyd George, 17 Nov. 1921, CAB 43/2; Stevenson Diary, 6, 8, 9, 11, 14 Nov. 1921, op. cit., 233-8; Cowling, 124-7; Curran (1980), 25; memo by Worthington-Evans, 12 Nov. 1921, CAB 43/2; Jones Diary, 12 Nov. 1921, Jones, 162-4.

14. Griffith to de Valera, 31 Oct. 1921, MP, P7/A/82; Griffith to de Valera, 11, 12 Nov. 1921, Childers Papers, 7790; memo on sub-conferences, 2-3 Nov. 1921, MP, P7/A/72; Griffith to de Valera, 8, 9, 22 Nov. 1921, ibid.; other letters from Griffith to de Valera, CP, 7790; Jones Diary, 8-9 Nov. 1921, Jones, 155-7; Lloyd George report, ibid., 160-1; Stevenson Diary, 6, 8, 9, 11, 14 Nov., op. cit., 233-8; Jones Diary, 14 Nov. 1921, Jones, 164; Childers Diary, 16 Nov. 1921, CP, 7814; Barton notes on sub-conferences, 5-6 Dec. 1921, Treaty Deb., appx.

15. Memos, 22, 28 Nov. 1921, Treaty Deb., 290-1; Griffith to de Valera, 29 Nov. 1921, CP, 7790; Childers Diary, 22, 23, 28 Nov. 1921, ibid., 7814; Jones Diary, 22, 28 Nov., 1921,

Jones, 169-72, 176; Collins to Art O'Brien, 23 Nov. 1921, Art O'Brien Papers, 8425;
Griffith to de Valera, 22, 23 Nov. 1921, MP, P7/A/72; Collins to Mulcahy, 23 Nov.
1921, ibid.; Pakenham, 195-7; Griffith to de Valera, 29 Nov. 1921, CP, 7790; Childers
Diary, 15, 16, 27, 28 Nov. 1921, ibid., 7814; Cabinet Minutes, 5 Dec. 1921, CAB 43/1;
memo from Jones to Lloyd George, 5 Dec. 1921, Jones, 180; *Treaty Deb.*, appx 4, 298;
Pakenham, 202, 204; Griffith to de Valera, 29 Nov. 1921, CP, 7790.
16. Childers Diary, 1 Dec. 1921 CP, 7814; *Treaty Deb.*, 301-3; SPO, DE 1/3; Childers
Diary, 3 Dec 1921, CP, 7814; de Valera to Lord Longford, 25 Feb. 1963, loc. cit.;
O'Connor (1965), 183; Blythe, *Treaty Deb.*, 192-5 (3 Jan. 1922); British Cabinet
Minutes, 5 Dec. 1921 CAB 23(2).
17. Pakenham, 212; Childers Diary, 4 Dec. 1921, CP, 7814; Childers notes, 4 Dec. 1921,
ibid., 7855; Pakenham, 215-16; Jones Diary, 4 Dec. 1921, Jones, 180; for British
knowledge of Dáil cabinet split see above and Pakenham, 218; memo from Jones to
Lloyd George, 5 Dec. 1921, Jones, 180-1; *Treaty Deb.*, appx, 304-5; Pakenham, 217-18;
Ó Muirthile Memoir, 168, MP, P7a/205; for Collins's attitude to Dominion status see
Collins to O'Kane, 2 Nov. 1921, Taylor (1958), 162-3, and his notes on the settlement,
c. 4 Dec. 1921, ibid., 176.
18. Barton notes on sub-conferences, 5-6 Dec. 1921, *Treaty Deb.*, appx; H. A. L. Fisher
Diary, 6 Dec. 1921, Gilbert (1977), 1684; Scott Diary, 2-5 Dec. 1921, Wilson, 406-12;
Pakenham, 229-42; Griffith's scribbled memo for 6 Dec. 1921, CP, 7790; Childers
Diary, 5-6 Dec. 1921, ibid., 7855; Childers note on Irish delegates' discussion of final
terms, 6 Dec. 1921, ibid., 7786.
19. Childers notes on discussion, 6 Dec. 1921, loc. cit.; Barton notes on sub-conferences, loc.
cit.; Pakenham, 243-4; Childers Diary, 6 Dec. 1921, loc. cit.; Collins comment, n.d.,
probably c. 23 Nov. 1921, MP, P7/A/72; Sturgis Diary, 8 Dec. 1921, loc. cit; *Daily
Chronicle*, cited in Morgan, 264; Taylor, (1958), 178; British press response, e.g. *Times,
Daily Telegraph, Daily Mail*, 7 Dec. 1921, and *Morning Post*, 8 Dec. 1921; Chamberlain to
Craig, 16 Dec 1921, CO 906/30; Jones Diary, 9 Dec. 1921, Jones, 187.

Chapter 4:
The Treaty Split (pp. 34-46)
1. O'Donoghue (1954), 196.
2. Mulcahy notes on Béaslaí (1926), ii, MP, P7/D/67; Pakenham (1935), 262-4; Longford
and O'Neill (1970), 167-8; de Valera to McGarrity, 27 Dec. 1921, NLI, McGarrity
Papers, 17440; O'Higgins, *Treaty Deb.*, 173 (15 Dec. 1921); Dáil Cabinet Minutes, 8 Dec.
1921, SPO, DE 1/3; Childers Diary, 8 Dec. 1921, CP, 7814; Childers notes of meeting,
ibid., 7819.
3. De Valera to McGarrity, 27 Dec. 1921, loc. cit.; Longford and O'Neill, 168; Seán
Fitzpatrick, O'MN, P17B/95; Harry Colley, ibid., P17B/97; Séamus Robinson, ibid.,
P17B/36; Andy Cooney quoted in Andrews (1979), 205; Cosgrave, *Treaty Deb.*, 108 (21
Dec. 1921), 118 (14 Dec 1921); Longford and O'Neill, 168; Robinson, loc. cit.
4. The one anti-Treaty newspaper was the *Connachtman:* see *Nationalist* (Clonmel), 21 Dec.
1921. *Times*, 30 Dec. 1921; *Cork Examiner*, 28 Dec. 1921, and 2, 5 Jan. 1922; *Irish
Independent*, 14 Dec. 1921; Fogarty to Childers, 8 Dec. 1921, CP, 7848; *Cork Examiner*, 30
Dec. 1921, 3 Jan. 1922; Griffith, *Treaty Deb.*, 20 (19 Dec. 1921).
5. Macready report for week ending 10 Dec. 1921, CAB 24/131; Celia Shaw Diary, Dec.
1921, NLI MSS, 23409; *Kilkenny People*, 24 Dec. 1921; *Meath Herald*, 31 Dec. 1921;
Collins to Kitty Kiernan, n.d. (early Jan. 1922), quoted in Forester (1971), 271; weekly
summary of state of Ireland, 7 Dec. 1921, CAB 24/131; TDs' change of attitude,
Macardle (1937), 573, and Longford and O'Neill, 175; de Valera to McGarrity, 27
Dec. 1921, loc. cit.; Maguire, O'MN, P17B/100, and in *Survivors*, 289.
6. Griffith, *Treaty Deb.*, 18 (19 Dec. 1921), 135-9 (14 Dec. 1921), 335-8 (7 Jan. 1922);
Collins, ibid. 30-6 (19 Dec. 1921), 303-4 (7 Jan. 1922); Mulcahy, ibid., 142-4 (22 Dec.
1921); Collins, ibid., 32-6 (19 Dec. 1921); Collins notes for public address, Aug. 1922,
MP, P7/B/28; Collins (1922), 31, 36; Horgan to Childers, 24 Aug. 1921, CP, 7848;
Griffith, *Treaty Deb.*, 21-2 (19 Dec. 1921); Béaslaí, ibid., 176-8 (3 Jan. 1921); Griffith,

ibid., 104-10 (14 Dec. 1921); Collins, ibid., 31-6 (19 Dec. 1921); Seán Milroy, ibid., 154 (15 Dec. 1921); Griffith, ibid., 104-5 (14 Dec. 1921); O'Higgins, ibid., 174-5 (15 Dec. 1921); Leahy, O'MN, P17B/100; Mrs Childers's notes to Basil Williams, CP, 7851: Collins to IRB, see Frank Thornton, O'MN, P17B/100; O'Donnell in *Survivors*, 28.

7. MacSwiney, *Treaty Deb.*, 248, 255 (17 Dec. 1921); Mrs Pearse, ibid., 221 (4 Jan. 1922): Mrs Clarke, ibid., 350 (9 Jan. 1922); Mrs O'Callaghan, ibid., 59 (20 Dec. 1921): Boland, quoted in Fanning (1983b), 5; Stack, *Treaty Deb.*, 27 (19 Dec. 1921); Mellows, ibid., 227-30 (4 Jan. 1922); Andrews, 201; O'Faolain, (1965), 150-1; Sinn Féin Funds Case, loc. cit.; for Rory O'Connor see p. 67 below; Fanning (1983b), 2, 3; for the suggested Dáil compromises see below.

8. De Valera, *Treaty Deb.*, 271, 346 (6, 7 Jan. 1922), 192 (16 Dec. 1921), 122-39 (14 Dec. 1921); 266-8, 273-4 (5-6 Jan. 1922); Connolly to McGarrity, 8 July 1922, McGarrity Papers, 17654; O'Faolain, 149; O'Hegarty (1924), 153; Dwyer (1981), 138; Fanning (1983b), 3; for de Valera's attempt to distance himself from the IRA see p. 70 below; Robinson, *Treaty Deb.*, 290-4 (6 Jan. 1922); Brugha, ibid., 325-34 (7 Jan. 1922), Christy Byrne, O'MN, P17B/95; Mrs. Wyse-Power Diary, 8 Jan. 1922, MP, P7/D/3; Griffith and de Valera, *Treaty Deb*, 261-8 (5 Jan. 1922).

9. NLI, O'Donovan Papers, 22301; O'Donovan, O'MN, P17B/31; Paddy Rigney, ibid., P17B/105; MacSwiney to McGarrity, 24 Apr. 1922, CP, 7835; Hayes in conversation with Mulcahy, 22 Oct. 1964, MP, P7/D/78.

10. Mulcahy talk on Collins, 29 Oct. 1963, MP, P7/D/66; Dáil cabinet meeting, 8 Dec. 1921, Childers Diary, 8 Dec., 1921, CP, 7814; O'Donovan Papers, loc. cit.; O'Hegarty (1924), 82; instructions to Cork TDs, 17 Dec. 1921, MP, P7/D/70; *Treaty Deb.*, 125-31 (14 Dec. 1921); O/C 1st S.Div. to C/S, 6 Jan. 1922, MP, P7/A/32; Hegarty to Lynch, 6 Jan. 1922, ibid.; *Times*, 27, 28 Dec. 1921; Robinson, *Treaty Deb.*, 288-92 (6 Jan. 1922).

11. Aiken to D/P, 18 Apr. 1924, CP, 7847; Moylan, *Treaty Deb.*, 268 (17 Dec. 1921); Hales, ibid., 263; Lynch to his brother, quoted in O'Donoghue (1954), 86; *DD*, 303-4 (27 Apr. 1922).

12. Lynch to Mulcahy, 4 Jan. 1922, P7/A/32; Mulcahy in conversation with Liam Deasy, Jan. 1963, ibid., P7/D/45; O/C Cork 1 to O/C 1st S. Div., 22 Nov. 1921, MP P7/A/31; Mulcahy notes on Béaslaí, ii, loc. cit.; Lynch to C/S, 4 Oct. 1921; Barry to D/O, 27 Sept. 1921; C/S to O/C 1st S. Div., 7 Oc. 1921, MP, P7/A/26; Sturgis Diary, 15 Dec. 1921, PRO 30/59; O'Malley (1936), 198; notes of conversation between Deasy and Mulcahy, 18 Oct. 1962, MP, P7/D/45; Lynch to I/O and Adjt 1st S. Div., 11 Dec. 1921, UCD, P21/1; 1st S. Div. resolution, 10 Dec. 1921, MP, P7/A/32; Deasy, O'MN P17B/86; O'Donoghue, ibid., P17B/95.

13. O'Malley (1936), 333, 339, 340; Sturgis Diary, 29 Nov. 1921; O'Malley (1978), 30-1; Robinson note, 22 Nov. 1921, MP, P7/D/70; Robinson, *Treaty Deb.*, 288-9 (6 Jan. 1922); Mulcahy notes on Liam Ó Briain's address, 20 Feb. 1964, MP, P7/D/3.

14. Report from Q/M W. Mayo Bde, 3 May 1921, MP, P7/A/38; Mulcahy conversation with Gen. McMahon, 15 May 1963, ibid., P7/D/3; for Sligo see p. 10 above; for removal of OCs in S. Roscommon and Kerry 1 see above; press despatch, 27 Apr. 1922, MP, P7/A/63.

15. AAC/S (O'Malley) to O/C 1st N. Div., 26 Sept. 1922, MP, P7a/81; Rumpf and Hepburn (1977), 57-62; Mary MacSwiney, 12 Mar. 1922, TCD, MacSwiney Papers, 7835; Sturgis Diary, 19 Jan. 1922.

16. Report of 1st W. Div. conference, 2 Sept. 1921, MP, P7/A/24; Brennan, *Clare Champion*, 12 Nov. 1922; note from Barrett, 28 Nov. 1921, and report of O/C 1st W. Div., 10 Nov. 1921, MP, P7/D/70; Liam Manahan, O'MN, P17B/106; Paddy McDonnell, ibid., P17B/130; Scully, ibid., P17B/102; Mulcahy notes on Béaslaí, ii, loc. cit.; Séamus Malone (Seán Forde), O'MN, P17B/103, and in *Survivors*, 98; Paddy O'Connor, O'MN, P17B/100-1; Jimmy Leahy, ibid., P17B/100; Ned O'Reilly, ibid., P17B/126; Mick Burke, ibid., P17B/108, 126; Mulcahy notes on P. S. O'Hegarty article in *Irish Times*, 15 May 1963, P7/D/1, 3; Mulcahy talk on Collins, 29 Oct. 1963, ibid., P7/D/66; Mulcahy notes on Béaslaí, ii, loc. cit.; Frank Henderson, O'MN, P17B/99; Harry Colley, ibid., P17B/97; Joe O'Connor, ibid., P17B/105; Seán Burke, ibid.,

P17B/34; Andy Doyle and Paddy O'Connor, ibid., P17B/101; Seán Smith, ibid.. P17B/122; Tom Burke, ibid., P17B/98; Paddy O'Brien and Paddy McDonnell, ibid.. P17B/114; British military report on situation in 6th Div. area, 8 Apr. 1922, CAB 24/136; for Hegarty and O'Donoghue going neutral see p. 93 below; Tom Brennan and Dinny Allen, O'MN, P17B/98.

17. De Valera to McGarrity, 27 Dec. 1921, loc. cit.; Mary MacSwiney to her brother Peter. 1 Jan. 1922, NLI, Hearn Papers, 15993; Brugha, *Treaty Deb.*, 467 (19 May 1922); Boland to Dillon, 27 July 1922, FitzGerald Papers; Manahan, O'MN, P17B/106; Brian O'Higgins, ibid., P17B/97; Ó Broin (1976), 200; Joe Sweeney, O'MN, P17B/98; Gearóid O'Sullivan at Army Enquiry, 1924, MP, P7/C/31; Mulcahy notes on Béaslaí, ii, loc. cit.; O'Muirthile Memoir, 172, MP, P7a/205.

18. Lynch to I/O and Adjt 1st S. Div., 11 Dec. 1921, UCD, P21/1; O'Donoghue (1954); 190-5; Ó Broin 1976); 196, 200; Ó Muirthile Memoir, 168, loc. cit.; Deasy, O'MN, P17B/34; Ranelagh (1976); Ó Muirthile at Army Enquiry, MP, P7/C/13; Mulcahy notes on Béaslaí, ii, loc. cit.; letter of 30 Jan. 1922 opposing Treaty, O'MN, P17B/34; Lynch to McGarrity, 21 Dec. 1922, McGarrity Papers, 17455. Col. Jephson O'Connell at Army Enquiry, MP, P7/C/27; Liam Manahan, O'MN, P17B/106; Brian O'Higgins, O'MN, P17B/97; Paddy Mullally, ibid., P17B/106; Dan Corkery, ibid., P17B/111; O'Donoghue (1954), 189-90; Liam Manahan, Tom Brennan, Dinny Allen, Harry Colley, Brian O'Higgins, Dan Corkery, O'MN, loc. cit.; Tom Maguire, ibid., P17B/100; J. J. Rice, ibid., P17B/38; Andrews (1979), 264; Frank Henderson, O'MN, P17B/99; Quill, ibid., P17B/102, 139; Séamus Robinson, ibid., P17B/95; Oscar Traynor, ibid.; 'Andy Mac', ibid., P17B/36, 100; Oscar Traynor, ibid., P17B/34; Maginiss, ibid., P17B/20; Mulcahy notes on Béaslaí, ii, loc. cit.

19. Brennan in conversation with Mulcahy, 1 May 1963, MP, P7/D/1; Sinn Féin Funds Case, PROI, 2B/82/116, item 19; O'Malley (1936), 144; Irish Labour Party and TUC Report for 1924, p. 120, quoted in Mitchell (1974), 143; O'Faolain, 146; Johnson, *Treaty Deb.*, 412-14 (10 Jan. 1922); for Labour peace efforts see below; O'Donnell in *Survivors*, 25; O'Malley (1978), 286; Mellows, *Treaty Deb.*, 227-32 (4 Jan. 1922).

Chapter 5:
The Irish Question in the United States (pp. 47-51)

1. O'Callaghan, *Private Sess.*, 9 (18 Aug. 1921); de Valera, ibid., 13-18; Carroll to MacSwiney, 28 Mar. 1922, UCD, MacSwiney Papers, P48a/116(1); AARIR membership claim, NLI, McGarrity papers, 17524(3); McGarrity report on split in the Clan, 13 Jan. 1921, ibid., 17424.

2. *Boston Globe* 7 Dec. 1921 (Phelan); *New York World*, quoted in *Times*, 7 Jan. 1922; *New York Times*, 5 Jan. 1922; Connolly Memoir, 301, UCD; *Irish Press* (Philadelphia), 10 Dec. 1922; Rossa F. Downing report on AARIR, 15 Aug. 1922, New York Public Library, McKim-Maloney Papers, Box 22; *Manchester Guardian*, 10 Dec. 1921.

3. *Gaelic American*, 17 Dec. 1922; Devoy to Collins, 16 Feb. 1922, quoted in Tansill (1924), 439; de Valera to McGarrity, 10 Sept, 1922, NLI, McGarrity Papers, 17440; FOIF circular, 31 Dec. 1923, McKim-Maloney Papers, Box 30; Connolly Memoir 34.

4. Walsh to C. J. France, 5 Jan. 1922, New York Public Library, Walsh Papers, Box 112; Walsh to Joseph Scott, 17 Jan. 1922, ibid.; Boland to Dillon, 25 Jan. 1922; Dillon to Boland, 20 Mar. 1922; Boland to McGarrity, 12 Apr. 1922, McGarrity Papers, 17424; Boland to Dillon, quoted in Cronin (1972), 114; MacSwiney to McGarrity, 29 Apr., 2 May 1922, TCD, MacSwiney Papers, 7835; McGarrity memo, Feb. 1922, McGarrity Papers, 17654; Ó Muirthile Memoir, 223, MP, P7a/205; McGarrity report on Clan convention at Philadelphia, 7 Aug. 1922, McGarrity Papers, 17525.

5. Chapter by Downing in W. G. Fitz-Gerald (ed.), *The Voice of Ireland* (1924); F. P. Walsh, ibid., 243; J. C. Walsh to Stephen O'Mara, NLI, O'Mara Papers, 21550.

6. *Nationalist* (Clonmel), 18 Feb. 1922; *New York Times*, 14 Feb. 1922; James E. Murray to Thomas W. Lyons, 12 July 1922, and Murray to Horgan, 20 July 1922; Murray to O'Hanlon, 1 Sept. 1922, MP, P7a/88; Daniel T. O'Connell in Fitz-Gerald, *Voice of Ireland*, op. cit.; Ó Muirthile Memoir, 224-9, including Collins to McGarrity, 23 Feb.

1922; note, 27 July 1922, UCD, MacSwiney Papers, P48a/37/3; Dennis McCullough to Luke Dillon, 21 June 1922; McGarrity to Lynch, 25 Jan. 1923, McGarrity Papers, 17445.

7. PG Minutes, 3 Mar. 1922, SPO, G1/1; *New York Times,* 18 Mar. 1922; Connolly Memoir, 310; correspondence between J. J. Hearn, de Valera and Collins, Mar. 1922, NLI, Hearn Papers, 15992-3; Smiddy to Minister for Foreign Affairs, Dublin, 5 Apr. 1922, MP, P7a/88; Lavelle (1961), 293-6; *New York Times,* 20 Mar. 1922; Joseph Scott to Mary MacSwiney, 10 May 1922, UCD, MacSwiney Papers, P48a/116(15).

Chapter 6:
The Political and Constitutional Background in Early 1922 (pp. 52-57)

1. O'Higgins address, 1924, entitled 'Three Years' Hard Labour', quoted in White (1948), 84.

2. February meeting British conference on Ireland, CAB 43/6; Curtis to Thomas Jones, 16 May 1922, quoted in Jones (1971), 200-1.

3. Macready report for week ending 31 Dec. 1921, CAB 24/131; Macready report for week ending 11 Feb. 1922, CAB 24/133; James Masterton-Smith to Secretary of State, 15 Feb. 1922, CO 739/4; Cope to Anderson, 14 Feb. 1922, CO 906/20; Churchill to Cope, 9 Feb. 1922, ibid.

4. McColgan (1983), 104; Churchill to Mrs Churchill, 4, 11 Feb. 1922, Gilbert (1977), 1752, 1768; Churchill in Commons, quoted by Brugha, *DD,* 141 (1 Mar. 1922); *Irish Independent,* 28 Feb. 1922; Churchill to Collins, 8 Apr. 1922, CO 739/14; general report by Churchill to cabinet, 5 Apr. 1922, CAB 23/30.

5. PG Minutes, 30 Jan. 1922, SPO, G1/1; conference on Ireland with Irish ministers, 5 Feb. 1922, CAB 43/6; PG Constitution Committee, memo, 24 Jan. 1922, UCD, Kennedy Papers, P4/169.

6. UCD, MS P24/43; *Treaty Deb.,* 269 (5 Jan. 1922); Mulcahy notes on Béaslaí (1926), ii, MP, P7/D/67; Collins, *Treaty Deb.,* 346-7 (7 Jan. 1922), 422 (10 Jan. 1922); Mac Néill, ibid., 417-21 (10 Jan. 1922).

7. O'Donoghue (1954), 201-3; O'Hegarty (1924), 109-13; Griffith, *Treaty Deb.,* 376 (9 Jan. 1922); Fanning (1983b), 9.

8. Ard-Fheis, report, MP, P7/A/75; NLI, McGarrity Papers, 17143; NLI, Stack Papers, 18550, including unsigned letter from Griffith to de Valera; Childers Diary, 21-23 Feb. 1922, CP, 7815; *Freeman's Journal,* 22 Feb. 1922; MacSwiney to Hegarty, n.d., TCD, MacSwiney Papers, 7835; Kingsmill Moore's summing up, Sinn Féin Funds Case, PROI, 2B/82/117, file 32; de Valera, ibid., file 35; Paddy O'Keeffe, ibid., file 41; Kevin O'Shiel and George Lyons, ibid., file 47; de Valera, ibid., 2B/82/116, item 4.

9. *Irish Times,* 23 Feb. 1922; conference of British and Irish ministers, 26 Feb. 1922, CAB 43/6, 26; Churchill to ?, 25 Feb. 1922, House of Lords Record Dept, Lloyd George Papers, F/102/40-54.

10. Kathleen O'Connor Diary, 22 Feb. 1922, quoted in Longford and O'Neill (1970), 184; de Valera to Stack, 31 Mar. 1922, quoted in Gaughan (1977), 201; de Valera at Sinn Féin Funds Case, loc. cit.

11. Garvin (1981), 132; report of Hanna Sheehy-Skeffington, Director of Organisation for Sinn Féin, MP, P7a/75; Kingsmill Moore, de Valera and others at Sinn Féin Funds Case, loc. cit.; Macardle (1937), 597; Longford and O'Neill, 184.

Chapter 7:
The Military Split (pp. 58-69)

1. Mulcahy memo, 26 Apr. 1922, NLI, MS 22808; J. J. O'Connell at Army Enquiry, 1924, MP, P7/C/3; J. J. O'Connell, 'Account of Events concerning setting up of National Army', NLI, O'Connell Papers, 15441; Mulcahy at Army Enquiry, MP, P7/C/10.

2. Andrews (1979), 205, 213; 'Address from the Soldiers of the Army of the Republic to their former Comrades in the Free State Army and the Civic Guard', MP, P7/B/87; Walsh, O'MN, P17B/122.

3. Anti-Treaty IRA members to Mulcahy, 11 Jan. 1922, MP, P7/B/191; C/S to all divisional B/Cs, 21 Jan. 1922, ibid.; statement from Mulcahy on 'genesis of Army situation', ibid.; Séamus O'Donovan memo 'in answer to a Questionnaire on the Army Split', NLI, O'Donovan Papers, 22310; Mulcahy to Traynor, 13 Jan. 1922, MP, P17/B/191.

4. Mulcahy statement on 'genesis of Army situation', loc. cit.; O'Donovan answer to questionnaire, loc. cit.; C/S to all divisional commandants, 21 Jan. 1922, loc. cit.; Dáil Cabinet Minutes, 12 Jan. 1922, SPO, DE 1/4; O'Malley (1978), 52; O'Connor to C/S, 18 Jan. 1922, MP, P7/B/191; Lynch to C/S, 13 Jan. 1922, ibid.

5. Mulcahy, DD, 351 (28 Apr. 1922); Mulcahy notes at Dáil meeting, 28 Feb. 1922, MP, P7/A/67; note of M/D for Dáil meeting of 28 Feb. 1922, ibid., P7/A/61; Desmond FitzGerald to Mulcahy, 24 Mar. 1922, MP, P7/B/191.

6. Minute of General Staff meeting, 24 Jan. 1922, MP, P7/A/66; History of Tipperary No. 3 Bde by C. F. Colmaille, O'MN, P17B/127; minute of General Staff meeting, 31 Jan. 1922, MP, P7/B/191; Director of Organisation's report, ibid.; O'Malley (1978), 54; Mulcahy, DD, 140 (1 Mar. 1922); Nationalist (Clonmel), 18 Jan. 1922; minute of GHQ meeting, 24 Jan. 1922, loc. cit.; Cork Examiner, 28 Feb. 1922; Cope to Churchill, 20 Feb. 1922, CO 906/20; report for week ending 27 Feb. 1922, CAB 24/234.

7. Dáil Cabinet Minutes, 12 Jan. 1922, DE 1/4; O'Malley (1978), 49; Gen. Seán MacMahon at Army Enquiry, MP, P7/C/14; J. J. O'Connell, 'Account of events . . .', loc. cit.; Childers Diary, 14 Mar. 1922, CP, 7815; Gen. Michael Costello at Army Enquiry, MP, P7/C/25; report on PG army by British source, CAB 24/134; 'Memo on Officers', submitted to Army Enquiry, MP, P7/C/42; Seán MacMahon at Army Enquiry, ibid., P7/C/33.

8. MacMahon at Army Enquiry, MP, P7/C/14; Hogan letter to Army Enquiry, ibid., P7/C/19; O'Sullivan at Army Enquiry, ibid., P7/C/31; Russell, ibid., P7/C/29.

9. MacMahon at Army Enquiry, MP, P7/C/14; Dalton in RTE television programme, Emmet Dalton Remembers; O'Duffy to M/D, 22 May 1922, MP, P7/B/92; Russell at Army Enquiry, ibid., P7/C/18, 20, 28, 29.

10. Interim Report of Army Enquiry, MP, P7/C/41; general notes used for Army Enquiry, ibid., P7/C/42; Russell at Army Enquiry, ibid., P7/C/20, 28, 29; MacMahon, ibid., P7/C/33; O'Sullivan, ibid., P7/C/12.

11. O'Connell, 'Account of Events . . .', loc. cit.; O'Sullivan at Army Enquiry MP, P7/C/32; Mulcahy, ibid., P7/C/36.

12. PGI Conclusions, 10 Mar. 1922, CO 739/11; Limerick Echo, 21 Feb. 1922; Times 20 Feb. 1922; Childers Diary, 23 Feb. 1922, CP, 7815.

13. Mulcahy memo, 26 Apr. 1922, NLI, MS 22808; Mulcahy notes on Béaslaí (1926), ii, MP, P7/D/67; Limerick Chronicle, 9, 11 Mar. 1922; O'Malley (1978), 55-62; Irish Times, 9 Mar. 1922; Childers Diary, 7 Mar. 1922, CP, 7815; O'Malley to O'Connor, 9 Mar. 1922, NLI, MS 15444(11); O'Connell, 'Account of Events . . .', loc. cit.; Cork Examiner, 9, 13 Mar. 1922.

14. Brennan to AC/S, 8 Mar. 1922, O'Connell Papers, 22127(111).

15. Blythe review of Younger (1968), UCD, Comerford Papers; notes for Army Enquiry, MP, P7/C/42; O'Donoghue (1954), 206; Lynch press statement, 27 Apr. 1922; de Valera to M/D, 6 Mar. 1922, MP, P7/B/191; Mulcahy's secretary to de Valera, 6 Mar. 1922, ibid.

16. O'Mara's meeting with Griffith, 9 Mar. 1922, MP, P7/B/191; scribbled note from O'Mara, received 10 Mar. 1922, ibid., P7/B/191; O'Connell, 'Account of Events . . .', loc. cit.; O'Connor to Childers, 11 Mar. 1922, NLI, MS 15444; Childers Diary, 11 Mar. 1922, CP, 7815; Oscar Traynor, O'MN, P17B/95.

17. Macready note to Churchill, 8 Mar. 1922, CO 739/11; O'Malley notes, NLI, MS 15444; extract from Macready letter, 21 Mar. 1922, CO 739/11; Churchill to Macready (with 'Not Sent' at the top), 22 Mar. 1922, ibid.; Churchill to Collins, 14 Mar. 1922, CO 739/14; O'Connell, 'Account of Events . . .', loc cit.

18. O'Connell, 'Account of Events . . .', loc. cit.; Jimmy Leahy, O'MN, P17B/100; O'Malley (1978), 73; Childers Diary, 13 Mar. 1922, CP, 7815; Gaynor, O'MN,

P17B/119; Dan Gleeson in *Survivors*, 267; Cope to Churchill, 1 Apr. 1922, CO 739/14; Cope to Churchill, 4 Apr. 1922, ibid.; Churchill to Cope, 31 Mar. 1922, CO 906/20; Churchill to Collins, 3 Apr. 1922, ibid.

19. *DD*, 140-1 (1 Mar. 1922), 333-5 (28 Apr. 1922); Mulcahy statement on 'genesis of Army situation', MP, P7/B/191; Rory O'Connor memo, ibid., P7/B/90; Griffith to M/D, n.d., probably mid-Mar. 1922, ibid., P7/B/191; Mulcahy to Collins, 15 Mar. 1922, ibid., P7/B/192; Dáil Cabinet Minutes, 15 Mar. 1922, SPO, DE 1/4.

20. Mulcahy to Collins, 15 Mar. 1922, MP, P7/B/192; Mulcahy's suggested resolutions for compromise to be put before a meeting of all divisional and brigade O/Cs to be held on 24 Mar. 1922, ibid., P7/B/191; Dáil Cabinet Minutes, 21 Mar. 1922, DE 1/4; memo, MP, P7/B/191; O'Duffy statement on 'genesis of Army situation', ibid.; *Irish Independent*, 26 Apr. 1922; Mulcahy, *DD*, 249 (26 Apr. 1922); pro-Treaty report, 26 Mar. 1922, MP, P7/B/191; *Irish Independent*, 23 Mar. 1922.

21. Mick Leahy, O'MN, P17B/108; Mulcahy to CS, 24 Mar. 1922, MP, P7B/192; O'Donoghue (1954), 220-2; Aiken, O'MN, P17B/93; O'Duffy statement in Irish newspapers, 29 Mar. 1922; O'Connor's reply, *Irish Independent*, 5 Apr. 1922.

22. Frank Thornton to M/D, 26 Mar. 1922, MP, P7/B/191; agenda for Convention, 25 Mar. 1922, ibid.; newspaper cutting, 27 Mar. 1922, ibid., P17/B/192a; Maguire in *Survivors*, 291; Maguire, O'MN, P17B/100; Traynor, ibid., P17B/98; Joe O'Connor, ibid., P17B/105.

23. Andrews, 218; O'Connor press statement, 5 Apr. 1922.

Chapter 8:
De Valera and the Military and Political Developments (pp. 70-71)

1. Tallents's talks with Bishop MacRory, 1 July 1922, CO 906/26; de Valera to C. O'M., 13 Sept, 1922, MP, P7/B/86; account of President's Committee on Policy, 8 Jan. 1922, CP, 7848; Childers Diary, ibid., 7815; Mrs Childers to de Valera, 28 Nov. 1940, giving her husband's account, ibid., 7848; de Valera, *DD*, 368 (3 May 1922).

2. *Irish Independent*, 17 Mar. 1922; *Irish Times*, 20 Mar. 1922; *Times*, 21 Mar. 1922; de Valera to *Irish Independent*, 23 Mar. 1922; Curran (1980), 174-5; de Valera to Hearn, 29 Apr. 1928, NLI, Hearn Papers, 15987; *Evening News*, 13 Apr. 1922; de Valera press statement, 1 May 1922; de Valera's interview with Dublin correspondent of the *Chicago Tribune*, 15 May 1922, MP, P7/A/73a.

Chapter 9:
Military Developments after the Army Convention (pp. 72-76)

1. J. J. O'Connell at Army Enquiry, 1924, MP, P7/C/3; O'Malley (1978), 67, 72, 75; Macardle (1937), 632; Cope to Churchill, 14, 17, 18 Apr. 1922, CO 739/14; letter to Secretary of Dáil, 14 Apr. 1922, FitzGerald Papers; Dáil Cabinet Minutes, 13 Apr. 1922, DE 1/4; Republican Army Executive to all TDs, 25 Apr. 1922, ibid.

2. Cope to Churchill 14, 17, 18 Apr. 1922, CO 739/14; Churchill to Collins, 12 Apr. 1922, SPO, S1322; Churchill to Cope, 17 Apr. 1922, CO 739/14; Macready to Churchill, 16 Apr. 1922, House of Lords Record Dept, Lloyd George Papers, F/10/2-67; Churchill to Macready, 17 Apr. 1922, CO 906/20; Lord Devonshire note, 22 Nov. 1922, CO 739/8; Macardle (1937), 641-2; Macready (1924), ii, 637; Macready reports for weeks ending 8 Apr. 1922 and 29 Apr. 1922, CAB 24/136; Churchill general report, Cabinet Minutes, 5 Apr. 1922, CAB 23 (30); meeting of British signatories to Treaty, CAB 431; Churchill in cabinet, 10 Apr., 16 May 1922, CAB 23/30; Churchill to Lloyd George, 12 Apr. 1922, Lloyd George Papers, F/10/2-63; cabinet economic and military sub-committees, i.e. SS (IC) Conference 1-8, 1 June 1922, SS (IC) 7th Minutes, 1-9, 2 June 1922, CAB 16/42; Churchill, 5 Apr. 1922, CAB 23 (30).

3. Casey, O'MN, P17B/102; Henderson, ibid., P17B/105; Mullally, ibid., P17B/106; O'Malley (1978), 75.

4. Curtis to Cope, 5 Apr. 1922; Curtis to Collins via Cope, 3 Apr. 1922, SPO, S1322; Collins to Churchill, 5 Apr. 1922, CO 739/5; Churchill to Cope for Collins, 5 Apr. 1922, SPO, S1322; *Irish Times*, 13 Mar. 1922; C-in-C, Queenstown, to Admiralty, 6 Apr. 1922;

Cabinet Committee Minutes, 3 Apr. 1922; Cope to Curtis, 5 Apr. 1922, CO 739/5; Cope to Churchill, 17 Apr. 1922; report on Cork, 7 Apr. 1922, CAB 24/136; Churchill to Collins, 2 Mar. 1922, CO 906/20; Curtis to Collins via Cope, 3 Apr. 1922, loc. cit.

5. British Cabinet Minutes, 8 Mar. 1922, CAB 27(29); Macardle (1937), 612; Cope to Churchill, 17 Apr. 1922; Cope to Masterson-Smith, 9 May 1922, CO906/20; O'Connor (1965), 190; *Irish Independent*, 26 April 1922; Childers Diary, 25 Apr. 1922, CP, 7815; Tom Burke (Brigade O/C in Offaly), O'MN, P17B/95; Dan Gleeson in *Survivors*, 269-70; Joe Byrne, O'MN P17B/122; Thomas Johnson to Mulcahy, 27 Apr. 1922, MP, P7/A/63.

6. O'Connell at Army Enquiry, loc. cit.; Childers Diary, 10, 11 Apr. 1922, CP 7815; Younger (1968), 255-7; Churchill to Cope, 31 Mar. 1922, CO 739/5; Cope to Churchill, 1 Apr. 1922, CO 739/14; Churchill to Cope, 31 Mar. 1922, CO 906/20; PG statement on genesis of the dispute, MP, P7/B/192a; Mulcahy notes on Béaslaí (1926), ii, ibid., P7/D/67; Gen. Seán MacMahon at Army Enquiry, ibid., P7/C/14; Harry Colley O'MN, P17B/97; Seán Lemass, ibid., P17B/94; Andrews (1979), 218-19.

7. Con Casey O'MN, P17B/102; PG Army Publicity Department report, MP, P7/A/63; Walter Mitchell in *Survivors*, 388; Andrews (1979), 223; Peter O'Connor, O'MN, P17B/95; Seán Gaynor, ibid., P17B/119; O'Connell at Army Enquiry, loc, cit.; Liam Mellows account of events leading up to Four Courts attack, FitzGerald Papers; *Kilkenny People*, 29 Apr., 6 May 1922; Macardle (1937), 635.

8. Collins to McGarrity, 5 Apr. 1922, NLI, McGarrity Papers, 17436; Childers Diary, 12, 26 Mar. 1922, CP, 7815; Collins to M/D, 14 Mar. 1922, MP, P7/B/191; Macready report for week ending 8 Apr. 1922, and British military report on Cork, 7 Apr. 1922, CAB 24/136; O'Connor (1965), 193; Younger, 275-6.

9. F. C. Nally, HQ 1st Bde, 3rd W. Div., to Griffith, 13 Apr. 1922, MP, P7/B/152; copy of note sent to Mac Eoin from McCabe, ibid.; Forester (1971), 300; Mellows account of events, loc. cit.; Frank Carty and Tom Scanlon, O'MN, P17B/128, 137; O'Connell at Army Enquiry, loc. cit.; Younger, 270-5; Sturgis to Churchill, 20 Apr. 1922, CO 739/16; *Times*, 21 Apr. 1922.

Chapter 10:
The North, from Treaty to Attack on the Four Courts (pp. 77-88)

1. Craig to Chamberlain, 15 Dec. 1921, CO 906/30; Lionel Curtis and Thomas Jones memo for PGI Committee, 25 Mar. 1922, CO 739/4; Craig to Devonshire, 6 Nov. 1922, CO 739/1.

2. Collins (1922), 13; Collins miscellaneous notes, MP, P7/B/28; O'Malley, O'MN, P17B/160; O'Hegarty (1952), 754; Lloyd George in Commons, 14 Dec. 1921, CO 739/23; Lloyd George in cabinet, 6 Dec. 1921, CAB 23(27); Birkenhead in House of Lords, 3 Mar. 1922, and Churchill in Commons, 16 Feb. 1922, quoted in Macardle (1937), 602-3, 623; Wedgwood Benn in Commons, 15 July 1922, CO 739/10 (reply drafted by J. Masterton-Smith); Colum (1959), 296-7; Conference of British and Irish Ministers, 5-6 Feb. 1922, and note from Jones and Curtis, CAB 43/6.

3. O'Shiel to members of Executive Council, 29 May 1923, SPO, S2027; 2nd N. Div. report, signed by Mulcahy, NLI, MS 17143; Mulcahy at meeting of North-Eastern Advisory Committee, 11 Apr. 1922, SPO, S1011; O'Higgins memo to PG ministers, White (1948), 92-4; de Valera address to meeting of Republican TDs, 7 Aug. 1924, UCD, MacSwiney Papers, P48a/290(56); *Belfast Newsletter*, 7 Dec. 1921; Craig to Churchill, 26 May 1922, CO 739/14; Craig in NI parliament, 23 May 1922, CO 906/26.

4. IFS report on 1922 Northern developments relating to claims for pensions etc., n.d., FitzGerald Papers; British Cabinet Minutes, 10 Feb. 1922, CAB 10(22), CAB 21/254; PGI Committee meeting, 14 Feb. 1922, CAB 21/254; Conference of Ministers with Griffith, 9 Feb. 1922, ibid.; detailed correspondence between British and Irish governments and Northern and British governments, CO 906/20; message from

Collins to Lloyd George, 8 Feb. 1922, and telegram from Collins to Lloyd George, 9 Feb. 1922, House of Lords Record Dept, Lloyd George Papers, F/10/61; *Cork Examiner*, 17 Jan. 1922; *Times*, 11 Feb. 1922; *Irish News*, 9 Feb. 1922; Tom Ketterick, O'MN, P17B/95; Macready report for week ending 13 Feb. 1922, CAB 24/133; Churchill to Craig, Lloyd George Papers, F/102/45; *Cork Examiner*, 14 Feb. 1922;correspondence between Churchill, Cope, Craig and Collins, 11-15 Feb. 1922, CO 906/20, CO 739/4, PRONI, CAB 8x2/1 and Lloyd George Papers, F/102/46; Churchill to Griffith (Conference of Ministers with Griffith), 9 Feb. 1922, CAB 21/254.

5. Churchill to Craig, 13 Feb. 1922, CO 739/4; Anderson to Cope, 13 Feb. 1922, CO 906/20; conclusion of meeting, 10 Feb. 1922, CAB 27/185; Churchill to Collins, 13 Feb. 1922, CO 739/4; Churchill to Craig, 11 Feb. 1922, CO 906/20;Collins to Churchill, 16 Feb. 1922, ibid.; Cope to Churchill, 1 Mar. 1922, ibid.; Collins to Churchill, 19 Feb. 1922, ibid.; Macready report for week ending 13 Feb. 1922, CAB 24/113; Cope to Churchill, 7 Mar. 1922, CO 906/20; Cope to Jones, 14 Feb. 1922, CAB 21/254; Griffith to Collins, 8 Feb. 1922, ibid.; IFS report, n.d., loc.cit.; Ketterick O'MN, P17B/95. Collins to Lloyd George, 9 Feb. 1922, CO 906/20; Churchill to Collins, 12 Apr. 1922, SPO, S1322.

6. Macready to Chief of Imperial Staff, 16 Feb. 1922, CO 739/4; Churchill to Craig, 14 Feb. 1922, ibid.; Churchill to Collins, 14 Feb. 1922, CO 906/20; Churchill to Cope for Collins, 3 May 1922, CO 739/5; Macready (1924), ii, 622-4; Macready report for week ending 4 Mar. 1922, CAB 24/134; H.J. Creedy to Curtis, 23 Mar. 1922, CO 739/10.

7. *Times*, 21 Mar. 1922; British army memo for 21-31 Mar. 1922, CAB 24/136; Macready to Churchill, 21 Mar. 1922, CO 906/20; Churchill to Collins and Griffith, 20 Mar. 1922, ibid.; Macready letter, 21 Mar. 1922, CO 739/11; Craig to Churchill, 21 Mar. 1922, CO906/20; Macready report for week ending 15 July 1922, CAB 24/138; IFS report, n.d., loc. cit.

8. Churchill to Collins, 24 Mar. 1922, CO 906/20; PGI Conclusions, 20 Mar. 1922, CO 739/4; list of 'outrages' in NI, PRONI, CAB 6/11; Tallents notes on Specials for his report, CO 906/27; Craig to Sir Henry Wilson, 3 Apr. 1922; Craig to Wilson, 3 Apr. 1922, PRONI, CAB 6/89; Spender to Wilson, 6 Apr. 1922, ibid.; letter from Stormont Castle to Churchill, 28 June 1922, ibid.

9. PG Minutes, 19 Jan. 1922, SPO, G1/1; Gilbert (1975), 686; terms of the agreement, SPO, S1801; PG Minutes, 23 Jan. 1922, loc. cit.; British Cabinet Conclusions, 23 Jan. 1922, CAB 23/29; *Cork Examiner*, 23, 27, 28 Jan. 1922; PG Minutes, 30 Jan., 2 Feb. 1922, loc. cit.; *Irish Times*, 2, 3, 4 Feb. 1922; *Irish News*, 3 Feb. 1922; *Cork Examiner*, 4 Feb. 1922.

10. PGI Committee meeting, CO 739/4; 'Heads of Agreement between the Provisional Government and the Government of Northern Ireland', CO 906/30; conference minutes, 29-30 Mar. 1922, CO 739/5; conference on pact, CAB 43/5; for favourable press reaction see *Irish Times*, 31 Mar. 1922, and *Times*, 31 Mar. 1922; for rare critical response see *Irish News*, 31 Mar. 1922; North-Eastern Advisory Committee meeting, 11 Apr. 1922, SPO, S1011; PG Minutes, 5 Apr. 1922, SPO, G1/2; Collins to Craig, 5 Apr. 1922, CO 906/29; Craig to Collins, 5 Apr. 1922, ibid.; Collins to Craig, 29 Apr. 1922, ibid.; Craig to Collins, 25 Apr. 1922, ibid.; Collins to Churchill, 27 Apr. 1922, CO 739/14; Tallents, 'Report on Agreement of 30 March', CO 739/16; Tallents notes, CO 906/30; Dawson Bates on limited powers of the Conciliation Committee, CO 906/23; Andrews to Craig, 17 May 1922, with other detailed information on the expelled workers issue, CO 906/23; Craig's address to Ulster businessmen's meeting, 3 Apr. 1922, CO 906/23.

11. North-Eastern Advisory Committee meetings, 11 Apr., 15 May 1922 (including memo by O'Shiel), SPO, S1011; PG Minutes, 6 Mar. 1922, SPO, G1/1; for reduction in IRA activity during the pact see IFS report, n.d., loc. cit., and Churchill to Lloyd George, 12 Apr. 1922, Lloyd George Papers, F, 10/2-55.

12. IFS report, n.d., loc. cit.; 2nd N.Div. report, NLI, MS 17143; Frank Aiken, O'MN, P17B/90; Johnny McNoy, ibid., P17B/116; Roger McCorley, ibid., P17B/98; Tom MacAnally, ibid., P17B/99, 142; Mick O'Hanlon, ibid., P17B/106; Lehane to Secretary of Military Service Pensions Board, 7 Mar. 1935, ibid., P17B/108; Rory

O'Connor letter revealing Mulcahy's involvement, *Poblacht na h-Éireann War News*, no. 121, 22 Dec. 1922; Charlie Daly, O'MN, P17B/132; Oscar Traynor, ibid, P17B/132.

13. IFS report, n.d., loc. cit.;Roger McCorley, Tom MacAnally, Johnny McNoy, O'MN, loc. cit.; Séamus Woods, ibid., P17B/107; O/C 3rd N. Div. to C/S, 19 May 1922, MP, P7a/173; North-Eastern Advisory Committee meeting, 15 May 1922, loc. cit.; Lt-Comdt Conroy to Mary MacSwiney, 11 May 1923, UCD, MacSwiney Papers, P48a/117; *Irish News*, 5 May 1922; O'Duffy statement, published in national press, 26 Apr. 1922; Lynch in *Irish Times*, 27 Apr. 1922; message from Gen. Solly-Flood, 27 June 1922, CO 906/23; Macready report for week ending 29 Apr. 1922, quoting Lynch's admission of the arms swap, CAB 24/134; Col. J. Brind report, 20 May 1922, ibid.

14. North-Eastern Advisory Committee meetings, 11 Apr., 15 May 1922 (including comments of Woods and Rev. John Hassen of Belfast), loc. cit.; Woods report on situation in No. 1 (Belfast) Bde, MP, P7/B/77.

15. Kevin O'Shiel report on visit by his representative, Hugh A. McCarthy, to S. and E. Down, 19 Apr. 1922, UCD, Kennedy Papers, P4/v/2, P4/L1/6; McCorley, O'MN, P17B/98; Donegan, ibid., P17B/108; 2nd N. Div. report, NLI, MS 17143; O'Shiel memo to each member of IFS government, 6 Oct. 1922, Kennedy Papers, P4/v/1; Cosgrave, *DD*, 86 (9 Sept. 1922).

16. Craig to Churchill, 23 May 1922, CO 906/20; Macready report for week ending 27 May 1922, CAB 24/137; Brind for Macready, report for 7 June 1922, ibid.; *Times*, 22, 24, 25 May 1922; Séamus Woods memo, 27 July 1922, MP, P7/B/1; report on No. 1 (Belfast) Bde, ibid., P7/B/77; Macready report for week ending 8 July 1922, CAB 24/138; Spender to Masterton-Smith, 17 Apr. 1922, CO 739/16.

17. O'Shiel/McCarthy report on S. and E. Down, 19 Apr. 1922, loc. cit.; Tom MacAnally, O'MN, loc. cit.; report on No. 1 (Belfast) Bde, loc. cit.; Aiken to D/P, 18 Apr. 1924, CP 7847; Máire Comerford's account in her memoir, 'The Dangerous Ground', UCD, Comerford Papers, LA18.

18. Report by Comdt Hogan, O/C PG troops, 7 June 1922, CO 739/15; Gen. Cameron's instructions, 1 June 1922, CAB 43/7; Craig to Churchill, 30 May 1922, CAB 21/254; Northern Border Commission report, 30 May 1923, CO 739/11; Churchill to Collins, 4 June 1922, CO 736/14; Churchill to Collins, n.d., probably 6 June 1922, ibid.; Collins to Griffith, 9 June 1922, SPO, DE 2/61; PGI Committee on operations in Pettigo area, Cameron report, 6 June 1922, CO 739/14; scribbled notes by Collins, with casualty figures, 9 June 1922, SPO, S1235; Collins to Griffith, 8 June 1922, ibid.; PGI Committee on operations in the Pettigo area, CAB 21/254; Churchill to Prime Minister, 7 June 1922, CAB 21/254; declaration of neutral zone by British troops, 29 June 1922, CO 739/10; Sweeney, O'MN, P17B/97; Collins to Griffith, 9 June 1922, SPO, S1235; PG Minutes, 9 June 1922, SPO, G1/2.

19. Lloyd George to Churchill, 8 June 1922, Gilbert (1977), 13-14; Conference of British and Irish Ministers, 10 June 1922, CAB 43/6; meeting of British signatories of Treaty, 9 June 1922, CAB 43/7; Cabinet Minutes, 1 June 1922, CAB 23/31; Jones (1971), 204-12.

20. PG Minutes, 3 June 1922, SPO, G1/2; Collins in *Daily Mail*, quoted in *Belfast Newsletter*, 30 June 1922.

21. Churchill to Craig, 30 May 1922, Lloyd George Papers, F/10/2; Cabinet Minutes, 30 May 1922, CAB 23/30; Craig to Churchill, 31 May 1922, CO 906/20; meeting of British signatories of Treaty, 9 June 1922, CAB 43/1; Churchill to Craig, 6 June 1922, PRONI, CAB 6/43; Macready report for week ending 10 June 1922, CAB 24/137; Curtis to Devonshire, 5 Apr. 1923, and report on Cushendall, with correspondence, CO 739/19; Tallents, 'Notes on Police' and other memoranda, CO 906/26, 27; British Cabinet Minutes, 24 July 1922, CAB 41/30; Curtis to Greer, 26 Mar. 1922, CO 739/15; memo of Churchill's meeting with the three Catholic businessmen, 2 June 1922, CO 906/25; meeting of British signatories of Treaty, 16 June 1922, CAB 43/7; Tallents report, CO 739/16.

22. Fanning (1983b), 26-7; Donnelly, 7 Apr. 1922, PROI, 2B/82/6, item 2; North-Eastern

Advisory Committee meeting, 15 May 1922, loc. cit.; Healy, 30 Sept. 1922, Kennedy Papers, P4/v/1.
23. O'Duffy report to all members of government, 22 Sept. 1924, UCD, Blythe Papers, 24/223; Milroy, *DD*, 248-9 (13 Sept. 1922); Loughnane to Curtis, 27 Feb. 1923, CO 739/20.

Chapter 11:
Social and Governmental Problems (pp. 89-92)
1. Andrews (1979), 208; report for week ending 2 Feb. 1922, CAB 24/132; O'Higgins, *DD*, 147 (1 Mar. 1922); Moylan, ibid., 340 (28 Apr. 1922); ibid. (26 Apr. 1922), appxs D, F; Mulcahy, ibid., 251 (26 Apr. 1922); Macardle (1937), 634; Johnson to Mulcahy, 27 Apr. 1922, MP, P7/A/63.
2. Midleton to Churchill, n.d., PRO, Midleton Papers, 30/67/49; Midleton to George V, 30 Apr. 1922, ibid., 30/67/50; record of meetings, Midleton and Andrew Jameson with Griffith, Duggan, Hogan and O'Higgins, 13, 19 Mar. 1922, ibid., 30/67/49.
3. Curran (1980), 182-3; *DD*, 39-95 (10 May 1922); Paddy Ruttledge, O'MN, P17B/142; Greaves (1971), 317, 330.
4. PG Minutes, 16 Jan. 1922, SPO, G1/1; for 1st S. Div. and Civic Guard see above; C-in-C (Collins) to C/S, 7 Aug. 1922, MP, P7/B/1; C-in-C to Acting Chairman PG, 6 Aug. 1922, ibid., P7/B/29; O'Duffy to C of GS, n.d., probably early Sept. 1922, ibid., P7/B/71; O'Higgins to O'Duffy, 4 Sept. 1922, and Mulcahy to O'Duffy, 5 Sept. 1922, ibid., P7/B/48; PG Minutes, 31 Aug. 1922, SPO, G1/1.
5. PG Minutes, 13 Feb. 1922, SPOI, G1/1; report of commission of inquiry into Civic Guard, 14 July 1922, FitzGerald Papers; Mulcahy, *DD*, 250 (26 Apr. 1922); Dáil Cabinet Minutes, 4 Apr. 1922, SPO, DE 1/4; O'Higgins to Mulcahy, 1 Sept. 1922, MP, P7/B/70; Prof. Hogan at Army Enquiry, 1924, ibid., P7/C/25; O'Malley (1978), 81-2; PG Minutes, 27 June 1922, SPO, G1/2; O'Shiel, report of commission of inquiry, loc. cit.; PG Minutes, 18, 22 Aug. 1922, ibid., G1/3; PG Minutes, 17 July, 1922, ibid., G1/2; Acting Chairman PG to C-in-C, 17 July 1922, MP, P7/B/29.

Chapter 12:
The Search for Unity (pp. 93-104)
1. Collins to Joe McGarrity, 5 Apr. 1922, NLI, McGarrity Papers, 17436; *Cork Examiner*, 10 Apr. 1922; MacEntee, *DD*, 345 (28 Apr. 1922); *Irish Times*, 12, 22, 27 Apr. 1922; Macardle (1937), 643-5; Mellows account of events leading up to Four Courts attack, FitzGerald Papers; O'Donoghue (1954), 227-8, 244-5; O'Malley, O'MN, 17B/90; for McGarrity's peace move see p. 50 above.
2. Ó Muirthile Memoir, 190-5, MP, P7a/201; O'Donoghue, O'MN, P17B/95; O'Donoghue (1954), 233-5; Brady, O'MN, P17B/95; Mulcahy memo submitted to Army Enquiry, 1924, MP, P7/C/42; Ó Muirthile Memoir 188, loc. cit.
3. For the statement see Irish Newspapers, 2 May 1922, memo 'The Army Truce: How it was brought about', MP, P7/B/142; article in UCD, MacSwiney Papers, P48a/438; meetings between the signatories and Collins, 22, 29 Apr. 1922, Collins notes, MP, P7a/45; Collins Diary, ibid., P7a/150; Breen to Paddy Daly, 27 Apr. 1922, ibid., P7/B/192; diary of developments and Moylan's suggested peace terms, ibid.; memo on Moylan's desire to compromise, 21 Apr. 1922, ibid., P7/B/152; Irish newspapers, 2 May 1922; memo 'The Army Truce', loc. cit.
4. Hegarty, *DD*, 355-9 (3 May 1922); Mellows, ibid., 360; Moylan, ibid., 363; de Valera, ibid., 366-7; truce terms, 4 May 1922, MP, P7/B/191; Collins notes, 5 May 1922, ibid., P7a/45; memo 'The Army Truce' loc. cit.; scribbled notes, probably by O'Duffy, 10 May 1922, MP, P7/B/192; Lynch to O'Duffy, 12 May 1922, ibid.; Peace Committee report presented to Dáil, 17 May 1922, p. 413; *Cork Examiner*, 23 May 1922.
5. Report of Dáil committee, 10 May 1922, including Boland's draft suggestions and the report of Republican delegates, 11 May 1922, 'Committee of 10: Draft Proposals of Supporters of Treaty', 5 May 1922, MP, P7/B/192; Mulcahy notes on Béaslaí (1926),

ii, ibid., P7/D/67; memo on Dáil debate on the committee, 10 May 1922, UCD, P24/459; Mellows, *DD*, 418 (17 May 1922); Boland, ibid., 422.

6. Memo 'Six-County Position in the Present National Crisis', sent to Griffith, de Valera, Collins, Brugha, etc. following a meeting in Dundalk, 15 May 1922, and letter from P. Lavery and Aiken, Newry, 12 May 1922, MP, P7a/145; Cosgrave to Mulcahy, 23 Dec. 1922, enclosing copy of *Poblacht na h-Éireann War News*, 31 Aug. 1922, containing O'Connor's claim about Mulcahy, MP, P7/B/87; Collins, *DD*, 434-9 (17 May 1922).

7. De Valera, *DD*, 439-40 (17 May 1922); Collins memo, MP, P7a/145; report of Collins–de Valera meeting, 18-19 May 1922, ibid.

8. Griffith, *DD*, 460 (19 May 1922); O'Higgins, ibid., 464; Mulcahy, ibid., 473; Collins, ibid., 478; Collins account of meeting, 19 May 1922, loc.cit.; Jones to Prime Minister, 17 May 1922, House of Lords Record Dept, Lloyd George Papers, F/26/1-31; *Times*, 22 May 1922; PGI Conclusions, 21 May 1922, CO 906/20; Boland to McGarrity, McGarrity Papers, 17424; O'Malley, O'MN, P17B/160; terms of pact, 20 May 1922, MP, P7a/145; O'Connor (1965), 195; memo, UCD, MacSwiney Papers, P48a/299(8); Stack to McGarrity, 27 Aug. 1922, McGarrity Papers, 17489; Anne MacSwiney, O'MN, P17B/112; Liam Manahan, ibid., P17B/117.

9. Churchill memo, 23 May 1922, CO 739/5; British Cabinet Minutes, 30 May 1922, CAB 23(30); Churchill in cabinet, 16 May 1922, ibid.; Blythe article and review of Younger (1968), UCD, Comerford Papers; Colum (1959), 339; Tierney (1980), 309-10; PG Minutes, 25 May 1922, SPO, G1/2; Mulcahy, *DD*, 172 (12 Sept. 1922); O'Higgins, ibid., 1286 (23 July 1923); *Sunday Times*, 26 May 1922; Boland to McGarrity, 30 May, 4 June 1922, McGarrity Papers, 17424; Seán T. O'Kelly to Art O'Brien, 21 Apr. 1922, NLI, Art O'Brien Papers, 8425; Mary MacSwiney to McGarrity, 29 Apr. 1922, McGarrity Papers, 17654; see also TCD, MacSwiney Papers, 7835, and UCD, MacSwiney Papers, P48a/300 (1); O'Malley (1978), 152.

10. De Valera at Sinn Féin Funds Case, PROI, 2B/82/118; Macready report for week ending 1 July 1922, CAB 24/137; Forester (1971), 306; Collins scribbled note, MP, P7a/145.

11. Peace Committee report presented to Dáil, 17 May, 1922, p. 413; *Cork Examiner*, 23 May 1922; note from M/D for Collins, MP, P7/B/192; chronological list of developments, ibid.; Mellows account of events leading up to Four Courts attack, loc. cit.; army unity proposals, MP, P7/B/192; Lynch's proposals to Collins, 8 May 1922, and Collins notes on meeting, ibid., P7a/145; O'Hegarty to M/D, 13 May 1922, ibid.; Mulcahy notes, ibid., P7/B/192; memo on Army Council proposals, ibid.; Liam Lynch to M/D, 7 June 1922, ibid.; O'Duffy's suggestions for distribution, ibid.; 'Discussion of Provisional Government Cabinet Meeting on Draft Agreement between the Two Sections of the IRA', 7 June 1922, SPO, S1322; PG decisions, 5, 7, 12 June 1922, SPO, S1233; PG Minutes, 5, 7, 12 June, SPO, G1/2; Mulcahy memo on army unification proposals, in 'Note on the Army position in June 1922', 29 Oct. 1963, MP, P7/D/1; Mick Murphy, O'MN, P17B/112; O'Duffy to Mulcahy, 22 May 1922, MP, P7/B/192; Lynch letter, 8 June 1922, ibid.

12. Greaves (1971), 326-7; memos to M/D, 15, 24 June 1922, MP, P7/B/192; Executive memo, 24 June 1922, ibid.; Mellows account of events, loc. cit.; O'Donoghue (1954), 244-6; M/D to Secretary, Four Courts Executive, 12 June 1922, MP, P7/B/192; Mulcahy notes on Béaslaí, ii, loc. cit.

13. Moylan, O'MN, P17B/94; O'Donoghue (1954), 228; Humphreys in *Survivors*, 342; Hegarty to *Cork Examiner*, 30 May 1922; Mulcahy to Hegarty, 12 May, 6 June 1922, MP. P7/B/192; Mulcahy Diary, 11, 12, 13 May 1922, ibid., P7/B/193.

14. J. J. O'Connell, 'Account of Events concerning setting up of National Army', NLI, O'Connell Papers, 15441; O'Connell to C/S (O'Duffy), 22 May 1922, and reply, 26 May 1922, NLI, MS 22130; O'Connell's copy of evidence, May 1922, ibid.

15. Twomey, 'Memo on Present Situation', 25 July 1922, MP, P7/B/90; Liam Lynch to O/C 1st S. Div., 6 Sept. 1922, ibid.; Dalton to M/D, 10 May 1922, ibid., P7/B/102; Mulcahy, *DD*, 166-73 (12 Sept. 1922); unsigned notes (possibly by Collins), MP, P7a/145; Ó Muirthile Memoir, 189.

Chapter 13:
The Constitution (pp. 105-108)

1. O'Kelly to Art O'Brien, 21 Apr. 1922, NLI, Art O'Brien Papers, 8425; Boland to McGarrity, 12 Apr. 1922, NLI, McGarrity Papers, 17424; MacSwiney, 'Message from America', UCD, MacSwiney Papers, P48a/378 (8); Churchill to Cope, 8 May 1922, CO 906/20.

2. For the three original drafts, MP, P7/A/65; Farrell (1970); Curran (1980), 201; Towey (1977); Douglas memo, *Daily News*, 4 Apr. 1922; memo on first meeting of Constitution Committee, 24 Jan. 1922, UCD, Kennedy Papers, P4/169; Hogan memo, 1 May 1922, MP, P7/D/65; O'Rahilly memo, 12 Apr. 1922, ibid.; Curran (1980), 204.

3. Cabinet Conclusions, 16 May 1922, CAB 23(30); Cope to Churchill, 23 May 1922, CO 739/14; interview between PM and others with Griffith and Collins, 27 May 1922, CAB 43/1; aide-memoire of meeting, CAB 43/3; Cabinet Minutes, 30 May, 1 June 1922, CAB 23/30; Lloyd George at British signatories' meeting, 26 May 1922, CAB 43/1; Curtis account of later interview between PM and Griffith and Collins, CAB 43/7; Jones (1971), 202-3, 206; FitzAlan at British signatories' meeting, 23 May 1922, CAB 43/1.

4. Curtis account, CAB 43/7; Jones, 205-7; Lloyd George at British signatories' meeting, 26 May, CAB 43/1; Lloyd George to Griffith, 1 June, 1922, House of Lords Record Dept, Lloyd George Papers, F/21/1; meetings of 26-27 May 1922, loc. cit.

5. Accounts of meeting by Curtis and Jones, loc. cit.; British signatories' meeting, 9 June 1922, CAB 43/1; Griffith to Lloyd George, 2 June 1922, Lloyd George Papers, F/21/1; PG Minutes, 2-3 June 1922, SPO, G1/2; Griffith to Collins, 9 June 1922, SPO, S1235; British signatories' meeting, 15 June 1922, CAB 43/1; Lloyd George at British signatories' meeting, 16 June 1922, ibid.

6. O'Higgins, *DD*, 477-8 (20 Sept. 1922): Towey (1977); Kohn (1932), 83; Collins draft article on constitution, MP, P7/B/27; O'Higgins, *DD*, 358 (18 Sept. 1922); Churchill at British ministers' meeting, 23 May 1922, CAB 43/1; Boland, 13 July 1922, McGarrity Papers, 17424.

Chapter 14:
The June Election and the Assassination of Sir Henry Wilson (pp. 109-114)

1. *Times*, 17 June 1922; Griffith at Conference of British and Irish Ministers, 10 June 1922, CAB 43/6; Boland, 13 July 1922, NLI, McGarrity Papers, 17424; *Irish Times*, 19 June 1922; Gallagher (1979); de Valera to McGarrity, 10 Sept. 1922, McGarrity Papers, 17440.

2. *Cork Examiner*, 15, 16 June 1922; *Freeman's Journal*, 15 June 1922; *Kilkenny People*, 17 June 1922; Mitchell (1974), 159; Gorey, *DD*, 26 (9 Sept. 1922); O'Brien, ibid., 164 (12 Sept. 1922).

3. Gallagher (1979); Macardle (1937), 657-8; Rumpf and Hepburn (1977), 59 (map), 61, 64; *Kilkenny People*, 17 June 1922; Conference of British and Irish Ministers, 10 June 1922, CAB 43/7; Mitchell (1974), 160-2.

4. Irish and British national newspapers, 23 June 1922; Billy Aherne, O'MN, P17B/99; Dinny Kelleher, ibid., P17B/107; Denis Brennan, ibid., P17B/100; Taylor (1961).

5. Joe Sweeney, O'MN, P17B/29, 97, and in *Curious Journey*, 281; Pa Murray, O'MN, P17B/89; Seán MacGrath, ibid., P17B/100; Frank Thornton, ibid.; Mick Murphy, ibid., P17B/112; Liam Tobin, ibid.; Seán MacBride in *Survivors*, 117; letters of Joe Dolan and Patrick O'Sullivan in *Sunday Press*, 27, 28 Sept. 1953, and ensuing correspondence in that paper between Joe Dolan and Florrie O'Donoghue; de Valera in NLI, Art O'Brien Papers, 8461.

6. Michael Cremins, O'MN, P17B/89; Bob Briscoe, ibid., P17B/99; Billy Aherne, ibid., P17B/99; Dinny Kelleher, ibid., P17B/107; George White, ibid., P17B/105; Frank Martin (of London IRA) evidence (undisclosed source); evidence on Dunne seeing O'Connor and Collins, Dunne testimony given to Frank Saurin, (undisclosed source); O'Malley, O'MN, P17B/23; O'Malley (1978), 85; Tobin, O'MN, P17B/94; Blythe

review of Younger (1968), UCD, Comerford Papers; Moylan, O'MN, P17B/94, 100; Macready (1924), ii, 651.

7. Conference of British Ministers, appx 1, CAB 21/255; Jim O'Donovan, O'MN, P17B/31; John Neary, ibid., P17B/122; Collins to Churchill, 21 Mar. 1922, CO 739/14; Collins to Craig, 27 Apr. 1922, CO 906/29; Dinny Kelleher, O'MN. P17B/107.

8. Pa Murray and Michael Cremins, O'MN, P17B/89; Ernie Noonan, ibid., P17B/94; George White, ibid., P17B/105; Bob Briscoe and Billy Aherne, ibid., P17B/99; Dinny Kelleher, O'MN, loc. cit.; Seán MacGrath and Denis Brennan, ibid., P17B/100; memo on IRA activities in Britain, O'MP, P17a/51; Stevenson Diary, 22 June 1922, Stevenson (1971); Conferences of British Ministers, 22-23 June 1922; and discussions on Four Courts, 22-25 June 1922, CAB 21/255; Lloyd George to Collins, 22 June 1922, CAB 35; Macready (1924), ii, 652; Kevin O'Higgins memo to ministers, quoted in White (1948), 91.

Chapter 15:
The Attack on the Four Courts (pp. 115-122)

1. Seán MacBride account of Army Convention written in Newbridge jail, July 1923, MP, P7/B/90; Andrews (1979), 225-6; O'Donoghue (1954), 246; Tom McEllistrim, O'MN, P17B/102; Brodie Malone, ibid., P17B/109; Mulcahy address to Donegal Men's Association, 11 Dec. 1964, MP, P7/D/70.

2. Conference of Ministers, 23-24 June 1923, CAB 21/255; Lloyd George scribbled notes, 24 June 1922, ibid.; Diarmuid O'Hegarty (Secretary to the Government) to Lloyd George, 22 June 1922, UCD, Blythe Papers, P24/27.

3. Conference of Ministers, 24-25 June 1922, and memo, 24 June 1922, CAB 21/255; Macready scribbled notes, 23 June 1922, ibid.; note from Hankey after receiving a telephone message from Churchill's private secretary, ibid.; Macready (1924), ii, 652-4; Churchill at cabinet meeting, 29 June 1922, Jones (1971), 213; Churchill to Collins, 7 July 1922, CO 739/6; Churchill in Commons, 26 June 1922, S1322; Times, 27 June 1922.

4. Manchester Guardian, 24 June 1922; PG Minutes, 27 June 1922, SPO, G1/2; Mulcahy talk on Collins, 29 Oct. 1963, MP, P7/D/66; O'Malley, O'MN, P17B/161; reports, 27, 28 June 1922, MP, P7/B/192; Thornton, O'MN, P17B/100; Moylan, ibid., P17B/94; O'Malley (1978), 88-90; memo, 28 June 1922, MP, P7/D/66; report from C/S, 28 June 1922, ibid., P7/B/106; Younger (1968), 322-3.

5. PG Minutes, 27 June 1922, SPO, G1/2; review of developments for 28 June 1922, MP, P7/D/66; Mulcahy talk on Collins, 29 Oct. 1963, ibid; Ernest Blythe review of Younger (1968), UCD, Comerford Papers; Cosgrave, DD, 65-77, (11 Sept. 1922); O'Higgins, ibid., 94-9; Mulcahy, ibid., 166-78 (12 Sept. 1922); O'Hegarty (1924), 123; Thomas Johnson, DD, 181-7 (12 Sept. 1922); O'Higgins, ibid., 1263-86 (23 July 1923); Blythe review of Younger, loc. cit.

6. Mulcahy comments, 17 Nov. 1967, MP, P7/D/63; Mulcahy talk on Collins, 29 Oct. 1963, loc. cit.; O'Connor (1965), 177; O'Hegarty (1924), 123; Cope to Curtis, 27 June 1922, CO 906/21; Churchill to Cope, n.d., probably 27 June 1922, ibid.

7. O'Donoghue (1954), 258; O'Malley note, 25 June 1922, O'MN, P17B/23; Tod Andrews, ibid., P17B/88; Connie Neenan in Survivors, 243; Humphrey Murphy in Kerry People, 29 July 1922; O'Donoghue (1954), 258; Deasy (1982), 45-6; O'Sullivan's comment in Colum (1959), 367; for the decision to allow 1st S. Div. leaders to return south see p. 135 below; Mulcahy talk on Collins, 29 Oct. 1963, loc. cit.

8. O'Donoghue (1954), 260-1; Macready report for week ending 15 July 1922, CAB 24/138; O'Malley, (1978), 91-4; Brennan (1950), 338; Máire Comerford, 'The Dangerous Ground', UCD, Comerford Papers; 'Events in connection with IRA leading up to attack on Four Courts', UCD, MacSwiney Papers, P48a/299(33).

9. Maguire, O'MN, P17B/100; O'Donoghue (1954), 230; Longford and O'Neill (1970), 195; Irish Labour Party and TUC Report, 1922; Churchill to Cope for Collins, 28 June 1922, CO 906/21.

10. Macready report for week ending 1 July 1922, CAB 24/137; Churchill's telephone conversation with Cope, 28 June 1922, CO 906/21; Cope to Curtis for Churchill, 28 June 1922, ibid.; Cope to Curtis, 28, 29 June 1922, ibid.; Macready (1924), ii, 655-6, 659; Dalton in RTE television programme *Emmet Dalton Remembers*; Collins to Churchill, 29 June 1922, CO 906/21; Churchill to Cope, 28 June 1922, ibid.; Churchill to Cope for Macready, 28 June 1922, ibid.; Cope to Curtis, 28 June 1922, ibid.; Cope to Churchill, 2 July 1922, CO 739/13; Gen. Seán MacMahon at Army Enquiry, 1924, MP. P7/C/14.

11. Correspondence between Churchill, Cope and Curtis, 28-29 June 1922, CO 906/21.

12. Andrews (1979), 230-1; Traynor, O'MN, P17B/95, 98, 142; Seán Mooney, ibid.. P17B/94; Moss Twomey, ibid., P17B/95; Frank Henderson, ibid,, P17B/99; O'Malley, ibid., P17B/101; Humphreys in *Survivors*, 430-7.

13. O'Malley (1978), 92-112; Peadar O'Donnell in *Survivors*, 25; Moss Twomey and Oscar Traynor, O'MN, loc. cit.; despatch from Desmond FitzGerald, No. 5, statement regarding surrender, MP, P7/B/60; memo from M/D after speaking to Gen. Daly, 30 June 1922, and another memo from M/D, and C/S to M/D, both 30 June 1922, ibid.; C/S's report, ibid., P7/B/106; Mulcahy notes, ibid., P7/B/107; Cope to Curtis, 30 June 1922, CO 906/21; Macready report for week ending 1 July 1922, CAB 24/137; O'Malley (1978), 113-19.

14. O'Malley (1978), 115-21; Dr Jim Ryan (of Wexford), O'MN, P17B/103; *The Plain People*, 2 July 1922; Twomey, O'MN, P17B/95; FitzGerald statement, loc. cit.; Doyle, O'MN, P17B/95; Smith, ibid., P17B/122; Brennan, ibid.

Chapter 16:
The Dublin Fighting (pp. 123-126)

1. Seán Mooney, O'MN, P17B/94; Frank Henderson, ibid., P17B/99; Oscar Traynor, ibid., P17B/98, 142; operation report, 2 July 1922, MP, P7/B/60; Hegarty for Collins, 2 July 1922, ibid.; list of posts occupied by Republican forces, 29 June 1922, ibid.; Comdt Thornton to AC/S, 2 July 1922, ibid., P7/B/106; lists of posts in the south of the city from 'I.O. Division', n.d., probably 2 July 1922, ibid.; Cope to Curtis for Churchill, 30 June 1922, CO 739/13; Máire Comerford in *Survivors*, 46, and *Curious Journey*, 283.

2. Madge Clifford (Comer), O'MN, P17B/103; Mulcahy note on Brugha, MP, P7/D/1; discussion between Deasy and Mulcahy, 18 Oct. 1962, ibid., P7/D/45; Brennan (1950), 343-7; Longford and O'Neill (1970), 196; *Poblacht na h-Éireann War News*, No. 3, 29 June 1922; *Irish Times*, 1 July 1922; de Valera to Brugha, 6 July 1922, UCD, MacSwiney Papers, P48a/255(1); Childers to Mrs Childers, 12 July 1922, TCD, CP, 7855.

3. Humphreys in *Survivors*, 43; Macready report for week ending 4 July 1922, CAB 24/137; Younger (1968), 334, 338; A/G to Collins, 2 July 1922, MP, P7/B/60; operation records, 2 July 1922, ibid.; Hegarty for Collins, 2 July 1922, ibid.; O/C 2nd E. Div. to AC/S, 3 July 1922, ibid.; PG army report, 3 July 1922, ibid.; report by Capt. Dalton, 3 July 1922, ibid.; Medical Officer, in charge of forces, to M/D, 3 July 1922, ibid.; PG army report, 5 July 1922, ibid.; PG Minutes, SPO, G1/2; Oscar Traynor, O'MN, P17B/95; Frank Henderson, ibid., P17B/99.

4. Two PG army reports, 5 July 1922, MP, P7/B/60; Fanning (1983b), 16; *Times*. 7 July 1922; Seán Mooney, O'MN, P17B/94; Ben Doyle, ibid., P17B/95; Longford and O'Neill (1970), 196; report by Capt. Dalton, 3 July 1922, MP, P7/B/106; Ned O'Reilly, O'MN, P17B/126; Longford and O'Neill, 196-7; de Valera to Brugha, 6 July 1922, UCD, MacSwiney Papers, P48a/255 (1); Harling in *Curious Journey*, 285-6; Walton. ibid., 283; Ketterick, O'MN, P17B/95; O'Donoghue (1954), 261; David Neligan in *Curious Journey*, 284; O'Malley (1978), 123-7.

5. Mulcahy address to Donegal Men's Association, 11 Dec. 1964, MP, P7/D/70; Florrie Begley, O'MN, P17B/111; Connie Neenan in *Survivors*, 244; pro-Treaty propaganda in *Limerick War News*, 18 July 1922; Mulcahy conversation with Deasy, 18 Oct. 1922, MP. P7/D/45; Deasy (1982), 49-51; Tom McEllistrim, O'MN, P17B/102; O'Donoghue (1954), 259-60; Seán Culhane, O'MN, P17B/108; *Cork Examiner*, 1 July 1922.

6. Churchill to Collins, 7 July 1922, CO 739/6; Birkenhead, 6 July 1922, quoted in Macardle (1937), 691; Churchill to Collins, 30 June 1922, CO 906/21.

Chapter 17:
The Military and Political Background to the Fighting (pp. 127–141)
1. Estimate of Republican troop numbers, MP, P7/B/140; Gen. Seán MacMahon at Army Enquiry, 1924, ibid., P7/C/14; Cope to Curtis for Churchill, 29 June 1922, CO 906/21.
2. For British arms supplies and regular Irish requests see CO 906/21; Collins memo to Acting Chairman of PG, 5 Aug. 1922, MP, P7/B/29; Boland to Luke Dillon, 27 July 1922, FitzGerald Papers.
3. McNoy, O'MN, P17B/94; Robinson, ibid., P17B/99; McHugh, ibid., P17B/110; Cooney, ibid., P17B/116; Máire Comerford Memoirs, UCD; Andrews (1979), 240.
4. O'Donnell in *Survivors*, 25; Robinson, O'MN, P17B/101; O'Connor, ibid., P17B/105; O'Duffy, n.d., probably mid-July 1922, MP, P7/B/69; Deasy to D/E, 9 July 1922, O'MP, P17a/87; O'Hanlon, O'MN, P17B/106; O'Connor (1958), 171-3; O'Malley to Lynch, 21 July 1922, MP, P7a/81; Twomey, 'Memo on Present Situation', 25 July 1922, O'MP, P17a/34; Robinson, O'MN, P17B/99.
5. Moloney's two notes, O'MP, P17a/15; D/O 1st S. Div. (?) to A/G, Fermoy, 1 Aug. 1922, Army Archives, A/0991/4; Hales, n.d., probably July 1922, ibid., A/0991/2; O'Malley (1978), 148-50.
6. Lynch to O/C 1st S. Div., 3 Sept. 1922, O'MP, P17a/17; O'Malley to DC/S, 21 July 1922, ibid., P17a/54; O'Malley to AO/C 1st E. Div., 19 Aug. 1922, ibid., P17a/55; Robinson, CP, 7851; A/G to O/Cs, 12 July 1922, O'MP, P17a/15.
7. Lynch to O/C 3rd S. Div., 5 Sept. 1922, O'MP, P17a/17; *Times*, 23 Aug. 1922; Hegarty to Lynch, 11 July 1922, FigzGerald Papers; for Aiken and 4th N. Div. see pp. 169-71 below; Maguire and Gilmore, O'MN, P17B/100; Seán Hennessy (O/C, 4th Batt., 4th Bde) to B/C Mid-Clare, 22 July 1922, Army Archives, Frank Barrett Papers, A/1012.
8. Sinn Féin Funds Case, PROI, 2B/82/117; de Valera to Eamonn Donnelly, 25 Oct, 1922, ibid., 2B/82/116; de Valera to Stack, 20 Sept. 1922, ibid.; Stack to de Valera, 1 Jan. 1923, SPO, 2B/82/119; Gaughan (1977), 217-30.
9. Longford and O'Neill (1970), 197; Brennan (1950), 349-52; de Valera to C.O'M., 12 Sept. 1922, MP, P7a/162; Boland-McGarrity correspondence, NLI, McGarrity Papers, 17424; Liam Pedlar to McGarrity, 3 Aug. 1922, ibid., 17478; Stack to McGarrity, 3 Aug. 1922, ibid., 17489; Diarmuid Brennan, n.d., UCD, Comerford Papers.
10. Childers Diary, 28 June–3 Nov. 1922, CP, 7818; Childers notes, 1 July 1922–10 Nov. 1922, ibid., 7855; Childers notes, 6 Sept., 20 Oct. 1922, and two pieces by Robinson, with his reminiscences of Childers and his memories of the Civil War, ibid., 7851; O'Connor (1958), 182-3; O'Duffy to C-in-C, 12 Aug. 1922, MP, P7/B/39; *Irish Times*, 6 Sept. 1922; *Times*, 19 Sept., 25 Nov. 1922; despatch from J. F. Carter, 18 Aug. 1922, with Home Office report on Childers's supposed movements, CO 739/9; *Times*, 25 Nov. 1922; Childers statement, CP, 7829.
11. Donnegan to O'Malley, quoted in Greaves (1971), 377; Twomey, 'Memo on Present Situation', 25 July 1922, O'MP, P17a/34; de Valera to Colivet, 17 Mar. 1923, Longford and O'Neill, 207; O'Connor to O'Malley, 12 Sept. 1922, O'MP, P17a/61; Lynch to Deasy, 1 Sept. ibid., P17a/17.
12. De Valera Diary, 13 Aug. 1922, Longford and O'Neill, 198; de Valera to Rev L. McKenna, S.J., 18 Jan. 1922, ibid., 210; Andrews, O'MN, P17B/88; Mick Mansfield, ibid., P17B/95; de Valera to McGarrity, McGarrity Papers, 17440; Cosgrave at meeting between Bonar Law and Irish ministers, 24 Oct. 1922, CO 739/7; Con Moloney (A/G) to Deasy (AC/S), 5 Sept. 1922, O'MP, P17a/61; Moloney to O'Malley, 5 Sept. 1922, ibid.; Lynch to Deasy, 6 Sept. 1922, MP, P7/B/90; Lynch to Deasy, 17 Sept. 1922, O'MP, P17a/18; Lynch to O'Malley, 17 Sept. 1922, MP, P7a/81; Mellows memos from prison, late Aug. and early Sept. 1922 (captured and published by PG), ibid., P7/B/86; Moloney to O'Malley, 5 Oct. 1922, O'MP, P17a/64.

13. PG Minutes, 3 July 1922, SPO, G1/2; *Times*, 5 July 1922; conference at Portobello Barracks, 17 July 1922, MP, P7a/56; PG Minutes, 26 Aug. 1922, G1/3; memo on establishment of War Council, 12 July 1922, MP, P7/B/177; Mulcahy at Army Enquiry, ibid., P7/C/10; PG Minutes, 1, 12 July 1922, G1/2; Collins to Griffith, 14 July 1922, MP, P7/B/177; PG to Collins, 15 July 1922, ibid., P7/B/29.

14. Collins memo, 21 July 1922, and Collins to Lt-Gen. O'Connell (Curragh Camp Operations Area), 20, 23 July 1922, MP, P7/B/17; for criticisms of Prout's command and Dalton's complaints see pp. 209, 201 below; MacManus to A/G, 18 Sept. 1922, and memo by him, n.d., O'MP, P17a/215; Mulcahy memo to Collins (referred to by Mulcahy at Army Enquiry), MP, P7/C/35.

15. MacMahon at Army Enquiry, MP, P7/C/14; Mulcahy, ibid., P7/C/7; for inspection staff and army training see pp. 224-5 below; O'Sullivan at Army Enquiry, MP, P7/C/12; *An tÓglach*, 11 Nov. 1922; O Muirthile at Army Enquiry, MP, P7/C/13; Russell, ibid., P7/C/29; Mulcahy, ibid., P7/C/37; Mulcahy, *DD*, 2432 (29 Nov. 1922).

16. Hogan at Army Enquiry, MP, P7/C/25; for poor relations between O'Duffy and Dalton see p. 201 below; Blythe, UCD, Blythe Papers, 24/223; Cathal O'Shannon, *DD*, 1618 (7 June 1923); PG Minutes, 26 Aug. 1922, G1/3; O'Sullivan at Army Enquiry, MP, P7/C/12; David Neligan, ibid. P7/C/17, 29; Charles Russell, ibid., P7/C/18, 20, 28; material for preparation of Interim Report of Army Enquiry, ibid., P7/C/41; general notes, ibid., P7/C/42; for Dalton and Ennis see pp. 201-3 below; Brennan to C-in-C, 15 May 1923, MP, P7/C/10.

17. Mulcahy, *DD*, 166-78 (12 Sept. 1922), 848 (27 Sept. 1922); Cope to Curtis for Churchill, 29 June 1922, CO 906/21; Cope to Curtis, 3 July 1922, CO 739/13; PG Minutes, 2-4 July 1922, G1/2; O'Sullivan at Army Enquiry, MP, P7/C/12, 31; PG Minutes, 14 July 1922, G1/2; PG decision, 2 July 1922, S1369; official memo, 2 July 1922, ibid.; PG Minutes, 8, 10 July 1922, G1/2; PG decision, 7, 24 July 1922, S1369; O'Higgins *DD*, 275-8 (14 Sept. 1922), 920 (28 Sept. 1922); Curtis to Sir John Chancellor, 4 Oct. 1922, CO 739/7; PG Minutes, 19 Sept. 1922, G1/3; proposed telegram, Churchill to Governors of Seychelles and St Helena, 28 Sept. 1922, CO 906/22; captured letter from Q/M 29 Sept. 1922, and D/I to M/D, 16 Dec. 1922, MP, P7/B/87; Cope to Curtis, 28 Sept. 1922, CO 906/22; PG Minutes, 30 Oct. 1922, S1369; letter to M/D, 20 Nov. 1922; President's Office to Bishop of Limerick, 13 Nov. 1922; memo on Limerick jail, S1369; telegram, 29 Aug. 1922, on burning of Maryborough jail, ibid.

18. PG decision, 14 July 1922, and Cosgrave to Collins, 14 July 1922, S1376; PG Minutes, 26 July 1922, G1/2; PG Minutes, 4 Sept. 1922, G1/3; Collins to Cosgrave, 25 July 1922, MP, P7/B/29; Collins to FitzGerald, 26 July 1922, ibid., P7/B/53; PG Minutes, 12 July 1922, G1/2; Curtis to Secretary of State, 5 Sept. 1922, CO 739/9; Midleton, 28 July 1922, PRO, Midleton Papers, 30/67/51; Hoare report on Ireland to British cabinet, 21 Sept. 1922, CO 739/15; Collins to Cosgrave, 21 Aug. 1922, NLI, MS 13539; PG Minutes, 29 July 1922, G1/3; O'Higgins, *DD*, 955-6 (29 Sept. 1922), 1294-6 (30 May 1923); O'Duffy to Mulcahy, 24 July 1922, MP, P7a/173; Fanning (1983b), 61.

19. PG Minutes, 24 July 1922, G1/2; Collins to Cosgrave, 21 Aug. 1922, NLI, MS 13539; Johnson, *DD*, 182 (12 Sept. 1922); Macready report for week ending 2 Sept. 1922, CAB 24/138.

Chapter 18:
The War in the Localities: July–August 1922 (pp. 142-171)

1. J. McGrath to Comdt-Gen. Ennis, 5 July 1922, MP, P7/B/106; material captured at Blessington, ibid.; Traynor, O'MN, P17B/95; Alfie White, ibid., P17B/110; History of Tipperary No. 3 Bde by C. F. Colmaille, ibid., P17B/127.

2. Doyle, O'MN, P17B/95; Traynor to C/S, 6 July 1922, MP, P7/B/106; Traynor to A/G, 3rd Batt., 2 July 1922, ibid; note from FGHQS.E. Command to Traynor, 14 July 1922, ibid; Traynor, O'MN, P17B/95; Vice-O/C O'Donovan to O/C from HQ 3rd Batt., 4 July 1922, MP, P7/B/106; PG army reports, 7, 9 July 1922, ibid.; Republican report

from Blessington to O/C Barracks, 8 July 1922, ibid., P7/B/60; Gilmore, O'MN, P17B/106.

3. O'Malley (1978), 133, 138; report of meeting of Republican IRA, GHQ Limerick, 5 July 1922, with review of military situation by C/S, FitzGerald Papers; PG army report for N.E. Command, MP, P7/B/60; report of Adjt E. Command, 6 July 1922, and various other reports, ibid., P7/B/106; Tommy Brennan and Dinny Allen, O'MN, P17B/98; O'Malley (1978), 132-42.

4. PG army report, 13 July 1922, MP, P7/B/60; Robinson, O'MN, P17B/99. Whelan and Clifford, ibid., P17B/103; Moylan to O'Malley from New Ross, 10 July 1922, ibid., P7/B/106; Moylan to O'Malley, n.d., ibid.

5. Two notes from Comdt McAllister, Wexford, 10 July 1922, MP, P7/B/16; C/S to M/D, 6 July 1922, ibid., P7/B/59; E. Command report, 7 July 1922, ibid., P7/B/61; E. Command report, 8 July 1922, ibid., P7/B/60; McAllister to C/S, from Enniscorthy, 7, 10 July 1922, ibid., P7/B/106.

6. Lynch to O'Malley, 10 July 1922, MP, P7/B/106; O/C Dublin (Traynor), 2 July 1922, ibid.; Traynor to C/S, from Blessington, 6 July 1922, ibid., P7/B/90; O'Malley to Deasy, 9 Sept. 1922, ibid.

7. Cullinan and Gilmore, O'MN, P17B/106; O'Malley to Lynch, 28 July 1922, MP, P7a/81; Andrews, O'MN, P17B/88; O'Malley to Lynch, 6 Aug. 1922, MP, P7a/81; *An tÓglach*, 20 Jan. 1923.

8. Acting O/C Dublin 1 to AAC/S, 30 Aug. 1922, O'MP, P17a/61; Alfie White, O'MN, P17B/110; Liam Nugent, ibid., P17B/88; John Cullinan, ibid., P17B/106; I/O 2nd E. Div. to D/I 7 Aug. 1922, MP, P7/B/4; I/O 2nd E. Div. to Command I/O 5 Aug. 1922, ibid., P7/B/59; O'Malley to Lynch, 9 Aug. 1922, ibid., P7/A/81; *Irish Times,* 8 Aug. 1922; Christy Smith, O'MN, P17B/109; Andrews (1979), 237.

9. Andrews, 237-9; Christy Smith, O'MN, P17B/109; Séamus Fox and Paddy Mullally, ibid., P17B/106; Frank Henderson, ibid., P17B/99.

10. Brennan quoted in Younger (1968), 370; MacSwiney to Deasy, 5 Feb. 1923, SPO S2210; O'Duffy memo, n.d., probably mid-July 1922, MP, P7/B/69; Dan Donovan, O'MN, P17B/95; Seán Hyde, ibid., P17B/101; Mick Murphy and Seán Murray, ibid., P17B/112; Lynch report from Limerick, 9 July 1922, O'MP, P17a/15; Co. Limerick truce, 4 July 1922, MP, P7/B/90; IRA Executive meeting, 5 July 1922, FitzGerald Papers; Jamie Managhan, O'MN, P17B/112.

11. PG army operation report, 7 July 1922, MP, P7/B/60; letters and reports from MacManus, 5-6 July 1922, ibid., P7/B/60, 61, 106; Younger, 371, 373; Dan Donovan, Seán Hyde, Paddy Coughlin, O'MN, loc. cit.; Lynch report from Limerick, 9 July 1922, O'MP, P17a/15; Frank Aiken, O'MN, P17B/93; IRA Executive meeting, 5 July 1922, loc. cit.; Limerick city agreement, MP, P7/B/106.

12. Younger, 370-8; Aiken O'MN, P17B/98; Lynch report from Limerick, 9 July 1922, loc. cit.; Lynch to AC/S, 18 Aug. 1922, ibid., P17a/61; Hyde and Coughlin, O'MN, loc. cit.; Moylan to Deasy, 6 July 1922, Army Archives, A/0991/2; MacSwiney to Deasy, 5 Feb. 1923, SPO, S2210; Bumstead, O'MN, P17B/112; Leahy and Sullivan, ibid., P17B/108.

13. Hogan from HQ 4th S. Div. to A/G, 12 July 1922, MP, P7/B/107; Seán MacMahon at Army Enquiry, 1924, ibid., P7/C/14; Republican A/G to AC/S, 13 July 1922, O'MP, P17a/60; Aiken, O'MN, P17B/98; *Cork Examiner,* 12 July 1922; *Limerick Chronicle,* 20 July 1922; Hyde to Deasy, 11 July 1922, Army Archives, A/0991/2; Lynch to O'Malley, 13 July 1922, O'MP, P17a/60; A/G to AAC/S, 19 July 1922, ibid.; Mulcahy to O/C 4th S. Div., n.d., MP, P7/B/69; O'Duffy to C-in-C, 21 July 1922, ibid.; O'Duffy note, 23 July 1922, ibid., P7/B/21.

14. Despatch from O'Duffy, n.d., MP, P7/B/69; Mulcahy to O/C 4th S. Div., n.d., MP, P7/B/21; O'Duffy report to C-in-C, n.d., c. 20 July 1922, ibid., P7/B/69; Managhan, O'Duffy report on Limerick operations, 21 July 1922, MP, P7/B/69; *Cork Examiner,* 22 July 1922; *Times,* 24 July 1922; *Limerick Chronicle,* July 1922; C-in-C (Collins) to Prout, 21 July 1922, MP, P7/B/63; Murphy and Managhan, O'MN, P17B/112.

15. A/G to AAC/S 19 July 1922, O'MP, P17a/60; Hogan to A/G, 15 July 1922, MP,

P7/B/21; O'Duffy report to C-in-C, n.d., c. 20 July 1922, ibid., P7/B/69; Managhan, O'MN, P17B/112; Moloney to O'Malley (A/G to AAC/S), 19 July 1922, O'MP. P17a/60; Patrick O'Donnell, O/C E. Limerick Bde. 9 Aug. 1922, ibid., P17a/107; Murray, O'MN, P17B/112; Deasy, ibid., P17B/34.

16. O'Duffy despatch from FGHQ Limerick, 23 July 1922, MP, P7/B/21; O'Duffy report to C of GS, 26 July 1922, ibid., P7/B/68; S. MacCarthy to Adjt 4th S. Div., 24, 25 July 1922, ibid.; O'Duffy report, 4 Aug. 1922, ibid.; O'Duffy to Mulcahy, n.d., early Aug. 1922, ibid., P7/B/71; report from Lt Kearns, 29 Aug. 1922, ibid., P7/B/113; report for Republican Director of Publicity, 20 July 1922, Army Archives, A/0991/2; O'Duffy to C of GS, 4 Aug. 1922, MP, P7/B/68; Moloney to Deasy, 19 July 1922, O'MP, P17a/60; Lynch to AC/S, 25 July 1922, MP, P7a/81.

17. A/G (Moloney) to AAC/S, 2 Aug. 1922, O'MP, P17a/60; Republican A/G to AC/S, 7 Aug. 1922, ibid.; O'Duffy report, 4 Aug. 1922, MP, P7/B/68; report by Comdt Flood, 3 Aug. 1922, ibid., P7/B/107; *Irish Times*, 4 Aug. 1922; for advance on Kilmallock front and Mulcahy's plans see MP, P7/B/69; O'Duffy, 4 Aug. 1922, ibid., P7/B/68; PG phone reports from Limerick, 5, 8 Aug. 1922, ibid., P7/B/107; O'Duffy to C of GS, n.d., early Aug. 1922, ibid. P7/B/71; intelligence report, ibid., P7/B/68; O'Duffy despatch, 7 Aug. 1922, ibid.; *Irish Times*, 4, 7 Aug. 1922; *Limerick War News*, 9 Aug. 1922; Republican IRA Divisional O/C to O/C Mid-Limerick Bde, 6 Aug. 1922, Army Archives, A/0991/4; Lynch to O'Malley, 9 Aug. 1922, MP, P7a/81.

18. PG army reports, 4 Aug. 1922, MP, P7/B/68; Republican A/G to AC/S, 7 Aug. 1922, O'MP, P17a/60; *Irish Times*, 4 Aug. 1922; McSweeney in Limerick to Mulcahy, MP, P7/B/107; correspondence from E. T. Whitehead, 8 Aug. 1922, and Mrs. Blennerhasset, 15 Aug. 1922, both from Adare, CO 739/6; PG Army reports, 4, 11 Aug. 1922, MP, P7/B/68, 72; O'Duffy to C/S, 10 Aug. 1922, ibid., P7/B/70.

19. Fitzpatrick (1977); *Clare Champion*, 26 Aug. 1922; *Irish Times*, 4 Oct. 1922; O'Duffy despatch to C-in-C, n.d., MP, P7/B/69; report from Intelligence Department, S.W. Command, to D/I, GHQ, 22 Aug. 1922, ibid., P7/B/71; *Limerick War News*, 31 July 1922, with O'Duffy's review of military situation; *Clare Champion*, 5, 12 Aug. 1922; S.W. Command report, 4 Aug. 1922, MP, P7/B/68; C of GS to O'Duffy, 31 Aug. 1922, ibid., P7/B/70; PG army report from 1st W. Div., n.d. (early September?), ibid., P7/B/113; O'Duffy report, 29 Aug. 1922, ibid.; PG army report, 11 Aug. 1922, ibid.; Hogan report, 20 Nov. 1922, ibid., P7/B/137; Hennessy to B/C Mid-Clare, Army Archives, Frank Barrett Papers, A/1012, lot 24; Hennessy to O/C No. 4 Bde, 24 July 1922, ibid.

20. Edwards in *Survivors*, 5; Macready report for week ending 15 July 1922, CAB 24/138; memo on Waterford for PG army, 8 July 1922, MP, P7/B/63; scribbled notes, ibid., P7/B/107; Divisional O/C to D/E FGHQ Limerick, 9 July 1922, ibid., P7/B/93; *Irish Independent*, 24 July 1922; report by an Inspector of the Local Government Department, MP, P7/B/106.

21. Whelan to O/C 1st S. Div., n.d., probably mid-July 1922, Army Archives, A/0991/3; Culhane, O'MN, P17B/108; Whelan to Adjt 1st S. Div., O'MP, P17a/96; Whelan, O'MN, P17B/95, 103.

22. Collins memo, 14 July 1922, MP, P7/B/18; Collins to Comdt McCarthy (Adjt 2nd S. Div.), 20 July 1922, ibid.; Thornton to D/I, 20 July 1922, ibid., P7/B/63; Thornton, O'MN, P17B/100.

23. GC of C to Prout, 21 July 1922, MP, P7/B/63; report by Comdt McCarthy, Kilkenny, 21 July 1922, ibid., P7/B/107; Whelan, O'MN, P17B/95; Deasy, ibid., P17B/86; Colmaille, ibid., P17B/127; Whelan to Republican C/S, n.d., Army Archives, A/0991/2; *Sunday Independent*, 23 July 1922; *Irish Independent*, 22, 24, 25 July 1922; Younger, 390-5.

24. Deasy to O/C Waterford, 19 July 1922, O'MP, P17a/87; Republican I/O, Carrick, to A/G Operations, 24 July 1922, ibid., P17a/34; Whelan, O'MN, P17B/103; Whelan to C/S (Lynch), n.d., Army Archives, A/0991/12; Colmaille, loc. cit.; Thornton to D/I, 20 July 1922, MP, P7/B/63; I/O 2nd S. Div. from FGHQ Limerick, 24 July 1922, O'MP, P17a/34; C of GS to Capt. P. Dalton, 21 July 1922, MP, P7/B/63; Dalton to M/D, 27 July 1922, ibid., P7/B/65; PG army memo, 26 July 1922, ibid.

25. Cooney, O'MN, P17B/107; Liam Lynch to O/C 3rd S. Div., 5 Sept. 1921, MP, P7/B/86; PG army report, 8 July 1922, ibid., P7/B/106; GC-in-C to Lt.Gen. O'Connell, 16 July 1922, ibid., P7/B/17; PG army report from 3rd S. Div., 4 July 1922, ibid., P7/B/106; PG army report, 12 July 1922, ibid., P7/B/60; memo on position of 3rd S. Div., n.d., probably mid-July 1922, ibid., P7/B/17; Tipp. No. 1 Bde report, ibid., P7/B/106; Gleeson in *Survivors*, 269; PG army report, 5 July 1922, MP, P7/B/106.

26. 3rd S. Div. report, 4 July 1922, MP, P7/B/106; GC-in-C to Lt-Gen. O'Connell, 14 July 1922, ibid., P7/B/17; memo on Curragh Operations Area, 23 July 1922, ibid., P7/B/19; GC-in-C to O/C Curragh Operations Area, 21, 26, 27 July 1922, ibid., P7/B/191; Collins to Lt-Gen. O'Connell, 16 July 1922, and Collins report from Roscrea, 17 July 1922, NLI, MS 22127(1); Mitchell in *Survivors*, 388; Gaynor to Robinson, from Birr, n.d., probably mid-July 1922, MP, P7/B/106; PG army report for Birr-Banagher area, 26 July 1922, ibid., P7/B/112.

27. Mac Eoin to Collins, 31 July 1922, MP, P7/B/145; GC-in-C to Acting O/C 3rd S. Command, 3 Aug. 1922, ibid., P7/B/19; reports, 11 Aug. 1922, ibid.; GC-in-C to Comdt-Gen. Price, 17 Aug. 1922, ibid.; PG army intelligence reports, n.d., probably end of Aug. 1922, ibid., P7/B/112; PG army report on Republican activities, 7 Aug. 1922, ibid., P7/B/68; notes by Comdt Gantley, 29 July 1922, ibid., P7/B/107; McGrath to C-in-C, forwarding account of Tonduff ambush, ibid., P7/B/19; C-in-C to PG, 29 July 1922, ibid., P7/B/29; Mitchell in *Survivors* 388.

28. C-in-C (Collins) reports, 23 July, 7 Aug. 1922, MP, P7/B/19; memo on Curragh Camp Operations Area, 23 July 1922, ibid.; C-in-C report, 31 July 1922, ibid.; GC-in-C to Acting O/C, 3rd S. Div., 8 Aug. 1922, ibid., P7/B/19; O'Malley to C/S, 9 Aug. 1922, ibid., P7a/81; O'Malley to Lynch, 24 Aug. 1922, ibid.; O'Malley to C/S, 3 Sept. 1922, ibid.; Gaynor, O'MN, P17B/119.

29. O'Malley to Lynch, 22 Sept. 1922, MP, P7a/81; Maguire, O'MN, P17B/109; Carty ibid., P17B/128; Carney, ibid., P17B/109; Tom Scanlon, ibid, P17B/133; Hunt, ibid.; Killilea, ibid., P17B/109; Kilroy, ibid., P17B/101; O'Malley, ibid., P17B/113.

30. PG army report, 7 July, 1922, MP, P7/B/60; PG army report, and report from Capt. Peadar Conlon, 5 July 1922, ibid., P7/B/133; John Greeley, O'MN, P17B/113; list of operations carried out by 1st Batt. Sligo Bde, NLI, O'Connell Papers, 22118; PG army report for C/S, 11 July 1922, MP, P7/B/106; Younger, 354-62; Scanlon, O'MN, P17B/133; PG army memo, 24 July 1922, MP, P7/B/72; *Times*, 20 July 1922; Mac Eoin to C-in-C, 31 July 1922, MP, P7/B/145.

31. Carty, O'MN, P17B/128; Maurteen Brennan, ibid., P17B/33; Mac Eoin report from Collooney, 15 July 1922, MP, P7/B/107; Col.-Comdt's note from Athlone, 15 Sept. 1922, ibid., P7/B/49; list of operations carried out by 1st Batt. Sligo Bde, loc. cit.; Macready report for week ending 15 July 1922, CAB 24/138.

32. Collins to Acting Chairman PG, 5 Aug. 1922, MP, P7/B/29; Mac Eoin to C-in-C, 31 July 1922, ibid., P7/B/145; *Irish Times*, 31 July 1922; Maguire, O'MN, P17B/100.

33. 'Western Command: Immediate Objectives of Expedition for Mulcahy's intelligence information', and memo on objectives of expedition, 17 July 1922, MP, P7/B/73; Adjt for Col.-Comdt O'Malley, from Westport, 25 July 1922, ibid.; QMG note, 23 July 1922, with list of materials used by the expedition, ibid.; C of GS to Mac Eoin, 27 July (two notes), 28 July 1922, ibid; intelligence report sent by Mac Eoin to Collins, and Mulcahy notes, ibid., P7/B/80; C of GS to Mac Eoin, 28 July 1922, ibid., P7/B/73;; *Irish Times*, 26, 31 July, 3 Aug. 1922; *Irish Independent*, 28 July 1922; Lawlor to Mac Eoin, 21 July 1922, MP, P7/B/107; Mac Eoin to C-in-C, 31 July 1922, ibid., P7/B/145; *Connaught Telegraph*, 29 July 1922.

34. Heavey, O'MN, P17B/120; *Irish Independent*, 28 July 1922; I/O Athlone Command to D/I, 10 Aug. 1922, Army Archives, file 37; report, MP, P7/B/4; *Irish Times*, 31 July 1922; Collins to Acting Chairman PG, 5 Aug. 1922, MP, P7/B/29; Mulcahy to MacEoin, 14 Aug. 1922, ibid., P7/B/73.

35. Daly, O'MN, P17B/132; Comdt-Gen. 1st N. Div., Republican IRA, 19 Sept. 1922, O'MP, P17a/63; O'Duffy, 3 July 1922, MP, P7/B/106; Sweeney, O'MN, P17B/97, and in *Curious Journey*, 287-8; Jack Fitzgerald, O'MN, P17B/112; Lehane to Daly, 10

Nov. 1922, MP, P7/B/86; Lehane note, n.d., O'MP, P17a/65.

36. O'Malley to C/S (Lynch), 28 July, 24 Sept. 1922, MP, P7a/81; O'Malley to O/C 1st N. Div., 26 Sept. 1922, ibid., Lehane to Daly, 10 Nov. 1922, ibid., P7/B/86; Daly, O'MN, P17B/132.

37. McHugh, O'MN, P7B/110; Begley, ibid., P7B/111; Lynch to O/C 1st S. Div., 1 Sept. 1922, O'MP, P7a/17; Tadhg O'Sullivan, O'MN, P17B/108; Managhan, ibid., P17B/112.

38. Chairman's Office to M/D, 11 July 1922, SPO, S1376; message sent on by H. C. Somerville to British Admiralty, 14 July 1922; report from Mrs Powell, sister of Michael Collins CO 739/3; Macready report for week ending 18 July 1922, CAB 24/138; *Cork Examiner* for the period; Tom Hales to O/C 1st S. Div., 19 July 1922, Army Archives, A/0991/2; Enright, O'MN, P17B/103; report on situation in Cork by M. O'Connell, 19 July 1922, MP, P7/B/40.

39. C of GS to O'Duffy, 7 Aug. 1922, MP, P7/B/69; memo from Ministry of Economic Affairs at Cork, n.d., probably early Aug. 1922, ibid.; C of GS, GHQ to Dalton, 3 Aug. 1922, ibid.; *Cork Examiner*, 12 Aug. 1922; *Irish Times*, 15 Aug. 1922; Hayes in conversation with Mulcahy, 22 Oct. 1964, MP, P7/D/78; O'Connor (1958), 180, 'Liam' to C-in-C, from Douglas, 10 Aug. 1922, MP, P7/B/20; PGI Conclusion No. 25, 1 Aug. 1922; note to War Office, 2 Aug. 1922; Churchill to Collins, 4 Aug. 1922, CO 739/10; Somerville, 9 Aug. 1922, CO 739/3; RTE television programme, *Emmet Dalton Remembers*; Crofts and Leahy, P17B/108; Barrett, ibid., P17B/111; Donovan, ibid., P17B/95; Lunch to AC/S, 18 Aug. 1922, O'MP, P17a/61; Lynch to O'Malley, 9 Aug. 1922, MP, P7a/81.

40. 'Liam' to C-in-C, from Douglas, 10 Aug. 1922, MP, P7/B/20; Lynch to AC/S, 9 Aug. 1922, ibid., P7a/81; *Irish Times*, 12, 15 Aug. 1922; Younger, 412-21; Murphy, O'MN, P17B/112; Murray, ibid., P17B/88; Dalton to C-in-C, 12 Aug. 1922, MP, P7/B/20.

41. Dalton to C-in-C, 11 Sept. 1922, Army Archives; *Irish Times*, 14, 16, 17, 21 Aug. 1922; S. W. Command report, 22 Aug. 1922, MP, P7/B/71; Deasy (1982), 72; O'Faolain (1965), 154.

42. Cahill to O/C Kerry 1, 15, 20 July 1922, O'MP, P17a/99; report from Kerry 1, 19 July 1922, ibid.; Murphy report, 13 July 1922, Army Archives, A/0991/2; Connors, Rice, Dennis Quill, O'MN, P17B/102; O'Duffy to C-in-C, n.d. probably mid-July 1922, MP, P7/B/69;*Daily Mail*, 3 July 1922; *Irish Independent*,8 July 1922; Deasy report at GHQ meeting in Limerick, 6 July 1922, FitzGerald Papers; Lynch report from Limerick, 9 July 1922, O'MP, P17a/15; Rice, O'MN, P17B/139.

43. McEllistrim, O'MN, P17B/102; Cahill to Murphy, 15 July 1922, O'MP, P17a/99; PG army reports, 4, 6 Aug. 1922, MP, P7/B/68; O'Duffy, *Irish Times*, 9 Aug. 1922; *Irish Independent*, 9 Aug. 1922; Brig. Daly report of the landing at Fenit, MP, P7/B/133; Michael Fleming, Billy Mullins, Johnny Connors, O'MN, P17B/102; Eamon Enright, ibid., P17B/103; P. J. McHugh, ibid., P17B/109; Stan Barry, ibid., P17B/111; J. J. Sheehy in *Survivors*, 358; Mullins (1983); 143; Republican A/G to AAC/S, 7 Aug. 1922, O'MP, P17a/60; O'Duffy to C of GS, n.d., MP, P7/B/68.

44. PG army report, 4 Aug. 1922, MP, P7/B/68; O'Duffy to C of GS, 12 Aug. 1922, ibid., P7/B/113; Connors, O'MN, P17B/102; O'Duffy to C of GS, 16 Aug. 1922, MP, P7/B/70; Daly, from Millstreet, 17 Aug. 1922, ibid., P7/B/43; O'Duffy report, 11 Aug. 1922, ibid.; Military Secretary (for O'Duffy) to C-inC, 19 Aug. 1922, ibid., P7/B/21; *Irish Times*, 15, 18 Aug. 1922.

45. Seán Fitzpatrick, O'MN, P17B/127; Micky Fitzpatrick, ibid., P17B/126; Robinson, ibid., P17B/49; Séamus Malone, ibid., P17B/103; C/S (Lynch) to O/C 1st S. Div., 10 July 1922, O'MP, P17a/15.

46. Colmaille, loc. cit.; review of situation in Kilkenny, Mid-Tipp., S. Tipp. and Waterford, MP, P7/B/106; report from Republican IRA GHQ, 6 July 1922, FitzGerald Papers; PG army report, 12 July 1922, MP, P7/B/106; *Cork Examiner*, 10, 14 July 1922; Lynch note from Limerick, O'MP, P17a/15; Seán Moylan to Robinson, 13 July 1922, ibid.; A/G to AAC/S. 13 July 1922, ibid., P17a/60; A/G to AC/S, 18 July 1922, ibid.; Jimmy Leahy, O'MN, P17B/100; Micky Fitzpatrick, ibid., P17B/114;

Mulcahy to Signals Officer, Kilkenny, MP, P7/B/106; report by Comdt William McCarthy, ibid., P7/B/107; 2nd S. Div. report, 20 July 1922, ibid., P7/B/107; for S. Tipp. Bde and the defence of Waterford see p. 155 above.

47. Seán Forde, O'MN, P17B/103; Micky Fitzpatrick, ibid., P17B/114; Colmaille, loc. cit.; Prout report, 4 Aug. 1922, MP, P7/B/18; *Irish Times*, 7 Aug. 1922; *Nationalist* (Clonmel), 12 Aug. 1922; O'Halloran, O'MN, P17B/114.

48. O'Duffy memo, 23 July 1922, MP, P7/B/21; Colmaille, loc. cit.; Comdt O'Connor report on Tipperary operations, n.d, probably late July/early Aug. 1922, MP, P7/B/68; C of GS to Capt O'Connor, 25 July 1922, ibid., P7/B/69; Collins to Ryan, 25 July 1922, ibid.; Republican A/G to AAC/S, 29 July, 2 Aug. 1922, O'MP, P17a/60; Younger, 395-6; 2nd S. Div. report, FitzGerald Papers; *Irish Independent*, 1, 2, 4 Aug. 1922.

49. A/G to AAC/S, 7 Aug. 1922, O'MP, P17a/60; PG army report by Adjt Kilkenny barracks, 3 Aug. 1922, and Post Office report on Carrick-on-Suir, 4 Aug. 1922, MP, P7/B/107; Colmaille, loc. cit.; Adjt O'Brien, Carrick, 4 Aug. 1922, MP, P7/B/107; 2nd S. Div. report, FitzGerald Papers; Prout to GHQ 4 Aug. 1922, MP, P7/B/118; wireless message, Prout to GHQ 10 Aug. 1922, ibid., P7/B/107; Séamus Forde, O'MN, P17B/103; Micky Fitzpatrick, ibid., P17B/114; *Nationalist* (Clonmel), 12 Aug. 1922; Lynch to AC/S, 9 Aug. 1922, MP, P7a/81; Deasy (1982), 69-70.

50. Andrews to O'Malley, n.d., probably early Aug. 1922, O'MP, P17a/60; Johnny McNoy, O'MN, P17B/94; Aiken to Mulcahy, 6 July 1922, O'MP, P17a/175; Aiken, O'MN, P17B/93; Aiken memo on 4th N. Div. from Jan. to July 1922, ibid.

51. Aiken, O'MN, P17B/93; McNoy, ibid., P17B/94, 116; Aiken memo, CP, 7847.

52. Aiken, O'MN, P17B/93; McNoy, ibid., P17B/94, 116; Aiken to Mulcahy, 15 July 1922, MP, P7/B/192; scribbled notes by Mulcahy, ibid.; Aiken to M/D from Dundalk jail, 23 July 1922, with annotation by Mulcahy, ibid., P7a/175.

53. Aiken to Mulcahy, 27 Aug. 1922, O'MP, P7a/178; *Irish Independent*, 27 July 1922; Andrews from HQ 4th N. Div., n.d., Aug. 1922, O'MP, P17a/60; Andrews, P17B/88; Andrews (1979), 239-45.

54. PG army D/I, 'Report on Situation', 14 Aug. 1922, MP, P7/B/59; Maj.-Gen. Hogan to GC of S, 17 Aug. 1922, ibid., P7/B/60; McNoy, O'MN, P17B/116; *Irish Independent*, 15, 16, 18 Aug. 1922; reports by Hogan, 18-20 Aug. 1922, MP, P7/B/59; Hogan to Capt. O'Hegarty, 23 Aug. 1922, ibid., P7/B/60.

55. O'Malley to C/S, 3 Sept. 1922, MP, P7a/81; see also C/S to O'Malley, 27 Aug. 1922, ibid.; C/S to O'Malley, 12 Sept. 1922, ibid.; O'Malley to C/S, 17 Sept. 1922, ibid.

Chapter 19:

The Opening of the Guerrilla Phase of the War (pp. 172-175)

1. C-in-C to Acting Chairman PG, 5 Aug. 1922, MP, P7/B/29; *Irish Times*, 15 Aug. 1922; C/S (Mulcahy) to Prout, 1 July 1922, MP, P7/B/63; O'Duffy, 22 Aug. 1922, ibid., P7/B/71; Moloney, ibid., P7/B/93; Deasy to O/C Cork 4, 12 Aug. 1922, ibid., P7/B/71; O/C 1st S. Div. (Deasy) to all O/Cs, 12 Aug. 1922, O'MP, P17a/87.

2. *Irish Times*, 20 Sept. 1922; Dalton to C-in-C, 11 Sept. 1922, Army Archives; Deasy to Brigade O/Cs, 13 Sept. 1922, O'MP, P17a/88; Divisional Adjt to Brigade O/Cs 1st S. Div., 4 Dec. 1922, Army Archives, A/0991/11; Adjt 1st S. Div. to C/S, n.d., probably early Jan. 1923, O'MP, P17a/22; Deasy, O'MN, P17B/86; O'Malley (1978), 148; Barry, MP, P7/B/140; Robinson, CP, 7851.

Chapter 20:

The Death of Collins (pp. 176-179)

1. Copy of notes from Collins's notebooks, 8-23 Aug. 1922, MP, P7a/62; Forester (1971), 333-4; Paddy O'Connor, O'MN, P17B/100; Sweeney in *Survivors*, 292; Taylor (1958), 240; Thornton, O'MN, P17B/31; Connie Neenan in *Survivors*, 246; Robinson memo, NLI, MS 18470; Malone, O'MN, P17B/29, and in *Survivors*, 98; O'Donoghue and Cathal O'Shannon, O'MN, P17B/95, 109; Deasy, ibid., P17B/86; Longford and O'Neill (1970), 199.

2. Collins notes, MP, P7/B/28; O'Connor, O'MN, P17B/100.

3. PG army report, 23 Aug. 1922, MP, P7/B/71; Deasy, O'MN, P17B/34; Crofts and Mick Leahy ibid., P17B/108; Dalton's account, Taylor (1958) and Feehan (1981).
4. Feehan (1981); Neeson (1968); Gen. M. J. Costello, *Irish Times*, 3 Sept. 1981; John Dowling, ibid., 22 Oct. 1981; Cormac Mac Carthaigh, *Irish Independent*, 24 Aug. 1963; correspondence between Máire Comerford and Prof. John A. Murphy, UCD, Comerford Papers; Prof. Liam Ó Briain's talk, MP, P7/D/66; Cormac Mac Carthaigh, *Agus*, Apr. 1968; *Cork Examiner*, 5 Nov. 1985; P. J. McHugh, O'MN, P17B/110; Jamie Managhan, ibid., P17B/112.
5. For British reaction see below; O'Donnell in *Survivors*, 28; Lynch to Deasy, 27 Aug. 1922, MP, P7a/81; Mick Leahy, O'MN, P17B/108.
6. For negotiations with O'Brien see p. 193 below; Lynch to O/C 1st S. DIv., Army Archives A/0991/13; Mulcahy's speech at funeral, MP, P7a/64; Mulcahy to Dalton, 23 Aug. 1922, CO 739/6; Gen. Seán MacMahon at Army Enquiry, 1924, MP, P7/C/14; reports in British Army Infantry Bde, Intelligence Summary for Aug. and Sept. 1922, MP, P7/B/86; Collins (1922); Hoare report to cabinet, 21 Sept. 1922, CO 739/15; Curtis to Churchill, 17 Sept. 1922, CO 739/14; unsigned letter, probably Curtis, to Churchill, 25 Aug. 1922, CO 739/6.

Chapter 21:
The Establishment of the Third Dáil (pp. 180-182)
1. PG Minutes, 25 Aug. 1922, SPO, G1/3; *DD*, 17 (9 Sept. 1922); White (1948), 108; Cosgrave to Craig, quoted in Curran (1980), 251; Belton to Midleton, 3 Oct. 1922, PRO, Midleton Papers, 30/67/51; O'Malley (1978), 176-7.
2. *DD*, 8-13 (9 Sept. 1922); ibid., 354 (18 Sept 1922); O'Higgins, ibid., 469-578 (19 Sept. 1922); Cope to Curtis, 5 Sept. 1922, CO 906/22.
3. *DD*, 806-82 (27 Sept. 1922); Mac Néill memo of government meeting, 17 Feb. 1923, MP, P7/C/42; PG decision, 4 Oct. 1922, SPO, S1785; PG Minutes, 3-4 Oct. 1922, SPO, G1/3; Blythe, *DD*, 837 (27 Sept. 1922); Mulcahy notes, MP, P7/D/80; Mulcahy note, 23 Sept. 1966, ibid., P7/D/88; Johnson and O'Shannon, *DD*, 812-17, 825-30 (27 Sept. 1922); Cosgrave, ibid., 874-80; MacMahon at Army Enquiry, 1924, MP, P7/C/14; for Cork see p. 202 below; Mulcahy, *DD*, 176-86 (12 Sept. 1922); O'Connor O'MN, P17B/101.
4. Brown (1981), 77, 8; Fanning (1983b), 18-19; for the pastoral see Irish newspapers, 11 Oct. 1922; de Valera to Mannix, 6 Nov. 1922, quoted in Longford and O'Neill (1970), 204.

Chapter 22:
Peace Initiatives (pp. 183-185)
1 Report to British government, 19 July 1922, CO 739/13; PG Minutes, 24 July 1922, SPO, G1/2; memo, 19 Aug. 1922, MP, P7/B/20; O'Brien (1969); NLI, William O'Brien Papers, 13972.
2. Mulcahy conversation with Vinny Byrne, 7 Jan. 1964, MP, P7/D/3; Mulcahy, *DD*, 1213 (30 Jan. 1923); de Valera Diary, 6 Sept. 1922, Longford and O'Neill (1970), 199; de Valera to McGarrity, 10 Sept. 1922, NLI, McGarrity Papers, 17440; conversation between Mulcahy and his son Risteárd, 19 Aug. 1963, MP, P7/D/69; PG Minutes, 5 Sept. 1922, SPO, G1/3.
3. Murray, O'MP, P17a/88; Deasy, O'MN, P17B/86; Lynch to Deasy, 6 Sept, 1922, MP, P7/B/90; Lynch to Deasy, 17 Sept. 1922, O'MP, P17a/18; IRA Executive meeting, 16-17 Oct. 1922, O'MP, P17a/12; document from IRA HQ Cork Bde, 30 Aug. 1922, with personal testimony of meetings, MP, P7/B/90; O/C 1st S. Div. (Deasy) to C/S, 5 Sept. 1922, O'MP, P17a/88; Lynch to Adjt 1st S. Div., 11 Oct. 1922, ibid., P17a/19; for 'Neutral IRA' see O'Donoghue (1954).

Chapter 23:
The Formation of the Republican Government (pp. 186-188)
1. O'Malley to Lynch, 21 July, 3, 24 Sept. 1922, MP, P7a/81; message from Oscar

Traynor, Barney Mellows, Eamon Corbett, Liam Pilkington, 9 Sept. 1922, ibid., P7a/162; two letters from Liam Mellows, 11 Sept. 1922 and n.d., ibid., P7/B/86; Lynch to O'Malley, 18 Sept. 1922, ibid., P7a/81; Lynch to O/C 1st S. Div., 17 Sept. 1922, O'MP, P17a/18; de Valera to Murphy, 7 Sept., 12 Sept. (two letters), 13 Sept. 1922, MP, P7/B/86.

2. IRA Executive meeting, 16-17 Oct. 1922, MP, P7a/81; de Valera to AAC/S, 25 Oct. 1922, and reply, 26 Oct. 1922, ibid.; Macardle (1937), 737; army proclamation, 26 Oct. 1922, MP, 7a/81; de Valera address to Republican TDs, 7 Aug. 1924, UCD, MacSwiney Papers, P48a/290 (56); Stack, 8 Aug. 1924, ibid., P48a/290(5); President (de Valera) to Art O'Brien, 3 Nov., 11 Dec. 1922, NLI, Art O'Brien Papers, 8424; de Valera to McGarrity, 19 Oct. 1922, NLI, McGarrity Papers, 17440; de Valera to MacSwiney, 14 Nov. 1922, TCD, MacSwiney Papers, 7835; MacSwiney at meeting of Republican government, 20 Dec. 1923, UCD, MacSwiney Papers, P48a/290/27.

Chapter 24:
The First Executions (pp. 189-192)

1. Notice on 7 Nov. 1922, signed by C-in-C, MP, P7/B/85; Kathleen O'Connor Diary, 17 Nov. 1922, quoted in Longford and O'Neill (1970), 205; O'Higgins, *DD*, 2267 (17 Nov. 1922).
2. Mrs. Childers, CP, 7851; Robinson memo on the war, ibid.; Childers protest, 19 Nov. 1922, ibid., 7829. Maj.-Gen. O'Sullivan to Mrs Childers, 24 Nov. 1922, ibid.; Childers notes, 20 Nov. 1922, ibid., 7855; Childers to Mrs Childers, 20 Nov. 1922, ibid.; Mrs Childers to Childers; 25 Aug. 1922, ibid., 7860; de Valera to Mrs Childers, Dec. 1922, ibid., 7848; de Valera to McGarrity, 28 Nov. 1922, NLI, McGarrity Papers, 17440.
3. Liam Lynch for Army Council to Ceann Comhairle, O'MP, P17a/19; Lynch to all Battalion O/Cs, 30 Nov. 1922, MP, P7a/83; Lynch memo, 4 Dec. 1922, ibid., P7a/85; Mulcahy in conversation with Senator Michael Hayes, ibid., P7/D/78.
4. Henderson, O'MN, P17B/99; de Valera to P. J. Ruttledge, 15 Dec. 1922, quoted in Longford and O'Neill, 208; for the killings see the national newspapers of the following day; message in Mulcahy's handwriting, MP, P7/B/85; Mulcahy conversation with Hayes, loc. cit.; White (1948), 131-3; Greaves (1971), 388; *Times*, 9 Dec. 1922; Johnson and O'Shannon, *DD*, 49-54 (8 Dec. 1922); O'Higgins, ibid., 73.
5. For Lynch's late orders see pp. 193-4, 235 below; Whelan and Smith, O'MN, P17B/103; Sheehy, ibid., P17B/104; O'Connor, ibid., P17B/101; Deasy to all Battalion O/Cs, O'MP, P17a/99.

Chapter 25:
The British Government and the Early Civil War (pp. 193-194)

1. Macready to Churchill, 20 Sept. 1922, CO 739/2; Curtis to FitzAlan, 9 Jan. 1923, CO 739/9; Curtis to Churchill, 25 Aug. 1922, CO 739/6; Infantry Bde Intelligence Summary, Aug-Sept. 1922, MP, 7/B/86; meeting between Bonar Law and Irish ministers, 24 Oct. 1922, CO 739/7; Amery memo, 24 Oct. 1922, quoted in Canning (1985), 69.
2. Cope to Masterton-Smith, 13 Oct. 1922, CO 739/2; Macready (1924), ii, 660; Churchill to Cope, 10 Oct. 1922, CO 906/22; Macready report on position of British troops in Southern Ireland, 4 Nov. 1922, CO 739/10; memo by Secretary of State for War, n.d., probably early Dec. 1922, CAB 24/140; Cope to Churchill, 16 Sept. 1922, CO 739/2; Curtis to Loughnane, 11 Dec. 1922, ibid.

Chapter 26:
The Southern Unionists and the Civil War (pp. 195-197)

1. Fitzpatrick (1977), 78; *A Record of Some Mansions and Houses Destroyed, 1922-23...*, PRO, Midleton papers, 30/67/52; Moloney to all O/Cs, 19 Aug. 1922, MP, P7/B/93; note to Adjt 1st S. Div., 21 Sept. 1922, Army Archives, A/0991/7; O'Connor (1964), 215; O'Sullivan (1940), 101-8; R. E. Kennedy, *The Irish - Emigration, Marriage and Fertility* (1975), 136, 215, quoted in Fanning (1983b), 40.

2. Sturgis to Churchill, 20 Apr. 1922, CO 739/16; O'Callaghan-Westropp to Lord Mayo, 28 Jan. 1920, quoted in Fitzpatrick (1977), 80; Sturgis to Cope, 19 July 1922, CO 906/21; Midleton to Prime Minister, 23 Aug. 1923, Midleton Papers, 37/60/53; Midleton letter, 28 July 1922, ibid., 30/67/51; 18th Infantry Bde, Intelligence Summary, 20 Aug. 1921, MP, P7/A/23.
3. Midleton to Jameson, 17 Nov. 1922, Midleton Papers, 30/67/52; Midleton letter, 24 Nov. 1922, ibid.; memo enclosed in Midleton letter, 28 July 1922, ibid., 30/67/51; Brown (1981), 77-8; Belton to Midleton, 1 Sept. 1922, Midleton Papers, 30/67/51; Bernard to Midleton, 20 Oct. 1922, ibid., 30/67/53; Gogarty to M/D, 4 July 1922, MP, P7/B/106.

Chapter 27:
The Civil War and the Railways (pp. 198-200)

1. Townshend (1979a); Pádraig Yeates, 'The Unsung War of the Iron Road', Sunday Press, 1 May 1983; notes for speech, possibly of Mulcahy's, MP, P7/B/179.
2. AC/S (O'Malley) to C/S, 3 Sept. 1922 (two letters), and Lynch to O'Malley, 12 Sept. 1922, O'MP, P17a/81; staff meetings, 28, 31 July 1922, ibid., P17a/15; Lynch to O'Malley, 4 Sept. 1922, MP, P7a/81; PG Minutes, 18 July 1922, SPO, G1/2; memo from Ministry of Economic Affairs, 18 July 1922, MP, P7/B/24; PG Minutes, 7, 22 July 1922, G1/2; Adjt N.E. Command to Secretary of Irish Engineering Union, SPO, S1573.
3. Lynch from Clonmel, 10 July 1922, MP, P7a/80; Lynch to O'Malley, 28 Sept. 1922, ibid., P7a/81; newspaper cutting, 25 July 1922, ibid., P7/B/59; C-in-C to PG, 26 July 1922, ibid., P7/B/30; letter from Maurice Healy enclosed in President to C-in-C, 29 Oct. 1922, ibid., P7/B/83; Col. Charles Russell, 3 Nov. 1922, ibid., P7/B/110; IFS army report, 2 Jan. 1923, ibid., P7/B/124; intelligence report, 29 Aug. 1922, ibid., P7/B/113.
4. D/E to 'Liam F', Engineering Inspector, 3rd S. Div., 29 Dec. 1922, Army Archives, A/0990/10-12, lot 2; PG army intelligence report, 29 Aug. 1922, MP, P7/B/113; Manchester Guardian, 8 Jan. 1923; IFS army report, 21 Jan. 1923, MP, P7/B/123; for destruction of Sligo station see above; IFS army report, 23 Jan. 1923, MP, P7/B/124.
5. Russell to C of GS, 25 Oct., 3 Nov. 1922, MP, P7/B/110; Mulcahy, DD, 2437 (29 Nov. 1922); PG Minutes, 1 Oct. 1922, G1/3; Tuam Herald, 21 Apr. 1923; Cosgrave, DD, 80 (13 Apr. 1923); An tÓglach, 21 Apr. 1923.
6. Davin, DD, 1607 (7 June 1923); Russell at Army Enquiry, 1924, MP, P7/C/28, 29; Ó Muirthile to C-in-C, 23 Jan. 1923, ibid., P7/B/67; for problems in Co. Wexford see p. 246 below; Defence Council minutes, 23 Apr. 1923, MP, P7/B/321; IFS army report, 26 May 1922, ibid., P7/B/139.

Chapter 28:
The War in the Localities: September 1922–January 1923 (pp. 201-220)

1. Crofts, O'MN, P17B/108; Dalton to C-in-C, 11 Sept. 1922, Army Archives; Dalton to C-in-C, 12 Aug. 1922, MP, P7/B/20; Dalton to C of GS, 2, 5 Sept. 1922, ibid., P7/B/71; Dalton to C-in-C, 18 Nov. 1922, ibid., P7/B/67; O'Duffy to C of GS, n.d., probably early Sept. 1922, ibid., P7/B/71.
2. Dalton to C-in-C and other GHQ members, MP, P7/B/67; P. J. Carney for Gen. Galvin, 29 Aug. 1922, ibid., P7/B/113; Doyle, O'MN, P17B/33; Deasy to O/C Cork 3, 3 Jan. 1923, O'MP, P17a/85; Mulcahy notes for Army Enquiry, 1924, MP, P7/C/42.
3. Mulcahy memo for Army Enquiry, MP, P7/B/195; O'Brien and Crofts, O'MN, P17/B/108; Adjt Cork 1 to Adjt 1st S. Div., 5 Sept. 1922, Army Archives, A/0991/5; Adjt 1st S. Div., 21 Sept. 1922, ibid., A/0991/7; Pa Murray to Div. Adjt, 30 Sept. 1922, ibid.; O/C Cork 1 to Adjt 1st S. Div., 8 Nov. 1922, ibid., A/0991/10.
4. Adjt 1st S. Div. to A/G, 13 Nov. 1922, O'MP, P17a/89; O/C Cork 5 to O/C 1st S. Div., 22 Sept. 1922, ibid., P17a/98, and Army Archives, A/0991/7; Adjt 1st S. Div. to C/S, 21 Oct. 1922, ibid., A/0991/9; Hales, 6 Sept. 1922, ibid., A/0991/5; O'Sullivan, O'MN, P17B/112; Crofts, ibid., P17B/108, 112.

5. MacSwiney letter, Army Archives, A/0991/8; Murray, 22 Sept. 1922, ibid., A/0991/7; Deasy note, 5 Sept. 1922, and C/S (Lynch) to O/C 1st S. Div., n.d., early Sept. 1922. ibid., A/0991/5; Jamie Managhan, O'MN, P17B/112; Tadhg O'Sullivan, ibid.. P17B/108; Divisional Adjt to C/S, 12 Sept. 1922, O'MP, P17a/88; Dalton to C/S, 2 Sept. 1922, MP, P7/B/71; Adjut Cork 1 to Adjt 1st S. Div., 4 Sept. 1922, ibid., P7/B/93; Mick Sullivan and Pat Corkery, O'MN, P17B/111; O'Connor (1958), 185-6; O'Faolain (1965), 157-8.

6. Div. Adjt to C/S, O'MP, P17a/22; O/C Cork 1 to O/C 1st S. Div., 22 Nov. 1922, ibid.. P17a/93; Tom Crofts, Charlie Brown, Seán Murray, P17B/112; Irish Independent, 4, 5 Oct. 1922; A/G's operation orders for early Sept. 1922, MP, P7/B/113; Tadhg O'Sullivan and Pat Corkery, O'MN, loc. cit.; Patsy Walsh, ibid., P17B/112.

7. Dalton to C-in-C, 18 Nov. 1922, MP, P7/B/67; Mulcahy (?) notes, 1 Feb. 1922, in general notes on Army Enquiry, ibid., P7/C/42; Col. Charles Russell at Army Enquiry, ibid., P7/C/20, 29; David Neligan, ibid.; O'Sullivan, ibid., P7/C/327; MacMahon, ibid., P7/C/35; C-in-C to Comdt Murphy, 14 Dec. 1922, ibid., P7/B/67; Mulcahy memo on reorganisation of Cork Command, ibid.; Ó Muirthile at Army Enquiry, ibid., P7/C/13; Ó Muirthile report, 23 Jan. 1923, ibid., P7/B/67.

8. Liam Lynch, O'MP, P17a/17; O'Duffy to C-in-C, 8 Sept. 1922, MP, P7/B/113; Divisional Adjt to O/C Kerry 1, 21 Aug. 1922, ibid.; S.W. Command Order No. 10, ibid.; Lynch memo, 18 Sept. 1922, Army Archives, A/0991/6; J. J. Rice, O'MN, P17B/102; Murphy weekly report to C-in-C, 18 Sept. 1922, MP, P7/B/113; Irish times, 27 Sept., 11 Oct. 1922.

9. Note from HQ 1st S. Div., 5 Sept. 1922, O'MP, P17a/88; J. J. Rice, O'MN, P17B/38, 102; Irish Times, 27 Sept., 4, 11 Oct. 14 Nov. 1922; O'Duffy to C-in-C, 29 Aug. 1922, MP, P7/B/113.

10. Charlie Daly, O'MN, P17B/132; note from HQ 1st S. Div., 5 Sept. 1922, O'MP, P17a/88; unsigned document, n.d., mid to late Nov. 1922, MP, P7/B/93; Irish Times, 27 Sept., 17 Oct. 1922.

11. Mulcahy conversation with Senator Michael Hayes, MP, P7/D/78; O/C Kerry 1 to I/O 1st S. Div., 12 Aug. 1922, O'MP, P17a/93; copy of report on killings, 16 Sept. 1922, MP, P7a/81; PG army report, 17 Oct. 1922, ibid., P7/B/120; Mullins (1983); Kingsmill Moore, Irish Times, 27 Sept. 1922; Rice, O'MN, P17B/102.

12. Note from HQ Kerry 1, n.d., O'MP, P17a/99; report from H. C. Somerville (British Naval Intelligence, Haulbowline), 8 Sept. 1922, CO 739/3; Adjt Kerry 2 to O/C 1st S. Div., 20 Sept. 1922, O'MP, P17a/99; Murphy, 16 Sept. 1922, Army Archives, A/0991/7; Murphy to O/C 1st S. Div., n.d., end of July or (more probably) early Aug. 1922, O'MP, P17a/99.

13. Barry, O'MN, P17B/111; Robinson report, 13 Sept. 1922, MP, P7/B/90; Robinson memoir, CP, 7851; O/C Operations to O/C 1st S. Div., 1 Sept. 1922, O'MP, P17a/88; shorter reports from the same source, MP, P7/B/93; O/C Kerry 2 to 1st S. Div., n.d., probably Sept. 1922, O'MP, P17a/99; J. J. Rice to Adjt 1st S. Div., n.d., probably Sept. 1922, MP, P7/B/93; Seán Hyde to GOC, 9 Sept. 1922, Army Archives, A/0991/5; Somerville report, 19 Sept. 1922, CO 739/3; Lynch to O/C 1st S. Div., 17 Sept. 1922, MP, P7/B/93.

14. Rice to O/C 1st S. Div., O'MP, P17a/99; Rice, O'MN, P17B/38; C-in-C message, 11 Sept. 1922, MP, P7/B/66; wireless message, 11 Sept. 1922, and Comdt Griffin, O/C Waterville, 9 Sept. 1922, ibid.; Kerry 1 report, 16 Sept. 1922, Army Archives. A/0991/6.

15. Robinson to Adjt 1st. S. Div., 29 Sept. 1922, O'MP, P17a/99; Robinson memoir, CP, 7851; Robinson report, 10 Oct. 1922, FitzGerald Papers; Hyde to O/C 1st S. Div., 29 Sept. 1922, Army Archives, A/0991/5; Adjt Kerry 2 to Adjt 1st S. Div., 13 Oct. 1922, ibid., A/0991/8; SNO Queenstown to Admiralty, 2 Oct. 1922, CO 739/3; Irish Times, 11 Oct. 1922; report from Col. W. Maxwell-Scott to C-in-C, 3 Oct. 1922, CAB 24/139; AA/G to O/C 1st S. Div., 4 Jan. 1923, O'MP, P17a/22.

16. PG army report, 'General Appreciation of the Military Situation as on November 28th', MP, P7/B/120; weekly report on Kerry situation for week ending 24 Nov. 1922,

ibid.; PG army report, 21 Nov. 1922, ibid., P7/B/123; *Irish Times*, 21 Nov. 1922; Gen. Murphy to C-in-C, 7 Dec. 1922, MP, P7/B/72; C-in-C to Murphy, 14 Dec. 1922, ibid.: Murphy to C-in-C, 14 Dec. 1922, 2 Jan. 1923, ibid.; Price to C-in-C, 6 Dec. 1922, ibid., P7/B/120; PG army report, 'Appreciation of Situation', ibid., P7/B/124.

17. Fitzpatrick, O'MN, P17B/114; Lynch to O/C 1st S. Div., 17 Sept. 1922, O'MP, P17a/18; History of Tipperary No. 3 Bde by C. F. Colmaille, O'MN, P17B/127; Deasy to Adjt 1st S. Div., 30 Nov. 1922, O'MP, P17a/19.

18. Fitzpatrick, O'MN, P17B/114, 126; Colmaille, loc. cit.; Lynch to O/C 1st S. Div., 10 Oct. 1922, O'MP, P17a/19.

19. Mulcahy (?) to 2nd S. Div., n.d., probably mid-Dec. 1922, MP, P7/B/64; PG army report, 13 Oct. 1922, ibid., P7/B/177; letter to Cosgrave, 11 Jan. 1923, ibid., P7/B/64; C-in-C, 11 Dec. 1922, with report from Phelan, I/O Waterford Bde, ibid., P7/B/64; Colmaille, loc. cit.; wireless reports from Kilkenny, 12, 17 Dec. 1922, MP, P7/B/64; *Irish Independent*, 12, 14 Dec. 1922; Prout to D/I, 17 Dec. 1922, MP, P7/B/64; D/I to C-in-C, n.d., probably mid or late Dec. 1922, ibid.; Micky Fitzpatrick O'MN, P17B/114; note of President's interview with Denis Gorey, TD, on military position in Kilkenny, MP, P7/B/64; Prout to C-in-C, 16 Dec. 1922, ibid.

20. President's interview with Gorey, and letter from Carrick resident, 26 Dec. 1922, MP, P7/B/64; C-in-C to Prout, 27 Dec. 1922, enclosing letter to Price, ibid.; Price report, n.d., probably Jan. 1923, ibid.

21. O'Duffy to C of GS, n.d., probably early or mid-Sept. 1922, MP, P7/B/71; Comdt-Gen. S.W. Command to O/C Troops, Newcastle West, 15 Sept. 1922, ibid., P7/B/112; PG army report from Mid-Tipp., n.d., ibid. P7/B/113; intelligence reports from various areas, ibid.; Lynch to O/C 1st S. Div., 10 Oct. 1922, O'MP, P17a/19; Gaynor, O'MN, P17B/119; Hynes, ibid., P17B/129; Comdt-Gen to C-in-C, 20 Nov. 1922, MP, P7/B/137; Carroll, O'MN, P17B/130; Ryan and Daly, ibid., P17B/112.

22. O'Malley (AAC/S) to C/S, 24 Aug. 1922, MP, P7a/81; O'Malley to C/S, 28 July 1922, ibid.; for CID see p. 225 below; Smith, O'MN, P17B/100; O'Malley to Lynch, 6 Aug., 3 Sept. 1922, MP, P7a/81; Lynch to O'Malley, 5 Oct. 1922, ibid.; O'Malley (1978), 145-6, 155, 172; *Poblacht na h-Éireann War News*, 27 Sept. 1922; Macardle (1937), 731.

23. O'Malley to Lynch, 28 July 1922, MP, P7a/81; George Gilmore, O'MN, P17B/106; Maj.-Gen. J. F. Dalton to A/G, 19 July 1922, MP, P7/B/107; O'Malley (1978), 155-8; Lynch to O'Malley, 5 Oct. 1922, MP, P7a/81; Col. Brind, 19 Sept. 1922, CAB 24/139; O'Malley (1978), 173-4; *Irish Times*, 9, 24 Nov. 1922; John Cullinan, O'MN, P17B/106; details of Dublin 2 strength at meeting of Dublin 1, 29 Oct. 1923, O'MP, P17a/58; Dublin 2 reports, ibid., P17a/82; Séamus Fox, O'MN, P17B/106; Mulcahy, *DD*, 134 (12 Sept. 1922); Cosgrave to C-in-C, 19 Aug. 1922, MP, P7/B/29.

24. Lynch to O'Malley, 5 Oct. 1922, MP, P7a/81; O'Malley to C/S, 24 Aug. 1922, ibid.; O'Malley to Divisional Engineer, 1st E. Div., 20 Sept. 1922, Army Archives, A/0989/4; O'Malley to D/E, 2 Nov. 1922, O'MP, P17a/59; O'Malley to Lynch, 31 July, 6 Aug. 1922, MP, P7a/81.

25. *Irish Times*, 6 Nov. 1922; O'Malley (1978), 179-89; phone message, Capt. H. S. Murray to Col.-Comdt Conroy, 14 Sept. 1922, Army Archives, A37; O'Malley, O'MN, P17B/101.

26. C-in-C to C of GS, 30 Sept. 1922, enclosing letter from Prof. Joseph Whelehan, TD, MP, P7/B/74; IFS intelligence, 21 Dec. 1922, Army Archives, B37; PG army I/O, 30 Oct. 1922, ibid., A37; O/C W. Command to 'Confidence', Dublin, 5 Sept. 1922, MP, P7/B/73.

27. Athlone Command radio message, 16 Oct. 1922, Army Archives, B37; Kiely intelligence report, 1 Nov. 1922, MP, P7/B/114; report from Area I/O Westport, 13 Oct. 1922, Army Archives, A37; W. M. Sears, TD, to Mulcahy, n.d., probably mid-Nov. 1922, MP, P7/B/75; W.A.P. (initials of the local Mayo source), 30 Oct. 1922, MP, P7/B/86; Kilroy, O'MN, P17B/101; intelligence reports by I/O 2nd W. Div., 20, 23, 24, 27, 29, 30 Oct. 1922, Army Archives, A37; Tommy Heavey, O'MN, P17B/120; Kiely intelligence reports, 25, 30 Oct., 4 Nov. 1922, Army Archives, B37; divisional intelligence report, 13 Nov. 1922, MP, P7/B/75; Castlebar I/O report, 13 Nov. 1922,

ibid.; Westport I/O report, 31 Oct. 1922, Army Archives, A37; Castlerea I/O report, 18 Oct. 1922, ibid.; I/O reports, 13, 23, 25 Oct. 1922, ibid., B37; phone message from W. Command, 24 Oct. 1922, MP, P7/B/74; note from Col.-Comdt A. MacCabe, Divisional Adjt, Ballymote, to Command Adjt, Athlone, Army Archives, B37.

28. Lynch to O/C 1st S. Div., 17 Sept. 1922, O'MP, P17a/18; phone message from Col.-Comdt Conroy, Athlone, 15 Sept. 1922, MP, P7/B/48; Kilroy's captured account, enclosed in letter from C-in-C to C/S, n.d., probably early Oct. 1922, and Kilroy despatch to Vice-Brigadier No. 5 Bde, 4th W. Div., 14 Sept. 1922, ibid., P7/B/87; Divisional Comdt 4th W. Div. (Kilroy) to O/C No. 3 Bde, 28 Sept, 1922, ibid., P7/B/90; Kilroy, O'MN, P17B/101; Matt Kilcawley, ibid., P17B/137; Jack Leonard, I/O 4th W. Div., to D/I No. 2 Bde, 18 Sept. 1922, MP, P7/B/93; Conroy to D/I, 13 Sept. 1922, Army Archives, A37.

29. O/C 4th W. Div. to Kilroy, 21 Sept. 1922, MP, P7/B/90; copy of document captured by Athlone Command, M. Mangan to Comdt-Gen. McDonnell, 4th W. Div., 15 Sept. 1922, ibid.; Jack Leonard note, loc. cit.; Matt Kilcawley, O'MN, P17B/137; Frank Carty, ibid., P17B/128; Kilroy, ibid., P17B/101; Christy Macken and Jack Feehan, ibid., P17B/113; PG army I/O Westport, 30 Oct. 1922, Army Archives, A37; I/O Claremorris, 1 Nov. 1922, ibid.; Irish Times, 1, 7 Nov. 1922. For information on these developments I am indebted to Michael MacEvilly.

30. Carty, O'MN, P17B/128; PG army report, 6 Dec. 1922, MP, P7/B/120; Conroy intelligence report, 22 Aug. 1922, Army Archives, A37; PG army report on general operations, 4 Nov. 1922, ibid., B37; W. Command report, 7 Nov. 1922, MP, P7/B/114; Conroy, Athlone, 26 Aug. 1922, Army Archives, A37; Comdt-Adjt Boyle to Div. Adjt, 18 Sept. 1922, ibid.; C-in-C to Mac Eoin, 5 Sept. 1922, MP, P7/B/73; phone message from Mac Eoin, 4 Sept. 1922, ibid.; Conroy to D/I, 4 Sept. 1922, Army Archives, A37; report by Adjt 2nd Batt. S. Leitrim, 15 Sept. 1922, ibid.

31. Phone message from Mac Eoin, 4 Sept. 1922, MP, P7/B/73; Carty, O'MN, P17B/128; Scanlon, ibid., P17B/133; Irish Times, 20 Sept. 1922; report by I/O 3rd W. Div., n.d., Army Archives, A37; PG army report, 19 Sept. 1922, ibid.; Maureen Brennan, O'MN, P17B/133; cipher message, Col.-Comdt O'Doherty, Ballyshannon, to 'Confidence', Dublin, 20 Sept. 1922, MP, P7/B/48; wire, Conroy, Athlone, to C-in-C, 18 Sept. 1922, ibid., P7/B/73; wireless message, Conroy to Mac Eoin, 21 Sept. 1922, with despatch from Lawlor, ibid., P7/B/74; Brennan, Carty, Scanlon, O'MN, loc. cit.; Irish Times, 20 Sept. 1922; report by I/O 3rd W. Div., n.d., Army Archives, A37; Younger (1968), 470; Lieut., FGHQ 3rd W. Div. to AA/G, 10 Jan. 1923, O'MN, P17B/134.

32. IFS army report, 15 Dec. 1922, Army Archives, A37; 3rd W. Div. report, 18 Dec. 1922, ibid.; information supplied by Michael MacEvilly; Mulcahy to C-in-C, 19 Oct. 1922, MP, P7/B/74; W. M. Sears, TD, to Mulcahy, n.d., probably mid-Nov. 1922, ibid, P7/B/75; interview with Dr O'Donnell, MD, of Co. Sligo, ibid.; C-in-C to Mac Eoin, 22 Dec. 1922, ibid.; Kiely note, 1 Nov. 1922, ibid., P7/B/114.

33. Conroy, Athlone, to D/I, 25 Oct. 1922, Army Archives, A37; Lawlor to O/C Troops, W. Command, 6 Oct. 1922, ibid.; Mac Eoin to A/G, 6, 9 Oct. 1922, ibid.; Lawlor to his mother, 9 Oct. 1922, MP, P7/B/87.

34. Telegram, O/C W. Command to 'Confidence', Dublin, 5 Sept. 1922, MP, P7/B/73; Q/M's Office to C-in-C, 6 Sept. 1922, ibid.; Mac Eoin to C-in-C, 12 Sept. 1922, ibid., P7/B/74; Reports Officer 3rd W. Div. to Reports Officer W. Command, ibid., P7/B/114; Lawlor's orders, 4 Dec. 1922, Army Archives, B37; Mulcahy to Mac Eoin, 22 Nov. 1922, and Mac Eoin to C-in-C, 23 Nov. 1922, MP, P7/B/45; phone message, Conroy to C-in-C, 24 Nov. 1922, ibid., P7/B/75; PG army report, 28 Nov. 1922, ibid., P7/B/120; W. Command report, 27 Nov. 1922, Army Archives, B37.

35. Macken, O'MN, P17B/113; Staff Captain for C-in-C to D/I, Jan. 1923, MP, P7/B/75; Lawlor report for Dec. 1922, enclosed in Mac Eoin report to C-in-C, 28 Dec. 1922, ibid.; Eamon Price to C-in-C, 6 Dec. 1922, ibid., P7/B/120; report from Newport, 26 Nov. 1922 to O/C W. Command, 26 Nov. 1922, and Lawlor's order, 4 Dec. 1922, Army Archives, B37; Lawlor to Mac Eoin, 21 Nov. 1922, MP, P7/B/75.

36. W. M. Sears, TD, to Mulcahy, 23 Dec. 1922, MP, P7/B/75; PG army report, 6 Dec.

1922, ibid., P7/B/120; Mac Eoin to C-in-C, 19 Dec. 1922, ibid., P7/B/75.
37. C. Ó Gaora to O/C 4th W. Div.; J.J.C. (O/C No. 3 Bde), 5 Jan. 1923, NLI, Art O'Brien Papers, 8460.
38. Coogan n.d.; Walter Mitchell in *Survivors*, 389; AO/C 1st E. Div. to AAC/S, 5 Aug. 1922, Army Archives, A/0989/4; O'Malley to Lynch, 28 July 1922, MP, P7a/81; O/C 1st E. Div. to AAC/S, 5 Aug. 1922, Army Archives, A/0989/4; Price to O'Malley, 20 Sept. 1922, ibid.; Lynch to O'Malley, 27 Aug. 1922, MP, P7a/81; O'Malley to Lynch, 24 Aug. 1922, ibid.; Lynch to AC/S, 4 Sept. 1922, ibid.; O'Malley to Lynch, 22 Sept. 1922, ibid.; Adjt 1st E. Div. to AAC/S, 27 Oct. 1922, Army Archives, A/0989/4; AO/C 1st E. Div. to AAC/S, 5 Aug. 1922, ibid.; Price, 21 Sept. 1922, ibid.; AO/C 1st E. Div. to AAC/S, 6 Oct. 1922, ibid.; *Irish Times*, 2 Dec. 1922.

Chapter 29:
The Free State—Government and Army: January–April 1923 (pp. 221-227)
1. IFS army report, 21 Jan. 1923, MP, P7/B/124; Loughnane to Curtis, 17 Mar. 1923, CO 739/18.
2. Executive Council Minutes, 10-11 Jan. 1923, SPO, G2/1; O'Higgins memo, 11 Jan. 1923, MP, P7/C/21; Hogan memo, 11 Jan. 1923; ibid., P7/B/321; Hogan, *DD*, 1062 (24 Jan. 1923); Hogan and O'Higgins, ibid., 897-900, 904-10 (17 Jan. 1923); O'Higgins at Army Enquiry, 1924, MP, P7/C/21.
3. Secretary of Executive Council to M/D, 31 Jan. 1923, MP, P7/B/177; Army Council decisions, 12 Feb. 1923, ibid., P7/B/178; to President from undeclared source, 1 Feb. 1923, ibid., P7/B/101; C-in-C to Comdt-Gen. O'Hegarty, 13 Dec. 1922, ibid.; *Irish Times*, 31 Jan. 1923; O'Connor (1964), 211.
4. IFS army report, 9 May 1923, MP, P7/B/139; O'Higgins at Army Enquiry, ibid., P7/C/33; O'Connell, ibid., P7/C/15; 27; O'Higgins memo to cabinet, 27 Mar. 1923, ibid., P7/C/42.
5. Mulcahy conversation with Senator Michael Hayes, 22 Oct. 1964, MP, P7/B/78; Mulcahy on IRB, 20 May 1924, ibid., P7/C/36; material for preparation of Interim Report of Army Enquiry, 10 June 1924, ibid., P7/C/41; Kennedy quoted in Fanning (1983b), 46.
6. Costello at Army Enquiry, MP, P7/C/25; MacMahon, ibid., P7/C/33; Healy to Beaverbrook, Jan. 1923, NLI, MS 23272; Mulcahy to Brennan, 8 Feb. 1923, MP, P7/B/76.
7. C-in-C to C/S, 12 Dec. 1922, MP, P7/B/153; Army Council meeting, 27 Dec. 1922, ibid., P7/B/177; Seán MacMahon at Army Enquiry, ibid., P7/C/14; Charles Russell, ibid., P7/C/28, 33; Mulcahy, ibid., P7/C/37; report for week ending 30 Dec. 1922, ibid., P7/B/137; *Observer*, 25 Feb, 1923; *Manchester Guardian*, 14 Mar. 1923.
8. MacMahon at Army Enquiry, MP, P7/C/14, 33; O'Connell, ibid., P7/C/19; Costello, ibid., P7/C/25; David Neligan, ibid., P7/C/17; letter from James Hogan to Army Enquiry, 9 May 1924, ibid., P7/C/19; Russell, at Army Enquiry, ibid., P7/C/7; O'Connell, ibid., P7/C/9, 15, 26.
9. Report to Desmond FitzGerald and Maj.-Gen. McGrath, 13 Oct. 1923, FitzGerald Papers; O'Higgins, *DD*, 1294-7 (30 May 1923); O'Higgins at Executive Council meeting, 25 May 1923, SPO, G2/2.
10. Ó Broin (1976), 207-8; O'Higgins, MP, P7/C/23; O'Connell, ibid., P7/C/5; Ó Muirthile, ibid., P7/C/13; Mulcahy, ibid., P7/C/36, 38; Russell, ibid., P7/C/18, 28; general notes on developments in the army, ibid., P7/C/42.
11. O'Duffy to M/D, Jan. 1923, MP, P7/B/194; MacMahon at Army Enquiry, ibid., P7/C/35; Brennan to Mulcahy, 15 May 1923, ibid., P7/C/10.
12. IFS army report, 21 Jan. 1923, MP, P7/B/124; for army numbers see p. 265 below; O'Higgins at Army Enquiry, MP, P7/C/21; Mulcahy, ibid., P7/C/35; Executive Council Minutes, 22, 27, 30 Mar., 9, 17 Apr. 1923, SPO, G2/1; Cosgrave, *DD*, 72-83 (13 Apr. 1923); Executive Council Minutes, 29 Mar. 1923, MP, P7/C/42; McCartan, Cosgrave and Mulcahy, *DD*, 58-63 (12 Apr. 1923); *Times*, 7 Apr. 1923; *Morning Post*, 9 Apr. 1923; *Manchester Guardian*, 10, 11 Jan. 1923; Executive Council Minutes, 30 Mar., 17

Apr. 1923, G2/1; Mulcahy to Cosgrave, 28 Mar. 1923, and reply, 9 Apr. 1923, MP. P7/C/42; Council of Defence minutes, 3, 9, 23 Apr., 3, 10, 16, 24, 29 May 1923, ibid., P7/B/321; memo on proposed scheme for Special Infantry Corps, ibid., P7/B/141; Mulcahy at Army Enquiry, ibid., P7/C/35.

Chapter 30:
The Republicans and the Civil War: January–April 1923 (pp. 228-238)

1. Letter to Pa[Murray], 13 Feb. 1923, MP, P7/B/89; Thomas Johnson, *DD*, 791 (10 May 1923); for prisons see p. 268 below; Macardle (1937): 913-14; O'Malley (1978), 221; report of 1st S. Div. meeting, 26 Feb. 1923, MP, P7/B/89; Scully, O'MN, P17B/102; C/S to James O'Donovan, 2 Apr. 1923, MP, P7/B/90.

2. C/S (Lynch) to all ranks of IRA, 9 Feb. 1923, O'MP, P17a/23; Lynch to A/G (Moloney), 2 Feb. 1923, ibid.; Henderson, O'MN, P17B/36; Andrews (1979), 268-9, 271-2; O'Donoghue (1954); O'Donovan to Lynch, 27 Jan. 1923, and reply, 31 Jan. 1923, NLI, MS 22306.

3. De Valera to McGarrity, 5 Feb. 1923, NLI, McGarrity Papers, 17440; Deasy (1982); Deasy, O'MN, P17B/86; Deasy statement, O'MP, P17a/22; Deasy to all battalions and O/Cs, 30 Jan. 1922, ibid., P17a/99.

4. Moss Twomey, O'MN, P17B/197; Lynch to O/Cs Commands, 2 Feb. 1923, O'MP, P17a/23; Lynch to A/G (Moloney), 29 Feb. 1923, ibid.; Madge Clifford, O'MN, P17B/89; Moylan to ?, 23 Feb. 1923, CO 739/21; MacSwiney to Deasy, 5 Feb. 1923, SPO, S2210; Frank Barrett, 5 Feb. 1923, ibid.; Frank Carty to Deasy, 6 Feb. 1923, ibid.; report from D/I's Office, 16 Jan. 1924, MP, P7/B/140; O'Malley to C/S, 10 Feb. 1923, O'MP, P17a/40; Bill Quirke on Deasy's court martial, O'MN, P17B/86.

5. O'Malley to C/S, 10 Feb. 1923, O'MP, P17a/40; Deasy to all battalions and O/Cs, 30 Jan. 1922, ibid., P17a/99; Executive Council Minutes, 16 Feb. 1923, SPO, G2/1; McLoughlin to Deasy, 7 Feb. 1923, O'MP, P17a/46; 'Seán F' to O/C 2nd S. Div., from Limerick prison, 6 Feb. 1923, ibid.; Denis Lacey to O/C Clonmel, 12 Feb. 1923, MP, P7/B/89; 1st S. Div. meeting, 26 Feb. 1923, ibid.; D/I to C/S, 31 Mar. 1923, ibid., P7/B/90; Rice, O'MN, P17B/102; Cork prisoner to Pa [Murray], 13 Feb. 1923, MP. P7/B/89; letter from a prisoner in 'hospital wing', 21 Feb. 1923, SPO, S1859; Paddy O'Sullivan, O'MN, P17B/112.

6. Memo, President (de Valera) to A/G, 28 Feb. 1923, MP, P7/B/89; 1st S. Div. meeting, 26 Feb. 1923, ibid.; IRA Executive meeting, 23 Mar. 1923, ibid.; A/G note, ibid., P7/B/91; letter from Donal O'Hannigan of Neutral IRA Members' Association, and de Valera's reply, *Daily Bulletin*, 22 Feb. 1923, in O'MP, P17a/140; Bill Quirke, O'MN, P17B/86; O'Donoghue (1954), 288-9; *Times*, 9 Mar. 1923.

7. P. J. Ruttledge, O'MN, P17B/86; Andrews, ibid., P17B/88; Madge Clifford, ibid., P17B/89; Ruttledge, ibid., P17B/90, 97; Lynch to A/G, 12 Mar. 1923, O'MP, P17a/24; Lynch statement at 1st S. Div. meeting, 26 Feb. 1923, MP, P7/B/89; Andrews, 267-79; Kathleen Barry, O'MN, P17B/86; President (de Valera) to A/G, 22, 28 Feb., 2, 5 Mar. 1923, MP, P7/B/89.

8. *Daily Bulletin*, 22 Feb. 1923; de Valera to A/G, 22 Feb. 1923, MP, P7/B/89; Neutral IRA Members' Association to de Valera, 24 Feb. 1923, ibid.; A/G to President, 20 Feb. 1923, ibid.; 1st S. Div. meeting, 26 Feb. 1923, ibid.; President to A/G, 22 Feb. 1923, ibid.; Lynch to de Valera, 28 Feb. 1923, and reply, 7 Mar. 1923, Longford and O'Neill, (1970), 215-16.

9. Churchill to Cope, 24 Aug. 1922, Jones (1971), 215-16; de Valera to Edith M. Ellis, 26 Feb. 1923, MP, P7/B/89; de Valera to Fahy, 12 Dec. 1922, Longford and O'Neill, 212; de Valera, *Daily Bulletin*, 27 Feb. 1923, in O'MP, P17a/140; President to Ministers, 19 Feb. 1923, NLI, Art O'Brien Papers, 8460; de Valera to Lynch, 7 Mar. 1923, Longford and O'Neill, 216; de Valera to A/G, 2 Feb. 1923, MP, P7/B/89; de Valera to MacSwiney, 14 Nov. 1922, TCD, MacSwiney Papers, 7835.

10. De Valera to McGarrity, 5 Feb. 1923, McGarrity Papers, 17440; de Valera to Lynch, 12 Dec. 1922, Longford and O'Neill, 208.

11. 1st S. Div. meeting, 26 Feb. 1923, MP, P7/B/89; Lynch to Moloney, 8 Mar. 1923,

O'MP, P17a/24; Moloney notes, 7 Mar. 1923, ibid.; Staff Captain to A/G, 8 Feb. 1923, O'MP, P17a/85.

12. Lynch to A/B (Moloney), 12 Mar. 1923, O'MP, P17a/24; IRA Executive meeting, 23-24 Mar. 1923, MP, P7/B/89; 1st S. Div. meeting, 26 Feb. 1923, ibid.; A/G to C/S, 2 Apr. 1923, O'MP, P17a/25.

13. Lynch to Moylan, 6 Feb. 1923, McGarrity Papers, 17466; Lynch to McGarrity, 5 Feb. 1923, ibid., 17445, also CO 739/21; Lynch to Moylan, n.d., CO 739/21; McGarrity to Lynch, 15 Jan., 14 Feb. 1923, McGarrity Papers, 17445; McGarrity memo on amount of arms planned, ibid., 17466; McGarrity to Stack, 26 Feb. 1923, ibid., 17489; Aiken at Executive meeting, O'MN, P17B/40.

14. Kathleen Barry, O'MN, P17B/86; Andrews, ibid., P17B/88; IRA Executive meeting, 23-24 Mar. 1923, MP, P7/B/89; Quirke, O'MN, P17B/86; Rice, ibid., P17B/102; O'Donoghue (1954), 299-301.

15. For Prout's sweep see p. 244 below; Col. Charles Russell at Army Enquiry, MP, P7/C/20; Andrews, O'MN, P17B/88 and Andrews, 285-8; *Irish Times*, 16 Apr. 1923.

16. O'Donoghue (1954), 304-6; Younger (1968), 502-4; Lynch to all Battalion O/Cs, 4 Apr. 1923, O'MP, P17a/25; Florrie O'Donoghue, O'MN, P17B/95; George Power, ibid., P17B/100; *Irish Times*, 11 Apr. 1923; IFS army report for week ending 21 Apr. 1923, MP, P7/B/139.

17. Paddy Browne, O'MN, P17B/116; P. J. Ruttledge, ibid., P17B/97; Executive Council Minutes, 17 Apr. 1923, SPO, G2/1.

Chapter 31:
The War in the Localities: January–April 1923 (pp. 239-247)

1. O/C 1st S. Div. (Crofts) to DC/S, 2 Mar. 1923, O'MP, P17a/90; Lynch to Div. I/O and Div. Adjt, 11 Dec. 1922, UCD, MS P21/1; Lynch to Liam Deasy, 7 Nov. 1922, ibid.; O'Donoghue note, 2 Dec. 1922, ibid.; Deasy note, 29 Dec. 1922, ibid.; O'Donoghue to Deasy, 2 Dec. 1922, ibid., P21/5; O'Donoghue to Lynch, 1 Jan. 1923, ibid.; Lynch to Deasy, 4 Jan. 1923, ibid.; Hegarty to Deasy, n.d., P21/8; for Barry's post-war amnesty effort see p. 260 below; Lynch to Adjt 1st S. Div., 3 Jan. 1923, MP, P7/B/89; Report of Strengths and Posts, 1 Apr. 1923, ibid., P7/B/141; DC/S to C/S, 6 Mar. 1923, O'MP, P17a/85.

2. Barry at Executive meeting, 20 Apr. 1923, O'MP, P17a/12; Crofts to Moylan, 1 Feb. 1923, ibid., P17a/160.

3. Crofts, O'MN, P17B/108; evidence from sundry areas, 1st S. Div. meeting, 26 Feb. 1923, O'MP, P17a/90; DC/S to C/S, 6 Mar. 1923, ibid., P17a/85; Murphy, O'MN, P17B/112; O'Sullivan, ibid., P17B/108.

4. For W. R. E. Murphy's remarks see p. 208 above; radio report from O/C Kerry Command, 25 Jan. 1923, P7/B/72; IFS army report, 26 Jan. 1923, ibid., P7/B/124; message from J. J. Rice, 9 Feb. 1923, Army Archives, A/0991/1; Humphrey Murphy, MP, P7/B/89 and O'MP, P17A/90; wireless message, O/C Kerry Command to Department of Military Statistics, 28 Jan. 1923, MP, P7/B/72; Kerry Command report, 19 Apr. 1923, ibid., P7/B/130; Kerry report at 1st S. Div. meeting, 26 Feb. 1923, O'MP, P17a/90 and MP, 7/B/89, IFS army report, 28 Feb. 1923, MP, P7/B/130; IFS army report for week ending 7 Apr. 1923, ibid., P7/B/139; *Irish Times*, 9 Jan. 1923.

5. J. J. Rice, O'MN, P17B/101; Charlie Daly, ibid., P17B/132; Johnny Connors and Dan Flavin, ibid., P17B/102; Macardle (1924); Col. Jephson O'Connell at Army Enquiry, 1924, MP, P7/C/15; O'Malley on Rice's testimony, O'MP, P17B/101.

6. IFS casualty list, in file on casualties of Kerry Command, Army Archives; Kerry Command message, 6 Mar. 1923, MP, P7/B/130; Kerry 1 report, 16 Mar. 1923, ibid., P7/B/99; O'Malley, O'MN, P17B/160; Daly message, 6 Mar. 1923, NLI, MS 22956.

7. Copy of enquiry into Ballyseedy killings, and Gen. Price's report, 11 Apr. 1923, NLI, MS 22956; Kerry Command report, 7 Mar. 1923, MP, P7/B/130; Kerry 1 reports, 7, 16 Mar. 1923, ibid., P7/B/99; Bill Baily, O'MN, P17B/94; Oscar Traynor, ibid., P17B/95; J. J. Rice, ibid., P17B/102; Charlie Daly, ibid., P17B/132; O'Malley, ibid., P17B/160; Sheehy in *Survivors*, 359; May Dalaigh, ibid., 367; *DD*, 125-95 (17 Apr. 1923):

Anne MacSweeney, O'MN, P17B/112; Kerry Command report, 13 Mar. 1923, MP. P7/B/130.

8. O'Malley, O'MN, P17B/160; Kerry 1 reports, 12, 16 Mar. 1923, loc. cit.; Ballyseedy enquiry, loc. cit.; John Joe Rice, O'MN, P17B/102; secret report, for President 'only', from Gen. Daly, with report following enquiry into Cahirciveen incident, MP. P7/B/322; DD, 125-95 (17 Apr. 1923); McHugh, O'MN, P17B/110; confidential information on Harrington's report; McCarthy quoted in Macardle (1937), 766.

9. Daly report on Cahirciveen, loc. cit.; IFS army messages, 5, 6, 7 Mar. 1923, MP. P7/B/130; casualty list for Kerry Command, Army Archives; Manchester Guardian, 19 Apr. 1923; letter from Daly, 27 Mar. 1923, MP, P7/B/130; Kerry Command report, 26 Mar. 1923, ibid., P7/B/138; Kerry Command reports, 17, 19 Apr. 1923, ibid.. P7/B/130; Macardle (1924).

10. Executive Council Minutes, 1 May 1923, MP, P7/B/322; IFS army reports, 15, 28 Apr., 5, 9 May 1923, ibid., P7/B/139; report on executions in Kerry Command, 25 Apr. 1923, ibid., P7/B/126.

11. For Lynch's optimism concerning the west see p. 236 above; Claremorris Command report, 31 Mar. 1923, MP, P7/B/139; A/G to D/Communications, 30 Mar. 1923, O'MP, P17a/24; Defence Council meeting, 23 Apr. 1923, MP, P7/B/321.

12. Letter from unidentified source, Claremorris, 8 Mar. 1923, MP, P7/B/75; uncatalogued file, Army Archives, summary of AC/S report, 24 Mar. 1923, O'MP, P17a/24; Claremorris Command report, 31 Mar. 1923, MP, P7/B/139; IFS army report for week ending 28 Apr. 1923, ibid., P7/B/321.

13. A/G to C/S, 26 Feb. 1923, O'MP, P17a/23; Daily Telegraph, 16 Feb. 1923; Times, 12 Mar. 1923; P. Brennan, O/C No. 3 Bde, to O/C 3rd W. Div., 17 Feb. 1923, Army Archives, A/0990/10-12, lot 2; captured document of No. 1 Bde, 3rd W. Div., MP, P7/B/91; Capt. Henry Boyle to O/C Reports, 3rd W. Div., 12 Jan. 1923, Army Archives, B37; No. 1 Bde, 3rd W. Div. report, 12 Jan. 1923, ibid., A/09901/10-12, lot 2; Irish Times, 12 Jan. 1923; Mulcahy, DD, 1143-4 (31 Jan. 1923); Times, 13 Feb. 1923; DD, 1353-1415 (7, 8 Feb. 1923).

14. Note from Divisional Comdt 4th W. Div., 8 Mar. 1923, Army Archives, A/0990/10-12; Hyde to A/G, 10 Mar. 1923, ibid.; Athlong Command report for week ending 29 Mar. 1923, MP, P7/B/138; Macken to O/C 4th W. Div., 1 Apr. 1923, ibid., P7/B/90.

15. O'Connor, O'MN, P17B/100-1; Andy Kennedy, ibid., P17B/114; History of Tipperary No. 3 Bde by C. F. Colmaille, O'MN, P17B/127; Nationalist (Clonmel), 27 Jan. 1923; A/G to C/S, 12 Mar. 1923, O'MP, P17a/24; M.T. [Twomey] to C/S, 2 Apr. 1923, ibid., P17a/25.

16. Ryan at Army Enquiry, MP, P7/C/8; O'Connor, O'MN, loc. cit.; IFS army report, 31 Mar. 1923, MP, P7/B/139; note from HQ 3 Command to A/G, 8 Feb. 1923, Army Archives, A/0991/15, lot 3; Colmaille, loc. cit.; A/G to C/S, 12 Mar. 1923, O'MP, P17a/24; 'C/S Department' to C/S, 6 Mar. 1923, ibid., P17a/85; Nationalist (Clonmel), 21 Feb. 1923; for Moloney's arrest see p. 236 above.

17. IFS army report 31 Mar. 1923, MP, P7/B/139; Glendon, O'MN, P17B/103; Fitzpatrick, ibid., P17B/114; Nationalist (Clonmel), 21 Apr. 1923; Paddy O'Connor, O'MN, loc. cit.; Colmaille, loc. cit.; IFS army reports, 23, 29, 31 Mar. 1923, MP, P7/B/138-9.

18. IFS army report for week ending 28 Apr. 1923, MP, P7/B/139; Comdt M. T. Gantley, O/C 2nd Batt., to Col. Lawlor, 2 Mar. 1923, ibid.; IFS army report, 31 Mar. 1923, ibid.; IFS army report, 23 Mar. 1923, ibid., P7/B/138.

19. Tom Brennan and Dinny Allen, O'MN, P17B/98; Andrews (1979), 262-6. I had several interviews with Dr Thomas O'Reilly, who had been O'Sullivan's Intelligence Officer and main assistant. IFS army report for week ending 28 Apr. 1923, MP, P7/B/139; note from C-in-C, 9 Dec. 1922, ibid., P7/B/111; Ryan at Army Enquiry, ibid., P7/C/8; unnamed IFS army officer, ibid.; John B. Fahy, DJ, and Thomas S. O'Kelly, State Solicitor, Co. Wexford, to C-in-C, 19 Feb. 1923, ibid., P7/B/64; IFS army report, with 'Note on Wexford' to C-in-C, 12 Feb. 1923, ibid., P7/B/138.

20. Ryan at Army Enquiry, loc. cit.; Brennan and Allen, O'MN, loc. cit.; IFS army report, 28 Apr. 1923, loc. cit.; inspection reports on Prout's Waterford Command, statement of

Col. Jephson O'Connell, MP, P7/C/9.
21. A/G to C/S, 10 Mar. 1923, O'MP, P17a/24; Moss Twomey to C/S, 5 Apr. 1923, ibid.,
    P17a/25; C/S's Operation Order No. 15, 22 Jan. 1923, ibid., P17a/22; Lynch to
    Twomey, 31 Mar. 1923 (two letters), ibid., P17a/24; summary of operations of Dublin 1
    for week ending 24 Feb. 1923, MP, P7/B/92; A/G to C/S, 26 Feb. 1923, O'MP,
    P17a/23; IFS army report for end of Mar. 1923, MP, P7/B/139.
22. Twomey report, 22 Mar. 1923, O'MP, P17a/24; IFS army report for end of Mar. 1923.
    loc. cit.; Twomey to C/S, 5 Apr. 1923, O'MP, P17a/25; A/G note, 13 Mar. 1923, ibid.,
    P17a/24; Fox, O'MN, P17B/106; Doyle, ibid., P17B/95; message from Reports
    Officer, Dublin Command, 15 Apr. 1923, MP, P7/B/131.

Chapter 32:
The North and the Civil War (pp. 248-252)
  1. *Times*, 26 Feb. 1923; CAB 45/30; Spender to Sturgis, 2 Aug. 1922, CO 906/21; Woods,
     O'MN, P17B/107; Woods memo, 27 July 1923, MP, P7/B/77; IFS army memo, n.d.,
     FitzGerald Papers; Lt-Comdt Conway to Mary MacSwiney, 11 May 1923, UCD,
     MacSwiney Papers, P48a/117(2)/4; Seán Lehane to Secretary, Military Service
     Pensions Board, 7 Mar, 1935, O'MN, P17B/108.
  2. Mulcahy to Collins, 24 July 1922, MP, P7/B/78; Woods memo, 29 Sept. 1922, SPO,
     S1801; Woods note, 3 Aug. 1922, MP, P7/B/79; IFS army memo, n.d., loc. cit.;
     MacAnally, O'MN, P17B/99; McCorley, ibid., P17B/98; Lt-Comdt Conway to Mary
     MacSwiney, 11 May 1923, loc. cit.
  3. O'Malley (1978), 169, and 3 Sept. 1922, MP, P7a/81; O'Malley to Lynch, 28 July
     1922, ibid.; Lynch to O'Malley, 12 Sept. 1922, ibid.; Bowman (1982), 77; O'Shiel
     memo to ministers, n.d., probably end of Nov. 1923, UCD, Blythe Papers, P24/171.
  4. PG Minutes, SPO, G1/3; Blythe Papers, P24/70; Cosgrave, *DD*, 16-17 (6 Dec. 1922);
     Curtis to Churchill, 17 Sept. 1922, reporting letter from Cope, CO 739/14; Cosgrave to
     Lord Devonshire, 10 Jan. 1923, CO 739/17.
  5. Woods memo, 29 Sept. 1922, loc. cit.; PG to a Law Officer, 1 Nov. 1922, UCD,
     Kennedy Papers, P4/v/1; PG Minutes, 30 Jan., 17 Feb., 3 Mar. 1922, SPO, G1/1; PG
     Minutes, 18 Apr., 10 May, 9 June, 27 July, 1922, G1/2; PG Minutes, 6 Nov. 1922, G1/3;
     PG Minutes, 12, 19 Mar. 1923, G2/1; Fanning (1983b); 27; Cope to Churchill, 16 Sept.
     1922, CO 739/2; Hugh A. McCarthy report, sent by Kevin O'Shiel to Executive
     Council, 6 Nov. 1923, UCD, MS, P24/203; Hughes, *DD*, 1222-3 (20 July 1923); Baxter,
     ibid., 697 (19 Sept. 1922).
  6. O'Shiel report, sent on by Cosgrave to Mulcahy, 25 Jan. 1923, MP, P7/B/101; Waller
     to Curtis, 21 Dec. 1922, CO 739/16; Cosgrave to Baldwin, 9 June 1923, Jones (1971),
     221; McCarthy report, loc. cit.; Kevin O'Shiel to all members of Executive Council, 19
     Apr. 1922, Kennedy Papers, P4/v/2, P4/L1/6; Anderson to Tallents, 31 Oct. 1923, CO
     739/20.
  7. Spender to Curtis, 28 June 1922, CO 739/16; O'Shiel to all members of Executive
     Council, 19 Apr. 1923, SPO, S2198; Craig to Wilson, 10 May 1922, PRONI, CAB
     6/89; Craig memo, 23 June 1922, CO 906/27; Cosgrave to Churchill, 20 Aug. 1922, CO
     906/21; Churchill to Craig, 31 Aug. 1922, ibid.; Churchill to Cosgrave, 2 Sept. 1922,
     CO 906/22; Cope to Curtis, 5 Sept. 1922, ibid.; Curtis to Churchill, 2 Sept. 1922, House
     of Lords Record Dept, Lloyd George Papers, F/10/3-2 42; Masterton-Smith to Craig,
     15 Aug. 1922, CO 739/6; Tallents to Curtis, 3 Nov. 1922, CO 739/1; further correspon-
     dence cited in Buckland (1979), 206-9; review of Heuston case and correspondence on
     the case, 22-26 Dec. 1922, CO 739/1; Loughnane to Curtis, 17 Apr. 1923, CO 739/18.
  8. Loughnane to Curtis 5 Mar. 1924, CO 739/26; Spender note on meeting of 10 Nov.
     1922, CO 739/8; Curtis, 30 July 1923, CO 739/20; Irwin, 12 Aug. 1922, quoted at Sinn
     Féin Funds Case, PROI, 2B/82/117.

Chapter 33:
Exile Nationalism: The United States and Britain in the Civil War (pp 253-255)
  1. *Clare Champion*, 26 Aug. 1922; Murray to Horgan, 20 July 1922, MP, P7a/88; Ó Broin

(1976). 222; interview with Joseph Connolly, 29 Dec. 1942, Sinn Féin Funds Case, PROI, 2B/82/116; Seán Moylan, 23 Feb. 1923, CO 739/21; McGarrity to de Valera, 27 Sept. 1922, 25 Mar. 1923, NLI, McGarrity Papers, 17440; McGarrity to de Valera, 22 Dec. 1923, ibid., 17608; McGarrity to Lynch, 15 Jan., 14 Feb. 1923, ibid., 17445; de Valera to Miss Broy, 12 Jan. 1923, FitzGerald Papers.

2. Boland to McGarrity, 27 July 1922, McGarrity Papers, 17424; Stack to McGarrity, 10 Sept. 1922, ibid., 17489; letter from Hanna Sheehy-Skeffington, New York, 6 Jan. 1923, MP, P7/B/87; de Valera to O'Kelly, 5 Feb. 1923, CO 739/2; de Valera to Ginnell, ibid.; meeting of delegates, 12 Sept. 1922, FitzGerald Papers; captured letter from Moylan, New York, 23 Feb. 1923, CO 739/21; Moylan at Clan meeting, McGarrity Papers, 17608; Moylan report, 20 Mar. 1923, ibid., 17466; Moylan to O/C 1st S. Div., 28 Dec. 1922, FitzGerald Papers, captured letter from Moylan, 23 Feb. 1923, CO 739/21.

3. Moylan to O/C Britain, 23 Mar. 1923, UCD, Blythe Papers, 24/223; Moylan to McGarrity, 10 May 1923, 19 Jan. 1925, McGarrity Papers, 17466; unsigned memo on Clan organisation, n.d., 1924 or 1925, ibid., 17525.

4. Report on revolutionary activities, 16 Mar. 1922, CAB 24/134; O'Brien to Boland, 6 Apr. 1922, NLI, Art O'Brien Papers, 8425; O'Brien memo to Minister for Home Affairs, 30 Jan. 1923, ibid.; for London IRA see above; Liam Lynch to O/C 1st S. Div., 3, 10 Sept. 1922, O'MP, P17a/17; Pa [Murray] to C/S, 5 Oct. 1922, ibid., P17a/51; Murray, O'MN, P17B/88.

5. Sturgis to Donnelly, 13 Jan. 1923, CO 729/19; O/C Britain to C/S, 30 Mar. 1923, MP, P7/B/91; notes on history of ISDL, Art O'Brien Papers, 8425; reports on revolutionary organisations, 15, 22, 28 Mar., 12 Apr. 1923, CAB 24/159; report on revolutionary organisations, 19 Apr. 1923, CAB 24/160; O'Higgins, *DD*, 2352 (20 Mar. 1923); *Times*, 16 Mar. 1923; C/S to O/C Britain, 5 Apr. 1923, O'MP, P17a/25; Twomey to C/S, 5 Apr. 1923, ibid.; Murray to C/S, 30 Mar. 1923, MP, P7/B/92; Lynch to O/Cs Commands, 2 Feb. 1923, O'MP, P17a/23.

Chapter 34:
The Ceasefire (pp. 256-258)

1. IRA Executive meeting, 20 Apr. 1923, O'MP, P17a/12; Republican Government and Army Council meeting, 20-27 Apr. 1923, ibid.; Ruttledge, O'MN P17B/97; message to all Battalion O/Cs, 24 Apr. 1923, O'MP, P17a/25; Aiken message to all officers, 28 May 1923, ibid.; memo, 28 Apr. 1923, MP, P7/B/90; de Valera proclamation, 27 Apr. 1923, ibid.; Executive Council Minutes, SPO, G2/2.

2. Jameson report of meeting of 3 May 1923, and Douglas memo on other interviews with de Valera, SPO, S2210; White (1948), 153; meeting of 13-14 May, O'MP, P17a/12; Aiken order, 24 May 1923, MP, P7/B/90; de Valera proclamation, 24 May 1923, ibid.; de Valera to MacSwiney, 26 May 1923, Longford and O'Neill (1970), 221.

Chapter 35:
The Republicans (pp. 259-262)

1. Aiken to O'Malley, 27 June 1923, Army Archives, A/1120; for O'Malley's views see p. 145 above; Bell (1970); Coogan (1970).

2. IFS army reports for weeks ending 12, 19, 26 May, 2 June 1923, MP, P7/B/139; report on Republican prisoners, sent to all members of Executive Council, 21 June 1924, UCD, Blythe Papers, P24/233.

3. Mary MacSwiney to de Valera, 10 Feb. 1923, UCD, Comerford Papers; for Barry's peace efforts in June see SPO, S2210; Mulcahy at Army Enquiry, 1924, MP, P7/C/10; Republican Government and Army Council meeting, 30 June 1923, O'MP, P17a/12. IRA Executive Council meeting, 11 July 1923, O'MN, P17B/93; de Valera to Republican Minister for Home Affairs (Ruttledge), 1 June 1923, NLI, MS 18375(15); de Valera to all ministers and C/S, 30 May 1923, ibid; Republican meeting, 7 Aug. 1924, UCD, MacSwiney Papers, P48a/290(56).

4. IFS army report from Limerick Command, 16 Aug. 1923, N.P, P7/B/131; Longford

and O'Neill (1970), 226-8; de Valera to Republican Election Organising Committee, 25 July 1923, NLI, MS 18375(15).

5. De Valera correspondence with Ruttledge, Dec. 1923 and Jan. 1924, MP, P7/B/140.

6. Macardle (1937), 789-90; Rumpf and Hepburn (1977), 60 (map), 61; O'Malley (1978), 237-8; Conor Maguire to Mrs Childers, 1 Sept. 1923, CP, 7849; MacEntee, Jan. 1924, UCD, MacSwiney Papers, P48a/290(56).

Chapter 36:
The Post-War Free State Government and Army (pp. 263-267)

1. O'Higgins, DD, 1984-6 (15 June 1923) 356-7 (20 Apr. 1923); Michael Costello to M/D, 1 Jan. 1924, MP, P7a/136; Comdt Egan, 1 Jan. 1924, ibid.; M/D to President, 2 Jan. 1924, ibid; Cosgrave note, 15 Jan. 1924, ibid.; Fitzgibbon, DD, 964 (16 May 1923); O'Higgins, ibid., 2308-9 (22 June 1923); O'Duffy to Executive Council, 5 July 1924, with reports for weeks ending 30 June, 8, 22, 30 Sept. 1924, UCD, Blythe Papers, P24/223; debate on second stage of Public Safety (Emergency Powers) Bill, DD, 2501-2606 (25 June 1923), 461-526 (10-11 July 1923), 565-881 (12-13 July 1923); Johnson, ibid., 791 (10 May 1923); Moore, Senate Deb., 1422-8 (26 July 1922); Johnson, DD, 739 (12 July 1923).

2. O'Higgins, DD, 2003 (2 July 1923), 357 (20 Apr. 1923); Garvin (1981), 146-7.

3. Maj.-Gen. Séamus Hogan at Army Enquiry, 1924, P7/C/6, 9, 19; Col. David Neligan, ibid., P7/C/17; Prof. James Hogan, ibid., P7/C/25; Col. Charles Russell, ibid., P7/C/20; Waterford Command report, 12 July 1923, ibid., P7/C/9; O'Higgins note, 22 Dec. 1923, ibid., P7/C/42; IFS army report, 9 Jan. 1924, ibid., P7/B/139; O'Duffy report to M/D, 29 Dec. 1923, ibid., P7a/134; Mulcahy to O'Duffy, 31 Dec. 1923, ibid.; note, 20 Feb. 1924, ibid., P7a/139; Costello report, 8 Jan. 1924, ibid., P7/B/140.

4. Memo on case, n.d., MP, P7/C/42; O'Higgins to Cosgrave, 17 Aug. 1923, ibid., P7a/133; Maj.-Gen. Séamus Hogan at Army Enquiry, ibid., P7/C/6; Mulcahy, ibid., P7/C/7; O'Higgins, ibid., P7/C/10; Col. Jephson O'Connell, ibid., P7/C/15; Hogan ibid., P7/C/24; Maj.-Gen. Cahir Davitt and Col. Charles Russell, ibid., P7/C/22; Gen. Seán MacMahon, ibid., P7/C/35; O'Duffy to M/D, 29 Dec. 1923, ibid., P7a/134; material for preparation of Army Enquiry's Interim Report, ibid., P7/C/41.

5. IFS government memo, MP, P7/C/10; note on plan for demobilisation of officers, ibid., P7/C/42; note on demobilisation and on O/Cs' meeting, 10, 15 Dec 1923, ibid., P7/B/179; memo on demobilisation and reorganisation, ibid., p7/B/141; note to D/I (IRA), 25 Oct. 1923, ibid., P7a/871. Evidence on demobilisation at Army Enquiry: Mulcahy, MP, P7/C/7; Nolan, ibid., P7/C/16; Neligan, ibid., P7/C/17; Costello, ibid., P7/C/25; Russell, ibid., P7/C/18, 28; Jephson O'Connell, ibid., P7/C/15; Ó Muirthile, ibid., P7/C/13; O'Higgins, ibid., P7/C/21-2; Prof. James Hogan, ibid., P7/C/25; Interim Report of Army Enquiry, ibid., P7/C/41; for formation of officers' associations see ibid., P7/B/140, P7/C/5.

6. Note, MP, P7/B/179; account of O/Cs' meeting, 15 Dec. 1923, ibid.; Interim Report of Army Enquiry, loc. cit.; for Barry's peace efforts see p. 260 above.

7. O'Higgins at Army Enquiry, MP, P7/C/21-2; O'Connell, ibid., P7/C/15; Prof. Hogan, ibid., P7/C/25; Costello, ibid.; for Mulcahy's dissatisfaction with Prout's and Mac Eoin's commands see pp. 209, 216 above; Russell at Army Enquiry, MP, P7/C/29; Mulcahy on IRB, ibid., P7/C/10, 38.

8. Mulcahy at Army Enquiry, MP, P7/C/7; Valiulis (1985); Russell at Army Enquiry, MP, P7/C/29.

Chapter 37:
The Republican Hunger-Strike, October-November 1923 (pp. 268-271)

1. O'Higgins at Army Enquiry, 1924, MP, P7/C/10; O'Donovan's jottings from jail, 22 Sept. 1923, NLI, O'Donovan Papers, 22306; Cullinan, O'MN, P17B/106; de Valera to prisoners, 18 July 1923, MP, P7/B/93; de Valera to Aiken, 22 June 1923, quoted in Longford and O'Neill (1970), 225.

2. Report from C/S to IRA Executive Committee, 10 Aug. 1924, O'MP, P17a/12;

Republican document from Sinn Féin HQ to Bishops, 24 Oct. 1923, MP, P7a/87a; Sinn Féin HQ appeal to TDs, 24 Oct. 1923, ibid.; appeal to TDs, ibid.; Kilroy, O'MN, P17B/101; intercepted prisoner's letter from Tintown No. 3 Camp, 7 Nov. 1922, *Irish Independent*, 23 Nov. 1923, and MP, P7a/87a.

3. Madge Clifford, O'MN, P17B/103; de Valera note from prison, 6 Dec. 1923, MP. P7/B/40, and another note, ibid., P7a/87a; C/S to O/Cs of all prisons and camps, 31 July 1923, ibid., P7/B/93; Aiken to O/C Prisoners, Kilmainham, 19 Nov. 1923, NLI, Stack Papers, 17091; IRA Executive meeting, 11-12 July 1923, O'MP, P17a/12.

4. Clifford, O'MN, P17B/103; O'Connor (1958), 209-15; O'Donnell in *Survivors*, 31; O'Donnell (1965), 193-203; note from 'A/P', and circulated note from D/Is, 12 Dec. 1923, MP, P7/B/140; 'S. Mac. S./Capt.' to C/S, 24 Oct. 1923, ibid., P7a/87a; O'Malley (1978), 255.

5. Aiken to Mountjoy hunger-strikers, 20 Nov. 1923, MP, P7a/87a; O'Malley to Mrs Childers, 19, 23 Nov. 1923, CP, 7850; NLI, Stack Papers, 22398; Aiken to O/C Kilmainham Prisoners, 19 Nov. 1923, NLI, MS 17091; C. Byrne order calling off strike, 28 Oct. 1923, SPO, S1859; Byrne note, 28 Oct. 1923, MP, P7a/87a; Cecil Ó Máille to O/C Prisoners, Tintown No. 1 Camp, 6, 7 Nov. 1923, ibid.; C/S report to IRA Executive Committee, 10 Aug. 1924, O'MP, P17a/12.

6. Aiken to Mountjoy hunger-strikers, 20 Nov. 1923, MP, P7a/87a; Dinny Daly, O'MN, P17B/102; letter from Henderson, 2 Nov. 1923, and statements by Gaynor and Robinson, 17 Nov. 1923, MP, P7a/87a; Eoin Mac Néill, UCD, MS P24/192B; Stack to 'Winnie', 22 Oct. 1923, and other Stack notes, 24 Oct., 12, 18 Nov. 1923, Stack Papers, 22398; O'Malley to Mrs Childers, 12, 19, 23, 24 Nov. 1923, CP, 7850; 'N' to O/C Kerry 1, 6 Nov. 1923, SPO, S1859; 'Steve' to 'Kit', 24 Nov. 1923, MP, P7a/87a; 'Kit' to 'Lil', n.d. (copy of document intercepted coming into Curragh), ibid.; 'Steve' to 'May', 29 Nov. 1923, ibid.

7. Sheehy, O'MN, P17B/104; Adjt Kerry 1 to O/C Kerry 1, 5 Nov. 1923, SPO, S1859; AC/S (Aiken) to 'M' (Mrs Childers), 24 Nov. 1923, CP, 7847; 'P' to 'A.P.', 2 Jan. 1924, MP, P7a/87a; O'Duffy to President, 5 July 1924, Blythe Papers, P24/223; report for period ending 30 June 1924, ibid.; O'Duffy to government, 8 Sept. 1924, ibid.

Conclusion (pp. 272-276)

1. Fanning (1983b), 108-10; Longford and O'Neill (1970), 274-6; Williams (1966) 117-18, 184.

2. *DD*, 1515-16 (6 June 1923), 1815 (13 June 1923); Curran (1980), 276; Neeson (1967), 173; Fanning (1983b), 39; O'Higgins, 14 Nov. 1924, quoted in Macardle (1937), 785; O'Sullivan (1940), 115; Curran (1980), 276; Cosgrave report on financial year, 1922-23, *DD*, 72-82 (13 Apr. 1923); army estimates, ibid., 1450-62 (1 June 1923); Mulcahy, ibid., 1636-40 (7 June 1923); T. J. Kiernan, 'Public Finance' in *Saorstát Éireann Official Handbook,* (1932), 86-7; Cathal O'Shannon, *DD*, 1648 (7 June 1923); ibid., 1717 (12 June 1923); O'Higgins, ibid., 2325 (22 June 1923); for rate and tax collection problems see p. 263 above; Blythe, *DD*, 2021 (6 Mar. 1923); Fanning (1983b), 39.

3. Cosgrave, *DD*, 80-1 (13 Apr. 1923); White (1948), 151.

4. Edwards (1977), 179, 245; Aiken, 3 Aug. 1922, MP, P7a/175; oral evidence from Dr Risteárd Mulcahy and Dr C. S. (Tod) Andrews.

5. Sinn Féin Funds Case, PROI, 2B/82/117; O'Higgins, *DD*, 1909 (1 Mar. 1923); O'Faolain (1965), 174; O'Connor (1958), 167.

6. Bowman (1982); Thomas Jones Diary, 9 Feb. 1923, Jones (1971), 219-20; Scott Diary, 31 Aug. 1922, Wilson (1970), 412; Moran quoted in MacDonagh (1983), 9.

Bibliography

PRIMARY SOURCES

DUBLIN
University College, Dublin, Archives
Ernest Blythe Papers
Máire Comerford Papers
Hugh Kennedy Papers
Mary MacSwiney Papers
Richard Mulcahy Papers
J. J. ('Ginger') O'Connell Papers
Ernie O'Malley Papers
Ernie O'Malley Notebooks
Other miscellaneous material

University College, Dublin, Library
Joseph Connolly Memoir (by permission of Father F. X. Martin)

Trinity College, Dublin, Records Office
Erskine Childers Papers
Mary MacSwiney Papers

National Library of Ireland
F. S. Bourke Papers
Michael Collins Papers
Michael Collins correspondence with Austin Stack
Frank Gallagher
Eva Gore-Booth letters, mainly to Constance Markievicz
Tim Healy correspondence with Lord Beaverbrook
John J. Hearn Papers
Thomas Johnson Papers
Joseph McGarrity Papers
Kathleen MacKenna Napoli Papers
Art O'Brien Papers
William O'Brien Papers
J. J. ('Ginger') O'Connell Papers
James L. O'Donovan Papers
James O'Mara Papers
Séamus Robinson Statement
Celia Shaw Diary
Austin Stack Papers
Material on military report into Ballyseedy killings

State Paper Office of Ireland
Material catalogued under 'DE' and 'S', i.e. Dáil Cabinet, Provisional Government and
Executive Council Minutes, together with government material.

Public Record Office of Ireland
Sinn Féin Funds Case, 1948

Army Archives
Inspection reports; local material; captured documents

Private
Desmond FitzGerald Papers

BELFAST
Public Record Office of Northern Ireland
Some Cabinet Papers and some material under 'Fin'

LONDON
Public Record Office
Cabinet Minutes and Papers
Colonial Office Papers
Anglo-Irish Treaty negotiations
Lord Midleton Papers
Mark Sturgis Papers
S. G. Tallents Papers

House of Lords Record Department
David Lloyd George Papers

UNITED STATES OF AMERICA
New York Public Library
McKim–Maloney Papers
Frank P. Walsh Papers

National Archives, Washington DC
State Department Files

ORAL TESTIMONY
My chief reliance has been on Ernie O'Malley's interviews with vast numbers of his
contemporaries—almost entirely Republicans. These are found in his notebooks. I had
conversations with C. S. ('Tod') Andrews, Colonel Dan Bryan, Máire Comerford and Dr T.
O'Reilly. Reminiscences of Risteárd Mulcahy (of his father) and León Ó Broin were invaluable.

DÁIL DEBATES
Private Sessions of Second Dáil (Dublin 1972)
Official Report: Debate on the Treaty between Great Britain and Ireland (Dublin 1922)
Dáil Debates (Dublin 1922-   )

NEWSPAPERS AND PERIODICALS
*Irish Times; Irish Independent; Freeman's Journal; Cork Examiner; Kerry People; Kilkenny People;
Meath Herald and Cavan Advertiser; The Nationalist* (Clonmel); *Connaught Telegraph; Clare
Champion; Limerick Echo; Limerick Chronicle*

Poblacht na h-Éireann War News (1922-23); *Republican War Bulletin* (10 Aug.-Dec. 1922); *The
Separatist* (18 Feb.-9 Sept. 1922); *Southern Bulletin* (6 Jan.-24 Feb. 1923)

Straight Talk (8 Nov.-28 Dec. 1922); *The Plain People* (1922); *The Nation* (1922); *The Irish People: War Special* (July-Aug. 1922); *The Free State; Limerick War News* (July-Aug. 1922)

Irish News (Belfast); *Belfast Newsletter; Northern Whig*
The Times; Manchester Guardian; Morning Post; The Observer
New York Times; Boston Globe; Gaelic American; Irish World; Irish Press (Philadelphia)

SECONDARY SOURCES

Andrews, C. S., *Dublin Made Me: An Autobiography* (Dublin/Cork 1979)

Barry, T., *Guerilla Days in Ireland* (Dublin 1949)

Barry, T., *The Reality of the Anglo-Irish War, 1920-21, in West Cork: Refutations, Corrections and Comment on Liam Deasy's 'Towards Ireland Free'* (Tralee 1974)

Béaslaí, P., *Michael Collins and the Making of a New Ireland*, 2 vols (Dublin 1926)

Beckett, J. C., *The Making of Modern Ireland, 1603-1923* (London 1966)

Bell, J. Bowyer, *The Secret Army: A History of the IRA, 1916-70* (London 1970)

Bew, P., Gibbon, P., and Patterson, H., *The State in Northern Ireland, 1921-72: Political Forces and Social Classes* (Manchester 1979)

Bowman, J., 'Sinn Féin's Perception of the Ulster Question: Autumn 1921', *The Crane Bag (Northern Issue)*, iv, 2 (1980)

Bowman, J., *De Valera and the Ulster Question, 1917-73* (Oxford 1982)

Boyce, D. G., *Englishmen and Irish Troubles* (London 1972)

Boyce, D. G., *Nationalism in Ireland* (London 1982)

Boyle, K., 'The Tallents Report on the Craig-Collins Pact of 30 March 1922', *Irish Jurist*, xii (1977)

Breen, D., *My Fight for Irish Freedom* (Dublin 1924)

Brennan, M., *The War in Clare, 1911-21* (Dublin 1980)

Brennan, R., *Allegiance* (Dublin 1950)

Brown, T., *Ireland: A Social and Cultural History, 1922-79* (London 1981)

Buckland, P., *Irish Unionism 1: The Anglo-Irish and the New Ireland, 1885-1922* (Dublin 1972)

Buckland, P., *Irish Unionism 2: Ulster Unionism and the Origins of Northern Ireland, 1886-1922* (Dublin 1973)

Buckland, P., *The Factory of Grievances: Devolved Government in Northern Ireland, 1921-39* (Dublin 1979)

Buckland, P., *James Craig* (Dublin 1980)

Buckland, P., *A History of Northern Ireland* (Dublin 1981)

Callwell, C. E., *Field-Marshal Sir Henry Wilson: His Life and Diaries* (London 1927)

Canning, P., *British Policy towards Ireland, 1921-41* (Oxford 1985)

Carroll, F. M., *American Opinion and the Irish Question, 1910-23* (Dublin 1978)

Casey, J., 'Republican Courts in Ireland, 1919-22', *Irish Jurist*, v (1970)

Casey, J., 'The Genesis of the Dáil Courts', *Irish Jurist*, ix (1974)

Churchill, W. S., *The World Crisis: The Aftermath* (London 1929)

Collins, M., *The Path to Freedom* (Dublin 1922)

Colum, P., *Arthur Griffith* (Dublin 1959)

Coogan, O., *Politics and War in Meath, 1913-23* (privately published n.d.)

Coogan, T. P., *The I.R.A.* (London 1970)

Cowling, M., *The Impact of Labour, 1920-24* (Cambridge 1971)

Cronin, S., *The McGarrity Papers* (Tralee 1972)

Curious Journey: An Oral History of Ireland's Unfinished Revolution, ed. K. Griffith and T. O'Grady (London 1982)

Curran, J. M., 'The Consolidation of the Irish Revolution, 1921-33', *University Review*, v (1968)

Curran, J. M., 'The Decline and Fall of the I.R.B.', *Éire-Ireland*, x (1975)

Curran, J. M., *The Birth of the Irish Free State, 1921-23* (Alabama 1980)

Dangerfield, G., *The Damnable Question: A Study in Anglo-Irish Relations* (London 1976)

Davis, R., *Arthur Griffith and Non-Violent Sinn Féin* (Dublin 1974)

Davis, R., 'The Advocacy of Passive Resistance in Ireland, 1916-22', *Anglo-Irish Studies*, iii (1977)

Deasy, L., *Towards Ireland Free: The West Cork Brigade in the War of Independence, 1917-21* (Cork 1973)

Deasy, L., *Brother Against Brother* (Dublin/Cork 1982)

Dwyer, T. Ryle, *Eamon de Valera* (Dublin 1980)

Dwyer, T. Ryle, *Michael Collins and the Treaty: His Differences with de Valera* (Dublin/Cork 1981)

Edwards, R. Dudley, *Patrick Pearse: The Triumph of Failure* (London 1977)

Fanning, R., *The Irish Department of Finance, 1922-58* (Dublin 1978)

Fanning, R., *The Four-Leaved Shamrock: Electoral Politics and the National Imagination in Independent Ireland* (Dublin 1983a)

Fanning, R., *Independent Ireland* (Dublin 1983b)

Farrell, B., 'The Drafting of the Irish Free State Constitution', *Irish Jurist*, v (1970)

Farrell, B., *The Founding of Dáil Éireann: Parliament and Nation-Building* (Dublin 1971)

Farrell, M., *Northern Ireland: The Orange State* (London 1975)

Feehan, J. M., *The Shooting of Michael Collins: Murder or Accident?* (Dublin/Cork 1981)

Figgis, D., *Recollections of the Irish War* (London 1927)

Fitzpatrick D., *Politics and Irish Life, 1913-21: Provincial Experience of War and Revolution* (Dublin 1977)

Fitzpatrick, D., 'The Geography of Irish Nationalism, 1910-21', *Past and Present*, lxxvii (1978)

Forester, M., *Michael Collins: The Lost Leader* (London 1971)

Gallagher, M., 'Socialism and the Nationalist Tradition in Ireland, 1798-1918', *Éire-Ireland*, xii (1977)

Gallagher, M., 'The Pact General Election of 1922', *Irish Historical Studies*, xxi, 84 (1979)

Garvin, T., 'The Destiny of the Soldiers: Tradition and Modernity in the Politics of de Valera's Ireland', *Political Studies*, xxvi (1978)

Garvin, T., *The Evolution of Irish Nationalist Politics* (Dublin 1981)

Garvin, T., 'The Anatomy of a Nationalist Revolution: Ireland 1858-1928', *Contemporary Studies in Society and History* (July 1986)

Gaughan, J. A., *Austin Stack: Portrait of a Separatist* (Dublin 1977)

Gaughan, J. A., *Thomas Johnson, 1872-1963* (Dublin 1980)

Gilbert, M., *Winston S. Churchill*, Vol. IV: *1916-22* (London 1975)

Gilbert, M., *Winston S. Churchill*, Vol. IV, Companion Volume, Part 3: *Documents, April 1921-November 1922* (London 1977)

Greaves, C. D., *Liam Mellows and the Irish Revolution* (London 1971)

Griffith, K., and O'Grady, T., see *Curious Journey*

Harkness, D., *The Restless Dominion* (Dublin 1969)

Harkness, D., *Northern Ireland since 1920* (Dublin 1983)

Hezlet, A., *The 'B' Specials: A History of the Ulster Special Constabulary* (London 1972)

Hopkinson, M. A., 'The Irish Question in American Politics from the End of the First World War to the Irish Civil War' (Ph.D. thesis, University of Cambridge, 1971)

Irish Boundary Commission, Report and Documents, intro. G. Hand (Shannon 1969)

Johnson, D., 'The Belfast Boycott, 1920-22', in J. M. Goldstrom and L. A. Clarkson (ed.), *Irish Population, Economy and Society: Essays in Honour of the late K. H. Connell* (Oxford 1981)

Jones, T., *Whitehall Diary*, Vol. III: *Ireland, 1918-25*, ed. K. Midlemas (London 1971)

Kee, R., *The Green Flag: A History of Irish Nationalism* (London 1972)

Kohn, L., *The Constitution of the Irish Free State* (London 1932)

Laffan, M., 'The Unification of Sinn Féin in 1917', *Irish Historical Studies*, xvii, 67 (1971)

Laffan, M., *The Partition of Ireland, 1911-25* (Dublin 1983)

Lawlor, S., 'Civil-Military Relations in Ireland, 1921-23' (Ph.D. thesis, University College, Dublin, 1976)

Lawlor, S., *Britain and Ireland, 1914-23* (Dublin 1983)

Lavelle, P., *James O'Mara: A Staunch Sinn Féiner, 1873-1948* (Dublin 1961)

Longford, Earl of, and O'Neill, T. P., *Eamon de Valera* (London 1970)

Lyons, F. S. L., *Ireland since the Famine* (London 1971; paperback ed. cited in notes)

Macardle, D., *Tragedies of Kerry* (Dublin 1924)

Macardle, D., *The Irish Republic: A Documented Chronicle* (London 1937; paperback ed. (1968) cited in notes)

McColgan, J., *British Policy and the Irish Administration, 1920-22* (London 1983)

MacDonagh, O., *Ireland: The Union and its Aftermath* (London 1977)

MacDonagh, O., *States of Mind: A Study of Anglo-Irish Conflict, 1780-1980* (London 1983)

Mac Eoin, U., see *Survivors*

Macready, C. F. N., *Annals of an Active Life*, 2 vols (London 1924)

Marreco, A., *The Rebel Countess: The Life and Times of Constance Markievicz* (London 1967)

Miller, D. W., *Church, State and Nation in Ireland, 1898-1921* (Dublin 1973)

Mitchell, A., 'Labour and the National Struggle, 1919-21', *Capuchin Annual*, xxxviii (1971)

Mitchell, A., *Labour in Irish Politics, 1890-1930: The Irish Labour Movement in an Age of Revolution* (Dublin 1974)

Morgan, K. O., *Consensus and Disunity: The Lloyd George Coalition Government, 1918-22* (London 1979)

Morrison, G., *The Irish Civil War: An Illustrated History* (Dublin 1981)

Moynihan, M. (ed.), *Speeches and Statements by Eamon de Valera, 1917-73* (Dublin 1980)

Mulcahy, Risteárd, 'The Development of the Irish Volunteers, 1916-22' (address to Irish Military History Society, 9 Nov. 1978)

Mullins, B., *Memoirs of Billy Mullins* (Tralee 1983)

Murphy, J. A., *Ireland in the Twentieth Century* (Dublin 1975)

Neeson, E., *The Civil War in Ireland 1922-23* (Cork 1966)

Neeson, E., *The Life and Death of Michael Collins* (Cork 1968)

Neligan, D., *The Spy in the Castle* (London 1968)

O'Brien, W., *Forth the Banners Go* (Dublin 1969)

Ó Broin, L., *Revolutionary Underground: The Story of the Irish Republican Brotherhood, 1858-1924* (Dublin 1976)

Ó Broin, L., *Michael Collins* (Dublin 1980)

Ó Broin, L. (ed.), *In Great Haste: The Letters of Michael Collins and Kitty Kiernan* (Dublin 1983)

O'Carroll, J. P., and Murphy, J. A. (ed.), *De Valera and his Times* (Cork 1983)

O'Connor, B., *With Michael Collins in the Fight for Irish Independence* (London 1929)

O'Connor, F., *An Only Child* (London 1958; paperback ed. (1971) cited in notes)

O'Connor, F., *The Big Fellow: Michael Collins and the Irish Revolution* (Dublin 1965)

O'Connor, U., *Oliver St John Gogarty* (London 1964; paperback ed. (1984) cited in notes)

O'Donnell, P., *There Will Be Another Day* (Dublin 1963)

O'Donnell, P., *The Gates Flew Open* (Cork 1965)

O'Donoghue, F., *No Other Law* (Dublin 1954)

O'Donoghue, F., 'Guerilla Warfare in Ireland', *An Cosantóir*, xxiii (1963)

O'Faolain, S., *Vive Moi: An Autobiography* (London 1965)

O'Farrell, P., *Ireland's English Question: Anglo-Irish Relations, 1534-1970* (New York 1971)

O'Hegarty, P. S., *The Victory of Sinn Féin* (Dublin 1924)

O'Hegarty, P. S., *A History of Ireland under the Union* (London 1952)

O'Higgins, K., *Civil War and the Events which Led to It* (Dublin 1922)

O'Malley, E., *On Another Man's Wound* (London 1936; paperback ed. cited in notes)

O'Malley, E., *The Singing Flame* (Dublin 1978; paperback ed. cited in notes)

O'Sullivan, D., *The Irish Free State and its Senate* (London 1940)

Pakenham, F., *Peace by Ordeal* (London 1935; paperback ed. (1962) cited in notes)

Ranelagh, J. O'Beirne, 'The IRB from the Treaty to 1924', *Irish Historical Studies*, xx, 77 (1976)

Riddell, Lord, *Intimate Diary of the Peace Conference and After, 1918-23* (London 1923)

Rumpf, E., and Hepburn, A. C., *Nationalism and Socialism in Twentieth-Century Ireland* (Liverpool 1977)

Ryan, D., *Seán Tracy and the Third Tipperary Brigade, I.R.A.* (Tralee 1945)

Schmitt, P., *The Irony of Irish Democracy: The Impact of Political Culture on Administrative and Democratic Development in Ireland* (Lexington 1973)

Sheehan, K., 'The Northern Policy of the Provisional and First Irish Free State Governments, 1922-24' (M.A. thesis, University College, Dublin, 1982)

Stevenson, F., *Lloyd George: A Diary*, ed. A. J. P. Taylor (London 1971)

Stewart, A. T. Q., *The Narrow Ground: Aspects of Ulster, 1609-1969* (London 1977)

Stewart, A. T. Q., *Edward Carson* (Dublin 1981)

Strauss, E., *Irish Nationalism and British Democracy* (London 1951)

Survivors, ed. U. Mac Eoin (Dublin 1981)

Tansill, C. C., *America and the Fight for Irish Freedom, 1866-1922* (New York 1924)

Taylor, R., *Michael Collins* (London 1958)

Taylor, R., *Assassination* (London 1961)

Tierney, M., *Eoin MacNeill, Scholar and Man of Action, 1867-1945* (Oxford 1980)

Towey, T., 'Hugh Kennedy and the Constitutional Development of the Irish Free State, 1922-23', *Irish Jurist*, xii (1977)

Towey, T., 'The Reaction of the British Government to the 1922 Collins–de Valera Pact', *Irish Historical Studies*, xxii, 85 (1980)

Townshend, C., *The British Campaign in Ireland, 1919-21: The Development of Political and Military Policies* (Oxford 1975)

Townshend, C., 'The Irish Railway Strike of 1920: Industrial Action and Civil Resistance in the Struggle for Independence', *Irish Historical Studies*, xxi, 84 (1979a)

Townshend, C., 'The Irish Republican Army and the Development of Guerrilla Warfare, 1916-21', *English Historical Review*, xciv (1979b)

Townshend, C., *Political Violence in Ireland: Government and Resistance since 1848* (Oxford 1983)

Valiulis, M. G., *Almost a Rebellion: The Irish Army Mutiny of 1924* (Cork 1985)

Van Voris, J., *Constance Markievicz: In the Cause of Ireland* (Amherst 1967)

Ward, A. J., *Ireland and Anglo-American Relations, 1899-1921* (London 1969)

White, T. de Vere, *Kevin O'Higgins* (London 1948; paperback ed. cited in notes)

Williams, T. D. (ed.), *The Irish Struggle, 1916-26* (London 1966)

Williams, T. D. (ed.), *Secret Societies in Ireland* (Dublin 1973)

Wilson, T. (ed.), *The Political Diaries of C. P. Scott, 1911-28* (London 1970)

Younger, C., *Ireland's Civil War* (London 1968)

Index